Age and Equality Law

The Library of Essays on Equality and Anti-Discrimination Law
Series Editor: Suzanne B. Goldberg

Titles in the Series:

Disability and Equality Law
Elizabeth F. Emens and Michael Ashley Stein

Sexuality and Equality Law
Suzanne B. Goldberg

Gender and Equality Law
Julie Goldscheid

Race and Equality Law
Angela P. Harris

Age and Equality Law
Michael Selmi

Religion and Equality Law
Nelson Tebbe

Age and Equality Law

Edited by

Michael Selmi

George Washington Law School, USA

ASHGATE

Published by
Ashgate Publishing Limited
Wey Court East
Union Road
Farnham
Surrey GU9 7PT
England

Ashgate Publishing Company
Suite 3–1
110 Cherry Street
Burlington
VT 05401-3818
USA

www.ashgate.com

British Library Cataloguing in Publication Data
Age and equality law. – (The library of essays on equality and anti-discrimination law)
1. Age discrimination in employment–Law and legislation.
I. Series II. Selmi, Michael.
344'.01398133-dc23

The Library of Congress has cataloged the printed edition as follows: 2012939435

ISBN 9781409437239

MIX
Paper from responsible sources
FSC® C018575
FSC www.fsc.org

Printed and bound in Great Britain by the
MPG Books Group, UK

Contents

Acknowledgements

Ashgate would like to thank our researchers and the contributing authors who provided copies, along with the following for their permission to reprint copyright material.

Chicago-Kent College of Law for the essay: Susan Bisom-Rapp, Andrew Frazer and Malcolm Sargeant (2011), 'Decent Work, Older Workers, and Vulnerability in the Economic Recession: A Comparative Study of Australia, the United Kingdom, and the United States', *Employee Rights and Employment Policy Journal*, **15**, pp. 43–121.

Chicago-Kent Law Review for the essay: Sara E. Rix (2006), 'The Aging of the American Workforce', *Chicago-Kent Law Review*, **81**, pp. 593–617.

Edward Elgar Publishing Ltd for the essay: Scott J. Adams and David Neumark (2006), 'Age Discrimination in US Labor Markets: A Review of the Evidence', in W.M. Rodgers (ed.), *Handbook on the Economics of Discrimination*, Cheltenham: Edward Elgar, pp. 187–211.

Japan Labor Review for the essay: Ryoko Sakuraba (2009), 'The Amendment of the Employment Measure Act: Japanese Anti-Age Discrimination Law', *Japan Labor Review*, **6**, pp. 56–75.

Joanna N. Lahey (2010), 'International Comparison of Age Discrimination Laws', *Research on Aging*, **32**, pp. 679–97. Copyright © 2010 Joanna N. Lahey.

Oxford University Press for the essay: Claire Kilpatrick (2008), 'The New UK Retirement Regime, Employment Law and Pensions', *Industrial Law Journal*, **37**, pp. 1–24. Copyright © 2008 Industrial Law Society.

Stetson University College of Law for the essay: Charmaine Spencer and Ann Soden (2007), 'A Softly Greying Nation: Law, Ageing and Policy in Canada', *Journal of International Aging, Law & Policy*, **2**, pp. 2–32.

Stewart J. Schwab (1993), 'Life-Cycle Justice: Accommodating Just Cause and Employment at Will', *Michigan Law Review*, **92**, pp. 8–62. Copyright © 1993 Stewart J. Schwab.

Texas Law Review for the essay: Christine Jolls (1996), 'Hands-Tying and the Age Discrimination in Employment Act', *Texas Law Review*, **74**, pp. 1813–46. Copyright © 1996 Texas Law Review Association.

University of Chicago Press for the essays: Edward P. Lazear (1979), 'Why is there Mandatory Retirement?', *Journal of Political Economy*, **87**, pp. 1261–84. Copyright © 1979 The University of Chicago; George Rutherglen (1995), 'From Race to Age: The Expanding Scope

Publisher's Note

The material in this volume has been reproduced using the facsimile method. This means we can retain the original pagination to facilitate easy and correct citation of the original essays. It also explains the variety of typefaces, page layouts and numbering.

Series Preface

What is discrimination in the twenty-first century? What is equality? The *Library of Essays on Equality and Anti-Discrimination Law* presents both classic and cutting-edge perspectives on these challenging questions. Across titles that focus on age, disability, gender, race, religion and sexuality, the *Library* is a robust introduction to the field for newcomers and an invaluable resource for experts.

Each volume in the series includes many of the most important, thought-provoking, and hard-to-find works in its area, together with an introductory essay by a leading scholar. This essay situates the volume's articles and chapters within the larger body of related scholarship, highlights cross-cutting themes, and provides a roadmap for readers to continue their explorations. The compiled selections then allow the field to unfold, at least in part, through side-by-side review of the works.

Strikingly, although each volume has its own identity-based focus, many of the most important inquiries cross disciplinary boundaries, with insights from one volume carrying over to the next. A careful read of the race discrimination volume, for example, will produce new insights regarding age discrimination, and vice versa. The same is true for the volumes on disability, gender, religion and sexuality.

Chief among the inquiries are questions about how best to conceptualize identity and distinguish between permissible different treatment and impermissible discrimination. As the works make clear, scholars' theories of discrimination and equality are at least as varied as their ideas about identity. Not surprisingly, a similar complexity runs through the regulations and policies that lawmakers produce. And the global perspective offered in the volumes reinforces that while geography inevitably plays a role, state lines – though important – are only one among many factors that influence the development of law and scholarship in this area.

Because law has such an ambivalent relationship to identity and discrimination, the fields that are this *Library*'s focus are defined at least as much by the questions scholars pose as by the answers they offer. The focus on inquiries, rather than outcomes, is important too because the political, social, and economic conditions that inform our understandings of discrimination and equality inevitably change over time. So, likewise, do our understandings of age, disability, gender, race, religion and sexuality and the relationships among these aspects of identity. Each volume in the series, both on its own and as part of the full collection, is thus an important source for the questions that help define the contours of each field, even as the underlying terrain continues to shift.

SUZANNE B. GOLDBERG
Columbia University, USA

Introduction

This volume explores the category of age discrimination, a common category of prohibited action but one that also tends towards less consensus than other non-discrimination categories, particularly when compared to race and gender. Within the United States, a federal prohibition on age discrimination became law in 1968 and since then the law has evolved to prohibit mandatory retirement in all but a few select industries. Indeed, with some exceptions, the Age Discrimination in Employment Act (typically referred to as the ADEA) has generally provided broad and robust protections to workers aged 40 and over. Prohibitions on age discrimination are a much more recent consideration in other parts of the world; indeed, within the European Union most of the legislative actions have occurred within the last decade. Despite the different origins, most countries are likely to confront the same issues that the United States legal system has addressed, in large part because of the ambivalence that surrounds prohibitions on age discrimination.

Protections against age discrimination will likely increase in importance over the next decade for several related reasons. As discussed in more detail below, older employees are especially vulnerable to lay-offs in a weak economy, given their generally higher salaries, and certainly in the United States there is substantial evidence of significant displacement among the older population. Not only are older workers prone to lay-offs but they are also subject to discrimination in the hiring process, and they often have a particularly difficult time obtaining new employment. Both of these phenomena – lay-offs and hiring discrimination – can lead to expensive and difficult litigation, and there has been a recent upsurge in age discrimination lawsuits filed in the United States. The global recession has also substantially decreased the value of many pensions, particularly those that are based on the performance of stock markets as is true with most American pensions today, but this concern extends far beyond the United States. Pension benefits that are tied to investment performance have left many older workers with insufficient income to carry on the kind of life they were expecting to experience in retirement, which has prompted many employees to work beyond their expected retirement date or to seek to return to the workforce (see Sara Rix, Chapter 7 in this volume) As should be apparent, these two concerns compound existing problems leaving older workers in an especially precarious position – they need to work longer in a difficult economy where their higher salaries make them vulnerable to cost-saving lay-offs. Interest in age discrimination will only increase over the next decade and this volume explores some of the many issues that are likely to arise, and also what makes age discrimination distinctly different from most other prohibited classifications.

* * *

In its simplest form, discrimination means treating two similar persons or entities differently, and in the context of anti-discrimination law we most commonly associate unlawful discrimination with animus or deep-seated bias. This is no doubt central to our concept of race discrimination where discrimination often stems from hatred or feelings of inferiority towards another. Gender discrimination, on the other hand, is more commonly associated not with bias so much as with perceptions regarding the proper roles for men and women, as well as views of competence that arise from those distinct roles. The source of age discrimination, however, is quite different.

Although it is always difficult to make broad generalizations, concerns with respect to age discrimination generally arise from misperceptions regarding the abilities of older workers rather than the kind of animus that often fuels race discrimination. This was the conclusion of the report that accompanied the passage of the ADEA in the United States, which concluded that while age discrimination was an entrenched labour market practice it arose primarily because employers assumed that the abilities of older workers had receded more than they actually had (Wirtz, 1965). This misperception remains true today but there is here a kernel of truth that also makes age discrimination qualitatively different from other protected categories of discrimination. It is widely recognized that abilities do, in fact, deteriorate with age – how much, how rapidly and how meaningful that deterioration is are all contested issues but there is little question that as workers age their abilities likewise change. Some of the changes are related to physical and mental deterioration that comes with age, while other changes are the product of the tedium that attends many jobs performed over a lifetime.

As a result, what is often described as age discrimination turns out to be overly broad generalizations about the abilities of older workers. Employers may, for example, assume that the abilities of all older workers deteriorate at a similar pace when, in fact, there is likely a tremendous variation among workers of all ages. Within the United States legislative system that protects against age discrimination this concern regarding group generalizations has been translated into a requirement that employers generally, though not always, must make an individualized determination regarding the abilities of older workers. The only exception to this individualized assessment is in the rare circumstance where the employer can demonstrate that an individualized determination is not feasible, but the primary concern that the courts have expressed with age-based determinations is that they are the product of stereotypical views of older workers rather than their actual abilities (*Hazen Paper Co.* case).[1] It is worth noting that, within the American system, an employer is able to take into account actual abilities and there is no requirement that an employer must give preference to older workers if that means accepting weaker performance. What an employer is prohibited from doing is basing employment decisions on assumptions regarding the abilities of older workers.

The American judicial system adds a particular cast to the interpretation of age discrimination laws. Within the federal judicial system, judges are appointed for life and many of them serve well into their seventies and even into their eighties. As of 2011, four of the nine Justices serving on the United States Supreme Court were at least 70 years old, and judges are often highly sceptical of employer claims that older workers cannot compete with their younger counterparts. But, and this has provided an unusual twist to the development of the case law, the Justices are also rather unsympathetic to claims from workers who are seeking some preference or advantage in the workplace, as the Justices themselves have proved an especially hearty group who frequently work through illnesses and chronic pain. Thus, the American cases are steeped almost entirely in the concern for broad generalizations, and to

1 *Hazen Paper Co.* v. *Biggins*, 507 U.S. 604 (1993).

the extent employers can demonstrate actual age-related differences they are more than likely to succeed in defending their actions.

There is another important but complicating aspect to the age discrimination cases. A peculiar but uniform feature of the labour market is an upward-sloping wage function. With few exceptions, salaries tend to increase over time, and continue to do so throughout one's career despite the decline in productivity that typically occurs later in one's career. As Christine Jolls discusses in Chapter 2, employees have come to expect wage increases over time and see annual increases (or at least not wage decreases) as a matter of fairness, and employers have responded in kind to this expectation. But to make this arrangement work – one where later in one's career the employer is paying more than necessary to secure a worker's services – there typically has to be an end point for the relationship. This was the point of the influential essay by Edward Lazear, included as Chapter 3 in this volume, which will be discussed in more detail shortly along with some of the legal analysis related to what has come to be defined as the life-cycle wage theory. The important point to emphasize here is that employers are reluctant to reduce individual salaries in the face of declining productivity and are more inclined, where feasible, to terminate those employees.[2] This reluctance to reduce wages should be distinguished from the common labour market tactic during weak economies in which employers engage in across-the-board wage cuts, often negotiated with unions, as a means of staying competitive in the world economy.

A word about the role of unions and age discrimination would be in order, and here it is important not to rely for comparative purposes exclusively on the United States, where unions are weaker than in most other parts of the world. Indeed, in many ways, statutory interventions in the market, such as the ADEA, have replaced protections once provided by American unions, who traditionally have ensured healthy pensions and a regulated workforce. A traditional hallmark of the union workplace is that promotions and salaries are closely aligned with seniority, which allows the unions to reduce competition among employees while also restricting the power of employers over labour management and, in turn, encouraging dedicated employment careers. Under this arrangement, age discrimination is generally not a significant concern, particularly when the seniority protections are combined with a workplace rule that allows terminations only for just cause, as is universally true in union workplaces. However, in a labour market where the power and presence of unions is sharply reduced, statutory protections become critical to ensuring that older workers are protected from arbitrary dismissals.

Another distinguishing feature of age discrimination is the need to define the protected class. Theoretically, a ban on age discrimination could involve any age, thus making it impermissible to take age into account in the employment process, as some countries such as Japan do with their employment statutes. Age discrimination laws might also seek to protect individuals during a certain period of their life, for example from ages 40 to 60, or might simply prohibit discrimination among all those over a certain age, 40 years old in the context of the United States. What protections a legal system provides will turn on the purpose that underlies the prohibition. To the extent a system seeks to bracket age from the employment process, it might protect all ages, and many contend that youthful workers are subject to forms of age discrimination akin to that older workers face. The United States,

2 For an extended discussion of this issue, see Bewley (1999).

on the other hand, prohibits discrimination against all those who are 40 years or over, which has created a number of difficulties for litigation arising under the statute. This is obviously a very broad category, capturing a large segment of the workforce, and likely protects many individuals who are not vulnerable to the primary harm the statute seeks to avoid. In particular, it seems unlikely that individuals in their forties, particularly their early forties, are commonly the victim of stereotypes that affect older workers, given that most people would not consider individuals in their forties to fall within the category of older workers. Similarly, individuals in their forties are likely to be able to obtain new employment much quicker than individuals who have obtained the age of 50 or above, thus mitigating one of the harms that attend to age-based decision-making.

Having no upper limit to the protection can also prove difficult and costly for employers. This has been especially true in the world of academia where the demands of the job typically allow many individuals to continue working into their seventies or beyond, and it can be difficult, and costly, for employers to justify terminations late in one's career. As a practical matter, this means that employers are most commonly forced to buy out the contracts of older professors through incentives that will induce earlier retirement. This has also created some disincentives to hire professors who have the right to tenure, creating increased pressure to hire individuals as adjunct professors with short-term appointments to avoid the problem of older workers staying on beyond their expected work period.

All of these factors render concerns with age discrimination distinct from other areas of anti-discrimination protection. The essays assembled in this volume address these and other issues related to protecting individuals from age discrimination. Some provide introductory and background information to the various issues, while others evaluate the evolution of the American system in its interpretation and enforcement of the ADEA. Further essays focus on the international scene, with contributions that explore issues of age discrimination in Canada, Japan, the United Kingdom, the European Union and Australia. The remaining portion of this Introduction will provide a brief summary of the collected works and explain how the various essays fit together to analyse the complexities of age discrimination.

* * *

Edward Lazear developed what has proved to be perhaps the most influential model relating to issues of age discrimination, although his model was designed to provide a theoretical understanding of the wage function in a long-term contractual relation. The model, which has come to be known as the life-cycle wage theory, posits that employers typically underpay workers through much of their early career, when employees are often still trying to establish themselves, and match that underpayment with overpayments later in their careers, after their productivity stagnates or begins to decline. This allows employers to provide wage increases throughout one's career and induces employees to invest in a long-term relationship with their employer. An essential component of the model is a fixed end date for the relationship, which allows employers to calculate the total cost of the employment relationship over a lifetime. Without that end date, an employer will be uncertain how to structure payments later in one's career, and the force of the model weakens considerably.

The essays by Stewart Schwab and Christine Jolls build on the Lazear model, but in slightly different ways. Chapter 5 by Professor Schwab is probably the best known essay within legal scholarship on the rationales for age discrimination laws, and he focuses on the period in the Lazear model when employers begin to overcompensate their long-term employees. This period, likely to arrive with a long-term employee in his late forties or early fifties, creates a particular vulnerability in the relationship that is ripe for exploitation. The novel part of Professor Schwab's essay is that he contends that common law courts have adopted a version of the life-cycle wage theory in their adjudication, and have paid particular attention to older workers who are subject to opportunistic firings by their employers. The common law courts have, according to Professor Schwab's interpretation, largely filled the gap in the at-will system by ensuring that older workers are not unfairly deprived of the bargain of long-term wages. Consistent with his argument, Professor Schwab demonstrates that courts are far less protective of mid-career employees (those, for example, in their forties) who are more mobile and thus less susceptible to advantageous firings.

In Chapter 2 Christine Jolls explores the various rationales for an age-based wage scale and seeks to justify the existing legal interventions. Like Schwab, she emphasizes the way back-loading employee wages can deter employees from shirking by increasing the potential punishment for misbehaviour since there is more to lose when wages are effectively deferred to a later date. Relying on work from behavioural economics, Professor Jolls also notes that workers typically express a preference for wages that show upward movement, even if the wage increases cumulatively are less than a worker might be able to secure in the labour market. This relationship, however, is difficult to enforce in an unregulated market, given that the wages are provided through an implicit, rather than explicit, contract. While employees might demand a contract, absent a union setting most individual employees will not have the power to make such demands, and are likely to discount the likelihood of a future opportunistic firing, and non-market sanctions, such as reputational effects, are not likely to prove a sufficient constraint on individual breaches of the contractual commitment. Professor Jolls then turns to the ADEA to assess its value as a hands-tying device to ensure that employers live up to their long-term commitments and contrasts the ADEA with the common law of wrongful discharge, the facet of the law celebrated by Professor Schwab. One important comparative advantage to the ADEA over the common law is that it prohibits discrimination in hiring and is better suited for the more mobile job market that defines many of the world's labour markets today.

Samuel Issacharoff and Erica Worth Harris, in Chapter 1, present the sceptical case for age discrimination, questioning whether what is typically defined as age discrimination is not really something quite different and primarily based on productivity differences. Like the previous two essays, this essay is also steeped in Lazear's life-cycle wage model, noting, in contrast to the other authors, that the economic vulnerability of late-career workers 'is the norm rather than the exception' (p. 3), which thus poses a restraint on opportunistic discharges. The real focus of concern is how the statute has been transformed into a wrongful discharge statute while providing relatively little protection for the original concern that animated the statute, namely hiring discrimination. Although barriers to entering the workforce were typically seen as the chief concern of the original statute, claims arising under the statute are far more likely to occur after discharge, in part because those claims are often worth considerably more than a hiring claim would be. The authors also explore the role of the main lobbying group for older workers, the American Association of Retired Persons (AARP), a once powerful force for legislation for older individuals.[3] In particular, the group was instrumental in pushing through a series of amendments to the statute that overturned restrictive Supreme Court decisions, ultimately providing a broad range of statutory protections for a large segment of the American workforce. These efforts included ending routine mandatory retirement and the creation of statutory guards for retirement incentive plans, a system that has spawned considerable litigation and helped transform the statute into what the authors label 'a benefits protection regulation for older workers' (p. 40).

Law professor and long-time commentator on the interests of older workers Michael Harper takes a very different approach in Chapter 9. Professor Harper's focus is on the discrepancies that exist in the protections provided to older workers compared to those protected by the statute known as Title VII, which proscribes discrimination based on race, gender, national origin and religion. One important difference between the work of Professor Harper and that of Issacharoff and Worth is the timing of the works, as Professor Harper is writing more than a decade later and documents a decline in the statutory protections afforded older workers as a result of a series of adverse Supreme Court decisions. Older workers are now more limited in the claims that they can bring, and the remedies they are afforded now are likewise weaker than Title VII provides, depending on the nature of the underlying claim. After documenting the disparities in statutory protections, Professor Harper calls for equalizing the legislation through statutory amendments. Additionally, as a way of encouraging employers to hire older workers, Professor Harper proposes a probationary period during which older workers would be unable to sue for age discrimination.

The next two contributions to be discussed seek to provide an empirical foundation to the enduring debates over the age discrimination statute in the United States. Economists are often sceptical of the power of statutory reform, given that making it more expensive to hire workers or more difficult to discharge them may create disincentives to hire workers, a concern that is certainly not unique to issues of age discrimination though the expected decline in productivity that accompanies the ageing process might add an additional rationale for limiting the hiring of older workers. In Chapter 8 Scott Adams and David Neumark present a comprehensive review of the many studies involving the experience of older workers in the American labour market and the related issue of the role age discrimination plays in that experience. The authors conclude that age is taken into account in many employment decisions and that older workers tend to be displaced more frequently and suffer longer bouts of unemployment than their younger counterparts. While it is notoriously difficult to assess the role of discrimination in these labour market effects – given the difficulty of isolating any single cause, including discrimination – the authors find a link between age discrimination and the adverse outcomes older workers encounter, even though some of the studies that rely on worker reports indicate relatively low levels of perceived discrimination. Overall, perhaps the best conclusion from the review is that a finding of prevalent age discrimination is consistent with the data, though it would always be important to qualify this conclusion by noting that the evidence is not overwhelming.

[3] The power of the AARP has waned over the last decade. As discussed by Issacharoff and Worth, the AARP was extremely successful in overturning Supreme Court decisions that were against the interests of older workers. However, as detailed in the essay by Michael Harper (Chapter 9), many recent Supreme Court decisions have largely gone unchallenged in the legislative process, a sign of the declining influence of the AARP.

George Rutherglen, in Chapter 4, takes up a different empirical task by analysing age discrimination litigation. Much of his data is now dated but his conclusions appear to remain sound and certainly have not been contradicted by any other published study. Perhaps the most revealing empirical finding was that most age discrimination plaintiffs are what would be defined as upper-income white men – individuals who lost relatively high-level jobs and who obtain relatively high success in the courts compared to race or gender discrimination plaintiffs. There are likely a couple of reasons for this superior success rate, one of which is the fact that upper-income plaintiffs are more likely to be able to attract quality attorneys because lost income is central to the damage claims of employment discrimination plaintiffs. The other reason is that jurors likely have an easier time identifying with age discrimination plaintiffs since it is a category we will all one day experience, and the fact that so many plaintiffs have lost high-level jobs also likely adds another sympathetic factor given that these are also the kind of jobs to which many jurors would likely aspire. Professor Rutherglen also demonstrates that age discrimination plaintiffs typically recover higher amounts than other discrimination plaintiffs, and he notes that age claims have a stronger resemblance to wrongful discharge claims than other forms of discrimination.

Overall, these works demonstrate that the experience of age discrimination in the United States has been complex but likely holds important lessons for other countries as they move towards a stronger system of protection against age discrimination. This will be particularly true in crafting protections against late-career opportunistic firings and countering the difficulties older workers have entering the workforce, keeping in mind that claims of hiring discrimination are often more difficult to prove since they commonly lack the comparative evidence that can be essential to proving discrimination. But there are other areas in which the American system is unlikely to prove much of a guide – this includes foremost the peculiar American system of at-will employment, which shifts many claims of what would otherwise be wrongful discharge claims into claims of discrimination. The American system of at-will employment allows employers to terminate employees without providing any justification, and the primary limitations on that exercise of an employer's will are the various statutory anti-discrimination protections. This has created a system in which employees who believe their firing was unjust often try to shape their claims as involving issues of discrimination so that they might take advantage of statutory protection. Similarly, the low rate of union presence increases the importance of court litigation, as opposed to the self-administered arbitration systems that characterize union-represented systems. Finally, the American prohibition on mandatory retirement in all but a few industries also makes claims of age discrimination more common and in some ways more difficult than in a system that permits mandatory retirement and provides adequate pensions for retired workers. The American pension system also differs from most other nations in that it is largely private, with some provision for public assistance in the form of social security, and dependent on investment returns to ensure an adequate income for retired workers.

Several of the essays explore the emerging area of age discrimination law in other countries. In many countries, prohibitions against age-based decision-making are relatively new, and generally too new to allow for broad interpretive guidance. This is true with respect to European Union Law, which is guided by a 2000 Directive requiring member states to create legislation designed to combat age discrimination (see Joanna Lahey, Chapter 10 in this volume). By 2007, all member states were in compliance, but decisions interpreting the various legislations are only now beginning to be issued though these early decisions indicate potentially robust protection that borrows freely from the American experience (see Colm O'Cinneide, Chapter 13 in this volume). An important facet of the EU mandate is that age discrimination, unlike other areas within the anti-discrimination arsenal, can be justified if an employer is able to demonstrate that its age restriction is designed to satisfy a 'legitimate aim'. That term, and its interpreting provisions, is considerably broader than the language that arises from the American age discrimination regime and may permit a broader array of age-based employment policies. The EU Directive also permits mandatory retirement while disallowing decisions based on age alone rather than focusing solely on older workers.

During the last decade Australia has been one of the few countries that has had a need for workers not so much because of a shortage of younger workers but due to a growing economy, and the government has been creating incentives to delay retirement and to increase part-time work for older workers. In Chapter 6 Susan Bisom-Rapp, Andrew Frazer and Malcom Sargeant provide a broad overview of the issues facing older workers in Australia, the United Kingdom and the United States, and they highlight the broadening participation of older workers, which they define as aged 55 and older, in Australia. At the same time, they note that older workers typically face significantly longer periods of unemployment. Although age discrimination legislation was implemented in 1993, the Australian law remains relatively underdeveloped given the rarity of court cases and the multiple means of protecting against discrimination on the basis of age, though the law is potentially far reaching, prohibiting compulsory retirement as well as decisions that are the product of indirect discrimination. As a member of the European Union, the United Kingdom has complied with the EU Directive but it also appears to be one of the countries more resistant to addressing discrimination against older workers. The United Kingdom, for example, introduced a default retirement age, which presumed retirement at age 65 but permitted workers to request to continue work, a request the employer was not required to grant (see Claire Kilpatrick, Chapter 14 in this volume). Several court challenges led to disparate rulings under the broad exception for pursuing legitimate aims, but the legislation was ultimately abolished in 2011.

As described by Ryoko Sakuraba in Chapter 12, the Japanese protections against age discrimination are a recent addition to the country's anti-discrimination legislation, taking effect only in 2007. This means that the legislation is too new to know exactly how it will be interpreted but the law was designed to address the pending crisis in the Japanese labour market, which, as in so many countries, is facing a shortage of younger workers in the near future. The problem is particularly acute in Japan given that employment in many sectors has traditionally commenced immediately out of college and lasted throughout one's career, thus leaving little room for older workers who have been displaced or younger workers who might not have followed the traditional path. For this reason, the Japanese legislation prohibits making age-based decisions generally and is not restricted to older workers.

In Chapter 11 Charmaine Spencer and Ann Soden explore the complex Canadian system as it relates to ageing, including the many programmes Canada has established that relate to the health and welfare of older workers. They detail the conditions of the elderly population in Canada, including their pensions, legal services, health care and the status of mandatory retirement, which while banned persists in some occupations where it can be justified as a bona fide occupational requirement. In all, the international essays reveal the relative infancy of most age discrimination regimes, as well as the growing importance of discrimination issues as they relate to older workers.

References

Bewley, T. (1999), *Why Wages Don't Fall During a Recession*, Cambridge, MA: Harvard University Press.

Wirtz, W. Willard (1965), *The Older American Worker: Age Discrimination in Employment, Report of the Secretary of Labor to the Congress under Section 715 of the Civil Rights Act of 1964*, Washington DC: US Department of Labor.

[1]

IS AGE DISCRIMINATION REALLY AGE DISCRIMINATION?: THE ADEA'S UNNATURAL SOLUTION

SAMUEL ISSACHAROFF*
ERICA WORTH HARRIS**

Through a series of reforms over the last two decades, the Age Discrimination in Employment Act (ADEA) has become the most far-reaching of the antidiscrimination statutes. In this Article, Professor Issacharoff and Ms. Harris provide a critical reexamination of both the ADEA itself and, more generally, the use of antidiscrimination law to address the problem of aging in employment. The authors distinguish the disadvantages that older employees face from classic claims of employment discrimination, noting the inapplicability of the antidiscrimination model underlying the ADEA to some of the problems associated with aging in employment. The authors then turn to the development of the ADEA and its amendments, examining the role of regulatory capture in the expansion of ADEA protections. They conclude that the broad use of antidiscrimination law to address the problem of aging in employment without accounting for the differences between classic claims of discrimination and the particular problems faced by older employees has resulted in a dramatic and unjustified shift in wealth toward older Americans. Accordingly, they propose a series of reforms designed to address both the specific problems faced by older employees and the reallocation of wealth imposed by recent ADEA amendments.

INTRODUCTION

The process of aging brings each organism closer to its eventual demise. Among advanced organisms, humans included, adaptation to aging and the approach of death marks a central feature of social organization. Such social responses are as diverse as the organisms that inhabit the planet, although the extremes are fairly recognizable. At one pole, we may identify complex societies, such as those found in parts of Asia, in which the aged are revered and care for the aged forms a central organizing feature of domestic life. At the other ex-

---

* Charles Tilford McCormick Professor of Law, University of Texas. B.A., 1975, State University of New York at Binghamton; J.D., 1983, Yale University.

** Law Clerk to the Honorable Lee Hyman Rosenthal, U.S. District Court for the Southern District of Texas; Olin Fellow and Lecturer in Law, University of Virginia School of Law, 1997-98. B.A., 1993, Rice University; J.D., 1996, University of Texas. The authors thank Cynthia Estlund, Jack Getman, Walter Kamiat, Douglas Laycock, George Loewenstein, Richard Pildes, Rip Verkerke, Finis Welch, and participants at the University of Texas School of Law faculty workshop for helpful suggestions. Chris Hoffman, David Horan, and Bret Tate provided valuable research support, as did David Gunn. The views expressed are those of the authors alone.

treme are societies that treat the invalid or near-invalid elderly as burdens. Aging Eskimos take it upon themselves to end their own lives before becoming a burden upon their young.[1]

Without descending into the anthropological smorgasbord of varying social organizations, we wish to posit a simple hypothesis: Unique among the complex and consuming confrontations with aging and the approach of death stands the legal regime developed in the United States for addressing the problem of aging in the workplace. The American contribution is to fold the question of aging into the undifferentiated welter of antidiscrimination law through the Age Discrimination in Employment Act (ADEA or Act).[2]

The elderly lack the critical features of disadvantaged group status that give some elementary coherence to an antidiscrimination model. Far from being discrete and insular, the elderly represent the normal unfolding of life's processes for all persons. As a group, older Americans do not suffer from poverty or face the disabling social stigmas characteristically borne by black Americans at the start of the civil rights era. Indeed, we shall look to extensive evidence that older Americans are a relatively privileged social group sharing none of the characteristics of groups to which society may owe an ongoing obligation of remediation.

This Article proceeds along several fronts. First, we look at the formal use of antidiscrimination law to address the problem of aging in employment. The ADEA draws its inspiration from the vivid image of hiring signs that limited applicants to those under forty-five, for example. This invocation of "Elders Need Not Apply" allowed the incorporation of many of the statutory mechanisms of Title VII's prohibition on race and sex discrimination. Nonetheless, even the initial proponents of the ADEA acknowledged that the parallels to other antidiscrimination commands were imperfect—a point that apparently has been lost along the evolutionary trail of the ADEA. In order to draw out the unique features of age in the workforce, we conclude Part I by examining the economic structure of career employment. By reviewing the employment "life-cycle," we show both the unique disadvantages that older employees face and the distinction between these disadvantages and classic claims of discrimination in employment.

We next turn to the two central points of our argument. First, the ADEA statutory scheme misconstrues the antidiscrimination model.

1 See Edward M. Weyer, The Eskimos 248 (1932) (discussing means employed by Eskimos to commit suicide). Professor Weyer also reports that this practice is sometimes accelerated by outright geronticide. See id. at 137-39.

2 29 U.S.C. §§ 621-34 (1994).

Antidiscrimination laws have proved most effective at breaking down formal barriers to entry in employment markets. When employers constrict the full range of employees they are willing to consider for hiring, this taste for discrimination imposes costs because employers predictably have to pay higher wages in order to satisfy their demand from a smaller supply of labor. Antidiscrimination laws that break down such inefficient preferences are remarkably successful in promoting rapid integration.[3]

Unfortunately, the source of concern for older employees is overwhelmingly at the tail end of a lifetime of employment, not at the hiring stage. The antidiscrimination model not only does a poor job of explaining the late-career vulnerability of older employees but also understates the prevalence of such vulnerability. At heart, the antidiscrimination model works best when addressing aberrant behavior that departs from rational market commands. By contrast, the economic vulnerability of late-stage career employees is the norm rather than the exception and is made all the more complicated by the clear economic incentives that run counter to the interests of such employees.

This first point leads to the second and no doubt more controversial part of our thesis. The disjunction between the source of employment vulnerability of older employees and the antidiscrimination model underlying the ADEA has had consequences far beyond the theoretical. By unleashing a politically evocative and litigation-tested antidiscrimination law into the arena of the workplace, Congress created an invitation to special interest capture of unjustified wealth. To demonstrate this capture, we make three points. First, we show that the ADEA on its terms failed to alter significantly the difficulties of older employees seeking to enter the workforce. Second, we demonstrate that, particularly after the emergence of the American Association of Retired Persons (AARP) as a powerful lobbying presence, advocates of expansive ADEA remedies essentially abandoned the issue of job acquisition that had been at the heart of the initial passage of the Act. Third, we turn to the amendments of the ADEA in 1986 and 1990 to reveal how the Act became, paradoxically, the most far-reaching of the antidiscrimination statutes. Through a carefully

[3] See James J. Heckman & Brook S. Payner, Determining the Impact of Federal Antidiscrimination Policy on the Economic Status of Blacks: A Study of South Carolina, 79 Am. Econ. Rev. 138, 173-74 (1989) (noting marked increase in number of blacks employed in textile industry in South Carolina after enactment of Title VII); James J. Heckman & J. Hoult Verkerke, Racial Disparity and Employment Discrimination Law: An Economic Perspective, 8 Yale L. & Pol'y Rev. 276, 290 (1990) (noting that enactment of Title VII dramatically expanded pool of available workers in southern textile plants and that "economic incentive for nondiscrimination created a powerful leverage effect for the law").

orchestrated assault on mandatory retirement and targeted employee retirement incentive programs, the AARP-inspired amendments of the ADEA provoked a significant one-time transfer of resources to the generation whose members are currently drawing to the close of their working careers.

The final part of this Article returns to the problem of the actual incentives operating against older workers within individual firms. We propose a system of contract protections and an easing of mandatory retirement to grant some additional opportunity and dignity to older workers. At the same time, we part company with the wealth grabbing components of the recent ADEA amendments. Thus, we argue that employers should be relieved of the obligation to contribute to pension plans for employees beyond the age at which pensions and benefits vest. We will also argue that what are euphemistically termed "negative salary increases" of employees beyond the expected retirement age should not serve as prima facie evidence of employment discrimination but, rather, should be expected as employee tenure advances.

Our goal in this paper is to find a middle ground between the loss of dignity and capture. With an increase in longevity and with the emergence of attachment to work as a central social institution, the portrayal of abrupt and mandatory removal from the workforce as an assault on the dignity of senior employees should come as no surprise. At the same time, the dramatic shift in wealth toward older Americans and the diminished job prospects of the young provoke grave concerns that a misguided antidiscrimination model has allowed a concerted and politically powerful group of Americans to engage in a textbook example of what economists would term "rent seeking."

I
Aging Under Employment Contracts

A. *The Original Understanding*

In 1967, half of all private job openings were barred to applicants over fifty-five, and a quarter to those over forty-five.[4] This "Elders Need Not Apply" attitude was found to be the cause of a growing

[4] See Age Discrimination in Employment: Hearings on H.R. 3651, H.R. 3768, and H.R. 4221 Before the Gen. Subcomm. on Labor of the House Comm. on Educ. and Labor, 90th Cong. 7 (1967) [hereinafter 1967 House Hearings] (statement of W. Willard Wirtz, Secretary of Labor). Some members of Congress had been urging age discrimination legislation since 1951, but Congress did not give the issue serious consideration until 1967. See S. Rep. No. 90-723, at 13 (1967) (individual views of Sen. Jacob V. Javits) (discussing history of efforts to legislate against age discrimination in employment).

problem among America's elderly: long-term unemployment.[5] Relying on a Department of Labor report, Congress found that the burden of unemployment was falling disproportionately on older workers,[6] that employers were operating under mistaken assumptions about the effects of aging,[7] and that age barriers to hiring were the root of the unemployment problem.[8] The Department of Labor's Commissioner on Aging reported that, although older workers were "frequently preferred over the younger"[9] workers when it came to promotions and treatment within the workplace, older *applicants* were treated with disdain.[10] Testimony before Congress condemned this type of age dis-

---

5 See 1967 House Hearings, supra note 4, at 61 (statement of Peter J. Pestillo, Labor Counsel, U.S. Chamber of Commerce) ("In 1965, unemployment for workers under 45 lasted an average of 13.1 weeks. Workers who were over 45, however, remained idle for 19.1 weeks."); id. at 151 (statement of Rep. Joshua Eilberg) (citing unemployment statistics for older workers); id. at 153-54 (statement of William D. Bechill, Commissioner on Aging) (noting problem of long-term unemployment amongst elderly); id. at 422 (statement of Rep. Claude Pepper) (reporting that numerous studies demonstrated problem of long-term unemployment among older workers).

6 See Amendments to the Age Discrimination in Employment Act of 1967: Hearing on H.R. 14879 and H.R. 15342 Before the Subcomm. on Equal Opportunities of the House Comm. on Educ. and Labor, 94th Cong. 40 (1976) (statement of W. Willard Wirtz, Secretary of Labor) (arguing that "[t]he unemployment costs of a distressed economy *must not* be thrown disproportionately on older people").

7 See 1967 House Hearings, supra note 4, at 7 (statement of W. Willard Wirtz, Secretary of Labor) (reporting that large part of age discrimination is due to "a failure on the part of employers to realize how technology and the life sciences have combined to increase the value of older people's work"); id. at 45 (statement of Norman Sprague, Director, Employment and Retirement Program, National Council on the Aging) (relating age discrimination "to the inaccurate views often held concerning the physical abilities, learning capacities, and psychological flexibility of older persons"); id. at 154 (statement of William D. Bechill, Commissioner on Aging) (stating that "stereotyped attitudes about the ability of older people . . . play a major role in barring older workers from fair employment consideration").

8 See id. at 7 (statement of W. Willard Wirtz, Secretary of Labor) (stressing that "it is *opportunity* which people want" and providing examples of older workers who could not find employment); id. at 60 (statement of Peter J. Pestillo, Labor Counsel, U.S. Chamber of Commerce) ("The underlying goal of the proposed legislation is a laudable one: that of opening up greater job opportunities to older people."); id. at 81-82 (statement of Dr. Harold L. Sheppard, Upjohn Institute for Employment Research) (discussing difficulties faced by older workers looking for work); id. at 84 (comments of Rep. John H. Dent) (discussing problem of older workers trying to find reemployment after layoff); id. at 155 (statement of William D. Bechill, Commissioner on Aging) (noting that ADEA would be "effective tool in reducing the incidence of this problem of discriminatory hiring practices based solely on chronological age"); see also United Air Lines, Inc. v. McMann, 434 U.S. 192, 203 n.9 (1977) (citing H.R. Rep. 90-805, at 4 (1967), reprinted in 1967 U.S.C.C.A.N. 2213) (noting primary purpose of ADEA was to promote hiring of older workers).

9 1967 House Hearings, supra note 4, at 154 (statement of William D. Bechill, Commissioner on Aging).

10 See id.

crimination as inhumane,[11] unjust,[12] and cruel.[13] This testimony called for legislation to break down stereotypes used by employers[14] and to open opportunities to older workers.[15] Although there was some variation amongst the proposed bills,[16] there was broad agreement that antidiscrimination legislation was the answer. At its most basic, the argument ran: "[T]o prohibit age discrimination in employment is so plainly and unarguably right, that to belabor it is to dull it, . . . nobody defends such discrimination, and . . . there is general agreement that it ought to be stopped."[17]

Thus, after little debate and even less public attention,[18] Congress passed the Age Discrimination in Employment Act of 1967.[19] Modeled on Title VII of the Civil Rights Act,[20] the ADEA made it illegal for an employer "to fail or refuse to hire or to discharge any individual or otherwise discriminate against any individual with respect to his compensation, terms, conditions, or privileges of employment, because of such individual's age."[21]

From the ADEA's inception, however, an unmistakable current recognized that, despite tracking the statutory form of Title VII, the

[11] See id. at 7 (statement of W. Willard Wirtz, Secretary of Labor) (characterizing problem of age discrimination in employment as "inhuman . . . *bad* business . . . [and] indecent").

[12] See id. at 156 (statement of William D. Bechill, Commissioner on Aging) (urging Congress to combat "arbitrary, unjust discrimination"); id. at 450 (statement of Rep. James A. Burke) (commenting that age discrimination is "unfair and inequitable").

[13] See id. at 9 (statement of W. Willard Wirtz, Secretary of Labor) (quoting President Johnson describing age discrimination as "cruel sacrifice in happiness and well-being"); id. at 404 (statement of Charles Rowan, Chairman, Jobs After 40 Committee, Fraternal Order of Eagles) (stating that "the cruel, senseless discrimination against older people in employment goes on unchecked").

[14] See id. at 155 (statement of William D. Bechill, Commissioner on Aging) (commenting on educational benefits of legislation).

[15] See id. at 60 (statement of Peter J. Pestillo, Labor Counsel, U.S. Chamber of Commerce) (citing opportunity as "underlying goal" of legislation).

[16] See id. at 55-56 (comments of Rep. Roman C. Pucinski) (reviewing proposal that employers be given tax credit for hiring older workers).

[17] Id. at 426 (statement of Francis O'Connell, Legislative Director, Transportation Workers Union); see also id. at 6 (statement of W. Willard Wirtz, Secretary of Labor) (making nearly identical comments).

[18] See Daniel P. O'Meara, Protecting the Growing Number of Older Workers: The Age Discrimination in Employment Act 14 (1989) ("[T]here was no significant opposition to the ADEA in Congress. The popular press paid very little attention to the bill.").

[19] Pub. L. No. 90-202, 81 Stat. 602 (codified as amended at 29 U.S.C. §§ 621-34 (1994)).

[20] See George Rutherglen, From Race to Age: The Expanding Scope of Employment Discrimination Law, 24 J. Legal Stud. 491, 496 (1995) (noting that "the ADEA simply paraphrases the corresponding prohibition in Title VII").

[21] Age Discrimination in Employment Act § 4, 81 Stat. at 603 (codified as amended at 29 U.S.C. § 623(a)(1) (1994)).

Act addressed something other than traditional discrimination.[22] The legislative history reflects Congress's understanding that "age discrimination in employment [is] a complex phenomena [sic] based on many interrelated factors."[23] Unlike the victims of traditional forms of discrimination, aging employees confront a question of "economics; it is not discriminatory or malice [sic], it is simply that it costs more money to employ [older workers]."[24] As one individual explained:

> The problem of age discrimination is a complex one because it is seldom a matter of blind or arbitrary prejudice which often exists for reasons of race, creed, color, national origin, or sex. Age discrimination is a more subtle series of problems based upon a combination of institutional factors and stereotyped thinking.[25]

Because age discrimination was considered to be independent of other forms of discrimination, Congress declined to place enforcement of the Act with the Equal Employment Opportunity Commission (EEOC). As originally codified, the ADEA applied to individuals aged forty to sixty-five[26] and was administered by the Department of Labor.[27]

From the very beginning, the most striking feature of the ADEA as applied, rather than as intended, was the marked disparity between the stated congressional aim of redressing barriers to job acquisition by older employees and the actual effect of the statute. While the Act had an immediate impact on formal barriers to employment, such as maximum age listings for job openings, the removal of these barriers failed to solve, or even reduce, the problem of long-term unemployment.[28] At the 1976 "Impact of the ADEA" hearings, the clear weight of the testimony was that the 1967 Act had no discernible im-

---

22 See Older Workers Benefit Protections Act: Joint Hearing on S. 1511 Before the Subcomm. on Labor of the Comm. on Labor and Human Resources and the Special Comm. on Aging, 101st Cong. 231 (1989) [hereinafter OWBPA Hearings] (statement of Mark S. Dichter, on behalf of the Association of Private Pension and Welfare Plans, U.S. Chamber of Commerce, National Association of Manufacturers, and ERISA Industrial Committee) (noting that in 1967, "Congress understood that age discrimination is by nature different from discrimination on the basis of race or sex").

23 1967 House Hearings, supra note 4, at 5 (comments of Rep. John H. Dent).

24 Id. at 69 (statement of Peter J. Pestillo, U.S. Chamber of Commerce).

25 Id. at 45 (statement of Norman Sprague, Director, Employment and Retirement Program, National Council on Aging).

26 See Age Discrimination in Employment Act § 12, 81 Stat. at 604 (codified as amended at 29 U.S.C. § 631(a) (1994)).

27 See id. § 6, 81 Stat. at 607 (codified as amended at 29 U.S.C. § 632 (1994)).

28 See O'Meara, supra note 18, at 22-23 (citing Bureau of Labor Statistics, U.S. Dep't of Labor, Unemployed Persons by Duration, Sex, Age, Color and Marital Status, Employment and Earnings 25 (1967)) ("The ADEA has ultimately failed at its primary purpose, the reduction of long-term unemployment among older workers.").

pact on the long-term unemployment problem for older employees.[29] Despite the growing number of ADEA suits,[30] long-term unemployment amongst the elderly had in fact increased by 2.8% between 1967 and 1976.[31]

B. The Life-Cycle Model

The ADEA failed in its stated objective because it rested on a misunderstanding of the sources of employment barriers for older workers. Employers' reluctance to hire older workers was not necessarily attributable to an inaccurate assumption of older workers' capabilities based on animus or lack of familiarity with a socially isolated group of potential employees. Rather, the barriers to employment stemmed from an accurate understanding of the relation between wages and age, borne out by the actual workplace experience of employers. That relationship is most accurately depicted by the life-cycle model of career employment.

Although detailed in several other articles (including some written by the authors), a brief overview of this model is necessary to communicate why the ADEA failed to fulfill its initial purpose. With the indulgence of readers already steeped in this literature, an understanding of the relation between pay scales and productivity over the employment career is, we propose, the central explanatory variable in identifying the unique employment hurdles facing older employees.

Employment markets have a unique feature that sets them apart from the neoclassical economic depiction of supply and demand curves dictating price. The typical long-term employment relationship that emerged in the American workplace after World War II featured a steady pattern of wage increases for employees up until the moment of retirement.[32] These wage increases persisted in cases where identifying any increase in productivity was impossible and even in circumstances where one could establish that productivity either leveled off earlier in the employee's career or was actually falling. The life-cycle

---

29 See, e.g., Impact of the Age Discrimination in Employment Act of 1967: Hearings Before the Subcomm. on Retirement Income and Employment of the Select Comm. on Aging, 94th Cong. 5 (1976) [hereinafter Impact Hearings] (statement of Norman Sprague, Director, New Life Institute) (stating that "for workers covered by this Act . . . the employment situation is still not at all good").

30 See id. at 25 (statement of Rep. William Randall) (stating that "backlog" of ADEA cases has increased every year).

31 See Bureau of Labor Statistics, U.S. Dep't of Labor, Unemployment Rate by Sex, Race and Age, 1947-1979 Handbook of Labor Statistics 67 (1980).

32 Although some dispute the effect of inflation on real wage structures, particularly after the 1970s, nominal wages (the actual dollar figure for wages) still follow the pattern of steady increases over time.

model was developed to explain the paradox of what economists would term the absence of wage elasticity or, simply, the failure of wages to fluctuate in response to the actual productivity of employees.[33]

If wages rise without a corresponding increase in productivity, what explains the willingness of employers in the late stages of an employee's career to pay more than the cost of obtaining cheaper substitute labor from a younger employee? In the absence of some external constraint introducing a monopoly-like distortion in the labor market,[34] no employer could pay wages above employee productivity without inviting market challenge from more efficient competitors. So long as one focuses exclusively on wages and productivity at a particular point or even a single day in the career of a senior employee, the

[33] This implicit contract was first described by Edward Lazear. See Edward P. Lazear, Why Is There Mandatory Retirement?, 87 J. Pol. Econ. 1261, 1262 (1979) (developing what is now recognized as the life-cycle model). Lazear's model of life-cycle employment has been generally accepted, receiving much empirical support. See, e.g., Robert Hutchens, Delayed Payment Contracts and a Firm's Propensity to Fire Older Workers, 4 J. Lab. Econ. 439, 440 (1986) (determining that certain jobs for which older workers are employed but not hired have characteristics associated with delayed payment contracts, in accordance with Lazear's life-cycle model); George Loewenstein & Nachum Sicherman, Do Workers Prefer Increasing Wage Profiles?, 9 J. Lab. Econ. 67, 68 (1991) (reporting that even in careers in which "productivity would seem to be relatively static, workers receive wages that rise substantially with tenure") (citing Robert F. Frank & Robert M. Hutchens, Feeling Good vs. Feeling Better: A Life-Cycle Theory of Wages (1988) (unpublished working paper, Cornell University, Department of Economics)); James L. Medoff & Katharine G. Abraham, Are Those Paid More Really More Productive? The Case of Experience, 16 J. Hum. Resources 186, 186 (1981) (summarizing results of empirical study showing that experience cannot adequately explain experience-earnings profile); Jacob Mincer & Boyan Jovanovic, Labor Mobility and Wages, in Studies in Labor Markets 21, 25-28 (Sherwin Rosen ed., 1981) (finding that wages within firm rise relative to alternative opportunities as job seniority increases); see also Stewart J. Schwab, Life-Cycle Justice: Accommodating Just Cause and Employment at Will, 92 Mich. L. Rev. 8, 11 (1993) (using life-cycle employment model to argue that contract protections should be provided for employees at beginning and end of cycle); Michael L. Wachter & George M. Cohen, The Law and Economics of Collective Bargaining: An Introduction and Application to the Problems of Subcontracting, Partial Closure, and Relocation, 136 U. Pa. L. Rev. 1349, 1356-64 (1988) (using life-cycle model of employment to analyze efficiency of internal labor markets). But see J. Hoult Verkerke, An Empirical Perspective on Indefinite Term Employment Contracts: Resolving the Just Cause Debate, 1995 Wis. L. Rev. 837, 912-13 (1995) (arguing that these implicit commitments should not be basis for implied contractual obligations).

[34] This concept is at the heart of the charge that unions inevitably seek monopoly rents by introducing a cartel in the labor market. See Richard A. Posner, Some Economics of Labor Law, 51 U. Chi. L. Rev. 988, 990 (1986) (arguing that "American labor law is best understood as a device for facilitating . . . the cartelization of the labor supply by unions"). This argument is somewhat undercut by matching actual union contracts to the career-wage pattern favored by both employees and many employers. See Richard B. Freeman & James L. Medoff, What Do Unions Do? 9-10 (1984); Paul C. Weiler, Governing the Workplace: The Future of Labor and Employment Law 74-76 (1990).

paradox of apparent overpayment is unresolvable. Shifting the focus to the entire worklife of a career-term employee, however, exposes that wages and marginal productivity are separated not only at the late stages of employment, but throughout a typical employee's career.

An illustration of the career-wage model helps clarify the issue:

Figure 1.

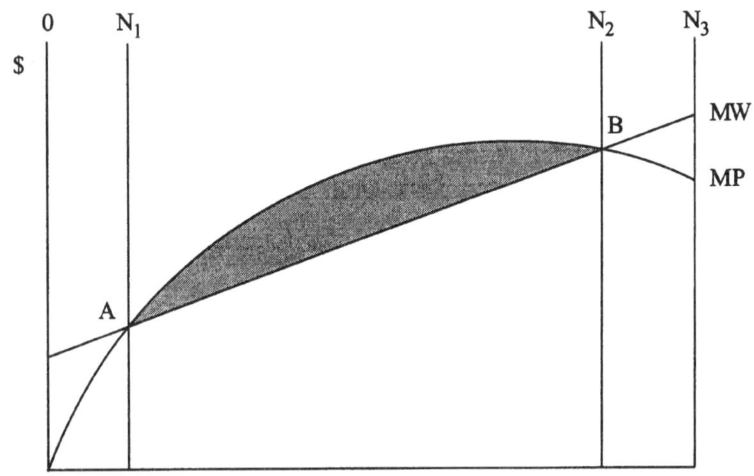

Legend

MW:	Marginal Wage of Employee
MP:	Marginal Product of Employee
Shaded Area:	Period in mid-career where employee's wage is less than employee's marginal productivity
$0–N_1$:	Training Period
$N_1–N_2$:	Mid-Career
$N_2–N_3$:	Later Career
A & B:	Cross Points

In simple economic terms, the model depicts the employee receiving a wage premium during the training stages of employment and again at the end stages of his or her career. During the middle stages, however, the employer is actually paying the employee less than the employee's marginal productivity. Accordingly, in order to ensure an increasing wage structure, employers paid workers more than their worth during the beginning and the ending phases of their careers.[35]

35 See Lazear, supra note 33, at 1264.

They were willing to suffer this loss in exchange for an intermediate period of superprofitability from the employee's services.[36]

This exchange depended on two further steps. First, the employer had to resist the temptation to discharge the employee in the late stages of employment. This discharge would be opportunistic because the employer would have already received the benefits of the bargain during the middle stages of employment. Furthermore, the employee would be in no position to recapture his or her legitimate late-stage compensation from any other employer.

Second, the system of mandatory retirement made the exchange possible by providing the necessary endpoint to the bargain.[37] The mandatory retirement age allowed for a predesignated moment at which the employment relationship could be revisited. In fields characterized by formal tenure, such as academia, this could mean that productive senior faculty would be termed emeritus but would continue teaching or conducting research on shorter-term contracts or grants. Viewed in this way, mandatory retirement provided not so much the compelled endpoint of employment but rather a prearranged point of renegotiation. This prearranged renegotiation provided career employees some security against constant reviews of productivity and some dignitary protection should their skills begin to ebb later in their careers. For employers, mandatory retirement afforded a point at which employees could be reevaluated without imposing the stigma of having been singled out for potential termination as nonperforming individuals. Mandatory retirement also enabled employers to avoid the corresponding costs to overall employee morale if employees were seen to be "picked upon" in their later years.[38] Without a clear termination point, no employer could afford to contract either expressly or implicitly for an open ended escalating wage

36 See id.

37 See id.; see also Samuel Issacharoff, Contractual Liberties in Discriminatory Markets, 70 Tex. L. Rev. 1219, 1248 (1992) (describing mandatory retirement as "integral element of a long-term contractual relationship").

38 One of the consequences of the end of mandatory retirement in academia has been renewed attention to periodic reviews of productivity throughout a professor's career. For example, the Texas A&M Board of Regents directed all 10 schools in the system to draft policies for removal of tenured professors whose annual reviews reflected poor performance. One draft by the Texas A&M University Faculty Senate proposed that professors be given six years to improve their performance before being fired. See A. Phillips Brooks, Tenure, Academia's Inviolable Code, Becomes Legislative Target, Austin Am. Statesman, July 8, 1996, at A1 (discussing allegations that legislative proposal to eliminate tenure would hurt Texas's universities' ability to hire best and brightest faculty); see also Nancy Youssef, U. Va. Wants More Reviews of Tenured Professors, The Virginian-Pilot, Apr. 23, 1995, at B3 (discussing University of Virginia proposal to review tenured professors every six years).

package that was neither tethered to actual productivity nor accompanied by more formal periodic reviews, a point to which we shall return in the concluding section of this Article.

Two alternative explanations illuminate the desirability of the life-cycle arrangement for employers and employees. Most economists who have looked at life-cycle employment emphasize the importance of this arrangement as a check against employee shirking.[39] By having rewards postponed, employees have a large investment in continued employment with the same firm, particularly as the employees age and become less marketable. This investment is particularly valuable in jobs where productivity is hard to measure and shirking is difficult to detect. By introducing an added measure of vulnerability, employees are given a strong disincentive to slack off, even if the actual chance of detection is small. A similar result obtains if the career exchange is examined from a psychological perspective focusing on the satisfaction of the preferences of the contracting parties. From the employee's side, a long-term upward salary trend appears to correspond to strong psychological desires for a sense of improvement over time and for the deferral of rewards—even when the aggregate economic return to the employee is no better than if payment were pegged directly to productivity.[40] There is also a sense of improved overall morale when employees can be retired with a celebratory party rather than at the tail end of a terminal review decision. The life-cycle arrangement thus appears to satisfy the contracting desires of both employers and employees through the major parts of an employee's worklife.

Unfortunately, the life-cycle employment model also illustrates the vulnerability of older employees and explains why employers do not want to hire older workers, independent of any matter of discrimination. An employee in an arrangement that holds out pay in excess of productivity in the later stages of an employee's career faces distinct risks. The primary risk is that an employer under financial stress may come to see an expensive senior employee as an unaffordable luxury, regardless of implicit contractual obligations. Consider, for example, the current age discrimination lawsuit against Westinghouse Electric Corp., an old-time manufacturer that has discovered greener

[39] See, e.g., Lazear, supra note 33, at 1264; Schwab, supra note 33, at 17.

[40] See Loewenstein & Sicherman, supra note 33, at 68. In experimental settings, Professors Loewenstein and Sicherman found that subjects placed in the position of new hires preferred an upwardly sloping wage scale even when clearly confronted with a situation in which the deferral of payment had negative aggregate effects because employees would be foregoing the time value of money paid immediately. See id. at 75.

pastures in its ownership of CBS, Inc.[41] A rather candid memo unearthed during discovery states simply, "In many of our businesses we have an older work force . . . Additionally, our low-growth businesses can strain opportunities for younger workers . . . We have to get the 'blockers' out of the way."[42]

A second risk directly tied to the first is that if an employee were to lose her employment, there would be a strong disincentive to any subsequent employer hiring her. Any new employer hiring a senior employee at her then-current wage scale would be assuming a wage premium for services delivered to another employer.[43] An older employee already at (or near) the end stage of the employment cycle would present an unduly expensive investment for a new employer. The employer would have to invest in firm-specific training of the older worker, the worker would expect a high wage, and the older employee might be retiring within a few years. For an employer to hire an older employee at the wage such an employee would normally command within the firm's employment scale simply would be economically irrational. Further, because a reduction in pay to a level approximating productivity would appear to be a dignitary affront to the employee and would be potentially disruptive within the firm, the life-cycle wage pattern has the predictable effect of freezing unemployed older workers out of the job market altogether.

Thus, the 1967 Act, which set its sights on express age discrimination in hiring, was insufficient to solve the problem of long-term unemployment. The "No Elders Need Apply" signs came down, but the reluctance to hire older workers remained.

---

41 See Paulette Thomas, Restructurings Generate Rash of Age-Bias Suits, Wall St. J., Aug. 29, 1996, at B1.

42 Id. (alteration in original).

43 An interesting example comes with demands for long-term contracts in professional sports. At their peak, sports stars routinely seek long-term contracts to protect against the risk of injury and to continue compensation even as their skills begin to decline. Teams, particularly those operating under salary caps, are quite eager to defer payment. For example, teams that want to keep their stars often give them the long-term contracts they demand but use a variety of methods including signing bonuses and structured payouts to insure that they will have room under the cap in the future. See Andrew E. Serwer, How High?, Sports Illustrated, Nov. 8, 1993, at 88, 88 (reporting terms of NBA forward Larry Johnson's 12-year, $84 million contract with Charlotte Hornets). These long-term obligations become an issue when teams attempt to trade aging stars. The result is that younger players with shorter-term contracts are more marketable than older players with several years left on sizeable contracts. See Clifton Brown, Davis Traded by Knicks to Raptors for '97 Pick, N.Y. Times, July 25, 1996, at B13 (reporting efforts of Knicks to trade excess shooting guard and ability to trade Hubert Davis with one remaining contract year rather than John Starks with four remaining contract years).

C. *The ADEA Plaintiff*

In 1967, Congress had a clear image of whom it sought to protect. The ADEA was for a common man, not old, but older, with gray at his temples and a few lines on his face, with years of experience in his field, who, upon reading the classifieds, found several jobs for which he was qualified but for which applications from those over forty were not accepted.

The actual ADEA plaintiff, however, has turned out to be radically different. Rather than challenging barriers to job seeking, the typical litigant is concerned about holding onto a job he or she already has.[44] Empirical studies of ADEA litigation show that 76% of ADEA cases involve employee termination, while only 9% involve a refusal to hire claim.[45] Other actions involve failure to promote (6.6%), demotion (6.3%), and compensation and benefits (1.9%).[46] The numbers are in complete conflict with what had been predicted by the original legislators and are inconsistent with the original intent of the ADEA. This trend was accentuated in 1986 with the amendment of the ADEA to forbid mandatory retirement for all but a small number of employees.[47] Without a natural termination point for long-term employment relations, employers faced increasing competitive pressures to remove older employees from their payrolls, which in turn prompted more ADEA litigation.

Once again, an understanding of the life-cycle model of employment could have predicted the outcome. Because older employees are being paid more than their marginal productivity at the end of the

---

44 See John J. Donohue III & Peter Siegelman, The Changing Nature of Employment Discrimination Litigation, 43 Stan. L. Rev. 983, 984 (1991) ("Although the authors and early architects of employment discrimination laws envisioned them as tools for opening employment opportunities to blacks, women, and other minorities, this is no longer their primary use. Instead, the antidiscrimination laws are predominantly used to protect the existing positions of incumbent workers."); Rutherglen, supra note 20, at 495 ("[M]ost claims of employment discrimination are now claims of discriminatory discharge. Litigation under the ADEA, which concerns such claims almost exclusively, exemplifies this trend in its most extreme form.").

45 See Michael Schuster & Christopher S. Miller, An Empirical Assessment of the Age Discrimination in Employment Act, 38 Indus. & Lab. Rel. Rev. 64, 64 (1984).

46 See Cathie A. Shattuck, ADEA Litigation Survey (1983), reprinted in Recipients of ADEA Settlements Are Mostly Long-Term Male Employees, 7 Daily Lab. Rep. (BNA) A-3 (Jan. 12, 1984); see also Billie Brandon & Robert A. Snyder, ADEA Update: Case Law And "Cost" as a Defense, Personnel Admin., Feb. 1985, at 116, 117-18 (finding similar results: termination – 73% (discharge – 56% and involuntary retirement – 17%); refusal to hire – 7%; failure to promote – 8%; demotion – 5%; involuntary transfer – 2%; employment conditions – 5%).

47 Age Discrimination in Employment Amendments of 1986, Pub. L. No. 99-592, § 2, 100 Stat. 3342, 3342 (1986) (codified as amended at 29 U.S.C. § 623 (1994)).

life cycle, they are at risk for opportunistic firings by their employer.[48] Having enjoyed the period of superprofitability during the intermediate phase of employment, an unscrupulous employer could fire an older worker in the final stage and, in essence, cut off a clear liability.[49] Traditionally, employers refrained from this opportunistic behavior because of the adverse impact on employee morale and the firm's reputation;[50] encouraging highly productive midstage employees to stay with the firm would be difficult if they observed widespread termination of employees at the next stage of employment.[51] Nonetheless, competitive pressures for downsizing in the 1980s and an increase in global competition provided sufficient incentive for employers to engage in such opportunistic breaches of long-term contract obligations.[52] The temptation to discharge long-term employees was compounded by the mergers and acquisitions boom of the 1980s as the management that inherited the obligations to long-term employees viewed itself as divorced from, and consequently not subject to the

[48] See Christine Jolls, Hands-Tying and the Age Discrimination in Employment Act, 74 Tex. L. Rev. 1813, 1821, 1830 (1996) (describing cost-based decisionmaking phenomenon at later stages of employment); Schwab, supra note 33, at 19 (noting that late-stage employees are paid more than they produce and become vulnerable to opportunistic firing).

[49] Richard Posner uncharacteristically misses this point in his insightful work on the effects of aging. He dismisses arguments in favor of the ADEA by claiming that "employers have their own incentives, unrelated to law, to avoid firing competent employees of any age, even if replacements are available. The employer has invested in the employee, and if the employee is still productive the employer is continuing to earn a return on the investment." Richard A. Posner, Aging and Old Age 334 (1995). Posner errs by confusing the concept of "productivity" with "profitability," the latter being adversely affected by the upward slope of the career-wage trajectory. As Christine Jolls clearly expresses, "[w]hen wages rise above marginal revenue product . . . the individual is no longer profitable, though from the employee's standpoint the high wages are simply restitution for low wages earned early on." Jolls, supra note 48, at 1821.

[50] The importance of reputation is summarized as follows: "[I]n the absence of an explicit contract, applicants will seek information from other workers about the employer's past performance. Applicants are obliged to judge the employer, in part, by reputation." Arthur M. Okun, Prices and Quantities: A Macroeconomic Analysis 51 (1981); see also Oliver E. Williamson, The Economic Institutions of Capitalism 259-61 (1985); Bengt Holmstrom, Contractual Models of the Labor Market, 7 Am. Econ. Rev. 308, 311-13 (1981).

[51] For an example of a defense of employment at will on the grounds that reputational interests of employers make cheating unlikely, see generally Richard A. Epstein, In Defense of the Contract at Will, 51 U. Chi. L. Rev. 947 (1984).

[52] For arguments that the reputational interests of employers are insufficient to overcome the temptation of opportunistic discharges, see Freeman & Medoff, supra note 34, at 9-10; Walter Kamiat, Labor and Lemons: Efficient Norms in the Internal Labor Market and the Possible Failures of Individual Contracting, 144 U. Pa. L. Rev. 1953, 1970 n.27 (1996); Schwab, supra note 33, at 26-27; Weiler, supra note 34, at 74-76. For a defense of the ADEA as a prohibition on such opportunistic discharges, see Jolls, supra note 48, at 1829-40.

obligations of, the management that had enjoyed the peak years of productivity of these same employees.

Moreover, the end-stage employees have the greatest incentive to bring suit. First, an opportunistic firing renders such individuals essentially unemployable because no other employer would assume the burden of the high-wage, late-stage employee. Second, "[a]n individual who is not hired will rarely build up the bitterness and hostility toward the prospective employer that is necessary to carry a suit through to trial."[53] Potential plaintiffs in discharge cases are far more likely to find lawyers since potential damages are higher than in refusal-to-hire cases.[54] Finally, refusal-to-hire cases are much more difficult to prove where the number of applicants outnumbers positions available and where many factors unknown to the potential litigant could have been taken into consideration. In contrast, a terminated employee has nothing to fear from and plenty of animosity toward his former employer, has a significant amount of damages, and can more readily build a case of discrimination.[55] Thus, the empirical evidence is hardly counterintuitive.

Those studies also reveal another interesting development in ADEA cases: Plaintiffs are mostly older white male professionals. Almost 86% of ADEA plaintiffs are male.[56] This discrepancy may be due to the greater number of males in the workforce, the greater likelihood that men have pushed through to the end stage of career-term employment,[57] or the ability of female plaintiffs to seek relief under alternative statutes. Regardless, the trend is notable. Moreover, more than 79% of plaintiffs are white-collar employees.[58] This overrepresentation may be a statistical artifact as well, reflecting the fact that employees in blue-collar employment are subject to greater physical strain and tend to be forced into retirement earlier;[59] again, however, the trend must be noted. Although the race of plaintiffs is not often reported, from the cases that do provide a description of the plaintiffs, apparently a disproportionately large number of ADEA

53 O'Meara, supra note 18, at 27.

54 See Posner, supra note 49, at 329 (arguing that monetary amounts and chances of winning are higher in discharge cases).

55 See O'Meara, supra note 18, at 27-28.

56 See Brandon & Snyder, supra note 46, at 41; Shattuck, supra note 46, at A-3.

57 For a discussion of the interruption in career-term employment caused by childbirth and childrearing by women, see generally Samuel Issacharoff & Elyse Rosenblum, Women and the Workplace: Accommodating the Demands of Pregnancy, 94 Colum. L. Rev. 2154 (1994).

58 See Shattuck, supra note 46, at A-3.

59 This proposition is advanced in Posner, supra note 49, at 344.

plaintiffs are white.[60] Finally, the majority of plaintiffs, 55%, are between fifty and fifty-nine years old.[61] Only 27% are over sixty and 18% are in the forty to forty-nine age bracket.[62]

This profile of both the typical ADEA plaintiff and the subject of litigation suggests that the ADEA has developed into a wrongful termination cause of action for employees entering the final stage of employment rather than the protection against categorical action based on the sort of invidious motivation generally associated with the term "discrimination" and originally envisioned by Congress.[63] Several commentators have noted that the ADEA has become "a wrongful discharge statue for white male professionals and managers."[64] Again, this evolution is not surprising. As discussed above, under the life-cycle contract, employers pay employees more than they are worth at the end of their life-cycle. At that stage, employers have a financial incentive to fire the older worker.[65] Without mandatory retirement, those financial incentives have increased exponentially. Because there is no universal protection against wrongful discharge in this country, older white male workers are turning to the one piece of legislation that protects them—the ADEA.[66]

60 See Schuster & Miller, supra note 45, at 68 (inferring from infrequency of reported decisions mentioning plaintiff's race that most are white); see also Rutherglen, supra note 20, at 496 (providing data showing that large majority of ADEA plaintiffs are white).

61 See Schuster & Miller, supra note 45, at 68; see also Shattuck, supra note 46, at A-3.

62 See Schuster & Miller, supra note 45, at 68.

63 We leave aside discussion of the apparently rising "contingent workforce" of individuals holding multiple part-time jobs, itinerant positions, or other employment lacking any prospect of lifetime tenure with one employer. See Richard S. Belous, The Rise of the Contingent Work Force: The Key Challenges and Opportunities, 52 Wash. & Lee L. Rev. 863, 868 (1995) (documenting sizable growth of temporary, part-time business service, and self-employed workers between 1980 and 1993, and estimating that 25-30% of workforce employed in contingent, nonpermanent jobs); Jonathan P. Hiatt, Policy Issues Concerning the Contingent Work Force, 52 Wash. & Lee L. Rev. 739, 743-53 (1995) (advocating broad-scale legal regulation of contingent employment market); Maria O'Brien Hylton, The Case Against Regulating the Market for Contingent Employment, 52 Wash. & Lee L. Rev. 849, 862 (1995) (arguing that regulation of contingent workforce is likely to be counterproductive due to little indication that regulation will cause incorporation of contingent workers into core workforce). The demographic profile of the ADEA shows that such employees are as unlikely to bring claims under the ADEA as they are under common law wrongful discharge laws. See O'Meara, supra note 18, at 25-26.

64 O'Meara, supra note 18, at 48; see also Jolls, supra note 48, at 1829-40 (justifying ADEA as protection against late-career opportunism); Rutherglen, supra note 20, at 496 (noting that justifications for the ADEA "have a surprising resemblance to the justification for recognizing claims for wrongful discharge").

65 See Schwab, supra note 33, at 43.

66 See id. ("At the end of their lifecycle, they often earn more than their current productivity. If they do, the employer has a financial incentive to terminate them .... The Age Discrimination in Employment Act provides one check against late-career opportunism."); see also Cynthia L. Estlund, Wrongful Discharge Protections in an At-Will World,

To the extent that the ADEA turned out to provide protection against terminations (be they discriminatory, arbitrary, or perhaps just undesired) rather than discriminatory refusals to hire, the Act foreshadowed the development of other antidiscrimination laws. The profile of cases litigated under Title VII reveals that the antidiscrimination laws are increasingly used to "protect the existing positions of incumbent workers."[67] Thus, the most comprehensive study of antidiscrimination litigation concludes that, "[w]hile most [Title VII] cases formerly attacked discrimination in hiring, today the vast majority of all litigation suits challenge discrimination in discharge."[68] Nonetheless, the ADEA stands apart in offering protection based on a category that does not correspond to the traditional indicia of discriminatory victimization.

D. *Antidiscrimination with a Difference*

In *Furnco Construction Corp. v. Waters*,[69] then-Justice Rehnquist articulated the justification for the relaxed use of presumptions of discrimination in favor of black plaintiffs:

> A prima facie case . . . raises an inference of discrimination only because we presume these acts, if otherwise unexplained, are more likely than not based on the consideration of impermissible factors. And we are willing to presume this largely because we know from our experience that more often than not people do not act in a totally arbitrary manner, without any underlying reasons, especially in a business setting. Thus . . . it is more likely than not the employer, whom we generally assume acts only with *some* reason, based his decision on an impermissible consideration such as race.[70]

Justice Rehnquist's attention in *Furnco* focused on the shifting of the burden of production upon a relatively minimal plaintiffs' showing, which is known as the *McDonnell Douglas* approach in Title VII law.[71] While the *Furnco* rationale may hold in the context of race or

74 Tex. L. Rev. 1655, 1671-74 (1996) (describing pressure on antidiscrimination statutes from discharged employees lacking other means of redress).

67 Donohue & Siegelman, supra note 44, at 984.

68 Id.

69 438 U.S. 567 (1978).

70 Id. at 577 (citation omitted).

71 See McDonnell Douglas Corp. v. Green, 411 U.S. 792, 802-03 (1973) (setting forth burden shifting under Title VII disparate treatment claims). But see St. Mary's Honor Ctr. v. Hicks, 509 U.S. 502, 506-12 (1993) (restricting *McDonnell Douglas* burden shifting by forcing plaintiff to prove ultimate issue of discriminatory treatment even where defendant has failed to discharge intermediate burden of production); Deborah C. Malamud, The Last Minuet: Disparate Treatment After *Hicks*, 93 Mich. L. Rev. 2229, 2232-35 (1995) (describing shift in *Hicks*).

even sex, it fails to justify a presumption of age discrimination.[72] First, and most simply, the ADEA is not concerned with a constitutionally protected class. Unlike race and sex,[73] age is not a suspect classification and no credible claim has ever been made that older Americans are subject to arbitrary state laws inspired purely by animus.[74] In *Massachusetts Board of Retirement v. Murgia*,[75] the Supreme Court explained that "old age does not define a 'discrete and insular' group . . . in need of 'extraordinary protection from the majoritarian political process.' Instead, it marks a stage that each of us will reach if we live out our normal span."[76] As summarized by Professor Rutherglen, the ADEA "cannot be justified in terms of opening opportunities to a historically disfavored group."[77]

Second, in age cases, as opposed to racial discrimination claims, the alternative explanation is everpresent. In simple doctrinal terms, courts have been forced to recognize that cost-based discrimination

---

72 Almost immediately after the decision in *Furnco*, courts began to question the applicability of a strict *McDonnell Douglas* test to age discrimination cases. As expressed by the Sixth Circuit, "[t]his factor of progression and replacement is not necessarily involved in cases involving the immutable characteristics of race, sex, and national origin. . . . Thus we do not believe that Congress intended automatic presumptions to apply whenever a worker is replaced by another of a different age." Laugesen v. Anaconda Co., 510 F.2d 307, 313 n.4 (6th Cir. 1975); see also Kelly v. American Standard, Inc., 640 F.2d 974, 980 (9th Cir. 1981) (holding that replacement of older employee by younger employee does not raise same presumption of discrimination as replacement of black employee by white employee). As a general matter courts developed a more demanding application of evidentiary presumptions in age cases. The resulting standard requires a plaintiff to establish a "nexus" that directly ties the age of the complainant to the complained of conduct, rather than a mere showing that an employee from a protected class was displaced. See Lovelace v. Sherwin-Williams Co., 681 F.2d 230, 238-41 (4th Cir. 1982) (developing nexus test). In O'Connor v. Consolidated Coin Caterers Corp., 116 S. Ct. 1307 (1996), the Supreme Court recently ruled that in order to establish a prima facie case, an ADEA plaintiff alleging unlawful discharge could not satisfy his prima facie burden merely by showing that he was replaced by an employee under 40. See id. at 1310. For example, a displaced 40-year-old employee could not satisfy his initial burden by showing that he was replaced by a 39-year-old from outside the protected class. Rather, the ADEA plaintiff must show that his replacement is "substantially younger." This holding contrasts with the *McDonnell Douglas* regime in place for other discrimination claims requiring proof that a discharged employee was replaced by someone from outside the protected class.

73 See, e.g., United States v. Virginia, 44 F.3d 1229, 1235 (4th Cir. 1995) (noting that classifications based on gender are held to heightened level of scrutiny).

74 This concept of state action that is comprehensible only on the grounds of class-based animus was the rationale by which the Supreme Court struck down a Colorado constitutional amendment limiting conferral of legal benefits to homosexuals. See Romer v. Evans, 116 S. Ct. 1620, 1623 (1996). The Court did so despite the fact that homosexuals as such do not enjoy constitutional protection as a discrete and insular group. See generally Bowers v. Hardwick, 478 U.S. 126 (1986).

75 427 U.S. 307 (1976) (per curiam).

76 Id. at 313-14 (citation omitted).

77 Rutherglen, supra note 20, at 521.

may serve as a defense to an age-based classification in circumstances in which comparable defenses would be unavailing were the challenged classification to be triggered by race or sex. For example, several courts have held that a legitimate business reason or economic purpose could justify a differentiation in benefits based on age.[78] The question of the relation between age and seniority-sensitive employee rights came to the fore in *Hazen Paper Co. v. Biggins*,[79] in which the Supreme Court ruled that "there is no disparate treatment under the ADEA when the factor motivating the employer is some feature other than the employee's age"[80]—even if that feature happens to correlate with age. *Hazen* seemed to doom attempts to prove a prima facie case of age discrimination by showing that employer reliance upon a proxy for age—such as seniority, income level, or pension status—was sufficient to establish the discriminatory intent necessary for liability under the Act.[81]

This result in turn exposes the paradox of the ADEA. Concern about employer opportunism against older employees is well founded. As demonstrated by the life-cycle model, employers have a significant incentive to breach their part of the implicit bargain. Having enjoyed the period of superprofits during the middle stages of employee careers, employers in economic straits may seek to evade the obligations that underlie the career-wage relationship. By providing older employees a legal remedy for an opportunistic breach, the ADEA has been recast from a statute providing access to the workplace for older Americans into the most dramatically far reaching of the antidis-

[78] See, e.g., Potenze v. New York Shipping Ass'n, 804 F.2d 235, 238 (2d Cir. 1986) (ruling that plan that offset Social Security benefits for those workers over 65 choosing to participate in employee retirement incentive program (ERIP) was not subterfuge because plan was justified by legitimate business reasons); Cipriano v. Board of Educ., 785 F.2d 51, 57-58 (2d Cir. 1986) (reasoning that ERIP with age ceiling would not constitute subterfuge to avoid ADEA if employer could provide legitimate reason for excluding workers over 60 from participating); Crosland v. Charlotte Eye, Ear & Throat Hosp., 686 F.2d 208, 215 (4th Cir. 1982) (holding that provision excluding workers over 55 from pension plan was not illegal if "the provision was motivated by a legitimate business or economic purpose which, objectively assessed, reasonably justified it"); see also 29 U.S.C. § 623(f)(2)(B) (1994) (allowing age-based discrimination when observing terms of bona fide employee benefit plan).

[79] 507 U.S. 604 (1993).

[80] Id. at 609.

[81] For an excellent discussion of the tension in ADEA law after *Hazen*, see Robert J. Gregory, There is Life in That Old (I Mean, More "Senior") Dog Yet: The Age-Proxy Theory After *Hazen Paper Co. v. Biggins*, 11 Hofstra Lab. L.J. 391, 427 (1994) (arguing that many ADEA claims cannot survive unless plaintiffs can rely on proxy theory to "challenge employment criteria that can readily mask age discrimination").

crimination statutes.[82] As a result, ADEA claims in the federal courts are mushrooming. In 1988, they accounted for more than 25% of the work of the EEOC, and between 1989 and 1993 the number of claims filed with the EEOC jumped 34%.[83]

While the ADEA may indeed serve the purpose of providing legal redress to one sector of the older workforce, whether antidiscrimination legislation is the proper vehicle for redressing this concern remains unclear. If the source of the risk to older workers is economics, in general, and opportunistic breaches, in particular, a real question emerges as to why this problem should be folded into the antidiscrimination rubric. Professor Jolls defends the Act as "handstying" by which employers are deterred from cheating on their implied contractual obligations.[84] Not only is this explanation a rather significant departure from the original stated purpose of the Act, but it constitutes a peculiar use of the antidiscrimination model. Protection of long-term employees could be accomplished by recognizing the important role of common law actions, as described by Professor Schwab;[85] by relaxing the at-will presumption found in the common law, as proposed by Professors Estlund[86] and Kamiat;[87] by creating a statutory abrogation of employment at will, as has already been done in Montana;[88] by creating compulsory arbitration over the termination

[82] See OWBPA Hearings, supra note 22, at 420 (introductory remarks of Sen. Metzenbaum) (describing reformed ADEA as "this Nation's fundamental civil rights law safeguarding older Americans in the workplace").

[83] See Posner, supra note 49, at 330 (citing EEOC reports); Bimal Patel & Brian H. Kleiner, New Developments in Age Discrimination, 45 Lab. L.J. 709, 712 (1994) (reviewing EEOC filing data from 1989-1993, originally compiled in Sara Marley, Age-Related Suits Increase, Bus. Ins., Jan. 17, 1994, at 1, 1); Rutherglen, supra note 20, at 507-08 (producing tables recording charges filed with EEOC); see also Jolls, supra note 48, at 1814 (reviewing data).

[84] Jolls, supra note 48, at 1829. Professor Jolls, however, seems to accept the view that "the ADEA cannot be justified on traditional distributive or rights-based grounds." Id. at 1814.

[85] See Schwab, supra note 33, at 43-47; Stewart J. Schwab, Wrongful Discharge Law and the Search for Third-Party Effects, 74 Tex. L. Rev. 1943, 1943-47 (1996) (noting that most states, with the "notable exception of New York," recognize the tort of wrongful discharge if the discharge violated public policy and arguing that analyzing third-party effects is the appropriate method for defining public policy); see also Mark P. Gergen, A Grudging Defense of the Role of the Collateral Torts in Wrongful Termination Litigation, 74 Tex. L. Rev. 1693, 1693 (1996) (defending employees' use of collateral torts such as intentional infliction of emotional distress and defamation on grounds that courts are capable of screening out nonmeritorious claims).

[86] See Estlund, supra note 66, at 1657 (arguing that at-will presumption undermines effectiveness of wrongful discharge law and frustrates important policy objectives).

[87] See Kamiat, supra note 52, at 1957-68 (suggesting that bargaining impediments between employers and individual employees show current contractual model is "broken").

[88] See Wrongful Discharge From Employment Act, Mont. Code Ann. §§ 39-2-901 to 2-915 (1995).

of long-term employees, as proposed by the Model Employment Termination Act;[89] or by establishing administrative mechanisms to deter employer misconduct.[90] Using the ADEA to substitute for a "for cause" rule of employment law provides only patchwork protection to a handful of successful plaintiffs. Additionally, those few plaintiffs who do succeed tend to be drawn disproportionately from the ranks of the most privileged employees.

Furthermore, the expense of this solution may very well overwhelm any stopgap protection that is obtained. The 1984 transfer of enforcement power over the ADEA from the Department of Labor to the EEOC[91] should not obscure the significant advantages available to ADEA plaintiffs over other antidiscrimination complainants. Unlike pre-1991 Title VII plaintiffs, ADEA plaintiffs received the right to jury trials and liquidated damages.[92] Although these changes were hardly noticed at the congressional hearings, they proved to be highly significant in the subsequent onslaught of litigation. The ADEA emerged as the most potent of the antidiscrimination statutes with remedies that included injunctive relief,[93] reinstatement,[94] front pay,[95] and reasonable costs and attorneys' fees.[96] Moreover, unlike the pre-1991 version of Title VII, the ADEA's right to back pay is not discre-

[89] See Model Employment Termination Act § 6, 7A U.L.A. 89-90 (Supp. 1996), reprinted in 9A Lab. Rel. Rep. (BNA) § 540:21, at 37-38 (1991). See generally Theodore J. St. Antoine, The Making of the Model Employment Termination Act, 69 Wash. L. Rev. 361, 376-79 (1994) (reporter for Acts Drafting Committee discussing rationale for Act's preference for arbitration as means of enforcement).

[90] See Samuel Issacharoff, Contracting for Employment: The Limited Return of the Common Law, 74 Tex. L. Rev. 1783, 1806-11 (1996) (proposing no-fault severance administrative model).

[91] See O'Meara, supra note 18, at 248-51.

[92] See 29 U.S.C. § 626(c)(2) (1994) (jury trials); 29 U.S.C. § 626(b) (1994) (liquidated damages); Rutherglen, supra note 20, at 496 (noting ADEA "allowed for the right to jury trial and for liquidated damages—procedures that were not available under Title VII as originally enacted"); see also T. Mark Sandifer, Casenote, No Exclusion for ADEA Claims Under I.R.C. § 104(a)(2): An Analysis of *Commissioner v. Schleier*, 47 Mercer L. Rev. 637, 640 (1996) ("[U]nlike the pre-1991 version of Title VII, the ADEA provides for jury trials and liquidated damages.").

[93] See 29 U.S.C. §§ 217, 626(b) (1994); see also Farkas v. New York State Dep't of Health, 554 F. Supp. 24, 28-29 (N.D.N.Y. 1982) (finding plaintiff met test for granting preliminary injunction because he made prima facie showing of age discrimination); Cannister v. FAA, 24 FEP Cases 1621 (D.D.C. 1979) (restraining employer from transferring employees).

[94] See 29 U.S.C. § 626(b) (1994).

[95] See, e.g., O'Donnell v. Georgia Osteopathic Hosp., 748 F.2d 1543, 1551 (11th Cir. 1984) (noting that "front pay is an available remedy under the ADEA"); EEOC v. Prudential Fed. Sav. & Loan Ass'n, 741 F.2d 1225, 1232 (10th Cir. 1984) (recognizing future damages), vacated on other grounds, 469 U.S. 1154 (1985); Cancellier v. Federated Dep't Stores, 672 F.2d 1312, 1319 (9th Cir. 1982) (same).

[96] See 29 U.S.C. §§ 216(b), 626(b) (1994).

tionary, it is a matter of right.[97] Liquidated damages provide double recoveries where the employer committed a willful violation of the statute,[98] and awards of back pay include damages for lost wages, pension benefits, insurance benefits, profit sharing benefits, and accrued sick leave.[99]

More critically, the relaxed reliance on the antidiscrimination model as a panacea for all employment problems served as an invitation to other forms of opportunistic behavior—this time by the beneficiaries of the ADEA statutory scheme.

II
Reforms and Capture

A. *The Emergence of an Interest Group Strategy*

The ADEA has had a long and complex history. Since 1967, there have been several series of initiatives, some successful, some not. The first significant amendment to the Act came as Congress began to examine seriously the condition of an aging workforce. In the early 1970s, Congress not only approved significant increases in Social Security benefits[100] and passed the Employee Retirement Income Security Act of 1974,[101] but also extended the ADEA to cover employees of federal and state governments.[102] By 1976, the Gray Lobby and its allies in Congress moved to eliminate the age cap of the ADEA altogether in both the public and private sectors.[103] In fact, one group wanted not only the end of mandatory retirement, but also affirmative action programs "comparable to those contained in Title VII."[104] More moderate proposals simply would have raised the statutory age

97 See Maureen E. McClain, Litigating an Age Discrimination Case: Special Litigation Problems and Techniques, in Advanced Strategies in Employment Law, 439, 451 (PLI Litig. & Admin. Practice Course Handbook Series No. 342, 1987) (citing Lorillard v. Pons, 434 U.S. 575 (1978)).

98 See 29 U.S.C. §§ 216(b), 626(b) (1994).

99 See Barbara L. Schlei & Paul Grossman, Employment Discrimination Law 522-23 nn.215-19 (2d ed. 1983).

100 See Michael D. Hurd, Research on the Elderly: Economic Status, Retirement, and Consumption and Saving, 28 J. of Econ. Lit. 565, 590 (1990) (projecting values of 1968, 1970, 1971, and 1972 changes in Social Security benefit schedule to represent 72% increase).

101 Pub. Law No. 93-406, 88 Stat. 829 (codified as amended at 29 U.S.C. §§ 1001-1461 (1994)).

102 See Joseph E. Kalet, Age Discrimination in Employment Law 3 (1986).

103 See Amendments to the Age Discrimination in Employment Act of 1967: Hearings on H.R. 65 and H.R. 1115 Before the Subcomm. on Employment Opportunities of the Comm. on Educ. and Labor, 95th Cong. 7 (1977) [hereinafter 1977 House Hearings] (statement of Rep. Claude Pepper) (introducing his bill, H.R. 65, which would prohibit discrimination on basis of age in both public and private employment).

104 1967 House Hearings, supra note 4, at 185.

cap from sixty-five to seventy,[105] a position that finally won out in the 1978 amendments to the Act.[106] In 1984, Congress transferred enforcement to the EEOC,[107] the enforcement agency for Title VII legislation, and held additional hearings on eliminating the age cap for private sector employees.[108] In 1986, these objectives were realized as all workers over the age of forty were brought under the statutory umbrella and, notably, virtually all mandatory retirement was eliminated.[109] Finally, in 1990, Congress passed the Older Workers Benefits Protection Act (OWBPA),[110] a far ranging statute prohibiting the use of many targeted retirement inducement programs, the implications of which we will discuss below.[111]

These amendments to the ADEA did not occur in a vacuum. Over the same twenty-five-year period, the number of older Americans increased,[112] their percentage of the national wealth soared,[113] and they brought a steadily increasing number of cases under the ADEA.[114] Interestingly, there is a stunning mismatch between the expansion of ADEA litigation and the dramatic improvement in the economic status of the elderly. For example, between 1970 and 1984, the median real income of households comprised of persons over sixty-five rose by 35%, compared to less than 1% for those comprised

---

105 See S. Rep. No. 95-493, at 31 (1977), reprinted in 1978 U.S.C.C.A.N. 504, 525 (additional views of Sen. Jacob K. Javits) (describing proposal to raise age cap to 70 as "the more conservative position").

106 See Age Discrimination in Employment Act Amendments of 1978, Pub. L. No. 95-256, § 3, 92 Stat. 189 (codified as amended at 29 U.S.C. § 631(a) (1994)).

107 The transfer was originally effected in 1978 pursuant to Reorganization Plan No. 1, which was authorized by the Reorganization Act of 1977, Pub. L. No. 95-17, 91 Stat. 29 (1977) (codified as amended at 5 U.S.C. §§ 901-12 (1994)). However, because of an unusual procedural mechanism that was subsequently determined to be unconstitutional, Congress had to reaffirm the transfer in a separate bill. See Act of Oct. 19, 1984, Pub. L. No. 98-532, 98 Stat. 2705 (codified as amended at 5 U.S.C. § 906 (1994)).

108 See generally Amendments to the Age Discrimination in Employment Act: Hearings on H.R. 2161, H.R. 3093, and H.R. 5310 Before the Subcomm. on Employment Opportunities of the House Comm. on Educ. and Labor, 98th Cong., 2d Sess. (1984).

109 See Age Discrimination in Employment Act of 1986, Pub. L. No. 99-592, § 2, 100 Stat. 3342 (1986) (codified as amended in 29 U.S.C. § 631 (1994)).

110 Pub. L. No. 101-433, 104 Stat. 978 (1990) (codified as amended at 29 U.S.C. §§ 623, 626, 630 (1994)).

111 For additional information, see Staff of Senate Comm. on Labor and Human Resources, 102d Cong., Legislative History of the Older Workers Benefit Protection Act (S. 1511 and Related Bills), pt. I (Comm. Print 1991) (detailing legislative background of OWBPA).

112 The elderly portion of the population has increased steadily. In 1900, only 4% of the population was 65 or older; in 1980, that number increased to 11%; by 2050, that figure is projected to reach 24%. See Hurd, supra note 100, at 565.

113 See id. at 585-88.

114 See O'Meara, supra note 18, at 29-33.

of persons aged twenty-five to sixty-four.[115] This increase reflects a steady and dramatic rise in individual income for senior citizens; between 1957 and 1990, the median income of persons in the over-sixty-five category more than doubled, a pace far outstripping the rate of the rest of the population.[116] With older Americans living longer and having more wealth and disposable time, we now confront a concern noted by Judge Posner:

> [Our] concern is that the increase in nonworking life expectancy associated with the growing fraction of elderly people implies a decline in the ratio of productive to consuming years over the life cycle, and that the elderly will use their political muscle to force the productive young to support the consuming old.[117]

This opportunity for capture by a specific group is significant given the power of the elderly in this country. Older persons are more likely than any other group to vote,[118] to write members of Congress, and to join public interest organizations.[119] As summarized by Representative Claude Pepper, the enthusiastic champion of ever greater benefits for senior citizens, "[t]hey have money and they have power."[120] The result has been that, since the 1970s, "the elderly have reaped a steadily increasing proportion of governmental benefit programs."[121] From

115 See Alan J. Auerbach & Laurence J. Kotlikoff, The Impact of the Demographic Transition on Capital Formation, in Demography and Retirement: The Twenty-First Century 163, 174 (Anna M. Rappaport & Sylvester J. Schieber eds., 1993).

116 See Posner, supra note 49, at 42. Judge Posner makes the critical additional observation that this increase is in actual income and does not include the imputed income from Medicare. It is possible to adjust this figure further by adding in the imputed income from owner occupied housing. Since the elderly are much more likely to live in their own homes and are likely to have less (if any) debt on these homes, imputing the income value of housing raises the expected living standard beyond that which would be projected from income stream alone. See Hurd, supra note 100, at 582 (noting imputation of income from housing equity increases income of elderly). As expressed by Professor Hurd, "[a] major finding of the research on economic status is that on average the elderly are as well off as the nonelderly and possibly much better off." Id. at 588.

117 Posner, supra note 49, at 36. Put less diplomatically, the question is whether the ADEA reforms are part of a larger problem of "[a] system in which the taxpayer supports the retiree rather than the retiree supporting himself out of his own deferral of consumption [that] invites each generation of old people to use their [sic] concentrated political might to plunder the young." Id. at 283.

118 See, e.g., Desda Moss, AARP Pushes Health-Care, Aging Issues, USA Today, May 10, 1988, at 1. See generally U.S. Census Bureau, Voting and Registration (last modified Aug. 16, 1996) <http://www.census.gov/population/socdemo/voting/votetab2.dat>.

119 See, e.g., Moss, supra note 118, at 1; Leigh Page, Seniors May Hold the Wild Card on Medicare Reform, Am. Med. News, Sept. 4, 1995, at 1. See generally U.S. Census Bureau, Voting and Registration (last modified Aug. 16, 1996) <http://www.census.gov/population/socdemo/voting/votetab2.dat>.

120 Moss, supra note 118, at 1.

121 Lawrence A. Frolik & Alison P. Barnes, An Aging Population: A Challenge to the Law, 42 Hastings L.J. 683, 707 (1991).

Medicare to Social Security, today's elderly comprise one of the most favored groups in the country with respect to legislative entitlements.[122] Unsurprisingly, that power clearly can be seen at play in the expansion of the ADEA.[123]

Most central has been the evolution of thinking about the problem of aging in the workforce. As we set out above, the image of the Act has changed from a reflection of a concern over entry barriers to a vehicle for addressing concerns at the end of an employee's worklife. No discussion of this transformation is possible, however, without addressing the critical role played by interest group pressures organized through the American Association of Retired Persons (AARP).[124] Although reforms of the ADEA may not appear as serious a problem as the viability of the Social Security system or the state of medical insurance, the reforms of the Act had every bit as much to do with an intergenerational struggle over societal goods. Moreover, while the changes in the Act's focus brought the ADEA in closer step with the problems identified by the life-cycle model, they also introduced the prospect of a direct financial benefit to an identifiable group of people.

B. Bad Statutes and the Invitation to Capture

Although the initial ADEA vision may have been misguided, there is no evidence that it offered direct financial benefits to its proponents. The original legislation was primarily an attempt to eliminate the offensive categorical restrictions on hiring older workers. As

122 See id. at 715 (noting increase in such areas as Social Security, medical care, property tax relief, and subsidized housing); Peter G. Peterson, Will America Grow Up Before it Grows Old?, Atlantic Monthly, May 1996, at 55, 57-60 (citing statistical change in demographics resulting in imminent "age wave" expected to hit American Social Security system); Neal R. Peirce & Peter C. Choharis, The Elderly as a Political Force—26 Million Strong and Well Organized, 1982 Nat'l J. 1559, 1559-1562 (quoting retired Rep. Dan Mica as noting elderly may receive more federal aid than necessary "because of political concerns").

123 See O'Meara, supra note 18, at 48 ("The continued expansion of the ADEA is also ensured by the involvement of special interest groups whose power in Congress is substantial."); Peirce & Choharis, supra note 122, at 1560 ("Elderly advocates . . . take some of the credit for . . . the 1978 law that repealed the mandatory retirement age for most federal workers and extended the retirement age from 65 to 70 for most private workers.").

124 See The Removal of Age Ceiling Cap Under the Age Discrimination in Employment Act: Joint Hearing Before the Subcomm. on Employment Opportunities of the Comm. on Educ. and Labor and the Subcomm. on Health and Long-term Care of the Select Comm. on Aging, 99th Cong. 46-47 (1986) (statement of Dr. Erling Johnson on behalf of AARP) (noting "sharply limited" opportunities for older workers); H.R. Rep. No. 99-756, at 7-8 (1986), reprinted in 1986 U.S.C.C.A.N. 5628, 5633-34 (quoting earlier testimony of Dr. Johnson of AARP, characterizing mandatory retirement as denial of older Americans' "basic rights to remain as productive members of society").

is so often the case in the antidiscrimination context, that which appeared as undoubtedly necessary to the eradication of a societal wrong proved over time to be insufficient to accomplish the task alone.[125] Nonetheless, as the Secretary of Labor testified in 1967, there was no Gray Lobby to motivate the original Act.[126] Because of that absence, the original Act was considered a measured approach,[127] and its framers predicted that it would result in fewer than 1000 charges annually.[128] In stark contrast, the legislation that evolved during the 1986 and 1990 reforms was clearly aimed to benefit a discrete group that served, not coincidentally, as its chief champion.

The absence of an active interest group lobbying on behalf of the initial ADEA dispels concerns that the statute in its origins was prompted by concerted self-interest. Ultimately, however, the presence of self-interest cannot be the touchstone for evaluating legislative initiatives.[129] All legislation needs a push, a form of institutional force to overcome the natural inertia present in all political orders. To disqualify legislation, or to subject it to a near universally fatal form of judicial review, on this basis would condemn the regulatory state. The converse, however, is also true: The mere ability to articulate a public-regarding purpose cannot insulate legislation from a real concern that it is an expression of rent seeking interests. Our collective experi-

125 The classic example comes with Griggs v. Duke Power, 401 U.S. 424 (1971). A scant seven years after Congress passed Title VII, the Court had to confront the fact that "built-in headwinds," themselves the product of years of de facto and de jure segregation, had left the black citizens of North Carolina as vulnerable to disparate impact exclusion from desired employment as they had been to categorical prohibitions on their job seeking under formal segregation. See id. at 432.

126 See 1967 House Hearings, supra note 4, at 7 (statement of W. Willard Wirtz, Secretary of Labor) (declaring that reason for no prior action to assure older employees opportunity was because "the 'has-beens' haven't a lobby").

127 See id. at 8 (statement of W. Willard Wirtz, Secretary of Labor) (arguing that H.R. 4221 demonstrated "conservative" but "determined" approach to age discrimination in employment).

128 See Age Discrimination in Employment: Hearings on S. 830 & S. 788 Before the Subcomm. on Labor of the Comm. on Labor and Pub. Welfare, 90th Cong. 46 (1967); see also O'Meara, supra note 18, at 14 ("In short, Congress was totally unaware of the impact the ADEA would ultimately have.").

129 For the contested positions on this issue, see James M. Buchanan & Gordon Tullock, The Calculus of Consent: Logical Foundations of Constitutional Democracy 283-95, 305 (1962) (introducing public choice argument that legislative arena is source of special interest capture); Frank H. Easterbrook, Statutes' Domains, 50 U. Chi. L. Rev. 533, 543 (1983) (arguing for strict literal construction of statutes in light of capacity for rent seeking behavior); Cass R. Sunstein, Naked Preferences and the Constitution, 84 Colum. L. Rev. 1689, 1731 (1984) (arguing for stricter judicial review of nonpublic-interest-protecting statutes).

ence from eyeglass prescriptions[130] to margarine availability[131] shows the ease with which claims of the public interest may be misappropriated on behalf of private gain.[132]

The experience of the ADEA suggests a somewhat different concern. Poorly crafted statutes, particularly those with significant remedial or redistributive potential, are open invitations to self-interested capture. Using an existing statutory vehicle for obtaining desired ends is simply easier than initiating the process of getting favorable legislation passed in the first place. Although this type of claim is difficult to "prove," there are several reasons to surmise that the claim is indeed true.

First, working through an existing statutory framework significantly lowers the entry barriers for strategic agitation. Not only does an existing statute provide a preexisting platform for making claims, but it vastly expands the available fora through which redress can be sought. In the absence of an existing statute, lobbying efforts must be directed at Congress to obtain an initial legal claim, or more uncertainly at the courts to read a new cause of action into existing law. A statute on the books, however, not only means that further legislative assistance can be sought, but also that advocacy groups can appeal to courts and regulatory agencies directly.[133] The Supreme Court confir-

130 See Williamson v. Lee Optical, 348 U.S. 483, 486-87 (1955) (discussing Oklahoma law that prohibited opticians from fitting "old glasses into new frames or supply[ing] a lens" without prescription from ophthalmologist or optometrist and upholding law even though it may "exact a needless, wasteful requirement in many cases").

131 For a classic discussion of the concerted efforts of dairy farmers to block and/or tax the sale of margarine, see Geoffrey P. Miller, Public Choice at the Dawn of the Special Interest State: The Story of Butter and Margarine, 77 Cal. L. Rev. 83 (1989).

132 One of our favorite examples occurs presently in Texas. Texas is the only state in the nation that does not permit home equity loans secured by a lien on the homestead. As a result, consumers with large equity in their homes are unable to secure credit that not only is available at lower rates, but also is the only form of consumer credit that is tax deductible. Consequently, homeowners in need of funds are forced to sell their homes and refinance a new home in order to tap their equity. The most vocal opponents of allowing homeowner equity loans are those well known champions of consumer rights: the Texas real estate lobby and the Texas homebuilders lobby. See Earl Golz, No Equity to Lend; Texas Law Still Prohibits Financing that Banks, Some Homeowners Want, Austin Am.-Statesman, Aug. 18, 1996, at H1. Detecting a tad of self-interest in such sudden invocations of the public welfare by these business interests is not difficult.

133 For examples of expansive regulatory interpretations of the ADEA, see, e.g., 29 C.F.R. §§ 1625.4(b), 1625.5 (1993) (stating that while using phrase "state age" in help-wanted advertisement or on employer application is not automatic violation of ADEA, possibility that this phrase may deter older workers will trigger close scrutiny to guarantee it is for lawful purposes only); 29 C.F.R. § 1625.7(c) (1993) (mandating that if age is used as "limiting criterion, the defense that the practice is justified by a reasonable factor other than age is unavailable"); 29 C.F.R. § 1625.12 (1993) (requiring that party asserting bona fide executive or high policy maker exemption bear burden of proof that elements have been met).

mation hearings of Justice Clarence Thomas provide an example. In defending his record as head of the EEOC, Thomas candidly described how the resources and energies of that agency had been shifted to age discrimination claims and away from the more traditional areas of concern—race and sex.[134] In addition, the presence of *federal* legislation enhances the rewards to be gained since the payoffs to successful agitation would be measured at the national rather than local level.[135]

Second, the presence of an established legislative format allows proponents of a particular agenda to adopt the posture of fighting a defensive battle for what is already theirs as opposed to an offensive battle for what they seek to obtain. As strategic thinkers going back to the time of Sun Tzu have recognized, defensive battles leverage the resources that may be delivered to battle.[136] Moreover, the capacity to pitch a claim as defending preexisting entitlements resonates with clearly developed legal principles granting a privileged position to rights already recognized. As expressed by Oliver Wendell Holmes:

> It is in the nature of man's mind. A thing which you have enjoyed and used as your own for a long time, whether property or an opinion, takes root in your being and cannot be torn away without your resenting the act and trying to defend yourself, however you came by it. The law can ask no better justification than the deepest instincts of man.[137]

134 See Nomination of Judge Clarence Thomas to be Associate Justice of the Supreme Court of the United States: Hearings Before the Senate Comm. on the Judiciary, 102d Cong. 315 (1991) (statement of then-Judge Clarence Thomas) (describing focus on age discrimination as "requir[ing] a redirection of an enormous amount of resources in the agency").

135 This understanding is somewhat different than Professor Miller's conclusion about the effect of a federal system on the efforts to deter margarine consumption: "The existence of a federal system benefitted the dairy lobby because the industry could initiate campaigns for state legislation, where free-rider and organization costs were low relative to national politics." Miller, supra note 131, at 86.

136 According to the great Chinese military strategist, "those skilled at making the enemy move do so by creating a situation to which he must conform; they entice him with something he is certain to take, and with the lures of ostensible profit they await him in strength." Sun Tzu, The Art of War 93 (Samuel B. Griffith trans., Clarendon Press 1963) (6th century B.C.). This tactic is part of the overall strategy by which "those skilled in war bring the enemy to the field of battle and are not brought there by him." Id. at 96.

137 Oliver W. Holmes, The Path of the Law, 10 Harv. L. Rev. 457, 477 (1897). For a review of the bases for legal recognition of preexisting entitlements, see Samuel Issacharoff, When Substance Mandates Procedure: *Martin v. Wilks* and the Rights of Vested Incumbents in Civil Rights Consent Decrees, 77 Cornell L. Rev. 189, 215-18 (1992). For explicit examples of such defensive posturing by the AARP allegedly to protect preexisting entitlements in the debates over employee benefits, see Has High Court Imperiled Older Workers' Benefits?, Occupational Hazards, Oct. 1989, at 115 (quoting AARP attorney Chris Mackaronis that "[The Supreme Court's decision in *Public Employees Retire-*

A clear example of this principle can be found among a group drawn from within the protected class of the ADEA. As a result of a regulatory anomaly, a finite group of individuals—the so-called notch babies—fell within two classes of eligibility that allowed them to claim what was in effect double Social Security benefits.[138] While no conceivable affirmative strategy would have allowed this group any sort of credible claim on enhanced benefits, the hue and cry over having something "taken away" allowed the notch babies to beat back attempts at regulatory ordering.[139] This understanding dovetails with Geoffrey Miller's conclusion that, in the context of organizing to thwart the challenge from margarine, dairy farmers were clearly "willing[ ] to pay more to protect a benefit they had than to purchase a benefit that they did not have."[140]

The notch babies also illustrate the third advantage of fighting from within a preexisting statutory scheme. Every effort to obtain goods from the political system requires organization and costs. Economic analyses of group activity predict that the greater the number of potentially affected parties, the greater the cost and difficulty of forming a stable organization or coalition to press for change.[141] In

ment System v. Betts] is incorrect" and "must be overturned through legislative action, thus explicitly restoring the rights older workers have had all along under the law").

138 "Notch babies" are so called because they were born between 1917 and 1921 and thus fell within a regulatory gulf erroneously created when Congress indexed Social Security benefits to keep up with inflation in 1972. In the 1972 law, Congress inadvertently granted Social Security recipients born between 1910 and 1916 double compensation for inflation. See Timothy Noah, Notch Babies: The Hidden Issue of the '86 Campaign, New Republic, Dec. 1, 1986, at 18, 20. Congress then tried to remedy this unintended windfall by tapering off excess payments for those born between 1917 and 1921. The claim of the notch babies was that although they received extra Social Security benefits which Congress never intended for them when revising the system in 1972, they did not receive as much extra as those born before them. See Julie Kosterlitz, Little Can Match a Notch Baby's Cry, 1988 Nat'l J. 1081, 1081.

139 The notch babies argued vociferously in Congress for added benefits to match fully the windfall received by those born in 1910-1916. Congress eventually capitulated on the issue, holding hearings on the notch issue and often addressing bills to mollify the notch babies' claims that Congress unjustly failed to "find enough money to pay [them] what is rightfully [theirs]." Julie Kosterlitz, Pension Penury, 1992 Nat'l J. 1809, 1809; see also Kosterlitz, supra note 138, at 1081 (discussing hearings on issue and influence of "vocal" notch babies on legislators); Susan Kellam, Social Security Riders Thrown From Senate Treasury Bill, 50 Cong. Q. Wkly. Rep., Sept. 12, 1992, at 2712, 2712 (noting that Senate was virtually evenly divided on whether to fund extra benefits for notch babies).

140 Miller, supra note 131, at 87.

141 See Mancur Olsen, Jr., The Logic of Collective Action: Public Goods and the Theory of Groups 53-65 (1965). See generally Daniel A. Farber and Philip P. Frickey, Law and Public Choice: A Critical Introduction (1991); Russell Hardin, Collective Action (1982). For a discussion of the specific problems of organizing coalitions to pursue legislative reforms, see Robert D. Tollison, Public Choice and Legislation, 74 Va. L. Rev. 339, 341-42 (1988).

the case of the notch babies, insuperable organizational barriers would prevent forming such a coalition to agitate for superbenefits. Even at the simplest level, defining the terms under which the preferred groups would be constituted would be impossible. Moreover, while a tremendous number of individuals would potentially benefit, no single prospective Social Security recipient would have a sufficient stake in the proposed benefits to undertake the arduous and expensive task of organizing a coalition to advocate such benefits. The presence of a preexisting statutory definition, however, gives an immediate organizational form to the affected group. In economic terms, the fact of a prior organization reduces the costs associated with group action. The group is defined externally and the problem of free riders is diminished because coalition members can be identified more readily and asked for assistance.[142]

C. *The Capture of the ADEA*

If, as we propose, the conceptual shortcomings of the ADEA's antidiscrimination scheme made it a walking invitation to capture, the missing ingredient was the agent that would accept that invitation. That agent proved to be the American Association of Retired Persons (AARP). Although the organization had been founded in 1958, the AARP did not emerge as the pivotal agent for older Americans until the early 1980s.[143] During the 1976 congressional hearings on the ADEA, for example, the AARP was still a secondary player.[144] The incremental change in the age cap from sixty-five to seventy was mainly the result of efforts by other organizations such as the National Council on Aging (NCOA) and the Council on Aging (COA).[145]

The radical transformation of ADEA legislative reforms is inseparable from the corresponding transformation of the AARP. After

142 See Gary S. Becker, A Theory of Competition Among Pressure Groups for Political Influence, 98 Q.J. Econ. 371, 380 (1983) (commenting on constant problem of free riding in political organization).

143 See Jonathan Peterson, 19 Million Members: Association of Retirees a Major Force, L.A. Times, Sept. 19, 1985, § 1, at 5 (counting only two million AARP members in 1971, but 12 million in 1981).

144 See David DeVoss, Empire of the Old: Old Age, Says the American Association of Retired Persons, is a Privilege, Not a Punishment, L.A. Times, Feb. 12, 1989, Magazine, at 8 (citing cash flow problems and declining membership as reasons for AARP's ineffectiveness).

145 See Peterson, supra note 143, at 5 (noting that in 1960s, the "AARP left it to other organizations, such as the National Council of Senior Citizens, to be the chief advocates"); Getting Rid of 65-and-Out, Bus. Week (Industrial ed.), Mar. 1, 1976, at 61 (citing "the militant Gray Panthers and the sedate American Association of Retired Persons" as being among opponents of mandatory retirement).

experiencing financial difficulties in the late 1970s,[146] the AARP began a vigorous marketing campaign to increase its membership.[147] In 1983, the AARP dropped its minimum membership age requirement from fifty-five to fifty, instantaneously adding thousands to its membership rolls.[148] By 1984, the AARP claimed "15% of the U.S. adult population."[149] That membership was quickly parlayed into a huge trust fund, which in turn was used to build "a public policy institute, [a team of] professional lobbyists, [and] a legal staff."[150] The AARP has grown to become the largest private, nonprofit, and nonpartisan membership organization in the world.[151] Today, its annual budget is over $386 million, $86 million of which comes from government funding,[152] and its membership includes nearly one of every five voters in the United States.[153]

As its membership grew, the AARP became a serious political presence with an agenda to transform the ADEA. By 1983, the AARP had announced its "global initiatives," which included its opposition to mandatory retirement.[154] In 1984, it began to pursue aggressively its political interests,[155] while advertising itself as "[a] strong, effective voice in Washington, . . . committed to opposing age

[146] See DeVoss, supra note 144, at 8.

[147] This campaign offered AARP members special group rates on products and services, including discounted insurance, travel, hotels, magazines, and prescriptions. See DeVoss, supra note 144, at 8; Eric Schurenberg & Lani Luciano, The Empire Called AARP, Money, Oct. 1988, at 128, 130; see also Business and Financial Practices of the AARP: Hearings before the Subcomm. on Social Security and Family Policy of the Comm. on Finance, 104th Cong. 90 (1995) (statement of Paul S. Hewitt) (noting relation between media flood and AARP power). By 1982, the AARP had "started aggressively promoting an expanded range of competitively priced financial services." DeVoss, supra note 144, at 8.

[148] See Peterson, supra note 143, at 5.

[149] Bryan D. Glass, Comment, The British Resistance to Age Discrimination Legislation: Is it Time to Follow the U.S. Example?, 16 Comp. Lab. L.J. 491, 532 (1995).

[150] Id.

[151] See AARP, All About the AARP: Its Programs, Its Services 12 (1987); see also Schurenberg & Luciano, supra note 147, at 128 (noting that AARP has 30 million members, which makes it second largest organization in the United States—second only to Roman Catholic Church).

[152] See Hearing on AARP Gives Preview of Lobby Reform Battle, Congress Daily, June 13, 1995, available in 1995 WL 10435462.

[153] See Schurenberg & Luciano, supra note 147, at 128-29.

[154] See Peterson, supra note 143, at 5 (noting increasingly bold goals, including containing health care costs and improving work conditions of older employees).

[155] See id. at 49 (quoting John Rother, Director of AARP's division of legislation, research, and public policy, on AARP's increased assertiveness in promoting interests of older workers in 1985: "We've been very conservative in the past about not wanting to push too hard . . . but we just can't walk away.").

discrimination in employment, modifying negative attitudes towards older persons and protecting our members' right to work."[156]

The power of "the nation's largest special-interest group"[157] has not gone unnoticed by Congress.[158] Despite increasing budgetary constraints in the 1980s and 1990s, the AARP has been at the forefront of a successful capture of an ever-increasing share of government welfare benefits[159] and has made entitlement programs like Social Security and Medicare political sacred cows.[160] Today's elderly, "who make up about 12.5% of the population, receive 60% of federal social spending."[161] The AARP's growth in power coincides neatly with the changing focus of the ADEA and the expansion of its statutory initiatives.

The first evidence of the AARP's political muscle came with Representative Pepper's 1986 legislative efforts to end mandatory retirement.[162] Although Representative Pepper and others had been trying to eliminate mandatory retirement since 1976, no action was taken until the AARP had accumulated enough power to get the legislation passed.[163]

Already having been a growing force in ADEA litigation through its role as a plaintiff,[164] the AARP was instrumental in Congress's decision to amend the statute. In the legislative history of the 1986

156 AARP's Internet Webpage (visited May 25, 1997) <http://www.aarp.org/advocacy.html>.

157 Margot Hornblower, Gray Power! AARP Emerges as the Nation's Most Powerful Special Interest Lobby, Time, Jan. 4, 1988, at 35, 35.

158 See id. (citing Congress's abandonment of proposal to scale down Social Security cost of living increases in response to pressure from senior citizens' lobby).

159 See Glass, supra note 149, at 532 (crediting AARP with helping elderly draw at least 72% of all federal expenditures); Peirce & Choharis, supra note 122, at 1560 (noting lobbying victories of elderly in preventing cuts in basic Social Security benefits and securing 1978 law that repealed mandatory retirement age for most federal workers and extended retirement age from 65 to 70).

160 See Peterson, supra note 143, at 5 (remarking on immense size of AARP and resultant political clout).

161 Michael D'Antonio, The New Generation Gap, L.A. Times, Mar. 14, 1993, Magazine, at 16.

162 See 29 U.S.C. § 631 (1994).

163 By 1983, the AARP boasted 14 million members and was considered "the great grandaddy of senior power in America." See Tom Morganthau, Legions of the Old, Newsweek, Jan. 24, 1983, at 23; see also Debate: Should Mandatory Retirement Be Outlawed?, N.Y. Times, Apr. 14, 1985, § 4, at 24 (showing increasing number of Americans aged 55 and older).

164 See Peterson, supra note 143, at 5 ("AARP carried its opposition to mandatory retirement to the Supreme Court, in separate briefs filed on behalf of public employees and Western Airlines flight engineers."); Debate: Should Mandatory Retirement be Outlawed?, supra note 163, at 24 (quoting AARP Executive Director Cyril F. Brickfield on mandatory retirement: "[A]ge discrimination cases are the largest category of cases now being handled by the Equal Employment Opportunity Commission.").

amendment, the AARP commanded nearly 200 pages of testimony. Thanks to this advocacy and Congress's rush to pass legislation in an election year, the bill, which in eliminating mandatory retirement fundamentally altered an entire system of career employment, was passed with relatively little discussion.[165] With the end of mandatory retirement in 1986, the AARP could lay claim to the fruits of "a campaign . . . that lasted almost a quarter of a century."[166] However, with the enactment of the OWBPA[167] in 1990, older Americans were given more than anyone could have imagined.[168]

Although the end of mandatory retirement was the most visible of the AARP's efforts, its role in the 1990 amendments to the ADEA may have been more critical yet. Reacting to the Supreme Court's decision in *Public Employees Retirement System of Ohio v. Betts*[169] which significantly expanded the scope of ADEA exceptions for early retirement and benefit plans,[170] the AARP pushed Congress to consider a new amendment to the ADEA: The Older Workers Benefit Protection Act. *Betts* was a particular source of concern for the AARP-led lobby because of its refusal to require purely symmetrical treatment of all employees for purposes of all employer benefit programs. The *Betts* plaintiff sought to require an employer undergoing a reduction in force to offer disability benefits to an employee who would already be receiving a fully vested pension.[171] The legislative history reflects that the OWBPA was intended to restore the pre-*Betts* status of the law;[172] however, significant debate took place over what that status was. The AARP acted quickly, and its self-interest became apparent in debates over three major issues: early retirement incentive plans, pension-severance offset programs, and supplemental unemployment benefits.

165 See O'Meara, supra note 18, at 18-19 (noting that amendments were passed in rush of legislation and that "there are no meaningful committee reports on the controversial provisions").

166 DeVoss, supra note 144, at 8; see also M.B. Christie, AARP Picks New Executive Director, Wash. Post, Aug. 17, 1987, at 7 (quoting AARP executive director Cyril F. Brickfield as citing elimination of mandatory retirement as one of AARP's "greatest past achievements"); John Furey, The Elderly: Soft Voice, Big Stick, San Diego Union Trib., May 28, 1986, at A1 (discussing lobbying power and tactics of AARP).

167 Older Workers Benefit Protection Act of 1990, Pub. L. No. 101-433, 104 Stat. 978 (codified as amended at 29 U.S.C. §§ 623, 626, 630 (1994)).

168 See infra text accompanying notes 179-82.

169 492 U.S. 158 (1989).

170 See id. at 177, 181.

171 See *Betts*, 492 U.S. at 163-64.

172 See OWBPA Hearings, supra note 22, at 3 (statement of Sen. Pryor) ("What we are trying to do is to restore by restatement the rules, regulations and law regarding the [ADEA]'s application to employee benefits.").

Early retirement incentive plans (ERIPs) are generally a one-time lump sum payment to induce an older worker to retire voluntarily.[173] ERIPs were industry's response to the 1986 amendments ending mandatory retirement. The idea that older workers could draw steadily increasing wages into the indefinite future was so entirely unrealistic in terms of the potential drain on available resources that employers had to contract around its provisions to maintain some fiscal integrity. As explained above, the life-cycle employment model rests on the assumption of some endpoint to the contract. The elimination of mandatory retirement destroyed that endpoint, leaving employers without a fixed point of closure to their implicit bargain for a long-term, escalating-wage contract.[174] Faced with indefinite contractual liability, employers searched for a means for accelerating the retirement age of the original set of workers approaching the previously accepted retirement age.[175] They quickly realized that early retirement incentives could induce costly older workers to retire before they became an unmanageable liability.[176] To minimize costs and

[173] See Kerry A. Brennan, Note, Early Retirement Incentives: "Golden Handshake" for Some, Age Discrimination for Others, 54 Brook. L. Rev. 927, 928 n.5 (1988) (reporting results from study concluding that 51% of surveyed employers offered cash payment as part of their ERIPs); Neill A. Borowski, Legislation May Board Shut "Windows" for Early Retirement, Chi. Trib., July 22, 1990, § 7, at 12B (describing ERIP amounting to two times worker's annual salary); Mike Causey, After the Buyouts, Wash. Post, Dec. 5, 1994, at D2 (reporting that one large scale ERIP offered buyouts of up to $25,000); Bill Sing, Look Before Leaping at Early Retirement Offers, L.A. Times, Jan. 13, 1991, at D4 (finding that ERIPs often eliminate pension reductions for early retirement, grant bonus years toward pensions, or give lump sum payment equal to six months' or one year's worth of pay or two weeks' pay for each year of service).

[174] See Erica Worth, Note, In Defense of Targeted ERIPs: Understanding the Interaction of Life-Cycle Employment and Early Retirement Incentive Plans, 74 Tex. L. Rev. 411, 420 (1995) (describing how end of mandatory retirement led to birth of ERIPs); see also OWBPA Hearings, supra note 22, at 321 (statement of Charles A. Corry, Chairman, USX Corp.) ("[T]he continuous stream of legislation and regulation makes it more and more difficult for employers and employees to plan retirement incomes, age of retirement, employee replacements, pension plan funding, pension cost, tax impact . . . .").

[175] See Worth, supra note 174, at 420 ("Faced with an indefinite obligation to pay excessive wages to older workers, employers searched for a way to escape unbounded liability without violating the ADEA . . . ."); see also Robert Lewis, "Downsizing" Taking a Higher Toll, AARP Bull., Nov. 1994, at 14, 14 (reporting view of older worker who noted that "the traditional employer-employee compact that rewarded performance and loyalty with job security no longer exists").

[176] See Edward P. Lazear, Pensions as Severance Pay, in Financial Aspects of the United States Pension System 57, 57 (Zvi Bodie & John B. Shoven eds., 1983) (noting that pensions are being used to induce older workers to retire); Charles A. Shanor, Age Discrimination Issues: Reductions in Force, Voluntary Separation Programs, and Severance Benefits Litigation, C669 ALI-ABA Course of Study Materials: Advanced Employment Law and Litigation 369, 385 (1991) (noting that plans offer lump sums and other incentives which augment existing retirement benefits in order to induce early retirement); Charles B. Craver, The Application of the Age Discrimination in Employment Act to Persons Over

maximize the effectiveness of ERIPs, however, employers often targeted the plans to a specific age group among the older workers.[177] Targeted ERIPs, even if costlier than the original life-cycle bargain, at least limited the employer's exposure to those employees who would not otherwise be induced to retire by the passage of time alone.

In 1990, the AARP set out to do away with these techniques for avoiding the most expensive effects of the 1986 amendments ending mandatory retirement. At first, the AARP lobbied heavily against targeted ERIPs as a whole, claiming that providing bonuses or added pension benefits only to workers under a certain age was a clear *per se* violation of the ADEA.[178] The intention was to eliminate the targeted nature of such plans, but the AARP argued its position too well. Thanks to the AARP's moving testimony regarding the inherently detrimental nature of ERIPs, Congress began to consider eliminating the exemption for ERIPs from the ADEA's prohibition on age classifications entirely. This step would have spelled the end for ERIPs given that no employer could afford to offer retirement inducements to its entire workforce. At this point, the AARP did an about-face and began to lobby heavily for the preservation of ERIPs.[179] The AARP argued that ERIPs benefited older workers so long as they

Seventy, 58 Geo. Wash. L. Rev. 52, 110 (1989) (observing that businesses that "may no longer rely upon mandatory retirement policies to terminate older employees . . . will be forced to resort to voluntary retirement incentives"); Frolik & Barnes, supra note 121, at 687 ("Employers who can no longer engage in mandatory retirement arrange pension benefits to encourage voluntary retirement in order to spare themselves the attempt at justifying forced retirement of a particular individual."); Gurus in Government, Economist, May 20, 1995, at 21, 22 ("Employment laws mean that sacking public workers is expensive . . . because senior people have to be 'bought out'. . . ."); Jeanne Saddler, Playing Favorites? Older Workers Sue Over Early Retirement Plans, Wall St. J., Aug. 14, 1987, § 2, at 17 (observing that early retirement incentive plans have "become one of corporate America's most widely used tools for pruning its work force").

177 See OWBPA Hearings, supra note 22, at 207 (statement of Association of Private Pension and Welfare Plans) ("In order to maximize the effectiveness of early retirement window plans, employers often . . . limit the program to an age band of five to fifteen years."); Shanor, supra note 176, at 385 (stating that because programs are related to retirement eligibility, in almost all cases they are targeted at employees within protected age group); see also Richard G. Kass, Early Retirement Incentives and the Age Discrimination in Employment Act, 4 Hofstra Lab. L.J. 63, 64 (1986) (noting that most ERIPs withdrew or severely reduced benefits after age 55); Saddler, supra note 176, at 17 (discussing debate over ERIPs that offer benefits only to younger workers and typically exclude workers over 65 from participating).

178 See, e.g., Saddler, supra note 176, at 17 (noting AARP's opposition to North Tonawanda, N.Y. school system program offering bonuses and added pension benefits to workers under certain age).

179 See OWBPA Hearings, supra note 22, at 173-75 (statement of Horace B. Deets, Executive Director, AARP).

were offered to everyone over a minimum age.[180] By abandoning the claim that all age classifications are inherently suspect, the AARP set out to salvage age classifications that work only to enrich older Americans. Unsurprisingly, the AARP won out. The OWBPA prohibits only "targeted" ERIPs; ERIPs are legal so long as employers include all employees over some minimum age.[181]

The resulting windfall to older workers is more than a simple adjustment and raises real concerns about political legitimacy. Whenever legal rules change, particular groups have the capacity for a one-time gain until affected market actors can adjust to the new legal baseline. Thus, for example, the Social Security Act of 1933 provided immediate benefits to all Americans, despite the fact that workers approaching retirement age at the time of enactment had not paid into the Social Security fund. Similarly, the passage of ERISA in 1974 immediately brought federal guarantees to underfunded pensions. The fact of previous underfunding should have freed up money for those employers to subsidize past higher wages than would otherwise have been available.[182] To some extent, therefore, ERISA provided a one-time windfall to employees whose prior wage demands had been cushioned by underfunded pension plans. In similar fashion, the elimination of mandatory retirement provided some initial, unexpected gains to the first generation of affected employees.

Nonetheless, the actual course of the debates around ERIPs demonstrates a far more self-conscious assertion of wealth-grabbing self-interest. The main ideological loadbearer was a demand for formal equal treatment of all employees, regardless of any economic considerations associated with age. When it came to benefiting older workers, however, delineations based on age and violations of the equal treatment principle proved to be more than just acceptable—they were required.[183]

---

180 See id. at 173 (statement of Horace B. Deets, Executive Director, AARP) (recognizing that ERIPs can benefit employers and employees); id. at 188-90 (AARP report to Congress) (discussing AARP's stance on ERIPs and impact of Benefit Protection Act on preexisting law).

181 In order to maintain a sufficient level of inducement for the younger older workers, the incentives were not devalued. Instead, employers suffered the increased cost of buyouts, the cost of which was ultimately borne by the next generation of employees through depressed wage rates. The huge commitment of resources was greater than anything that could have been expected under the original life-cycle contracts.

182 See Richard A. Ippolito, Pension Security: Has ERISA Had Any Effect?, 11 Reg. 15, 19-20 (1987) (arguing that unionized workers' demands for higher wages were met by underfunding pensions).

183 See OWBPA Hearings, supra note 22, at 38-40 (statement of Robert F. Laufman) (describing circumstances of three elderly retirees who would get more money if OWBPA were in place to guarantee benefits); id. at 54 (statement of R. Gaull Silberman, Vice

The AARP demonstrated the same form of opportunism on the issue of pension-severance offset programs. Most employers offer workers a variety of benefit plans, including pension, severance, and disability benefit plans. However, most employers also provide for offsets between these plans. For example, in an involuntary reduction in force, those employees who are eligible to receive pension benefits would not receive full severance benefits; the pension benefits received would offset the severance benefits they would otherwise be qualified to receive. Thus, in the *Betts* case, the plaintiff employee was given her pension benefits, but was not eligible for disability benefits. These offsets were customary across industries. When the issue was raised at the 1990 hearings, the AARP contended that older workers deserved both pension and severance benefits.[184]

The AARP argued that, because younger workers who received severance pay would still have 100% of their pension benefits at retirement (assuming they were rehired after a temporary layoff), older workers should also receive both forms of benefits.[185] To deny older workers severance benefits was "age discrimination in its purest form."[186] The AARP reasoned that because severance pay was intended to tide a worker through an extended period of unemployment until suitable employment is located, older workers, who endure long periods of unemployment, are the most in need of severance benefits.[187]

The reality is just the contrary. Severance pay is meant to "provide[ ] funds to those with insufficient service or age to receive immediate pensions."[188] Severance pay is not just an extra bonus; it is an attempt to soften the financial impact of an involuntary termination. When an older employee has a pension, he has "available a stream of income over his remaining life"[189] and does not need the severance

Chairman, EEOC) (declaring that OWBPA would bring benefits back); see also Has High Court Imperiled Older Workers' Benefits?, supra note 137, at 116 (quoting AARP attorney Chris Mackaronis, who maintained that *Betts* must be overturned through legislative action to restore older workers' legal rights).

184 See OWBPA Hearings, supra note 22, at 171 (statement of Horace B. Deets, Executive Director, AARP) (maintaining that severance and pension benefits are fundamentally different); id. at 222 (Burton D. Fretz, Executive Director, National Senior Citizens Law Center) (noting that denial of benefits hits older workers hardest).

185 See id. at 171 (statement of Horace B. Deets, Executive Director, AARP).

186 Id. at 172 (statement of Horace B. Deets, Executive Director, AARP).

187 See id. at 222 (statement of Burton D. Fretz, Executive Director, National Senior Citizens Law Center) (noting that, at time of hearing, less than half of older workers who lost their jobs became re-employed).

188 Id. at 315 (statement of ERISA Industry Committee, by James D. Short, Vice President).

189 Id.

benefits. By prohibiting the use of offset provisions, older employees would be effectively double dipping into the company's benefit reserves.[190] Because those reserves are finite, an extra bonus would translate into smaller benefits for employees who are severed later.[191] Yet, AARP Executive Director Cyril F. Brickfield argued that pension-severance offset programs have "a particularly devastating impact on the older worker who must remain in the work force because his or her pension is inadequate."[192] Although this would provide favored treatment for elderly workers over younger unemployed workers who receive no pension at all while out of work, Brickfield abandoned the AARP's favored arguments for equal treatment when extra benefits for the elderly are at stake.

Employers responded with force at the 1990 hearings, but had no power to stop the processes that had been set in motion nearly a decade before.[193] Representatives from several businesses argued that prohibiting offsets would result in a windfall to older workers and a reduction of benefits for everyone else.[194] The efforts were too little too late; the AARP had the floor and the Congressmen by that time. The legislative history reflects this balance of power; the AARP alone managed to secure 225 pages worth of testimony,[195] while the combined interests of state pension funds, industry, and unions are represented by fewer than 80 pages of testimony.[196] The elimination of targeted ERIPs passed without amendment, and, although the integrated benefits issue was "compromised," employers had clearly lost.

Supplemental unemployment benefits (SUBs) were similarly seized by the AARP. SUBs were the outgrowth of the steel mill closures in the midwest.[197] In an effort to cushion the blow of massive

[190] See id. at 385 (letter of Dick Warden, Legislative Director, United Auto Workers) (asserting that integrated benefit programs are essential to assuring continuation of coverage for lives of workers and their families); see also id. at 322 (statement of C.A. Corry, Chairman, USX Corp.) (explaining that OWBPA would result in double benefits for some workers at expense of others).

[191] See Donald R. Stacy, A Possibility of Avoiding "Double Dipping" into Severance and Pension Payments, 5 Lab. Law. 1, 2-3 (1989) (noting additional point that while pension-eligible individuals tend to be older, this will not be so in every case).

[192] Cyril F. Brickfield, Pension Policy: Economic and Political Forces, 1980 Nat'l J. 2004, 2007.

[193] See Legislative History of the Older Workers Benefit Protection Act, 136 Cong. Rec. H10020 (daily ed. Oct. 18, 1990) (comments of Rep. Clay).

[194] See OWBPA Hearings, supra note 22, at 197 (statement of Association of Private Pension and Welfare Plans) (noting also that prohibition of integrated plans would prevent fair allocation of benefits).

[195] See id. at 165-390.

[196] See id. at 321-403.

[197] See Donald B. Thompson, Big Steel Doesn't Think Pact is Anemic, Industry Wk., Mar. 21, 1983, at 19.

factory shutdowns, industry executives and labor unions agreed to additional unemployment benefits.[198] These benefits were designed to be expressly deductible against pension benefits in order to preserve greater benefits for the younger unemployed workers who would suffer from "involuntary retirement" more severely than their pension-eligible counterparts.[199] The plans were approved by the IRS and under ERISA law as "neither arbitrary nor capricious."[200]

Once again, the AARP stepped in at the 1990 hearings. Using the same reasoning applied to severance benefits, the AARP argued that older workers had just as much right to the unemployment benefits as younger workers.[201] Falling back on its most welcome position, the AARP argued that any offset provision would be presumptively invalid as a classification based on age.[202] Once again, industry responded that prohibiting offsets would violate the meaning and purpose of SUBs and would allow older employees to double dip at the expense of younger workers.[203] This time, Congress created an entirely new provision within the ADEA, section 4(l)(1)(B), specifically exempting SUBs from pension offsets and allowing the older employees to claim another group of benefits.[204]

By the time of the 1990 amendments to the ADEA, the transformation of the statute was complete. The ADEA is now primarily a benefits protection regulation for older workers. The original impetus toward facilitating integration into the workplace is all but forgotten. The ADEA now codifies an express double standard: classifications based on age are presumptively discriminatory, unless they benefit older workers. This results in rather open ended obligations to provide older workers lump sum buyouts, dual pension and severance benefits, and supplemental unemployment benefits without giving any consideration to the economic rationale for these programs.

198 See Stacy, supra note 191, at 3.

199 See id.

200 Id.

201 See Betts Bills Revised, Pensions & Investment Age, Dec. 11, 1989, at 33, 33 (noting labor unions' concerns that bills could threaten legality of early retirement plans and integrated benefits programs).

202 See Nicole Weisenee, States News Service, Mar. 28, 1990 (noting AARP's position).

203 See OWBPA Hearings, supra note 22, at 385 (statement of Dick Warden, Legislative Director, United Auto Workers).

204 See John H. Langbein & Bruce A. Wolk, Pension & Employee Benefit Law 376 (2d ed. 1995).

III
Decoupling Nondiscrimination from Wealth Grabs

A. *Identifying the ADEA's Mischief*

1. *Mandatory Retirement*

We confess to a strong temptation to argue for the straightforward reintroduction of mandatory retirement. At its most fundamental, crediting the argument that mandatory retirement is a form of discrimination of any meaningful sort is problematic. Because mandatory retirement is imposed by society on all members of society, at least potentially, it entails neither the stigmatization nor victimization associated with the imposition of constraints on discrete and insular groups. By way of example, labeling as just a society that declares that women or black citizens cannot hold certain jobs because of their membership in those particular subclasses is difficult. In such a case, the more powerful group or groups in society have imposed a legal disability on a finite subset of the population.[205] On the other hand, imagining a society claiming the mantle of justness that declares that the working lives of its members shall run from twenty to sixty-five and then offers postemployment security in the form of generous health and retirement programs is perfectly plausible.[206] Coherently applying the label of discrimination to an obligation borne equally by all working members of the society is impossible.

Moreover, a strong contractual argument can be made that employees subject to mandatory retirement after a career-term relationship with an employer are simply getting their return on a prearranged bargain. Older employees may argue that in their younger incarnation they had not anticipated the harms that would befall them as they approach the end of their work lives. Such an argument would ring true in terms of the general inability of people to correctly discount the impact of remote future events in planning a present course of

---

205 This of course refers to the classic *Carolene Products* argument defining membership in a "discrete and insular group." Carolene Prods. Co. v. United States, 304 U.S. 144, 153 n.4 (1938). Walter Kamiat helped us with the formulation of this argument.

206 On one view, that is already the basic state of affairs in the United States:

> A retired American today is probably the freest human being ever to walk the earth. Assuming that basic needs are met by a pension, Social Security, Medicare and investment income, the retiree lives in a perpetual paradise of leisure and recreation. If the retiree stays healthy, this special status can be enjoyed for 15 to 20 years. There is time to fish all day and golf every afternoon.

Kingsley Davis, Our Idle Retirees Drag Down the Economy, N.Y. Times, Oct. 18, 1987, at A31; see also Adam Gopnick, The Chill, New Yorker, Mar. 17, 1977, at 64 (chronicling French political agitation for mandatory retirement age of 55).

action.[207] Nonetheless, this argument sweeps too broadly. Just as the seventy-year-old of tomorrow must live with the tattoos fancied by the twenty-year-old of today, so too does the law recognize that the contractual obligations of the young adult may bind the same person in a more wizened state.

The best argument against enforcement of mandatory retirement is that the societal baseline has changed so dramatically since the current generation of near-retirees entered the workforce that continued enforcement of across the board terminations required by mandatory retirement would be unfair.[208] Americans not only live considerably longer than in past generations, but they do so with greater health and vitality.[209] Americans may also be more attached to the workplace, particularly with the advent of two-career families and the increased integration of the workforce, than at the time when the current generation of potential retirees first began working. While we find these arguments incomplete, we accept their logic for now—particularly since the effort to roll back the end of mandatory retirement appears politically futile.

What will the end of mandatory retirement mean? Most likely its demise will force a confrontation with the unreliability of the common defense of ADEA reforms, which claims that, "as an overall matter, the performance of older workers [is] at least as good as that of younger workers."[210] This argument suffers from a terrible selection bias: Those workers who are still in the workforce past normal retirement age are not a random sample of their age cohorts.[211] Given the

---

207 See generally Choice Over Time (George Loewenstein & Jon Elster eds., 1995) (presenting empirical and experimental literature on skewed perceptions of risk and reward over time).

208 Strikingly, this argument did not emerge in the legislative debates over the 1986 amendments to the ADEA. Instead, the simpler invocation of antidiscrimination carried the day.

209 See Hurd, supra note 100, at 567 tbl.1, 568 tbl.2. These data, derived from the *Current Population Reports* of the U.S. Bureau of the Census, show, for example, that between 1900 and 1990, the percentage of Americans aged 55 and above increased from 9% to 20%. In addition, the life expectancy of those aged 65 increased from 11.3 to 14.9 years for men and from 12.0 to 19.2 years for women. Perhaps more striking is the phenomenon aptly described by Judge Posner: "Forty years ago, most 60-year-olds and all 70-year-olds were thought, by themselves and others, 'old.' Today a great many people retain a reasonable simulacrum of 'youth' (more precisely of middle age) until their late seventies." Posner, supra note 49, at 49. Posner then adds: "Of course, the shift has costs. One is the cost in medical care of keeping young. Another is the added burden of elder care on young and middle-aged adults, for along with a shift from old to not-old has come a shift from dead to old." Id.

210 EEOC v. Wyoming, 460 U.S. 226, 230-31 (1983) (listing conclusions of Secretary of Labor, confirmed through "extensive factfinding," which led to creation of ADEA).

211 This argument is supported by Posner, supra note 49, at 63 (claiming that those who live to old age "are apt to be healthier than average, of course, but also more intelligent,

trends toward earlier retirement, the toils exacted in manual labor, and the overall desire of management to remove older employees, those senior employees still in the workforce are those who for some reason have withstood the pressures toward exit. In addition, such employees are most likely clustered in areas of the workforce in which monitoring costs make precise estimations of productivity difficult. By contrast, earlier employee attrition is the norm in occupations with greater physical demands or more routinized measures of performance. One does not see seventy-five-year-old assembly line workers any more readily than one sees forty-five-year-old running backs in the National Football League. As expressed by Professor Epstein in the inimitable University of Chicago style, "production ceases at death or incapacitation, and it may well fall before that."[212]

The confrontation with the end of mandatory retirement will not take place across the employment spectrum. A steady move toward earlier retirement has accompanied the increased longevity of Americans. Between 1957 and 1987, for example, the percentage of men aged fifty-five to fifty-nine in the workforce fell from 91.4% to 79.7%; the comparable percentages for men aged sixty to sixty-four fell from 82.9% to 54.9%.[213] The same trend is found among women, although the data are somewhat more complicated to analyze because of the heavy influx of women into the labor force during this period.[214] The reasons for earlier retirement are varied. In occupations requiring heavy physical toil, laborers tend to wear out. In other occupations, the military being the extreme example, retirement packages induce very early departures from the workforce—oftentimes with the expectation of a second, more limited, career.[215]

better educated, and more affluent, since health, income, education, and intelligence are all positively correlated").

212 Richard A. Epstein, Forbidden Grounds: The Case Against Employment Discrimination Laws 449 (1992).

213 See Hurd, supra note 100, at 572 tbl.7.

214 Instead of measuring total percentage of women in the workforce, it is necessary to measure the rate at which women who are in the workforce are retiring. This measure is statistically termed the "retirement hazard rate," which simply denotes the likelihood with which women in the workforce will retire during defined periods of time. See id. at 571. For women aged 55 to 64, the hazard rate increased from .207 to .364 from 1957 to 1987. See id. at 572 (noting that by 1987 "the hazards of men and women were about the same").

215 A clear example of the early retirement phenomenon is government employees. Federal employees can retire fully vested in very generous pensions after age 55 and 30 years of service; most state and local governments also tend to provide more generous benefits than private systems. See James H. Schulz, The Economics of Aging 247-48, 250 (5th ed. 1992). One study found that in fiscal 1978, 59% of male civil service employees who retired were 60 or younger. See id. at 236. These figures are completely out of line with the private sector. See Herman B. Leonard, The Federal Civil Service Retirement System: An Analysis of Its Financial Condition and Current Reform Proposals, in Pen-

One area where the end of mandatory retirement will have a marked effect is among managerial and professional employees. This group alone has resisted the trend toward earlier retirement.[216] Judgments of performance in this area are based on the worker's experience and the work product tends to be highly valued. As a result, careers "peak" relatively late. Perhaps because the perquisites of power and influence come late, and perhaps because the wage profiles may be steeper, the end of mandatory retirement provides a sudden opportunity for this group to perpetuate itself in office. As may be suspected, this phenomenon is compounded in fields in which productivity is hardest to measure—university professors, for example.[217]

As we have already demonstrated, the ADEA's casual introduction of the antidiscrimination norm into the career-wage relationship has significantly damaged the life-cycle arrangement. Despite the antidiscrimination gloss, the elimination of mandatory retirement is a benefit overwhelmingly to employees drawn from the most privileged sectors of the workforce. These employees have already received the greatest benefits from the life-cycle arrangement: a steady upward swing of wages, a relaxed form of productivity review during their working careers, and a strong likelihood of generous pension protections. In short, they have realized all their contractual claims. The ADEA's abolition of mandatory retirement now provides them with a chance for a second dip at the benefits of employment.

Perhaps the most troublesome aspect of the invocation of antidiscrimination rhetoric in this context is the obfuscation of the clear redistributive consequences of the end of mandatory retirement. If employees at the tail end of their productivity are to be kept in the workforce, and if they are to remain there at salary levels in excess of productivity, they impose costs to be borne by others.

Besides the loss of labor predictability and the introduction of double dipping, the most obvious cost of the end of mandatory retire-

sions, Labor, and Individual Choice 399, 413 (David A. Wise ed., 1985) (noting that only 7% of private sector employees retire before reaching 60).

216 The divergent trends can be derived from the tables in the Appendix. These tables examine workforce participation trends by age and educational level. While more precise data is hard to obtain, these tables clearly show an accelerated decline in workforce participation over time for the four education levels that are surveyed. Evidently, while all groups (of males) have had an earlier rate of withdrawal from the labor force, that trend is far less pronounced for the more educated sectors of the workforce.

217 The ADEA's prohibition on mandatory retirement in the university setting went into effect on December 31, 1993. Good data on the impact on universities are therefore difficult to obtain. One study at the University of Chicago predicted that up to 30% of the instructional budget was likely to be redirected as a result of the ADEA into either increased salary for expensive senior faculty that would have retired or costly buyouts of contracts. See Epstein, supra note 212, at 468-70.

ment is the redirection of firm income to older workers. Clearly, no firm can continue the pattern of promising an upward slope of wages indefinitely. In order to accommodate the expanded and unanticipated liability to older workers, the next generation's wage rates must be depressed. In addition, the conceptual foundations of a career-wage relation must be recast. We would expect firms to be less inclined to grant formal permanence to employees in a manner similar to a greater reluctance to grant tenure in the universities.[218]

An example from the University of Texas School of Law may help illustrate this issue. The Law School has been extremely fortunate to have loyal alumni who have endowed faculty chairs. While there are a significant number of these, the number is still finite. The Law School's official practice had been to award the chairs on a one-year basis, but in fact, chairs are granted on a career basis to its most successful mid- and senior-level professors. Once awarded, a chair remained in the hands of its recipient until retirement (or until the awarding of another chair deemed more desirable). With the end of mandatory retirement came the end of predictability in the turnover of chairs and the rewarding of newer faculty members. As a result, the Law School adopted a policy of awarding all prospective chairs for a finite period of time: ten years with a full review prior to an award for an additional five years. Thus current chairholders are entitled to hold their positions well beyond the original age of mandatory retirement, while new chairholders will have fixed terms of only ten to fifteen years.

2. *Pension Benefits*

The problems caused by the end of mandatory retirement are compounded by the ongoing shift from defined-benefit to defined-contribution pension plans. While the range of retirement programs is vast, and the governing regulatory regime is of mind-numbing complexity, a thumbnail sketch may help focus our discussion.[219] Under

---

[218] There is evidence of increasing pressure on the institution of tenure at universities across the country, although the links to the end of mandatory retirement are speculative at present. See Dr. William H. Cunningham, Tenure Revisited; Careful Peer Reviews No Threat to Freedom, Austin Am.—Statesman, Sept. 2, 1996, at A11 (reporting statement of University of Texas Chancellor on need to allay public concerns over faculty productivity); Mary Ann Roser, Tenure at UT is Under Review, Austin Am.—Statesman, Aug. 31, 1996, at A1 (reporting efforts by University of Texas to reevaluate tenure protections in light of legislative initiatives toward greater professor accountability).

[219] For a systematic comparison of defined-benefit and defined-contribution pension plans, see Zvi Bodie et al., Defined Benefit Versus Defined Contribution Pension Plans: What are the Real Trade-offs?, in Pensions in the U.S. Economy 139, 139-62 (Zvi Bodie et al. eds., 1988).

defined-benefit plans, a vested employee is entitled to a fixed pension that is typically calculated on the basis of length of service or a formula based on average earnings at the end of the employee's career. The benefits are based on actuarial assumptions about the workforce, and the employer is responsible for ensuring the integrity of the pension fund's assets. In defined-contribution plans, by contrast, the employer is responsible only for paying a contractually-based amount into a retirement fund for each employee. The contribution is made each year, oftentimes each quarter or each paycheck, and exhausts the employer's obligations. The employee, either individually or through a group representative, is responsible for the management of the assets accumulated in a retirement account.

Defined-benefit plans hold out only mild incentives toward late retirement. To the extent that these incentives are present, they derive from the fact that defined-benefit plans are usually not indexed for inflation[220] and instead typically substitute a formula based on the last year or years of an employee's career. Because of the career-wage slope, additional years of working will have the predictable effect of increasing the wage from which pension benefits are calculated. However, this effect is significantly limited by the fact that employees seeking to increase the size of their retirement benefits must still work an additional year rather than receive benefits.[221] Thus, the discounted future benefit rate must be offset against the year-by-year tradeoff of working instead of retiring on a pension. In addition, employers are still able to limit ongoing pension escalations by capping the number of years of service that can be included in benefit calculations.[222] In this fashion, the concept of the Normal Retirement Age (NRA) that is a foundation of ERISA can be protected from ADEA attack.[223]

---

220 See Posner, supra note 49, at 300 (comparing such plans to defined-compensation plans, which, not being paid until retirement, can be invested to be protected from inflation).

221 Additionally, employers may cap benefit levels based on the salary achieved after a set number of years of service. See 29 U.S.C. § 623(i)(2) (1994).

222 Under the relevant provision of ERISA, "A plan shall not be treated as failing to meet the requirements of this subparagraph solely because the plan imposes (without regard to age) a limitation . . . on the number of years of service or years of participation which are taken into account for purposes of determining benefit accrual under the plan." 29 U.S.C. § 1054(b)(1)(H)(ii) (1994) (also codified at 26 U.S.C. § 411(b)(1)(H)(ii) (1994)). Since capping defined benefits by a fixed number of years of service or by a fixed amount and did not employ an age classification, it avoided the strictures of the ADEA. For a general discussion of ERISA benefits, see Langbein & Wolk, supra note 204, at 384-85.

223 ERISA defines NRA as whatever is provided by the plan, or the later of age 65 or the fifth anniversary of the participant's participation in the plan as the default. See 29 U.S.C. § 1002(24) (1994). However, the NRA may not exceed 65. See id.

Whereas defined-benefit plans were once the norm, employers have shifted toward defined-contribution plans. Such plans now constitute the majority of pension plans in the United States,[224] although defined-benefit plans still hold more total assets.[225] Most critically, defined-contribution plans alter the incentives that substantially affect retirement decisions.[226] The effect is clearest in examining the concept of the NRA, which pension law defines as "the earliest age at which eligible participants are permitted to retire with full benefits."[227] Traditionally, if a participant wanted to retire before the NRA, he or she would receive reduced benefits.[228] Conversely, if a participant wanted to retire past the NRA, he or she would neither receive any additional benefits nor suffer a decrease in the rate of benefit accrual. The EEOC approved of this approach. Thanks to AARP involvement, however, the Omnibus Budget Reconciliation Act of 1986 amended ERISA to forbid any "cessation or reduction of benefit accrual 'because of attainment of any age.'"[229] While employers could avoid the consequences of this amendment in the defined-bene-

224 This move was spurred by the requirement of greater levels of minimum employer funding of defined-benefit plans following the enactment of ERISA and the Pension Protection Act of 1987. ERISA created the Pension Benefit Guarantee Corporation (PBGC), which serves as a public guarantor of underfunded defined-benefit pension plans. By 1993, the PBGC had incurred $5 billion in liabilities, a figure that the federal government budget for fiscal year 1995 projected would increase to between $45 billion and $70 billion. The PBGC has responded by tightening the funding rules and increasing insurance fees for defined-benefit plans which, in turn, has encouraged the transition to defined-contribution plans. See Randall P. Mariger, Public Policy Toward Pensions: Why Defined Contribution Pensions Dominate Government-Insured Defined Benefit Pensions, 95-3 Finance and Economics Discussion Series 1-3 (1995). Another factor in the push toward defined-contribution as opposed to defined-benefit plans was the ERISA requirement that pensions vest after 10 years, which was subsequently reduced to five years by the 1986 Tax Reform Act. See Laurence J. Kotlikoff & David A. Wise, The Wage Carrot and the Pension Stick: Retirement Benefits and Labor Force Participation 9 (1989). This requirement eliminated much of the Ponzi-scheme quality of defined-benefit plans that assumed high rates of attrition before vesting after 25 years, for example.

225 See B. Douglas Bernheim & John B. Shoven, Pension Funding and Saving, in Pensions in the U.S. Economy, supra note 219, at 88 (finding that in 1978, although 71.9% of pension plans were defined-contribution, 72.3% of all assets in pension plans were in defined-benefit plans); Kotlikoff & Wise, supra note 224, at 9; Pension and Welfare Benefits Admin., Abstract of 1990 Form 5500 Annual Reports, Private Pension Plan Bull., Summer 1993.

226 See Kotlikoff & Wise, supra note 224, at 97 (analyzing data from defined-benefit plans to show how employee retirement decisions are affected by incentive structure of pension plans).

227 Langbein & Wolk, supra note 204, at 376.

228 See id. at 379-80 (describing actuarial reductions that result from early retirement).

229 Id. at 384-85 (quoting and citing amendments to ERISA contained in Omnibus Budget Reconciliation Act of 1986, Pub. L. No. 99-509, § 9202(a), 100 Stat. 1874 (codified as amended at 29 U.S.C. § 1054(b)(1)(H) (1994))).

fits context by using non-age-based caps on benefit accrual, no such mechanism is available in the case of defined contributions.

This amendment significantly alters the comparative retirement incentives for defined-contribution as opposed to defined-benefit plans. Not only may benefit accrual be capped in a defined-benefit plan, but because defined benefits run the life of the pensioner (or the pensioner's surviving spouse), bequest considerations are not included in the pension plan.[230] The prospective retiree faces a classic "use it or lose it" tradeoff if retirement is postponed.

Prior studies have shown that retirement benefits that cannot be cashed out have an important effect on an employee's decision to retire.[231] For example, early research showed that Social Security was a more significant factor than the amount of saved assets in triggering retirement decisions.[232] The rationale was that, because Social Security avails to the benefit of the potential recipient alone and will not pass through the estate,[233] the employee would view foregone Social Security retirement benefits essentially as a wasting asset. Additional observations that older employees tailored their hours of work to fall under the maximum allowable to receive Social Security retirement benefits confirmed the conclusion.[234] Subsequent studies further revealed that defined-benefit pension plans, when available to a prospective retiree, are likely to outstrip the value of Social Security and are instead the best determinant of retirement decisions.[235]

Combining the observations about employee responses to incentive structures under Social Security and defined-benefit plans yields a troubling conclusion about defined-contribution plans: Defined-contribution plans as now structured under the ADEA and ERISA amendments clearly create incentives toward late retirement. There is no "use it or lose it" wasting asset element to defined-contribution

230 See id. at 382 (arguing that defined-benefit plans encourage earlier retirement than defined-contribution plans).

231 See generally Alan L. Gustman & Thomas L. Steinmeier, An Analysis of Pension Benefit Formulas, Pension Wealth, and Incentives from Pensions, in 10 Research in Labor Economics 53, 53-106 (Ronald Ehrenberg ed., 1989); Richard Ippolito, Toward Explaining Earlier Retirement After 1970, 43 Indus. & Lab. Rel. Rev. 556 (1990).

232 See James Schulz, Economics of Aging 77 (1988).

233 See Michael J. Boskin, Social Security and Retirement Decisions, 15 Econ. Inquiry 1, 13 (1977) (noting reasons why effect of Social Security benefits are more important than effect of income from other assets on probability of retirement).

234 See Gary Burtless & Robert A. Moffitt, The Joint Choice of Retirement Age and Postretirement Hours of Work, 3 J. Lab. Econ. 209, 230 (1985) (arguing that impact of Social Security on retirement probabilities and hours of work grows rapidly once individual reaches late 50s); Hurd, supra note 100, at 592 ("Apparently, many who work part-time after retirement choose hours close to the exempt amount in the earnings test.").

235 See Kotlikoff & Wise, supra note 224, at 97 (analyzing data from defined-benefit plans to reach this conclusion).

pension plans. Each year that an employee delays retirement not only postpones that employee's drawing down of his or her retirement fund, but increases the amount of the fund by the additional employer contributions. That increased level can either be used to subsidize a more lavish or simply more secure retirement, or to pass on to prospective heirs. To the extent that a particular job allows an older employee to coast, that employee can simply choose to defer the time to tap retirement savings. In practice, defined-contribution plans look more like tax deferred saved assets than actual retirement plans.[236]

3. *Employee Review and Salary*

By condemning mandatory retirement, the ADEA, paradoxically, may undermine the life-cycle model of employment. While reinforcement of employee expectations or "hands-tying" is arguably the best normative defense of the ADEA,[237] the extension of the ADEA to preclude employers from acting at the conclusion of the life-cycle contract may be the most lasting impact of the statute. We have already explored, in the first part of this section, what we consider to be the unjustified redistributive consequences caused by the ADEA's assault on mandatory retirement. Particularly in light of the demonstrated propensity of American workers to seek earlier retirement, the notion that a central (not to mention the prime) manifestation of the legal disability of the aged is mandatory retirement is worth rethinking.

We now turn to the paradox of this feature of the ADEA. All too often legal reforms are hampered by the lack of a systematic understanding of the means by which altered legal rules have effects that spill over beyond the precise focus of regulation. Thus, we propose that the likely effect of the ADEA, once internalized in employer con-

236 This feature of defined-contribution plans has not escaped notice. Complicated tax regulations require that some withdrawals begin at age 70½. Furthermore, accelerated taxes on excess withdrawals limit the ability of individuals to draw down defined-contribution pensions in a short period. In addition, estate taxes on the unused portion of a retirement fund are levied prior to the collection of outstanding income tax liability. The effect for the unfortunate or unsophisticated is that the combination of estate taxes and deferred-tax liability can wipe out virtually the entire reserved savings at death. This is in turn offset by a congressional penchant for creating windows for withdrawals in which individuals may draw down their retirement assets without being subject to the accelerated taxes on excessive withdrawals. See generally Peter Passell, Economic Scene: Be Thrifty and Invest Well, and Then Wait for the Huge Tax Bill, N.Y. Times, Nov. 21, 1996, at D2 (discussing implications of 1996 law suspending 15% tax on "excess distributions" from retirement savings).

237 See Jolls, supra note 48, at 1844 (arguing that "ADEA is likely to be a better means of achieving desirable hands-tying than other legal doctrines potentially suited to that function").

duct, will be to undermine further the income progression and relatively relaxed form of senior employee review that characterized the proper functioning of the life-cycle arrangement. Rather than cement the loose joints of a life-cycle contractual scheme, this aspect of the ADEA threatens to undo the entire structure.

Mandatory retirement may turn out to be a misnomer. There is ample anecdotal evidence of individuals past the formal retirement age for their fields who continued to be employed. In the field most readily at hand—legal academia—schools such as Hastings and New York Law School regularly buttressed the ranks of their teaching faculty with professors who had reached emeritus status at their home institutions. Mandatory retirement served primarily as a prearranged point at which an employer could sever a longstanding contractual relationship with a particular employee without in any sense "proving" that the employee was no longer capable. At its most basic, the mandatory retirement age spared most employees the distress and possible embarrassment of a late-stage review and the real possibility of being deemed unfit after a lifetime of service.[238] As expressed by Professor Epstein in assessing the academic context:

> There has to be some way to end the lifetime contract in order to preserve the vitality and productivity of the institution. Mandatory retirement is the only possible system that allows that to be done. The *automatic* termination rule avoids the endless evaluations of personnel and scholarship, the invidious and delicate comparisons between colleagues and friends that drove universities to take refuge in tenure in the first place.
>
> . . . With age, the risk of rapid decline, even for the ablest of academics, is too serious to ignore. The hiring of skilled older academics on short-term contracts would allow them to teach and research as long as they were able without putting them into the governance structure of the institution.[239]

Furthermore, there was a serious cost consideration for employers. Mandatory retirement spared the employer the time and expense necessary to establish to the satisfaction of fellow employees that a senior

[238] Constant productivity review will result in a loss of dignity for older workers who would have been removed without stigma under the traditional mandatory retirement policies. See 1977 House Hearings, supra note 103, at 84 (statement of Harold P. Coxon, Jr., Director of Labor Law, U.S. Chamber of Commerce) (arguing that prohibiting mandatory retirement age forces employers to terminate for cause in place of mandating stigma-free retirement for all employees at a certain age).

For-cause terminations necessarily entail an ugly exit for the older worker when the basis for that termination is the presumed exhaustion of one's individual abilities. But see id. at 8 (statement of Rep. Claude Pepper) (arguing that workers are not stigmatized by competency-based retirement).

[239] Epstein, supra note 212, at 462-63.

employee was no longer up to snuff. So long as the end of employment was uniform, there was no threat that termination would be seen as unjust, vindictive, or arbitrary in any one case.

What do we expect employers to do in anticipation of having to continue to employ senior employees who choose not to retire but whose skills have declined appreciably? In order to be able to move out senior employees no longer able to function effectively and at the same time avoid an ADEA challenge, employers must document the diminution in ability to the satisfaction of potential court review. Performance reviews of senior employees themselves, however, would appear to violate the ADEA's requirement of symmetrical treatment of all employees, regardless of age. The likely result is an expansion of employee monitoring and performance evaluations across the age spectrum. This expansion, in turn, will create costs, presumed efficiency losses in those worksites where formal monitoring is expensive,[240] and loss of freedom in institutions (such as universities) in which a significant measure of employee autonomy is considered indispensable to the mission of the enterprise.[241]

Greater investment in performance reviews, in turn, will place grave pressure on life-cycle wage arrangements. One of the key reasons for additional employee evaluations will be to terminate the pattern of steady wage increases that would otherwise continue even as productivity ebbs. To the extent that marginal employee productivity can indeed be measured, there is every reason to believe that long-term, more highly compensated employees will be increasingly vulnerable. These employees, who currently have expectations of wages above marginal output, will appear to be an unaffordable luxury in highly competitive markets.[242]

240 See Schwab, supra note 33, at 23-24 & nn.52-59 (summarizing economic literature on costs of employee monitoring and suggesting substitutes for direct employee review).

241 On the end of mandatory retirement necessitating "for cause" terminations, see 1977 House Hearings, supra note 103, at 81 (statement of Harold P. Coxon, Jr., Director of Labor Law, U.S. Chamber of Commerce) (noting that "if people could not be retired at a certain date, employers would be forced to look for 'cause' as a basis for retirement or discharge in order to avoid bias charges"). Those determinations force employers to engage in increased monitoring of all employees. See Michael Schrage, Why a Multimedia Big Brother Looms over the Future of Work, Wash. Post, July 29, 1994, at B3 (discussing increased surveillance of all levels of employees in workplace).

One consequence of increasing the number of "for cause" terminations is a likely increase in the number of ADEA suits. See 1977 House Hearings, supra note 103, at 102 (statement of Daniel E. Knowles, Director of Personnel, Grumman Aerospace Corp.) (arguing that without objective criteria, industry will be subjected to swell in charges of discrimination).

242 It is important to recall that the life-cycle arrangement serves to defer compensation from the most productive middle years to later stages of an employee's career when output would not independently justify an increased wage pattern. For those employees whose

The combination of the end of mandatory retirement and the ADEA's insistence on equal treatment of all senior employees, therefore, is likely to increase the wage pressure on all senior employees, not just those approaching normal retirement age.

B. *Restoring Order*

We have set out to show that what loosely passes for age discrimination in employment is a complex set of institutional arrangements, recognized even from the beginning of the ADEA as demonstrably different than the animus-based discrimination aimed prototypically at black Americans.[243] Perhaps more fundamentally, we have questioned the normative assumptions behind claims of age-based discrimination. Unlike restrictions that target isolated and vulnerable members of the society, limitations attending to age are those that, even if today placed on others, are ones that we shall later endure ourselves.[244] With the emergence of powerful political actors asserting expansive claims on behalf of older workers, however, all sense of limits seems to have dropped out of the ADEA picture.

Although these differences were acknowledged in the 1967 hearings, by 1990, the concern for the vulnerability of older workers at the end of the life-cycle had been replaced by an inflexibly reactive approach which made any age classification presumptively invalid. Neither the cases nor the legislative history of the OWBPA, however, explain why age classifications should trigger this kind of scrutiny. America's most expansive antidiscrimination law has emerged in the context of a group that has neither suffered historical discrimination nor lacked political power. On the contrary, American elderly have

---

output versus salary was not measured carefully during their most profitable years, the sudden introduction of greater scrutiny threatens to destabilize the implicit contractual understanding of a career-term relationship.

243 See OWBPA Hearings, supra note 22, at 231 (statement of Mark S. Dichter on behalf of the Association of Private Pension and Welfare Plans, U.S. Chamber of Commerce, National Association of Manufacturers, and ERISA Industry Committee) ("In considering age discrimination legislation back in the 1960s, Congress understood that age discrimination is by its nature different from discrimination on the basis of race and sex."); id. at 231-32 (citing The Older American Worker: Age Discrimination in Employment, Report of the Secretary of Labor to the Congress Under Section 715 of the Civil Rights Act of 1964, at 2 (1965), reprinted in EEOC, Legislative History of Age Discrimination in Employment Act of 1967, at 20 (1981) (explaining that employers' reluctance to hire older workers was primarily due to "institutional arrangements—such as pension, seniority, insurance, and promotion-from-within policies")).

244 See Massachusetts Bd. of Retirement v. Murgia, 427 U.S. 307, 313-14 (1976) (per curiam) ("Instead, [old age] marks a stage that each of us will reach if we live out our normal span."); Frolik & Barnes, supra note 121, at 711 (describing programs that favor elderly, such as Social Security, as efforts to "ameliorate" old age since "we do not want to be old" ourselves).

done amazingly well at capturing significant benefits through the political process.[245] Whatever the arguments that might be mustered on behalf of the elimination of mandatory retirement, we are simply at a loss to construct an argument for redirecting such significant social resources towards the most privileged of senior employees who readily assume the role of ADEA plaintiff.

We now turn to a series of modest proposals that will not, of themselves, cure the mischief caused by the ADEA. Rather these suggestions are intended as a springboard toward remedying some of the more bizarre incentives created under current law. We have deliberately tried to keep these proposals narrow in order to conform them where possible to existing law. As will be evident, however, many of these require a revisiting of recent ADEA reforms.

1. *Eliminate employer contributions to defined-contribution plans for employees working past the normal age of retirement*

This proposal seeks to conform the operation of defined-contribution and defined-benefit plans. Under current law, employers with defined-benefit programs may already cap the maximum retirement draw of employees by pegging the maximum retirement rate to the salary reached after a fixed number of years. The result is that the employer's obligation to the funding of the pension plan does not increase for any employee beyond the plan's Normal Retirement Age (NRA)—which by law can be no later than age sixty-five. No policy justification exists for continuing employer contributions to defined-contribution plans past the NRA given that the employer's obligations may equally be thought to have been discharged fully at that point. Further, this proposal could be combined with a corresponding elimination of tax deferral for employee contributions to a retirement fund after the NRA.[246]

The elimination of additional payments to defined-contribution plans will remove one incentive, secondary though it may be, for retirement age employees to stay on in the workforce. If a worker chooses to work past the NRA, then, at the very most, he or she should receive 100% of the benefits that have vested by the time he or she reaches age sixty-five, but no more. Such a phase-out will not harm the individual who wants to continue working, but will effec-

245 See Peterson, supra note 122, at 70 ("[E]lderly Americans now have the highest level of per capita household wealth of any age group . . . ."); id. at 74 ("Today's seniors, represented by powerful lobbies and voting in disproportionate numbers compared with the young, are already a potent political force"); id. ("[P]er capita federal spending on the elderly towers eleven to one over federal spending on children.").

246 This second step was suggested by Doug Laycock.

tively remove any incentive for an older worker to "hold out" for more of the pie.

2. *Offset employee wages by some proportion of the amount drawn down from defined-contribution plans*

Although defined-benefit plans are statutorily required to set an NRA no later than age sixty-five, defined-contribution plans have no direct equivalent. The closest parallel is the requirement that annuity-based retirement plans begin to pay out no later than age 70½.[247] For those employees still in the workforce at age 70½, some reduction in the employee benefit from the employer contribution equivalent to what happens in defined-benefit plans should be available. This reduction could be accomplished by offsetting salary by the percentage of the yearly annuity that represents the employer's share of the retirement contributions. For example, if an employee had a retirement plan in which the employer contributed half the retirement amount (matched by pretax payroll withholdings), and if the annuity payments beginning at age 70½ were $2000 per month, the employer should be entitled to reduce monthly salary by $1000. At a conceptual level, it is possible to think of the defined-contribution plan being "overfunded" for the employee who works beyond the point where annuity payments begin, in much the same fashion as a defined-benefit plan would be actuarially overfunded if an employee chose to work beyond the age of retirement eligibility.[248]

3. *Repeal the prohibition of targeted ERIPs or allow a set-off of ERIPs by pension eligibility*

Under current law, employers are allowed to implement only untargeted ERIPs, which are offered to all employees over a certain age. The problem with such plans is that they result in a one-time transfer of wealth to older employees at the expense of younger ones.[249] In

---

247 See Max J. Schwartz, Distributions from Qualified Retirement Plans—The Basic Rules, in Understanding ERISA 337, 349 (Joseph R. Simone ed., 1995).

248 This proposal would have no impact on employees whose defined-contribution plans call for a lump sum payment upon retirement. Whether this proposal would induce employees to switch over to riskier equity investments rather than annuity programs is a subject fit for debate. This proposal might also make the employer, in effect, an insurer for employees who pursue more aggressive and riskier investment strategies by not penalizing them if their investments do not pan out. While this effect is possible, it is not clear that the investment decisions of employees throughout their careers are subject to a rational calculus of subsidizing risky investments by being able to work into their seventies at the employer's expense.

249 See Worth, supra note 174, at 426-29 (providing detailed explanation of how untargeted ERIPs create intergenerational transfer of wealth).

the past, funds invested in targeted ERIPs could be rationalized as the amount of money the employer still owed the employee under the original life-cycle contract. With untargeted ERIPs, however, the employer must appropriate funds to those employees sixty-five and over who were owed nothing under the life-cycle contract. Because those employees were supposed to have retired at sixty-five under the original life-cycle contract, they receive a pure windfall when they accept an ERIP past the age of sixty-five and a more modest one depending on how close they are to retirement age. Ultimately, the money used to induce those workers over sixty-five to retire comes at the expense of decreased wages for the next generation.[250]

This windfall could easily be eliminated by mandating that any accepted ERIP would offset dollar for dollar any vested pension benefits in a defined-benefit plan or any annuities that *may* be collected from a defined-contribution plan.[251] Such a policy will effectively nullify any incentive for those workers over sixty-five; however, it will preserve the value of ERIPs for those younger older workers, who deserve some additional payment under the original life-cycle contract. This integrated approach will eliminate the double dipping and the incentives for wealth capture by the oldest workers. Instead of having employers entice older workers to retire by offering overly expensive buyouts or by engaging in costly monitoring programs, older workers will remain free to choose their own retirement date. Without any extraordinary incentives to work past sixty-five, only those workers who truly want to work for working's sake will stay on. More important, groups like the AARP will have no incentive to fight for even larger ERIPs and pension contributions. The incentive for capture would effectively be eliminated. Furthermore, to the extent that older workers need protection against opportunistic firings, they will continue to have it. The elimination of mandatory retirement will be undisturbed, and older workers will continue to have the choice to work past sixty-five.[252]

---

250 See Issacharoff, supra note 37, at 1248-49 (arguing that Epstein's analysis of mandatory retirement supports author's theory that applying ADEA to mandatory retirement rules results in wealth transfer to senior generation of employees).

251 This suggestion is broader than the salary set-off in the prior proposal. This ERIP reduction would be triggered by the total amount of annuity benefit available to the employee, even if the employee were under age 70½ and had not yet begun to draw down on his pension.

252 This proposal is not as radical as it seems. Congress has already agreed to phase in a higher age for Social Security benefit eligibility, evidencing an intent to phase out the windfalls being captured by the oldest workers. See Peterson, supra note 122, at 76.

4. Do not apply disparate impact analysis to the consequences on senior employees of regular employer review of all employees

Applying disparate impact analysis is the painful, and we fear inevitable, byproduct of the end of mandatory retirement. Employers will now be in the unenviable position of having to document declining productivity of older employees in order to avoid potential ADEA liability if senior employees have to be fired. This concern is of course a matter for each individual firm to address on its own terms. One important legal policy issue, however, is that the institution of employee review processes should not be allowed to serve as a proxy for proof of discriminatory intent, even if the most significantly affected group is the class protected under the ADEA. Regular employee reviews will be a natural consequence of the ADEA's recent expansions and should not be misinterpreted as a basis for disparate impact evidence of discrimination.

5. Do not apply disparate impact analysis to "negative salary increases" of senior employees

This suggestion follows directly from the fourth proposal. Because there is no reason to anticipate an ever-escalating level of employee productivity, and much reason to suspect the contrary, there is no reason for a constant upward slope of an employee's wage curve across his entire career. As we have set forth, that upward slope is best explained by career-length arrangements, which include a predetermined stopping point. With the end of mandatory retirement, employers should be expected to protect themselves against end-of-career exposures by documenting employee productivity and adjusting salaries downward for those employees with the greatest gulf between actual pay and present output. In some worksites, such monitoring undoubtedly will be highly inefficient. But where it is undertaken, the likely upshot will be a reduction in senior employee wages. Again, the law has a role to play here. Despite the lack of clearly established disparate impact liability under ADEA case law, there are constant pressures on this front from "pattern and practice" claims that seek to prove discriminatory motive based on broad statistical inferences.[253] No presumption of discrimination should be cre-

---

[253] See, e.g., Markham v. Geller, 451 U.S. 945, 948 (1981) (Rehnquist, J., dissenting from denial of certiorari) ("This Court has never held that proof of discriminatory impact can establish a violation of the ADEA . . . ."); EEOC v. Francis W. Parker Sch., 41 F.3d 1073, 1077 (7th Cir. 1994) (holding that decisions "which merely tend to affect workers over the age of forty more adversely than workers under forty are not prohibited" by ADEA); Hiatt v. Union Pac. R.R., 859 F. Supp. 1416, 1433-36 (D. Wyo. 1994) (finding disparate

ated by diminishing salaries of older employees. Instead, both the EEOC and the courts should anticipate this pattern as the employment norm and accord it no weight in an age discrimination case.

Conclusion

The battles over the ADEA are part of a broader confrontation with the elusive concept of intergenerational equity. An issue of claims to societal resources is present whenever there is a tradeoff to be had between investments for tomorrow and consumption for today. The sources of such tradeoffs range from environmental preservation to the competing demands for medical care for the elderly to additional educational resources for the young.[254]

As a general matter, broad questions of societal equities fit uncomfortably within standard legal discourse. The law can offer few concrete answers with regard to how much a society should invest in defense, housing, or medical care for the elderly. Legal commentators may opine on the changes from generations past that invested in such massive public works as the construction of the interstate highway system, the electrification of rural America, or the reconstruction of war ravaged Europe. Further, we may express concern or even dismay over the retreat from a commitment to broader conceptions of the public good in the political calculus of the day. Our expertise in these areas, however, is no broader than our capacity to marshal information and argue in the public sphere.

By contrast, legal commentators have much to offer when the debate shifts from abstract questions of broad societal duties to concrete applications of policy through statutes and judicial opinions. Here legal analysis holds sway in understanding the application of, and the incentives created by, new laws. The ADEA emerged from the 1986 and 1990 amendments as the most potent of antidiscrimination laws. Through relentless effort by special interest lobbyists, the antidis-

impact liability not available under ADEA). A line of cases, however, accepts, more or less without analysis, the availability of disparate impact analysis under the ADEA. See, e.g., EEOC v. Local 350, Plumbers & Pipefitters, 998 F.2d 641, 648 n.2 (9th Cir. 1992); Wooden v. Board of Educ., 931 F.2d 376, 379 (6th Cir. 1991); MacPhereson v. University of Montevallo, 922 F.2d 766, 770-71 (11th Cir. 1991). For a thoughtful discussion of the relation between disparate impact liability and the ADEA, see Evan H. Pontz, Note, What a Difference ADEA Makes: Why Disparate Impact Theory Should Not Apply to the Age Discrimination in Employment Act, 74 N.C. L. Rev. 267, 288-320 (1995) (arguing absence of statutory basis for establishing disparate impact theory under ADEA).

254 See Matthew Miller, Agitpol, New Republic, July 8, 1996, at 16-17 (quoting then-presidential candidate Richard Lamm as arguing, "[m]y aging body can prevent your kids from going to college. . . . We as a society spend more money turning 80 year olds into 90 year olds than we do 6 year olds into educated 16 year olds").

crimination model was captured for the benefit of a group that is not socially reviled, not penurious, neither discrete nor insular, not cut off from the mainstream of society, and not marked by the unmistakable badge of social opprobrium. The ADEA amendments forced a self-conscious wealth transfer not to society's victims or even its unfortunates, but to some of its most advantaged and secure. We cannot escape the conclusion that the use of antidiscrimination law and rhetoric to accomplish this aim is simply deplorable.

APPENDIX

Table 1: Percentage of Men in Population Aged 45–49 in Workforce by Education Level

Year	Non-High School Graduates	High School Graduates	Some College	College Graduate or Greater
1970	85.9	91.8	88.9	93.2
1980	80.2	89.9	89.6	94.9
1990	73.1	90.6	90.6	92.1
1994	62.6	88.2	88.2	92.1

Table 2: Percentage of Men in Population Aged 50–54 in Workforce by Education Level

Year	Non-High School Graduates	High School Graduates	Some College	College Graduate or Greater
1970	83.3	90.6	92.3	90.9
1980	74.5	86.6	89.9	93.1
1990	69.1	84.4	87.0	90.7
1994	65.8	81.6	85.0	90.3

Table 3: Percentage of Men in Population Aged 55–59 in Workforce by Education Level

Year	Non-High School Graduates	High School Graduates	Some College	College Graduate or Greater
1970	79.8	85.6	87.8	86.9
1980	69.7	79.9	84.2	89.5
1990	64.4	74.1	80.7	84.0
1994	56.0	73.1	75.6	82.3

Table 4: Percentage of Men in Population Aged 60–64 in Workforce by Education Level

Year	Non-High School Graduates	High School Graduates	Some College	College Graduate or Greater
1970	66.3	77.8	81.0	84.7
1980	50.4	59.5	63.4	69.4
1990	44.4	54.5	54.7	61.5
1994	39.5	46.6	50.2	60.4

Table 5: Percentage of Men in Population Aged 65–69 in Workforce by Education Level

Year	Non-High School Graduates	High School Graduates	Some College	College Graduate or Greater
1970	31.2	37.8	40.3	48.8
1980	19.1	24.3	32.0	36.8
1990	17.2	19.6	22.0	36.3
1994	14.1	20.8	23.8	33.4

These disparities can be observed in women in the workforce as well, although the trends are complicated by the influx of women into the workforce.

Table 6: Percentage of Women in Population Aged 55–59 in Workforce by Education Level

Year	Non-High School Graduates	High School Graduates	Some College	College Graduate or Greater
1970	36.1	45.9	49.5	56.8
1980	29.5	43.7	48.3	54.8
1990	30.9	47.2	50.9	61.6
1994	32.3	48.3	55.1	61.8

Table 7: Percentage of Women in Population Aged 65–69 in Workforce by Education Level

Year	Non-High School Graduates	High School Graduates	Some College	College Graduate or Greater
1970	11.1	16.9	19.9	21.8
1980	8.8	11.6	15.3	16.6
1990	9.0	12.2	14.0	18.3
1994	6.2	12.2	16.0	22.0

Sources: All data are from the March, Annual Demographic Supplements, Current Population Survey, Bureau of Labor Statistics. These data were drawn from the Census data tapes by Professor Finis Welch of Texas A&M University. We are deeply grateful to Professor Welch for his help.

[2]

Hands-Tying and the Age Discrimination in Employment Act

Christine Jolls*

Title VII's prohibitions on discrimination based on race, gender, religion, and national origin are typically justified on grounds other than economic efficiency. These prohibitions reflect, for many of us, a basic normative judgment that different outcomes for equally qualified employees of different races or other protected categories are simply wrong, wholly apart from their efficiency.[1] This argument is more difficult to sustain with regard to age discrimination, the subject of the Age Discrimination in Employment Act of 1967 (ADEA).[2] As the Supreme Court noted in *Massachusetts Board of Retirement v. Murgia*,[3] holding that age is not a suspect classification under the Equal Protection Clause: "[O]ld age does not define a 'discrete and insular' group . . . in need of 'extraordinary protection from the majoritarian political process.' Instead, it marks a stage that each of us will reach if we live out our normal span."[4] Old age has a temporal and, most critically, a universal element (almost universal at least) that is lacking in the categories covered by Title VII. These features mean that distributive or other gains for older workers are likely to come at the expense of these same workers in earlier years, making rules against age discrimination difficult to justify on traditional distributive or rights-based grounds.

While the normative foundation of the ADEA remains uncertain, the Act is as important a feature of the employment discrimination landscape

---

* Assistant Professor of Law, Harvard Law School (on leave 1995-97) and Faculty Research Fellow, National Bureau of Economic Research. B.A. 1989, Stanford University; J.D. 1993, Harvard University; Ph.D. (Economics) 1995, Massachusetts Institute of Technology. I thank David Charny, Samuel Issacharoff, D. Bruce Johnson, Avery Katz, Richard Posner, David Reiser, Alan Schwartz, Steven Shavell, Stephen Williams, and Jonathan Zittrain for helpful comments. I have also benefitted from the suggestions of participants in the *Texas Law Review* Symposium on The Changing Workplace and workshop participants at George Mason University, George Washington University, Georgetown University, and the University of Toronto. Finally, I am indebted to Mike Offner and Brian Schafer for excellent research assistance.

1. Title VII may also be efficient. *See* John J. Donohue III, *Is Title VII Efficient?*, 134 U. PA. L. REV. 1411, 1430-31 (1986).

2. 29 U.S.C. §§ 621-634 (1994).

3. 427 U.S. 307 (1976).

4. *Id.* at 313-14.

as is Title VII's traditional antidiscrimination command. Age discrimination claims accounted for 51% of the monetary damages obtained in employment discrimination cases brought by the Equal Employment Opportunity Commission (EEOC) between 1984 and 1988 and for approximately 25% of the EEOC's caseload over that period.[5] Likewise, ADEA claims filed with the EEOC grew 34% between 1989 and 1993 and nearly 200% over the 1980-1984 period.[6] Against the backdrop of the growing empirical significance of the ADEA, my contribution to this Symposium attempts to deepen our normative understanding of the Act.

I accept, for the most part, the premise that the ADEA cannot be justified on traditional distributive or rights-based grounds. The project is then to meet the challenge posed by the concluding passage of a recent empirical analysis of the ADEA: "[The ADEA] cannot be justified in terms of opening opportunities to a historically disfavored group. . . . It is therefore necessary to turn to other justifications for the ADEA. These have yet to be supplied . . . ."[7] I examine the possibility of an efficiency-based argument in favor of the ADEA, one that links the Act to a market failure potentially remedied by it. Drawing on this analysis, I suggest that common efficiency-based criticisms of the ADEA are misguided.[8] I do not purport to offer anything like a full-fledged efficiency defense of the ADEA; the ultimate desirability of the Act from an efficiency perspective turns on difficult empirical questions to which we do not yet have good answers. Likewise, I do not suggest (nor do I believe) that the ADEA was enacted to serve the efficiency function I argue may be ascribed to it. My goal is the more limited one of identifying and defending a particular efficiency-based argument in favor of the ADEA—an argument that, I suggest, makes sense of the ADEA cases, enjoys substantial empirical support, and corrects the prevailing view among economically oriented commentators that the ADEA has no redeeming virtues from an efficiency perspective.

The efficiency argument developed below arises out of the difficulty of achieving desirable "hands-tying" in the employer-employee relation-

---

5. George Rutherglen, *From Race to Age: The Expanding Scope of Employment Discrimination Law*, 24 J. LEGAL STUD. 491, 505, 507-08 (1995) (Tables: Charges Filed with the EEOC & Outcome in Cases Filed by the EEOC). The EEOC itself brings only a modest fraction of all age discrimination cases, but it brings them in rough proportion to initial claims filed with the agency, *see id.* at 509, and initial claims in turn reflect the overall body of employment discrimination cases (due to the requirement that the plaintiff exhaust administrative remedies), *see id.* at 501.

6. Bimal Patel & Brian H. Kleiner, *New Developments in Age Discrimination*, 45 LAB. L.J. 709, 712 (1994) (1989-1993 period); ROBERT J. FLANAGAN ET AL., ECONOMICS OF THE EMPLOYMENT RELATIONSHIP 269 (1989) (1980-1984 period).

7. Rutherglen, *supra* note 5, at 521.

8. For examples of such criticisms, see RICHARD A. EPSTEIN, FORBIDDEN GROUNDS: THE CASE AGAINST EMPLOYMENT DISCRIMINATION LAWS 441-71 (1992) and RICHARD A. POSNER, AGING AND OLD AGE 319-51 (1995).

ship. Hands-tying refers to a commitment not to engage in behavior that is attractive in the short term but ultimately destructive of long-term goals.[9] Such a commitment may be desirable in the employment setting for several reasons, some familiar and others less so, and, as explained below, may be facilitated by legal limits on age discrimination in employment. An important theme in the analysis to follow is the role of labor market mobility in an efficiency-based analysis of the ADEA. I suggest that whatever one believes about the need for legal intervention to remedy shortcomings of private contracting between employers and employees known to be in long-term relationships—the focus of much of the contemporary literature in employment law—job mobility creates an independent and possibly more broadly compelling basis for legal involvement.

The hands-tying perspective on the ADEA is grounded in a striking empirical regularity in the ADEA cases: older workers are often terminated or otherwise disfavored because they command higher wages than younger workers capable of performing the same job. As Part I explains, this empirical regularity is difficult to explain on the basis of the human capital considerations on which previous economically oriented analyses of the ADEA have focused.[10] The empirical regularity in the cases seems to put the efficiency costs of the Act (interpreted to prohibit the employer's behavior) in stark relief: society is forced to pay more for goods and services than in the absence of the prohibition. As Part I argues, however, this perspective on cost-based decisions about older workers fails to ask the obvious question raised by the pattern observed in the cases and corroborated by empirical evidence in the economics literature: *why* do older workers tend to be paid more than younger workers capable of performing the same jobs? Wages, after all, are determined in the market, not handed down from above. Yet higher pay based on age—wholly apart from either productivity or seniority at a particular firm—seems to be a fairly robust empirical fact about our economy. Why does the market produce such a situation, and what, if anything, does the answer suggest about the ADEA?

Part II sketches an answer to the first of these questions, concerning why the market might produce wages that rise with workers' age. The first and most familiar explanation for age-based wages (which I treat fairly

9. *See* Henry Hansmann & Reinier Kraakman, *Hands-Tying Contracts: Book Publishing, Venture Capital Financing, and Secured Debt*, 8 J.L. ECON. & ORGANIZATION 628, 629 (1992); Christine Jolls, *Contracts As Bilateral Commitments: A New Concern About Contract Modification*, 26 J. LEGAL STUD. (forthcoming Jan. 1997).

10. *See* POSNER, *supra* note 8, at 321, 328-30, 333-35, 337; Rutherglen, *supra* note 5, at 500-01; Peter H. Harris, Note, *Age Discrimination, Wages, and Economics: What Judicial Standard?*, 13 HARV. J.L. & PUB. POL'Y 715, 718 (1990); *see also* Metz v. Transit Mix, Inc., 828 F.2d 1202, 1217 (7th Cir. 1987) (Easterbrook, J., dissenting) (linking higher wages for older workers to higher productivity); EPSTEIN, *supra* note 8, at 451-52 (discussing human capital considerations).

briefly on that account) links such wages to incentive problems in the employment relationship. On this view, rewarding employees with higher wages later in life is desirable because it encourages them to work hard even when their efforts cannot be directly monitored. A second explanation for rising wages focuses on individuals' psychological preference for improvement in their earnings over time. Here rising wages are better than flat ones even if total earnings across the life-cycle are the same in present value terms; people like to feel that they are doing better over time. These two theories together seem to explain at least part of the rise in wages with workers' age.

The fact that age-based wages may be desired by labor market participants leads naturally to the question whether these parties face limits on their ability to put such wages into practice. If they do not, then legal intervention, including the ADEA, would be difficult to justify on efficiency grounds. As Part III explains, however, private solutions may be limited by employers' inability to *commit* to plans of rising wages, where the incentive to renege in the high-wage phase is great. Explicit or implicit contracts may help to mitigate the commitment problem, but in a world in which individuals often change jobs over the course of their working lives, contractual solutions are likely to be imperfect. As explained below, job mobility, though valuable in many respects, creates a species of inter-employer externality that cannot readily be solved by conventional private contracts. Legal limits on cost-based decisions about older workers represent a possible solution to this externality problem; such limits tie employers' hands and prevent them from reneging on the payment of age-based wages. Evidence on wages negotiated by unions—entities that may help to address the contracting barriers created by job mobility—seems to provide some support for the view that legal limits on cost-based decision-making may help to replicate the arrangements parties would choose in the absence of contracting barriers.

Part IV examines the implications of the hands-tying analysis for the ADEA. It explains that hands-tying considerations argue in favor of ADEA liability for cost-based decisions about older workers—and thus in favor of "disparate impact" liability under the Act. I also discuss reasons that the ADEA may be a better means of facilitating desirable hands-tying than other legal doctrines potentially suited to that purpose. I emphasize, however, that while disparate impact liability under the ADEA may be desirable in principle, it raises serious implementation issues and may entail considerable administrative cost. Part IV concludes with a discussion of whether and to what extent employees should be permitted to waive ADEA provisions as to events that may occur in the future. Hands-tying considerations imply that such waivers, now prohibited, should be permitted if knowing and voluntary—conditions that may, however, be unlikely to be satisfied in practice.

I. The Age-Wage Relationship

A. *ADEA Cases*

The paradigmatic ADEA claim arises from an employer's decision to replace an older worker with a younger, cheaper employee capable of performing the same job.[11] Thus, for example, in *Metz v. Transit Mix, Inc.*,[12] the court held that an employer violated the ADEA when, in seeking to cut its costs, it replaced the fifty-four-year-old plaintiff with a forty-three-year-old employee earning little more than half the plaintiff's salary.[13] Judge Easterbrook, in dissent, strenuously disputed the majority's conclusion: "It is hard to imagine how the use of wages could *not* be [a valid business measure]; wages correspond precisely to the costs of doing business, and hence to profitability."[14] Similarly, the Second Circuit's holding in *Geller v. Markham*[15] that a school board violated the ADEA when it passed over a fifty-five-year-old applicant on cost grounds elicited a spirited rebuke from then-Justice Rehnquist, who dissented from denial of certiorari on the ground that the school board's cost-cutting policy, which made no specific reference to age, did not constitute *age* discrimination in violation of the Act.[16]

The myriad cases involving cost-based decisionmaking under the ADEA arise when older workers are disfavored as a result of the high pay (in the form of wages or other benefits) they command. Of course, an expensive worker need not always be less attractive than a cheaper one; the critical issue is whether the higher cost of the more expensive worker is

11. *E.g.*, Hazen Paper Co. v. Biggins, 507 U.S. 604, 607 (1993); EEOC v. Francis W. Parker Sch., 41 F.3d 1073, 1075 (7th Cir. 1994), *cert. denied*, 115 S. Ct. 2577 (1995); Anderson v. Baxter Healthcare Corp., 13 F.3d 1120, 1125 (7th Cir. 1994); Bay v. Times Mirror Magazines, Inc., 936 F.2d 112, 114-16 (2d Cir. 1991); White v. Westinghouse Elec. Co., 862 F.2d 56, 58-59, 62 (3d Cir. 1988); *Metz*, 828 F.2d at 1203-05 ; Tice v. Lampert Yards, Inc., 761 F.2d 1210, 1212 (7th Cir. 1985); Dace v. ACF Indus., 722 F.2d 374, 375, 378 (8th Cir. 1983), *aff'd on reh'g*, 728 F.2d 976 (1984); Leftwich v. Harris-Stowe State College, 702 F.2d 686, 691 (8th Cir. 1983); Williams v. General Motors Corp. 656 F.2d 120, 130 n.17 (5th Cir. Unit B Sept. 1981), *cert. denied*, 455 U.S. 943 (1982); Geller v. Markham, 635 F.2d 1027, 1030 (2d Cir. 1980), *cert. denied*, 451 U.S. 945 (1981); Diamantopulos v. Brookside Corp., 683 F. Supp. 322, 325 (D. Conn. 1988); Wilson v. Popp Yarn Corp., 680 F. Supp. 208, 212 (W.D.N.C. 1988); Gelof v. Papineau, 648 F. Supp. 912, 921 (D. Del. 1986), *modified on other grounds*, 829 F.2d 452 (3d Cir. 1987); Green v. Edward J. Bettinger Co., 608 F. Supp. 35, 42 (E.D. Pa. 1984), *aff'd*, 791 F.2d 917 (3d Cir. 1986), *cert. denied*, 479 U.S. 1069 (1987); Franci v. Avco Corp., 538 F. Supp. 250, 259 (D. Conn. 1982); Marshall v. Arlene Knitwear, Inc., 454 F. Supp. 715, 730 (E.D.N.Y. 1978), *aff'd in part, rev'd in part, remanded without opinion*, 608 F.2d 1369 (2d Cir. 1979); Mastie v. Great Lakes Steel Corp., 424 F. Supp. 1299, 1318 (E.D. Mich. 1976).

12. 828 F.2d 1202 (7th Cir. 1987).

13. *Id.* at 1204-05, 1211.

14. *Id.* at 1219 (Easterbrook, J., dissenting) (emphasis in original).

15. 635 F.2d 1027 (2d Cir. 1980), *cert. denied*, 451 U.S. 945 (1981).

16. Markham v. Geller, 451 U.S. 945, 947 (1981) (Rehnquist, J., dissenting from denial of certiorari).

matched by higher productivity. Judge Easterbrook's *Metz* dissent puts the point nicely: "There is no 'qualified [worker]' in the abstract . . . . To say that someone is 'qualified' to manage the [defendant's] plant is to say that he can handle the manufacture and sale of concrete well enough that he adds to the value of the enterprise at least the cost of his salary."[17] When an older, more expensive employee is terminated or otherwise disfavored on cost grounds relative to a younger worker, the older worker's wage-productivity combination must have proven less attractive to the employer than that of the younger individual; otherwise the older worker would not have been disfavored. The wage pattern tentatively suggested by the cases is therefore one of increasing wages with age *even after controlling for productivity*.

The suggestion about the wage pattern is tentative because ADEA cases reflect an obviously circumscribed set of circumstances: only employees over forty are protected by the ADEA, and age discrimination will be difficult to prove unless the successful candidate is younger than the plaintiff.[18] However, the wage evidence described in the following section suggests that the cost-based decisionmaking observed in the ADEA cases may indeed reflect higher wage-productivity ratios for older workers than for younger ones.

B. Wage Evidence and the Limits of Human Capital Theory

Empirical evidence shows that wages tend to rise with age, sometimes dramatically. Regular wage payments often increase automatically with each additional year in the labor force; annual merit raises, for example, are typically above the rate of inflation even for the worst-performing individuals.[19] Likewise, employee compensation often includes a pension component, leading to spikes in the employee's total wage when benefits vest. Pension benefits may be a significant component of a worker's lifetime earnings; for example, in 1992 the average level of benefits (in present value terms) was $180,000, or fourteen percent of the total discounted value of earnings from the hire date to normal retirement age.[20]

17. *Metz*, 828 F.2d at 1213 (Easterbrook, J., dissenting).

18. *See, e.g.*, Roper v. Peabody Coal Co., 47 F.3d 925, 926 (7th Cir. 1995) (holding that to make out a prima facie case under the ADEA, the plaintiff must show that younger employees were treated more favorably than the plaintiff); Rinehart v. City of Independence, 35 F.3d 1263, 1265 (8th Cir. 1994) ("[T]he plaintiff [must] be replaced by a younger person" to make out a prima facie case under the ADEA), *cert. denied*, 115 S. Ct. 1822 (1995). The Supreme Court approved this approach in O'Connor v. Consolidated Coin Caterers Corp., 116 S. Ct. 1307, 1310 (1996).

19. FLANAGAN ET AL., *supra* note 6, at 289 & n.22; CHARLES A. PECK, PAY & PERFORMANCE: THE INTERACTION OF COMPENSATION & PERFORMANCE APPRAISAL 14 (Conference Board Research Bulletin No. 155, 1984).

20. Alan L. Gustman et al., *The Role of Pensions in the Labor Market: A Survey of the Literature*, 47 INDUS. & LAB. REL. REV. 417, 418 (1994).

Moreover, wage growth and pensions are empirically correlated, in the sense that the same individuals tend to have both, which suggests that the two phenomena arise from the same underlying influence.[21] The increase in workers' earnings with time in the labor force does not depend on their having long tenure with a particular employer; the increase is primarily a function of the total time spent in the labor force.[22]

It does not necessarily follow from this pattern of rising pay that wages rise with age *even after controlling for productivity*—the pattern tentatively suggested by the ADEA cases. The increase in wages with age might simply reflect increases in workers' productivity as they gain experience, accumulate human capital, and take on additional supervisory and training roles. Empirical evidence suggests that over eighty percent of companies provide on-the-job training, which is likely to result in greater productivity for workers with more experience.[23] Likewise, workers' wages appear to increase most rapidly in periods in which they are receiving training from their employers, suggesting that rising wages are at least a partial function of enhancements in human capital.[24] The human capital explanation for rising wages predicts that wages and productivity will rise in tandem, not diverge as workers grow older.

The picture is a bit more complex, but not qualitatively different, once the relationship-specific nature of human capital is accounted for. Employees' productivity often will be higher at their current employer than at a different firm because the training provided by the company, though typically not useless at a different firm, also would not be as valuable as at the original firm.[25] Both employer and employee thus gain by staying together; the employer gets a worker who is more productive than an outsider lacking specialized training would be, and the employee commands a higher wage than what he or she could get at an outside firm. The precise division of the surplus from staying together will depend on the relative bargaining power of the parties, but unless the employer has no bargaining power at all (a highly unlikely scenario), employees' wages will

21. *See* Edward P. Lazear, *Why Is There Mandatory Retirement?*, 87 J. POL. ECON. 1261, 1280 (1979) (Table: Logit and OLS Results).

22. *See* Katharine G. Abraham & Henry S. Farber, *Job Duration, Seniority, and Earnings*, 77 AM. ECON. REV. 278, 288-90 (1987); Joseph G. Altonji & Robert A. Shakotko, *Do Wages Rise with Job Seniority?*, 54 REV. ECON. STUD. 437, 442-46 (1987). These studies show that previous findings of a wage-tenure relationship were artifacts of the correlation between tenure and other explanatory variables (such as the quality of the job match) that in turn are correlated with wages but were omitted from the analysis.

23. HARRIET GORLIN, PERSONNEL PRACTICES I: RECRUITMENT, PLACEMENT, TRAINING, COMMUNICATION 41 (Conference Board Information Bulletin No. 89, 1981) (Table: On-Site Training or Education).

24. James N. Brown, *Why Do Wages Increase with Tenure? On-the-Job Training and Life-Cycle Wage Growth Observed Within Firms*, 79 AM. ECON. REV. 971, 971 (1989).

25. *See generally* GARY S. BECKER, HUMAN CAPITAL 40-51 (3d ed. 1993).

be below their "marginal revenue product" at the firm—the amount they add to the firm's revenue.[26] (Their wages at the present firm will be *above* their marginal revenue product at an outside firm, so the employees are still better off (wage-wise) with the current employer.)

With wages below marginal revenue product at the firm, the employer has no incentive to get rid of older workers in *Metz*-style terminations; these workers are adding more to the employer's revenue than they are costing in terms of wages.[27] Focusing on human capital considerations therefore leads to the conclusion (advanced by Richard Posner and others) that cost-based termination of older workers is an unlikely event—a conclusion that seems difficult to reconcile with the frequency in practice of *Metz*-style claims.[28] Rather, as explained above, the paradigmatic cost-based decisionmaking case makes sense only if the wage of the older worker is higher than the worker's marginal revenue product at the firm; only in this situation will the employer have an incentive to discharge or refuse to hire the older individual. The human capital explanation for rising wages may also be difficult to square with empirical evidence suggesting (tentatively) that relatively little of the increase in earnings with age is attributable to tenure at a particular firm as opposed to overall labor market experience.[29]

Consistent with the tentative suggestion in the ADEA cases (and contrary to the prediction of human capital theory), wage evidence supports

---

26. *See id.* at 41-44; FLANAGAN ET AL., *supra* note 6, at 55. In the version of the human capital model developed in Lorne Carmichael, *Firm-Specific Human Capital and Promotion Ladders*, 14 BELL J. ECON. 251 (1983), the wages of older workers are *above*, not below, their marginal revenue product at the firm. *See id.* at 252. However, as noted just below, even in this model employers have limited incentive to discharge older workers.

27. FLANAGAN ET AL., *supra* note 6, at 274; POSNER, *supra* note 8, at 333-35; Stewart J. Schwab, *Life-Cycle Justice: Accommodating Just Cause and Employment at Will*, 92 MICH. L. REV. 8, 15-16 (1993). In the Carmichael version of the human capital model noted in the preceding footnote, wages are above marginal revenue product for older workers, but the employer's incentive to fire these individuals is limited nonetheless, as firing a worker simply causes a high-wage job to "revert to the worker one rung down on the seniority ladder." Carmichael, *supra* note 26, at 252.

28. *See* POSNER, *supra* note 8, at 334. Posner supports his claim by reference to evidence that ADEA plaintiffs in reported cases are typically unsuccessful. *Id.* at 335. However, without any indication of how plaintiffs fare in cases brought under Title VII or other employment disputes, it is difficult to tell whether ADEA plaintiffs are an especially unfortunate group or, rather, plaintiffs do relatively poorly in all types of employment and civil rights litigation. In fact, the evidence suggests that age discrimination plaintiffs do substantially better than plaintiffs in race and gender discrimination cases. *See* Rutherglen, *supra* note 5, at 512 (Table: Outcome of Cases).

29. *See* Abraham & Farber, *supra* note 22, at 289-90, 295; Altonji & Shakotko, *supra* note 22, at 442-46. *See generally* Victor P. Goldberg, *A Relational Exchange Perspective on the Employment Relationship*, *in* FIRMS, ORGANIZATION, AND LABOUR 127 (Frank H. Stephen ed., 1984) (arguing that the importance of relationship-specifie human capital in the employment setting has been over-emphasized). *But see* Robert Topel, *Specific Capital, Mobility, and Wages: Wages Rise with Job Seniority*, 99 J. POL. ECON. 145, 147-48 (1991) (finding that increases in earnings over time are in fact attributable in significant part to tenure at a particular firm).

the view that at least some of the increase in pay levels with age cannot be explained by increased productivity. First, time in the labor force (whether or not with a single employer) appears to be a much greater factor in wage levels than rated performance, which is correlated at least to some degree with the employee's productivity.[30] Moreover, employers tend to go to great lengths to force or encourage older workers to retire, something they would have no incentive to do if older workers' productivity matched their wages. Mandatory retirement—the most extreme form of induced exit—was common prior to its abolition by Congress in 1986.[31] In the post-mandatory retirement era, employers have relied on carrots rather than sticks by, for example, structuring pension plans in such a way that workers can take early retirement while still obtaining full pension benefits.[32] "Open-window" offers of early retirement, which reward workers for leaving the firm "voluntarily," represent another means of inducing the departure of older employees, who, after all, are most likely to be interested in retirement.[33] Standing alone, mandatory retirement and exit-incentive programs could be consistent with wages equal to productivity until the age of retirement or early retirement, followed by a sharp drop-off in productivity at that age (hence the need for induced retirement, or else a sharp cut in wages). However, neither the prevalence of cost-based discharge of middle-aged employees in the ADEA cases, nor the empirical evidence on wages and productivity over the life-cycle, is consistent with this alternative explanation.

The wage-productivity relationship suggested by the cases and the empirical evidence is depicted graphically in Figure 1. The figure shows both wages and productivity (the latter measured by the employee's marginal revenue product at the firm) rising with age, but at different rates; wages rise faster than productivity. When wages are below marginal revenue product, the employer profits from having the employee on the payroll. When wages rise above marginal revenue product, however, employing the individual is no longer profitable, though from the employee's standpoint the high wages are simply restitution for low wages earned early on. It is precisely the divergence between wages and productivity in later years that gives rise to the cost-based decisionmaking observed in the ADEA cases.

30. James L. Medoff & Katherine G. Abraham, *Experience, Performance, and Earnings*, 95 Q.J. ECON. 703, 704 (1980); James L. Medoff & Katherine G. Abraham, *Are Those Paid More Really More Productive? The Case of Experience*, 16 J. HUM. RESOURCES 186, 204 (1981).

31. Age Discrimination in Employment Amendments of 1986, Pub. L. No. 99-592, 100 Stat. 3342 (codified as amended at 29 U.S.C. § 631(a) (1994)); Lazear, *supra* note 21, at 1261 (noting the prevalence of mandatory retirement).

32. Gustman et al., *supra* note 20, at 432.

33. Michael C. Harper, *Age-Based Exit Incentives, Coercion, and the Prospective Waiver of ADEA Rights: The Failure of the Older Workers Benefit Protection Act*, 79 VA. L. REV. 1271, 1277 (1993).

Figure 1

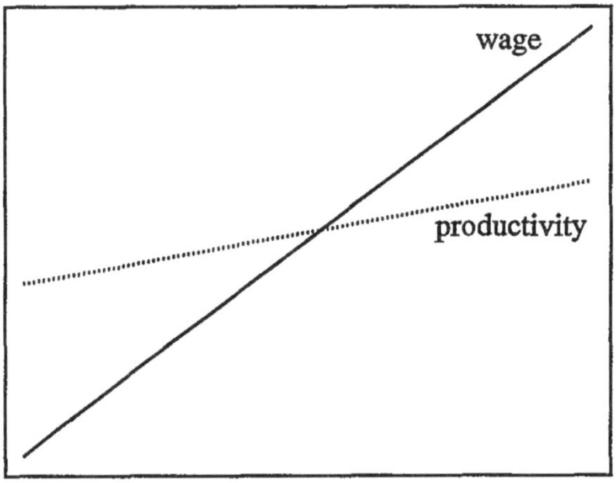

years in the labor force

A few clarifying comments may be helpful at this point. First, throughout the analysis below productivity is measured within the firm at which the employee works; as discussed above, productivity at an outside firm may be lower. Second, while the figure focuses on the rise in wages and productivity with age, at some point both may begin to fall as a consequence of aging. This would produce an inverted U-shaped curve for wages and productivity. Alternatively, it is sometimes suggested that productivity (but not wages) follows an inverted U-shaped pattern, beginning below wages, then rising above wages after the employee has been with the firm for a few years, and ultimately falling below wages again—perhaps because productivity levels off when an employee reaches middle age.[34] Regardless of these nuances, however, the central fact of a rising wage-productivity relationship over a significant portion of a worker's lifetime is supported by both the ADEA cases and the empirical evidence.

C. *Implications*

If, as the cases and the empirical evidence suggest, older workers have higher wage-productivity ratios than younger employees, how could it ever be efficient to force an employer to stick with its older employees? At first

34. Michael L. Wachter & George M. Cohen, *The Law and Economics of Collective Bargaining: An Introduction and Application to the Problems of Subcontracting, Partial Closure, and Relocation*, 136 U. PA. L. REV. 1349, 1362-63 (1988).

glance, such an outcome would appear to be at odds with any plausible notion of efficiency. Employers would be holding onto older workers to perform jobs that younger, cheaper candidates could do as well or better relative to their cost. Society would pay more for goods and services, and younger workers would sacrifice more in their early years than they would gain later on. Plants would be shut down,[35] the need for cost-cutting policies would be frustrated,[36] and the options of governmental bodies seeking to deal with shrinking budgets would be severely limited.[37]

This gloomy view, however, fails to consider *why* it might be that older workers are paid so generously. Wages are determined in the market, not handed down from above. Thus, if employers and employees are opting for age-based wages, presumably there is some reason for their doing so. The sensibility of prohibiting cost-based decisions about older workers cannot be assessed without consideration of the parties' reasons for getting themselves into the high-wage situation in the first place. Reasons that age-based wages may be efficient and therefore desired by market actors are the focus of Part II.

II. Explanations for Age-Based Wages

The view that forcing firms to retain older, more expensive workers is necessarily inefficient reflects a purely static conception of efficiency. From a static perspective, paying an input more than its marginal revenue product is clearly inefficient; neoclassical theory predicts that firms will hire workers up to the point at which marginal revenue product just equals the wage.[38] But the world is more complicated than this. The analysis below explains that once we move beyond the static perspective, age-based wages may be desired by market actors either as a response to incentive problems in the employment relationship or due to employees' psychological preference for increased earnings over time. Other factors may also contribute to age-based wages, but the two explanations discussed below have been tested and shown to have empirical support. The evidence suggests that at least part of the phenomenon of age-based wages is due to incentive considerations and the preference for increased earnings over time.

---

35. Metz v. Transit Mix, Inc., 828 F.2d 1202, 1212 (7th Cir. 1987) (Easterbrook, J., dissenting).

36. Steven J. Kaminshine, *The Cost of Older Workers, Disparate Impact, and the Age Discrimination in Employment Act*, 42 FLA. L. REV. 229, 233 (1990).

37. Markham v. Geller, 451 U.S. 945, 948 (1981) (Rehnquist, J., dissenting from denial of certiorari); *see also* Note, *The Age Discrimination in Employment Act of 1967*, 90 HARV. L. REV. 380, 399 (1976) (contending that there is no reason to construe the ADEA to prohibit firing older workers on cost grounds).

38. FLANAGAN ET AL., *supra* note 6, at 100.

A. *Incentive Problems in the Employment Relationship*

A classic problem in the employment setting is that workers may tend not to work hard when they are paid on the basis of time worked rather than performance. This moral hazard problem is potentially serious because almost ninety percent of employees in the United States are paid on time-worked basis.[39] Direct oversight of workers can alleviate the problem, but such oversight often imposes substantial costs of its own. While some individuals may work hard even apart from any personal financial reward (because they enjoy their work or believe that putting in an honest effort is the right thing to do), for other individuals the absence of a financial reward for hard work may affect behavior. This is true not only for workers in low-level jobs but also for top executives, as suggested by the push to tie these individuals' pay to corporate performance.[40]

A widely-noted solution to the moral hazard problem involves offering workers *delayed* rewards for good behavior.[41] Even if detailed monitoring of employees' effort or output levels is prohibitively costly (so that performance-based wages are not realistic), detecting the simple fact of "shirking" of some sort, with some probability, may be feasible.[42] Alternatively, assuming the infeasibility of cost-effective monitoring on a day-by-day or month-by-month basis, it may nevertheless be possible to infer something about employees' devotion and loyalty from their behavior over a longer period.[43] In either case, back-loading employees' wages reduces their incentive to shirk by increasing the potential punishment associated with such behavior. With back-loaded wages, much of the reward from not shirking comes later in the employee's working life. Thus, shirking may be punished—severely—by firing the wayward employee and depriving him or her of the back-loaded reward. The potential cost of shirking at any point is therefore higher than it would be if wages did not rise over time.[44]

---

39. *Id.* at 251.

40. *See generally* Michael C. Jensen & Kevin J. Murphy, *Performance Pay and Top-Management Incentives*, 98 J. POL. ECON. 225 (1990).

41. Lazear, *supra* note 21, at 1264; Edward P. Lazear, *Agency, Earnings Profiles, Productivity, and Hours Restrictions*, 71 AM. ECON. REV. 606, 615 (1981). Analyses that draw on or acknowledge (explicitly or implicitly) the incentive explanation for age-based wages include Harper, *supra* note 33, at 1288-89; Kaminshine, *supra* note 36, at 269-70; Schwab, *supra* note 27, at 15-19; Wachter & Cohen, *supra* note 34, at 1362-63; and Erica Worth, Note, *In Defense of Targeted ERIPs: Understanding the Interaction of Life-Cycle Employment and Early Retirement Incentive Plans*, 74 TEX. L. REV. 411, 416-20 (1995).

42. Lazear, *supra* note 21, at 1267; Lazear, *supra* note 41, at 614-15.

43. FLANAGAN ET AL., *supra* note 6, at 260, 264; Oliver Hart & Bengt Holmström, *The Theory of Contracts*, *in* ADVANCES IN ECONOMIC THEORY—FIFTH WORLD CONGRESS 71, 97-103 (Truman F. Bewley ed., 1987).

44. Lazear, *supra* note 21, at 1267; Lazear, *supra* note 41, at 607. The specifics of Lazear's model structure may be open to criticism in certain respects, *see* Peter Kuhn, *Wages, Effort, and*

The incentive explanation for age-based wages suggests that both employers and employees are made better off (financially) by the use of such wages. By mitigating the moral hazard problem, age-based wages raise workers' productivity over their years in the labor force and thus increase the surplus created by the employment relationship. The precise division of the extra surplus will depend on the nature of the market in question (employees will capture all of the surplus in a perfectly competitive market, in which lifetime wages and productivity are equalized[45]), but employers and employees are necessarily better off as a unit, and there is no reason to think that *employees* as a group would be made worse off. Incentive considerations therefore represent one reason why age-based wages may be desired by market participants.

Empirical confirmation of the incentive theory of age-based wages is complicated by the fact that jobs in which monitoring of employees is difficult (and, thus, back-loaded wages are desirable on incentive grounds) may also tend to be jobs in which wages increase over time due to accumulation of human capital. If this is true, then wage increases with age may reflect human capital rather than incentive considerations. The conflation poses a problem because the underlying phenomenon of interest—wages that are upward-sloping even after controlling for productivity—is difficult to observe directly.

Notwithstanding these complications, several pieces of evidence are suggestive. First, wages of older workers are higher—even after controlling for education, union status, race, region, and other characteristies—in jobs not involving repetitive tasks (defined as "repetitive or short cycle operations carried out according to set procedures or sequences"), where monitoring difficulties are likely to give rise to moral hazard issues, than in jobs involving repetitive tasks, where moral hazard should be less severe.[46] The comparison is possible because some jobs in the "repetitive task" category are skilled occupations that attract the same sorts of workers as are found in jobs not involving repetitive tasks.[47] A second piece of

---

Incentive Compatibility in Life-Cycle Employment Contracts, 4 J. LAB. ECON. 28, 35-38 (1986), but these criticisms do not go to the basic intuition behind Lazear's conclusion.

45. FLANAGAN ET AL., *supra* note 6, at 55.

46. Robert Hutchens, *A Test of Lazear's Theory of Delayed Payment Contracts*, 5 J. LAB. ECON. S153, S161, S163 (1987).

47. *Id.* at S161. Nevertheless, an important limit on the reliability of the finding is that employees may differ along dimensions that affect wages and are not captured by the education, union status, race, region, and other controls. What the evidence says is that an older worker with a given education level, union status, and so forth earns more in old age in a job not involving repetitive tasks than in a job involving such tasks. However, employees in jobs not involving repetitive tasks may be paid more in old age, or throughout their lives, even after controlling for education, union status, and other worker qualities, simply because of factors (including human capital) that cannot adequately be controlled for in the analysis.

evidence for the incentive explanation of age-based wages is that pension plans are more common in jobs not involving repetitive tasks, where monitoring may be difficult, than in jobs involving repetitive tasks, again controlling for differences in observable characteristics of employees.[48] Pensions are also more common among workers with demographic characteristics linked to job level (and, hence, at least arguably to monitoring difficulties).[49] Finally, mandatory retirement, which signals a divergence between wages and productivity, was most common (before its abolition) in jobs not involving repetitive tasks, and among workers with demographic characteristics linked to job level.[50]

B. *Psychological Preference for Increased Earnings over Time*

A second possible explanation for age-based wages is a psychological preference for improvement in earnings over time. Human beings appear to prefer increasing quantities of good things over time, as compared to constant streams or decreasing quantities.[51] This may reflect in large part a tendency to evaluate options based on whether they represent upward movement from an initial status quo.[52] Thus, for example, earning $20,000 one year, $22,000 the next, and $24,000 the year after that would typically be preferred to earning $22,000 each year. The former path entails repeated upward movement relative to the previous year's benchmark and is more attractive on that account.

Evidence from experimental economics studies suggests the existence of just this type of preference for improvement over time. In the context of job earnings specifically, one study found that individuals asked to choose between wage profiles that declined over time and wage profiles that increased over time overwhelmingly preferred the latter, even though the discounted present value of wage payments was higher with the former.[53] This preference existed despite discounting of future events (which would imply a preference for declining profiles) in other contexts. Subjects asked why they preferred increasing wage profiles gave, as the most common explanation, "pleasure from increase," followed by

48. *Id.* at S163.

49. Lazear, *supra* note 21, at 1280 (Table: Logit and OLS Results).

50. Hutchens, *supra* note 46, at S163; Lazear, *supra* note 21, at 1280 (Table: Logit and OLS Results).

51. George Loewenstein & Nachum Sicherman, *Do Workers Prefer Increasing Wage Profiles?*, 9 J. LAB. ECON. 67, 71-75 (1991); George Loewenstein & Drazen Prelec, *Negative Time Preference*, 81 AM. ECON. REV. (PAPERS & PROC.) 347, 347 (1991).

52. *See* Daniel Kahneman & Amos Tversky, *Prospect Theory: An Analysis of Decision Under Risk*, 47 ECONOMETRICA 263, 263 (1979); *see also* RICHARD H. THALER, THE WINNER'S CURSE: PARADOXES AND ANOMALIES OF ECONOMIC LIFE 100 (1992).

53. Loewenstein & Sicherman, *supra* note 51, at 71-75.

"aversion to decrease."[54] The preference for increasing profiles was less pronounced, although still present, in the case of rental income earned from ownership of an apartment building, a context in which improvements to the status quo are less likely to be attributed to actions taken by the individual.[55] These results may reflect what psychologists have called "mastery"—the idea that people derive satisfaction from the perception that they have mastered their environment, and for this reason prefer steady improvements to a flat path over time.[56]

Studies outside the wage context have produced similar findings. For example, subjects asked to choose between a free dinner at a French restaurant and a free dinner at a Greek restaurant typically preferred the former, and those who preferred the French dinner also preferred to receive it in one month's time rather than two.[57] This latter ordering indicates a general inclination towards having good things sooner rather than later; future events are discounted in value. However, when those who preferred the French dinner were told that they would receive both a French dinner and a Greek dinner, the majority preferred to have the Greek rather than the French dinner first—the opposite of what conventional present-value discounting analysis would predict.[58]

The experimental findings thus suggest that people prefer increasing quantities of good things over time. Age-based wages may be a real-world counterpart to the psychological evidence, either because productivity is flat while rising wages are preferred or because the rise in productivity is slower than the preferred rate of increase in wages. Either way, if the suggestion about age-based wages here is correct, then their use increases the surplus to be divided between employers and employees and makes these parties better off as a unit. (Also, as above, there is no reason to think that employees as a group would be made worse off.)

Wages satisfy what seems to be an important element in the preference for increasing sequences: they exhibit "integrity," which refers to the extent to which the events that comprise a sequence are of a similar type,

---

54. *Id.* at 78.

55. *Id.* at 74-75.

56. *Id.* at 69; Robert W. White, *Motivation Reconsidered: The Concept of Competence*, 66 PSYCHOL. REV. 297, 302 (1959). To check whether subjects were simply confused about the choice between declining and increasing profiles, Loewenstein and Sicherman explained that accepting a declining wage or rental income profile would yield higher monetary returns by allowing the individual to invest the front-loaded payments and earn positive returns in the form of interest. They also presented the subjects with the psychological explanation for preferring increasing profiles. Subjects' choices among profiles were qualitatively unchanged. *See* Loewenstein & Sicherman, *supra* note 51, at 75-76.

57. Loewenstein & Prelec, *supra* note 51, at 348.

58. *Id.*

are regularly spaced, and are not stretched too far apart.[59] If a sequence lacks integrity in this sense, then the preference for improvement over time may disappear. This occurs, for example, in sequences consisting of two dissimilar events, one a week off and the other twenty-six weeks off.[60] Wage sequences, in contrast, are comprised of similar, regularly spaced, and relatively frequent events.

I am not aware of any direct economic tests of the posited link between age-based wages and the psychological preference for improvement over time. Age-based wages do seem to be observed in jobs in which *incentive* considerations may be relatively unimportant; an example is airline pilots, whose wages increase sharply with age without any apparent increase in productivity, and whose "shirk[ing] on (say) safety [is] amply punished by nature."[61] On the other hand, it is possible that use of age-based wages where incentive considerations seem unimportant may reflect something other than a psychological preference for increased earnings over time.[62]

---

59. *Id.*

60. *Id.* at 349.

61. THALER, *supra* note 52, at 102; *see also* Robert H. Frank & Robert M. Hutchens, *Wages, Seniority, and the Demand for Rising Consumption Profiles*, 21 J. ECON. BEHAV. & ORGANIZATION 251, 252-53, 257 (1993).

62. An independent explanation for age-based wages, not considered in the text, is workers' desire to commit themselves to saving for retirement or higher anticipated expenses (including college tuition for children) in middle age. If willpower to save were not an issue, workers could simply take any "extra" pay earned in their early years and put it in the bank; age-based wages would not be necessary. If, however, workers are concerned about having the willpower to engage in an adequate level of saving, they may want to "bind themselves to the mast" through age-based wages, just as Ulysses, fearing the temptation of the Sirens' song, did in Homer's *Odyssey*. *See* HOMER, THE ODYSSEY 214 (Robert Fitzgerald trans., Anchor Books 1963). In effect, age-based wages facilitate saving for retirement or middle age by delaying the payment of the necessary funds until the appropriate point in the life-cycle. On this view, age-based wages may be efficient, in the sense of making the individual better off at each point in time. *See* E.S. Phelps & R.A. Pollack, *On Second-Best National Saving and Game-Equilibrium Growth*, 35 REV. ECON. STUD. 185, 188-89 (1968). Alternatively, they may make some "temporal selves" better off and others—those who want to engage in momentary splurges rather than futuristic saving for retirement or middle age—worse off, a distributive consequence that is probably salutary.

The retirement-saving theory, like the theories linking age-based wages to incentive issues and a psychological preference for increased earnings over time, explains why such wages may be desired by market actors. However, unlike the two theories examined in the text, the retirement-saving theory does not explain why age-based wages must be linked to the employment relationship in an ongoing way. Suppose that a worker leaves one employer and begins a new relationship with another. If the back-loaded wage entitlements the worker has accumulated at the first firm are packaged as a portable pension that follows the worker to the new firm, then the purpose of age-based wages has been fulfilled, without any need for a continuing link to the employment relationship. This feature of the retirement-saving explanation means that the rationale, developed more fully in Part III, for affording legal protection to employees' age-based wage entitlements on hands-tying grounds does not apply when age-based wages reflect retirement-saving considerations. While such considerations may provide a partial explanation for age-based wages, the empirical evidence described in the text suggests that the two theories I emphasize also play a significant role.

III. The Role of the Law: Hands-Tying

The preceding Part described two theories of age-based wages that, individually or together, seem to provide at least a partial account of the wage pattern suggested by the ADEA cases and the empirical evidence. One question raised by these theories is whether legal limits on cost-based decisions about older workers might contribute to private parties' ability to make use of age-based wages. If parties are readily able to reach their preferred solution on their own, then legal involvement is probably unnecessary. As this Part explains, however, private parties may be limited in their ability to rely on age-based wages in a world in which individuals often change jobs at least once over the course of their working lives. Labor market mobility, though certainly valuable on balance, creates a species of inter-employer externality that interferes with parties' ability to use contracts or other market mechanisms to commit to age-based wages. Commitment is essential because employers will be tempted to renege on their side of the bargain when wages rise above marginal revenue product, as illustrated by the claims of cost-based decisionmaking under the ADEA.

Legal limits on cost-based decisions about older workers represent a possible solution to the inter-employer externality problem arising from labor market mobility. They facilitate commitment by tying employers' hands and preventing them from reneging on age-based wages when the back-loaded portion of those wages comes due. The law may thus play a desirable hands-tying role in a setting in which the unregulated market is unable to ensure the satisfaction of employers' and employees' preferences for age-based wages.

The structure of the analysis in this Part reflects the conventional structure of analyses of legal rules from an efficiency perspective. I describe a potential market failure and then discuss whether legal intervention could conceivably help. The second step in the analysis proceeds at a highly general level at this stage. Thus, I ask whether and how an ideal legal regime governing cost-based decisions about older workers

A further explanation for age-based wages links them to employers' desire to attract the type of employee who is likely to stay with the firm for an extended period. *See* Joanne Salop & Steven Salop, *Self-Selection and Turnover in the Labor Market*, 90 Q.J. ECON. 619, 620 (1976). Here again, though, the proposed explanation for age-based wages is inconsistent with the rationale set forth in Part III for protecting employees' age-based wage entitlements. Central to the employee-selection theory (as developed by Salop and Salop) is the idea that job mobility is harmful to employers and must be discouraged by the choice of an appropriate wage structure. In contrast, the desirability and practical importance of mobility are central to the role of legal rules envisioned in Part III. If the employee-selection theory were modified to focus on attracting employees with desirable attributes other than long expected tenure at the firm (for example, ability to do the job well), then the theory would fit well with the argument in Part III. However, because the employee-selection theory (in any of its variants) has not, to my knowledge, been subjected to the same degree of empirical scrutiny as the two theories considered in the text, I do not pursue its implications here.

might remedy the market failure I describe. This generalized and idealized inquiry falls far short of an endorsement of the specific contours of any real-world regime, including that established by the ADEA. The inquiry is meant to show conceptually how legal limits on cost-based decisionmaking might address the externality problem I identify. Part IV returns to the specific context of the ADEA and grapples with the match between the ideal legal regime of this section and the recalcitrant reality of employment discrimination litigation.

A. *Market Solutions to the Commitment Problem*

The central constraint on age-based wages in an unregulated market—by which I mean a market governed solely by contract, property, and other common-law rules—is the difficulty of achieving commitment to such wages on the part of employers. Once employees' wages exceed their marginal revenue product, it is in the short-term interest of the firm not to employ them. They are no longer producing as much as they cost in wages, though from their perspective the high wages are merely restitution for low wages earned early on. Termination or failure to hire in these circumstances is precisely the sort of employer behavior underlying the paradigmatic cost-based decisionmaking claim under the ADEA.

The incentive to deviate from age-based wages implies the need for some form of commitment mechanism if such wages are to be feasible in an unregulated market. A useful typology of commitment mechanisms distinguishes between legally enforceable contracts, which commit parties by subjecting them to legal penalties for breach, and nonlegal sanctions, which commit parties by penalizing deviations through informal or extra-legal means.[63] Each of these forms of commitment represents a possible means of fostering the use of age-based wages in an unregulated market, but, as described below, each is subject to significant limits, in major part due to labor market mobility.

1. Legally enforceable contracts.—Legally enforceable contracts are perhaps the most obvious means of commitment. Entry into a contract can deter the parties from engaging in various forms of opportunistic behavior—such as terminating older employees whose wages exceed their marginal revenue product.[64] For this reason contracts make parties better off—paradoxically by allowing them, when it serves their interests, to limit their own future choices. Employment contracts illustrate the phenomenon well: by enabling employers to commit to high pay at the end of the life-

63. *See* David Charny, *Nonlegal Sanctions in Commercial Relationships*, 104 HARV. L. REV. 373, 376-78 (1990).

64. *See* RICHARD A. POSNER, ECONOMIC ANALYSIS OF LAW 89-91 (4th ed. 1992).

cycle, they make it possible for employers and employees to rely on age-based wages. Without a contract, discharging an employee earning more than marginal revenue product may be desirable for the employer; with a contract, the employer will keep the employee on because of a contractual obligation to do so. The prospects for contracting should be especially bright in the long-term relationships on which the contemporary employment law literature has focused, as employees in such relationships can contract while young for job protection when they are old.[65]

Economically oriented commentators who discount or dismiss contractual solutions to commitment problems in employment relationships often do so on the ground that transaction costs (broadly defined) preclude parties from writing even reasonably complete agreements.[66] However, the transaction costs of writing complete contracts in long-term relationships typically justify only default rules—rules that attach only if a contract is made, and only if the contracting parties do not explicitly contract around them. Legal regulation of employment discrimination clearly does not fall into this category. Thus, for example, a protection against age discrimination that did not attach until an employment relationship had been established and only then if the parties to the relationship had not contracted around the protection would bear little resemblance to antidiscrimination law as we know it. An individual would have no entitlement at all not to be discriminated against at the hiring stage because at that stage no employment relationship, and thus no protection against discrimination, would exist. Where transaction costs are the barrier to optimal contracting by private parties, it is the exception rather than the rule that creating an entitlement, rather than merely specifying a default term for an established relationship, makes rational contractors better off.[67]

A distinct and important source of contracting failure in employment relationships is imperfect information on the part of employees.[68] If imperfect information gives rise to a contracting failure, then a rule creating an entitlement may well yield efficiency gains, even relative to the alternative of providing employees with more information. Thus, for

65. For discussions of long-term employment relationships, see EPSTEIN, *supra* note 8, at 448-49; PAUL C. WEILER, GOVERNING THE WORKPLACE: THE FUTURE OF LABOR AND EMPLOYMENT LAW 63-64 (1990); Samuel Issacharoff, *Contractual Liberties in Discriminatory Markets*, 70 TEX. L. REV. 1219, 1247-48 (1992) (reviewing EPSTEIN, *supra* note 8); Samuel Issacharoff, *Reconstructing Employment*, 104 HARV. L. REV. 607, 621-24 (1990) (reviewing WEILER, *supra*); Rutherglen, *supra* note 5, at 500-01; and Schwab, *supra* note 27, at 13.

66. *E.g.*, Schwab, *supra* note 27, at 19-20.

67. Benjamin E. Hermalin & Michael L. Katz, *Judicial Modification of Contracts Between Sophisticated Parties: A More Complete View of Incomplete Contracts and Their Breach*, 9 J.L. ECON. & ORGANIZATION 230, 232-33 (1993).

68. *See, e.g.*, Samuel Issacharoff, *Contracting for Employment: The Limited Return of the Common Law*, 74 TEX. L. REV. 1783, 1799 (1996).

example, if employees' failure to appreciate the threat of cost-based discharge in their later years leads them not to insist on contractual protection against such behavior, then some form of legal intervention may be desirable on efficiency grounds. Information failures have not, however, been the focus of economically oriented commentators' analyses of employment relationships—perhaps in part because of the divergence in these commentators' views of the importance of the problem.

Transaction costs and information failures are not the only barriers to successful contracting in an unregulated market. Job mobility represents an additional—and possibly more broadly compelling—ground for questioning the efficacy of contractual means of commitment. Employees in long-term relationships with particular firms may be able to contract in advance for protection against cost-based discharge, but the contractual entitlements will protect them only as long as they stay in their original jobs. The entitlements are not portable to new employers. Thus, if an employee wants or needs to change jobs—because his or her productivity is higher at a different firm, or because he or she needs to move away from the job or the region for some reason—the employee will no longer be protected by the original contractual entitlement.

Mobile employees would be able to rely on contracts to achieve commitment to age-based wages if contracting in advance with every potential future employer were feasible. In that case, the employee would enjoy the same contractual protection as he or she would have in a long-term contractual relationship with a single employer. Such extensive ex ante contracting, however, is unlikely to be realistic. The more interesting question is whether the parties can somehow replicate what would occur if complete ex ante contracting were feasible. Contracting with the initial employer should be feasible, so the question then becomes whether the employee can leverage the original contractual entitlement not to be discharged when wages exceed marginal revenue product into an entitlement not to be disadvantaged on cost grounds at a new firm.

Numerous barriers to this sort of leveraging exist. As an initial matter, it is the first employer, not the second, who has captured the benefits of paying low wages early on in the relationship. The second employer will have no reason to agree to pay wages above marginal revenue product to an employee from whom the employer has not been able to recoup the back-loaded wages early on. One response to this problem is severance pay; the original employer should be willing to compensate the employee for giving up the right to a wage above marginal revenue product by moving to another company, as the employer saves money by removing the obligation to pay the employee the high wage.[69] However, the

69. Lazear, *supra* note 21, at 1272-73.

severance-pay strategy, without more, would *undo* for the future whatever benefit was sought to be achieved by age-based wages. Under the severance-pay strategy, the employee receives a lump-sum payment and then a wage equal to his or her marginal revenue product at the new employer. The back-loaded payment has already been made. Thus, whatever the reason for age-based wages in the first instance—whether incentive issues or a psychological preference for increased earnings over time—the intended function of such wages is no longer being served.

The intended function of age-based wages would continue to be served if the first employer somehow arranged for the second to cover the excess wages of the employee in the later years of the life-cycle, or continued to cover these excess wages itself. However, each of these solutions would require new contractual relationships, distinct from the traditional employer-employee one, and would thus impose additional transaction costs and informational difficulties. Furthermore, it is doubtful whether payment of a wage supplement by an individual's former employer (whether done indirectly through the new employer, or directly in the form of an annuity from the former employer) would respond to the psychological preference for increased earnings over time in the same way that payment of increasing wages over time by the current employer does.

An alternative means of leveraging the original contractual arrangement would involve coupling the severance-pay strategy with some form of up-front payment by the employee to the new employer, who would then pay out wages above marginal revenue product just as the original employer would have done. This type of employee bonding is not the sort of contractual arrangement we typically observe in practice. Indeed, if such an arrangement were feasible, then it is unclear why parties would ever need to rely on age-based wages for *incentive* purposes in the first place, as desirable incentives could be created (at least up to the point at which liquidity constraints kick in) by forcing employees to post bonds that would be forfeited in the event of employee misbehavior. Furthermore, it is doubtful whether the employee-bonding strategy would satisfy the psychological preference for improvement in earnings over the life-cycle, as increases in pay over time would simply reflect reimbursement of the bond posted by the employee.

At a minimum, then, each of the potential strategies for leveraging the original contractual arrangement will do so only imperfectly. The surplus created by employment relationships will be lower than it would be if employees could contract in advance with all potential future employers, thereby solving the inter-employer externality problem arising from job mobility. This is not to say that mobility is undesirable on balance; if that were true, mobility would not occur. The point is simply that in a world of mobile employees, contracting will not suffice to permit reliance on the age-based wages that employers and employees appear to prefer.

The empirical evidence suggests the practical significance of job mobility. While many employees remain with their employers for long periods,[70] a substantial fraction of employees moves around, even after many years in the labor force. Thus, for example, interview evidence from the 1980s suggests that 50% of mid-level computer positions and 28% of high-level sales positions are filled by outside hires.[71] Likewise, in the economy as a whole, 18% of workers aged 35 to 44, and 13% of workers aged 45 to 54, have been in their current jobs less than a year.[72] Fewer than one-third of employees aged 35 to 44, and fewer than one-half of employees aged 45 to 54, have been in their jobs more than 10 years.[73] These patterns are not new; an earlier study of the 1967-1973 period found, for example, that 12% of employees aged 35 to 49 changed jobs in a typical two-year period.[74] It is unclear whether mobility has increased over time, as media reports often suggest, or is holding constant, but it *is* clear that mobility is a significant feature of modern labor markets.[75]

The practical importance of job mobility is also indirectly suggested by the attention it has received in law reform efforts. For example, the passage of the 1986 amendments to the Employee Retirement Income Security Act of 1974 (ERISA), which require vesting of pension benefits after five years with an employer,[76] may have reflected a response to the prevalence of mobility among employees. Likewise, a major focus of the 1993 debate over health care reform was the barrier to job mobility created by preexisting condition clauses in employer-sponsored plans.[77]

The mobility figures and other evidence do not tell us whether mobility among workers is voluntary or involuntary (or somewhere in between).

---

70. Robert E. Hall, *The Importance of Lifetime Jobs in the U.S. Economy*, 72 AM. ECON. REV. 716, 718-20 (1982).

71. Paul Osterman, *White-Collar Internal Labor Markets*, *in* INTERNAL LABOR MARKETS 163, 172 (Paul Osterman ed., 1984) (Table: Openness of Job Ladders).

72. HENRY S. FARBER, ARE LIFETIME JOBS DISAPPEARING? JOB DURATION IN THE UNITED STATES: 1979-1993 (Princeton University Industrial Relations Section Working Paper No. 341, 1995) (Table A5: Fraction with Job Duration of One Year or Less).

73. *Id.* (Table A6: Fraction with Job Duration of More Than Ten Years).

74. Jacob Mincer & Boyan Jovanovic, *Labor Mobility and Wages*, *in* STUDIES IN LABOR MARKETS 21, 25 (Sherwin Rosen ed., 1981) (Table: Mobility by Experience and Tenure).

75. For evidence that mobility has increased over time, see Kenneth A. Swinnerton & Howard Wial, *Is Job Stability Declining in the U.S. Economy?*, 48 INDUS. & LAB. REL. REV. 293, 296-97 (1995), and Kenneth A. Swinnerton & Howard Wial, *Is Job Stability Declining in the U.S. Economy? Reply to Diebold, Neumark, and Polsky*, 49 INDUS. & LAB. REL. REV. 352, 355 (1996). For contrary findings, see FARBER, *supra* note 72, at 2, and Francis X. Diebold et al., *Comment on Kenneth A. Swinnerton and Howard Wial, "Is Job Stability Declining in the U.S. Economy?"*, 49 INDUS. & LAB. REL. REV. 348, 348 (1996).

76. Tax Reform Act of 1986, Pub. L. No. 99-514, 100 Stat. 2085 (codified at 26 U.S.C. § 411(a)(2) (1994)).

77. *See* Steven Pearlstein, *Reform's Economic Side Effects: Clinton's Prescription Runs the Risk of Slowing Recovery*, WASH. POST, May 2, 1993, at A1, A22.

For the most part, however, it does not matter for my argument. What matters is that employees change jobs—sometimes frequently—over the life-cycle. Whether this occurs because employees choose to move around or instead because (say) their firm goes bankrupt, employers and employees will not be able to rely on contracts to achieve commitment to age-based wages.

Under certain circumstances, mobility may not pose particularly significant problems. Thus, for example, job changes among workers receiving age-based wages for incentive reasons may be relatively uncommon in practice due to the inability of potential future employers to determine with accuracy whether a job loss was voluntary on the employee's part or instead represents a discharge for malfeasance (for which loss of the back-loaded portion of wages was the contemplated punishment). But while mobility may not spell the demise of contractual commitment across the board, it certainly suggests important limits on such commitment, particularly where job changes are not likely to reflect malfeasance or age-based wages are desired because of employees' psychological preference for increased earnings over time.

2. *Nonlegal Sanctions*.—Nonlegal sanctions represent an alternative to legally enforceable contracts for achieving commitment to age-based wages. Nonlegal sanctions for deviating from an informal understanding include termination of the relationship, loss of profitable future opportunities with other parties, and individual or social condemnation.[78] The first type of sanction provides no protection against employer deviation from age-based wages because termination of the relationship is precisely what the employer is seeking. The second type of sanction, in contrast, is of clear practical importance in the employment setting. Employers that fire older employees will gradually gain reputations for doing so and, thus, will not be trusted to follow through on age-based wages. Their inability to make credible offers of age-based wages will prevent them from using such wages to address incentive problems or attract employees seeking to satisfy a preference for increased earnings over time. The third type of sanction, individual or social condemnation, may also constrain employers (or, more likely, their decisionmakers).

While nonlegal sanctions are clearly important, they also have significant limitations, as suggested by employment law reforms such as ERISA and the erosion of the employment at will doctrine (though, of course, these legal developments may also reflect other, less benign influences).[79]

78. Charny, *supra* note 63, at 392-94.

79. *See* MARK A. ROTHSTEIN & LANCE LIEBMAN, CASES AND MATERIALS ON EMPLOYMENT LAW 1222-23 (3d ed. 1994) (tracing the enactment of ERISA to shortcomings of the private-sector pension

Upon close examination, the economic models in which the threat of losing profitable future opportunities (the type of nonlegal sanction emphasized in the preceding paragraph) is an effective means of commitment depend on strong assumptions. First, the threat of losing future opportunities can constrain an actor's behavior only if that behavior is observable (at least to some degree) to outside parties.[80] The greater the "noise" in outsiders' observation of an actor's behavior, the harder it is to constrain that behavior by the threat of loss of future opportunities. Employees face obvious barriers to perfect observation of the behavior of firms, and the problem is likely to be exacerbated by employees' need, in a world of labor market mobility, to make assessments about firms with which they have had little or no prior contact.

The second key assumption behind economic models in which the threat of losing future opportunities constrains an actor's behavior is that the time horizon for the actor's market participation is infinite or uncertain, or, alternatively, potential trading partners have incomplete information about the actor's incentives to misbehave (as distinguished from the actor's actual behavior).[81] Without either an infinite or uncertain horizon or incomplete information, all players will know that as the end of the horizon approaches, the threat of losing future opportunities will not be an effective deterrent. Reasoning backwards, this knowledge in turn implies that the deterrent will be ineffective to begin with.[82] With an infinite or uncertain horizon, in contrast, the players will never be aware that the end of the horizon is approaching. Likewise, with incomplete information, the actor has an incentive to establish a reputation as the "type" of player that adheres to its promises—though if in fact it is only masquerading as that type of player, it will still deviate from these promises as the end of the horizon approaches.[83] Reputational constraints are therefore effective only so long as parties do not foresee an end to an actor's market participation and, in the case of a finite and certain horizon, only if the additional requirement of incomplete information about the actor's incentives to mis-

system); Schwab, *supra* note 27, at 45-47 (arguing that incursions on employment at will reflect responses to opportunistic behavior by employers). *But see* Richard A. Ippolito, *A Study of the Regulatory Effect of the Employee Retirement Income Security Act*, 31 J.L. & ECON. 85, 87-100, 116-19 (1988) (rejecting arguments for ERISA based on failures in private pension markets, and offering an interest group explanation for the Act).

80. *See* DREW FUDENBERG & JEAN TIROLE, GAME THEORY 146-48 (1991) (discussing games in which players' actions are observable by their opponents, who condition their future play on these actions); *id.* at 182-97 (discussing games in which the public outcomes that players act upon provide only imperfect information).

81. Hart & Holmström, *supra* note 43, at 143.

82. R. DUNCAN LUCE & HOWARD RAIFFA, GAMES AND DECISIONS: INTRODUCTION AND CRITICAL SURVEY 97-102 (1957); Ronald J. Gilson & Robert H. Mnookin, *Disputing Through Agents: Cooperation and Conflict Between Lawyers in Litigation*, 94 COLUM. L. REV. 509, 514-20 (1994).

83. Hart & Holmström, *supra* note 43, at 144.

behave is met. Judge Easterbrook's dissent in *Metz v. Transit Mix, Inc.* explicitly recognizes as much: "When the firm encounters economic trouble or for some other reason plans to shrink, it need not worry about scaring away bright new employees; it is out of that market."[84]

The limitations on nonlegal sanctions suggest that they leave important gaps in the ability to commit to age-based wages in an unregulated market. Thus, as with legally enforceable contracts, it is possible that nonlegal sanctions are usefully complemented by legal means of tying the parties' hands to age-based wages.

B. Hands-Tying Through Legal Rules

The limits on market mechanisms for committing to age-based wages lead to the question whether legal rules could conceivably help to mitigate the failure of the private market. I begin by addressing this question in a general way, asking whether and how an ideal legal regime governing cost-based decisions about older workers might remedy the inter-employer externality problem that arises with contractual means of commitment. Part IV below adopts a more pragmatic approach to the problem, one that attempts to situate the conceptual analysis offered here within the real world of employment discrimination litigation.

I begin by considering whether legal limits on cost-based *discharge* of older workers might solve the inter-employer externality problem. I then address legal limits on cost-based *failure to hire* older candidates. In each instance, I suggest that legal rules have a potential role to play in achieving commitment to age-based wages.

1. Legal Limits on Cost-Based Discharge of Older Workers.—A threshold question about legal limits on cost-based discharge of older workers concerns the appropriate scope of such limits. Would employers be permitted to substitute lowering the wages of expensive older workers for discharging these individuals on cost grounds?[85] In theory, this is an important question, but in practice it is relatively unimportant for the simple reason that employers are extremely reluctant to cut their workers' pay, fearing adverse consequences for dedication and morale.[86] Thus, the important issue in practice is the degree to which cost-based discharge of older employees is limited by legal rules. I assume in what follows that older workers will not be vulnerable to wage cuts, either because of the

84. 828 F.2d 1202, 1221 (7th Cir. 1987) (Easterbrook, J., dissenting).

85. *Cf. id.* at 1209-10 (discussing similarities and differences between the two approaches).

86. Truman F. Bewley, *A Depressed Labor Market As Explained by Participants*, 85 AM. ECON. REV. (PAPERS & PROC.) 250, 253 (1995). Bewley's conclusions are based on an extensive set of interviews, which will be discussed more fully in a forthcoming book. *See id.* at 252.

practical considerations militating against such action or because of legal rules against it.

Legal limits on cost-based discharge of older workers address the central problem emphasized above with contractual means of commitment to age-based wages. As described above, labor market mobility impedes parties' ability to rely on contractual means of commitment because of the infeasibility of contracting in advance for protection against cost-based discharge with every potential future employer. The inability to contract in advance in this way means that an employee who has changed jobs has no contractual entitlement to continued employment once wages have risen above marginal revenue product. Legal limits on cost-based discharge of older workers respond to the limits on contractual solutions by reaching beyond the limits of any single employment relationship. Unlike contracts, they commit employers that have not entered into contracts with particular employees. In effect, legal rules replicate the contractual terms parties would bargain for were they contracting in advance with all potential future employers. Lcgal limits on cost-based discharge thus mitigate the job-mobility barrier to contractual means of commitment and effectively tie the parties' hands where contracts cannot.

2. *Legal Limits on Cost-Based Failure To Hire.*—The hands-tying argument for legal limits on cost-based decisions about older workers applies not only to decisions to discharge older workers but also to decisions not to hire these individuals. Legal limits on cost-based failure to hire provide the mobile employee with an entitlement to age-based wages at a new firm—assuming the employer does not have an independent ground for refusing to hire the individual. Legal rules thus replicate the arrangement the parties would have bargained for were ex ante contracting feasible. The only qualification of the previous argument is that legal protection against wage cuts may be more important in the case of hiring than in the case of discharge, as in the latter case employers' reluctance to impose wage cuts may be greater. Apart from this distinction, the argument for legal limits on cost-based failure to hire tracks that for limits on cost-based discharge. In both instances, legal rules tie the parties' hands where contracts cannot. The discharge and hiring contexts differ from one another in other respects—a point to which I return in Part IV—but conceptually the hands-tying argument is the same in the two settings.

Richard Posner has argued that legal limits on failure to hire older workers are unlikely to have much practical force because of the insubstantial economic damages suffered by disappointed job applicants, as distinguished from workers who are discharged after having accumulated significant relationship-specific human capital.[87] As described above, however, older workers appear to be paid more than younger ones simply because of their age—at least up to some point.[88] It follows that an older worker who is refused a job at a wage greater than marginal revenue product has in fact suffered substantial economic damages as a consequence of the employer's behavior.

C. *Empirical Confirmation*

The hands-tying argument for legal limits on cost-based decisionmaking suggests that imposing such limits will increase the feasibility, and therefore the use, of age-based wages. This prediction is one that is testable in principle. For example, if certain states were to adopt legal limits on cost-based decisionmaking during a particular period while other states did not adopt such limits, then the relative change in the use of age-based wages in the two groups of states might provide some insight into the effect of the legal change. If, however, legal limits on cost-based decisioumaking are imposed at the national level (as with the ADEA), then empirical confirmation of the hands-tying argument is difficult. Changes (or lack thereof) in the use of age-based wages accompanying the change in the legal regime may reflect not the legal innovation but instead some other change in the surrounding environment. For example, if the change in the regime coincided with a decrease in the effectiveness of reputational means of commitment to age-based wages, then any increase in the use of such wages as a consequence of the legal innovation might be cancelled out by the decrease in the use of such wages because of reduced effectiveness of reputational constraints on employer behavior. This observation has particular salience in the context of the ADEA; even if we had good evidence about the relative frequency of age-based wages before and after enactment of the Act (which, as far as I am aware, we do not), it would be difficult to disentangle the effects of the ADEA from those of other changes in the labor market—including changes in the effectiveness of reputational constraints on employer behavior—occurring over the same period.

Indirect means of corroborating the hands-tying argument are somewhat more promising. One means of testing the argument is to look to the wages negotiated by unions—institutions that may help to address the inter-employer externality problem that arises with job mobility. Whereas an employee who changes jobs at a point at which wages exceed marginal revenue product may be unlikely to earn age-based wages at a nonunion-

87. POSNER, *supra* note 8, at 329.
88. *See supra* notes 30-34 and accompanying text.

ized firm, a unionized firm needing experienced workers may find it difficult to employ them except at the wage level specified by the union. The union thus in effect mimics the ex ante contracting that would enable the parties to solve the inter-employer externality problem. In this way, unions may help to mitigate the shortcomings of private contracting—which of course persist to some degree in a market with imperfect restraints on employer behavior, such as those imposed by the ADEA. Whether unions actually perform this function is another question. It is, however, empirically true that unionized employees are more likely to have pensions, and were more likely to be subject to mandatory retirement, than their nonunionized counterparts, consistent with the suggestion of greater feasibility of age-based wages in the unionized sector.[89]

As a final observation, the fact that job mobility plays an important role in the hands-tying analysis developed above does not imply that only highly-mobile employees should avail themselves of legal protection against cost-based discharge or failure to hire. Given the existence of such protection, employees in long-term relationships, who might otherwise rely on contract terms for protection, may find it easier (less costly) to rely on legal rules. The off-the-shelf approach economizes on negotiating, drafting, and other transaction costs, and it permits the employee to capture the benefits, such as predictability, of using terms that have already been extensively litigated and interpreted by courts.[90] The empirical evidence indicates that many ADEA plaintiffs have been with their current employers for substantial periods,[91] suggesting that employees who are not highly mobile do indeed rely on legal means of protection.

IV. ADEA Implications

This Part focuses on the doctrinal implications of the hands-tying analysis developed in Part III. An important threshold issue is the degree to which the efficiency considerations underlying that analysis properly influence the project of interpreting the ADEA. Different theories of statutory interpretation would answer this question differently, and it is not my goal to defend any particular conception of the judicial role in the interpretive project. Rather, I pose the following question: given a possible normative basis for the ADEA (hands-tying), how should courts wishing to reach decisions congruent with that normative basis resolve doctrinal issues arising under the Act? The primary issue I consider is the avail-

89. *See* POSNER, *supra* note 8, at 350 n.59; Hutchens, *supra* note 46, at S164.

90. *Cf.* Michael Klausner, *Corporations, Corporate Law, and Networks of Contracts*, 81 U. VA. L. REV. 758, 774-89 (1995) (noting the advantages of using standard terms in corporate charter contracts).

91. Rutherglen, *supra* note 5, at 509.

ability of "disparate impact" analysis under the ADEA. I explain that hands-tying considerations argue in favor of ADEA liability for cost-based decisions about older workers—and thus in favor of disparate impact analysis. I also describe reasons that the ADEA is likely to be a better means of facilitating desirable hands-tying than other legal doctrines potentially suited to that purpose. I emphasize, however, that while disparate impact liability under the ADEA may be desirable in principle, it raises serious implementation issues and may entail considerable administrative cost. Part IV concludes by discussing whether and to what extent workers should be permitted to waive ADEA provisions, either as to past or current events or as to events that may occur in the future.

A. Disparate Impact Liability Under the ADEA

The most basic form of age discrimination occurs when an employer's behavior is directly motivated by the age of the affected employee. Such behavior is prohibited under antidiscrimination law's "disparate treatment" rubric. The employer behavior on which my analysis has focused, however, is not directly motivated by the employee's age; rather, it is motivated by an independent factor—cost—that is correlated with age. While several appeals courts upheld disparate treatment challenges to cost-based decisionmaking prior to the Supreme Court's decision in *Hazen Paper Co. v. Biggins*,[92] the conclusion that discrimination motivated by cost is discrimination motivated by age seems false almost by definition. *Hazen Paper* set the record straight on this point, holding that "there is no disparate treatment under the ADEA when the factor motivating the employer is some feature other than the employee's age."[93] The following section focuses on an alternative basis for legal limits on cost-based decisionmaking.

1. The Case for Imposing Disparate Impact Liability.—The "disparate impact" rubric in antidiscrimination law applies to employment practices that disproportionately burden a protected group but are not directly motivated by the protected characteristic.[94] Disparate impact analysis originated under Title VII, and its application in the ADEA context remains uncertain. The Court in *Hazen Paper* expressly reserved the question of the availability of disparate impact analysis under the ADEA, and appeals

92. 507 U.S. 604 (1993). Cases upholding the application of disparate treatment analysis to cost-based decisionmaking include White v. Westinghouse Elec. Co., 862 F.2d 56 (3d Cir. 1988) and Metz v. Transit Mix, Inc., 828 F.2d 1202 (7th Cir. 1987). In light of *Hazen Paper*, these cases are no longer good law. *See, e.g.*, Anderson v. Baxter Healthcare Corp., 13 F.3d 1120, 1125-26 (7th Cir. 1994).

93. 507 U.S. at 609.

94. *See* Griggs v. Duke Power Co., 401 U.S. 424, 431 (1971).

courts since then have split on the question.[95] The hands-tying analysis offered above provides a possible policy argument for imposing disparate impact liability: cost-based decisions about older employees—which the disparate treatment rubric cannot reach—may reflect a market failure remediable by legal involvement. Hands-tying thus argues in favor of disparate impact liability for cost-based decisionmaking.

Judge Easterbrook's *Metz* dissent ironically provides support for imposing disparate impact liability on hands-tying grounds. The dissent notes, "The distressed or shrinking firm may try to dispose of higher paid, older employees, cheating them out of the high compensation at the end of their careers. A disparate impact approach under the ADEA might help to curtail this opportunism."[96] Judge Easterbrook did not pursue this suggestion because he found it inapplicable to the facts of the case. However, the suggestion—though difficult to reconcile with the tenor of his opinion as a whole—is squarely in line with the hands-tying analysis developed above. Judge Posner has similarly recognized the possible desirability of limiting cost-based decisions about older workers, but he goes on to reject the idea out of hand, reasoning that "maybe because [it] would make it difficult for firms to take rational steps to reduce their costs when they find, for whatever reason, that they are paying wages in excess of the market, the Supreme Court has rejected this approach."[97] *Hazen Paper* is cited in support of the concluding assertion, but, as noted above, the implications of that decision for disparate impact liability under the ADEA are somewhat murkier than Posner suggests. From a policy perspective, hands-tying considerations provide an argument in favor of the approach of circuits that have upheld disparate impact liability under the ADEA.

2. *The "Discrimination" Label and Other Caveats.*—On first glance, labeling a cost-based discharge or refusal to hire "age discrimination" may

95. *See Hazen Paper Co.*, 507 U.S. at 610 ("[W]e have never decided whether a disparate impact theory of liability is available under the ADEA, and we need not do so here." (citation omitted)). Since *Hazen Paper*, the Seventh and Tenth Circuits have rejected disparate impact liability under the ADEA. *See* EEOC v. Francis W. Parker Sch., 41 F.3d 1073, 1076-77 (7th Cir. 1994), *cert. denied*, 115 S. Ct. 2577 (1995); Ellis v. United Airlines, Inc., 73 F.3d 999, 1006-10 (10th Cir. 1996). In contrast, the Eighth and Ninth Circuits have permitted disparate impact claims. *See* Houghton v. Sipco, Inc., 38 F.3d 953, 958-59 (8th Cir. 1994); EEOC v. Local 350, 998 F.2d 641, 648 n.2 (9th Cir. 1993). Justice Kennedy apparently did not find the *Hazen Paper* majority's statement about reserving the disparate impact question sufficiently reassuring, as he wrote a separate concurrence, joined by Chief Justice Rehnquist and Justice Thomas, emphasizing that he joined the Court's opinion only on the understanding that nothing in it incorporated disparate impact analysis into the ADEA context. *Hazen Paper Co.*, 507 U.S. at 618 (Kennedy, J., concurring). For a list of cases and commentary on disparate impact liability under the ADEA, see *Francis W. Parker Sch.*, 41 F.3d at 1079 & nn.1-2 (Cudahy, J., dissenting).

96. *Metz*, 828 F.2d at 1221 (Easterbrook, J., dissenting).

97. POSNER, *supra* note 8, at 337.

seem incongruous. After all, the employer is acting not on the basis of age but on the basis of cost. The observation has particular salience in the case of discharge of a recently-hired older employee or refusal to hire an older candidate, as here the employer has not benefitted from payment of low wages early on. On the other hand, these are precisely the situations in which private contracts are least effective (as job movement has occurred) and, thus, in which the hands-tying argument for legal involvement has the greatest force.

Several considerations support labeling cost-based discharge or failure to hire "age discrimination." First, the employer's behavior is based on the simple fact of the employee's position on the wage trajectory, which in turn is directly related to the employee's age. Second, in a world in which (because of legal or other constraints) employers typically do not engage in cost-based decisionmaking even as to older employees on whom they have not capitalized during low-wage periods, an employer that *does* engage in such decisionmaking will in effect reap the benefits of low wage payments without paying the full costs.

Apart from the labeling concern, imposition of disparate impact liability for cost-based decisions about older workers raises serious issues of implementation and may entail considerable administrative and other costs. To begin, courts may often be unable to distinguish between cases of cost-based discharge or refusal to hire an older worker and cases in which the worker is unattractive on independent grounds. Second, the behavior targeted by legal limits on cost-based decisionmaking is a deviation from the age-based wages desired by market participants. Identifying departures from a benchmark that is not itself easily identifiable presents obvious difficulties.

Courts might respond to the latter problem by looking to other firms in an employer's industry or in other industries to formulate rough age-wage benchmarks against which to assess the employer's behavior. Yardstick competition of this sort is used routinely by utility regulators seeking to uncover firms' underlying cost structures, much as courts here must seek to uncover underlying age-wage relationships.[98] Yardstick competition can also be used to guard against the imposition of liability for adverse decisions on an employer to whom, for some reason, older workers tend to flock—a response that is desirable on both fairness and efficiency grounds.

These observations hardly suffice (and in some cases do nothing) to dispel the concern that courts applying disparate impact analysis to cost-based decisions about older workers impose costs greater than any con-

98. *See* Paul L. Joskow & Richard Schmalensee, *Incentive Regulation for Electric Utilities*, 4 YALE J. ON REG. 1, 34-35 (1986).

ceivable benefit. My argument is simply that hands-tying considerations provide a possible argument for imposing disparate impact liability. Contrary to the suggestion of several courts and commentators, imposition of liability for cost-based decisionmaking is not inefficient as a matter of basic economics.[99] Instead, imposition of such liability may facilitate the use of age-based wages and is potentially desirable on that ground.

B. *Why the ADEA?*

An important question is whether the ADEA is likely to be a better means of achieving desirable hands-tying than other legal doctrines potentially suited to that function. The most obvious alternative to the ADEA, and the alternative on which I focus here, is the law of wrongful discharge, which, as its name suggests, imposes limits on employers' ability to discharge employees without cause.[100] Wrongful discharge law looks much like the ADEA in terms of the demographic characteristics of plaintiffs.[101] Moreover, several commentators on wrongful discharge law have focused on the precise features of wages and productivity emphasized above in the analysis of the ADEA.[102]

I offer two arguments about the suitability of the ADEA on hands-tying grounds, one comparative (involving the ADEA and wrongful discharge law) and the other a purely affirmative argument for the ADEA. As to the comparative issue, I want to suggest that, in two specific respects, the ADEA provides a better fit with the underlying problem than does wrongful discharge law. First, wrongful discharge law applies only to discharge, and not to refusal to hire an older candidate. Thus, wrongful discharge law does nothing to facilitate contract-like protection for employees who find it necessary to search for new jobs during the life-cycle. Second, tenure with a particular firm may be a significant factor in an employee's ability to prevail on a wrongful discharge claim (which will often rest on a notion of implied contract). Thus, again, wrongful discharge law fails to protect many of the individuals—this time, individuals who have recently joined new firms—who would be protected by the ADEA. These gaps in protection under wrongful discharge law are problematic because, as documented above, it is *age*, not tenure at a particular firm, that produces the wage-productivity disparity that in turn drives cost-based decisions about older workers. Wrongful discharge law is incomplete because it is fundamentally predicated upon the model of the employment relationship as a long-term relationship between employer and

99. For a list of courts and commentators seeming to suggest the opposite, see *supra* notes 35-37.

100. *See, e.g.*, Schwab, *supra* note 27, at 8-9.

101. Rutherglen, *supra* note 5, at 516-17.

102. *See* WEILER, *supra* note 65, at 67; Schwab, *supra* note 27, at 15-19.

employee—a model that, as described above, has animated much of the existing literature but fails to account for the conceptually and practically important phenomenon of job mobility.

The affirmative argument for the ADEA is in some sense just a recasting of the comparative argument. The affirmative version of the argument is that the ADEA makes pivotal the precise feature of an employee that makes contract-like protection desirable. According to the hands-tying analysis developed above, it is age, not time with a particular employer, that gives rise to a need for protection, and it is age that gives rise to protected status under the ADEA.

C. *ADEA Waivers*

A major issue in ADEA litigation has been whether and to what extent ADEA protections may be waived by their beneficiaries. Waivers of claims arising from past or contemporaneous events are explicitly permitted (subject to certain safeguards) by current law.[103] This section focuses on waivers of claims that have not yet arisen. Title VII precedent suggests that "prospective" waivers of this sort are generally prohibited.[104]

The hands-tying perspective implies that permitting prospective waivers of ADEA claims might be desirable on efficiency grounds. Operationally, employees would waive ADEA provisions prospectively by contracting out of these protections with their current employers. Such waivers would need to bind employees in future employment relationships as well, for otherwise an individual who waived ADEA protections as a young worker—and thereby perhaps obtained wages equal to, rather than less than, marginal revenue product in the early years of the life-cycle—might later be able to claim the right to wages above marginal revenue product at a different firm.

The basic efficiency argument in favor of prospective waivers is that they allow parties for whom age-based wages are not desirable—or at least not sufficiently desirable to warrant the costs of imposing legal liability for cost-based decisions about older workers—to avoid unnecessary and costly regulation of their private affairs. The most serious concern about permitting prospective waivers is that young employees may lack complete information on the costs and benefits of waiver. However strong the argument for permitting prospective waivers if knowing and voluntary, these conditions may be difficult to satisfy in practice.

---

103. Older Workers Benefit Protection Act of 1990, 29 U.S.C. § 626(f) (1994).

104. Alexander v. Gardner-Denver Co., 415 U.S. 36, 51-52 (1974).

V. Conclusion

The ADEA factors as significantly in employment discrimination litigation as does Title VII's traditional antidiscrimination command. However, normative analysis of the Act has lagged behind. I have attempted to deepen our normative understanding of the ADEA by tracing the contours and major implications of a hands-tying analysis of the Act. The hands-tying perspective is grounded in an empirical regularity apparent in ADEA cases and confirmed by empirical evidence: older workers are often paid more than younger workers capable of doing the same job. My analysis considers two possible explanations for age-based wages and identifies the impediments to the use of such wages in an unregulated market. I conclude that the ADEA may be understood in part as a hands-tying device enabling employers that wish to commit to age-based wages to do so. Viewing the ADEA in this light marks a departure from the distributional or rights-based focus of normative analysis under Title VII.

[3]

Why Is There Mandatory Retirement?

Edward P. Lazear

University of Chicago and National Bureau of Economic Research

This paper offers an explanation of the use of mandatory-retirement clauses in labor contracts. It argues that the date of mandatory retirement is chosen to correspond to the date of voluntary retirement, but the nature of the optimal wage profile results in a discrepancy between spot wage and spot VMP (value of the worker's marginal product). This is because it is preferable to pay workers less than VMP when young and more than VMP when old. By doing so, the "agency" problem is solved, so the contract with mandatory retirement is Pareto efficient. A theory of agency is presented and empirical evidence which supports the hypothesis is provided.

Mandatory retirement has recently become an important issue. Congress has enacted legislation that extends coverage under the Age Discrimination in Employment Act to workers up to age 70 rather than to age 65 as it previously stood. This essentially outlaws the use of mandatory retirement at age 65, a common practice. Furthermore, Congress is considering the extension of the Age Discrimination Act such that exemption would be eliminated entirely. The current legislation already does this for federal workers. In order to understand whether or not legislation outlawing mandatory retirement would benefit society, it is first essential to ask why this institution exists. The primary task of this paper is to offer an analysis of that institution, with testable implications, and then to discuss policy proposals that are consistent with and implied by this analysis. As an outgrowth, a

The author wishes to thank Charles Brown, Dennis Carlton, Linda Edwards, Victor Fuchs, Nathaniel Gregory, Victoria Lazear, Jacob Mincer, Sam Peltzman, Melvin Reder, Sherwin Rosen, and Lester Telser for useful suggestions. Victoria Lazear provided substantial assistance in solving the problem discussed in Section IA of the text.

theory of agency is presented which provides insight on how to compensate an agent in a manner that creates a harmony of interest between the principal and the agent.

There are many defenses and explanations of mandatory retirement. Most rely on the notion that a worker's productivity declines significantly after some age, say 65, and that mandatory retirement is the employer's way to deal with this reduced productivity. Yet, there is a significant diversity of talent in the labor force. No one claims that only the most talented individuals are the ones who can find jobs. Instead, economists believe that differences in wage rates reflect differences in productivity. The same is true of older workers. If older workers are less productive than younger workers, employers in a competitive labor market would be forced to pay older workers a lower wage rate than they pay younger workers. There is no necessity to lay off the older workers simply because their productivity is not as high as the younger workers'. In fact, very young workers earn less than middle-aged workers as a reflection of their lower productivity. Yet, we do not find researchers arguing that the minimum age for employment should be 45. The correct question then is, Why does employment rather than wage adjust?

Some have argued that morale would be adversely affected by lowering the wages of older workers. But it is not obvious that terminating workers rather than lowering their wages will improve the morale of the remaining work force. A 60-year-old worker who is faced with approaching termination is not necessarily going to have a better attitude than one who knows his wage rate will be lowered 5 years from now. Another view often expressed is that one cannot judge the decrease in productivity so that it would be impossible to adjust wages accordingly. But laying off a worker adjusts his wage rate to zero. This is a poorer approximation of his true productivity decline than any smooth wage adjustment. Furthermore, employers face the problem of gauging productivity for all workers. There is nothing unique about 65-year-olds in this regard. Thus, a productivity decline is not a sufficient explanation for the existence of mandatory retirement. One must ask why the productivity decline is dealt with by terminating the worker rather than by reducing his wages.[1]

Another "explanation" is that a uniform retirement policy avoids the disadvantage of discrimination between employees. Two questions arise. First, there is nothing that requires that a uniform retirement policy be one that has a provision for mandatory retirement. One could easily set up a flexible retirement scheme, where payment varies with length of service, that is invariant across individuals but

[1] See Gordon (1960), Kreps (1961), National Industrial Conference Board (1964), and U.S. Department of Health, Education, and Welfare (1976) for some commonly offered explanations of mandatory retirement.

does not require mandatory retirement at any given age. The second problem is that employers discriminate between employees at every level: some are promoted, others are terminated, others experience wage gains while others do not, and the existence of differences between workers is dealt with in many ways. Why should employers or employees favor a system that reduces the ability of the employer to compensate workers differentially?

Another "explanation" is that mandatory retirement creates promotion possibilities for younger workers. This explanation ignores at least two factors: First, young workers know that they will become old workers at some date in the future. They care about the present value of some lifetime wage path rather than the present value of any segment of it. Although they would prefer to be promoted when young, they also would, if their retirement is truly mandatory, prefer to continue working when old. Second, promotion may be interpreted as an increase in one's wage rate (and perhaps a change in the accompanying job title) that occurs as one's productivity rises over the life cycle. The firm will, in competition, pay the worker his marginal product, no matter how old he is. Thus, there would be no incentive for a firm to mandatorily retire a worker whose marginal product was equal to or greater than his wage rate to "promote" a younger worker.

Needless to say, none of the so-called explanations satisfactorily describes why it is optimal to terminate a worker at a certain age rather than reduce his wages accordingly and in a continuous fashion. In fact, explanations of mandatory retirement suffer from the same drawback as explanations of layoffs. Economists have been puzzled by layoffs as an alternative to spot VMP payments as well. I suggest that the two phenomena are linked.

The purpose of this paper is to give a theoretical explanation for the existence of mandatory retirement that is consistent with economic theory and then to test this theory empirically. Before proceeding, it is important to make clear what is meant by "mandatory retirement." The phenomenon that we wish to explain has the following characteristics: First, there is a definite date when a contract (either explicit or implicit) ends. Second, at that date there will be some workers who will wish to remain with the firm at their previous wage rates, but whom the firm will not choose to employ at that wage.[2]

[2] Given this definition, the institution of term contracts with up-or-out employment arrangements (i.e., arrangements where the worker is either promoted or forced to leave the firm) is a form of mandatory-retirement contract. The model to be presented in this paper could be applied to the analysis of that problem as well. In a recent theoretical paper by S. Freeman (1977), retirement and promotion decisions are linked. His model will not, per se, yield mandatory retirement, however. The reason is that in his framework there is no reason to distinguish between lump sums at critical time points and smooth payment streams with the same present value. The former will not yield mandatory retirement as it is commonly used.

Thus, mandatory retirement has the characteristic that at some time T, the worker earned some wage $\overline{W}$. But at $T + \epsilon$, the firm is no longer willing to employ the worker at wage $\overline{W}$, nor is the firm's wage-offer function continuous at that point (i.e., it takes a discrete jump downward for some workers). This story, by definition, implies that at T the firm is paying some workers more than the value of their marginal products. This is a necessary condition for the firm to desire to terminate the worker, and this is the bottom line to virtually all explanations of mandatory retirement. The argument here will be that, for reasons discussed below, it will be optimal for firms and workers to have a payment scheme such that the worker receives less than his marginal product when young and more than his marginal product when old. This implies that there be some date at which the firm is no longer willing to pay the worker his current wage. He is, therefore, mandatorily retired.

In some recent work, Feldstein (1976) has employed the notion that a worker's commitment to the firm tends to be permanent. He presents evidence which reveals that a large proportion of total job separations consist of layoffs, and, further, that layoffs are, in large part, temporary. That is, the worker is reemployed by the same firm which has laid him off in the first place. The lifetime commitment to the firm is the starting point from which we attempt to explain the existence of mandatory retirement. A sketch of that explanation follows.

Workers care about the present value of their wage stream over the lifetime (i.e., their wealth), whereas firms care about the present value of the worker's marginal product over his lifetime. Other things equal, a worker would be indifferent between a wage path which paid him a constant dollar amount over his lifetime and another one which had the same present value but paid him less when he was young and more when he was old. Other things equal, the firm would be indifferent between paying the two streams. But other things are not equal. It will be shown that a wage profile which pays workers less when they are young and more when they are old will allow the worker and firm to behave in such a way as to raise the present value of marginal product over the lifetime. For example, by deferring payment a firm may induce a worker to perform at a higher level of effort. Both firm and worker may prefer this high wage/high effort combination to a lower wage/lower effort path that results from a payment scheme that creates incentives to shirk. Thus, it may pay the firm and worker to set up a scheme such that the worker is paid less than his marginal product when he is young and more than his marginal product when he is old to compensate.

The efficiency condition for retirement is that the value of the worker's marginal product is just equal to his reservation wage. This will determine the optimal date of retirement. But if workers are paid less than their marginal products when they are young and more when old, their wage rate at T (the optimal retirement date) will exceed VMP and, therefore, the reservation wage. Although this is the efficient and equilibrium date of retirement (the date such that the present value of the lifetime marginal product equals the present value of the lifetime wage payment), the worker will not voluntarily retire at this date because wage exceeds reservation wage. Wage exceeds reservation wage at this point because that payment scheme produces a superior lifetime profile which workers prefer ex ante. Therefore, mandatory retirement is required to induce them to leave the firm at the optimal date. Thus, the existence of mandatory retirement is optimal from the worker's point of view. The worker is actually better off as the result of a contract which specifies a mandatory termination date. This allows the worker's present value of marginal product to be higher than it would be in the absence of such a contract, and these "rents" will spill over to the worker.

I. The Model

Consider an individual who has a value of marginal product over his lifetime, $V^*(t)$, and a wage rate $W^*(t)$ as illustrated in figure 1. This worker is receiving an amount less than his VMP for $t < t^*$ and an amount greater than his marginal product for $t > t^*$. Let T be the point such that

$$V^*(T) = \tilde{W}(T), \tag{1}$$

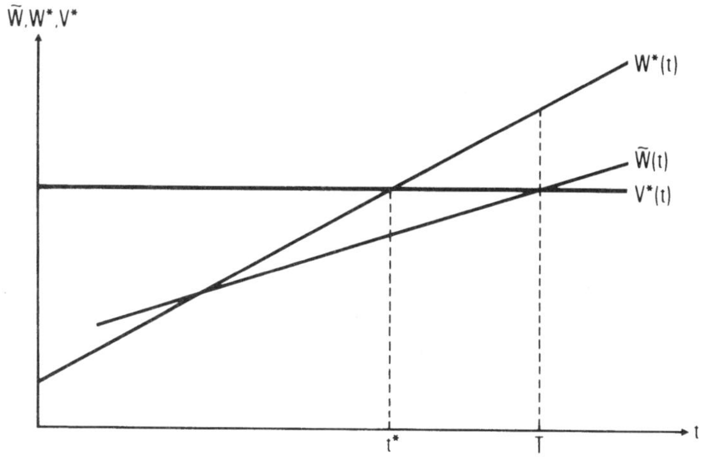

FIG. 1

where $\tilde{W}(t)$ is the individual's reservation wage at t. Any $W^*(t)$ path that satisfies the condition that

$$\int_0^T W^*(t)e^{-rt}dt = \int_0^T V^*(t)e^{-rt}dt$$

will be an equilibrium path.[3] That is, other things equal, a worker is indifferent between a path which pays him his spot VMP at each point in time and one which pays him a wage less than VMP initially and more than VMP later. As long as each path yields the same present value, workers have no preference. The argument in this paper, however, is that other things are not equal. A path which pays less than VMP when young and more than VMP when old may yield the worker a higher lifetime wealth. The reason is that a steeper path reduces the worker's incentive to cheat, shirk, and engage in malfeasant behavior. That is, it affects the amount of output per hour worked by altering the worker's incentive structure. This generates a preference for a path that has a wage greater than VMP at the date when VMP equals the reservation wage. Since this is the point when retirement should occur, and since workers would not voluntarily leave at this point (since $W^* [T] > \tilde{W} [T]$), "mandatory" retirement is a necessary consequence. But what is important here is that retirement is "mandatory" only in an ex post sense. It is negotiated in advance and is part of an optimal contractual arrangement which insures that firm-worker separation occurs at the appropriate time.[4]

A. *Incentives-induced Mandatory Retirement*

A steeper-than-VMP wage path is generated when we consider the notion of optimal effort, honesty, and malfeasance on the job.[5] These

[3] This assumes that the worker can borrow and lend at rate r. To the extent that this does not hold, a utility-maximizing framework must replace the wealth-maximizing one. The fundamental analysis and its conclusions, although somewhat more complex, remain essentially the same.

[4] That is, the worker is "mandatorily retired" at T. This is not the same as saying that the worker leaves the firm at T. He is retired from his old contract, but not necessarily from his old firm. For example, at age 65 many professors are mandatorily retired from their former contracts and renegotiate a new contract frequently called "emeritus." The wage rate changes, as do the working conditions. In this case, the worker stays with the former firm. In most cases, however, "mandatory retirement" will be coupled with firm-worker separation as well. The reason is that at T when renegotiation occurs, it is no longer necessarily the case that the worker-firm match and corresponding working conditions (hours, flexibility, effort, etc.) that were optimal between 0 and T will also be optimal between T and retirement (or death). For example, older workers may want shorter and more flexible hours with limited responsibility (or they may want zero hours of work, i.e., retirement). This is not necessarily the type of work conditions/wage trade-off that they would choose between 0 and T. If not, T will be characterized by a reshuffling of workers among firms. What is crucial is the termination of the former contract.

[5] Papers which have dealt with this issue are Becker and Stigler (1974) and Stiglitz (1975).

are treated symmetrically because performing at a level of effort lower than expected is merely a special type of worker "cheating."

Let a worker's marginal product at time t be given by $V^*(t)$; his reservation wage is $\tilde{W}(t)$, and the optimal wage path is $W^*(t)$ (as defined above). Worker "cheating" is assumed to be detectable immediately and the worker is dismissed when he cheats.[6] A worker will cheat when the present value of cheating exceeds the cost of cheating. The major cost of cheating is the loss of the current job which carries with it earnings greater than the individual's reservation wage. This immediately suggests that if wage paths are steeper than VMP paths (and reservation wage paths as the result), this will discourage cheating by workers since it raises the costs of termination. Stated otherwise, a firm which withholds payment until the end of an individual's work life is less likely to experience worker cheating than one that pays workers more at the beginning and less at the end of the worker's career. But if the former path discourages cheating, it results in a higher expected lifetime value of the marginal product. Thus, workers produce more and are paid more if their wage paths are steeper than VMP. But this implies that $W^*(T) > \tilde{W}(T)$. Given that, the worker would not choose to retire at T. Since his VMP is equal to his reservation wage at T, however, it is optimal for him to leave the firm. Therefore, both worker and firm will, at $t = 0$, agree on a "mandatory" retirement date of T. I reiterate that it is only mandatory in the sense that, once at T, the worker would prefer to continue working at $W^*(T)$ if it were available. It is not available because his VMP is less than $W^*(T)$, his reservation wage equals his VMP at that point, and he has been paid exactly the full present value of his lifetime VMP at point T. Time T is the date of ex post mandatory, but ex ante voluntary, retirement.

In order to determine the exact shape of the $W^*(t)$ path, it is necessary to formalize the model: To make the model completely general, we start out with the possibility not only of worker cheating, but of firm cheating as well. Firm "cheating" takes the form of promising a worker a stream $W^*(t)$ from 0 to T, but dismissing the honest worker at some $t < T$ and depriving him of the promised wage stream. The firm's cheating may be intentional or may be "unintentional," if, for example, the firm goes bankrupt before T.[7] Initially, let us assume that firm cheating is unintentional or exogenous and that the distribution of dates t at which the firm "cheats" on the worker is known

[6] This is a result rather than an assumption. It is true because any worker who finds it optimal to cheat at $t = t_0$ will cheat with certainty at $t > t_0$. Therefore, the firm gains by replacing him with a worker whose probability of cheating is less than one at that point.

[7] "Unintentional" is in quotes because the value of bankruptcy depends upon how much the firm owes workers and so is at least in part endogenous.

and given by $\tilde{g}(t)$. Exogeneity of $\tilde{g}(t)$ will be dropped below, but it is useful to adopt the assumption for comparison's sake.

Let the ith worker be assigned a $\theta_i \sim f(\theta_i)$, where θ is defined as the benefit that the worker derives from cheating. It may reflect the utility increase he derives when he works at a low effort level rather than the high effort level promised, or it may reflect something as tangible as revenue from the sale of stolen merchandise. For simplicity, assume that θ_i is constant over the worker's lifetime. If the worker "cheats," assume that he is caught with certainty and that as a result he is terminated. (The problem is complicated somewhat if there is a time lag for detection. As it turns out, that will necessitate pensions as part of the optimal wage path. For now this is ignored.)[8] The expected rent to a worker at time t is

$$R(t) = e^{rt}\int_t^T \Big\{ W^*(\tau) - \tilde{W}(\tau) - \tilde{g}(\tau)e^{r\tau}\int_\tau^T [W^*(\delta) - \tilde{W}(\delta)]e^{-r\delta}d\delta \Big\} e^{-r\tau}d\tau. \quad (3)$$

This rather complicated expression is the value in period t dollars of nominal rents to the worker $[W^*(t) - \tilde{W}(t)]$ minus the probability that the firm will cheat on the worker in the form of early termination ($\tilde{g}[\tau]$) times the cost to the worker of that cheating ($e^{r\tau}\int_\tau^T [W^*(\delta) - \tilde{W}(\delta)]e^{-r\delta}d\delta$). The worker cheats at time t if $\theta_i > R(t)$. From this, $\tilde{f}(t)$, the probability of worker cheating at time t, is derived:

$$\tilde{f}(t) = \begin{cases} F[R(0)] & \text{for } t = 0, \\ f[R(t)][R'(t)] & \text{for } R' < 0 \text{ and } t > 0, \\ 0 & \text{for } R' > 0 \text{ and } t > 0, \end{cases} \quad (4)$$

where $F \equiv 1 - \int_{-\infty}^R f(\theta)d\theta$. That is, at $t = 0$, some individuals, $F[R(0)]$, will have $\theta > R(0)$ and will choose to cheat. If $R'(t) > 0$, then those who did not cheat at $t = 0$ are even less likely to do so now or $\tilde{f}(t) = 0$. If $R'(t) < 0$, some individuals who did not cheat at zero, namely, $f[R(t)]\,[R'(t)]$, will now find it profitable to cheat, so $\tilde{f}(t) = f[R(t)]\,[R'(t)]$.

The problem then for the firm is to choose T and $W^*(t)$ so as to maximize the payment to the worker subject to the constraints that lifetime earnings equal lifetime expected VMP and that T is efficient. This can be written:

[8] It is a trivial extension of the model to allow the worker a probability of detection less than one. In the terminology below, $R(t)$ is merely replaced by $R(t)\cdot P$, where P is the probability of detection.

maximize over T, $W^*(t)$

$$\text{wealth} = \int_0^T \Big\{W^*(t) + \tilde{f}(t)\Big[\theta - e^{rt}\int_t^T W^*(\tau)e^{-r\tau}d\tau\Big] - \tilde{g}(t)e^{rt}\int_t^T W^*(\tau)e^{-r\tau}d\tau\Big\}e^{-rt}dt \qquad (5)$$

subject to

$$\text{wealth} = \text{expected VMP} = \int_0^T \Big[V^*(t) - \tilde{f}(t)e^{rt}\int_t^T V^*(\tau)e^{-r\tau}d\tau - \tilde{f}(t)c(t) - \tilde{g}(t)e^{rt}\int_t^T V^*(\tau)e^{-r\tau}d\tau\Big]e^{-rt}dt - \xi, \qquad (6)$$

where ξ are hiring costs and the boundary condition is

$$V^*(T) - \tilde{f}(T)c(T) = \tilde{W}(T). \qquad (7)$$

Equation (5) says wealth is equal to the wage rate ($W^*[t]$) plus the probability of worker cheating, $f(t)$, times the gain from worker cheating to the worker (θ) minus the cost to the worker ($e^{rt}\int_t^T W^*[\tau]e^{-r\tau}d\tau$), minus the probability of firm cheating, $[\tilde{g}(t)]$, times the cost to the worker ($e^{rt}\int_t^T W^*[\tau]e^{-r\tau}d\tau$). Expected VMP consists of nominal VMP, $\lfloor V^*(t)\rfloor$, minus the costs imposed by worker cheating equal to the sum of the loss of his output between t and T ($e^{rt}\int_t^T V^*[\tau]e^{-r\tau}d\tau$), and exogenous costs imposed on the firm, $c(t)$,[9] times the probability that the worker cheats, $[\tilde{f}(t)]$, minus the probability that the firm cheats, $[\tilde{g}(t)]$, times the effect on marginal product ($e^{rt}\int_t^T V^*[\tau]e^{-r\tau}d\tau$), minus hiring costs, ξ. Equation (7) says that net VMP at T must equal the reservation wage $\tilde{W}(t)$ for efficiency. The complete solution to the problem is complicated and relegated to an appendix.[10] We merely sketch the solution here.

If $\tilde{g}(t)$ is exogenous, that is, the probability of the firm cheating on the worker is independent of $W^*(t)$, the solution boils down to choosing $W^*(t)$ so as to set $\tilde{f}(t) = 0$, that is, completely eliminating worker cheating. Payment should be weighted sufficiently toward the end of the career so that at every point t it does not pay for the worker to cheat. The exact form of the solution depends upon the distribution of θ_i. In the simplest case, where all workers have $\theta_i = \bar{\theta}$, the solution is indeterminate, but it has the characteristic that at $W^*(T)$, $W^*(T) - \tilde{W}(T) \geqslant \bar{\theta}$, and that $V^*(T) = \tilde{W}(T)$.[11] The intuition behind this solution

[9] The $c(t)$ may be zero or positive. One example is the loss suffered when the worker takes customers with him upon his departure.

[10] Available from author upon request.

[11] The Becker-Stigler (1974) solution is a special case of this general form.

is clear: If the worker cheats, he imposes cost $c(t)$ on the firm, but receives $\bar{\theta}$. Therefore, the cheating lifetime net VMP and wealth is

$$\int_0^T V^*(t)e^{-rt}dt + [\bar{\theta} - c(t^*)]e^{-rt^*}$$

if the worker cheats at t^*. If he never cheats, his lifetime VMP and wealth is simply $\int_0^T V^*(t)e^{-rt}dt$. As long as $c(t) > \bar{\theta}$, the cost imposed on the firm by worker cheating exceeds the value of cheating to the worker (stolen machines sell at a price less than the replacement cost to the firm) and the zero-cheating path will be preferred. The zero-cheating equilibrium is produced by paths having $R(t) > \theta$ for all t.

Figure 2 illustrates some possible $W^*(t)$ paths. One path is *ABP*. Here the worker receives a constant amount less than his VMP over his lifetime, but receives a large lump sum at T to set present values of payment and marginal products equal. There is no worker cheating because $R(t)$ is always greater than $\bar{\theta}$; it never pays to cheat. Another possibility is the more conventional *LQ* curve. Again, there is no worker cheating, and at T the worker receives more than his marginal product. Again, of course, present values of lifetime earnings and marginal products are equal. Another possibility is *LKHQ*. This is the Becker-Stigler (1974) solution where the worker posts a "bond" equal to *LM*, is paid interest on it (*KM*), and gets back the principal at T (*HQ* = *LM*). A fourth possibility is *LHNX*. Here the worker is paid less than his VMP initially, more at T, and receives a pension equal to *NX*. As long as the present value of remaining rent exceeds $\bar{\theta}$ and the present

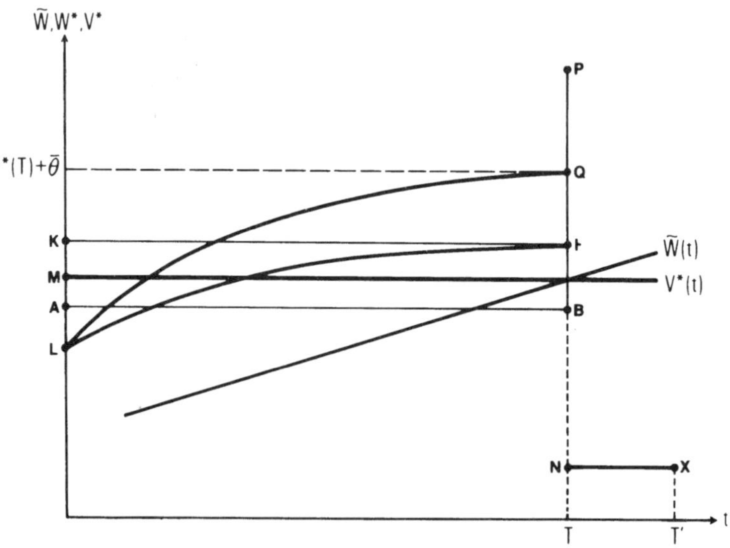

FIG. 2

value of earnings equals present value of payments, this will be an optimal path. This path is probably the most typical.

The important point that comes out of the above analysis is that in all these cases, $W^*(T) > \tilde{W}(T)$. That is, if the worker could continue to earn $W^*(T)$, he would not choose to retire. If he were paid $V^*(T)$, on the other hand, he would choose to retire. Mandatory retirement is warranted because it is optimal for the worker to retire at T, but paying him a wage that would induce him to do so voluntarily would result in more than the optimal amount of cheating. Thus, a path that is optimal from a cheating point of view coupled with mandatory retirement is superior for both worker and firm.

Without going into the details of the analysis, suffice it to say that when $\tilde{g}(t)$, the probability of firm cheating, is endogenous and influenced by the amount owed to the worker, the indeterminacy disappears (as it does for certain distributions of θ_i). The complete analysis is contained in an appendix.[12] The sense of the main result is this: As the amount owed to the worker above his marginal product increases, the gains to the firm from cheating on the worker increase. Therefore, minimizing the sum of cheating costs (which is essentially what [5] does) will trade off reduced worker cheating against increased firm cheating as $W^*(t)$ becomes more end weighted. This eliminates the indeterminacy and tends to reduce the end weighting of the payment stream. Mandatory retirement will still be required, however, since $W^*(T) > \tilde{W}(T)$.

As an aside, it is interesting to ask whether or not $\tilde{g}(t)$ is endogenous. That is, does the firm have a greater incentive to cheat when it owes the worker more? In a world of perfect (or unbiased)[13] information and infinitely lived firms, the answer appears to be "No." In that case, any cheating by the firm would affect the next generation of workers' assessments of $\tilde{g}(t)$. This would raise the wage that the firm has to pay to attract workers, and this cost should just offset the benefit. However, if either of these assumptions is dropped, $\tilde{g}(t)$ may well become endogenous.[14]

A second result is that as firm cheating becomes more profitable and $\tilde{g}(t)$ increases, T declines. That is, mandatory retirement should occur at earlier ages in industries where the incentive for firms to cheat on their workers is higher. This is because the left-hand side of equation (7) is reduced as $\tilde{f}(t)$ increases and less end weighting of the wage path produces a higher $\tilde{f}(t)$.

[12] Again, available from the author upon request.

[13] See Fama (1978) on this point.

[14] This suggests that a firm with an unanticipated decrease in its horizon will be more likely to cheat on workers. Thus, one may expect to find that the incidence of pension default and early termination is higher in declining industries.

One final and important implication results from the analysis: Other things constant (including education, ability, etc.), workers who have steeper profiles are more likely to have entered a long-term contract designed to prevent cheating. A necessary consequence of this contract is mandatory retirement. Therefore, individuals whose lifetime wage growth rate is higher than anticipated are more likely to have mandatory retirement. This somewhat counterintuitive implication that the high-performing, honest workers, with high wage growth rates, are more likely to have mandatory retirement is tested in the empirical section. The prediction is unequivocally supported by that evidence.

Note that pensions are a possibility, but not a necessity up to this point. Path *LHNX* in figure 2, for example, is one possible path. Two added considerations make pensions part of the optimal determinate wage path. The first, and most obvious, is a progressive income tax structure which makes a lump-sum payment at T less desirable than a smooth pension flow from T to T'. The second is relaxation of the assumption that cheating is observed immediately. If there were a lag time required for detection, then it would be optimal to withhold some payment until after T, or until the results were in, as it were. Pensions would act as such a holdback. This argument is somewhat less compelling than the first, however, because it requires that firms be allowed to terminate pension payments after they have already begun to make them. As an empirical phenomenon, the significance of midstream termination is doubtful.[15]

B. *Stochastic Variation*

Another consideration is important. There is a potential inefficiency in this model which is tied to the question of early retirement. One observes that individuals sometimes leave the firm before T, the date of mandatory retirement. Does this suggest a mistake or inefficiency implicit in the lifetime contract? The answer is no. Consider figure 3.

Suppose that we introduce a stochastic component to the analysis such that at time t^*, the worker receives an unexpected offer of $\tilde{W}_{t^*}$ from another firm. Under these circumstances, the worker would not leave the original firm, because $W^*(t^*) > \tilde{W}_{t^*}$. However, if $\tilde{W}_{t^*}$ mea-

[15] An alternative justification for a wage profile which rises more steeply than VMP is risk aversion coupled with uncertainty about VMP. If some workers will have low VMPs in the future relative to others, but neither workers nor firms can identify these workers initially, workers will prefer to buy "insurance" from the firm. This notion, which is described in detail in an earlier version of this paper, is related to the insurance ideas of Baily (1974), Azariadis (1975), Grossman (1977), and the self-selection analyses of Rothschild and Stiglitz (1976) and Salop and Salop (1976). The empirical evidence, however, is at odds with this view and so I only mention it in passing.

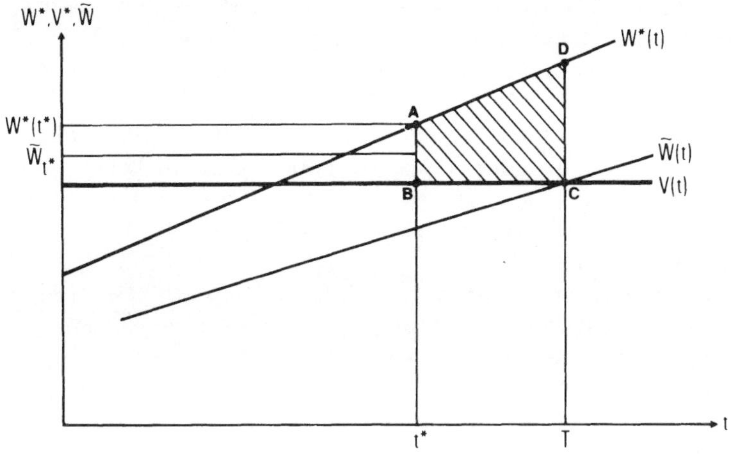

FIG. 3

sures his VMP in the alternative firm, it is inefficient for him to remain with the original firm since $\tilde{W}_{t*} > V(t^*)$. That is, his social value is greater at the alternative firm, yet he remains with the original firm only because his wage rate is higher there. This is clearly inefficient, and it is unnecessary. An appropriate severance payment will eliminate the inefficiency which seems at first glance to be a necessary consequence of long-term contracts. At t^*, the original firm still "owes" the worker area *ABCD* as payment (with interest) for service rendered between 0 and t_0. If the firm were to make a lump-sum payment to the worker at t^* equal to area *ABCD* in t^* dollars, the firm would have paid out over the worker's lifetime an amount exactly equal to the present value of his marginal product. This is the equilibrium condition for the firm's payment through T, so the firm suffers no loss by allowing the worker to quit at t^* with severance pay. The worker, however, is better off. As the result of taking the job at the alternative firm and receiving severance pay, he will receive the present value of $W(t)$ from 0 to T plus the present value of the difference $\tilde{W}(t^*) - V(t)$ from t^* to T. That is,

$$\begin{aligned}\text{the present value of earnings} &= \int_0^{t^*} W^*(\tau)e^{-r\tau}d\tau + \int_{t^*}^{T}[W^*(\tau) - V^*(\tau)]e^{-r\tau} \\ &\quad + \int_{t^*}^{T}\tilde{W}(t^*)e^{-r\tau}d\tau \\ &= \int_0^{T} W^*(\tau)e^{-r\tau}d\tau - \int_{t^*}^{T} V^*(\tau)e^{-r\tau}d\tau \\ &\quad + \int_{t^*}^{T}\tilde{W}(t^*)e^{-r\tau}d\tau \\ &= \int_0^{T} W^*(\tau)e^{-r\tau}d\tau + \int_{t^*}^{T}[\tilde{W}(t^*) - V^*(\tau)]e^{-r\tau}d\tau,\end{aligned}$$

which exceeds his earnings at the original firm $\left[= \int_0^T W^*(\tau)e^{-r\tau}d\tau\right]$ by the difference between $\tilde{W}(t^*)$ and V^* for the appropriate period. Thus, the worker and firm behave efficiently as long as severance pay is permitted.

One form that the severence-pay arrangement may take is increased pension benefits. Thus, we expect that workers who retire early would receive a larger expected pension than those who work through T. This is a characteristic of many pension plans (as will be discussed below).

The qualification raised in the last few paragraphs is an important one because it reconciles the phenomenon of early retirement with the lifetime payment scheme suggested earlier. It is also important because it means that unexpected changes either in the alternative use of time (as another employment offer or a change in the value of leisure, say, due to poor health) or in the value of the marginal product at the original firm (say, due to business-cycle conditions) do not result in an inefficiency. This long-term contract carries no immobility costs as long as severance pay (or pension adjustment) is permitted.

C. The Choice of T

The past few pages have argued that mandatory retirement is the necessary consequence of an optimal wage scheme which makes both workers and firms better off. There, the existence of some T or date of mandatory retirement was determined optimal. But one important issue remains: The formal model presented in Section A yields a solution for T given the parameters. However, one observes that the actual distribution of T is not as smooth as one might expect from that model. That is, the reservation wage functions are likely to be smooth, and this would imply a smooth distribution of T. The real world seems to be characterized by a set of T's that take particular values. One source (Banker's Trust 1975), which sampled firms which employed a total of 8.4 million workers (about 10 percent of the civilian labor force) in 1970–75, reports that of firms which stated an age of mandatory retirement, over 87 percent had that age equal to 65. This suggests that there is some exogenous factor which pulls T to age 65. An obvious candidate for prime mover is the social security provision which becomes available at age 65. Consider the reservation wage function in figures 1 and 2. If at 65 an individual becomes eligible for a social security subsidy to leisure, the reservation wage $\tilde{W}(t)$ is likely to take a discrete jump upward at 65. This means that voluntary retirement takes a discrete jump at age 65 as well, which implies that the choice of T such that age equals 65 is most likely. An implication of this argument is that before social security, the distribution of mandatory-retirement ages among firms with mandatory retirement would have been more dispersed. Unfortunately, no data are available on this point.

Social security is one possible determinant of T. There may be others as well. Social security payments do not affect all individuals in the same way. High-wage workers, for example, may find the social security subsidy to leisure relatively less attractive than do low-wage workers. As a result, ages of mandatory retirement might vary by the characteristics of the workers. An obvious determinant of retirement date is education. If education increases the value of work by more than the value of leisure, one would expect more educated workers to retire later (Bowen and Finegan [1969] find this positive relationship). If, as this paper claims, mandatory retirement is the outgrowth of an optimal long-term contract, we might then expect that conditional upon having mandatory retirement, education and the age of mandatory retirement will be positively correlated. This is explored in the empirical analysis below. In addition, anything that affects $\tilde{f}(t)$ and $\tilde{g}(t)$ will affect the choice of T. If either probability of cheating is higher, T will be lower. Thus, the age of mandatory retirement will be negatively related to the probability of early termination.

II. Some Implications of the Model

In the previous section, a model was presented which has implications for the incidence of mandatory retirement by job and demographic characteristics. In this section I will explore these implications in greater detail and outline the empirical tests which will be discussed in the next section.

The first and most important implication of the model is that mandatory retirement is more likely to be found where job tenure is long. That is, we portray mandatory retirement as the consequence of an optimal long-term contract between a worker and firm. If contracts are short term, say week by week or even year by year, profiles where wages are below VMP early in life and above VMP late in life are infeasible. Mandatory retirement is only useful in a long-term context.

Another implication, already discussed, is that unanticipated wage growth and the existence of mandatory retirement should be positively correlated. This, too, can be tested easily. By looking at an individual's work history and corresponding wage growth one can see how it relates to mandatory retirement. The argument on wage growth relates to the part that is unobservable at $t = 0$. Some differences are anticipated. We know, for example, from the outset that more educated workers learn more rapidly than the less educated. We therefore want to compare two individuals with the same observable characteristics.[16] The one with the most rapid wage growth, given these characteristics, is then the one with the higher probability of mandatory retirement under the incentives view. We therefore expect the probability of mandatory retirement to be positively related to the difference between actual wage growth and predicted (at time $t = 0$) wage growth.

Wage growth and job tenure are not exogenous variables. They are themselves the result of a choice process that is based on lifetime optimization. This suggests that mandatory retirement will be correlated with those variables that underlie wage growth and job tenure determination. That is, a reduced form, as well as structural approach, may prove interesting. For example, to the extent that whites have longer job tenure than nonwhites, whites should have a higher incidence of mandatory retirement. Similarly, if males enjoy longer job tenure than females, they will experience more mandatory retirement. Similarly, union workers, who have longer job tenure than nonunion workers (see Medoff 1976), should be more likely to experience mandatory retirement. It should be noted that these implications are the opposite of those derived from a queue or discrimination theory. If mandatory retirement were a way to reduce the labor force and make room for the younger, more desirable workers, one would expect that blacks, females, and the poorly educated would be the most affected. (They are the workers who suffer most from layoffs—the phenomenon that queue theory was formulated to explain.) The hypothesis in this paper, where mandatory retirement is viewed as the result of optimal lifetime contracting, suggests that it is the more favored rather than least favored workers who face mandatory retirement.[17]

Pensions are one way to compensate the worker at T. It was argued above that if there is a progressive tax structure which taxes lump-sum payments at a higher rate than it does pensions, or if cheating is detected with a lag, pensions will be part of the optimal path. Thus, pensions should be positively correlated with mandatory retirement since they both are manifestations of the same contractual arrangement. Also important is that it is necessary to have some type of severance pay in order to avoid the inefficiencies of a long-term contract. As argued above, paying higher pensions to those who retire

[16] What is observable to the economist may be much more limited than that which is observable to the employer. It is the latter that is relevant. We are, unfortunately, restricted to the former.

[17] It has been suggested that this view explicitly characterizes the Japanese labor market. Mandatory retirement takes place at age 55 after a long-term contract with the firm has been completed. Often, renegotiation takes place and the worker remains with the firm after 55 (see, e.g., Hashimoto [1977]).

before T is one such arrangement. Burkhauser (1976) finds that workers who leave the firm before the normal retirement date receive a pension, the actuarial value of which is a monotonic increasing function of the years to normal retirement. This is strong support for the long-term contract view.

This model reinforces the implication of many firm-specific labor models that older workers, if laid off, will have a difficult time finding another job at the same wage. If wage exceeds VMP for older workers, a new firm will be unwilling to pick this worker up at his previous wage.

An additional implication comes from considering types of compensation. Since the steep wage path which necessitates mandatory retirement is seen as the result of an agency problem, piece-rate workers are unlikely to experience mandatory retirement. Mandatory retirement was the necessary consequence of a payment scheme which induced workers to perform optimally. A piece-rate compensation scheme is a substitute. Under this type of payment scheme, workers always have an incentive to reveal their true ability or effort.[18]

The explanation of mandatory retirement provided in this paper also suggests a particular life-cycle pattern of preference for mandatory retirement. In this scheme workers at $t = 0$ prefer the payment arrangement that implies mandatory retirement. Firms prefer this arrangement as well. At time T, however, given that the worker and firm have followed the mandatory-retirement plan, firms favor mandatory retirement for the old worker, but the worker may oppose it vehemently, even though he favored it when he was young. That is, his lifetime wealth is higher with the mandatory-retirement scheme than without it, but given the wage path, his wealth would be even higher if he could continue to work at $W^*(T)$ beyond T. Thus, firms will oppose laws that restrict the use of mandatory-retirement contracts (explicit or implicit). Labor, in general, will also oppose these laws. Old workers, however, will push for legislation that makes mandatory retirement illegal since they can increase their wealth levels by doing so, given that they enjoyed wage paths $W^*(t)$ from $t = 0$ to $t = T$. This closely parallels the demographic breakdown of support of revisions to the Age Discrimination in Employment Act. Both business and organized labor opposed raising the age of exemption to 70. Major support, however, came from lobbying groups which represent the interests of the elderly.[19]

[18] Unfortunately, data on piece-rate vs. time-rate compensation are very difficult to obtain. They are unavailable in the data set used below in this study.

[19] It should be pointed out, however, that there are many other models of mandatory retirement which generate the same structure of preferences. On the other hand, Ehrenberg (1978) finds that firefighters and policemen who have mandatory-retirement provisions also obtain higher wages. This is consistent with this model.

III. An Empirical Model

In this section, the implications discussed above will be given specific functional form and will be tested empirically. Let MR be a dummy which equals one if the individual in question has a mandatory retirement provision on his current job, and zero otherwise.[20] Let E be the number of years that the worker has been employed with his current firm. Let AWG be the average level of wage growth over the individual's lifetime. Then the theory above predicts that

$$\text{prob}\ (MR = 1) = \frac{1}{1 + \exp\{-[\alpha_0 + \alpha_1 E + \alpha_2(AWG - \hat{AWG})]\}}, \quad (9)$$

where $\hat{AWG}$ is the predicted level of wage growth from a wage growth regression. Further, there will be equations for the determination of E and AWG as well:

$$E = \beta_0 + \beta_1 \text{ Male} + \beta_2 \text{ White} + \beta_3 \text{ Ed} + \beta_4 \text{ Urban} + \beta_5 \text{ Married} + \beta_6\ AFJ, \quad (10)$$

where Male, White, Urban, and Married are zero-one dummies, and Ed is the years of schooling completed; AFJ is the age of first job. (This corrects for vintage and inflation effects.)

$$AWG = \gamma_0 + \gamma_1 \text{Male} + \gamma_2 \text{ White} + \gamma_3 \text{ Ed} + \gamma_4 \text{ Urban} + \gamma_5 \text{ Married} + \gamma_6\ AFJ. \quad (11)$$

Alternatively, one can specify the following reduced-form equation:

$$\text{prob}\ (MR = 1) = 1/\{1 + \exp[-(\eta_0 + \eta_1\text{Male} + \eta_2\text{White} + \eta_3\text{Ed} + \eta_4\text{Urban} + \eta_5\text{Married} + \eta_6 AFJ)]\}. \quad (12)$$

The signs of the coefficients in (14) should be the same as the product of the sign on the corresponding variable in (12). This is because α_1 is positive and because $AWG - \hat{AWG}$ should not vary with any of these variables if (13) is specified correctly.

The same set of equations can be estimated with MR replaced by PP, where PP is a dummy equal to one if there is a pension plan. Thus,

$$\text{prob}\ (PP = 1) = \frac{1}{1 + \exp\{-[\delta_0 + \delta_1\text{Ed} + \delta_2(AWG - \hat{AWG})]\}}. \quad (13)$$

[20] This variable actually understates the true incidence of mandatory retirement. Some retirement is mandatory as a result of pension schemes which essentially prevent anyone from continuing to work past 65. For example, mandatory retirement is likely to be unnecessary in a firm that offers no pension to individuals who leave the firm after age 65, and a full salary pension to those who leave at 65. This points out that the mandatory-retirement response is itself a function of price. Some attempt to deal with response bias is made below.

If δ_1 and δ_2 have the same signs as α_1 and α_2, we might expect a positive simple correlation between *PP* and *MR*.

The data used in this analysis came from the Longitudinal Retirement History Survey, 1969–71. This is a panel study of about 11,000 individuals who were 58–63 years old in 1969. A follow-up survey was done in 1971, and the data used in this analysis are derived from that wave. Only those working in 1971 were used so that data on wages could be obtained.

All were asked whether or not their firm had a mandatory-retirement provision which applied to them. An affirmative answer to this question was coded as $MR = 1$. The wage rate, W, is the hourly (actual or derived) wage rate on the current job. The measure of job tenure used, E, is the difference between the question date and the date at which the individual reports to have started his current job. Average wage growth, AWG, is constructed as follows: Individuals were asked what their wage rates were on their first full-time jobs. (The starting wage on their current job was not reported.) They also reported the age at which they took this job. Thus, define

$$AWG \equiv \frac{W_t - W_{t_0}}{t - t_0}, \tag{14}$$

where t_0 is the age of first job and t is the individual's current age. All other variables were defined above.

IV. Results

First and most important, it should be noted that both job tenure and wage growth affect mandatory retirement positively. This is seen in equation (9) in table 1. Individuals who have longer job tenure and more rapid unanticipated wage growth are the ones who are most likely to face mandatory retirement. This finding, although consistent with the theory of this paper, is hard to reconcile in terms of queue or discrimination theories of mandatory retirement. Note that the effect of $AWG - \hat{AWG}$ is positive and substantial. This is consistent with the incentives or agency view of mandatory retirement. Second, note that the reduced-form coefficients in equation (12) go in the direction predicted by this theory but seem inconsistent with theories of discrimination. Note in particular that males and highly educated workers are the ones most likely to have mandatory retirement.[21]

It is interesting that the pension-plan equation (13) and the mandatory-retirement equation (9) are very similar and that the reduced-form versions are not very different. The theory related to

[21] The reversal in signs on the urban variable may reflect the fact that information is easier to obtain in small towns and there is, therefore, less need for payment schemes which require mandatory retirement.

TABLE 1

Logit and OLS Results

	Eq. (9): MR			Eq. (10): E	Eq. (11): AWG	Eq. (12): MR			Eq. (13): PP			PP		
	Logit	$\frac{\partial \bar{MR}}{\partial X_i} \cdot \frac{X_i}{\bar{MR}}$	$\frac{\partial \bar{MR}}{\partial X_i}$	OLS	OLS	Logit	$\frac{\partial \bar{MR}}{\partial X_i} \cdot \frac{X_i}{\bar{MR}}$	$\frac{\partial \bar{MR}}{\partial X_i}$	Logit	$\frac{\partial \bar{PP}}{\partial X_i} \cdot \frac{X_i}{\bar{PP}}$	$\frac{\partial PP}{\partial X_i}$	Logit	$\frac{\partial PP}{\partial X_i} \cdot \frac{X_i}{\bar{PP}}$	$\frac{\partial PP}{\partial X_i}$
E	.02727	.31	.006	...	...	...	...	...	.02958	.28	.007	...	...	...
	(.00249)								(.00249)					
$AWG-A\hat{W}G$	2.8992	*	.661	...	...	...	...	...	5.8557	*	1.46	...	...	...
	(.502)								(.5791)					
Male	...	...	...	2.25	.0640	.2268	†	.051	...	...	...	.3451	†	.086
				(.87)	(.0135)	(.1398)						(.1345)		
White	...	...	...	1.00	.0118	.0757	†	.017	...	...	...	.2650	†	.066
				(.77)	(.0119)	(.1299)						(.1231)		
Ed	...	...	...	.153	.0084	.0963	.655	.021	...	...	...	.0945	.51	.023
				(.062)	(.0009)	(.0100)						(.0097)		
Urban	...	...	...	−.289	.0183	.2254	†	.051	...	...	...	.3492	†	.087
				(.423)	(.0065)	(.0672)						(.0652)		
Married	...	...	...	1.015	−.0201	−.0244	†	−.007	...	...	...	.0221	†	.006
				(.769)	(.0118)	(.1230)						(.1185)		
AFJ	...	...	...	−.174	.0014	.0011	.014	.0002	...	...	...	−.0129	−.14	−.003
				(.030)	(.0004)	(.0049)						(.0048)		
DMR	...	...	...	...	...	...	...	...	...	...	...	...	...	...
Constant	−1.1067	...	...	16.1	−.0833	−1.9852	...	...	−.5582	...	...	−1.4727	...	...
	(.057)			(1.2)	(.0194)	(.2105)			(.0545)			(.200)		
SEE	...	...	...	13.27	.205	...	...	...	...	...	...	...	...	...
N	4,123	...	...	4,123	4,123	4,123	...	...	4,123	...	...	4,123	...	...
−2 log λ	186.7	...	...	...	...	119.9	...	...	324.9	...	...	180.7	...	...
R^2	...	...	...	.025	.029	...	...	...	...	...	...	...	...	...

Note.—Standard errors are in parentheses.

*$AWG - A\hat{W}G = 0$ by construction; $\overline{AWG} = .088$.

†Dummy variables; $\bar{MR} = .352$, $\bar{PP} = .485$.

lifetime labor force contracts predicts that this would be the case (note that the mean value of *MR* is .35 and the mean value of *PP* is .49). The exogenous variables seem to have virtually the same effect on the existence of mandatory retirement as they do on the existence of pension plans. Furthermore, the correlation between mandatory retirement and pension plans in a simple sense is extremely high. In this sample, 62 percent of those with a pension plan have mandatory retirement. Further, 86 percent of those who have mandatory retirement also have a pension plan. This finding is important. It is strong support for the coupling of mandatory retirement and pensions. The theory above suggests that they should be linked directly as each is the outcome of the same optimal contract. That is, in a world where the tax rate is higher on a lump-sum payment than on a smooth flow of income with the same present value, or in a world where cheating is detected with a lag, all wage paths that have mandatory retirement will also have pensions.

As mentioned above, there may be reporting bias associated with the *MR* variables. New workers, for example, may be less aware of the rules of the firm and less likely to report the existence of mandatory retirement. To treat this, individuals with tenure levels in the twentieth percentile were separated from the rest of the sample, and the estimation contained in table 1 was repeated for each group separately. (The low-tenure group had $0 \leqslant E \leqslant 4.3$; the high-tenure group had $4.3 \leqslant E \leqslant 59.0$.) The results, only summarized here for the sake of brevity, reveal the same basic story as table 1. Deletion of the low-tenure individuals leaves the results for the top 80 percent essentially unchanged. In addition, the results for the low-tenure group were similar to those for the high-tenure group. The only notable difference is that for this group, married workers were less likely to face mandatory retirement than unmarried ones.

Some empirical evidence can be obtained on variations in T, the age of mandatory retirement, across individuals. Earlier it was suggested that more highly educated individuals would have optimal dates of retirement later in their lifetimes. If the skills which they acquired in school were relatively more useful in the labor market, then they would have an incentive to continue working longer than less educated workers. It follows, then, that if mandatory retirement is a manifestation of an optimal long-term contract, more educated workers should have older ages of mandatory retirement.

In table 2, a regression is presented in which the age of mandatory retirement is regressed on demographic variables, education, and job tenure. The sample contains only those who face mandatory retirement. The first point is that education has an important (in size and precision of estimate) effect on the age of mandatory retirement. It

TABLE 2

REGRESSION AND LOGIT RESULTS

	MR Age OLS
Male	−.093 (.256)
White	−.387 (.246)
Ed	.118 (.017)
Urban	−.133 (.120)
Married	.198 (.225)
AFJ	−.005 (.009)
E	−.032 (.004)
Constant	66.4 (.4)
R^2	.066
N	1,429
SEE	2.25

NOTE.—Standard errors are in parentheses.

appears as though more educated workers make contracts which end at a later point in their life cycles. This is consistent with the notion that they choose to retire later voluntarily as well.

Second, note that job tenure has a negative effect on the age of mandatory retirement. In the context of this sample of old workers, all of whom are about the same age, job tenure is a proxy for the date at which the employment contract was made. Holding age about constant, those workers with fewer years of job tenure also have more recently made a "contract" with the employer than those with longer tenure. The results suggest that more recent contracts specify a later age of mandatory retirement. Individuals who have made more recent contracts may have done so either because the value of their leisure did not rise as rapidly as they expected ($\tilde{W}[t]$ is flatter than had been anticipated) or because they ended up being more productive in the labor force than expected ($V^*[t]$ is higher than anticipated). In either case, it is optimal for them to be "bought out" of their previous contract (through severance pay or early pensions) and to negotiate a new one. The new one will have a later date of mandatory retirement because, as equation (6) shows, the higher is $V^*(t)$ or the flatter is $\tilde{W}(t)$, the later will be the date of mandatory retirement.

Third, the coefficient on White is negative. Other things constant, whites have earlier ages of mandatory retirement than blacks. Although the explanation of this phenomenon is not obvious, let us conjecture. Even holding education and urbanization constant, whites have substantially higher income than blacks. This is especially true of nonwage income. Thus, if the education effect captures most of the wage variation, the white variable may well proxy higher property income. Since the income effect on leisure is positive, holding education constant yields an increase in the demand for leisure via income effects, so whites are richer individuals with the same wage rate. As such, whites prefer to work less and therefore set up contracts with earlier retirement dates.

V. Summary and Conclusions

This paper provides an explanation of the institution of mandatory retirement that is derived from optimizing behavior on the part of both workers and firms. The theory, simply stated, is that it pays both parties to agree to a long-term wage stream which pays workers less than their VMPs when young and more than the VMPs when old. By using this payment schedule, the worker's lifetime VMP is higher than it would be in the absence of that scheme because this provides valuable incentives to the worker which would otherwise be lost to moral hazard. A necessary consequence of this payment schedule is mandatory retirement, that is, a date at which the contract is terminated and the worker is no longer entitled to receive a wage greater than his VMP. Its mandatory nature is illusory, however. The date of mandatory retirement is the social and private optimum date of retirement.

This theory has some perhaps counterintuitive implications. It suggests that the long-tenured and most able workers will face mandatory retirement rather than the least tenured. It predicts that the highly educated, white, male workers are the ones most likely to be mandatorily retired. These predictions are borne out in the empirical section.

The most important implication of this theory is that workers and firms all benefit from the existence of mandatory retirement. Although older workers may be unhappy about this provision when the retirement day draws near, their lifetime wealth levels are increased as the result of being able to enter into these kinds of contracts. What they lose by being mandatorily retired is more than offset by what they have gained during working years as the result. As mandatory retirement is made illegal before age 70 and the social security payment age is not raised accordingly, there will be an efficiency loss as voluntary and mandatory retirement ages diverge. If the ability to enter into mandatory-retirement contracts is eliminated through legislation, this analysis argues that current older workers will enjoy a small once-and-for-all gain at the expense of a much larger and continuing efficiency loss that affects all workers and firms adversely.

References

Azariadis, Costas. "Implicit Contracts and Underemployment Equilibria." *J.P.E.* 83, no. 6 (December 1975): 1183–1202.

Baily, Martin N. "Wages and Employment under Uncertain Demand." *Rev. Econ. Studies* 41 (January 1974): 37–50.

Banker's Trust Company. *1975 Study of Corporate Pension Plans.* New York: Banker's Trust, 1975.

Becker, G., and Stigler, G. "Law Enforcement, Malfeasance, and Compensation of Enforcers." *J. Legal Studies* 3, no. 1 (1974): 1–18.

Bowen, W. G., and Finegan, T. A. *The Economics of Labor Force Participation.* Princeton, N.J.: Princeton Univ. Press, 1969.

Burkhauser, R. "Early Pension Decision and Its Effect on Exit from the Labor Market." Ph.D. dissertation, Univ. Chicago, 1976.

Ehrenberg, Ronald. "Retirement System Characteristics and Compensating Wage Differentials in the Public Sector." Unpublished paper, Cornell Univ., 1978.

Fama, Eugene. "Agency Problems and the Theory of the Firm." Mimeographed. Univ. Chicago, 1978.

Feldstein, Martin. "Temporary Layoffs in the Theory of Unemployment." *J.P.E.* 84, no. 5 (October 1976): 937–57.

Freeman, S. "Wage Trends as Performance Displays Productive Potential: A Model of Application to Academic Early Retirement." *Bell J. Econ.* 8, no. 2 (Autumn 1977): 419–43.

Gordon, M. S. "Older Workers and Retirement Policies." *Monthly Labor Rev.* 83, no. 6 (June 1960): 577–85.

Grossman, H. "Risk Shifting, Layoffs, and Seniority." Working Paper no. 76-7, Brown Univ., 1977.

Hashimoto, M. "Variable Wages, On-the-Job Training, and Lifetime Employment in Japan." Unpublished paper, Univ. Washington, September 1977.

Kreps, J. "A Case Study of Variables in Retirement Policy." *Monthly Labor Rev.* 84, no. 6 (June 1961): 587–91.

Medoff, J. "Layoffs and Alternatives under Trade Unions in United States Manufacturing." Discussion Paper no. 525, Harvard Inst. Econ. Res., 1976.

National Industrial Conference Board, Inc. *Corporate Retirement Policies and Practices.* Studies in Personnel Policy, no. 190. New York: NICB, 1964.

Rothschild, Michael, and Stiglitz, Joseph. "Equilibrium in Competitive Insurance Markets: An Essay on the Economics of Imperfect Information." *Q.J.E.* 90, no. 4 (November 1976): 629–49.

Salop, Joanne, and Salop, Steven. "Self-Selection and Turnover in the Labor Market." *Q.J.E.* 90, no. 4 (November 1976): 619–27.

Stiglitz, J. "Incentives, Risk, and Information: Notes toward a Theory of Hierarchy." *Bell J. Econ.* 6, no. 2 (Autumn 1975): 552–79.

U.S. Department of Health, Education, and Welfare. *Reaching Retirement Age.* Social Security Administration Research Report no. 47. Washington: Government Printing Office, 1976.

[4]

FROM RACE TO AGE: THE EXPANDING SCOPE OF EMPLOYMENT DISCRIMINATION LAW

*GEORGE RUTHERGLEN**

ABSTRACT

The Age Discrimination in Employment Act (ADEA) goes beyond the model of racial discrimination in prohibiting discrimination on a ground not recognized in the Constitution. As a consequence, the individuals protected by the ADEA differ sharply from those protected by earlier statutes such as Title VII of the Civil Rights Act of 1964. An examination of empirical data reveals that claims under the ADEA are brought predominantly by white males who hold relatively high-status and high-paying jobs. These claims mainly allege discriminatory discharge and result in recovery of money judgments several times higher than other claims of employment discrimination. As a whole, claims under the ADEA more closely resemble claims for wrongful discharge than other claims of employment discrimination. It follows that the ADEA cannot be justified, either doctrinally or empirically, because it protects a disfavored and relatively powerless minority group from discrimination.

THE law of employment discrimination was, and to a large extent still is, modeled on the constitutional law of racial discrimination. Segregation in employment, just like segregation in public education, was at the heart of what Title VII of the Civil Rights Act of 1964 prohibited.[1] Title VII simply extended the constitutional prohibition from public employment, which the Constitution covered of its own force, to private employment. Public employers were already forbidden from discriminating on the basis of race or national origin; Title VII imposed the same prohibitions on

* O. M. Vicars Professor of Law, University of Virginia School of Law. This article was prepared during my tenure as the John V. Ray Research Professor of Law and with the assistance of a grant from the Fund for Labor Relations Studies. I would like to thank Saul Levmore, Richard Posner, Glen Robinson, Rip Verkerke, and the participants in a discussion at the University of Virginia School of Law for comments on an earlier draft of this article. Special thanks are due to John Donohue, who supplied much of the data and the statistical analysis summarized in the tables in the article and who made detailed comments on earlier drafts.

[1] Civil Rights Act of 1964 § 703(a)–(d), 42 U.S.C. § 2000e-2(a) to (d) (1988).

private employers. The Age Discrimination in Employment Act (ADEA)[2] was the first enduring departure from the constitutional model of employment discrimination law. Unlike the prohibitions in Title VII, including those against discrimination based on religion and gender,[3] the ADEA plainly went beyond any constitutional claim. There has never been any form of heightened judicial review of government classifications on the basis of age.[4]

In prohibiting discrimination on the basis of age, the ADEA also moved employment discrimination law further from the nearly absolute constitutional and statutory prohibitions against racial discrimination. These prohibitions allow an exception mainly for affirmative action,[5] and the other prohibitions in Title VII are subject to an important exception only for bona fide occupational qualifications,[6] but the ADEA is subject to a broad array of exceptions.[7] These raise the question whether the ADEA should be interpreted and applied like the nearly absolute prohibitions against racial discrimination in the Constitution and Title VII.

Cases under the ADEA also anticipated developments under Title VII in two respects: first, plaintiffs under the ADEA have always had a right to jury trial;[8] and second, most plaintiffs have advanced far enough in their jobs to make a claim for discriminatory discharge worthwhile.[9] Plaintiffs who allege claims of age discrimination have much to gain and little to fear from jury trial.[10] And indeed, the crucial decision in most claims under the ADEA is on the question whether the plaintiff has sub-

[2] 29 U.S.C. §§ 621–34 (1988).

[3] The Supreme Court recognized a constitutional prohibition against sexual discrimination a few years after enactment of Title VII. See Reed v. Reed, 404 U.S. 71 (1971).

[4] See Massachusetts Board of Retirement v. Murgia, 427 U.S. 307 (1976).

[5] See, for example, United States v. Paradise, 480 U.S. 149 (1987); United Steelworkers v. Weber, 443 U.S. 193 (1979). The Constitution also allows racial classifications in a genuine emergency, such as a prison riot. See Lee v. Washington, 390 U.S. 333 (1968) (per curiam). Title VII explicitly allows preferences in favor of Native Americans. See Civil Rights Act of 1964 § 703(i), 42 U.S.C. § 2000e-2(i) (1988); see also Civil Rights Act of 1964 § 701(b)(1), 42 U.S.C. § 2000e(b)(1) (1988) (excluding Native American tribes from the coverage of the statute).

[6] Civil Rights Act of 1964 § 703(e)(1); 42 U.S.C. § 2000e–2(e)(1) (1988). The prohibition against religious discrimination is subject to additional exceptions, again mainly derived from the Constitution. See Civil Rights Act of 1964 §§ 701(j), 702, 703(e)(2), 42 U.S.C. §§ 2000e(j), 2000e-1, 2000e-2(e)(2) (1988).

[7] See text around notes 26–39 *infra*.

[8] Lorillard v. Pons, 434 U.S. 575 (1978); 42 U.S.C. 626(c)(2) (1988).

[9] See Tables 1 and 2.

[10] See text around notes 55–58 *infra*.

TABLE 1

CHARACTERISTICS OF PLAINTIFFS

	Non-ADEA Cases		All ADEA Cases		ADEA-Only Cases		ADEA-Plus Cases	
	%	Number	%	Number	%	Number	%	Number
Plaintiffs who were:								
Management and professional	30	244	64	73	68	57	52	16
Technical, sales, other support	26	211	25	29	21	18	36	11
Service	15	126	7	8	6	5	10	3
Operator and fabricator	22	177	2	2	1	1	3	1
Precision production	7	59	3	3	4	3	0	0
White males	5	38	57	26	74	20	32	6
Average age	39	373	55	115	55	87	52	28
Average job tenure (in years)	5.3	652	15.1	103	15.5	82	13.6	21
Average annual salary (Consumer Price Index for urban consumers, 1982–84 = $1.00)	$18,323	166	$35,528	21	$33,327	15	$41,030	6
Total number of cases		981		128		94		34

SOURCE.—American Bar Foundation Employment Discrimination Litigation Survey. For conversion to constant dollars, see the Statistical Abstract of the United States (1994), table 746.

NOTE.—Percentages are calculated based on the number of cases in which a characteristic (such as race) was reported, not necessarily on the total number of cases.

TABLE 2

CHARACTERISTICS OF CLAIMS

	NON-ADEA CASES		ALL ADEA CASES		ADEA-ONLY CASES		ADEA-PLUS CASES	
	%	Number	%	Number	%	Number	%	Number
Lag between violation and filing (in quarters)	9.0	844	5.6	123	5.4	92	6.2	31
Claims included discrimination in:								
Hiring	23.1	227	8.6	11	7.4	7	11.8	4
Firing	62.2	610	85.9	110	89.4	84	76.5	26
Pay	24.5	240	3.1	4	2.1	2	5.9	2
Demotion or promotion	39.0	383	20.3	26	16.0	15	32.4	11
Conditions of employment	44.8	439	12.5	16	10.6	10	17.6	6
Alleged violation was discrete	42.1	392	74.6	94	79.6	74	60.6	19
Plaintiff sought:								
Reinstatement, hiring, or promotion	49.1	457	62.3	76	67.8	61	46.9	15
Back pay	75.5	703	70.5	86	71.1	64	68.8	22
Punitive damages	55.9	520	71.3	87	73.3	66	65.6	21
Liquidated damages	.4	4	13.1	16	14.4	13	9.4	3
Pension or other benefits	9.9	92	33.6	41	37.8	34	21.9	7
Total number of cases		981		128		94		34

SOURCE.—American Bar Foundation Employment Discrimination Litigation Survey.

NOTE.—Percentages are calculated based on the number of cases in which a characteristic (such as the discrete or continuous nature of the violation) was reported, not necessarily on the total number of cases.

mitted sufficient evidence to get the case before the jury.[11] Likewise, it was supporters of Title VII, not opponents, who obtained a right to jury trial in the recently enacted Civil Rights Act of 1991.[12] In the years immediately after enactment of Title VII, by contrast, it was opponents of Title VII who sought to create a right to jury trial for claims under that statute, in the hope, presumably, that southern juries would not be sympathetic to claims of racial discrimination.[13] A second contrast with litigation in the years immediately after enactment of Title VII is that most claims of employment discrimination are now claims of discriminatory discharge.[14] Litigation under the ADEA, which concerns such claims almost exclusively, exemplifies this trend in its most extreme form.

This article examines the empirical evidence of the departures from the constitutional model of racial discrimination. Section I is a brief survey of the substantive and procedural differences between the ADEA and Title VII. Section II reports the results of an empirical study of employment discrimination cases in seven cities around the nation. Section III examines the similarity between patterns of litigation under the ADEA and litigation of state law claims of wrongful discharge.

I. Changing Prohibitions and Procedures

Both the substantive and the procedural provisions of the ADEA are unique. It established the first federal prohibition against discrimination on the basis of age[15] but also subjected this prohibition to an unprecedented number of exceptions. The coverage provisions of the statute compounded the effect of these substantive provisions. With several exceptions, the ADEA covers all employees at or above the age of 40,

[11] See generally Catharine J. Lanctot, The Defendant Lies and the Plaintiff Loses: The Fallacy of the "Pretext-Plus" Rule in Employment Discrimination Cases, 43 Hastings L. J. 57 (1991); Comment, The Age Discrimination in Employment Act: Handling the Element of Intent in Summary Judgment Motions, 38 Emory L. J. 523 (1989).

[12] Pub. L. No. 102-166, § 102, 105 Stat. 1071, 1073 (1991), codified as 42 U.S.C. § 1981a(c) (Supp. IV 1992).

[13] See Minna J. Kotkin, Public Remedies for Private Wrongs: Rethinking the Title VII Back Pay Remedy, 41 Hastings L. J. 1301, 1369–70 (1990); R. Wayne Walker, Title VII: Complaint and Enforcement Procedures and Relief and Remedies, 7 B.C. Indus. & Com. L. Rev. 495, 509 (1966); Note, The Right to Jury Trial under Title VII of the Civil Rights Act of 1964, 37 U. Chi. L. Rev. 167, 167 (1969).

[14] See John J. Donohue III & Peter Siegelman, The Changing Nature of Employment Discrimination Litigation, 43 Stan. L. Rev. 983, 1015–16 (1991); see also Michael Schuster & Christopher S. Miller, An Empirical Assessment of the Age Discrimination in Employment Act, 38 Indus. & Lab. Rel. Rev. 64, 70–71 (1984).

[15] The Age Discrimination Act, 42 U.S.C. § 6101 *et seq.* (1988), which prohibits age discrimination by recipients of federal funds, was enacted only in 1975.

regardless of race or sex.[16] Although Title VII nominally has equally broad coverage, it was intended mainly to protect racial minorities, women, and other traditional victims of discrimination;[17] claims of reverse discrimination by white males are the exception under Title VII, not the rule. What the reported cases reveal, and what the empirical evidence confirms, is that white males have been the principal beneficiaries of the ADEA.[18] Whatever the justification for protecting white males age 40 or over, it cannot be that they have been excluded from political and economic power. The justification for the ADEA must therefore be based on entirely different grounds. These turn out to have a surprising resemblance to the justification for recognizing claims for wrongful discharge.

In addition to extending the principle against discrimination beyond its traditional justification, the ADEA also created distinctive procedures for enforcement.[19] Essentially, the statute combined the procedures under the Equal Pay Act,[20] which themselves were taken from the Fair Labor Standards Act,[21] with the procedures under Title VII.[22] The net result was a procedural hybrid that allowed for the right to jury trial and for liquidated damages—procedures that were not available under Title VII as originally enacted. Although jury trials and damages have long been available for claims of racial discrimination under section 1981,[23] it was only recently, in the Civil Rights Act of 1991,[24] that similar procedures were made available to claims under Title VII. Because most claims under the ADEA concern discharges from employment, the provisions for compensatory and punitive damages further reinforce the similarity to claims for wrongful discharge.

A. *Substantive Prohibitions and Exceptions*

The basic prohibition in the ADEA simply paraphrases the corresponding prohibition in Title VII, substituting "age" for "race, color, religion,

[16] 29 U.S.C. § 631 (1988).

[17] Francis J. Vaas, 7 B.C. Ind. & Com. L. Rev. 431, 441–42 (1966).

[18] See Table 1; Schuster & Miller, *supra* note 14, at 68.

[19] 29 U.S.C. § 626 (1988).

[20] 29 U.S.C. § 206(d)(1) (1988).

[21] 29 U.S.C. §§ 215–18, 251–62 (1988).

[22] Civil Rights Act of 1964 § 706(g), 42 U.S.C. § 2000e-5 (1988).

[23] Setser v. Novack Investment Co., 638 F.2d 1137, 1140 (8th Cir. 1981), cert. denied, 454 U.S. 1064 (1981); see Johnson v. Railway Express Agency, Inc., 421 U.S. 454, 460 (1975).

[24] Pub. L. No. 102-166, § 102, 105 Stat. 1071 (1991), codified as 42 U.S.C. § 1981a (Supp. IV 1992).

sex, or national origin."[25] This prohibition is then subject to a wide variety of exceptions. In addition to a bona fide occupational qualification for age, modeled on that for sex under Title VII,[26] the ADEA contains a general exception for "reasonable factors other than age"[27] and a number of special exceptions for high-level employees[28] and certain aspects of fringe benefit and retirement plans.[29]

The multitude of exceptions under the ADEA has not figured in most of the litigation under the statute. As the empirical evidence makes clear, ADEA cases usually concern a discharge from employment, or less frequently, denial of promotion or refusal to hire.[30] These cases are decided under the same structure of proof as claims of racial or sexual discrimination under Title VII.[31] Indeed, one exception under the ADEA, for employment decisions based on "reasonable factors other than age,"[32] simply codifies the most common defense to claims of intentional discrimination under Title VII, a "legitimate, nondiscriminatory reason for the employee's rejection."[33]

The exceptions to the ADEA of greatest practical significance concern the ways in which age can be taken into account in retirement, pension, disability benefits, and medical insurance plans.[34] These exceptions routinely affect millions of employees and only rarely give rise to litigation. Faced with the related and highly technical requirements of the Employment Retirement Income Security Act,[35] employers have hired specialists to adapt their fringe benefit plans to the requirements of the ADEA as

[25] Compare 29 U.S.C. § 623(a)(1),(2) (1988) with 42 U.S.C. § 2000e-2(a)(1),(2) (1988). The ADEA also adds a provision, from the Equal Pay Act, requiring employers to eliminate discrimination in compensation by raising wages of the lower paid group. Compare 29 U.S.C. § 623(a)(3) (1988) with 29 U.S.C. § 206(d)(1) (1988).

[26] 29 U.S.C. § 623(f)(1) (1988).

[27] *Id.* This provision resembles the exception to the Equal Pay Act for differentials in pay "based on any other factor other than sex." See 29 U.S.C. § 206(d)(1)(iv) (1988).

[28] 29 U.S.C. § 631(c) (1988). An exception for mandatory retirement of firefighters, police officers, and college professors lapsed at the end of 1993. See Pub. L. No. 99-592, 100 Stat. 3344 (1986).

[29] 29 U.S.C. § 623(f)(2), (g), (i) (1988).

[30] See Table 2.

[31] Mack A. Player, Proof of Disparate Treatment under the Age Discrimination in Employment Act: Variations on a Title VII Theme, 17 Ga. L. Rev. 621, 634 (1983).

[32] 21 U.S.C. § 623(f)(1).

[33] McDonnell Douglas Corp. v. Green, 411 U.S. 792, 802 (1973); Howard Eglit, The Age Discrimination in Employment Act's Forgotten Affirmative Defense: The Reasonable Factors Other than Age Exception, 66 B.U. L. Rev. 155 (1986).

[34] 29 U.S.C. § 623(f)(2), (g), (i) (1988).

[35] Pub. L. No. 93-406, 88 Stat. 829 (1974), codified in 29 U.S.C. § 1000 *et seq.* (1988) and scattered sections of 26 U.S.C. (1988).

well.[36] The most controversial of these exceptions has been for retirement and insurance plans, which has twice been given a fairly broad interpretation by the Supreme Court and twice amended by Congress to further narrow its scope.[37]

What is notable about these exceptions is not how detailed they are, or how rarely they are subject to litigation, but the fact that they exist at all. Pension, and medical and life insurance plans must take account of age, if only because life expectancy and health decrease as age increases. The most recent federal legislation on this subject explicitly acknowledges this defense to considering age in fringe benefit plans.[38] Yet a similar correlation between sex and life expectancy was found inadequate to support consideration of sex in pension plans under Title VII.[39] The exceptions to the ADEA do not prove the rule, but the opposite: how limited the rule really is.

The prohibition against age discrimination is likely to remain narrower than the prohibitions against race and sex discrimination so long as age is a more acceptable basis for decisions in public and economic life. For the young, age serves as a restriction on such common activities as voting, driving, and employment;[40] and for the old, it figures in the eligibility for and cost of a variety of insurance and social welfare programs.[41] As the Supreme Court said in *Massachusetts Board of Retirement v. Mur-*

[36] See generally John H. Langbein & Bruce A. Wolk, Pension and Employee Benefit Law, at 322–51 (1990); Bruce J. Brafman, Issues in Early Retirement: Voluntary Early Retirement and Separation Incentive Plans, Practicing Law Institute Litigation and Administrative Practice Course Handbook Series, Litigation, Handling Corporate Employment Problems (1991); Charles S. Mishkind & Akusin B. Marshall, A Management Perspective on Reductions in Force: ADEA, ERISA and Related Litigation, Practicing Law Institute, Corporate Law and Practice Course Handbook Series, Employment Discrimination Litigation (1991).

[37] United Air Lines, Inc. v. McMann, 434 U.S. 192 (1977), overruled by Age Discrimination in Employment Act Amendments of 1978, Pub. L. No. 95-256, 92 Stat. 189 (1978); Public Employees Retirement System v. Betts, 492 U.S. 158 (1989), overruled by the Older Workers Benefit Protection Act, Pub. L. No. 101-433, 104 Stat. 978 (1990).

[38] The Older Workers Benefit Protection Act, Pub. L. No. 101-433, § 103, 104 Stat. 978 (1990); see 2 Howard Eglit, Age Discrimination §§ 4–12 (1981 & Supp. 1991); Paul T. Shultz & Douglas J. Tormey, Congress Responds to *Betts:* The Older Workers Benefit Protection Act of 1990, 16 Employee Rel. L. J. 533, 533–39 (1991); Niall A. Paul, The Older Workers' Benefit Protection Act: Forcing a New Look at Early Retirement Incentives and Waivers, 17 Employee Rel. L. J. 29, 34–41 (1991).

[39] City of Los Angeles Department of Water & Power v. Manhart, 435 U.S. 702 (1978).

[40] U.S. Const. amend. XXVI, § 1 (right to vote protected only for those at least 18 years old); 29 U.S.C. § 203(l) (1988) (restrictions on child labor below age 16); Va. Code § 46.2-334 (Michie 1950) (driving license available only to those at least 16 years old).

[41] See Peter H. Schuck, The Graying of Civil Rights Law: The Age Discrimination Act of 1975, 89 Yale L. J. 27, 31–32, 82–85 (1979).

gia,[42] the case rejecting age as a suspect classification under the Equal Protection Clause: "But even old age does not define a 'discrete and insular' group . . . in need of 'extraordinary protection from the majoritarian political process.' Instead, it marks a stage that each of us will reach if we live out our normal span." In constitutional law, there is no need to protect the old from the rest of the population, most of whom will live to the same age. So, too, in employment, there is no evidence that older workers on the whole are worse off than younger workers, although the earnings of unskilled workers do tend to decrease before retirement.[43]

Nor can discrimination against older workers be condemned as an inefficient form of statistical discrimination. According to the statistical theory of discrimination, personal characteristics such as race are used to select employees for the job.[44] Although these generalizations may be accurate in the short run—perhaps because of the effects of past discrimination—they create inefficiencies over the long run by discouraging members of racial minorities from developing the qualifications and applying for jobs from which they are excluded. A statistical theory of age discrimination would have to establish that the balance of efficiency lies with prohibiting generalizations on the basis of age. This conclusion is implausible for several reasons: first, everyone's physical and mental abilities decline at some point with age, more steeply for some individuals than others and more steeply in some jobs than others; second, the countervailing benefits of age, such as experience and judgment, do not invariably outweigh the loss of these abilities; third, the period over which older workers can gain and utilize new skills necessarily is shorter than for younger workers; and fourth, more accurate methods of evaluation, such as individualized testing, may cost enough to outweigh the gain in accuracy that they achieve. Some employers in some circumstances might find generalizations on the basis of age to be efficient; others might not. There is no reason to believe that efficiency, even over the long run, dictates a single solution to this problem for all employers and all jobs.

[42] *Murgia, supra* note 4, at 307, 313–14 (per curiam).

[43] Even before the enactment of the ADEA, the earnings of most workers increased until the then-standard retirement age of 65. See Herbert S. Parnes, Avril V. Adams, Paul Andrisani, Andrew I. Kohen, & Gilbert Nestal, The Pre-retirement Years 21 (Manpower Research and Development Monograph No. 15, U.S. Dep't of Labor, Manpower Administration 1975) (longitudinal data reflect steady increase in the average annual incomes of preretirement-age men, although cross-sectional data do not, probably because of lower levels of education of older cohorts).

[44] Edmund S. Phelps, The Statistical Theory of Racism and Sexism, 62 Am. Econ. Rev. 659 (1972).

Instead of being based on a constitutional theory of discrete and insular groups, or the economic theory of statistical discrimination, the ADEA is more plausibly based on the life cycle theory of earnings. Although the coverage of the ADEA extends to all employees at or over the age of 40, the justification for the statute is limited to specific abuses of individual employees. Under the life cycle theory of earnings, an employee's compensation at first exceeds his productivity because the employee receives on-the-job training from the employer.[45] Although an employee's compensation gradually increases with seniority and with promotions, productivity increases even faster. At some point, the employee's productivity exceeds his compensation, so that the employer profits from the training that it has given to the employee. As the employee grows old, however, his productivity again sinks below his compensation. According to the life cycle theory of earnings, the employer's profits during the middle period should compensate it for its losses in the earlier and later periods. Although there are dangers of opportunism by both the employer and employee throughout the relationship, the life cycle earnings theory tends to emphasize opportunism by the employer in the later period. During that period, the employer can do better for itself simply by terminating the employee. The employee, on the other hand, having developed skills specific to his job and to his existing employer, will have difficulty finding an equally attractive job with another employer.

The life cycle theory of earnings supports arguments for protecting employees from dismissal without good cause late in their careers. These arguments figured in the debates over the ADEA and led to its enactment, although not as prominently as the subsequent litigation over discharges would lead one to expect.[46] Whether or not they are compelling as a matter of overall efficiency, or as a matter of fairness to individual employees, these arguments differ dramatically from the arguments for remedying long-standing discrimination against racial minorities and women or for the inefficiency of statistical discrimination against older workers. Indeed, they presuppose one form of explicit discrimination against older workers: mandatory retirement when the surplus value conferred on the employer during the employee's productive middle period has been exhausted. With this qualification, these arguments are simply versions of the arguments for allowing claims for wrongful discharge, restricted to

[45] Stewart J. Schwab, Life-Cycle Justice: Accommodating Just Cause and Employment at Will, 92 Mich. L. Rev. 8, 14–15 (1993). For a judicial endorsement of the theory, see Metz v. Transit Mix, Inc., 828 F.2d 1202, 1211–22 (7th Cir. 1987) (Easterbrook, J., dissenting).

[46] Secretary of Labor, The Older American Worker: Age Discrimination in Employment: Report to Congress under Section 715 of the Civil Rights Act of 1964, at 5–20 (1965).

employees within the coverage of the ADEA.[47] Both kinds of claims are mainly concerned with protecting the investment that long-term employees have made in developing skills specific to their jobs. For this structural reason, we should expect claims under the ADEA to closely resemble claims under the developing law of wrongful discharge.

B. Procedures for Enforcement

The procedures under the ADEA further enhance the similarity to the law of wrongful discharge. Although the ADEA adopted some of the requirements for exhaustion of state and federal administrative remedies from Title VII, it reduced their significance considerably. The most important procedures under the ADEA are those adopted from the Equal Pay Act, and in particular, those which provide for the right to jury trial and for the award of liquidated damages.[48] These procedures allow plaintiffs to bring their claims before a jury composed mainly of employees like themselves or their spouses and to seek a limited form of punitive damages. Likewise, the restrictions on class actions under the ADEA,[49] requiring each plaintiff to opt affirmatively into any private action on her behalf, have restricted litigation under the statute almost entirely to individual actions, departing from the model of "across-the-board" class actions prominent in the first decade of litigation under Title VII.[50] With the diminished requirements for exhaustion of administrative remedies, these procedures ensure that claims for age discrimination are litigated in much the same way as claims for wrongful discharge.

The requirements for exhaustion of administrative remedies under the ADEA, although superficially similar to those under Title VII, are both easier to satisfy and less significant. Like Title VII, the ADEA requires plaintiffs to file charges of discrimination with suitable state or local agencies and with the Equal Employment Opportunity Commission (EEOC).[51] Unlike the procedures under Title VII, however, both sets of administrative remedies can be exhausted at the same time; they can even be exhausted after an action has been commenced; and they delay the action

[47] For a version of this argument, see Paul C. Weiler, Governing the Workplace: The Future of Labor and Employment Law 63–67 (1990).

[48] Compare 29 U.S.C. § 626(c)(2), (b) (1988) (ADEA) with 29 U.S.C. § 216(b) (1988) (Equal Pay Act). The right to jury trial was first implied from the provisions in the ADEA modeled on or referring to the FLSA. See *Pons, supra* note 8, at 575, 580-85.

[49] 29 U.S.C. § 626(b), 216 (1988).

[50] See George Rutherglen, Title VII Class Actions, 47 U. Chi. L. Rev. 688, 706–13, 720–21 (1980).

[51] Civil Rights Act of 1964 § 706(c)–(f), 42 U.S.C. § 2000e-5(c)–(f) (1988).

for only 60 days, instead of at least 180 days under Title VII.[52] Not only are plaintiffs allowed to get to court faster,[53] they are less encumbered than plaintiffs under Title VII by a complex, multitiered system of state and federal enforcement. By jumping quickly through only a few procedural hoops, they can get to court almost as easily as a plaintiff with an ordinary common-law claim.

The right to jury trial gave plaintiffs under the ADEA an even more important advantage, only recently conferred on plaintiffs under Title VII. Plaintiffs who alleged racial discrimination under section 1981 have always been entitled to a jury trial,[54] but they faced more difficulties in obtaining a sympathetic jury than plaintiffs under the ADEA. Plaintiffs who allege racial discrimination are usually from minority groups. Unless they sue in a federal district consisting predominantly of a central city, such as Washington, D.C., members of their own group are not likely to make up most of the jury. Plaintiffs under the ADEA are typically white, or so the empirical evidence strongly suggests.[55] It is correspondingly easier for them to obtain a jury largely of the same race and age and from the same economic class. A representative jury is more likely to be composed of employees or their dependents than it is of employers and managers.

For this reason, defendants in ADEA cases have sought strenuously to avoid jury trials, usually by motions for summary judgment, or if those fail, motions for directed verdict or judgment notwithstanding the verdict.[56] These motions might, of course, be explained on other grounds: motions for summary judgment by the defendant's interest in bringing the litigation to a quick conclusion, or at least obtaining a preview of the plaintiff's case, and motions for directed verdict and judgment notwithstanding the verdict by the defendant's desire to exhaust all means of

[52] Compare 29 U.S.C. § 626(d) (1988) (ADEA) with 42 U.S.C. § 2000e-5(f)(1) (1988) (Title VII); see Oscar Mayer & Co. v. Evans, 441 U.S. 750, 757–59 (1979).

[53] Plaintiffs also used to have a longer statute of limitations in which to go to court: 2 years, or in the case of willful violations, 3 years (29 U.S.C. §§ 626(e)(1), 255(a) (1988)). Delays by the EEOC, however, in processing charges under the ADEA prevented plaintiffs from complying with the statute of limitations. Congress initially responded to this problem by extending the limitation period to accommodate claims that would otherwise have been barred. See Pub. L. No. 100-283, 102 Stat. 78 (1988), as amended by Pub. L. No. 101-504, 104 Stat. 1298 (1990). More recently, the Civil Rights Act of 1991 replaced the old limitation period under the ADEA with the 90-day limitation period from Title VII, which begins to run only on receipt of a right-to-sue letter after the EEOC has completed its proceedings (29 U.S.C. § 626(e) (Supp. IV 1992)).

[54] *Johnson v. Express*, *supra* note 23.

[55] See Table 1.

[56] Lanctot, *supra* note 11.

avoiding an unfavorable judgment. Plaintiffs might also seek jury trials because of the increasing proportion of conservative federal judges appointed during the 1980s.[57] The little empirical evidence that there is suggests that juries are no more favorable to plaintiffs on the issue of liability than judges, although they might make larger awards of damages once they find liability.[58] Even if the sympathies of juries are suspended somewhere between professional lore and empirical confirmation, what cannot be doubted is that the right to jury trial under the ADEA strengthens the resemblance to claims of wrongful discharge. Whatever the actual behavior of juries, it is not likely to differ systematically between the two kinds of cases.

The remedies available under the ADEA are more limited than those for a claim of wrongful discharge, but they are in some respects more certain. A successful plaintiff under the ADEA is entitled to back pay (including lost fringe benefits), reinstatement, and attorney's fees.[59] If the jury finds that the defendant's violation was "willful," in the sense that it was committed in "reckless disregard" of the Act, the plaintiff is also entitled to an award of liquidated damages equal to the amount of back pay.[60] If the plaintiff is not reinstated, she may also receive an award of front pay. The award of back pay and liquidated damages, and in some circuits, the award of front pay, are made by the jury. Reinstatement and attorney's fees are awarded by the judge.[61] This package of remedies does not include nonpecuniary damages, such as those for emotional distress, or unlimited punitive damages, as are available for tort claims for wrongful discharge.[62] However, it is somewhat more generous than the remedies for simple contract claims for wrongful discharge, which do not include any form of nonpecuniary damages or punitive damages, or an award of attorney's fees.

[57] As of 1991, about 70 percent of sitting federal judges have been appointed by Presidents Reagan or Bush. See Ruth Marcus, Bush Quietly Fosters Conservative Trend in Courts, Wash. Post, Feb. 18, 1991, at A1.

[58] Harry Kalven, Jr., The Dignity of the Civil Jury, 50 Va. L. Rev. 1055, 1065–67 (1964); Eglit, *supra* note 33, at 205 n.238. A more recent study has found still fewer systematic differences in the outcomes and the amount of awards in cases tried to a judge and to a jury (Kevin M. Clermont & Theodore Eisenberg, Trial by Jury or Judge: Transcending Empiricism, 77 Cornell L. Rev. 1124, 1137–38, 1140–41 (1992)). Nevertheless, the data also showed that plaintiffs prevailed in civil rights cases on employment twice as frequently before juries as they did before judges. See Clermont & Eisenberg, *supra*, at 1175.

[59] 29 U.S.C. §§ 626(b), 216(b) (1988).

[60] Trans World Airlines, Inc. v. Thurston, 469 U.S. 111 (1985).

[61] There is a conflict among the circuits on whether awards of front pay should be made by the judge or jury. Comment, The Role of the Jury and the Court in Assessing Front Pay Awards under the Age Discrimination in Employment Act, 58 U. Chi. L. Rev. 1475 (1991).

[62] Steven L. Willborn, Stewart J. Schwab, & John F. Burton, Jr., Employment Law: Cases and Materials 147 (1993).

Paradoxically, the similarities between claims under the ADEA and claims for wrongful discharge have led courts to emphasize their differences. As many opinions have reiterated, the plaintiff's burden under the ADEA is not just to prove that the employer's offered reason for discharging the plaintiff was insufficient; the plaintiff must prove that it was a pretext for considering age.[63] The fact that courts insist on this distinction suggests that it is one that is easily blurred in practice. Discrediting the reason offered by the defendant often gives rise to an inference of age discrimination, but, as the cases strain to make clear, it is not identical to proving it.[64] The similarities between these claims cannot be further refined at the level of legal doctrine. Instead, it is necessary to look at the actual patterns of litigation under the ADEA.

II. Empirical Evidence

Litigation under the ADEA exemplifies trends that are apparent in other claims of employment discrimination. The decline in class actions under Title VII, for instance, has minimized the significance of the ADEA's restriction of class actions to opt-in classes. So, too, the increase in claims of discriminatory discharge, to about 86 percent of charges filed with the EEOC, has made all of employment discrimination law look more like the law of wrongful discharge.[65] What is distinctive about litigation under the ADEA is how far it carries forward this trend.

There are two sources of data about cases filed under the ADEA: statistics published by the EEOC about the large volume of charges of employment discrimination and about the very much smaller number of actions filed by the EEOC itself;[66] and the American Bar Foundation (ABF) Survey on employment discrimination claims in seven cities across the nation.[67] These sources of data have complementary strengths. The

[63] Texas Dep't of Community Affairs v. Burdine, 450 U.S. 248 (1981); Villanueva v. Wellesley College, 930 F.2d 124 (1st Cir. 1991); Lanctot, *supra* note 11.

[64] St. Mary's Honor Center v. Hicks, 113 S. Ct. 2742, 2748–49 (1993).

[65] Donohue & Siegelman, *supra* note 14, at 1015–16.

[66] 19 EEOC Ann. Rep. 8, 18 (1984); 20 EEOC Ann. R. 21 (1985); EEOC Combined Ann. Rep. Fiscal Years 1986, 1987, 1988, at 24 (1990).

[67] The data set is described in more detail in Donohue & Siegelman, *supra* note 14, at 985 n.3:

> [T]he American Bar Foundation Employment Discrimination Litigation Survey, Computer File (1990) (on file with the authors) contains the results of a detailed study of some 1250 employment discrimination cases in 7 cities (Atlanta, Chicago, Dallas, New Orleans, New York, Philadelphia, and San Francisco). Over the period from 1972 to 1987, just under 20% of all federal employment discrimination cases were filed in these seven cities. Although the cities were not selected randomly, the sample of cases chosen was randomly drawn from all cases filed in these cities between 1972 and 1987. We believe that the sample of cities contains enough internal variation to make it a useful, albeit imperfect, proxy for the U.S. caseload as a whole.

data from the EEOC provide information on virtually the entire universe of administrative charges of discrimination, but almost none at all about private litigation. The ABF survey fills this gap with a useful sample of about 20 percent of employment discrimination cases from 1972 to 1987. Other sources of data, such as the reports of the Administrative Office of the U.S. Courts, do not disaggregate employment discrimination claims from all civil rights actions. Another study, by Michael Schuster and Christopher S. Miller, examines published opinions in ADEA cases,[68] but without correcting for the selection of these cases from the universe of all cases that are filed.[69] The data from the EEOC and from the ABF together yield consistent conclusions about the number and character of claims under the ADEA.

The annual reports of the EEOC cover all charges filed with the EEOC itself and with state and local agencies that enforce similar laws against employment discrimination. These reports reveal that, in quantitative terms, charges of age discrimination have not dominated the caseload of these agencies. During the fiscal years 1984–88, the last 5-year period that largely overlaps with the ABF survey, charges of age discrimination filed with state agencies grew from 15.8 percent in 1984 to 18.0 percent in 1986 and then remained steady at 18.3 percent and 18.2 percent in 1987 and 1988. Over the same period, charges of age discrimination filed with the EEOC grew from 22.7 percent to 25.3 percent.[70]

The apparent value of these claims is more remarkable than their number. The EEOC brought claims under the ADEA in this 5-year period in nearly the same proportion as charges under that statute. Over the entire period, 24.7 percent of the actions it brought were under the ADEA.[71] A slightly different statistic, for cases closed during this period, reveals that 23 percent of cases were brought under the ADEA. By contrast, 51.0 percent of the monetary benefits secured through litigation by the EEOC were collected in ADEA cases.[72] Thus, the average recovery for each

[68] Schuster & Miller, *supra* note 14.

[69] Peter Siegelman & John J. Donohue III, Studying the Iceberg from Its Tip: A Comparison of Published and Unpublished Employment Discrimination Cases, 24 Law & Soc'y Rev. 1133 (1990).

[70] These percentages include both charges filed only under the ADEA and charges filed under the ADEA and Title VII. See Tables 3 and 4.

[71] *Id.* This percentage does not include mixed actions, brought under more than one statute, which are not broken down by the EEOC into those with an ADEA claim and those without. If all the mixed actions are counted as ADEA cases, the percentage rises to 30.2 percent. These percentages are also calculated without including any subpoena enforcement actions, in either the numerator or the denominator.

[72] See Table 5. Aggregating the numbers for each year, approximately 24.5 percent of the cases the EEOC resolved through litigation during the 5-year period were brought under the ADEA, while the monetary benefits secured through litigation under the ADEA totaled 51.0 percent of all monetary benefits received through litigation.

TABLE 3

CHARGES FILED WITH STATE AGENCIES

	FY 1984		FY 1985		FY 1986		FY 1987		FY 1988	
	Number	%	Number	%	Number	%	Number	%	Number	%
Non-ADEA cases	39,345	84.2	43,691	83.1	41,539	82.0	43,800	81.7	48,355	81.8
All ADEA cases	7,385	15.8	8,885	16.9	9,106	18.0	9,842	18.3	10,728	18.2
ADEA-only cases	5,871	12.6	7,045	13.4	6,947	13.7	7,782	14.5	7,743	13.1
ADEA-plus cases	1,514	3.2	1,840	3.5	2,159	4.3	2,060	3.8	2,985	5.1
Total	46,730		52,576		50,645		53,642		59,083	

SOURCES.—Computed from data in 19 Equal Employment Opportunity Commission (EEOC) Ann. Rep. 8, 18 (1984); 20 EEOC Ann. Rep. 21 (1985); EEOC Combined Ann. Rep. Fiscal Years 1986, 1987, 1988, at 24 (1990).

TABLE 4

CHARGES FILED WITH THE EQUAL EMPLOYMENT OPPORTUNITY COMMISSION (EEOC)

	FY 1984		FY 1985		FY 1986		FY 1987		FY 1988	
	Number	%	Number	%	Number	%	Number	%	Number	%
Non-ADEA cases	53,360	77.3	55,218	76.7	51,379	74.7	46,953	75.6	43,971	74.7
All ADEA cases	15,614	22.7	16,784	23.3	17,443	25.3	15,121	24.4	14,882	25.3
ADEA-only cases	12,489	18.1	13,601	18.9	13,854	20.1	11,627	18.7	11,454	19.5
ADEA-plus cases	3,125	4.6	3,183	4.4	3,589	5.2	3,494	5.6	3,428	5.8
Total	68,874		72,002		68,822		62,074		58,853	

SOURCES.—Computed from data in 19 EEOC Ann. Rep. 8, 18 (1984); 20 EEOC Ann. Rep. 21 (1985); EEOC Combined Ann. Rep. Fiscal Years 1986, 1987, 1988, at 24 (1990).

TABLE 5

OUTCOME IN CASES FILED BY THE EQUAL EMPLOYMENT OPPORTUNITY COMMISSION (EEOC)

	FY 1984		FY 1985		FY 1986		FY 1987		FY 1988	
	Number	%	Number	%	Number	%	Number	%	Number	%
Cases resolved:										
Non-ADEA	186	79.5	159	81.5	155	77.9	224	72.3	322	79.1
ADEA	48	20.5	36	18.5	44	22.1	86	27.7	85	20.9
Total	234		195		199		310		407	
Money recovered in all cases (in thousands; Consumer Price Index for urban consumers, 1982–84 = $1.00):										
Non-ADEA	$14,984	38.7	$25,596	71.0	$33,950	68.6	$8,588	21.0	$20,021	47.4
ADEA	$23,739	61.3	$10,442	29.0	$15,520	31.4	$32,232	79.0	$22,177	52.6
Total	$38,723		$36,038		$46,470		$40,820		$42,198	

SOURCES.—19 EEOC Ann. Rep. 18 (1984); 20 EEOC Ann. Rep. 21 (1985); EEOC Combined Ann. Rep. Fiscal Years 1986, 1987, 1988, at 25 (1990). For conversion to constant dollars, see Statistical Abstract of the United States (1994), table 746.

ADEA action brought by the EEOC (regardless of the number of private parties who benefited from the action) was two-and-one-half times the average recovery in each Title VII case and over four times the average recovery in each case under the Equal Pay Act.

Because claims brought by the EEOC are usually thought to be more meritorious than claims by private litigants,[73] the figures on back pay awards may overstate the value of ADEA claims relative to other claims. They are based on a very small proportion of the charges, less than .7 percent, filed with the EEOC during the same period. Nevertheless, the EEOC does not bring ADEA claims in disproportion to their number among initial charges of discrimination. Nor is it likely to have any special expertise or incentive to bring only the most valuable ADEA claims, since it received authority to enforce the statute only in 1979,[74] after it had enforced the prohibitions against race, national origin, and sex discrimination in Title VII for over a decade.

The inferences about the greater value of ADEA claims are borne out by the more detailed data from the ABF Survey. It contains information about the character of plaintiffs under the ADEA, the nature of their claims, and the damages they receive. The survey covered over 1,100 cases, of which 128 involved claims under the ADEA. Like most civil cases, only a small proportion of cases in the sample reached trial. A total of 179 cases were tried, and only 24 cases with a claim under the ADEA. Accordingly, the inferences from the data about the nature of the plaintiffs and their claims are stronger than the inferences about the outcome of trials.

By every measure, plaintiffs in ADEA cases are better off than plaintiffs in other employment discrimination cases. As Table 1 reveals, they are much more likely to be managerial and professional employees (64 percent of the plaintiffs whose job was identified in the sample) than other plaintiffs (30 percent of plaintiffs). They are, of course, likely to be older than other plaintiffs and to have a longer tenure on the job (over 15 years for ADEA plaintiffs and a little more than 5 years for other plaintiffs). It is therefore not surprising to find that the average salary of ADEA plaintiffs is almost twice the average salary of other plaintiffs. (This figure nevertheless must be used with some caution because it is based on the small subsample of tried cases and because both averages conceal wide variations among plaintiffs.)

[73] Theodore Eisenberg, Litigation Models and Trial Outcomes in Civil Rights and Prisoner Cases, 77 Geo. L. J. 1567, 1598–1601 (1989).

[74] Responsibility for enforcement of the ADEA was transferred from the Department of Labor to the EEOC on July 1, 1979. See Reorg. Plan No. 1 of 1978, 3 C.F.R. 321 (1978), reprinted in 5 U.S.C. app. at 1366–69 (1988) and in 92 Stat. 3781 (1978).

Among ADEA cases alone, 73 percent bring claims only under the ADEA. The remaining 27 percent, who also bring claims under other statutes, are more likely to be minorities or women. Only 19 percent of the plaintiffs in these cases were identified as white males. For all ADEA cases in which the race and sex of the plaintiff were identified, 57 percent were white males. (By contrast, only 5 percent of plaintiffs who did not bring ADEA claims were identified as white males.) The 57 percent figure, however, is likely to understate the proportion of white males, since sex or race went unstated in over half of the ADEA cases, and this is most likely to occur in cases brought by white males.[75] It is also plausible to assume that only relatively few women and minorities are likely to allege age discrimination alone and that only a few white men are likely to allege national origin discrimination or reverse discrimination. We can safely infer that a majority, and perhaps a large majority, of ADEA plaintiffs are white males. Apart from this difference in racial and sexual composition, however, there are no large differences among the occupational status, age, job tenure, and salary between these two groups of ADEA plaintiffs.

The claims that are brought by ADEA plaintiffs differ both in substance and in procedure from the claims brought by other plaintiffs. These differences are most striking in the cases brought only under the ADEA. For almost all of the entries in Table 2, the figures for "ADEA-Plus Cases" fall between those for "Non-ADEA Cases" and "ADEA-Only Cases." (For some of these entries, however, the number of "ADEA-Plus Cases" is so small that the difference between them and "ADEA-Only Cases" is not statistically significant.) Plaintiffs who bring ADEA claims alone are more likely than other plaintiffs to bring claims of discrimination in firing. They did so in 89 percent of the cases, whereas non-ADEA plaintiffs did so in 62 percent of cases. They are therefore less likely to bring claims of discrimination in hiring, pay, demotion or promotion, or conditions of employment. Corresponding to this difference in disputed employment decisions is a difference in the discrete or continuous nature of the alleged violation. Claims under the ADEA are more likely to concern particularized violations rather than systematic practices. Plaintiffs who bring only ADEA claims are also more likely to seek reinstatement and pension or other benefits, but again, these differences are smaller for plaintiffs who bring ADEA claims with other claims, as Table 2 reveals.

Other differences in the claims brought by ADEA plaintiffs result from

[75] For a similar inference, see Schuster & Miller, *supra* note 14, at 68–69.

the different procedures and remedies available under the statute. As noted earlier, ADEA plaintiffs can get to court more quickly than plaintiffs under Title VII,[76] a difference borne out by the shorter time between violation and filing for ADEA cases in Table 2. Plaintiffs under the ADEA can also seek liquidated or punitive damages, which were until recently only available to other plaintiffs who filed claims under section 1981 or the Equal Pay Act, but not under Title VII. The entries in Table 2 reveal more frequent requests for both kinds of relief under the ADEA than under other statutes.

The differences in outcomes between ADEA cases and other cases are even more dramatic than the differences between plaintiffs. Again, these differences are most striking for cases concerned only with claims under the ADEA. The most astonishing difference, in monetary recoveries, however, is the least well documented. Plaintiffs who bring claims only under the ADEA and whose recovery is reported in court records receive over seven times as much as plaintiffs who do not bring ADEA claims, over $83,600 as compared to $11,500. As Table 6 states, this comparison is based on a sample of only 10 cases brought only under the ADEA, and although the difference between recoveries in these cases and in cases under other statutes is statistically significant, the variance for both figures is very large. Both figures are heavily influenced by a few large recoveries that greatly exceed the average. Nevertheless, the difference between the two figures is consistent with the recoveries obtained by the EEOC in cases brought under the ADEA. The general question raised by Table 6 is whether the large recoveries reported in a small fraction of ADEA cases yield any inference about the large proportion of cases that are settled.

These recoveries are consistent with the higher status, longer job tenure, and higher salaries of ADEA plaintiffs in the much larger sample of all cases that are brought. Higher status and longer job tenure should be correlated with higher salary, as they are in the figures in Table 1. Under the life cycle theory of earnings, salary should increase with tenure on the job, as employees advance within a firm's internal system of seniority and promotions. The salaries of ADEA plaintiffs are almost twice as high as the salaries of plaintiffs in other cases. Because back pay is the principal component of monetary awards in employment discrimination cases, salaries in all cases should be correlated with recoveries, not just in the few cases in which recoveries are reported.

For more subtle reasons, status and job tenure should also affect the

[76] See text around notes 51–53 *supra*.

TABLE 6

OUTCOME OF CASES

	NON-ADEA CASES		ALL ADEA CASES		ADEA-ONLY CASES		ADEA-PLUS CASES	
	%	Number	%	Number	%	Number	%	Number
Settled	46.5	445	57.9	73	55.9	52	63.6	21
Defendant won:	47.0	451	26.3	33	25.8	24	27.3	9
Plaintiff dropped the case	13.9	133	4.8	6	4.3	4	6.0	2
On summary judgment	6.6	63	5.6	7	4.3	4	9.1	3
On some other pretrial motion	12.5	121	3.2	4	2.2	2	6.1	2
At trial	14.0	134	12.7	16	15.0	14	6.1	2
Plaintiff won at trial	2.2	21	6.3	8	8.6	8	.0	0
Other disposition	4.3	41	9.5	12	9.7	9	9.1	3
Total number of cases		958		126		93		33
Reported recoveries by plaintiffs (Consumer Price Index for urban consumers, 1982–84 = $1.00):								
Average money judgment recovered	$11,517	87	$68,785	10	$83,575	8	$9,623	2
Average attorney's fees recovered	$27,311	29	$53,174	2	$53,174	2	$0	0

SOURCE.—American Bar Foundation Employment Discrimination Litigation Survey. For conversion to constant dollars, see Statistical Abstract of the United States (1994), table 746.

rate and amount of settlements. Cases under the ADEA, whether or not they include other claims of discrimination, are settled more frequently than other cases, 58 percent of the time, as opposed to 47 percent. This figure suggests that settlements are easier to reach in ADEA cases, either because the parties are more likely to agree on the outcome of litigation or on an appropriate settlement. Because of the plaintiff's longer tenure on the job, both parties are more likely to have extensive information about the plaintiff's performance and the defendant's employment practices. The higher status of ADEA plaintiffs is also likely to increase their knowledge of the defendant's employment practices. For similar reasons, the plaintiff is likely to have vested pension rights or the right to severance pay which can be used by the defendant to increase its settlement offer. This inference is supported to some extent by the increased frequency of requests for pension and other benefits by ADEA plaintiffs, set forth in Table 2, and the greater average age of ADEA plaintiffs, to be found in Table 1.

Despite the higher settlement rate for ADEA cases, defendants still prevail much more frequently than plaintiffs in litigated cases, although they prevail less frequently on ADEA claims than on other claims. In cases brought only under the ADEA, defendants prevail 25.8 percent of the time, and plaintiffs 8.7 percent of the time. (Most of the remaining cases are settled.) Even if we confine the statistics only to decisions at trial, defendants prevail 15.0 percent of the time, or almost twice as often as plaintiffs. According to the well-known theory of George Priest and Benjamin Klein, we should expect cases that are seriously litigated to be decided equally often for the plaintiff and for the defendant.[77] An important exception to this principle is for actions in which the stakes are not evenly balanced, when, for instance, the defendant has more to lose than the plaintiff has to win. Evidently, this is true of ADEA claims.

But if so, the stakes are even more unbalanced on other claims. In non-ADEA cases, defendants prevail 47.0 percent of the time, and plaintiffs only 2.2 percent, with most of the remaining cases settled. Again, if we confine the comparison to cases at trial, defendants prevail 14.0 percent of the time, for a six-to-one differential. (In cases that combine ADEA claims and other claims, defendants won 6.1 percent of the cases that were tried, but plaintiffs did not win at all, partially no doubt because of the small sample of such cases.) In non-ADEA cases, the stakes seem to be even more lopsided for the defendant than in pure ADEA cases. What accounts for these lopsided stakes?

[77] George L. Priest & Benjamin Klein, The Selection of Disputes for Litigation, 13 J. Legal Stud. 1 (1984).

An obvious imbalance in the stakes results from fee-shifting statutes. These have been interpreted in employment discrimination cases to require a losing defendant almost always to pay the attorney's fees of a prevailing plaintiff. A losing plaintiff, however, hardly ever has to pay the fees of a prevailing defendant.[78] This explanation has some force if we consider only the plaintiff's incentives to go to trial, although it is doubtful that it accounts for all of the six-to-one ratio of victories in favor of defendants. The limited data on attorney's fees suggest that it is, at most, double the average monetary recovery in a non-ADEA case. Such large attorney's fees, if they are representative of the many cases in which fees are not reported, probably reflect the value of reinstatement or fringe benefits, which can be used to justify a larger award of attorney's fees. Indeed, under existing law, attorney's fees could not consistently be a large multiple of the total recovery and still be reasonable.[79] If so, they cannot explain the large differential in favor of the defendant at trial.[80]

The most plausible remaining explanation for the imbalance in stakes is that the defendant needs to maintain managerial control over its own employment practices, particularly against threats of litigation by other employees. On this explanation, an employer who loses one case may face many similar cases in the future. One disgruntled employee who prevails will encourage others to challenge the employer's personnel decisions. The defendant therefore faces the risk that a loss in one case will result in a cascade of cases. The employer may also have other interests in prevailing which are more or less closely related to preserving managerial control: preventing the plaintiff from obtaining reinstatement and returning as a discontented worker, preserving the benefits from the partic-

[78] Christiansburg Garment Co. v. EEOC, 434 U.S. 412 (1978).

[79] Farrar v. Hobby, 113 S. Ct. 566, 574 (1992); Hensley v. Eckerhart, 461 U.S. 424, 436 (1983); Charles Silver, Incoherence and Irrationality in the Law of Attorneys' Fees, 12 Rev. Lit. 301, 323 (1993) ("To my knowledge, no study has found that enhanced or unenhanced lodestar fee awards systematically or even frequently exceed customary contingent percentage fees."). In an exceptional case, in which the degree of success cannot easily be reduced to money damages, the award of attorney's fees may far exceed the damages awarded to the plaintiff (City of Riverside v. Rivera, 477 U.S. 561, 585–86 (1986) (opinion of Powell, J.)).

[80] However, one-way shifting of attorney's fees might explain some of the reduced differential in favor of the defendant in cases tried only under the ADEA. In the two cases in which attorney's fees are reported, the awarded fees are about half the average monetary award in all ADEA cases. If these figures could be generalized, the small size of awarded fees relative to the plaintiff's average recovery would dampen the effect from one-way shifting of attorney's fees, which in turn would explain some of the greater success that ADEA plaintiffs have as compared to other plaintiffs. This speculation, however, rests on a very small sample of only two cases.

ular employment practice in dispute, or protecting its general reputation as a nondiscriminatory employer. Each of these explanations is plausible; none of them is excluded by the evidence.

These explanations are also consistent with the defendants' lower rate of success in cases tried only under the ADEA. Under the Priest-Klein theory, we can infer from the defendant's lower rate of success that the stakes are less imbalanced in pure ADEA cases than in other cases and mixed cases. This suggestion is supported by the higher recoveries reported by plaintiffs in such cases. Although a higher recovery for the plaintiff also means greater exposure for the defendant, it will also disproportionately increase the plaintiff's stakes relative to the defendant's if the plaintiff is risk averse.[81] Since the plaintiff's job is usually his principal financial asset, we should expect plaintiffs to be risk averse in most cases alleging discriminatory discharge. A plaintiff with higher status, longer job tenure, and a higher salary is also likely to receive a higher settlement offer, which includes severance pay or pension benefits. Accordingly, we should expect ADEA plaintiffs to settle more of their cases, as they do. We should also expect ADEA plaintiffs to be more risk averse about rejecting settlement offers and going to trial; if settlement offers are more generous, risk averse plaintiffs have more to lose by going to trial. This effect is likely to be particularly pronounced for plaintiffs who are near the age of retirement. Severance and retirement benefits for ADEA plaintiffs, with an average age of 55, are more likely to approximate reinstatement than for plaintiffs under other statutes, with an average age of 39.

Moreover, many of the defendant's costs in settling an ADEA case are attributable to sources other than the plaintiff's recovery, in particular, costs to its managerial control over personnel decisions. These costs will not be confined only to ADEA cases, but to employment decisions that can be challenged on other grounds and so are independent of the high recoveries under the ADEA. The defendant's costs of losing are more or less constant across all employment discrimination cases, but the plaintiff's stakes increase in ADEA cases, enough to reduce the defendant's rate of success from six to one to less than two to one.

This explanation, although inevitably speculative, is consistent with the evidence for cases brought only under the ADEA, but not for mixed cases brought under the ADEA and other statutes. When these cases are litigated, plaintiffs appear to have a much lower rate of success and to obtain lower recoveries than in pure ADEA cases. Yet plaintiffs in these

[81] Priest & Klein, *supra* note 77, at 27–28.

cases have higher average salaries and only slightly lower job tenure than the plaintiffs who sue only under the ADEA. The outcome in mixed cases resembles the outcome in pure ADEA cases only in the similar rate of settlement. The remaining differences might be dismissed as not statistically significant because of the small number of mixed cases in which outcomes are reported. It is possible, however, that mixed cases are weaker because the plaintiff has not been able to identify what was wrong with the employer's adverse decision. By alleging so much, they might admit that they know too little. Alternatively, it might be that the judge or jury is less sympathetic to these plaintiffs because they are, as we have seen, predominantly women or minorities. Whatever the explanation, the relatively unfavorable results in these cases do not detract from, and may reinforce, the distinction between claims brought only under the ADEA and claims under other employment discrimination statutes.

From the evidence we have, claims under the ADEA are worth more than other claims: the plaintiff has a greater chance of settling, probably for a larger amount of money, and if the case is litigated, the plaintiff has a greater chance of winning and winning a larger amount of money. The plaintiff is also more likely to be a white male, more likely to have a high status occupation with a higher salary, and more likely to have raised a claim of discriminatory discharge. These similarities to general claims for wrongful discharge and their implications are taken up in the next section of the article.

III. A Comparison with Claims of Wrongful Discharge

The resemblance between claims under the ADEA and claims for wrongful discharge is borne out by the only major empirical study of wrongful discharge cases, conducted by the Rand Corporation in a survey of 120 cases tried in Los Angeles Superior Court in 1986 and 1987.[82] This study predated a leading decision of the California Supreme Court, *Foley v. Interactive Data Corp.*,[83] which restricted defendants' liability for wrongful discharge. For this reason, and because it is limited to a city with a reputation for generous verdicts, it probably overstates the amount that plaintiffs actually recovered. It is less likely to distort the characteristics of plaintiffs, which bear a striking resemblance to the characteristics of ADEA plaintiffs.

The plaintiffs in the Rand Study were overwhelmingly white, 89.3 per-

[82] James N. Dertouzos, Elaine Holland, & Patricia Ebener, The Legal and Economic Consequences of Wrongful Termination 4–12 (1988) (hereinafter cited as Rand Study).

[83] Foley v. Interactive Data Corp., 47 Cal. 3d 654, 254 Cal. Rptr. 211, 765 P.2d 373 (1988).

cent, and predominantly male, 68.6 percent. These figures are similar to the percentage of white males among plaintiffs who sued only under the ADEA, 74 percent. The plaintiffs in the Rand Study were also similar in occupation; 53.4 percent were executives or middle managers, while 68 percent of the plaintiffs in pure ADEA cases were in the broader category of managers or professionals. The job tenure of wrongful discharge plaintiffs, however, was lower; only 23.1 percent had served with the employer for over 15 years, while the average for plaintiffs under the ADEA was over 15 years. Despite the effect of job tenure on salary, the average salary of the two groups remained similar: $36,254 for wrongful discharge plaintiffs and $33,327 for plaintiffs who sued only under the ADEA.[84] And as we have seen, 89.4 percent of these claims concerned discriminatory discharge.

Despite the similarity in plaintiffs and claims, the recoveries reported in the Rand Study are larger than the recoveries under the ADEA, perhaps because awards in California are especially generous. The Rand Study is particularly valuable in its detailed analysis of verdicts and amounts actually paid to plaintiffs and their attorneys, but because the study was confined almost entirely to cases tried to a jury, it contains no information about dismissals. It does indicate that 95 percent of wrongful discharge cases were settled for an average of $30,000 for all cases filed.[85] Plaintiffs in the Rand Study prevailed in 67.5 percent of the cases, for a two-to-one ratio of victories in their favor, just the opposite of the ratio in cases involving only the ADEA. These verdicts, however, were set aside or reduced in posttrial proceedings so that plaintiffs were slightly less likely to prevail than defendants and very likely to have the jury verdict reduced. Further proceedings in the trial court and on appeal and further settlement negotiations reduced the average award to the plaintiff by more than half, from an average jury verdict for the plaintiff of $646,900 to a final average payment of $307,600.[86]

The success rate reported in the Rand Study is probably not as stable as the success rate under the ADEA. Uncertainty about the evolving law of wrongful discharge affected the success rate of plaintiffs in the years before 1986,[87] and the restrictive decision in *Foley v. Interactive Data*

[84] Rand Study, *supra* note 82, at 20–21. The Rand data apparently are reported in nominal dollars for the period 1980–86 (*id.* at 19). This is closely comparable to the dollar figures reported in the tables in this article, which are in constant dollars for the Consumer Price Index for urban consumers (CPI-U) averaged over the period 1982–84.

[85] *Id.* at 47–48.

[86] *Id.* at 26, 33–37, 40.

[87] *Id.* at 15–16.

Corp. undoubtedly reduced it thereafter.[88] By contrast, individual claims under the ADEA were governed by the structure of proof under *McDonnell Douglas Corp. v. Green*[89] over the entire period covered by the ABF data, 1972–87.[90] Developments under the ADEA, although significant, have not been of nearly the same magnitude as the changes that caused many states to depart from the common-law doctrine of employment at will.[91] Most states have recognized claims for wrongful discharge in one of its various forms, although as the law in California illustrates, the nature of the claim and the extent of the defendant's liability often take some time to be clarified.

Other doctrinal differences between the law of wrongful discharge and the ADEA also account for the larger recoveries reported in the Rand Study. A plaintiff who has prevailed on a claim of wrongful discharge is not ordinarily entitled to an award of attorney's fees, so that his net recovery is usually reduced by the amount of his attorney's contingent fee. All of the plaintiffs' attorneys were compensated by contingent fees, with almost two-thirds charging a fee of at least 40 percent of the recovery.[92] Contingent fees reduced the prevailing plaintiff's average net payment to $188,520.[93] Of this amount, 39.9 percent was attributable to punitive damages, which were awarded in about half of the cases in which plaintiffs obtained verdicts in their favor.[94] I do not have figures for the amount of liquidated damages awarded in ADEA cases, but the total amount of damages in ADEA cases is likely to be lower, since recovery is limited to back pay and an equal amount of liquidated damages. In a tort claim for wrongful discharge, which was generally available in California during the years covered by the Rand Study, the plaintiff could recover nonpecuniary damages for emotional distress and an unlimited amount of punitive damages.[95] The authors of the Rand Study also caution that the figures on average awards, just like those in the ABF data,

[88] For empirical evidence that supports this conclusion, see Samuel R. Gross & Kent D. Syverud, Getting to No: A Study of Settlement Negotiations and the Selection of Cases for Trial, 90 Mich. L. Rev. 319, 373–77 (1991). For doctrinal analysis of the decision, see David J. Jung & Richard Harkness, Life after *Foley:* The Future of Wrongful Discharge Litigation, 41 Hastings L. J. 131 (1989); Note, Employment-at-Will and the Aftermath of *Foley v. Interactive Data Corp.*, 34 St. Louis U. L. J. 695 (1990) (remedies for wrongful discharge).

[89] McDonnell Douglas Corp. v. Green, 411 U.S. 792 (1973).

[90] See Player, *supra* note 31.

[91] Weiler, *supra* note 47, ch. 2.

[92] Rand Study, *supra* note 82, at 38.

[93] *Id.* at 40. This average counts only cases in which the plaintiff obtained a jury verdict in his favor.

[94] *Id.* at 25–26.

[95] See note 88 *supra*.

are heavily influenced by a small number of very large awards.[96] They conclude that the median payment for all plaintiffs, whether or not they obtained a jury verdict in their favor, was only $30,000, which amounted to a severance payment of 6 months' salary.[97]

The magnitude of the recoveries reported in the Rand Study might be exaggerated, but the existence of a significant difference from employment discrimination cases is not. Plaintiffs who get to a jury on claims of wrongful discharge are more likely to recover, and more likely to recover larger judgments, than plaintiffs who get equally far with claims of employment discrimination, including claims under the ADEA. The recoveries reported in the Rand Study extend a pattern found in the ABF data: larger recoveries by plaintiffs are correlated with a higher success rate at trial. This correlation lends some support to my inference from the Priest-Klein theory that increasing the plaintiff's recovery evens out the stakes between plaintiffs and defendants. It also places claims under the ADEA midway between other claims of employment discrimination and claims of wrongful discharge. Although the figures from the Rand Study and from the ABF data are difficult to compare precisely, they yield the following pattern: in non-ADEA cases, plaintiffs win about one-seventh of the trials and winning plaintiffs recover an average of $11,500; in cases only under the ADEA, they win about one-third of the trials and recover an average of $83,600; and in wrongful discharge cases, they win two-thirds of the cases and ultimately obtain a net average recovery of $188,500.

With the passage of the Civil Rights Act of 1991, other employment discrimination claims should come to resemble ADEA claims more closely, but only to a degree. The act extended the right to jury trial and the right to compensatory and punitive damages to all claims of intentional discrimination.[98] These were formerly available only for claims of racial discrimination under section 1981 and, as liquidated damages, under the ADEA. Under the new act, damages are limited according to the size of the employer, but these limits roughly and imperfectly approximate the limits on liquidated damages under the ADEA.[99] What the act

[96] Rand Study, *supra* note 82, at 25–26.

[97] *Id.* at 39.

[98] Pub. L. No. 102-166, § 102, 105 Stat. 1071 (1991), codified as 42 U.S.C. § 1981a(b),(c) (Supp. IV 1992).

[99] The limits under the new act range from $50,000 to $300,000 depending on the size of the employer. The limits apply to future pecuniary losses, nonpecuniary losses, and punitive damages (Pub. L. No. 102-166, § 102, 105 Stat. 1071 (1991), 42 U.S.C. § 1981a(b)(3) (Supp. IV 1992)). By way of comparison, the ADEA allows an award of liquidated damages in an amount equal to an award of back pay for willful violations (29 U.S.C. §§ 626(b), 216(b) (1988)).

cannot change are the characteristics of plaintiffs who bring different kinds of discrimination claims and how sympathetic a jury is likely to be toward them. The few data available on claims under section 1981 suggest that the effective limits on damages do not arise solely from legal doctrine. Plaintiffs on these claims recover money judgments in almost the same percentage of filed cases as plaintiffs under Title VII.[100] From a broader sample of all constitutional tort cases, it appears that plaintiffs under section 1981 recover more than plaintiffs under Title VII, but less than half of what plaintiffs recover under the ADEA alone.[101]

Claims under the ADEA bear a far stronger resemblance to wrongful discharge claims than other claims of employment discrimination precisely because they are not claims on behalf of a discrete and insular group in our society.[102] Like wrongful discharge claims, they are usually brought by white males, and they can usually be avoided only by employers who establish general safeguards against unjust dismissal. The institutional reform stimulated by the ADEA, apart from changes in retirement and benefits policies, is indistinguishable from the reform caused by the law of wrongful discharge. In the latter, a major issue is how far such claims should go beyond the express or implied terms of the employment contract,[103] and a fundamental issue in both fields is how far the judge or jury should second-guess the employer's reasons for discharging the plaintiff.[104]

IV. Conclusion

The ADEA may be characteristic of trends in the law of employment discrimination, but only if those trends are eroding the distinctive characteristics of the field. The ADEA is part of a growing list of negative prohibitions, telling employers what they may not consider in hiring and firing employees. Someday this list might have the same effect as an affirmative command, telling them what they must consider, not just what they must exclude from consideration. As prohibitions against discrimination multiply to reach additional grounds, they have the same cumulative effect as an affirmative obligation only to discharge for good cause. They

[100] Theodore Eisenberg & Stewart Schwab, The Importance of Section 1981, 73 Cornell L. Rev. 596, 600–01 (1988).

[101] Theodore Eisenberg & Stewart J. Schwab, What Shapes Perceptions of the Federal Court System? 56 U. Chi. L. Rev. 501, 529–30 (1989).

[102] See *Murgia, supra* note 4, at 307, 313–14 (per curiam).

[103] Weiler, *supra* note 47, at 25–26, 70–78.

[104] Lanctot, *supra* note 11, at 64–67; Player, *supra* note 31, at 656; Eglit, *supra* note 33, at 168, 226.

also lose their moral force as absolute prohibitions when they are subject to multiple exceptions, as in the ADEA. Protection against wrongful discharge may—or may not—be justifiable, but if it is, it is on grounds only distantly related to the original aims and purposes of employment discrimination law.

Today, 25 years after enactment of the ADEA, and soon after the passage of the Americans with Disabilities Act of 1990 and the Civil Rights Act of 1991, it is difficult to imagine that the increasing scope of employment discrimination law can be reversed. Yet the customary justification for this body of law can no longer be applied, if it ever could, to all of the prohibitions against different forms of discrimination. The ADEA, in particular, cannot be justified in terms of opening opportunities to a historically disfavored group. Those 40 years old or older are not politically powerless and do not, as a group, suffer from economic disadvantages. On the contrary, those who sue under the ADEA tend to be white males who are relatively well off in status, positions, and pay. It is therefore necessary to turn to other justifications for the ADEA. These have yet to be supplied, and if they are not, both the breadth of and the need for the ADEA must be reexamined.

[5]

LIFE-CYCLE JUSTICE: ACCOMMODATING JUST CAUSE AND EMPLOYMENT AT WILL

*Stewart J. Schwab**

"You're fired!" Most American workers hearing these words have no legal recourse under traditional employment law. Unless they have specific protection in a contract — and few nonunion workers do — or evidence that the firing violates a specific antidiscrimination statute, workers are treated at will. Under this traditional view, an employer can fire them for a good reason, a bad reason, or no reason at all.[1]

Yet, as any employer who has recently tried to fire a worker will complain, the traditional doctrine is now full of holes. In the past decade or two, courts increasingly have become receptive to worker claims of unjust dismissal. Still, the protections remain patchwork and the trend uneven. No state court has proclaimed a general right of employees against arbitrary dismissal, although the Montana court has come close.[2] Indeed, the Supreme Courts of California and Michigan, long considered to be among the leading innovators in this area, have recently issued major decisions signaling hesitation with ever-expanding protections for employees.[3] On the legislative side, only

---

* Professor of Law, Cornell University. B.A. 1975, Swarthmore College; J.D. 1980, Ph.D. (Economics) 1981, University of Michigan. — Ed. For wonderful discussions and comments I thank Greg Alexander, Lynn Baker, Chris Bruce, Jim Brudney, John Donohue, Ron Ehrenberg, Bob Hillman, Bob Hutchens, Susan Koniak, Saul Levmore, Tom Rowe, Theodore St. Antoine, Bob Scott, John Siliciano, Kathy Stone, Steve Thel, Steve Willborn, and workshop participants at the University of Virginia Law School Faculty Workshop, the Labor Economics Workshop at Cornell University's Industrial and Labor Relations School, and the annual meetings of the American Law and Economics Association and the Canadian Law and Economics Association. I thank Mike Holden for his fine research assistance.

1. The classic statement of the at-will doctrine comes from the Supreme Court of Tennessee in Payne v. Western & Atl. R.R., 81 Tenn. 507 (1884):

> All may dismiss their employees at will, be they many or few, for good cause, for no cause or even for cause morally wrong, without being thereby guilty of legal wrong. . . . The sufficient and conclusive answer to the many plausible arguments to the contrary, portraying the evil to workmen and to others from the exercise of such authority by the great and strong, is: They have the right to discharge their employees. The law cannot compel them to employ workmen, nor to keep them employed.

81 Tenn. at 519-20.

2. *See* Crenshaw v. Bozeman Deaconess Hosp., 693 P.2d 487, 492 (Mont. 1984) ("Employers can still terminate untenured employees at-will and without notice [but] simply may not do so in bad faith or unfairly . . . .").

3. Foley v. Interactive Data Corp., 765 P.2d 373 (Cal. 1988) (denying tort remedies for firings that breach an implied covenant of good faith and fair dealing); Rowe v. Montgomery Ward

Montana, reacting to its extreme court decisions,[4] has a statute requiring employers to have good cause before firing a worker.[5] However, the Commissioners on Uniform State Laws have recently passed a Model Employment Termination Act that would finally abolish the at-will doctrine for most employees,[6] and we can expect further debate over employment at will as legislatures confront the model act.

Snapshot examinations of current unjust dismissal law have led employment law commentators to see only chaos, a set of cases with little internal coherence or rationale. A view of the decisions in their historical sweep causes commentators to see evolution: in the beginning was employment at will,[7] now chaos exists, the natural ending point will be just cause. Most commentators applaud the trend, urge its completion, and bemoan any hesitation or backsliding by the courts.[8] Their continual refrain is that the United States lags behind

& Co., 473 N.W.2d 268 (Mich. 1991) (finding that oral statements and handbook did not create legitimate expectation that discharges would only be for cause).

4. *See* LeRoy H. Schramm, *Montana Employment Law and the 1987 Wrongful Discharge from Employment Act: A New Order Begins,* 51 MONT. L. REV. 94, 108-10 (1990) (noting that an association of defense lawyers and insurance companies drafted bill that eventually became the Montana Wrongful Discharge from Employment Act).

5. Montana Wrongful Discharge from Employment Act of 1987, MONT. CODE ANN. §§ 39-2-901 to -914 (1991).

6. MODEL EMPLOYMENT TERMINATION ACT OF 1991, 7A U.L.A. 66 (Supp. 1993). The Model Act was controversial even among the commissioners. They rejected an attempt to pass a uniform act that would have required the commissioners to urge their respective legislatures to adopt the law. *See id.* prefatory note, 7A U.L.A. at 69-70 (Supp. 1993).

7. Legal historians have debated whether employment at will was truly "the beginning," or whether that presumption itself was a radical departure from earlier, status-based conceptions of employment. Much of the debate has focused on whether Horace Wood "invented" employment at will in his 1870 treatise or accurately was describing legal doctrine of the nineteenth century. *Compare* Jay M. Feinman, *The Development of the Employment at Will Rule,* 20 AM. J. LEGAL HIST. 118 (1976) *with* Mayer G. Freed & Daniel D. Polsby, *The Doubtful Provenance of "Wood's Rule" Revisited,* 22 ARIZ. ST. L.J. 551 (1990). *See also* Jay M. Feinman, *The Development of the Employment-at-Will Rule Revisited,* 23 ARIZ. ST. L.J. 733 (1991).

8. The strongest prediction of the demise of employment at will comes from Professor Peck, who begins his important article by noting:

> At times one is tempted, despite the hazards, to make predictions concerning the law of the future. The prediction made in this article is one of the safest that can be made. Indeed, it may be wrong to characterize what is said here as a prediction. So strong are the forces for the change that it may be only the details of an inevitable development that remain undisclosed. The prediction is that American courts will abandon the principle that, absent some consideration other than the services to be performed, a contract of employment for an indefinite term is to be considered a contract terminable at will by either party, with the consequences that an employer may discharge an employee for any cause, no cause, or even a bad cause.

Cornelius J. Peck, *Unjust Discharges from Employment: A Necessary Change in the Law,* 40 OHIO ST. L.J. 1, 1 (1979); *see also* Alfred W. Blumrosen, *Strangers No More: All Workers Are Entitled to "Just Cause" Protection Under Title VII,* 2 INDUS. REL. L.J. 519 (1978); Joseph Grodin, *Toward a Wrongful Termination Statute for California,* 42 HASTINGS L.J. 135 (1990); Gary Minda & Katie R. Raab, *Time for an Unjust Dismissal Statute in New York,* 54 BROOK. L. REV. 1137 (1989); Theodore J. St. Antoine, *A Seed Germinates: Unjust Discharge Reform Heads Toward Full Flower,* 67 NEB. L. REV. 56 (1988); Clyde Summers, *Individual Protection Against Unjust Dismissal: Time for a Statute,* 62 VA. L. REV. 481, 484 (1976) ("[T]he anachronistic legal

the rest of the world on this issue.[9] At the other extreme, some conservatives, most prominently Richard Epstein, hearken back to the heyday of employment at will as the ideal state of employment law.[10] Such observers lament every move away from a strict presumption that all employment contracts can be terminated at will by either party.

The fundamental problem with these perspectives is that they criticize current law but they do not understand or explain it, except in the crudest way. The just-cause boosters simply applaud every pro-employee decision and decry the others as backsliding responses to conservative political pressures. The at-will zealots simply cheer and boo the other way. Neither perspective appreciates the apparent vacillation of current courts, which erode the at-will presumption without rejecting it.

Current termination law does have an underlying coherence. We should recognize this coherence before we reject the contemporary common law system for either the Model Act's futuristic scheme of arbitrating just cause or a return to the heyday of employment at will. This paper attempts to articulate the coherence of current doctrine. Reacting to the almost uniform polarization on this issue, I argue both positively and normatively for an intermediate position. The current intermediate position of the common law balances two conflicting problems. A career-employment relationship faces two types of opportunism: opportunistic firings by an unfettered employer and shirking by employees with job security. An extreme legal rule can handle either problem alone, but only by ignoring the other. Thus, a legal presumption of employment at will handles the shirking problem well but gives no protection against opportunistic firings. A just-cause regime has the opposite virtue and flaw. The legal challenge is to find an intermediate rule that provides the optimal check against both dangers.

The common law has groped towards such a rule by recognizing

rule that employees can be discharged for any reason or no reason should be abandoned."); Note, *Protecting At-Will Employees Against Wrongful Discharge: The Duty To Terminate Only in Good Faith,* 93 HARV. L. REV. 1816 (1980).

9. *See* Samuel Estreicher, *Unjust Dismissal Laws: Some Cautionary Notes,* 33 AM. J. COMP. L. 310, 311 (1985) ("We seem to stand virtually alone among the nations of the Western industrialized world in not providing general protection against unjust discharge for private-sector employees who either cannot or do not choose unionism.").

10. Richard A. Epstein, *In Defense of the Contract at Will,* 51 U. CHI. L. REV. 947 (1984); *see also* Susan L. Catler, *The Case Against Proposals To Eliminate the Employment At Will Rule,* 5 INDUS. REL. L.J. 471 (1983); Larry S. Larson, *Why We Should Not Abandon the Presumption that Employment Is Terminable At-Will,* 23 IDAHO L. REV. 219, 253 (1986-1987) (any presumption other than at will "would only open a Pandora's box of new issues"); Richard W. Power, *A Defense of the Employment At Will Rule,* 33 DEF. L.J. 199 (1984).

that the relative magnitudes of the two problems vary over the life cycle of the worker. The danger of employer opportunism is greatest for late-career workers, and it is also a problem for some beginning-career employees. By contrast, the greater problem at midcareer is shirking. In response, the courts have begun to offer contract protections for workers at the beginning and end of the life cycle, while maintaining a presumption of at-will employment for midcareer employees. In arguing for the wisdom of this approach, I, like the courts, refrain from making a categorical statement that at-will or just-cause employment should never — or should always — be the governing presumption.

Let me sketch at the outset the boundaries of my inquiry. Using an internal-labor-markets model of career employment, this paper examines whether courts should presume, in the absence of any express contractual provision about job security, that an employee is at will or protected by just cause. This paper therefore skirts the fascinating contract issues involved in employee handbooks and other arguably express agreements about the standard of discharge. Nor will it evaluate the appropriate scope of tort limitations on employment at will.[11] The goal of this article is to articulate a coherent framework for understanding the default rules for employment termination. While most observers see chaos here, I find a certain logic in the leading cases. The courts have been boldest when job protection is most appropriate, and they have hesitated precisely when at will plays its most useful role.

An initial caveat about methodology is appropriate. When applying the model to the case law, I will not survey every termination case, or even most or many of the thousands of cases. Rather, my method is to use "leading" cases — those that may indicate trends in the law — and argue how these leading cases might fit together in a coherent structure. Leading cases rarely typify the mass of cases, and counter-examples certainly exist. Leading cases are worth studying, however, particularly in a rapidly evolving subject area, because they often give greater hints about the appropriate normative structure of law than

11. The tort of wrongful discharge in violation of public policy — applying more or less traditional concerns of tort law — attempts to protect outsiders to the employment relationship. *See* Stewart J. Schwab, Tort Limitations on At-Will Employment: Searching for Third-Party Effects (1991) (unpublished manuscript, on file with author). Protection of an employee fired for serving on jury duty provides a paradigm example. *See* Nees v. Hocks, 536 P.2d 512 (1975). By contrast, the contract law doctrines analyzed in this article regulate relations between employer and employee, regardless of whether outsiders are directly affected. Despite my sharp division between tort and contract limits on employment at will, I agree with Peter Linzer that the division is often artificial. *See* Peter Linzer, *The Decline of Assent: At-Will Employment as a Case Study of the Breakdown of Private Law Theory*, 20 GA. L. REV. 323 (1986).

would an exhaustive study of the hidebound mass of cases. Nevertheless, because of its reliance on leading cases, my inquiry must blend positive and normative analysis. Perhaps the question addressed here should be phrased as whether the leading employment-termination cases can fit into a coherent structure that has normative appeal.

One final caveat before we begin. One could argue that we should scrap common law litigation over employment terminations as not worth the cost of litigation.[12] Whatever rationality the current common law lines might draw, the argument goes, its advantages are swamped by the costs of deciding on what side of the line a particular employee falls. To my mind, this litigation-cost argument is the strongest argument for taking a polar position. By itself, however, it does not point clearly toward either pole. Supporters of a rigid at-will presumption emphasize that fewer employees will challenge terminations under their standard — thus saving on litigation costs.[13] At the other pole, proponents of just cause, worried about the feasibility of courts reviewing every dismissal, typically link their proposals to arbitration rather than litigation as the method of enforcement.[14] In any event, courts themselves are poor judges of the metadecision about whether to have common law enforcement of employment terms. Reacting to the cases they see, courts have attempted to create a coherent doctrine. Before rejecting their efforts on grounds of cost, one should appreciate the balance they are trying to achieve. Until now, no one has attempted to find the method behind the current madness. While the intermediate solution of the current common law inevitably will have detractors on both sides, much can be said on its behalf. The goal of this article is to present that defense.

I. Employment as a Relational Contract

Workers have many types of jobs and many types of relationships with employers. Younger workers typically try several jobs before beginning a long-term attachment to one employer.[15] This variety of

12. For an empirical analysis of the litigation costs, see James N. Dertouzos, The End of Employment-At-Will: Legal and Economic Costs (1988).

13. *See* Epstein, *supra* note 10, at 970-73 (an "enormous advantage" of the contract at will is that it is "very cheap to administer").

14. *See, e.g.*, Model Employment Termination Act § 6 (establishing arbitration); William B. Gould IV, *The Idea of the Job as Property in Contemporary America: The Legal and Collective Bargaining Framework*, 1986 B.Y.U. L. Rev. 885, 908-10 (arguing that arbitration should be the "first basic ingredient" of legislation to provide just cause).

15. *See* Robert E. Hall, *The Importance of Lifetime Jobs in the U.S. Economy*, 72 Am. Econ. Rev. 716, 720, 722 tbl. 3 (1982) (noting that the average worker holds 10 jobs during lifetime; 28% of workers are currently in jobs that will last 20 years or more; 23% are in jobs that will last less than two years); *see also* John T. Addison & Alberto C. Castro, *The Importance of Lifetime*

relationships may in itself counsel against a uniform legal approach to employment terminations. I will return to this issue at the end of this article,[16] but most of my analysis will concentrate on the career employee. Termination of the career employee provides the fact pattern for many leading cases in the erosion of employment at will.

A. *The Specific Human-Capital Story*

The key feature of the career employment relationship is that both sides are locked into it. The easiest explanation for lock-in comes from a human-capital story that emphasizes "asset specificity."[17] Under the basic human-capital model, workers become more productive as they learn the ways of the firm. Because the gains exceed the costs of training, these firm-specific skills are worth learning. In contrast to general skills, however, these skills are not useful to other firms.[18]

The issue becomes whether the employer and employee can decide how to share the costs and benefits so that this desirable training will occur. This issue can be resolved in a number of ways. One possibility is for the employer to pay for the firm-specific training and to receive the benefits of the greater productivity by paying the worker throughout his work life a wage equal to the wage he could get outside the firm. The problem is that the worker has no incentive to stay with the firm because he earns no more than he could get elsewhere, and so the employer risks losing the employee before it can recoup its training

Jobs: Differences Between Union and Nonunion Workers, 40 INDUS. & LAB. REL. REV. 393, 402 (1987) (unionized workers have longer job tenure than nonunion workers, but nonunion workers "enjoy considerable lifetime tenure after the job shopping years").

16. *See infra* Part V.

17. The term *asset specificity* comes from Oliver E. Williamson, OLIVER E. WILLIAMSON, THE ECONOMIC INSTITUTIONS OF CAPITALISM 52-56 (1985), who calls asset specificity the most important dimension for transaction-cost economics — the study of the "rational economic reasons for organizing some transactions one way and other transactions another." *Id.* at 52. As Williamson puts it, "asset specificity is the big locomotive to which transaction cost economics owes much of its predictive content." *Id.* at 56; *see also* Douglas L. Leslie, *Labor Bargaining Units,* 70 VA. L. REV. 353, 366-67 ("The key premise of the relational contract model of labor markets is that many job skills are learned on the job and are specific to the firm. Employees work in teams, and tasks are complex.").

18. A basic conclusion of Gary Becker's classic analysis, GARY S. BECKER, HUMAN CAPITAL (2d ed. 1975), is that workers rather than employers will pay for general training. If employers were to pay for training that was useful to other firms, workers after training would leave for other employers who, having incurred none of the training expenses, could afford higher wages. This is most obvious for the most general training, which is called "education." Employers rarely pay to educate workers because of the difficulty of ensuring the worker will stay for a reasonable length of time. Only employers like the U.S. Army, who have better means of enforcing student promises to work for them later, will pay for general training. Workers also can pay implicitly for on-the-job general training by accepting lower wages than they would receive from a job that did not give them the training.

investment. Another possible resolution is for the worker to pay for the training, perhaps by accepting a lower wage during the training period, and for the employer to pay the worker a higher wage once trained. The mirror image of the earlier problem occurs in this situation: the firm has an incentive to underpay the worker once he is trained, and the worker has no recourse — because the training is worthless elsewhere — as long as he is paid at least the outside wage.

The best solution is for the employer and worker to share both the costs and benefits of firm-specific training. Figure 1 gives a stylized

FIGURE 1

HUMAN-CAPITAL STORY

Sharing Throughout Life Cycle

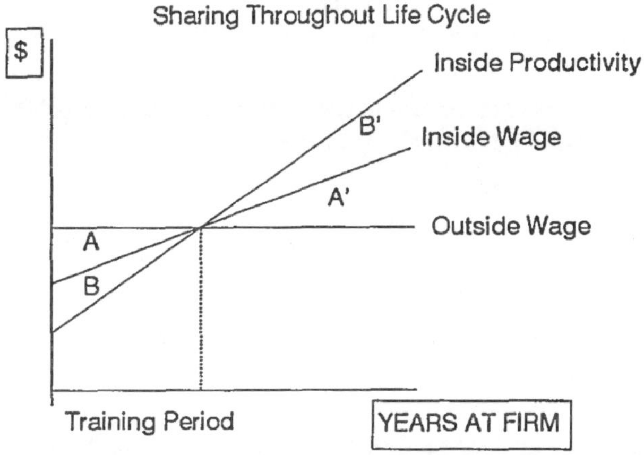

view of the situation. The outside wage is constant, equaling productivity based on general skills.[19] In the training period at the firm, the worker accepts less than the outside wage, thereby paying for some of the training, but the employer pays him more than his productivity during the training period, thereby paying for some of the training. After training, the worker receives more than the outside wage, thereby reaping some of the benefits of training, but the employer does not pay the worker for his full productivity, thereby allowing the employer to reap some of the benefits of training. The worker will agree to this arrangement if the higher post-training wages, when appropriately discounted, are at least as large as the lower training wages —

19. Outside productivity based on general skills remains constant because it is assumed that general skills remain constant over the working life. One could make the sketch more realistic by assuming that experience and maturity would increase outside productivity over time. Such complications would not further the basic insight of the model, which is that employers and workers share in both the costs and benefits of specific training, nor would it alter the specific conclusion that late-career workers receive more than the outside wage but less than their current productivity.

that is, if A' is at least as large as A. The employer will agree as long as the gains to it (B') are at least as large as its training costs (B).[20]

In practice, these higher post-training wages take the form of seniority-based wages and late-vesting pensions, which induce workers to stay with the firm after training.[21] Compared with the life cycle of otherwise similar workers, the model predicts that workers who receive substantial on-the-job training will receive higher pay in later years. Considerable empirical evidence supports this steep age-earnings profile of career employees and its relationship to training early in the career.[22]

A critical part of this simple human-capital story is the self-enforcing feature of the relationship. Because the parties share the costs and benefits of training throughout the employee's work life, both parties want to continue the relationship. The employer pays employees less than their full value later in their career. This protects employees from discharge because a discharge would harm the employer as well. The late-career wage exceeds, however, the outside wage the employee could receive, thereby discouraging the employee from quitting.

B. *The Efficiency-Wage Story and the Potential for Opportunism*

Gary Becker's human-capital theory[23] explained why wages rise with seniority, but puzzles arose that caused commentators to question the theory that workers would receive less than their value late in their career.[24] One such puzzle was mandatory retirement, which covered some thirty-five percent of the workforce before it was prohibited in 1986 by amendments to the Age Discrimination in Employment Act (ADEA).[25] Why would an employer, who is paying older workers less than they are worth, demand that such workers retire? A related puzzle is the presence of actuarially unfair pensions, which even after the 1986 ADEA amendments lawfully encourage older workers

20. Competition among employers and employees will ensure that, in equilibrium, A=A' and B=B'.

21. *See* RONALD G. EHRENBERG & ROBERT S. SMITH, MODERN LABOR ECONOMICS 160-63, 410, 425-37 (4th ed. 1991).

22. *See, e.g.*, James N. Brown, *Why Do Wages Increase with Tenure? On-the-Job Training and Life-Cycle Wage Growth Observed Within Firms*, 79 AM. ECON. REV. 971 (1989).

23. *See generally* BECKER, *supra* note 18.

24. For a superb account of these puzzles and their impact on human-capital theory, see Robert M. Hutchens, *Seniority, Wages and Productivity: A Turbulent Decade*, J. ECON. PERSP., Fall 1989, at 49.

25. Age Discrimination in Employment Amendments of 1986, Pub. L. No. 99-592, § 2(c)(1), 100 Stat. 3342, 3342 (codified at 29 U.S.C. § 631(a) (1988)). The mandatory retirement and actuarially unfair pension puzzles were first discussed by Edward P. Lazear, *Why Is There Mandatory Retirement?*, 87 J. POL. ECON. 1261 (1979).

to retire. The present value of many pensions declines if older workers keep working.[26] Again, why would an employer establish pension plans that encourage retirement if, as the human-capital model suggests, the employer makes money on older workers? A final puzzle stems from studies that suggest that workers' pay relative to others in their job grade increases with seniority but their relative productivity does not.[27] This evidence conflicts with Becker's hypothesis that productivity increases faster than wages. These puzzles suggest that employers want to end the relationship with late-career workers at some point, probably because employers perceive their wages as exceeding current productivity.

To explain the puzzles, economists have developed an efficiency-wage model.[28] The basic insight behind efficiency-wage models is that workers often work harder when the job pays more.[29] High "efficiency wages"[30] increase worker effort by making the job more valuable to the worker. Because workers want to keep the valuable job, they will work hard to avoid being dismissed. In effect, high wages increase the penalty for being dismissed — a dismissed worker forgoes the large payout. Because workers labor harder than otherwise, the firm can afford the higher compensation. An early version of the

26. For example, Lazear's study using 1980 data of large pension plans revealed that the expected present value of pension benefits was $79,476 for a worker with a salary of $25,000 and 40 years tenure retiring at age 65, but would have been $158,225 if that same worker had retired 10 years earlier. Edward P. Lazear, *Pensions as Severance Pay, in* FINANCIAL ASPECTS OF THE UNITED STATES PENSION SYSTEM 57, 72 tbl. 3.3 (Zvi Bodie & John B. Shoven eds., 1983).

27. James L. Medoff & Katharine G. Abraham, *Are Those Paid More Really More Productive? The Case of Experience,* 16 J. HUM. RESOURCES 186 (1981); James L. Medoff & Katharine G. Abraham, *Experience, Performance, and Earnings,* 95 Q.J. ECON. 703 (1980).

28. The distinction between efficiency-wage and human-capital models is not as sharp as the text suggests. Variants of the human-capital model, for example, suggest that late-career workers may be paid more than their current productivity. *See* H. Lorne Carmichael, *Reputations in the Labor Market,* 74 AM. ECON. REV. 713 (1984). For a good discussion of the distinction between human-capital and efficiency-wage models, see Robert Hutchens, *A Test of Lazear's Theory of Delayed Payment Contracts,* 5 J. LAB. ECON. S153 (1987).

29. *See* EHRENBERG & SMITH, *supra* note 21, at 425-26.

30. The term *efficiency wage* refers to raising the wage above the level workers can earn elsewhere until the marginal benefit from the resulting harder work just equals the extra wage. *Id.* at 423. Economists initially applied the efficiency-wage model to developing countries. Studies showed that a higher wage could lead to greater nutrition and health, which lead to greater productivity. Since then, economists have used the efficiency-wage model to explain wage rigidity in the face of involuntary unemployment, a central feature of Keynesian macroeconomic theory. Firms will not reduce the efficiency wage even when job applicants are willing to work for less because full employment would increase shirking. *See* Carl M. Campbell III, *Do Firms Pay Efficiency Wages? Evidence with Data at the Firm Level,* 11 J. LAB. ECON. 442 (1993) (finding evidence confirming an efficiency-wage model in which higher wages reduce turnover as well as induce greater productivity). *See generally* EFFICIENCY WAGE MODELS OF THE LABOR MARKET (George A. Akerlof & Janet L. Yellen eds., 1986). *But see* Brown, *supra* note 22, at 971 (finding that most within-firm wage growth is attributable to productivity increases rather than to "contractual" factors).

model[31] assumed that a firm employing this strategy[32] raised wages by a constant amount throughout a worker's life cycle. One problem with the early, flat-wage version of the model is that workers nearing retirement would care less about losing their high-wage job and would therefore be less deterred from shirking.[33]

Later versions of efficiency-wage models suggest that compensation will rise over a worker's career to induce effort throughout.[34] The implicit contract promises large payouts for senior workers, but it promises this reward only for hard-working employees.[35] The firm recognizes that day-to-day monitoring of a worker's effort may be difficult, but over a period of years the firm hopes to spot and weed out shirkers. The threat of being fired before the large payoff keeps employees working hard. Because employees work harder than otherwise, the firm can afford the higher compensation. Large law firms epitomize this model.

A related literature emphasizes that firms may conduct internal tournaments to induce high effort by junior and midlevel management employees.[36] Tournaments are especially likely when firms cannot monitor actual effort or output but can evaluate relative performance. A firm may (implicitly) tell an incoming class of workers that the best worker will win the grand prize of C.E.O. A single prize may be insufficient inducement, however, so the firm may (implicitly) offer several runner-up prizes of cushy vice-president jobs for those who try hard but fail. This model likewise suggests an implicit agreement whereby firms pay late-career employees more than their current productivity.

31. Carl Shapiro & Joseph E. Stiglitz, *Equilibrium Unemployment as a Worker Discipline Device,* 74 AM. ECON. REV. 433 (1984).

32. It has been suggested that Henry Ford's famous introduction of the five-dollar-a-day wage was an early example of an efficiency-wage strategy. On January 12, 1914, Ford Motor Company raised the wage by over 100%, from $2.34 to $5, while reducing work hours from nine to eight. Productivity rose so dramatically that labor costs per car rose by only 43%, material costs fell by 19%, and total costs per car fell 3.5%. *See* Daniel M.G. Raff & Lawrence Summers, *Did Henry Ford Pay Efficiency Wages?,* 5 J. LAB. ECON. S57 (1987). The authors reject alternative explanations for the cost reductions, such as reductions in turnover or ability to hire more productive workers as the wage rose.

33. Technically, the Shapiro-Stiglitz model avoids this difficulty by assuming an infinite working life for workers. *See* Shapiro & Stiglitz, *supra* note 31, at 435 n.5.

34. Considerable empirical evidence documents the incentive explanation for a life-cycle rise in earnings. *See, e.g.,* Hutchens, *supra* note 28. *See generally* Hutchens, *supra* note 24.

35. For an excellent, nontechnical synthesis of the efficiency-wage and related literature, see CHRISTOPHER J. BRUCE, ECONOMICS OF EMPLOYMENT AND EARNINGS (1990). Bruce distinguishes between the basic efficiency-wage model, in which a firm raises wages above competitive levels for all workers, and the wage-gradation model, in which a firm initially "underpays" a worker but later in the career overpays the worker. *See id.* at 100-05.

36. *See* Edward P. Lazear & Sherwin Rosen, *Rank-Order Tournaments as Optimum Labor Contracts,* 89 J. POL. ECON. 841, 848-49 (1981); James M. Malcomson, *Work Incentives, Hierarchy, and Internal Labor Markets,* 92 J. POL. ECON. 486 (1984).

Figure 2 grafts the efficiency-wage story to the human-capital model. As in the human-capital story, the outside wage is flat[37] and

FIGURE 2

EFFICIENCY-WAGE STORY

Opportunism Possible

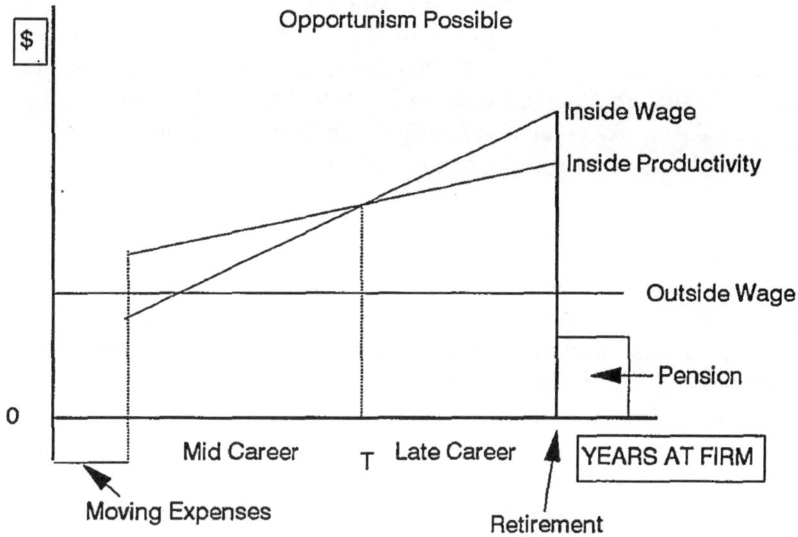

equal to outside productivity. The inside wage may be initially lower than the outside wage,[38] but then rises. Inside productivity rises as job-specific training occurs. Inside productivity is above outside productivity at all stages, even before much training, to emphasize the efficiency-wage story that harder work results in greater productivity throughout. Figure 2 adds two other wrinkles that will become important later. First, because I will specifically address the case law of employees who change employers, Figure 2 includes a preemployment "moving" period. In this stage, an employee quits the outside job and incurs moving expenses, thus having a negative wage. Figure 2 also explicitly illustrates a postretirement pension.

37. The flatness assumption is not critical to the story. Some writers draw the outside productivity as first increasing as the worker learns general skills and then decreasing as these skills atrophy. *See* Katherine V. Stone, *Employees as Stakeholders Under State Nonshareholder Constituency Statutes*, 21 STETSON L. REV. 45, 50 (1991). A flat curve is used here for simplicity. *Cf.* Michael L. Wachter & George M. Cohen, *The Law and Economics of Collective Bargaining: An Introduction and Application to the Problems of Subcontracting, Partial Closure, and Relocation*, 136 U. PA. L. REV. 1349, 1362-63 (1988).

38. Under the straight human-capital story, it is critical that early in the career the inside wage be below the outside wage because this is the worker's investment in training. Under the efficiency-wage story, the inside wage could be above the outside wage throughout the career if greater effort makes inside productivity higher throughout.

The critical point of the expanded story is that the implicit contract is not always self-enforcing. As Figure 2 illustrates, after point *T*, firms pay late-career employees more than they currently produce. At this point, late-career employees become vulnerable to opportunistic firing[39] because the general self-interest check on arbitrary firings does not exist; firing such a worker does not hurt the employer but is instead in its immediate economic interest. One can see a role for law in improving this situation. By policing against opportunism, the law can make the employment relationship more secure for and valuable to both sides. To understand fully the role law can play, we must examine the concept of opportunism more closely.

C. *Contracting Problems in Career Employment*

One solution to the problem of opportunism is for the parties entering into career employment to negotiate detailed contracts, enforceable by courts, that specify appropriate behavior by both sides. Unfortunately, three contracting challenges make detailed contracts an unsatisfactory solution. First, the parties cannot easily anticipate the future contingencies, or states of the world, that will influence the relationship.[40] Will demand for the product stay strong? Will the firm shift its focus from the employee's specialty to other areas that require more general skills? While all predictions of the future are difficult, anticipating events twenty or thirty years in advance is an exceptional challenge for employers and employees.

Second, even if parties can anticipate a future event, they may have difficulty specifying in detail the appropriate contractual response,[41] particularly when one party has access to relevant information that the other cannot easily observe.[42] A key element in the employment relationship is whether the employee is working hard, or, from the em-

39. Some readers might think that a clear tipping point between profitable and unprofitable employees does not exist. Employees approaching the critical *T* are less profitable to employers than employees earlier in their careers. Why not replace these more senior workers with junior workers, even before time *T*? Readers with this objection must implicitly adopt a model (perhaps based on imperfect capital markets) in which firms are prevented from undertaking all profitable activities open to them. If firms are not so constrained, a profit-maximizing employer would retain employees until age *T* before firing them because such employees are producing more than their wage and therefore add to profits. *Cf.* Robert Hutchens, *Delayed Payment Contracts and a Firm's Propensity to Hire Older Workers*, 4 J. LAB. ECON. 439, 445 (1986) ("If . . . the firm faces a form of fixed costs, it will wait until the last possible moment to cheat on one worker and hire another.").

40. Goetz and Scott call this "the problem of uncertainty in relational contracts." Charles J. Goetz & Robert E. Scott, *Principles of Relational Contracts*, 67 VA. L. REV. 1089, 1092 (1981).

41. Goetz and Scott call this "the complexity problem of relational contracting." *Id.*

42. *See* Alan Schwartz, *Relational Contracts in the Courts: An Analysis of Incomplete Agreements and Judicial Strategies*, 21 J. LEGAL STUD. 271, 278-79 (1992).

ployee's perspective, whether the employer is dismissing him for failure to work hard or for an unfair, opportunistic reason. When monitoring is difficult, two alternatives emerge. First, the parties may decide not to make any part of the contract contingent on difficult-to-monitor behavior. An at-will clause would accomplish this goal by making worker efforts irrelevant to the permissibility of discharge. Alternatively, the parties may write a vague "best efforts" or "good faith" clause for the contingency.[43] While this solution invites later court or arbitrator supervision over the meaning of the terms, that supervision may be preferable to contractual language that straitjackets parties' future options.

Finally, having anticipated a future problem and specified the contractual response, a party may be unable to prove a breach in court. Economists term this problem an *unverifiable contract.*[44] Unverifiability is particularly problematic when the contractual language is vague — as it will often be in relational contracts. Both employer and employee might know that the employee is not working as hard as "best efforts" require, but the employer cannot assemble sufficient objective evidence to convince a court or arbitrator of this fact. If the parties cannot turn to outside enforcement, they must develop self-enforcing mechanisms for any agreement to be effective. But, as we have seen, career-employment contracts — particularly those following the efficiency-wage model — are not fully self-enforcing.[45]

D. *Potential for Opportunism*

In the absence of enforceable, detailed contracts that regulate behavior, parties to a long-term relationship become vulnerable to opportunism. They cannot easily leave the relationship because they would have to repeat the investments or forgo their value.[46] The existence of "sunk costs" for one party creates a potential for opportunistic behavior by the other side. A firm can pay workers less than they are worth or treat them more harshly than the initial agreement contem-

43. Goetz and Scott suggest that many parties in long-term relational contracts introduce vague clauses. Goetz & Scott, *supra* note 40, at 1092-93. Employment contracts rarely have such clauses, however.

44. *See* Schwartz, *supra* note 42, at 279-80.

45. *See supra* note 39 and accompanying text.

46. Economists have termed the gap between the gains of the relationship and the next-best activity an "appropriable quasi-rent." The gap is a "rent" because it is more than the amount necessary to keep the worker in that job. It is only a "quasi"- rent, rather than a fixed or permanent rent, because, viewed at the beginning of the employee's career, the net return including investment costs may be no greater than other job alternatives. The gap is "appropriable" because, after the firm-specific investments are made, one side can capture the gains for itself without causing the other side to leave.

plated, knowing they cannot easily move. The employees can produce less than their skills allow, knowing the employer cannot easily replace them.

The law can sometimes help monitor opportunistic behavior, thereby increasing the parties' overall gains from the relationship. If the law can enforce promises not to exploit the other side's vulnerability, the parties can more confidently invest and the relationship will be more rewarding to both sides. The law has limits, however, because the contractual language often will be general and vague, as we have seen.[47] More importantly, because both employer and employee are investing, both can be exploited. A legal rule favoring one side would leave much opportunism by the other unchecked. To curb opportunism adequately, courts must engage in difficult, case-by-case assessments or create more flexible presumptions. As we will see, courts have responded by adopting presumptions that vary with an employee's life cycle.

1. *Employer Vulnerability to Shirking*

As the human-capital model indicates, employers make heavy investments in recruiting and training workers.[48] To ensure an adequate return on their investment, employers want workers to stay and produce for them after training. Some scholars focus on employer recruitment and training costs in emphasizing employer vulnerability to employees quitting, but this is not the true problem of opportunism. The basic human-capital model suggests that employers can adopt delayed-payment schemes to discourage quitting, thus making the contract self-enforcing. Late-vesting pensions and seniority-based wages can tell workers: "If you stick around, you will do well."

The greater risk to employers comes from employee shirking. The efficiency-wage model highlights the shirking problem. Even if pensions and seniority wages discourage workers from quitting, an employer still faces problems when workers stay. Workers often do not work as hard as they would under a fully specified and monitored contract. Economists label this behavior shirking.[49] A fully specified op-

47. *See supra* note 43 and accompanying text.

48. *See* Paul C. Weiler, Governing the Workplace 145-47 (1990).

49. As economic labels are wont to do, the term *shirking* offends many workers, and the class of behavior economists consider as shirking is broader than the literal term shirking might imply. While goofing off or engaging in pranks would certainly be shirking, it also includes failure to think creatively about workplace problems, failure to stay current in one's area of expertise with personal reading, and the like. As Alan Hyde nicely puts it, shirking is the failure to make "[an] active contribution to improving firm productivity." Alan Hyde, *In Defense of Employee Ownership*, 67 Chi.-Kent L. Rev. 159, 183 (1991).

timal contract would designate an optimal level of effort. Workers would agree to exert this effort because they prefer the higher wages that accompany it to an easier work life; the employer would agree because the greater productivity is worth the higher wages. Once hired, however, an employee may shirk from this optimal effort if employers have difficulty monitoring or replacing workers. Indeed, it is irrational for workers to work up to "optimal" levels if they prefer coasting a little. Workers know that the employer will have to spend money to catch shirkers and that, if it fires a shirker, the employer will have to recruit and train a replacement. As long as workers perform better than a rookie would — considering the costs of monitoring, recruiting, and training — the firm must accept less than optimal efforts from its workers.

Much of the debate over at-will employment addresses whether parties can write effective contracts to overcome the shirking problem. To put it bluntly, the real question is whether the threat of firing for cause is sufficient to deter substandard performance by workers. Proponents of at will emphasize the unverifiability of the performance standard in many employment contracts. The employer may know the worker is shirking but cannot convince a court or arbitrator that the conduct amounts to shirking. Oliver Williamson has emphasized the difficulty in distinguishing a consummate performance from a perfunctory performance: "Consummate cooperation is an affirmative job attitude whereby gaps are filled, initiative is taken, and judgment is exercised in an instrumental way. Perfunctory cooperation involves working to rules and in other respects performing in a minimally acceptable way."[50] One problem employers have in documenting a "perfunctory performance" is that particular instances of misconduct often seem trivial. Concluding that they add up to a significant problem requires acknowledging that the whole problem exceeds the sum of the parts. The heart of the employment-at-will argument is that proving cause under what is essentially an unverifiable agreement against shirking places too great a burden on employers, preventing them from effectively using efficiency wages to deter shirking.

Some may argue that commentators overstate this shirking problem because the employee's desire for a good reputation deters shirking. Even if shirking is possible in a just-cause world, this counterargument runs, benefits accrue to employees with a reputation for hard work. Not only may the incumbent employer reward hard work with promotions and pay raises, but employees with good repu-

50. WILLIAMSON, *supra* note 17, at 262-63.

tations are most attractive to outside employers. Nevertheless, this reputation argument, in both its inside and outside reputation forms, ignores several important facts. First, an individual worker with a good inside reputation may not reap major rewards. As we saw, employers often establish pay and promotion ladders that do not depend on current individual productivity in order to discourage quits with promises of big paydays in the future.[51] In such internal labor markets, pay scales attach to jobs rather than workers, and seniority rather than merit often determines who gets the jobs.[52] Promoting individual workers simply because of individual hard work may not be worth the disruptions in the general progression system. In these internal labor markets, then, unusually good effort may not be rewarded even though unusually bad effort is punished by firing.[53] Second, an employee may find it hard to acquire a good outside reputation if his skills are firm-specific. An academic whose publications are useful to many potential employers can obtain an outside reputation. Indeed, some might argue that the major inside job of the academic is to acquire an outside reputation. An engineer working on a classified defense project finds it more difficult — and therefore has less incentive — to obtain an outside reputation for hard work. The reluctance of employers to give candid references, itself a response to defamation law, exacerbates the difficulty for employees seeking to establish outside reputations.

A second response to the shirking argument involves a quick comparative law lesson. In the rest of the industrialized world, at-will employment is unknown,[54] yet workers manage to work hard without the threat of firing.[55] As Jack Beermann and Joseph Singer lament, why

51. *See supra* notes 30-31 and accompanying text.

52. This internal-labor-market model has been well depicted by Douglas Leslie: "Wage rates attach to particular jobs, and jobs, not workers, carry marginal products. Hirings occurs only at the entry level .... Seniority ladders control promotion, with the limitation that an employee may be punished if the firm discovers poor work habits." Leslie, *supra* note 17, at 368. For general discussions of the internal-labor-market model, see PETER B. DOERINGER & MICHAEL J. PIORE, INTERNAL LABOR MARKETS AND MANPOWER ANALYSIS 13-63 (1971); Wachter & Cohen, *supra* note 37, at 1353-67; and Oliver E. Williamson et al., *Understanding the Employment Relation: The Analysis of Idiosyncratic Exchange,* 6 BELL J. ECON. & MGMT. SCI. 250 (1975).

53. Even though the employer may not reward unusually hard workers, the employer will punish unusually lax workers by kicking them off the career ladder — that is, by firing them. Unlike sudden promotions, these terminations do not disrupt the seniority ladder for the remaining workers.

54. *See* Estreicher, *supra* note 9, at 311; Jack Stieber, *Protection Against Unfair Dismissal: A Comparative View,* 3 COMP. LAB. L. 229 (1980).

55. The point is forcefully argued by Beermann and Singer, who state:

> People in our society have come to view the world through ideological lenses that make them disbelieve claims that workers would be productive without the insecurity of the at-will rule. To paraphrase Mark Kelman, it is only through a miracle, or quirky cultural

does our society assume it can trust employers not to abuse the power of arbitrary firings while it refuses to trust employees protected by just cause?[56] Of course, one can overdramatize the comparative lesson. Industrial tribunals in Europe, having found a dismissal to be unjust, usually award modest severance pay that rarely exceeds six months duration.[57] Further, commentators of "Eurosclerosis" would caution against using Europe as a model for productive labor markets.[58]

Ultimately, the verifiability problem involves a question of degree, and the problem is greater for some jobs than for others. To the degree that clear contracts against shirking are difficult to write, monitor, and enforce, opportunistic behavior by employees will remain a threat.

2. *Employee Vulnerability*

As both the human-capital and efficiency-wage models emphasize, employees invest heavily as they pursue a career with a single employer. First, they obtain training that is more useful for their own employer than it would be elsewhere — what economists term *job-specific human capital.*[59] Second, they join the company's career path. This path, as we have seen, ties pay, promotions, and benefits to sen-

differences, that workers in the rest of the industrialized world, where the at-will rule is not in force, work at all.

Jack M. Beermann & Joseph W. Singer, *Baseline Questions in Legal Reasoning: The Example of Property in Jobs,* 23 GA. L. REV. 911, 933 (1989).

56. As Beermann and Singer put it:

> There is an irony in the assumption that owners and managers can be trusted to operate the business rationally while workers need insecurity to induce them to work. . . . The assumption that those doing the firing can be trusted with firing decisions while those being fired cannot be trusted to act responsibly on the job classifies those being fired as different from those doing the firing. Yet in many of these cases, the two parties come from the same social class and will have similar values. Thus, even if it were true that managers could be trusted and that workers could not be trusted to work hard and be productive, the prevailing assumptions underlying the employment-at-will doctrine fail to explain why discharged managers, as well as discharged workers, are subject to arbitrary firings.

Beermann & Singer, *supra* note 55, at 934. As I suggest in the text, the explanation is not one of class distinctions between managers and workers, but one found in the self-bonding protection against arbitrary terminations. The self-interest of employers, rather than societal faith in them, checks arbitrary firings of productive workers. There is no equivalent self-interest check that deters employee shirking in the absence of employer monitoring.

57. Ronald G. Ehrenberg, *Workers' Rights: Rethinking Protective Labor Legislation, in* RESEARCH IN LABOR ECONOMICS 285 (Ronald G. Ehrenberg ed., 1986); Stieber, *supra* note 54.

58. For an analysis of Europe's persistent unemployment problems, see Olivier J. Blanchard & Lawrence H. Summers, *Unemployment Beyond the National Rate Hypothesis,* 78 AM. ECON. REV., May 1988, at 182 (papers and proceedings); Richard B. Freeman, *Evaluating the European View that the United States Has No Employment Problem,* 100 AM. ECON. ASSN. PROC. 294 (1988). For a discussion of the term *Eurosclerosis,* see, for example, Alan Riding, *Europe in Turmoil,* N.Y. TIMES, Sept. 20, 1992, at A1; Hobart Rowen, *Germany: High-Tech Laggard,* WASH. POST, July 8, 1993, at A17.

59. *See* BECKER, *supra* note 18, at 18-26 (discussing specific training).

iority and generally forbids lateral entry.[60] A major cost of pursuing a career with one firm is that one forgoes other ladders and must start over at the bottom if one leaves the firm. Additionally, as they plan for a lifetime with an employer, workers put down roots, establish networks of friends in the workplace and the community, buy homes within commuting distance of the job, and build emotional ties to the community.

Losing these investments, roots, and ties can be devastating. Many studies document how even impersonal plant closings lead to increases in "cardiovascular deaths, suicides, mental breakdowns, alcoholism, ulcers, diabetes, spouse and child abuse, impaired social relationships, and various other diseases and abnormal conditions."[61] Being singled out and fired may be even more devastating.[62]

Because of these tremendous costs, no employee wants to lose his job involuntarily. Further, these investments, roots, and ties are sunk costs that trap the worker in his current firm, inhibiting him from departing voluntarily. Even if the career does not proceed as anticipated, the employee is reluctant to quit because the job remains preferable to alternative jobs. Such trapped workers are vulnerable to opportunism. The employer might pay them less than the implicit contract requires or work them harder, knowing they cannot easily quit.

By itself, this potential for opportunism does not justify a just-cause standard. Employers want such exploited workers to stay, not to leave. Only when conditions become so intolerable that the employee prefers to quit for another job might termination law come into play. In the economist's framework, this situation occurs when the employer has appropriated all the gains from the relationship, making the career no longer better than alternative jobs. Lawyers label these intolerable conditions a *constructive discharge.*

Defenders of at will contend that employer self-interest protects productive employees from discharge.[63] An employer hurts itself by arbitrarily terminating a productive worker or by causing him to quit

60. An early recognition in the legal literature of the significance of the ties, particularly pension and seniority protections, binding the employee to the job, is Mary Ann Glendon & Edward R. Lev, *Changes in the Bonding of the Employment Relationship: An Essay on the New Property,* 20 B.C. L. REV. 457, 475-83 (1979). Glendon and Lev emphasize two social trends of the late twentieth century: the strengthening of work ties over family ties, and the tendency for social standing and security to depend on workplace benefits backed up by the government rather than on family relationships. The inroads on employment at will, suggest Glendon and Lev, reflect and interact with these social trends.

61. St. Antoine, *supra* note 8, at 67.

62. *Id. See generally* KATHERINE S. NEWMAN, FALLING FROM GRACE (1988).

63. *See, e.g.,* Ehrenberg, *supra* note 57, at 292-93; Epstein, *supra* note 10, at 968.

because it wastes the recruiting and training investment in the employee. To avoid its own sunk-cost losses, an employer wants to keep good workers and fire only workers who fall below the standard of new entrants. Figure 1 illustrates this self-enforcing feature. After the training period, workers' productivity exceeds their wages, and the employer would lose this gain by firing such workers.[64]

While employers can make mistakes, the self-enforcing feature should minimize firing of productive workers. Employees do not need the grand and expensive apparatus of the law for further protection, claim at will's defenders. Indeed, its very expense harms employees as well as employers, for wages will inevitably fall as terminations become more expensive.

Opponents of at-will employment remain skeptical. A major concern is that an employer is not a monolith but rather a hierarchy of high-level managers and low-level supervisors. Often low-level supervisors make the decision to fire, and the factors influencing their decisions are often not perfectly aligned with the profit-maximizing interest of shareholders. Thus, while shareholders may not want employees to be fired arbitrarily, supervisors might. Personality conflicts and power trips may lead supervisors to fire valuable and productive employees.

Again, one can overstate the dangers of front-line supervisors running amok. The firm has incentives voluntarily to reduce supervisor mistakes so long as the gains in employee satisfaction outweigh the costs of supervising the supervisors. Just-cause advocates cannot make their point simply by showing that agency costs exist. They must show further that employers will not take cost-effective steps to ensure that they treat their employees fairly.

One check on such opportunism — emphasized in the efficiency-wage literature — is the employer's concern for its reputation. If word gets out that an employer routinely fires older workers, it will be harder for the employer to recruit entrants into career jobs. Perhaps more damaging than its outside reputation is its inside reputation with fellow employees when older, productive workers are fired.[65] This loss of collegiality may encourage other workers to quit. Problematically

64. Even in the training period, an employer has a profit motive to retain workers. Once training has begun, the employer will fully recoup its investment only by keeping the worker until retirement. In technical terms, once training costs have begun to be sunk, the employer earns a quasi-rent by retaining the worker.

65. Epstein persuasively argues that the greater reputational check against employer opportunism will be the demoralizing effect on the current workforce. Epstein, *supra* note 10, at 968.

for the employer, the most productive workers likely have the greatest opportunities for moving elsewhere.

In many situations, reputation is unlikely to check fully the employer's incentive to fire late-career workers. Young job entrants cannot easily assess an employer's reputation for how it handles senior workers.[66] Great problems arise in passing on knowledge of a firm's opportunistic firings between generations of workers.[67] These problems are particularly acute in small or new firms,[68] where much of the workforce works.[69] Finally, a reputation for harsh personnel policies may not greatly harm declining firms that are not hiring many new workers.[70]

Because reputation is not a full check on opportunism, firms must compensate workers for the risk that the delayed bonanza may not accrue. Early-career wages, or the late-career bonuses and pensions, must be higher than they would have to be were reputations more secure. Court scrutiny of opportunistic firings may offer another method of policing long-term contracts. Such third-party scrutiny may allow employers to offer efficiency-wage contracts at lower overall cost. The danger, of course, is that court intervention will diminish the employer's flexibility in firing workers whose shirking a court can-

66. *See* WEILER, *supra* note 48, at 74 ("[T]he worker who is shopping for a job will find it very difficult to learn (and certainly will not want to ask) about the actual dismissal risks in the firms being interviewed."). Weiler emphasizes the psychological tendency to underestimate the dangers of low-probability, high-cost events such as being fired. *Id.*

67. *See* WILLIAMSON, *supra* note 17, at 406-07. For a mathematical model of the role of reputation in labor markets, suggesting that reputation by itself will not enforce efficient behavior by firms, see Carmichael, *supra* note 28.

68. For an argument linking firm size to reputation, see Donald Parsons, *The Employment Relationship: Job Attachment, Work Effort, and the Nature of Contracts, in* 2 HANDBOOK OF LABOR ECONOMICS 789, 800-01 (Orley Ashenfelter & Richard Layard eds., 1986). The basic point is that even a "bad" small firm may have too few terminations for an outsider to detect a general pattern.

69. BUREAU OF THE CENSUS, U.S. DEPT. OF COMMERCE, STATISTICAL ABSTRACT OF THE UNITED STATES: 1992, at 526, tbl. 837 (112th ed. 1992) (indicating that 24% of workers — excluding government, railroad, self-employed, and other categories — work for firms of fewer than 20 workers, and that another 26.8% work for firms of 20 to 99 workers); *see also* Nancy E. Dowd, *Maternity Leave: Taking Sex Differences into Account,* 54 FORDHAM L. REV. 699, 711 (1986) (indicating that almost 40% of all employees work for businesses with fewer than 50 employees).

70. Some have argued that new management coming in after a corporate takeover might breach implicit contracts with impunity, doing such things as terminating pension plans that were the prize for working hard early in the life cycle. *See* John C. Coffee, Jr., *Unstable Coalitions: Corporate Governance as a Multi-Player Game,* 78 GEO. L.J. 1495, 1521-28 (1990); Andrei Shleifer & Lawrence H. Summers, *Breach of Trust in Hostile Takeovers, in* CORPORATE TAKEOVERS: CAUSES AND CONSEQUENCES 33 (Alan J. Auerback ed., 1988). This possibility is a further risk employees take in relying on reputation to ensure employers will not behave opportunistically at the end of the life cycle. The empirical importance of this motive in corporate takeovers has been questioned by Roberta Romano, *A Guide to Takeovers: Theory, Evidence, and Regulation,* 9 YALE J. ON REG. 119 (1992).

not verify. The question is whether court intervention can be limited to opportunistic firings, rather than to a broader supervision against unfair firings in general.

II. An (Inconclusive) Appeal to Empiricism

We see, then, that both the employer and employee are vulnerable to opportunism. Which is the greater problem — shirking or unjust firings? Or, more precisely, what legal rule can best reduce the problems? The choice is highly political. Those sympathetic to workers will feel their exploitation is the greater problem and favor just-cause. Others who instinctively rely on private markets may see a greater need to curb worker shirking and so favor at will.

Some scholars have looked at actual practices to help resolve the debate.[71] It is useful to sketch these appeals to empiricism before rejecting them as inconclusive and moving to the life-cycle theory of career employment.

A. *The Pervasiveness of At-Will Employment*

Certainly, at-will employment is the legal norm for the vast majority of American workers. As a long-repeated practice by many players negotiating many contracts, at-will employment is a plausible candidate for being the optimal arrangement, in the sense that the overall gains, which primarily accrue to the employer, outweigh the costs of potentially arbitrary firings, which are borne primarily by employees. Both sides can share this net gain by increasing the wage to compensate workers for the risk of firing. Richard Epstein uses this empirical observation to bolster his argument for the desirability of at-will employment: "The survival of the contract at will, and the frequency of its use in private markets, might well be taken as a sign of its suitability for employment relations."[72]

The empirical claim that most private employees are at will is rarely disputed.[73] One needs some faith in the efficiency of labor markets, however, to infer that this proves that at-will employment is effi-

71. An extensive inquiry by Mayer G. Freed & Daniel D. Polsby, *Just Cause for Termination Rules and Economic Efficiency*, 38 Emory L.J. 1097 (1989), concludes that a mandatory tenure system is less efficient than an at-will rule.

72. Epstein, *supra* note 10, at 948. Epstein concedes that employment at will has been in retreat in the common law but does not suggest that this weakens his empirical claim that survival implies suitability.

73. One recent survey of employment practices suggests, however, that perhaps 20% of nonunion employers offer grievance procedures leading to arbitration. John Delaney et al., Human Resource Policies and Practices in American Firms tbl. 26 (1989). Certainly, many employee handbooks contain limitations on at-will dismissal, and the courts are increasingly enforcing these handbooks. Thus, while clearly true until recently, the blanket statement

cient, in the sense that the costs to employers from a switch to just cause would outweigh the gains to workers. Unequal-bargaining-power theorists are unlikely to have such faith.

The noted institutional economist John Commons put it well long ago in disputing the claim that the employer and the at-will employee have equal freedom to quit the relationship:

> If the corporation has 10,000 employees it loses only one ten thousandth part of its working force if it chooses to not-employ the man, and cannot find an alternative man. But the man loses 100 per cent of his job if he chooses to not-work and cannot find an alternative employer.[74]

Commons's observation envisions an employer with market power, perhaps a monopsonist or even a company town. Even a monopsonist, however, would not insist on at-will employment if it harmed employees more than it helped the monopsonist. A monopsonist can increase its profits by offering cost-effective fringe benefits because employees would agree to work for a lower wage.[75] If employers had unlimited bargaining power, an employer would only pay workers a subsistence wage.[76] This does not accord with the reality of the labor market for most American workers.

In any event, the monopsony model is inapt. Most employees today have alternative job options,[77] at least at the beginning of a relationship, which limits the monopsony power of employers. If at will presents a serious danger of exploitation and beginning employees see the danger, they will require higher wages before they accept the danger. Refusing to concede that workers will receive benefits for which

---

that private nonunion employees overwhelmingly are subject to dismissal at will needs some qualifications today.

74. John R. Commons, Legal Foundations of Capitalism 72 (1924).

75. This argument breaks down for workers near the minimum wage, who legally cannot agree to work for lower wages even if they would receive greater job security in return.

76. Epstein makes a similar argument. He writes:

> Indeed if such an inequality did govern the employment relationship, we should expect to see conditions that exist in no labor market. Wages should be driven to zero, for no matter what their previous level, the employer could use his (inexhaustible) bargaining power to reduce them further, until the zero level was reached. Similarly, inequality of bargaining power implies that the employee will be bound for a term while the employer (who can pay the peppercorn consideration) retains the power to terminate at will. Yet in practice we observe both positive wages and employees with the right to quit at will.

Epstein, *supra* note 10, at 973. Peter Linzer makes a nice rebuttal to Epstein's point. "That workers got some of the greatly enlarged pie . . . is hardly proof that they would not have got more if they had had a stronger bargaining position. That they are not reduced to slavery or starvation is no proof that they are not exploited." Linzer, *supra* note 11, at 415. Still, Linzer refuses to make operational his concept of unequal bargaining power with a coherent theory of what it means, and in particular what its limits are, arguing instead that Epstein's theory can fall of its own weight because it is "based on fantasy or unproved assumptions." *Id.*

77. *See* Ehrenberg & Smith, *supra* note 21, at 78 ("Examples of pure monopsony in the labor market are difficult to cite . . . ."). Ehrenberg and Smith cite articles suggesting that the market for nurses in a small town with one hospital may be partially monopsonized. *Id.*

they are willing to pay, unequal-bargaining-power enthusiasts shift their argument away from the existence of a monopoly to the absence of real bargaining. Even if workers have several entry-level job options, the argument runs, workers have no real choice because every employer offers at-will employment on a take-it-or-leave-it basis. Duncan Kennedy, hardly an unabashed enthusiast of the economics vision, provides the best response to this argument.[78] As Kennedy realizes, one cannot test whether buyers as a class influence compensation packages by studying whether individuals dicker over terms.[79] The analogous argument would be that consumers have no influence over breakfast cereals because they cannot bargain with the grocery store manager over the terms of sale.[80]

Of course, as I have been emphasizing, both employer and employee gain more from the long-term relationship than they would by starting over with others. This relationship surplus must be divided between them. There is no clear theory or evidence about how the parties should divide the surplus.[81] Importantly, though, even an employer who captures most of the surplus has an incentive to promise just-cause terminations if that is the efficient promise. The fact that we virtually never see employers make such promises is some indication that at will is the efficient relationship, especially when at will is supported by a plausible model of its efficiency.

B. *The Unionized Just-Cause Standard as Counterfact*

Rather than resort to inequality of bargaining power to refute the

78. Duncan Kennedy provides the best general critique on inequality of bargaining power as a coherent justification for market intervention. Recognizing that unequal bargaining power is a phrase of many meanings, Kennedy finds several subtests:

> [T]he industry is "public"; the terms were drafted by the seller and offered on a take-it-or-leave-it basis; the seller is a bigger entity than the buyer; the sellers have monopoly power in the relevant market; the commodity in question is a necessity; and there is a shortage which permits sellers to exploit buyers.

Duncan Kennedy, *Distributive and Paternalist Motives in Contract and Tort Law, with Special Reference to Compulsory Terms and Unequal Bargaining Power,* 41 MD. L. REV. 563, 616 (1982). Kennedy finds all of these subtests inadequate, even if the goal behind them is to help the weak at the expense of the strong. In the text I concentrate on the monopoly power and take-it-or-leave-it subtests.

79. As Kennedy explains:

> There may be no bargaining because bargaining is expensive, and buyers as a group are unwilling to pay the increased cost of individualized transactions. Further, in a truly competitive market, no one gets to negotiate terms with anyone else. You can't argue that market power skews bargains and then object in those very situations where, because of competition, no one gets any individualized say at all.

Kennedy, *supra* note 78, at 616.

80. *See* WEILER, *supra* note 48, at 17.

81. Epstein gives several arguments to explain why either the employer or the employee might obtain most of the surplus. Epstein suspects that the surplus would be divided more or less evenly. Epstein, *supra* note 10, at 975-76.

significance of at will's pervasiveness, a weightier rebuttal[82] emphasizes that the just-cause standard always governs terminations among unionized workers.[83] Free-market proponents might attempt a quick dismissal of this fact by saying that unions distort the market; one cannot expect the unionized market to reflect efficiency.[84] But this response is too hasty.

The competitive market may reflect the preferences of marginal workers, but it does not necessarily reflect the wishes of inframarginal workers.[85] In a competitive labor market, employers learn how to structure their employment package from the ease with which they fill positions. They rely, in other words, on signals from workers they are trying to recruit, or workers who are deciding whether to quit. If these workers do not reflect the interests of inframarginal workers, the competitive market will not reach an efficient result.

The inframarginal workers — the career employees upon whom we have been focusing — are locked in. They have made significant investments in the workplace and cannot easily leave. In a competitive market that relies on exit and entry to register preferences, locked-in employees will not be included in the calculus. This is not a problem unless their preferences differ in some dimension from the preferences of marginal workers less tied to the firm. It is quite plausible, however, that the average worker has significantly greater preference for job security than does the marginal worker. The marginal worker is typically young and in the process of trying out several jobs before

82. Professor Weiler makes an excellent argument against at-will employment along these lines. WEILER, *supra* note 48, at 71-78.

83. Another major sector in which just-cause protection is the norm is the public sector. One explanation for this phenomenon might be the greater need of public employees for protection from arbitrary dismissal because the usual self-monitoring features against firing productive workers are muted for government employers. As public choice theorists emphasize, the goal of government employers may not be productive workers but workers willing to use the power of government to favor the latest election winners. Another explanation for just-cause protection of public employees is that, when political factors make it difficult for government employers to give highly visible wage increases, they increase compensation less obviously through fringe benefits, including job protection.

The other major area in which just cause is the predominant standard is for the university. A possible explanation for the existence of tenured university employees is the divergence between the overall social good in promoting a vigorous debate on ideas — which requires some debaters with wacky, unpopular, or unpleasant views, and often the personalities to match — and the local institutional goals that include not only college prestige but also collegiality. By granting tenure, the college binds itself to ignore the local costs in unpleasantness from tolerating an employee pursuing unpopular, unpleasant views. Colleges can afford to take this larger view of the common good because they are either nonprofit organizations or publicly subsidized.

84. This approach is reflected in Richard A. Posner, *Some Economics of Labor Law*, 51 U. CHI. L. REV. 988, 1000 (1984) ("Although some empirical support has been marshaled for this productivity-enhancement theory of unionization, the theory is extremely hard to accept.").

85. *See* WEILER, *supra* note 48, at 76; Leslie, *supra* note 17, at 358.

finally settling on a firm with which to establish a career.[86] This marginal worker may not recognize or value fully the firm's reputation for job security and may not realize that he may one day be locked into a career with this firm.[87]

In short, termination standards from the nonunion market, responding largely to the exit of young workers, may not reflect the aggregate costs and benefits as well as the union collective-choice mechanism, which reflects the preferences of average workers. On the other hand, also unwarranted is the bolder statement that the collective choice outcome is clearly a superior way of toting up the costs and benefits. As with many analyses, showing the flaws of a market mechanism does not, by itself, demonstrate the superiority of other solutions. In this case the problems with union median-voter solutions are well known.[88]

Ultimately, then, an appeal to empiricism cannot provide a universal answer to whether at will or just cause is the optimal standard. Each standard has costs and benefits, and the balance may shift depending on the situation. Those who debate the issue too frequently ask whether at will or just cause should be the presumption in all employment relationships. A universal answer cannot be found. The next section attempts to break down the inquiry into parts of the life cycle, and to explain the inherent logic of the common law solution.

III. Legal Supervision of Opportunistic Firings

It is time to examine the employment termination cases. In explaining the common law approach, I will first show that courts have attempted to police opportunistic firings by employers. I will then attempt to fit their efforts into the efficiency-wage framework.

A. *Ad Hoc Judicial Scrutiny of Employer Opportunism*

A party to a long-term relationship is most vulnerable to opportunism when the party has substantially performed while the other side has not.[89] The other side, having received most of its benefit, has an

86. See Hall, *supra* note 15, for evidence that young workers try out several jobs and then tend to have a long relationship with one employer.

87. *See* Weiler, *supra* note 48, at 75-76.

88. *See* Barry T. Hirsch & John T. Addison, The Economic Analysis of Unions 23-29 (1986), for a discussion that the median-voter solution may not provide a more efficient outcome than a competitive-market solution, even when average and marginal workers differ in their preferences for job security.

89. As Epstein writes:

> [C]ontract at will works only where performance on both sides takes place in lockstep progression. This condition will be satisfied where neither side has performed or where the

incentive to terminate the relationship to avoid paying out its side of the bargain. Contract doctrine generally imposes a duty of good faith upon parties, in part to protect against such opportunistic behavior. Section 1-203 of the Uniform Commercial Code (U.C.C.), for example, mandates good faith in commercial transactions.[90] While good faith defies simple definition,[91] for our purposes an appropriate meaning is that a party to the contract cannot deprive the other party of the benefit of the bargain.[92]

Courts have hesitated in imposing a generalized good-faith standard upon at-will employment relationships. The courts fear that a nebulous legal standard will make the delicate relationship too rigid or legalistic.[93] Nevertheless, some courts have made good-faith inroads

---

> worker's past performance has been matched by appropriate payment from the employer. . . . Where the sequence of performance requires one side to perform in full before the other side begins performance, this bonding mechanism will break down because there are no longer two unperformed promises of roughly equal value to stand as security for each other.

Epstein, *supra* note 10, at 979.

90. U.C.C. § 1-203, 1 U.L.A. 109 (1989) states: "Every contract or duty within this Act imposes an obligation of good faith in its performance or enforcement." U.C.C. § 1-102(3), 1 U.L.A. 12 (1989), while generally allowing the parties to waive U.C.C. provisions, forbids parties from disclaiming the obligation of good faith, although it allows the parties to determine the standards by which to measure good faith, if "not manifestly unreasonable."

91. Professor Robert Summers insists that good faith cannot be defined. As he writes:

> [To ask what good faith means] misconceives good faith. Good faith, as judges generally use the term in matters contractual, is best understood as an "excluder" — a phrase with no general meaning or meanings of its own. Instead, it functions to rule out many different forms of bad faith. It is hard to get this point across to persons used to thinking that every word must have one or more general meanings of its own — must be either univocal or ambiguous.
>
> . . . .
>
> . . . In most cases the party acting in bad faith frustrates the justified expectations of another. . . . [T]he ways in which he may do this are numerous and radically diverse. Moreover, whether an aggrieved party's expectations are justified must inevitably vary with attendant circumstances. For these reasons it is not fruitful to try to generalize further. It is easy enough to formulate examples of bad faith and work from them. Besides, any general definition of good faith, if not vacuous, is sure to be unduly restrictive, especially if cast in statutory form.

Robert S. Summers, *"Good Faith" in General Contract Law and the Sales Provisions of the Uniform Commercial Code*, 54 VA. L. REV. 195, 262-63 (1968).

92. *Cf.* 2 E. ALLAN FARNSWORTH, FARNSWORTH ON CONTRACTS § 7.17a (1990) (detailing the history of attempts to define "good faith" and offering alternatives to the definition in the text). Professor Lillard has described the benefit-of-the-bargain definition as the most popular definition of good faith in employment law cases. *See* Monique C. Lillard, *Fifty Jurisdictions in Search of a Standard: The Covenant of Good Faith and Fair Dealing in the Employment Context*, 57 MO. L. REV. 1233, 1249 (1992).

93. *See, e.g.*, Magnan v. Anaconda Indus., 479 A.2d 781, 789 (Conn. 1984) ("We decline the invitation of plaintiff to transform the requirement of good faith into an implied condition that an employee be dismissed only for good cause. To hold otherwise would render the court a bargaining agent for every employee not protected by statute or collective bargaining agreement."); Parnar v. Americana Hotels, Inc., 652 P.2d 625, 629 (Haw. 1982) (implying "a duty to terminate in good faith would seem to subject each discharge to judicial incursions into the amorphous concept of good faith. We are not persuaded that protection of employees requires such an intrusion on the employment relationship or such an imposition on the courts."); Moriss v. Cole-

on at-will employment. Although the courts rarely articulate it in these terms, they tend to make these inroads when investment asymmetries make the employee particularly vulnerable to opportunistic firings.

A leading example of a good-faith inroad is *Fortune v. National Cash Register Co.*,[94] in which the court imposed a good-faith limitation on an employer's ability to fire a salesperson about to receive a commission. Orville Fortune was a salesperson under a written at-will contract that entitled him to a bonus for equipment orders placed in his territory and an additional bonus when the equipment was installed in his territory. One day after Fortune signed a $5 million order, National Cash Register (NCR) fired him, depriving him of the installation part of the commission.[95] The Massachusetts Supreme Judicial Court, in upholding a jury verdict for Fortune, recognized that NCR had paid Fortune all the bonus to which he was entitled under the express contract. The court found NCR had breached, however, an implied covenant to act in good faith.[96]

Richard Epstein has attacked the *Fortune* decision as "wrong in principle."[97] He points to the important fact that NCR did not keep the disputed commission for itself, but rather paid it to an installations employee.[98] Epstein argues, therefore, that "[t]he case is not simply one where a strategically timed firing allowed the company to deprive a dismissed employee of the benefits due him upon completion of per-

man, 738 P.2d 841, 851 (Kan. 1987) ("[T]he principle of law stated in Restatement (Second) of Contracts § 2-5, that every contract imposes upon each party a duty of good faith and fair dealing in its performance and its enforcement, is overly broad and should not be applicable to employment-at-will contracts); Melnick v. State Farm Mut. Ins. Co., 749 P.2d 1105, 1111 (N.M.) ("Employers are entitled to be motivated by and serve their own legitimate business interests .... Protection of employees does not require such a restriction on an employer's discretion in managing his work force or such an imposition on the courts."), *cert. denied*, 488 U.S. 822 (1988); Thompson v. St. Regis Paper Co., 685 P.2d 1081, 1086-67 (Wash. 1984) (arguing that a good-faith exception would result in unwarranted judicial intrusion into each discharge decision and that "such an intrusion into the employment relationship is merely a judicial substitute for collective bargaining which is more appropriately left to the legislative process"). For an excellent 50-state survey of good-faith employment-termination cases, see Lillard, *supra* note 92.

94. 364 N.E.2d 1251 (Mass. 1977). For an analysis of the *Fortune* case similar to mine, see WEILER, *supra* note 48, at 67.

95. 364 N.E.2d at 1254. After discussing the "firing" with his branch manager, Fortune was allowed to stay in a "sales support" position until the employer ultimately fired him 18 months later. Fortune received his order bonus commission for machines delivered over the next 18 months, but he was denied the delivery bonus. He received neither the order or delivery bonus for machines delivered after his ultimate firing. While these developments after the initial "firing" complicate the story, the basic point remains true that NCR fired Fortune after he had done the work on the sale but before he could reap the full commission for his efforts.

96. 364 N.E.2d at 1255-56.

97. Epstein, *supra* note 10, at 981-82.

98. *Id.* at 981. The court, but not Epstein, notes that paying an installations employee departed from NCR's usual policy of paying bonuses only to salespeople. 364 N.E.2d at 1254.

formance."[99] Rather, "[t]he contractual provisions concerning commissions represent a rough effort to match payment with performance where the labor of more than one individual was necessary to close the sale."[100]

We should heed Epstein's warning against applying the good-faith principle without carefully considering the incentive and bonding devices the parties have created. Perhaps the *Fortune* decision is wrong in application. By paying all of the commission to some employee or other, the company avoided the temptation of an opportunistic termination. But the *Fortune* case is not wrong in principle. The valid principle, for which *Fortune* is usually read to stand, is that courts should scrutinize opportunistic firings in which the employee has largely performed his side of the bargain but has yet to reap his reward. Salespeople on commission are classic examples of persons who can find themselves in that situation.

Another classic example of a good-faith analysis occurs when an employer fires an employee shortly before he qualifies for a pension. Again, the usual self-interest check on an employer's decision to fire a productive employee is missing. An employer can save itself considerable money by exercising its at-will discretion just before a pension vests. A routine practice of firing all employees before their pensions vest might have severe reputation costs. But the occasional firing for this reason might be less damaging. The issue arose in *Ingersoll-Rand Co. v. McClendon,*[101] in which an employee with nine and three-quarters years of service was fired four months before his pension was to vest. Such a firing clearly violates the good-faith notion that an employer must give the employee the benefit of the bargained-for pension. The Texas Supreme Court allowed a common law tort action for wrongful discharge in violation of public policy. The U.S. Supreme Court did not disagree with the underlying rationale but reversed the Texas Supreme Court. It held that the employee must bring this claim under section 510 of the Employee Retirement Income Security Act (ERISA), which clearly prohibits an employer from discharging a worker "for the purpose of interfering with the attainment of any right to which [the worker] may become entitled under the [pension] plan."[102]

99. Epstein, *supra* note 10, at 981.

100. *Id.*

101. 111 S. Ct. 478 (1990).

102. 29 U.S.C. § 1140 (1988), *quoted in* 111 S. Ct. at 485; *see also* Hazen Paper Co. v. Biggins, 113 S. Ct. 1701, 1707 (1993) (to "fire an employee in order to prevent his pension benefits from vesting . . . is actionable under § 510 of ERISA").

Employer opportunism can occasionally surface when a worker quits rather than is fired. Again, the law must decide whether to regulate opportunism. An example is *Jordan v. Duff and Phelps, Inc.*,[103] a well-known case due to the disagreement between two law-and-economics-oriented judges about the application of the good-faith duty to employment at will. The majority opinion by Judge Easterbrook emphasized that courts should scrutinize situations in which opportunism is a danger. Jordan was an at-will employee of a close corporation who acquired one percent of the company's stock as part of his compensation plan. When Jordan resigned, he sold his stock for book value, as required under the plan. The company's chairman accepted his resignation without telling him of a possible merger that would increase his share's value from $23,000 to over $600,000. When Jordan learned of the merger, he filed a 10b-5 action alleging fraud in the purchase of corporate securities.[104] The majority opinion by Judge Easterbrook reversed a summary judgment for the employer, distinguishing between an employer who is "thoughtless, nasty, and mistaken" from one who engages in "[a]vowedly opportunistic conduct."[105] While the employer perhaps could have fired Jordan for any reason,[106] reasoned Judge Easterbrook, it could not cash out the stock option on the eve of its appreciation.[107] Judge Posner, in dissent, noted that "the possibility that corporations will exploit their junior executives . . . may well be the least urgent problem facing our nation."[108] Judge Posner argued that business executives would rather rely on their employer's good will and interest in reputation, and on their own bargaining power, than "pay for contract rights that are difficult and costly to enforce."[109]

Although leading examples of recent trends, the cases discussed so far do not illustrate the general hesitancy of courts to adopt an across-

103. 815 F.2d 429 (7th Cir. 1987).

104. 815 F.2d at 432-33.

105. 815 F.2d at 438.

106. In the actual case, Jordan resigned rather than was fired. The issue was whether a close corporation owes a duty to inform a shareholder-employee of the possible merger. But, if the closely held corporation-employer could fire Jordan for any reason, including a desire to capture the pending price rise on stock owned by Jordan, then it would have no duty to inform Jordan of the possible merger. The pivotal issue in the case thus becomes whether Jordan could be fired for this reason.

107. Judge Easterbrook imagined a little note from the employer: " 'There will be a lucrative merger tomorrow. You have been a wonderful employee, but in order to keep the proceeds of the merger for ourselves, we are letting you go, effective this instant. Here is the $23,000 for your shares.' " Judge Easterbrook said the court did not "suppose for a second" that the firm could fire an employee for this reason. 815 F.2d at 439.

108. 815 F.2d at 449 (Posner, J., dissenting).

109. 815 F.2d at 448.

the-board good-faith standard for termination of employment. This hesitancy is clearest in New York, where the highest court has declared that any good-faith requirement is inconsistent with employment at will. In *Murphy v. American Home Products Corp.*,[110] a company fired an accountant after he told top management that corporate officers had illegally manipulated the accounts of secret pension reserves. Conceding he was an at-will employee, Murphy complained that the employer breached the covenant of good faith by firing him simply for doing his job — which was, after all, to disclose accounting improprieties. The court of appeals rejected his claim, reasoning that the good-faith covenant was inconsistent with the employer's unfettered right to terminate employment at any time.[111]

The *Murphy* holding is consistent with the asymmetric-investment rationale for policing terminations. Admittedly, Murphy was between a rock and a hard place: be fired for being a poor internal auditor or be fired for being a vigorous internal auditor. The firing seems arbitrary and unfair, but it is not an example of employer opportunism.[112] The company will suffer if it wrongly chooses to smooth internal politics at the cost of chilling vigorous internal audits. Society suffers no injury other than that borne by the company.[113] Because the dangers of contract opportunism and third-party effects are absent, courts do not need to police the situation. To intervene in a situation like *Murphy* would leave no room for employment at will.

Even in Massachusetts, from which the seminal *Fortune*[114] case on good faith originated, courts have been careful to limit good-faith protection to situations of asymmetric investments. An employee has no

110. 448 N.E.2d 86 (N.Y. 1983).

111. 448 N.E.2d at 89-90.

112. The court recounted in the facts that Murphy had 23 years of service and was 59 years old when fired. 488 N.E.2d at 87. As I explain below, *infra* section III.B.1, courts should be sensitive to the exploitation claims of long-term employees. But the *Murphy* court nowhere used the length of tenure in its analysis of his age discrimination claim, although it reversed the lower court's dismissal on statute of limitation grounds. 488 N.E.2d at 93. Gary Minda reports that Murphy lost his age discrimination claim after a 10 day jury trial in 1988. A decade after his firing he was still in litigation. *See* Gary Minda, *Employment Law*, 42 SYRACUSE L. REV. 491, 493 n.8 (1991).

113. Murphy also brought a tort claim of wrongful discharge in violation of public policy. 488 N.E.2d at 90-91. The court emphatically denied the existence of such a cause of action. Such an extreme view is, in my judgment, unwise because the tort action is needed to control third-party effects of terminations. *See* Schwab, *supra* note 11. My point here is that the good-faith rationale, which requires one to allow the other party the benefit of the bargain, does not help Murphy. Other courts have equated the good-faith obligation with the tort of wrongful discharge in violation of public policy. *See, e.g.*, Brockmeyer v. Dun & Bradstreet, 335 N.W.2d 834, 840-41 (Wis. 1983). This is likewise an unwise limitation on the good-faith doctrine. The tort claim focuses on third-party effects, but the good-faith claim regulates opportunistic conduct between the parties, even if no one other than the employer and employee are directly affected.

114. 364 N.E.2d 1251 (Mass. 1977).

claim for a "bad faith" termination unless the employer intended "to benefit financially at the [employee's] expense, such as for the purpose of retaining for itself sales commissions or pension benefits which would otherwise be due to the [employee]."[115] For example, in one case employees sued when the employer changed its evaluation policy to a "Bell Curve," thus assuring that some employees would receive low ratings and be constructively discharged.[116] The Supreme Judicial Court found no violation of the good-faith standard, reasoning that the employees were merely complaining they had lost the opportunity for "future compensation for future services"[117] rather than being denied compensation "specifically related to a particular past service."[118] Only the latter termination is a form of opportunism, whereby the employer is firing an employee who has largely performed his side of the bargain without receiving benefits.

B. *Regulating Opportunism Over the Life Cycle*

These cases represent classic but ad hoc examples of courts protecting employees against opportunistic terminations. In *Fortune* an employee was fired before a commission came due. In *Ingersoll-Rand* an employee was fired before a pension vested. In *Jordan* an employer repurchased a terminated employee's stock just before it enormously increased in value. One can easily justify legal intervention on good-faith grounds. Employees can invest in the relationship more freely, making the relationship more valuable to both sides, when courts are available to ensure that employers will not exploit their investments. Likewise, *Murphy* illustrates the limits of a good-faith analysis. Without the potential for opportunism, courts should be reluctant to intercede in the relationship.

Unfortunately, an ad hoc "opportunism" test is unsatisfying for several reasons. Courts may have difficulty identifying opportunism when they see it. Even if courts can identify opportunism after the fact, an ad hoc test gives limited prospective guidance to employers and employees. Finally, the amorphous nature of an ad hoc opportu-

115. Siles v. Travenol Lab., Inc., 433 N.E.2d 103, 106 (Mass. App. Ct. 1982) (affirming judgment for employer notwithstanding jury verdict for $250,000). The court also declared that a "bad faith" termination claim would arise if the employer's reason for the discharge was contrary to public policy. *Siles*, 433 N.E.2d at 106. Such public policy claims are essentially based on tort principles. As stated earlier, they are beyond the scope of this article. *See supra* text accompanying note 11.

116. McCone v. New Eng. Tel. & Tel. Co., 471 N.E.2d 47 (Mass. 1984).

117. *McCone*, 471 N.E.2d at 50 (quoting Gram v. Liberty Mut. Ins. Co., 461 N.E.2d 796, 798 (Mass. 1984)).

118. *McCone*, 471 N.E.2d at 50.

nism test may mean it becomes so broadly applied that it is indistinguishable from a just-cause requirement for all terminations. This would weaken the deterrence of employee shirking — the prime rationale for employment at will.

If we recall the life cycle of the career employee, we can identify a more systematic pattern of legal intervention. Over the life cycle of a career employee, a sequence of possibilities for opportunism exists. A career employee is particularly vulnerable to opportunism at the beginning and end of his career. By contrast, employers are especially vulnerable to opportunism at the employee's midcareer. The cases suggest that courts are sensitive to this life cycle. Courts are most likely to scrutinize firings at the beginning and end of the life cycle. Courts do not get involved during midcareer unless they see an obvious case of particular opportunism, such as a firing before a pension vests or a sales commission is due.

1. *Beginning-Career Opportunism*

Employees face a risk of opportunistic termination at the beginning of the life cycle. The risk arises because employees commit irretrievable investments to the relationship before the employer does.[119] Usually the beginning-career cases involve employees who have moved to take a job or quit another job in reliance on a job offer.

Grouse v. Group Health Plan, Inc.[120] provides an example of a court protecting a beginning-career employee from opportunistic termination. A drugstore pharmacist resigned with two weeks notice in reliance on a job offer from a health clinic. When he called to begin work at the clinic, however, the employer told him that it had filled the position. The pharmacist was unemployed for some time. The court allowed the employee to recover under a promissory estoppel theory.[121] It determined that the employee had reasonably relied on the job offer and that justice required that the court hold the employer to its promise. The employer had argued it would be incongruous to

119. Figure 2 illustrates how early-career employees may make investments before the employer does. An employee starting his career may incur relocation costs. Further, the beginning wage may be lower than the wage he could get elsewhere and lower than his productivity, which is another form of asymmetric investment by the employee. I should note that a beginning wage below the alternative wage is not an essential feature of the efficiency-wage model and is often contrary to fact.

120. 306 N.W.2d 114 (Minn. 1981).

121. The court explicitly relied on § 90 of the *Restatement of Contracts,* which states: "A promise which the promisor should reasonably expect to induce action or forbearance . . . on the part of the promisee and which does induce such action or forbearance is binding if injustice can be avoided only by enforcement of the promise." RESTATEMENT OF CONTRACTS § 90 (1932), *quoted in Grouse,* 306 N.W.2d at 116.

provide a remedy for firing someone the day before work begins when the employee, being at will, would have no remedy for being fired the day after work began. The court agreed that such a result would be incongruous, but it resolved this contradiction by suggesting that an employee might also have a reliance claim if the employer fired him shortly after beginning work.

Other courts have used a theory of additional consideration to give employees who moved to a new job a reasonable time to recoup their investment before being arbitrarily dismissed. While many courts hold that merely working is insufficient consideration to make a just-cause promise enforceable, some additional detriment to the employee or benefit to the employer may lead to an enforceable promise. In *Veno v. Meredith,*[122] for example, a newspaper fired an editor eight years after he quit a prior job and moved from Newark to Pennsylvania to accept a position. The court, citing *Corbin on Contracts,*[123] declared that an employer could not arbitrarily discharge an employee for a reasonable time commensurate with the hardship the employee had endured.[124] The court upheld a directed verdict against the employee, however, declaring that after eight years the reasonable length of time "ha[d] surely passed."[125] In denying the employee's claim, the court distinguished a prior case that upheld an employee's verdict for breach of a "permanent" employment contract when he was fired three days into a job after moving from New York to Philadelphia.[126]

Some courts have held that relocating or leaving secure jobs is evidence that the parties must have agreed on a fixed-term contract rather than at-will employment. In *Lanier v. Alenco,*[127] a worker "with a wife and four children[ ] left a secure and well-paying position with General Electric, a position that he had held for eleven years," to

122. 515 A.2d 571 (Pa. Super. Ct. 1986), *appeal denied,* 616 A.2d 986 (Pa. 1992).

123. 3A Arthur A. Corbin, Corbin on Contracts § 684 (1960).

124. In the words of the court:

> When sufficient additional consideration is present, an employee should not be subject to discharge without just cause for a reasonable time. The length of time during which it would be unreasonable to terminate, without just cause, an employee who has given additional consideration should be commensurate with the hardship the employee has endured or the benefit he has bestowed.

515 A.2d at 580 (citations omitted).

125. 515 A.2d at 580 n.4.

126. Lucacher v. Kerson, 45 A.2d 245 (Pa. Super. Ct.), *affd.,* 48 A.2d 857 (Pa. 1946). *Lucacher* found a breach of a valid "permanent" contract of employment. *Veno* suggested the *Lucacher* court should have found the promise of permanent employment to be too vague to be a valid contract. Instead, said the *Veno* court, the *Lucacher* court should have "*inferred* a contract for a reasonable length of time based solely on the sufficient additional consideration." 515 A.2d at 580 n.4.

127. 459 F.2d 689 (5th Cir. 1972) (applying Louisiana law).

take a new job.[128] The court found it "unlikely" that the worker would have left without substantial assurances of job security, and it held that this fact corroborated evidence of a fixed one-year contract.[129]

Similarly, in *Miller v. Community Discount Centers, Inc.*,[130] a worker left his family in Toledo and moved to Chicago after he received a letter from his new employer stating he had "a rewarding and satisfying career ahead of [him]" and confirming the employer would pay one-half of his moving expenses immediately and the balance after one year.[131] The employer dismissed the worker after three months. The court upheld his claim for breach of a definite one-year contract, finding it "inconceivable that a man of plaintiff's age would leave his home to come to Chicago for the mere possibility that he would have a permanent position."[132]

We see, then, that courts sometimes allow claims by beginning-career employees who are arbitrarily fired after moving or quitting a prior job.[133] Some courts use a promissory estoppel or reliance theory, some find an implied contract for a reasonable time to allow the employee to recoup his expenses, and some simply use the decision to move or to quit as evidence of an actual definite-term agreement. Regardless of the theory for recovery, one can explain these cases as attempts to regulate opportunistic firings early in the life cycle. Employers have not yet invested in the relationship and thus are not hurt if they arbitrarily dismiss the new employee. This means that the relationship is not self-enforcing, as it is when both parties have incurred sunk costs.

Nevertheless, protection for beginning-career employees is far from universal. Many or even most courts refuse to find that reliance on an at-will job offer is reasonable.[134] In these cases, an employee

---

128. 459 F.2d at 692.

129. Louisiana is one of the few states without a statute of frauds requirement that contracts that cannot be completed within a year must be in writing. Instead, Louisiana requires that oral contracts with greater than $500 value be proved by corroborating circumstances. The issue in *Lanier* was whether quitting the prior job could be a corroborating circumstance.

130. 228 N.E.2d 113 (Ill. App. Ct. 1967).

131. 228 N.E.2d at 114-15.

132. 228 N.E.2d at 115. The opinion never reveals the employee's age.

133. In addition to the cases discussed in text, see Cashdollar v. Mercy Hosp., 595 A.2d 70 (Pa. Super. Ct. 1991) (holding that a professional moving his pregnant wife and child to a different state and leaving a job paying $82,000 annually creates sufficient hardship to protect against at-will firing).

134. Representative examples of cases refusing to uphold opportunism claims of early-career employees include: Ferreyra v. E.&J. Gallo Winery, 41 Cal. Rptr. 819 (Ct. App. 1964); Schoen v. Caterpillar Tractor Co., 243 N.E.2d 31 (Ill. App. Ct. 1968); and Romack v. Public Serv. Co., 499 N.E.2d 768 (Ind. Ct. App. 1986), *revd.*, 511 N.E.2d 1024 (Ind. 1987). In *Ferreyra*, an

quits another job or moves to a new job at his own risk.

The ambivalence of courts in this area is understandable. For at least three reasons, the opportunistic termination rationale for protecting employees is weaker in these beginning-career cases than it is later in the life cycle. First, very often the employer also makes substantial investments early in the relationship. Recruiting and training new employees can be a major cost to many firms. As Paul Weiler describes recruiting costs:

> The recruiting process itself imposes significant costs on the firm; not merely on the personnel department, which must do the initial advertising and screening, but also on the operating divisions, which must interview and judge the suitability of candidates. The magnitude of these costs can vary widely, depending on the nature of the job, the skills required, the number of applicants, and so on, but on occasion they can be substantial indeed.[135]

One study estimated that a typical firm spends 160 hours in hiring and training a new worker in the first three months on the job, and that these costs are nearly thirty percent of the value of an experienced coworker during the three-month period.[136] If the employer as well as the employee sustain heavy early costs, the risk of opportunistic termination is smaller. An employer that arbitrarily or unjustifiably fires an employee hurts itself as well, for it wastes the expenses of recruiting.

Second, even if recruiting costs are insignificant — as they will be in many cases — so that arbitrarily firing the employee does not penalize the employer, the employer gains nothing from firing a person early in his career. Thus, while employees often suffer no penalty from an arbitrary beginning-career firing, they gain no benefit from them either. This fact distinguishes beginning-career from late-career firings, in which the employer can gain from firing employees whom it pays more than their current output.

Argentinian worker gave up his job and moved his family to the United States to become a crew boss of a Gallo pruning and irrigation crew. The court held this was not sufficient consideration to protect against firing without cause. In *Schoen*, Caterpillar told the employee he must quit his present job to work for Caterpillar. The court held that the employee might still be fired at will because his quitting did not create sufficient consideration to make the new employment contract binding. Finally, in *Romack*, a police captain with 25 years of experience left a permanent position to take a job as a security manager. He also sold his old house to buy a new one within the community at his new employer's request. The court held that the captain was not protected against at-will firing.

135. WEILER, *supra* note 48, at 146. Weiler cites a study by Daniel J.B. Mitchell & Larry J. Kimbell, *Labor Market Contracts and Inflation*, *in* WORKERS, JOBS, AND INFLATION (Martin N. Baily ed., 1982), which reports that a 1979 survey of Los Angeles employers found that recruitment and initial training costs ranged from over $2000 for each office worker to over $3500 for production workers to over $10,000 for salary-exempt workers. WEILER, *supra* note 41, at 146 n.26.

136. *See* EHRENBERG & SMITH, *supra* note 21, at 142-44 (citing sources).

A final problem with job protection for new employees is that employers often need a probationary period to sort out hiring mistakes, wherein they can fire employees without explanation or extensive documentation of their reasons. Relevant here is the fact that competitive firms, largely responding to the entry and exit of early-career employees, virtually always contract for at-will dismissal.[137] Even the Model Employment Termination Act, which calls for general good-cause protection for employees, refuses to protect employees with less than a year of service.[138]

In sum, in many situations employer opportunism against beginning employees is either a trivial threat or outweighed by legitimate needs to maintain employer flexibility. In these situations, courts do not scrutinize the sudden termination. Still, the potential for opportunistic employer offers is real. An employer engages in opportunistic behavior when it hires a better person before training anyone but after the first job applicant has relied on the offer. Courts protect beginning employees from such opportunism.

2. *Late-Career Opportunism*

Late-career employees face the greatest danger of opportunistic firings. At the end of their life cycle, they often earn more than their current productivity. If they do, the employer has a financial incentive to terminate them, even if it violates an implicit promise to allow the employee to reap the rewards of hard work earlier in his career.

The Age Discrimination in Employment Act provides one check against late-career opportunism. By prohibiting employers from firing workers above the age of forty because of their age, the ADEA protects older workers from discharges based upon stereotypes that lead employers to underestimate their productivity. "We need new blood" and "Doe is slowing down a notch" are classic statements that create age discrimination lawsuits.

However, the ADEA may offer only limited protection against the central concern of the life-cycle model — opportunistic firings when salary and forthcoming benefits outweigh current productivity. In *Hazen Paper Co. v. Biggins,*[139] the Supreme Court unanimously held that an employer did not violate the ADEA when it fired a sixty-two-

137. *See supra* Part II.

138. Section 3(b) of the Model Employment Termination Act states that the good-cause protections "appl[y] only to an employee who has been employed by the same employer for a total period of one year or more and has worked for the employer for at least 520 hours during the 26 weeks next preceding the termination." MODEL EMPLOYMENT TERMINATION ACT, 7A U.L.A. 74 (Supp. 1993).

139. 113 S. Ct. 1701 (1993).

year-old employee just before his tenth anniversary with the company in order to keep his pension benefits from vesting. Although the Court agreed that the firing was actionable under section 510 of ERISA, it held "that an employer does not violate the ADEA just by interfering with an older employee's pension benefits that would have vested by virtue of the employee's years of service."[140] Justice O'Connor, writing for the Court, emphasized that age is not the same as years of service.[141] "The ADEA only requires an employer to ignore an employee's age; it does not specify *further* characteristics that an employer must also ignore."[142] Under the life-cycle model, the employee becomes vulnerable to opportunism with years of service, not with age. The ADEA is therefore of little help.

A recent Second Circuit case, consistent with but not cited in *Hazen Paper,* shows even more clearly the limitations of the ADEA in protecting workers from late-career opportunistic firings. In *Bay v. Times Mirror Magazines, Inc.*,[143] a fifty-four-year-old publisher who made nearly $200,000 per year brought an ADEA claim after being fired from his position at *Field and Stream.* The employee thought he had a "smoking gun" when he produced an internal memorandum from the company's chairman stating that the employee's salary alone mandated his dismissal. The employee asserted the memo established his "high salary was a critical factor in the decision," and that the high salary was "a direct function of his longevity, experience, seniority or periodic salary raises."[144] The Second Circuit, without disputing these assertions, affirmed summary judgment for the employer. Conceding that "high salary and age may be related," the court declared that "nothing in the ADEA . . . prohibits an employer from making employment decisions that relate an employee's salary to contemporaneous market conditions . . . and concluding that a particular employee's salary is too high."[145]

Other cases interpret the ADEA more expansively. In *Metz v. Transit Mix, Inc.*,[146] for example, the Seventh Circuit reversed a trial court judgment for an employer who had replaced a fifty-four-year-old, highly paid manager with a younger, cheaper colleague. The court emphasized that an employer cannot assess the costs of employ-

140. *Hazen,* 113 S. Ct. at 1707-08.
141. 113 S. Ct. at 1707.
142. 113 S. Ct. at 1707.
143. 936 F.2d 112 (2d Cir. 1991).
144. 936 F.2d at 117.
145. 936 F.2d at 117.
146. 828 F.2d 1202 (7th Cir. 1987).

ing an older worker when deciding whom to terminate because pay is a " 'proxy' for age."[147] Under this interpretation, which received an enigmatic citation from the Supreme Court in *Hazen,*[148] the ADEA protects older workers fired because their salary exceeds current productivity. Because of the close connection between a worker's age and time he spends with the company, the ADEA indirectly protects late-career employees as well.

Greater protection may come from common law courts, which in recent years have begun policing opportunistic firings of late-career employees.[149] The leading case is *Pugh v. See's Candies, Inc.,*[150] in which a thirty-two-year employee was abruptly fired after working his way up from dishwasher to corporate vice president. The employee never had a clear agreement about job security, although managers had given him encouraging evaluations over the years.[151] The court held that this career pattern, including the length of service and the policies and practices of the company, could establish an implied-in-fact promise against arbitrary dismissal.[152] *Pugh* epitomizes the effi-

147. 828 F.2d at 1208. Judge Easterbrook, in dissent, emphasized that pay is only a rough proxy for age except in the rare cases in which a firm uses a lock-step compensation system based on age. 828 F.2d at 1220. Easterbrook noted that another situation in which pay could differ from current productivity was with firms using life-cycle implicit contracts whereby employees would be paid less than productivity early in their career and more than current productivity late in their career. 828 F.2d at 1220-21. This is precisely the model analyzed in this article. Easterbrook recognized the potential for employer opportunism in this situation and suggested the ADEA might provide a remedy based on a disparate impact approach. 828 F.2d at 1221.

148. In *Hazen,* the Supreme Court did not preclude the possibility that the ADEA protects workers from an employer who fires workers with a certain pension status as a "proxy" for age, in the sense that the employer may suppose a correlation between the two factors and act on the basis of pension status to get at age. The court then gave a *"cf."* citation to *Metz,* saying that the case used " 'proxy' to mean statutory equivalence." Hazen Paper Co. v. Biggins, 113 S. Ct. 1701, 1707 (1993). It is unclear what degree of support this signals for the *Metz* case.

149. For an excellent discussion of the various legal theories by which courts uphold job security based on longevity of service, see Linzer, *supra* note 11, at 354-68, 383-86.

150. 171 Cal. Rptr. 917 (Ct. App. 1981).

151. As the court described it:

> When Pugh first went to work for See's, Ed Peck, then president and general manager, frequently told him: "if you are loyal to (See's) and do a good job, your future is secure." [The company's president] had a practice of not terminating administrative personnel except for good cause.... During the entire period of his employment, there had been no formal or written criticism of Pugh's work.

171 Cal. Rptr. at 919. Some read these statements as amounting to a company policy of just cause and categorize the case that way. *See* Linzer, *supra* note 11, at 345-55. I find the statements so general that almost any long-term employee could supply proof of similar assurances. The critical feature of *Pugh* is not these assurances, but the longevity of his tenure. Linzer does not disagree. *Id.* at 367.

152. The appellate court therefore reversed the trial court's dismissal at the end of the plaintiff's case and remanded for a second trial. At the second trial, the jury found for the employer, and the judgment was upheld on appeal. Pugh v. See's Candies, Inc., 250 Cal. Rptr. 195 (Ct. App. 1988). Thus, the employee whose case symbolizes court protection of late-career workers himself ultimately was fired without legal protection.

ciency-wage story and its end-game dangers. Pugh committed himself to a single firm, worked hard to gain promotions to the promised easy life, but then was terminated. *Pugh* also demonstrates the effect of the arrival of new management on job security. In *Pugh,* new management arrived a year before Pugh's firing. Such major corporate changes may diminish the reputational check on firings of late-career employees.

Length of service is the key element that motivates courts to scrutinize a late-career firing. Most opinions, like *Pugh,* also examine oral statements and the company's general procedures. But a Montana case, *Flanigan v. Prudential Federal Savings & Loan Association,*[153] starkly illustrates the centrality of longevity. In that case, a bank fired Mildred Flanigan without notice or a hearing after twenty-eight years of service. The Montana Supreme Court affirmed a nearly $1.5 million judgment for Flanigan, declaring that her "28 years of employment by Prudential gave her a secure and objective basis for believing that, if her work was satisfactorily performed, her employment would continue."[154] In its decision, the court quoted extensively from a California appellate case, *Cleary v. American Airlines, Inc.,*[155] which also emphasized longevity of service as a key element of a bad faith claim. In *Cleary,* the court upheld a claim brought by an employee dismissed without cause after eighteen years of service. The court declared that "[t]ermination of employment without legal cause after such a period of time offends the implied-in-law covenant of good faith and fair dealing contained in all contracts including employment contracts."[156]

Occasionally, an employee faces the danger of beginning-career and late-career opportunism at the same time. This situation occurs when a long-time employee agrees to a job transfer. A prominent example is *Foley v. Community Oil Co.,*[157] in which a thirty-year employee was fired three years after accepting a job transfer to another state. The court's explicit rationale in finding the employee had stated a claim tracks the life-cycle theory. The court first noted that "uprooting and moving a family" could give rise to a contractual claim.[158] The court then declared that "[l]ongevity of service can also give rise to an implied contract right."[159] Tracking the lock-in problem with

153. 720 P.2d 257 (Mont. 1986).

154. 720 P.2d at 262.

155. 168 Cal. Rptr. 722 (Ct. App. 1980).

156. 168 Cal. Rptr. at 729.

157. 64 F.R.D. 561 (D.N.H. 1974) (applying New Hampshire law).

158. 64 F.R.D. at 563.

159. 64 F.R.D. at 563.

which we have wrestled, the court explained that "[t]he employee, in providing long-term employment to a single employer substantially diminishes his economic mobility."[160]

In sum, one can explain these cases as attempts to monitor and enforce the implicit life-cycle employment contract. Late in an employee's career, the usual checks against opportunistic firings unravel. Courts enter to monitor the bargain. The bargain does not give late-career employees complete job security. They can be dismissed for cause, because otherwise the shirking problems would be immense, but the employer does not prove cause simply by proving that salary exceeds current productivity. That is the typical life-cycle pattern that both sides to career employment anticipate and, ex ante, it is in the interests of both sides.

3. *Midcareer Shirking*

Once the employer has begun to make substantial, asset-specific investments in an employee, the risk of arbitrary firing diminishes. The greater danger of opportunistic behavior — at least, behavior that an appropriate dismissal standard could limit — comes from the employee's side. Because the employer does not want to repeat recruiting and training costs with another employee, the incumbent employee has an opportunity to shirk without fear of dismissal. Shirking at midcareer can occur even if the employer has the right to dismiss at will, but the shirking problem can be exacerbated if the employer must also surmount the hurdle of proving just cause.

This is not to say that the employer cannot exploit the midcareer employee. Indeed, as I emphasized above,[161] being trapped by investments in firm-specific capital and in community roots can make a midcareer employee ripe for exploitation. But the exploitation will not take the form of firing because the employer is making money from the relationship. Rather than fire a midcareer employee, an employer may pay him less than would be called for under a fair division of the gains from the long-term relationship or make his workload or working conditions more onerous. Just cause cannot protect the midcareer employee from these abuses. Better, then, for the law to focus on something it can handle, which is deterrence of shirking by midcareer employees.

The courts seem to have intuited this fact by refusing, in general, to create contract protections against arbitrary terminations for mid-

160. 64 F.R.D. at 563.

161. *See supra* notes 59-60 and accompanying text.

career workers. Midcareer employees have made the fewest contributions to the doctrinal erosion of at-will employment.[162]

The most detailed data on wrongful termination plaintiffs come from a Rand study[163] of 120 California jury trials[164] in the early 1980s. Over half the plaintiffs in this sample were early-career employees, with five or fewer years of job tenure.[165] Nearly a quarter of the plaintiffs had over fifteen years of tenure,[166] with the remaining quarter of the plaintiffs being midcareer employees with six to fifteen years tenure.[167] This sample of jury trials suggests that midcareer employees are a minority of wrongful termination plaintiffs, and many of these may be bringing public policy and other tort claims not inconsistent with the life-cycle model.[168]

The leading cases also suggest to some extent the courts' reluctance to protect midcareer employees. One case that typifies this hesitation is *Rowe v. Montgomery Ward & Co.*[169] The case is especially significant because Michigan courts have been leaders in eroding the at-will presumption. In *Rowe,* a salesperson with eight-years tenure was fired for leaving the store one day without explanation. The employee sued, claiming she had been orally told she would have a job as long as she met her sales quota, and pointing out that when she was hired she had signed a "Rules of Personal Conduct" that enumerated only four reasons — all involving theft, dishonesty, or immorality —

---

162. Of course, it is hard to demonstrate convincingly a negative statement like "cases of this type rarely occur," especially when the methodology is to examine "leading" cases rather than systematically to examine all reported cases. Counterexamples do exist. In the text I discuss Foley v. Interactive Data Corp., 765 P.2d 373 (Cal. 1988), the most prominent counterexample. Still, I remain convinced as a positive matter that courts are not inclined to scrutinize terminations of midcareer employees, and the life-cycle model suggests the wisdom of their hesitation as a normative matter.

163. *See generally* JAMES N. DERTOUZOS ET AL., THE LEGAL AND ECONOMIC CONSEQUENCES OF WRONGFUL TERMINATION (1988).

164. The sample of 120 wrongful termination jury trials in California between 1980 and the first quarter of 1986 includes perhaps 65 to 70% of all wrongful termination trials in California during that time. *Id.* at 19 & n.1. One must use extreme caution in extrapolating from facts about tried cases to statements about all cases, including settled cases. Tried cases are likely to be a biased sample of all cases. *See generally* George L. Priest & Benjamin Klein, *The Selection of Disputes for Litigation,* 13 J. LEGAL STUD. 1 (1984); Stewart J. Schwab & Theodore Eisenberg, *Explaining Constitutional Tort Litigation: The Influence of the Attorney Fees Statute and the Government as Defendant,* 73 CORNELL L. REV. 719 (1988).

165. Some 18.2% of all plaintiffs had under one year of tenure, and another 34.2% had one to five years of tenure. DERTOUZOS ET AL., *supra* note 163, at 21 tbl. 4.

166. *Id.* (the precise number is 23.1%).

167. Some 15.7% of the plaintiffs had 6 to 10 years of tenure, and only 8.3% of the plaintiffs had 11 to 15 years of tenure. *Id.*

168. By contrast, according to the 1980 census, only 14.5% of workers had worked 15 or more years in their current jobs, while 60.1% had worked five or fewer years. *See* Robert E. Hall, *The Importance of Lifetime Jobs in the U.S. Economy,* 22 AM. ECON. REV. 716, 717 (1982).

169. 473 N.W.2d 268 (Mich. 1991).

for immediate discharge. The Michigan Supreme Court denied her claim,[170] emphasizing that the words of assurance were "more akin to stating a policy"[171] than offering an express contract, and noting that nothing in Montgomery Ward's "Rules of Personal Conduct" suggested that the enumerated conduct was the only basis for dismissal.[172] The *Rowe* court distinguished *Toussaint v. Blue Cross & Blue Shield,*[173] a leading employee-rights case, by emphasizing that *Toussaint* involved actual negotiations over job security by high-level employees.[174] *Rowe* evoked a spirited dissent by the author of *Toussaint,* who insisted that an enforceable promise was equally present for the low-level salesperson.[175]

The Court in *Rowe* did not rely heavily on her moderate job tenure but simply disallowed her claim because it found the circumstances were insufficient to infer an implied-in-fact contract.[176] One can only speculate that the court would have viewed Rowe's claim more sympathetically if she had thirty-years tenure rather than eight. Under the life-cycle model, the case would be dramatically different if Rowe had been a late-career employee.

The most prominent counterexample to my claim about midcareer employees not receiving protection is *Foley v. Interactive Data Corp,*[177] in which the California Supreme Court upheld an implied-in-fact contract claim as well as an implied-in-law breach of good-faith claim brought by an employee who served the company just six years and nine months before he was terminated. The *Foley* case is remarkable for at least two reasons. First, and ironically, most commentators view the decision as a dramatic cutback on employee rights because the court refused to grant tort damages for employees claiming a breach of the covenant of good faith. Second, and more pertinent to our analysis, *Foley* pushes the limits for defining a "late-career" employee. Basing an employee's just-cause claim on less than seven years of service cannot realistically be viewed as an attempt to deter opportunistic firing of late-career employees whose seniority-based earnings outrun their current productivity.[178] Indeed, the court recognized

170. The Court reversed a trial court judgment on a jury verdict of $86,500 plus interest. 473 N.W.2d at 281.

171. 473 N.W.2d at 275.

172. 473 N.W.2d at 275.

173. 292 N.W.2d 880 (Mich. 1980).

174. 473 N.W.2d at 274.

175. 473 N.W.2d at 289-308 (Levin, J., dissenting).

176. 473 N.W.2d 273-75.

177. 765 P.2d 373 (Cal. 1988).

178. When discharged in 1983, Foley was a branch manager in a Los Angeles subsidiary of

that short tenure might weaken Foley's implied contract claim.[179] It emphasized, however, three additional factors: (1) Foley alleged (rather vague) oral assurances of job security and consistent promotions and salary increases;[180] (2) Foley alleged breach of written "Termination Guidelines" that suggested self-imposed limitations on the employer's right to terminate employees;[181] and, (3) unlike Pugh, Foley had "supplied the company valuable and separate consideration" by signing a promise not to compete against the employer for one year after termination.[182] Many employees can allege the first two factors. The third factor is less common, although far from unique. Perhaps these other elements explain why *Foley* is not consistent with the general claim that courts rely on longevity of service and scrutinize only late-career terminations for opportunism. More realistically, *Foley* probably reflects a general move in California toward a good-faith standard for all terminations.[183]

In summary, my argument is that the general pattern of good-faith and implied-contract cases reflects an intuitive understanding by the courts that employees are subject to opportunistic discharge at the end, and less consistently at the beginning, of the life cycle. Courts are reluctant, however, to give general protection against arbitrary dismissal to midcareer employees. The economic self-interest of employers should keep such dismissals in check. The greater concern is with employee shirking.

To clarify the distinction I draw between scrutinizing opportunistic late-career terminations and scrutinizing all employment decisions under a just-cause standard, let me return to the facts of *Murphy v. American Home Products.*[184] Murphy, like the California Foley, was an internal whistleblower who reported to upper management wrongdoing by immediate supervisors.[185] While bucking the corporate hier-

---

Chase Manhattan Bank that markets computer-based decision-support services, making an annual salary of $56,164. In addition, as the court points out, he received a $6762 merit bonus two days before his discharge. 765 P.2d at 375. The court's opinion never mentions Foley's age. Based on these characteristics, it seems hard to characterize Foley as anything but a midcareer employee.

179. 765 P.2d at 377-78.

180. 765 P.2d at 383, 388.

181. 765 P.2d at 388.

182. 765 P.2d at 388.

183. The court several times declared that it was not disturbing the general at-will presumption, *see, e.g.*, 765 P.2d at 384, which indeed is codified in CAL. LAB. CODE § 2922 (West 1989). It simply held that the parties had reached a contrary implied agreement in this case. 765 P.2d at 383.

184. 448 N.E.2d 86 (N.Y. 1983).

185. Foley had informed a company vice president that Foley's immediate supervisor was under investigation by the FBI for embezzling from his prior employer. After Foley was fired,

archy often gets employees into trouble, courts are hesitant to referee the resulting turf fights.[186] Internal whistleblowing resembles too closely legitimate, but practically unverifiable, concerns that an employee is not a team player or that an employee creates difficulty in the office. Legal limning of these situations is probably not worth the costs.

Thus, I would have greater sympathy for Murphy if he claimed that he was fired after twenty-three years of service[187] because he was no longer pulling his weight or earning his salary. Unless the parties have clearly agreed to at-will dismissals throughout the life cycle, such a firing smacks of an employer opportunistically firing an employee who has committed the best years of his life and should reap, based on the norms of seniority, the benefits of a career commitment to the employer. In fact, Murphy did claim age discrimination — a claim that was still being litigated a decade after his discharge.[188] But a legitimate defense might be that opportunism had nothing to do with the termination; he was fired because he attempted to buck the corporate system. Of course, when an employer fires an older worker allegedly for such a reason, the proof problems in sorting out the real reason for discharge are enormous. This dilemma quite likely will make employers wary of firing older workers. My point, in short, is that just-cause protection should be limited to an inquiry into whether the employee was fired in breach of the life-cycle commitment to pay seniority-based wages and benefits or for other opportunistic reasons.

IV. Default Rules

"Aren't we done now?" the dear reader might ask. Not quite. We have seen that a life-cycle rule may be the best way for employer and employee to minimize the dangers of opportunism on each side of the employment relationship. One might still argue, however, that parties seeking this arrangement should put an explicit life-cycle rule in the contract. If they do not, courts should presume the contract is at will

the supervisor pled guilty in federal court to a felony count of embezzlement. 765 P.2d at 375 n.13.

186. I do see a valid role for legal scrutiny, in a tort guise, of terminations that may adversely affect public policy. Firing a whistleblower of illegal corporate acts often fits this category. *See* Schwab & Eisenberg, *supra* note 164.

187. The court in *Murphy* recounts in the facts that he had 23 years of service with his employer, 448 N.E.2d at 87, but nowhere uses his longevity in its analysis. The court also notes that Murphy was 59 years old when he was discharged and overturns the lower court's dismissal, on statute of limitations grounds, of his age discrimination claim. 448 N.E.2d at 92-93.

188. *See* Minda, *supra* note 112, at 493 n.8 (indicating that, although Murphy lost a subsequent trial on the age discrimination claim, the case was reversed and remanded upon appeal and is awaiting retrial).

or just cause. The final step in my argument, then, explains why the life-cycle rule should be the default rule for courts, even though the parties could choose any rule by explicit contract.

A. *Minimizing Transaction Costs*

The traditional law-and-economics literature on default rules suggests that courts do and should choose rules that minimize transaction costs. Two sometimes conflicting tests come from this approach. First and most prominent is the "mimic the market" or "would have wanted" test, whereby courts supply the default contract term that most parties would put in the contract were they bargaining without costs and with full information. This test saves most parties from the costs of acquiring information and bargaining over the term. The trick in applying this test is to determine which rule maximizes joint gains by helping one party more than it hurts the other. In general, a complex default rule is likely to "mimic the market" better than a simple rule, in that parties who were bargaining costlessly would probably agree to share risk and minimize opportunism on both side. The second test, the "improve bargaining that occurs" approach, urges a default rule that lowers costs for those who must bargain rather than allows most parties to avoid bargaining.[189] A simple, clear default rule may be easier for the parties to bargain around, and it may thus lower transaction costs for parties who will actually bargain over the particular term.[190]

Luckily, in our situation both tests point in the same direction.[191]

189. *See* Robert Cooter, *The Cost of Coase*, 11 J. LEGAL STUD. 1 (1982).

190. Mark Kelman has noted this ambivalence in law and economics between rules that lower bargaining costs and rules that mimic the market. He finds that clear rules are generally favored under the first criterion and complex rules under the second. *See* MARK KELMAN, A GUIDE TO CRITICAL LEGAL STUDIES 123-24 (1987).

191. Scholars recently have proposed an alternative criterion for default rules. Labeled "penalty default" rules or "information-forcing" default rules, these default rules are designed to be so onerous that one party will want to write around it, in the process revealing information that allows for a superior bargain. *See* Ian Ayres & Robert Gertner, *Filling Gaps in Incomplete Contracts: An Economic Theory of Default Rules*, 99 YALE L.J. 87, 91 (1989); Ian Ayres & Robert Gertner, *Strategic Contractual Inefficiency and the Optimal Choice of Legal Rules*, 101 YALE L.J. 729 (1992); Lucian A. Bebchuk & Steven Shavell, *Information and the Scope of Liability for Breach of Contract: The Rule of* Hadley v. Baxendale, 7 J.L. ECON. & ORGANIZATION 284 (1991); Melvin A. Eisenberg, *The Principle of* Hadley v. Baxendale, 80 CAL. L. REV. 563 (1992); Jason S. Johnston, *Strategic Bargaining and the Economic Theory of Contract Default Rules*, 100 YALE L.J. 615 (1990). Applied to our context, unfortunately, the penalty default model does not point definitely to either just cause or at will, and the model does not work at all when a third alternative such as a life-cycle default is possible. For example, suppose that at will is the efficient contract for most workers. The few job applicants for whom just cause is appropriate cannot risk being labeled a shirker by requesting just cause. The model might suggest that just cause should be the default, forcing employers — who arguably are not penalized by being labeled an arbitrary, unfair employer — to insist on an at-will clause. But because employers probably are penalized by a reputation for unfairness, an at-will default might be needed to keep

First, under the would-have-wanted default test, our previous analysis suggests that a life-cycle termination standard would be optimal for most career employees; by minimizing opportunism on both sides, it allows for the most productive relationship. Because it maximizes the overall gains to the relationship, most parties bargaining under low transaction costs would opt for the life-cycle rule.

Second, the lower-bargaining-costs approach also favors a life-cycle default rule because it is easier for parties to bargain away from than toward the life-cycle rule. At-will clauses are easy to compose.[192] Just-cause clauses are also straightforward to write, although the phrase "just cause" is a rich and complex term of art in labor arbitration.[193] In Professor Rose's marvelous terminology, these are "crystal" rules.[194] By contrast, a life-cycle rule would be hard to draft because it would be difficult to specify at the outset of a relationship exactly when the relative vulnerability switches from employer to employee. Rose would call the life cycle a "muddy" rule.[195] The parties cannot easily articulate at the time of initial hire the proper governing structure for their future relationship. They may prefer to rely on courts' often bumbling and instinctive judgment about relative vulnerabilities. Under the life-cycle default, parties can simply say nothing too explicit in the contract and count on courts to apply the life-cycle approach. In short, the parties can easily draft away from a life-cycle default if they choose, but they cannot easily draft away from an at-will or just-cause presumption toward a life-cycle rule.

Indeed, the ambiguity in the timing of a life-cycle default rule may be itself desirable. Suppose a contract explicitly called for at-will em-

---

"good" at-will employers from being lumped together with bad ones. The formal penalty default model requires that a majority of contracts clearly favor one rule. *See* Bebchuk & Shavell, *supra*, at 292 & n.22 (emphasizing that the fraction of high valuation buyers determines whether limited or unlimited liability is the optimal rule). As discussed *supra* in Part II, it is unclear whether the optimal termination clause in most cases would be at will or just cause. Indeed, the argument of this article is that the optimal clause shifts back and forth over the career of each worker. Because of the problems with the penalty default model in this context, the discussion of it is relegated to a footnote.

192. Richard Epstein puts it succinctly: "the phrase 'at will' is two words long and has the convenient virtue of meaning just what it says, no more and no less." Epstein, *supra* note 10, at 955.

193. *See generally* Roger I. Abrams & Dennis R. Nolan, *Toward a Theory of "Just Cause" in Employee Discipline Cases*, 1985 DUKE L.J. 594.

194. Carol M. Rose, *Crystals and Mud in Property Law*, 40 STAN. L. REV. 577, 577-78 (1988) (defining as "crystalline" those often arbitrary property law rules that attempt to delimit rights in unambiguous terms, so as to create clear expectations in those who are subject to the rules — for example, the rule allowing a subsequent real estate purchaser to take property free of any unrecorded preexisting claim).

195. *Id.* at 578 (defining as "mud" amorphous legal doctrines that make it difficult for parties to know their rights in advance — for example, nuisance law).

ployment for the first fifteen years of the relationship but just cause thereafter. The employer would have a strategic incentive to review an employee at fourteen years and eleven months and terminate if forecasts of future performance were not rosy, even if current performance were adequate. The costs of termination to an employee after nearly fifteen years are tremendous.[196] But under the more malleable life-cycle default, the strategic doomsday evaporates. An employer, unsure when the at-will standard changes to just cause, is more likely to act in good faith.

Under either approach, then, a life-cycle default rule is optimal. To reiterate, under a life-cycle default, the court presumes that mid-career employees have an at-will relationship with their employer because that contractual structure best deters opportunistic behavior by the parties. Late-career employees, by contrast, are ripe for opportunistic termination, and so courts require good cause for terminating such employees. The optimal standard for new employees is more nuanced. On the one hand, employees who have quit other jobs or who have significant moving expenses perhaps should have a reliance damages default. On the other hand, employers often need a probationary period to sort out poor matches. Perhaps a default probationary period should be presumed, absent unusual reliance expenditures by the beginning employees.

B. *Relational Contract Default Rules*

Recently, the literature on default rules has examined long-term relational contracts. The debate centers on whether simple or complex rules are better able to deter opportunistic behavior in the relationship. Some have argued that complex default rules that consider the particular circumstances of the parties better control the strategic behavior problems of relational contracts.[197] Certainly the life-cycle default, which is premised on the fact that both employer and employee can exploit the other's sunk costs, attempts to control strategic behavior on both sides. In this way it is a complex default rule.

In contrast, Robert Scott has noted that most default rules in commercial relational contracts tend to be simple, categorical, and winner-

196. We do see contracts, particularly collective bargaining contracts, that explicitly call for a switch from at will to just cause after a probationary period. As I have suggested, these probationary periods create an incentive to review the employee immediately before just cause vests. Almost invariably, however, probationary periods are short — three months, six months, one year — and thus regulate beginning employees. The short time horizon limits the sunk costs the employee has at stake.

197. Clayton P. Gillette, *Commercial Relationships and the Selection of Default Rules for Remote Risks*, 19 J. LEGAL STUD. 535 (1990).

take-all.[198] Scott cautions that these prevailing default rules may have normative force, so that concocting a complex default may be a misguided attempt to control strategic behavior.[199] As he emphasizes, legal rules "are both a threat and a temptation."[200] Legal attempts to prevent opportunism by one side invite evasive responses from the other side. Certainly this is true for employment relations. Preventing employer opportunism by a just-cause standard invites increased employee shirking. Scott concludes by emphasizing that legal sanctions are not the only control on opportunism.[201] Social forces of reciprocity and honesty, particularly when benefits accrue to a good reputation, are powerful deterrents. Rather than legally enshrining these social norms, which may destroy the informality that makes them so effective, the optimal structure may rely on clear, harsh, legal defaults combined with social sanctions against failure to cooperate.

Scott's argument against complex, contextualized defaults is powerful in the commercial context in which he uses it, but its lessons may justify a life-cycle default here. First, the life-cycle default may not fall on the complex side of Scott's spectrum. Although parties could not easily agree on the tipping points, the life-cycle default does call for a categorical legal winner at every point in the relationship. In that sense, the default is clearer than a default rule that calls for sharing. Second, to the extent a life-cycle default is complex, its complexity arises from the common law, albeit still in embryonic form; Scott objects to complex default rules that the common law has ignored or rejected. Thus, like Scott, I am using the common law to provide both a positive description and a normative base for a life-cycle default rule. Finally, Scott's argument focuses on commercial relationships of indefinite or permanent length. The opportunism can come at any time by either side, usually in response to exogenous shocks to the relationship. While random shocks can also disturb employment relationships, the inevitable life cycle of the employment relationship presents clear end-game and beginning-game problems, in which the employer's potential for opportunism becomes predictable and one-sided. In midcycle, by contrast, the self-interest of the employer in not firing productive workers provides a nonlegal check on arbitrary firings, so the law should focus on the possible opportunism by employees. Given this predictable cycle, the legal default rule for employment ter-

198. Robert E. Scott, *A Relational Theory of Default Rules for Commercial Contracts*, 19 J. LEGAL STUD. 597 (1990).

199. *Id.* at 611.

200. *Id.* at 613.

201. *Id.* at 615.

minations can focus more precisely on opportunistic threats than can a default rule in the usual commercial relationship.

V. The Variety of Employment Relationships

A. *Who Are the Life-Cycle Workers?*

At the beginning of this article, I noted the great variety of employment relationships. In subsequent sections, I concentrated on the career employment relationship with two defining characteristics: (1) both sides invest heavily in the relationship in ways that will be lost if the relationship is severed prematurely;[202] and (2) contracting problems prevent easy monitoring of work performance or verification of poor performance to outsiders. It is time to consider what workers fit the life-cycle model. Table 1 provides the framework.[203]

Table 1
Types of Employment Relationships and Optimal Termination Standards

	General Investments	Specific Investments
Verification Easy	(1) Standard Unimportant	(3) Just Cause
Verification Hard	(2) At Will	(4) Life Cycle

We must determine whether just cause or at will is the preferable standard for a particular type of job. The employer's perspective depends on which row of the table applies. When verification is easy (top row), a just-cause presumption does not harm employers. An employer can simply show a court or arbitrator it has just cause for firing a shirking worker. By contrast, when verification is hard (bottom row), a just-cause standard makes employers vulnerable to opportunism by shirking workers because the employer cannot verify to a court or arbitrator the reasons it suspects shirking.

202. These asset-specific investments can themselves be of two types. They may be skills that are valuable only to the particular employer, as modeled in Gary Becker's human-capital model, *see supra* note 18, and illustrated in Figure 1. They can also be the employee's decision to climb the career ladder, whereby hard work, even using general skills, is rewarded by late-career perks and bonuses. This is the efficiency-wage model as depicted in Figure 2.

203. Oliver Williamson presents a similar table in Williamson, *supra* note 17, at 247, but he uses it to reach more general conclusions about employment-governance structures.

The employee's perspective depends on which column applies. When workers have made only general investments (left column), their skills are transferable to another firm. Even if they are terminated from one firm, they are not hurt greatly because other firms are willing to pay them comparable wages. Because terminations are less costly to employees in this column, at-will protection is adequate. By contrast, when workers have made firm-specific investments, which include entering an individual firm's career ladder (right column), they suffer greatly from termination.

These observations lead to easy conclusions for the off-diagonal boxes (2) and (3). The employer and employee perspectives clash more directly in boxes (1) and (4). In box (1), neither party is vulnerable, so the discharge standard is less important. I have spent the bulk of the article addressing box (4) and will simply reiterate that a life-cycle rule best accommodates the mutual vulnerability.

The more challenging task is pigeonholing a worker or job in a particular box. One dichotomy is between general investments and specific investments. Jobs in which both sides have made only general investments are nearly an empty set among workers with more than a few years' experience. Importantly, investments are broader than job skills. Many, perhaps most, workers have skills that many firms value and are thus general. These general skills make them less vulnerable to opportunism. But most workers develop specific ties to their workplace — familiar faces and routines — that they will lose if they leave. Often, workers enter a career job ladder with a particular firm, assuming that hard work will lead to promotions and future rewards. If one defines workers with specific investments as workers who will suffer from job loss, most experienced workers fall into this category.[204]

It is harder to draw the line that separates jobs in which acceptable job performance is easy to monitor and verify from jobs in which monitoring and verification is hard. Perhaps common law courts can draw the line — as they draw so many others — on an intuitive, case-by-case basis. This approach would be acceptable if the courts kept the function of the line in mind. The line is supposed to separate jobs in which a just-cause requirement will not create severe shirking problems from jobs in which an employer cannot easily prove objectionable employee behavior to a court and so employers cannot credibly threaten to fire shirking employees.

Some have suggested that high-level as opposed to low-level jobs

204. Construction workers, with their transient job sites, are perhaps an exception.

present such a dichotomy. An employer may only have an unprovable sense that a high-level worker is not performing adequately. Such jobs have many intangible characteristics, such as the ability to motivate and work with others. By contrast, low-level jobs usually involve the performance of tangible and verifiable tasks. Even such a staunch and eloquent advocate of just cause as Professor St. Antoine has suggested that high-level employees should be exempt from a comprehensive just-cause scheme.[205] He has suggested that we should draw an indirect line excluding from just-cause protection employees entitled to a pension above a certain amount or employees who have fixed-term contracts of two years or more.[206]

One must be careful of class myopia in making such proposals. Most jobs, even the most unskilled or menial, require complex mental states to perform them well. Boredom, frustration, and low morale can impair performance on any job. While sometimes this fact manifests itself in objective, verifiable ways, many times it does not. Certainly job status and job complexity do not correlate well. Nevertheless, a duality exists between jobs requiring simple, repetitive tasks and those requiring complex, varied tasks. If the tasks are simple and repetitive, "successful job performance is relatively easy to define and measure in ways that virtually every reasonable person would consider fair, accurate, thorough, and objective."[207]

Courts and commentators have thoroughly debated the analogous issue in employment discrimination law; few tests for job applicants have survived a challenge of bias. If objective tests cannot be found to evaluate job applicants, we should not expect employers to be able to provide objective evidence of cause when they fire a worker for not performing adequately. Mark Kelman has noted this tension.[208] In advocating a near ban on employment testing for applicants because objective criteria for hiring cannot be found, he recognizes that employers must be given greater leeway in dismissing workers who do not live up to the admittedly subjective standards of the job.[209] In

205. *See* St. Antoine, *supra* note 8, at 72 ("In the higher ranges of management, one official's evaluation of another's business judgment may become so intertwined with questions of fair personal treatment that the two cannot be separated."). Interestingly, the management advisors to the Model Employment Termination Act (META), for which Professor St. Antoine was the reporter, wanted high-level workers to be covered in order to get the advantage of displacing common law actions. Under the META they are covered.

206. *Id.*

207. Barbara Lerner, Washington v. Davis: *Quantity, Quality and Equality in Employment Testing,* 1976 SUP. CT. REV. 263, 280-81.

208. Mark Kelman, *Concepts of Discrimination in "General Ability" Job Testing,* 104 HARV. L. REV. 1157 (1991).

209. Kelman, *supra* note 208, at 1233 (the main problem in abolishing screening tests is that

other words, the law cannot simultaneously squeeze both the hiring and firing decisions.

I have noted already that unionized employees are universally governed by a just-cause standard while nonunionized private employees generally are not.[210] One explanation for this difference is that unionized jobs are typically more routine or repetitive, thus making objective measures of performance easier and lowering the burden of showing cause. On the other hand, unions may demand regulation and rules precisely to facilitate objective evaluation of workers.[211] If objective evaluation is feasible, the problem of unverifiable shirking is reduced and the just-cause requirement becomes less burdensome for employers.

Finally, in considering what jobs fit the life-cycle model, we must recognize that the model may apply differently to female workers than to male workers because the career-employment pattern differs. For many women, the end of the life cycle is not the period of greatest vulnerability. Rather, their time of concern is the middle period, when many women leave the workforce temporarily to have children. A common employment pattern is for women to "prove themselves" by working hard early in their career in exchange for implicit promises that the employer will give them greater flexibility in early child-rearing years. Having performed their end of the bargain, women face the danger that an employer will behave opportunistically by dismissing them rather than giving them the promised flexibility. The law regulates these opportunistic firings under Title VII and other antidiscrimination laws. Although our general analysis against opportunistic firings applies to this situation, the common law rules we have analyzed apply more often and more cleanly to "traditional," that is male, life-cycle patterns.[212] Certainly, men have brought most of the leading life-cycle wrongful discharge cases.

B. *The Rise (and Fall?) of Career Employment*

If legal intervention at the end of the life cycle is so wise, a critical

there "would be pressure to loosen controls on discharge . . . as a practical response to the needs of the employer").

210. *See supra* Part II.

211. *See* Leslie, *supra* note 17, at 369-70.

212. *See generally* Kathryn Abrams, *Gender Discrimination and the Transformation of Workplace Norms*, 42 VAND. L. REV. 1183, 1221 (1989) (workplace norms "reflect their history as institutions shaped by and for men"); Martha Minow, *The Supreme Court, 1986 Term — Foreword: Justice Engendered*, 101 HARV. L. REV. 10, 41 (1987) (asking whether pregnancy leave violates equal treatment because it "treat[s] men as the norm and presume[s] a workplace designed for men (or nonpregnant persons)").

reader might ask, why did it take courts so long to get it? Or, alternatively, one might ask whether this sudden judicial rush to protect some workers suggests an unwise departure from the wisdom of the past. In response, I would emphasize that career employment is relatively recent in our economy, becoming common only after World War II. Thus, only in the last decade or two have employers and workers played out the end game of career employment. Therefore, courts have only recently had the opportunity to respond to opportunistic behavior at the end of the life cycle.

Certainly, career employment was less prominent fifty or seventy-five years ago. Henry Ford introduced his five-dollar-per-day pay in 1914 in large part to counter the phenomenal turnover in his River Rouge factory, which exceeded 2000% per year.[213] Much of the rise in career employment can be attributed to the growth of firm size and the increasing costs of employee turnover and lack of discipline.[214] Immigration and reverse migration before the 1920s delayed a sense of community and roots among workers, diminishing a desire for job security.[215] Not until after World War II did pensions — a key bonding feature of career employment — become prevalent. In short, until the last few decades few workers spent their lives in a single career employment.

Because of the recent rise in career employment, I need not dispute Richard Epstein's claim that at will was the optimal rule to regulate the employment relationship for much of this century.[216] Whether it was or not, times have changed, and the common law has changed with it. With the rise of career employment has come the life-cycle doctrine in employment law.

Some commentators suggest that career employment is becoming a thing of the past.[217] One bit of evidence for this claim is the decline in

213. *See* ALLAN NEVINS, FORD: THE TIMES, THE MAN, THE COMPANY 512-41 (1954); *supra* note 32.

214. *See* DOERINGER & PIORE, *supra* note 52; Victor P. Goldberg, *A Relational Exchange Perspective on the Employment Relationship, in* FIRMS, ORGANIZATION AND LABOUR 127 (Frank H. Stephen ed., 1984).

215. *See* Sanford M. Jacoby, *Industrial Labor Mobility in Historical Perspective*, 22 INDUS. REL. 261, 267 (1983) (between 1920 and 1950, workers gradually "became more attached to their employers" and "employers became more committed to their workforce"); Sanford M. Jacoby, *The New Institutionalism: What Can It Learn from the Old?*, 29 INDUS. REL. 316, 327 (1990) ("Workers born in the U.S. were more likely than mobile immigrants to value attachments to particular employers and communities.").

216. *See* Epstein, *supra* note 10.

217. *See* BENNETT HARRISON & BARRY BLUESTONE, THE GREAT U-TURN: CORPORATE RESTRUCTURING AND THE POLARIZING OF AMERICA (1988); RICHARD S. BELOUS, THE CONTINGENT ECONOMY: THE GROWTH OF THE TEMPORARY, PART-TIME AND SUBCONTRACTED WORKFORCE (1989).

pension coverage in the 1980s.[218] If life-cycle contracts decline in importance, one might expect parties to call on courts less frequently to enforce perceived opportunism. As career employment ebbs, so too may lawsuits ebb whose underlying theories rest on a breach of a long-term relationship.

Conclusion

The argument of this article has a classic form — it puts court decisions in an area of law into a framework and thereby declares them to have some coherence. In this case, the declaration is that courts, with their embryonic life-cycle doctrine, are reacting wisely to the issues litigants present to them. The life-cycle framework that courts have developed provides the parties in a career employment relationship a legal structure that checks opportunistic behavior. Its fundamental premise is that both employer and employees can act opportunistically. Consequently, a life-cycle analysis does not categorically condemn or celebrate employment at will. It supports, in broad outline, the contract law inroads that have been made on the at-will doctrine, particularly at the beginning and the end of an employee's career, and it explains the continued vitality of the at-will rule for mid-career employees. The current position of the courts is superior to a dogmatic insistence on the old at-will regime, which creates an excessive risk of opportunistic terminations for long-term, and sometimes beginning-career workers. Moreover, the current hesitant, intermediate position may also be superior to a general just-cause standard, which would lead to excessive shirking by midcareer workers.

The life-cycle framework therefore makes coherent the seemingly schizophrenic behavior by courts in employment termination cases. Within the framework, courts will protect employees when the danger of employer opportunism is high, but they will retain the at-will presumption when the employer is more vulnerable. One can thus argue that the courts are reacting appropriately to the employment-termination cases they encounter.

This coherence in the common law is internal to the system. In particular, it assumes that common law litigation is the chosen method of resolving these disputes, and that the courts largely do not consider the systemic costs of litigation. It may be preferable, all things considered, to opt for an administrative or arbitration system that requires just cause for all employment terminations. But it is unfair, in arguing

218. *See* David E. Bloom & Richard B. Freeman, *The Fall in Private Pension Coverage in the United States*, 82 Am. Econ. Rev., May 1992, at 539 (papers and proceedings documenting decline in pension coverage in 1980s).

for such a change, to portray the current common law as hopeless chaos. Far from being chaotic, the current common law provides optimal rules for regulating employment terminations.

[6]

Decent Work, Older Workers, and Vulnerability in the Economic Recession: A Comparative Study of Australia, the United Kingdom, and the United States

Susan Bisom-Rapp, Andrew Frazer and Malcolm Sargeant

I. INTRODUCTION

The International Labour Organization (ILO) has made "decent work" the cornerstone of its recommended strategy for recovery from the global economic crisis.[1] Launched in 1999, years before the recession,[2] the ILO's decent work agenda seeks for workers not only "the creation of jobs of acceptable quality"[3] but also protection "from the vulnerabilities and contingencies which take people out of work, whether these arise from unemployment, loss of livelihood, sickness or old age."[4]

This article is addressed to the final listed vulnerability – old age. In countries with aging populations, the global recession and its aftermath present unique challenges for older workers, and compels an assessment of how they are faring. To this end, the ILO's concept of decent work provides a useful metric or yardstick.[5] Decent work, a multifaceted concept, assists in revealing the interdependence of policy measures needed to secure human dignity across the course of working lives. With this in mind, in three English-speaking, common law countries – Australia, the United Kingdom (U.K.), and the United States (U.S.) – we consider several decent work principles applicable to older workers and provide evaluations in light of them. The three countries provide a useful comparison because all are "liberal market economies" with similarities in their patterns of labor

* Susan Bisom-Rapp is Professor of Law at Thomas Jefferson School of Law, San Diego, California (U.S.A.). Andrew Frazer is Senior Lecturer in the Faculty of Law, University of Wollongong, Wollongong, New South Wales (Australia). Malcolm Sargeant is Professor of Labour Law, Middlesex University Business School, London (United Kingdom). Susan Bisom-Rapp wishes to thank Abigail Kiernan, her research assistant, for excellent support. The authors wish to thank Mike Zimmer for comments on an earlier draft.

1. *See, e.g.*, International Labour Organization [ILO] Director-General, *Recovery and Growth with Decent Work* (2010), *available at* <http://www.ilo.org/wcmsp5/groups/public/---ed_norm/---relconf/documents/meetingdocument/wcms_140738.pdf> [hereinafter *Recovery and Growth*]; ILO Director-General, *Tackling the Global Jobs Crisis: Recovery through Decent Work Policies* (2009), *available at* <http://www.ilo.org/wcmsp5/groups/public/---ed_norm/---relconf/documents/meeting document/wcms_106162.pdf> [hereinafter *Decent Work Policies*]; RAYMOND TORRES, ET AL., INT'L INST. FOR LABOUR STUDIES, THE FINANCIAL AND ECONOMIC CRISIS: A DECENT WORK RESPONSE (2009), *available at* <http://www.ilo.org/public/libdoc/ilo/2009/109B09_59_engl.pdf> [hereinafter A DECENT WORK RESPONSE]; *see also* ILO, *Recovering From the Crisis: A Global Jobs Pact*, at 2 (June 19, 2009), *available at* <http://www.ilo.org/public/libdoc/ilo/2009/109B09_192_engl.pdf> ("Action must be guided by the Decent Work Agenda and commitments made by the ILO and its constituents in the 2008 Declaration on Social Justice for a Fair Globalization.").

2. *See* Francis Maupain, *New Foundation or New Façade? The ILO and the 2008 Declaration on Social Justice for a Fair Globalization*, 20 EUR. J. INT'L L. 823, 838-39 (2009).

3. ILO Director-General, *Report of the Director General: Decent Work* (1999), *available at* <http://www.oit.org/public/english/standards/relm/ilc/ilc87/rep-i.htm> [hereinafter *Decent Work*].

4. *Id.*

5. *See* Juan Somavia, *Older Workers and the Crisis: Towards an Integrated and Decent Work Perspective*, THE JOURNAL: AARP INT'L, Summer 2009, at 36.

regulation, though pursued through different forms and traditions.[6] Relevant to the analysis is the role workplace law plays in each country in ameliorating or exacerbating older worker vulnerability.

As initially articulated, decent work was an intentionally malleable construct, whose content remained purposefully vague.[7] The decent work agenda enumerated four pillars – fundamental rights at work, fostering employment, expanding and improving social protection, and promoting social dialogue[8] – but left it to national governments to determine their meaning.[9] In 2008, the Declaration on Social Justice for a Fair Globalization reaffirmed support for the four pillars, reordering them and declaring them "inseparable, interrelated and mutually supportive."[10] In other words, ILO members must, in order to implement the agenda, pursue these inseparable objectives simultaneously since inattention to any one jeopardizes achievement of the others.[11]

Reviewing the situation confronting older workers, however, three of the four objectives are especially pertinent: employment promotion, social protection, and fundamental rights. With respect to the first, Francis Maupain, former ILO legal advisor and key drafter of the 2008 Declaration, argues that member countries must foster conditions "for increasing the creation and development of work" in a way that enables individuals to benefit from "changing possibilities."[12] To gauge the present status of older

6. *See* VARIETIES OF CAPITALISM: THE INSTITUTIONAL FOUNDATIONS OF COMPARATIVE ADVANTAGE (Peter A. Hall & David Soskice eds., 2001); Juan C. Botero et al., *The Regulation of Labor*, 119 Q.J. ECON. 1339 (2004); Meredith Jones & Richard Mitchell, *Legal Origin, Legal Families and the Regulation of Labour in Australia*, *in* VARIETIES OF CAPITALISM, CORPORATE GOVERNANCE AND EMPLOYEES 60, 86 (Shelley Marshall et al. eds., 2008) [hereinafter *Legal Origin*]; (arguing that despite its very different history of interventionist regulation, labor conditions in Australia are closer to those in liberal market economies than co-ordinated market economics). For critiques of the "legal origins" literature regarding labor law see Beth Ahlering & Simon Deakin, *Labor Regulation, Corporate Governance and Legal Origin: A Case of Institutional Complementarity?* 41 LAW & SOC'Y REV. 865 (2007); David E. Pozen, *The Regulation of Labour and the Relevance of Legal Origin*, 28 COMP. LAB. L. & POL'Y J. 43 (2007).

7. *See* Maupain, *supra* note 2, at 838.

8. *See* Gillian MacNaughton & Diane F. Frey, *Decent Work, Human Rights, and the Millennium Development Goals*, 7 HASTINGS RACE & POVERTY L.J. 303, 316-17 (2010).

9. Maupain, *supra* note 2, at 838. The ILO, however, has conducted significant research into and discussion of the methods by which member states can measure progress toward achieving decent work. *See, e.g.*, ILO Tripartite Meeting of Experts on the Measurement of Decent Work, Geneva, Switz., Sept. 8-10, 2008, *Measurement of Decent Work: Discussion Paper for the Tripartite Meeting of Experts on the Measurement of Decent Work*, TMEMDW-R-[2008-08-0062-1]-En.doc/v2 (2008), *available at* <http://www.ilo.org/wcmsp5/groups/public/---dgreports/---integration/---stat/documents/meetingdocument/wcms_100335.pdf>.

10. McNaughton & Frey, *supra* note 8, at 321. The order of the objectives as set forth in the 2008 Declaration is: employment promotion; social protection; social dialogue; and fundamental rights. *Id.*

11. Maupain, *supra* note 2, at 838.

12. *Id.* at 834.

workers vis-à-vis this objective, we review data from Australia, the U.K., and the U.S. on employment, unemployment, and other measures of economic health or hardship, such as underemployment and worker discouragement. We also consider the extent of legal job security protection in each country, protections which might forestall rising unemployment and facilitate greater employment and income opportunities.

Regarding the second objective, ILO members have agreed, via the 2008 Declaration, to pursue measures of social protection – including sufficient unemployment insurance and income security in old age[13] – which minimize the effects of unpredictable and traumatic events such as the global recession.[14] This system of "positive social protection," also called "dynamic security," requires creating an environment whereby workers obtain "a fair share of the benefits of progress."[15] In assessing the condition of older workers with respect to this goal, we review information on retirement security and unemployment benefits.

Finally, on fundamental rights, this article is most concerned with the elimination of discrimination.[16] The status of the prohibition on age discrimination as a fundamental right is unclear.[17] International human rights instruments, including the ILO's fundamental anti-discrimination instruments, Convention No. 111 (Discrimination (Employment and Occupation)) and Convention No. 100 (Equal Remuneration), do not expressly list age as a prohibited basis for differentiation.[18] Yet age has been identified as an emerging new ground, and countries, including Australia, have in their adoption of Convention No. 111 added age as a prohibited basis via Article 1(1)(b) of that convention.[19] To address the issue of age discrimination, this article reviews the legal protections against age bias in each of the three countries profiled.

13. *See* ILO Gender Promotion Programme, *Realizing Decent Work for Older Women Workers*, at 9 (2000), *available at* <http://natlex.ilo.ch/wcmsp5/groups/public/---dgreports/---gender/documents/publication/wcms_079196.pdf> [hereinafter *Decent Work for Older Women Workers*] ("Decent work . . . leads to basic security in old age and adversity."); Somavia, *supra* note 5, at 39.

14. Maupain, *supra* note 2, at 835.

15. *Id.*

16. *See* Int'l Labour Conference, Declaration on Fundamental Principles and Rights at Work, International Labour Organisation [ILO], 37 I.L.M. 1233 (June 18, 1998) [hereinafter 1998 Declaration].

17. *See* Monika Schlachter, General Report to the XVIIIth International Congress of Comparative Law: The Prohibition of Age Discrimination in Labour Relations 4-5 (July 25-Aug. 1, 2010) (on file with author).

18. *Id.* at 4; *see also Decent Work for Older Women Workers*, *supra* note 13, at 37 ("Currently there exists no legally binding universal instrument calling for national policies to eliminate and outlaw discrimination in access to employment, training and work conditions on the grounds of age.").

19. *Decent Work for Older Women Workers*, *supra* note 13, at 38.

In short, this article gauges how each of the three countries performed during the economic crisis in terms of employment promotion, social protection, and fundamental rights, with a particular focus on older workers. Although the recession affected each country to a different extent, and the response of national employers to the crisis varied significantly, the effects of the financial crisis on older workers are strikingly similar. The recession has affected the quality of work for older workers; for many, employment has become more fragile, inconstant, and insecure. Additionally, in all three nations, the recession compromised older workers' ability to plan for and secure a key decent work precept, a dignified retirement.

Greater national differences emerge when evaluating labor regulation affecting older workers. While all three countries prohibit age discrimination to varying degrees, during an economic crisis such prohibitions do not sufficiently contribute to employment security for older workers. General labor standards, like those restricting termination and layoff or requiring severance pay, and the provision of a robust safety net, are just as important in forestalling older worker vulnerability. While none of the three countries pursues its labor market policy with an eye toward achieving decent work, by using that ILO concept as a touchstone, and looking broadly at the intersecting factors that contribute to older worker insecurity, the outlines of needed policy reforms become clear. In particular, we conclude that market principles are a poor mechanism for pursuing decent work for older workers, a fact apparent in the U.S., for example, as the effects of the crisis have continued even though the recession technically ended in June 2009.

Before undertaking country-specific analyses, one should note that older worker employment has been growing in all three countries, though the increase over the last decade has been more notable in Australia and the U.K. than in the U.S. For example, in 1999, the percentage of the older population (ages fifty-five to sixty-four) in employment was in Australia, the U.K., and the U.S., respectively: 44.3, 49.4, and 57.7.[20] By 2009, the percentages in Australia, the U.K., and the U.S., respectively, had risen to: 59.0 (+14.7), 57.5 (+8.1), and 60.6 (+2.9).[21] Thus, all three countries at the present time have comparable rates of older workers engaged actively in work.

20. *See How Do OECD Labour Markets Perform?*, OECD, <http://www.oecd.org/document/22/0,3343,en_2649_39023495_43221014_1_1_1_1,00.html> (last updated Jul. 6, 2010) (scroll to "employment to population ratios" table, second on the page).

21. *Id.*

Also noticeable, however, are dramatic differences in the overall unemployment rates of the three countries and their changes over time. Turning to 1999, the unemployment rates in Australia, the U.K., and the U.S., respectively, were: 7.0, 6.0, and 4.3.[22] In 2009, the rates for Australia, the U.K., and the U.S. were: 5.7 (-1.3), 7.8 (+1.8), and 9.4 (+5.1).[23] Thus, while the global economic crisis affected all three countries, it affected U.S. workers much more severely in terms of job loss. To better understand why this is so and the particular conditions of older workers, this article continues in three discrete sections. Part II covers Australia, Part III describes conditions for older workers in the U.K., and Part IV reviews the U.S. The article concludes with Part V, which briefly reviews the decent work lessons gleaned from the economic downturn.

II. AUSTRALIA

From the mid-1990s until 2009, Australia experienced its longest-ever period of sustained economic growth, fuelled in large part by minerals exports to the growing Asian economies.[24] The Australian economy was virtually unaffected by the East Asian economic crisis of the late 1990s and the mild global downturn of the early 2000s. Between 2003 and 2007, Australia's economy clearly showed a new trajectory. Previously, the country's economic fortunes followed closely those of the western economies, particularly the U.S. However with the persistence of high growth, the view became widespread that Australia's economy had become "decoupled" from the western economies and was now strongly allied with East Asian growth. By 2006-07 sustained growth reached a point where capacity constraints became apparent, as infrastructure and investment were unable to meet the potential for growth. Between 2006 and 2008, the official unemployment rate fell from 4.6 percent to 3.9 percent, the lowest for thirty years and considered to be below the effective rate for full employment.[25] Reports of labor shortages became widespread in many

22. *Id.* (scroll to "unemployment rates and long-term unemployment" table, first on the page).

23. *Id.*

24. Australia's economy ranks as the thirteenth largest in the world, despite having a population of twenty-two million and a labor force of eleven million. See *GDP (current US$)*, THE WORLD BANK, <http://data.worldbank.org/indicator/NY.GDP.MKTP.CD> (last viewed Mar. 4, 2011).

25. Alison Preston & Therese Jefferson, *Labour Markets and Wages in 2008*, 51 J. INDUS. REL. 313, 315 (2008). The non-accelerating-inflation rate of unemployment (NAIRU), the highest rate at which unemployment is supposed to occur without producing inflation, is currently estimated to be between 4.5 percent and 5 percent for Australia. *See* Steven Kennedy et al., *Examining Full Employment in Australia Using the Phillips and Beveridge Curves*, 41 AUSTL. ECON. REV. 286 (2008); G.C. Lim et al., *Phillips Curve and the Equilibrium Unemployment Rate*, 85 ECON. RECORD 371, 376 (2009).

industries, and inflation began to rise.[26] Governments and business gave increased attention to the need for more effective training schemes to meet the need for skilled labor.

The boom led to appreciation of the need for more effective workforce utilization, with attention being given to measures for increasing participation by older workers through delayed retirement and part-time work. The earlier publication of the Australian Treasury's *Intergenerational Reports* from 2002 onward[27] had brought the economic and social consequences of an aging population into public focus. While Australia's population is aging, this is happening more slowly than in comparable countries.[28] The age profile of Australia's population has been moderated by a historically high and increasing migration intake, drawn mainly from younger ages, and a rise in the domestic birth rate over the last decade.[29]

Although Australia actually has a less age-skewed population profile than most other developed countries, the effect in particular of an aging workforce in reducing long-term labor force supply and participation prompted government and employer organizations to focus on the need for policies to increase employment participation among older workers by delaying retirement and greater use of part-time work.[30] Employers were repeatedly told from many quarters about the need to dismantle informal barriers preventing the hiring and retention of older workers in order to meet the anticipated gap in labor supply.[31] However it was only with the labor shortage that age discrimination as a barrier to increased participation received close attention by policy-makers, with government and industry

26. Harry Perlich, *The Impact of the GFC on Australia as a "Dual Economy"*, J. AUSTL. POL. ECON., Dec. 2009, at 65, 73-78.

27. COMMONWEALTH OF AUSTL., INTERGENERATIONAL REPORT 2002-03 (2002), *available at* <http://www.budget.gov.au/2002-03/bp5/download/BP5_Combined_PDF.zip>. Since then, two further reports have been published: COMMONWEALTH OF AUSTL., INTERGENERATIONAL REPORT 2007 (2007), *available at* <http://www.treasury.gov.au/documents/1239/PDF/IGR_2007_final_report.pdf>; and COMMONWEALTH OF AUSTL., AUSTRALIA TO 2050: FUTURE CHALLENGES (2010), *available at* <http://www.treasury.gov.au/igr/igr2010/report/pdf/IGR_2010.pdf>; *see also* PRODUCTIVITY COMM'N, COMMONWEALTH OF AUSTL., ECONOMIC IMPLICATIONS OF AN AGEING AUSTRALIA: PRODUCTIVITY COMMISSION RESEARCH REPORT (2005), *available at* <http://www.pc.gov.au/__data/assets/pdf_file/0020/69401/ageing.pdf>.

28. *See* Maggie Walter et al., *Keeping Australia's Older Workers in the Labour Force: A Policy Perspective*, 43 AUSTL. J. SOC. ISSUES 291, 292 (2008).

29. See ACCESS ECON. PTY LTD., ACT AND REGION DEMOGRAPHICS AND TRENDS ii-iii, 3-5, 12-15 (2007), *available at* <http://www.cmd.act.gov.au/__data/assets/pdf_file/0009/119718/act-region-demographics-trends.pdf> (reporting on the population trends for the Australian Capital Territory and Australia as a whole).

30. Walter et al., *supra* note 28, at 292.

31. Derek Parker, *Skills Shortage: Crisis Ahead*, MGMT. TODAY, Aug. 2004, at 26-29; Walter et al., *supra* note 28.

programs being developed to promote recognition of the value of older workers among employers.[32] Employers now realized that retaining and retraining older workers was one of the most important ways of overcoming skill shortages.[33]

At the same time, November 2007 saw the election of a Labor government at the national level, one committed to the reintroduction of protective and collectivist labor legislation as well as interventionist industry policy and investment directed at "nation building" projects.[34] The new government was elected on a promise to dismantle the "WorkChoices" legislation which the conservative Howard government had implemented in 2006.[35] The conservative legislation had been designed to reduce both collective bargaining and the system of awards which set minimum wages and conditions across industries.[36] This legislation also significantly undermined the federal unfair dismissal provisions, implemented in 1994 and the only significant legal measure providing job protection. Up to 80 percent of the workforce was excluded from the coverage of the unfair dismissal legislation, while for the remainder of the workforce redundancies, known in the U.S. as "layoffs," were made significantly easier to implement as employers could remove workers simply by citing "operational reasons" for their retrenchment.[37]

The WorkChoices legislation began to be removed by a transitional system introduced by the Labor government in March 2008. It was followed by the *Fair Work Act 2009* which reinstated award protections against reduction of wages and conditions, while restoring coverage of the unfair dismissal provisions.[38] While some of the reforms had been implemented by transitional legislation which came into force at the end of 2008, the reintroduction of unfair dismissal and award protection did not commence until January 2010. However, the changes were publicized well in advance and may be regarded as having operated *de facto* from at least the middle of 2009, particularly as enforcement of labor standards had

32. Parker, *supra* note 31; Walter et al., *supra* note 28.

33. AUSTL. INDUS. GRP., SKILLING THE EXISTING WORKFORCE: FINAL PROJECT REPORT 7-8 (2008), *available at* <http://www.aigroup.com.au/portal/binary/com.epicentric.contentmanagement.servlet.ContentDeliveryServlet/LIVE_CONTENT/Publications/Reports/2008/skilling_existing_workforce.pdf>.

34. Andrew Stewart & Anthony Forsyth, *The Journey from Work Choices to Fair Work*, *in* FAIR WORK: THE NEW WORKPLACE LAWS AND THE WORK CHOICES LEGACY 1, 7-8 (Anthony Forsyth & Andrew Stewart eds., 2009).

35. *Id.* at 2-8.

36. *Id.* at 3-6.

37. *Id.* at 4.

38. Carolyn Sutherland, *Industrial Legislation in 2008*, 51 J. INDUS. REL. 297 (2009); Stewart & Forsyth, *supra* note 34, at 8-13.

already been strengthened by changes to legislation and policy since 2007.[39]

A. The Australian Economy and the Recession

The emergence of the global financial crisis in mid-2008 therefore came at a time when Australia could not have been better placed to respond. The financial crisis was initially anticipated as likely to have a major impact on employment and living standards in Australia, with consequent increase in demand for government social services and assistance by charities.[40] Public expectations of economic performance and consumer spending declined markedly in the second half of 2008, and while spending had largely recovered by the middle of 2009, public perceptions remained pessimistic until the end of the year, particularly among older Australians.[41] In 2008, economists were conservatively predicting that the unemployment rate would increase to 5.4 percent in 2009 and over 6 percent in 2010.[42]

The financial crisis produced a brief economic downturn, with negative growth in late 2008 followed by low growth (1 percent) in 2009.[43] So, technically, Australia did not experience a recession, although the rapid slowing of growth affected many businesses and families. The decline in equity prices reduced the wealth of Australian households by nearly 10 percent by March 2009.[44] In one survey conducted in mid-2009, 43 percent of working respondents aged fifty-five and over reported that they were worse off financially compared with a year before.[45] Construction activity

39. Tess Hardy, *A Changing of the Guard: Enforcement of Workplace Relations Laws Since Work Choices and Beyond*, *in* FAIR WORK, *supra* note 34, at 75; Tess Hardy & John Howe, *Partners in Enforcement? The New Balance Between Government and Trade Union Enforcement of Employment Standards in Australia*, 22 AUSTL. J. LAB. L. 306 (2009).

40. ACCESS ECONOMICS, THE IMPACT OF THE GLOBAL FINANCIAL CRISIS ON SOCIAL SERVICES IN AUSTRALIA (2008), *available at* <http://www.accesseconomics.com.au/publicationsreports/getreport.php?report=183&id=235>.

41. COMMONWEALTH BANK, VIEWPOINT: ECONOMIC VITALITY REPORT, Sept. 2010, at 5-6.

42. CONSENSUS ECONOMICS, ASIA-PACIFIC CONSENSUS FORECASTS, Nov. 2008; ACCESS ECONOMICS, *supra* note 40, at 11.

43. *See Statistical Tables: Output and Labour: Gross Domestic Product - G10*, RESERVE BANK OF AUSTL., <http://www.rba.gov.au/statistics/tables/xls/g10hist.xls?accessed=0803-09:02:30> (last viewed Mar. 7, 2011).

44. AUSTL. BUREAU OF STATISTICS, 2009-10: YEAR BOOK AUSTRALIA 687 (2010) [hereinafter 2009-10: YEAR BOOK AUSTRALIA], *available at* <http://www.ausstats.abs.gov.au/Ausstats/subscriber.nsf/0/AC72C92B23B6DF6DCA257737001B2BAB/$File/13010_2009_10.pdf>; Paul Bloxham & Thomas Betts, Reserve Bank of Austl., *The Composition and Distribution of Household Wealth in Australia*, RESERVE BANK BULLETIN, Apr. 2009, at 13, *available at* <http://www.rba.gov.au/publications/bulletin/2009/apr/pdf/bu-0409-2.pdf>.

45. Kate O'Loughlin et al., *Impact of the Global Financial Crisis on Employed Australian Baby Boomers: A National Survey*, 29 AUSTRALASIAN J. AGEING 88, 91 (2010) (calculated from tables 1 and

slowed considerably, however the economy as a whole experienced only a mild downturn. This was due to a combination of prompt economic stimulus by the federal government, sustained resource export demand, and only mild falls in consumer sentiment.

While job vacancies began to decline in the latter part of 2008, unemployment did not begin to rise until the following year. Official unemployment rates rose from 4.2 percent in May 2008 to a peak of 5.8 percent in August 2009, falling to 5.2 percent in May 2010.[46] This compared most favorably with an official unemployment rate of 10.5 percent at the peak of the previous recession in February 1993.[47] The overall employment rate (percentage of civilian population employed) declined from 64.5 percent at the end of 2008 to 63.1 percent in mid-2009, with a very slight pick-up in 2010.[48] By July 2009, employment was again rising, and it was appearing that the worst of the downturn had been weathered. However underemployment, gauged by labor utilization rates, increased more substantially from 8.9 percent in May 2008 to 11.5 percent in February 2010.[49]

A key reason for the subdued rise in unemployment was a shift from full-time to part-time employment. Not only were most new jobs created during 2008-09 part-time, but part-time work replaced full-time work.[50]

2).

46. *See* AUSTL. BUREAU OF STATISTICS, 6202.0, LABOUR FORCE AUSTRALIA: MAY 2010, at 1, *available at* <http://www.ausstats.abs.gov.au/ausstats/meisubs.nsf/0/CBB5B08A0F9DF57FCA25773D00184AB4/$File/62020_may%202010.pdf>.

47. *See* AUST'L BUREAU OF STATISTICS, 6202.0 LABOUR FORCE AUSTRALIA: DECEMBER 1994 at 10 tbl 5 (seasonally adjusted revised estimate for February 1993) *at* <http://www.abs.gov.au/AUSSTATS/abs@.nsf/DetailsPage/6202.0Dec%201994?OpenDocument.>.

48. These figures were calculated by the authors using data from *GM1 – Labour Force Status and Gross Changes (flows) by Sex, State, Age*. The data can be downloaded from *6202.0 – Labour Force, Australia, May 2010*, AUSTL. BUREAU OF STATISTICS (Oct. 6, 2010, 11:30 AM), <http://www.abs.gov.au/AUSSTATS/abs@.nsf/DetailsPage/6202.0May%202010?OpenDocument> (scroll to the bottom of the page and select the "GM1 – Labour Force Status and Gross Changes (flows) by Sex, State, Age" .srd file).

49. CTR. OF FULL EMP'T AND EQUITY, UNIV. OF NEWCASTLE, LABOUR UNDERUTILISATION 1-2 (May 2010), *available at* <http://e1.newcastle.edu.au/coffee/pubs/CLMI/2010/CLMI_total_May_2010.pdf>.

50. *See, e.g.*, AUSTL. BUREAU OF STATISTICS, 6202.0, LABOUR FORCE AUSTRALIA: JANUARY 2008, at 1 (Feb. 14, 2008), *available at* <http://www.ausstats.abs.gov.au/Ausstats/subscriber.nsf/0/C60CAE877261455CCA2573EE0018F63E/$File/62020_jan%202008.pdf> (reporting a monthly decrease in full-time employment of 7800 but an increase in part-time employment by 34,600); AUSTL. BUREAU OF STATISTICS, 6202.0, LABOUR FORCE AUSTRALIA: DECEMBER 2008, at 1 (Jan. 15, 2009), *available at* <http://www.ausstats.abs.gov.au/Ausstats/subscriber.nsf/0/81BA0B35D2A2009BCA25753E00136A35/$File/62020_dec%202008.pdf> (reporting a monthly decrease in full-time employment of 43,900 and an increase in part-time employment of 42,800); AUSTL. BUREAU OF STATISTICS, 6202.0, LABOUR FORCE AUSTRALIA: DECEMBER 2009, at 1 (Jan. 14, 2010) [hereinafter LABOUR FORCE AUSTRALIA: DECEMBER 2009], *available at* <http://www.ausstats.abs.gov.au/ausstats/meisubs.nsf/0/3D60FEAFC4F51E5BCA2576AA001256B5/$File/62020_Dec 2009.pdf> (reporting a monthly increase in full-time employment of 7300 but an increase in part-time employment 27,900).

Aggregate monthly hours worked in full-time employment fell by 3.3 percent between 2008 and 2009, while the decline in part-time hours was only 2.5 percent.[51] However this was only a short-lived change: when the economy rebounded in 2010, full-time hours increased by 3.4 percent while hours worked part-time rose by only 2.6 percent.[52] With the downturn expected to be short-lived, employer associations and consultants were widely reported as advising employers not to cut their workforces or else they would again face labor shortages when the downturn ended.[53] There were strong anecdotal reports that, rather than lose skilled workers, employers were reducing the hours worked. Many workplaces adopted the unusual approach of moving to a four-day week or shorter working days.[54] However a substantial part of the shift to part-time employment appears to have been the result of full-time workers being replaced by part-time or casual workers. This also produced a shift in the gender balance, with a net gain of jobs for women.[55]

Survey research suggests that the decline in hours worked (2.3 percent between June 2008 and July 2009) was due more to a reduction in movement from part-time to full-time work as the economy slowed than to a downgrading of jobs from full-time to part-time. Workers seeking jobs with greater hours were less likely to find them, while new job-takers were more likely to find part-time than full-time employment.[56]

Another significant factor which has been proposed is an increase in

51. *See* LABOUR FORCE AUSTRALIA: DECEMBER 2009, *supra* note 50, at 4.

52. *See* AUSTL. BUREAU OF STATISTICS, 6202.0, LABOUR FORCE AUSTRALIA: MAY 2010, at 3 (June 10, 2010), *available at* <http://www.ausstats.abs.gov.au/ausstats/meisubs.nsf/0/CBB5B08A0F9DF57FCA25773D00184AB4/$File/62020_may%202010.pdf>. Part-time workers as a proportion of all employed persons rose from 28.4 percent in May 2008, to 29.3 percent in May 2009, and 29.7 percent in May 2010. *See* AUSTL. BUREAU OF STATISTICS, 6105.0, AUSTRALIAN LABOUR MARKET STATISTICS: JULY 2010, at 34 tbl.1.1 (July 16, 2010) [hereinafter LABOUR MARKET STATISTICS: JULY 2010], *available at* <http://www.ausstats.abs.gov.au/Ausstats/subscriber.nsf/0/549DB4631937A23DCA2577610014F952/$File/61050_july%202010.pdf> (providing the raw figures for the numbers employed full-time, part-time, and both). Part-time work is defined as normally working less than thirty-five hours per week. *Id.* at 99.

53. *See* MERCER, WORKPLACE 2012: BEYOND THE GLOBAL FINANCIAL CRISIS 2, 8, 11 (2008), *available at* <http://www.mercer.com.au/attachment.dyn?idContent= 1329160&filePath=/attachments/English/Mercer_Au_Workplace2012_ResearchReportUpdate_Dec08.pdf> (recommending that employers work to retain older workers to counteract skills shortages).

54. Media Release, Australian Chamber of Commerce and Industry, Labour Market Flexibility Curtails Job Losses (Aug. 6, 2009) (on file with authors).

55. Guay C. Lim et al., *Review of the Australian Economy 2009-10: On the Road to Recovery*, 43 AUSTL. ECON. REV. 1, 5-6 (2010); Guay C. Lim et al., *Review of the Australian Economy 2008-09: Recessions, Retrenchments and Risks*, 42 AUSTL. ECON. REV. 1, 7 (2009).

56. Bruce Bradbury, *Are Employers Using Part-Time Work to Hang onto their Workers?*, CLUB TROPPO (Aug. 12, 2009, 12:15 PM), <http://clubtroppo.com.au/2009/08/12/are-employers-using-part-time-work-to-hang-onto-their-workers/>.

workers taking paid leave.[57] When the financial crisis began, employers were advised to pressure workers into taking paid leave.[58] Since workers in Australia (particularly older workers, who are more likely to be in secure jobs with leave entitlements) tend to hoard their paid leave as a form of insurance against redundancy,[59] or layoff, the taking of paid leave represents a reduction of wealth by such workers and a decline in their longer-term income security.

The effect of the financial crisis on the labor force generally in Australia was therefore limited. The greatest effects were a decline in youth employment as new entry positions dried up, a reduction in average hours worked (particularly for full-time workers), and a shift in employment levels from full-time to part-time work.[60] The latter two effects actually improved the employment chances of older workers, who are more likely to work part-time;[61] however this was at the cost of lower incomes and underemployment for many.

B. Older Workers Employment and Participation Rates

In common with other industrialized countries, older workers in Australia have experienced an increase in employment and participation in the last two decades, with increasing proportions in work, higher levels of hours worked and later average retirement ages. During the economic boom, participation rates for older workers in Australia increased at higher rates than for younger age groups (which had neared effective full employment), and this continued through the economic crisis. Labor force participation rates for older workers actually increased during 2008-09. Using the May quarter for each year (March-May), the average employment rate (labor force as a percentage of the civilian population) increased marginally for older age groups while declining slightly for younger ages.

57. BRIGID VAN WANROOY ET AL, AUSTRALIA AT WORK: IN A CHANGING WORLD 36 (Workplace Research Ctr., Univ. of Sydney, 2009), *available at* <http://sydney.edu.au/documents/future_students/1259186125-australia-at-work-in-a-changing-world.pdf>.

58. *See id.*

59. *See id.*

60. Michael Plumb et al, , *The Labour Market during the 2008-2009 Downturn*, RESERVE BANK BULLETIN, March 2010, at 2-3, 5, *available at* <http://www.rba.gov.au/publications/bulletin/2010/mar/pdf/bu-0310-1.pdf>.

61. AUSTL. BUREAU OF STATISTICS, 4102.0, AUSTRALIAN SOCIAL TRENDS SEPTEMBER 2010: OLDER PEOPLE AND THE LABOUR MARKET 1-2 (2010) [hereinafter OLDER PEOPLE AND THE LABOR MARKET], *available at* <http://www.ausstats.abs.gov.au/ausstats/subscriber.nsf/LookupAttach/4102.0Publication29.09.104/$File/41020_OlderWorkers.pdf>.

Table 1

Employment Rate by Age, May Quarter:
Labor Force as a Percent of Civilian Population[62]

Age Group	May 2007 Qtr	May 2008 Qtr	May 2009 Qtr	May 2010 Qtr
20-24	78.4	78.6	75.8	75.0
25-44	80.3	81.1	79.8	79.1
45-54	80.5	81.2	80.7	80.7
55-64	57.4	57.6	59.9	60.9
65+	8.8	9.7	10.9	11.1
all ages	63.5	64.3	63.5	63.2

This has been attributed to workers deciding to stay in the workforce longer in response to their shrinking retirement savings.[63] However the increase was in keeping with strong growth in employment participation by older workers which began earlier in the decade. The age-related changes in employment participation in Australia over the period of the recession are associated more with longer term changes in labor demand and attitudes of older workers than with fluctuations caused by economic downturn. Employment participation by older male workers has been increasing since the 1990s, reversing a previous trend towards earlier retirement.[64]

One explanation for this change is that the destruction of low-qualification "blue collar" male jobs which began in the early 1980s reached its nadir and was eclipsed by the improved availability of jobs for older workers (as the youth workforce fell proportionately) in combination with government policies aimed at increasing incentives to work longer.[65]

62. These figures were calculated by the authors using data from *GM1 – Labour Force Status and Gross Changes (flows) by Sex, State, Age*. The data can be downloaded from *6202.0 – Labour Force, Australia, July 2010*, AUSTL. BUREAU OF STATISTICS (Aug. 12, 2010, 11:30 AM), <http://www.abs.gov.au/AUSSTATS/abs@.nsf/DetailsPage/6202.0Jul%202010?OpenDocument> (scroll to the bottom of the page and select the "GM1 – Labour Force Status and Gross Changes (flows) by Sex, State, Age" .srd file).

63. AUSTL. BUREAU OF STATISTICS, 6202.0, LABOUR FORCE AUSTRALIA: JULY 2010, at 4 (Aug. 12, 2010), *available at* <http://www.ausstats.abs.gov.au/ausstats/meisubs.nsf/0/99D0F 2ED2D274087CA25777C001734CC/$File/62020_jul%202010.pdf>.

64. *See* OLDER PEOPLE AND THE LABOR MARKET, *supra* note 61, at 1.

65. Michael Keating, *Increasing Labour Force Participation*, *in* COMM. FOR ECON. DEVELOPMENT OF AUSTL., GROWTH 51: AUSTRALIA'S AGEING POPULATION 66 (2004).

For older men, the improvement in job fortunes since the beginning of this century has involved a sharp rise in full-time participation; part-time employment for this group has been increasing at a steadier but much slower rate.[66] It appears that these changes are associated with shifting attitudes towards working patterns by the "baby boomer" generation, who tend to have longer participation in work (though at lower overall participation rates) than predecessor generations.[67]

The greatest change in participation by older workers, however, has been among older female workers. This shift appears to be a long-term change, rather than one associated with a particular birth cohort or short-term economic impact: employment participation by women is increasing for all ages, but the increase is strongest among older age groups who have traditionally had the lowest levels of participation.[68] This change may itself be a reflection of vulnerability as older women have had relatively low income security in the form of accrued benefits and savings as a result of low participation in paid employment over the life-course. The "added worker effect" may also be involved, as older women take up jobs to replace the income of other household members who have lost work.[69] During the recession, part-time jobs replaced full-time jobs to some extent; and, because women workers predominate in the part-time job market, opportunities increased for women – including those seeking to replace the income lost by unemployed male partners.

Over the period of the economic crisis, the most significant short-term increase in participation has been among women aged sixty to sixty-four: between 2007 and 2010 their participation rate climbed from 46 percent to 52 percent, an increase of 12 percent.[70] Within the sixty to sixty-four age groups, women took up work at double the rate for men and accounted for over half the increase in employment.[71] Within the fifty-five to fifty-nine

66. Steven Kennedy & Alicia Da Costa, *Older Men Bounce Back: The Re-Emergence of Older Male Workers*, AUSTL. TREASURY ECON. ROUNDUP, Spring 2006, at 32, 34, *available at* <http://www.treasury.gov.au/documents/1190/PDF/Economic_Roundup_Spring_2006.pdf>.

67. *Id.* at 39.

68. *Id.* at 36.

69. The "added worker effect" is not considered to be very strong in Australia. PRODUCTIVITY COMM'N, *supra* note 27, at 55.

70. Calculated from data on Labour Force Status by Social Marital Status, Age, and Sex, available for download from *6291.0.55.001 – Labour Force, Australia, Detailed – Electronic Delivery, Jun 2010*, AUSTL. BUREAU OF STATISTICS, <http://www.abs.gov.au/AUSSTATS/abs@.nsf/DetailsPage/6291.0.55.001Jun%202010?OpenDocument> (last updated Aug. 18, 2010) (scroll to Time Series Spreadsheets and select "Table 01. Labour force status by Social marital status, Age and Sex" to download either the .xls or .zip file) (using May quarter averages).

71. Calculated from data on Labour Force Status by Social Marital Status, Age, and Sex, available for download from *6291.0.55.001 – Labour Force, Australia, Detailed – Electronic Delivery, Jun 2010*, AUSTL. BUREAU OF STATISTICS, <http://www.abs.gov.au/AUSSTATS/abs@.nsf/DetailsPage/6291.

age group, employment rose by 9 percent, with women making up two-thirds of the increase.[72] Women now comprise 44 percent of the employed in the fifty-five to sixty-four age cohort.[73] In Australia, as in the U.K., the relatively strong employment participation of older workers, both during the recession and over the longer term, is due largely to increasing participation by older women in part-time employment.

C. Part-Time, Self-Employment, and Atypical Work

Other measures of employment vulnerability reveal few short-term changes among *employed* older workers in Australia which can be attributed to the recession. Although part-time employment increased overall at the expense of full-time jobs, there were only slight age-related variations in the part-time employment rate (as a percentage of all employed); nor were there any significant gender differences in the rate changes, although the differences between men and women remained substantial. The short-term changes were most noticeable for younger age groups, although there were significant increases in part-time employment rates among men aged sixty to sixty-four and women aged forty-five to fifty-four.[74] However these variations are most likely associated with longer-term patterns.

Older Australians are working part-time at increasing rates. This is a long-term trend towards a more gradual transition to retirement, particularly among older men (older women have long been concentrated

0.55.001Jun%202010?OpenDocument> (last updated Aug. 18, 2010) (scroll to Time Series Spreadsheets and select "Table 01. Labour force status by Social marital status, Age and Sex" to download either the .xls or .zip file) (using May quarter averages).

72. Calculated from data on Labour Force Status by Social Marital Status, Age, and Sex, available for download from *6291.0.55.001 – Labour Force, Australia, Detailed – Electronic Delivery, Jun 2010*, AUSTL. BUREAU OF STATISTICS, <http://www.abs.gov.au/AUSSTATS/abs@.nsf/DetailsPage/6291.0.55.001Jun%202010?OpenDocument> (last updated Aug. 18, 2010) (scroll to Time Series Spreadsheets and select "Table 01. Labour force status by Social marital status, Age and Sex" to download either the .xls or .zip file) (using May quarter averages).

73. Calculated from data on Labour Force Status by Social Marital Status, Age, and Sex, available for download from *6291.0.55.001 – Labour Force, Australia, Detailed – Electronic Delivery, Jun 2010*, AUSTL. BUREAU OF STATISTICS, <http://www.abs.gov.au/AUSSTATS/abs@.nsf/DetailsPage/6291.0.55.001Jun%202010?OpenDocument> (last updated Aug. 18, 2010) (scroll to Time Series Spreadsheets and select "Table 01. Labour force status by Social marital status, Age and Sex" to download either the .xls or .zip file) (using May quarter averages).

74. These figures were calculated by the authors using data from *GM1 – Labour Force Status and Gross Changes (flows) by Sex, State, Age*, *supra* note 62. Between the May 2007 and May 2010 quarters, the part-time employment rate for prime-age men the rate fell very slightly (staying at around 7 percent for thirty-five to forty-four-year olds and 9 percent for forty-five to fifty-four-year olds). For older men aged sixty to sixty-four the part-time employment rate rose from 23.8 percent to 24.6 percent. Among women workers, part-time employment increased from 41.8 percent to 42.6 percent for women aged forty-five to fifty-four, but there were no significant changes for other age groups. *Id.*

in part-time work).[75] This trend toward part-time work has been developing over the last decade and is associated with higher labor force participation rates by older workers.[76] Most of this trend is voluntary: involuntary part-time employment declines with age from age fifty-five onwards and comprises less than one-quarter of such older workers.[77] An increasing proportion of older workers are deliberately moving into semi-retirement, taking part-time work to supplement their retirement savings and pensions. The economic crisis does not appear to have contributed to this shift to part-time work. However the shift towards part-time work is a sign of increased vulnerability among older workers. In Australia, part-time jobs tend also to be casual in status, and casual jobs are considerably more precarious than permanent ones: casual workers have no paid annual or sick leave and low job security; they also tend to be paid less than permanent workers. Over 58 percent of all part-time jobs have no paid leave entitlements, the usual definition of a casual job in Australia.[78] We should not assume, however, that casual status is invariably associated with precarious tenure. Casual status is a legal construct, the result of the award system, and about half of all casual workers are employed in ongoing positions with stable wages.[79] Older casual workers in particular tend to spend longer periods with their current employer than younger age groups.[80] However by comparison with the job security associated with full-time permanent employment, the shift to part-time casual work

75. John Spoehr et al., Australian Institute for Social Research, Experience Works: The Mature-Age Employment Challenge 5 (2009), *available at* <http://www.productiveageing.com.au/userfiles/file/Experience%20works-full%20reportFINAL_web.pdf>; *see also* Joanna Abhayaratna et al., *Part-Time Employment: The Australian Experience* 119 (Austl. Productivity Comm'n Staff Working Paper, 2008), *available at* <http://www.pc.gov.au/__data/assets/pdf_file/0020/81065/part-time-employment.pdf>.

76. Kennedy & Da Costa, *supra* note 66, at 34-35 ; Andrew Frazer & Malcolm Sargeant, Older Workers as Vulnerable Workers in the New World of Work, Paper for the International Industrial Relations Association 15th World Congress: The New World of Work, Organisations & Employment 4 (Aug. 24-27, 2009), *available at* <http://ro.uow.edu.au/cgi/viewcontent.cgi?article=1070&context=lawpapers>.

77. Abhayaratna et al., *supra* note 75, at 142-43. However a study based on a different survey sample found for older males aged fifty-five to sixty-four the probability of involuntary part-time work higher than for prime-age groups. *See* Roger Wilkins, *Personal and Job Characteristics Associated with Underemployment*, 9 Austl. J. Lab. Econ. 371, 379 (2006).

78. *See* Austl. Bureau of Statistics, 6359.0, Forms of Employment: November 2009, at 29 tbl.7 (Apr. 29, 2010) [hereinafter Forms of Employment: November 2009], *available at* <http://www.ausstats.abs.gov.au/Ausstats/subscriber.nsf/0/FFFDDE1422B6216ECA25771300111FC5/$File/63590_november%202009.pdf>.

79. Greg Murtough & Matthew Waite, *The Growth of Non-Traditional Employment: Are Jobs Becoming More Precarious?* 9 (Austl. Productivity Comm'n Staff Research Paper, 2000), *available at*: <http://www.pc.gov.au/__data/assets/pdf_file/0009/8010/nontrademp.pdf>.

80. Productivity Comm'n, Commonwealth of Austl., The Role of Non-Traditional Work in the Australian Labour Market 71-72 (2006), *available at* <http://www.pc.gov.au/__data/assets/pdf_file/0016/8431/nontraditionalwork.pdf>.

represents an increase in precariousness for many older workers.

Older workers tend to move from direct employment to self-employment as either independent contractors or business operators. At the end of 2009, only 67 percent of people working at age fifty-five or over were employees, compared with 82.9 percent of the prime-age workers aged twenty-five to forty-four.[81] The shift to self-employed status is associated with vulnerability since self-employed workers must provide their own means of income security. The statistics on independent contractors and business operators show a decline in the proportion of older workers who were self-employed in 2008 and 2009 in some older age groups.[82] This may be a reflection of the greater precariousness of the older self-employed in economic downturns, since such workers tend to leave the labor force rather than report as unemployed. The most significant change was a rise (from 45 percent to 48 percent) in the proportion of working people aged sixty-five and over who were employees. This suggests that some of the oldest group of workers may have remained in employment rather than become self-employed.[83]

D. Unemployment, Underemployment and Discouraged Workers

Over the period of the crisis, older workers experienced an increase in unemployment similar to that for other adult age groups. Between 2007 and 2009, unemployment for men aged fifty-five to sixty-four rose from 2.6 percent to 3.9 percent, a 50 percent increase. The increase in the unemployment rate for men aged forty-five to fifty-four was slightly higher. Older women fared better, experiencing a lower proportionate rise than younger female workers.[84]

81. *See* FORMS OF EMPLOYMENT: NOVEMBER 2009, *supra* note 78, at 17 tbl.3. Workers aged fifty-five and over comprised 26 percent of all independent contractors and 31 percent of all business operators. *Id.* at 6-7.

82. *Compare* AUSTL. BUREAU OF STATISTICS, 6359.0, FORMS OF EMPLOYMENT: NOVEMBER 2007, at 15 tbl.2 (Apr. 28, 2008) [hereinafter FORMS OF EMPLOYMENT: NOVEMBER 2007], *available at* <http://www.ausstats.abs.gov.au/Ausstats/subscriber.nsf/0/F8430DD3E08953CFCA257435001196C9/$File/63590_nov%202007.pdf> *with* AUSTL. BUREAU OF STATISTICS, 6359.0, FORMS OF EMPLOYMENT: NOVEMBER 2008, at 18 tbl.2 (June 12, 2009) [hereinafter FORMS OF EMPLOYMENT: NOVEMBER 2008], *available at* <http://www.ausstats.abs.gov.au/Ausstats/subscriber.nsf/0/8C62E3501983EC5BCA2575D2001B01AE/$File/63590_nov%202008.pdf> *and* FORMS OF EMPLOYMENT: NOVEMBER 2009, *supra* note 78, at 17 tbl.3.

83. FORMS OF EMPLOYMENT: NOVEMBER 2008, *supra* note 82, at 18 tbl.2; FORMS OF EMPLOYMENT: NOVEMBER 2009, *supra* note 78, at 17 tbl.3. Comparable figures before 2008 are not strictly commensurable because of definitional changes after 2007.

84. LABOUR MARKET STATISTICS: JULY 2010, *supra* note 52, at 34 tbl.1.1. The raw data can be downloaded from *6105.0 – Australian Labour Market Statistics, July 2010*, AUSTL. BUREAU OF STATISTICS, <http://www.abs.gov.au/AUSSTATS/abs@.nsf/DetailsPage/6105.0July%202010?OpenDocument> (last updated Oct. 7, 2010) (scroll to data cubes and select "Table 1.1. Extended labour

It is with the duration of unemployment where we see significant age-related effects. Long-term unemployment (over one year) remains markedly higher for older workers than for younger ages. The proportion of older unemployed who remain out of work for a year or more has been declining over the last decade: for the fifty-five and older group, the long-term proportion of total unemployed has decreased from 49 percent in 1999 to 25 percent in 2009.[85] However during the economic crisis we see the same pattern as for previous recessions: older workers who lost their jobs remained out of work for longer than younger workers, and their level of unemployment has remained high long after employment for the general workforce recovered. With the downturn, the older unemployed stayed out of work for longer than younger groups, and continued to do so after unemployment declined in 2010. Long-term unemployment for older workers has persisted after the recovery.

Table 2

Unemployment: Mean Duration of Unemployment, by Age Groups, 2007-10[86]

	25-34	35-44	45-54	55+
2007	34	34	48	70
2008	30	44	54	51
2009	26	32	39	47
2010	33	31	48	59

force underutilization rate" to download the .xls file) [hereinafter Extended Underutilisation].

85. AUSTL. BUREAU OF STATISTICS, 6105.0, AUSTRALIAN LABOUR MARKET STATISTICS: APRIL 2010, at 13 (Apr. 1, 2010), *available at* <http://www.ausstats.abs.gov.au/Ausstats/subscriber.nsf/0/9E0CFE203CFECA18CA2576F700154B6B/$File/61050_apr%202010.pdf>.

86. LABOUR MARKET STATISTICS: JULY 2010, *supra* note 52, at 58 tbl.3.1 (reporting results for May); AUSTL. BUREAU OF STATISTICS, 6105.0, AUSTRALIAN LABOUR MARKET STATISTICS: JULY 2009, at 67 tbl.3.1 (July 3, 2009) [hereinafter LABOUR MARKET STATISTICS: JULY 2009], *available at* <http://www.ausstats.abs.gov.au/Ausstats/subscriber.nsf/0/CB629C2C74A77E1BCA2575E800229285/$File/61050_jul%202009.pdf> (same); AUSTL. BUREAU OF STATISTICS, 6105.0, AUSTRALIAN LABOUR MARKET STATISTICS: JULY 2008, at 79 tbl.3.1 (July 3, 2008) [hereinafter LABOUR MARKET STATISTICS: JULY 2008], *available at* <http://www.ausstats.abs.gov.au/Ausstats/subscriber.nsf/0/C13A89556EEE7941CA25747A00116F59/$File/61050_jul%202008.pdf> (same); AUSTL. BUREAU OF STATISTICS, 6105.0, AUSTRALIAN LABOUR MARKET STATISTICS: JULY 2007, at 53 tbl.3.1 (July 6, 2007) [hereinafter LABOUR MARKET STATISTICS: JULY 2007], *available at* <http://www.ausstats.abs.gov.au/Ausstats/subscriber.nsf/0/808C70323C0E2B43CA25730F00177FF6/$File/61050_jul%202007.pdf> (same).

Table 3

Long-Term Unemployment: Percent of Total Unemployed Who Were out of Work for Fifty-Two Weeks or Longer, by Age Groups, 2007-10[87]

	25-34	35-44	45-54	55+
2007	14	16	25	27
2008	15	20	23	26
2009	15	17	17	22
2010	17	19	27	31

Labor underutilization – enforced idleness among those who would prefer to work more hours – is a growing problem in the Australian labor market.[88] While most strongly associated with younger workers, the problem has grown among the mature labor force as well. Underemployment (measured by the percentage of part-time workers who would prefer to work more hours) rose substantially (from 4.5 percent to 5.2 percent) for older workers between 2007 and 2009, and remains at this high level. Most of the increase was among men. However older workers did not experience greater proportionate increases in underemployment than other age groups.[89]

Older workers have longer periods of underemployment. During the downturn, they experienced persistently higher levels of long-term underemployment than younger groups, with 45 percent of those aged fifty-five and over remaining underemployed for more than a year (compared with 35 percent for the prime thirty-five to forty-four age group), but the rate did not change over the period.[90] The median duration of insufficient

87. *See* LABOUR MARKET STATISTICS: JULY 2010, *supra* note 52, at 58 tbl.3.1 (reporting results for May); LABOUR MARKET STATISTICS: JULY 2009, *supra* note 86, at 67 tbl.3.1 (same); LABOUR MARKET STATISTICS: JULY 2008, *supra* note 86, at 79 tbl.3.1 (same); LABOUR MARKET STATISTICS: JULY 2007, *supra* note 86, at 53 tbl.3.1 (same).

88. Iain Campbell, *Pressing Towards Full Employment? The Persistence of Underemployment in Australia*, 61 J. AUSTL. POL. ECON. 136 (2008).

89. Calculated from the raw data available to be downloaded from *6202.0 – Labour Force, Australia, July 2010*, *supra* note 62 (scroll down and select "Table 21. Labour Underutilisation by Age and Sex – Trend, Seasonally Adjusted and Original" to download either the .xls or .zip file).

90. AUSTL. BUREAU OF STATISTICS, 6265.0, UNDEREMPLOYED WORKERS AUSTRALIA: SEPTEMBER 2009, at 17 tbl.4 (Feb. 23, 2010) [hereinafter UNDEREMPLOYED WORKERS AUSTRALIA: SEPTEMBER 2009], *available at* <http://www.ausstats.abs.gov.au/Ausstats/subscriber.nsf/0/0234F5869C8CAAC0CA2576D20013A485/$File/62650_sep%202009.pdf>; AUSTL. BUREAU OF STATISTICS, 6265.0, UNDEREMPLOYED WORKERS AUSTRALIA: SEPTEMBER 2007, at 19 tbl.5 (Feb. 25, 2008)

work for older workers actually declined (from fifty to thirty-four weeks) between 2007 and 2009, while remaining relatively constant for other adult age groups.[91] This pattern of underemployment suggests that a "discouraged worker effect" is operating for older underemployed workers.[92] In 2009, over half of all discouraged job seekers were aged fifty-five and over. Among the discouraged, 26 percent were aged fifty-five to sixty-four, a proportion which stayed constant between 2007 and 2009.[93] Total underutilization rates fell in 2008, but climbed again the following year, with the greatest impact felt among both younger and older groups.[94] The crisis seems therefore to have resulted in longer periods of underemployment for older workers, but no significant changes in the level of underutilization apart from a slight increase among the oldest group.

E. Labor Market Regulation Affecting Older Workers

Legislation prohibiting discrimination on the ground of age in employment (along with other areas) was introduced in the Australian states and territories progressively during the 1980s and 1990s.[95] The use of compulsory retirement ages by employers was specifically prohibited by legislation about the same time. By 1999 all states had prohibited both age discrimination and compulsory retirement.[96] A court decision had

[hereinafter UNDEREMPLOYED WORKERS AUSTRALIA: SEPTEMBER 2007], *available at* <http://www.ausstats.abs.gov.au/Ausstats/subscriber.nsf/0/A44F2FA22AAB4309CA2573F700102BC7/$File/62650_sep%202007.pdf>.

91. UNDEREMPLOYED WORKERS AUSTRALIA: SEPTEMBER 2009, *supra* note 90, at 17 tbl.4; UNDEREMPLOYED WORKERS AUSTRALIA: SEPTEMBER 2007, *supra* note 90, at 19 tbl.5.

92. UNDEREMPLOYED WORKERS AUSTRALIA: SEPTEMBER 2009, *supra* note 90, at 17 tbl.4; UNDEREMPLOYED WORKERS AUSTRALIA: SEPTEMBER 2007, *supra* note 90, at 19 tbl.5. The discouraged worker effect is supported by a 21 percent decline in the mean duration of underemployment for the fifty-five and older group over 2007-09, contrasted with an increase for all other age groups. UNDEREMPLOYED WORKERS AUSTRALIA: SEPTEMBER 2009, *supra* note 90, at 17 tbl.4; UNDEREMPLOYED WORKERS AUSTRALIA: SEPTEMBER 2007, *supra* note 90, at 19 tbl.5.

93. AUSTL. BUREAU OF STATISTICS, 6220.0, PERSONS NOT IN THE LABOUR FORCE: SEPTEMBER 2009, at 7, 14 tbl.3 (Mar. 24, 2010) [hereinafter PERSONS NOT IN THE LABOUR FORCE: SEPTEMBER 2009], *available at* <http://www.ausstats.abs.gov.au/Ausstats/subscriber.nsf/0/38F947FA13716DD2CA2576EF00159779/$File/62200_sep%202009.pdf>; AUSTL. BUREAU OF STATISTICS, 6220.0, PERSONS NOT IN THE LABOUR FORCE: SEPTEMBER 2007, at 16 tbl.3 (Mar. 25, 2008) [hereinafter PERSONS NOT IN THE LABOUR FORCE: SEPTEMBER 2007], *available at* <http://www.ausstats.abs.gov.au/Ausstats/subscriber.nsf/0/4C2C7019CB72D012CA257412001A3216/$File/62200_Sep%202007.pdf>. The proportion of discouraged job seekers aged fifty-five and over actually fell from 63 percent in 2007. PERSONS NOT IN THE LABOUR FORCE: SEPTEMBER 2009, *supra* at 19 tbl.7; PERSONS NOT IN THE LABOUR FORCE: SEPTEMBER 2007, *supra* at 21 tbl.7.

94. Extended Underutilisation, *supra* note 84. Total (extended) underutilization includes unemployed, underemployed, discouraged job-seekers and those with marginal attachment to the labor force (i.e. engaged in intermittent work). 2009-10: YEAR BOOK AUSTRALIA, *supra* note 44, at 258.

95. Sol Encel, *Age Discrimination in Law and in Practice*, 3 ELDER L. REV. 13 (2004).

96. *Id.*

previously held that the use of gender-differentiated retirement ages constituted unlawful sex discrimination.[97] In 2004 the Australian federal parliament passed the *Age Discrimination Act*, which operates alongside the state and territory legislation and which prohibits discrimination on the ground of age.[98] However this legislation was not much used because, unlike other anti-discrimination legislation, it required that the complainant prove that age was the dominant reason for his or her adverse treatment.[99] This was altered by legislation in 2009 so that age need now only be shown to be an operative cause of the treatment.[100]

Despite this legislation, there is considerable anecdotal and survey evidence of widespread continuing discrimination against older people in Australia in the field of employment. There is statistical evidence that compulsory retirement policies persisted at many workplaces for at least five years after they became unlawful, and it is still common for older workers to be pressured to retire at or before the traditional age of sixty-five.[101] Discrimination based on age is particularly prevalent in recruitment.[102] Because such discrimination is usually covert or unconscious, it is difficult to measure its extent or changes over time. Research conducted before the global financial crisis found that older Australian workers have much more pessimistic expectations about their ability to find another job following redundancy than do younger workers: the average perceived probability of finding a similar job was over 50 percent for prime age workers but fell to 36 percent for those aged fifty-five to sixty-four.[103] In early 2009, 20 percent of unemployed workers aged forty-five and over reported being "considered too old by employers" as the main reason for difficulty in finding work, and this was by far the most

97. *Allders Int'l Pty Ltd v Anstee* (1986) 5 NSWLR 47 (Austl.).

98. *Age Discrimination Act 2004* (Cth) s 18.

99. *See Act 68 of 2004* (Cth) s 16, *available at* <http://www.comlaw.gov.au/Details/C2004C01379>.

100. *Age Discrimination Act 2004* (Cth) s 16.

101. Rachael Patterson, *The Eradication of Compulsory Retirement and Age Discrimination in the Australian Workplace: A Cause for Celebration and Concern*, 3 ELDER L. REV. 1, 8 (2004). A survey of workers who retired in 1997 showed that 18 percent of workers aged sixty to sixty-four, and 65 percent of workers aged sixty-five and over gave the reason for their retirement as "reached compulsory age." AUSTL. BUREAU OF STATISTICS, AUSTRALIAN SOCIAL TRENDS 2000, at 131 (2000), *available at* <http://www.ausstats.abs.gov.au/Ausstats/subscriber.nsf/0/0061403922BF6F55CA2569110080BA2C/$File/41020_2000.pdf>.

102. Lynne Bennington, *Prime Age Recruitment: The Challenges for Age Discrimination Legislation*, 3 ELDER L. REV. 27 (2004); Sol Encel & Helen Studencki, *Older Workers: Can they Succeed in the Job Market?* 23 AUSTRALASIAN J. AGEING 33 (2004); Chris Kossen & Cec Pedersen, *Older Workers in Australia: the Myths, the Realities and the Battle over Workforce "Flexibility"*, 14 J. MGMT. & ORG. 73 (2008).

103. Jeff Borland, *What Happens to the Australian Labour Market in Recessions?*, 42 AUSTL. ECON. REV. 232, 240 (2009).

common reason given in that age group.[104] Similarly, 20 percent of people not in the labor force reported that being "considered too old" was the main reason for their not looking for work: more than those who reported that they did not need to work or had retired.[105]

In the three largest jurisdictions over the period of the financial crisis, there was a significant increase in both the number of formal complaints concerning age discrimination in employment, and an increase in the proportion which such complaints contributed to all discrimination complaints in the area of employment.

104. AUSTL. BUREAU OF STATISTICS, 6222.0, JOB SEARCH EXPERIENCE: JULY 2009, at 19 tbl.7 (Dec. 21, 2009), *available at* <http://www.ausstats.abs.gov.au/Ausstats/subscriber. nsf/0/C7F8B45F33 DBEFEFCA257690000F114A/$File/62220_jul%202009.pdf>. The proportion fluctuated from 24 percent in 2007 to 16 percent in 2008. AUSTL. BUREAU OF STATISTICS, 6222.0, JOB SEARCH EXPERIENCE: JULY 2008, at 19 tbl.7 (Jan. 12, 2009), *available at* <http://www.ausstats.abs.gov.au/Ausstats/subscriber.nsf/0/FB963D6DCA437057CA257539000D1844/$File/62220_jul%202008.pdf>; AUSTL. BUREAU OF STATISTICS, 6222.0, JOB SEARCH EXPERIENCE: JULY 2007, at 20 tbl.7 (Dec. 7, 2007), *available at* <http://www.ausstats.abs.gov.au/Ausstats/subscriber.nsf/0/AAF26AF7A7E83 A05CA2573A9001B46AA/$File/62220_jul%202007.pdf>

105. AUSTL. BUREAU OF STATISTICS, 6239.0, BARRIERS AND INCENTIVES TO LABOUR FORCE PARTICIPATION: JULY 2008 TO JUNE 2009, at 27 tbl.7 (Dec. 8, 2009), *available at* <http://www. ausstats.abs.gov.au/Ausstats/subscriber.nsf/0/7E777A58003E9246CA25768500158F23/$File/62390_ju l%202008%20to%20jun%202009.pdf>. This was a decline from the previously reported rate of 27 percent in 2007. *See* AUSTL. BUREAU OF STATISTICS, 6239.0, BARRIERS AND INCENTIVES TO LABOUR FORCE PARTICIPATION: JULY 2006 TO JUNE 2007, at 26 tbl.7 (Dec. 19, 2007), *available at* <http://www.ausstats.abs.gov.au/Ausstats/subscriber.nsf/0/AF76E535F8283C0DCA2573B5000A775C/ $File/62390_jul%202006%20to%20jun%202007.pdf>.

Table 4

Age Discrimination in Employment Complaints: Commonwealth, New South Wales and Victoria, 2006-07 to 2008-09[106]

Year	Age Complaints in Employment	Age as a Percent of All Employment Complaints
2006-07	219	5.5%
2007-08	285	6.7%
2008-09	265	5.7%

Because formal complaints are only a small fraction of the discrimination actually experienced, it is notable that the number of informal inquiries made to the federal agency concerning older age discrimination and compulsory retirement peaked in 2007-08, increasing by 13 percent over the previous year before declining to previous levels in 2008-09.[107]

106. AUSTL. HUMAN RIGHTS COMM'N, ANNUAL REPORT 2008-09, at 78-80 (2009) [hereinafter AHRC, ANNUAL REPORT 2008-09], *available at* <http://www.hreoc.gov.au/pdf/about/publications/annual_reports/2008_2009/ar09_complete.pdf>; AUSTL. HUMAN RIGHTS & EQUAL OPPORTUNITY COMM'N, ANNUAL REPORT 2007-08, at 74-76 (2008) [hereinafter AHRC, ANNUAL REPORT 2007-08], *available at* <http://www.hreoc.gov.au/about/publications/annual_reports/2007_2008/AR_2007_2008_complete.pdf>; AUSTL. HUMAN RIGHTS & EQUAL OPPORTUNITY COMM'N, ANNUAL REPORT 2006-07, at 80-81 (2007) [hereinafter AHRC, ANNUAL REPORT 2006-07], *available at* <http://www.hreoc.gov.au/about/publications/annual_reports/2006_2007/pdf/hreoc_ar2006-07.pdf>; ANTI-DISCRIMINATION BD. OF NEW S. WALES, ANNUAL REPORT 2008-09, at 16 (2009) [hereinafter ADBNSW ANNUAL REPORT 2008-09], *available at* <http://www.ipc.nsw.gov.au/lawlink/adb/ll_adb.nsf/vwFiles/ADBAnnualReport0809.pdf/$file/ADBAnnualReport0809.pdf>; ANTI-DISCRIMINATION BD. OF NEW S. WALES, ANNUAL REPORT 07-08, at 18 (2008) [hereinafter ADBNSW ANNUAL REPORT 2007-08], *available at* <http://www.ipc.nsw.gov.au/lawlink/adb/ll_adb.nsf/vwFiles/ADBAnnualReport0708V2.pdf/$file/ADBAnnualReport0708V2.pdf>; ANTI-DISCRIMINATION BD. OF NEW S. WALES, ANNUAL REPORT 2006-07, at 16 (2007) [hereinafter ADBNSW ANNUAL REPORT 2006-07], *available at* <http://www.ipc.nsw.gov.au/lawlink/adb/ll_adb.nsf/vwFiles/ADBAnnualReport06-07.pdf/$file/A D BAnnualReport06-07.pdf>; VICTORIAN EQUAL OPPORTUNITY & HUMAN RIGHTS COMM'N, ANNUAL REPORT 2008/09, at 16-17 (2009) [hereinafter VEOHRC ANNUAL REPORT 2008-09], *available at* http://www.equalopportunitycommission.vic.gov.au/pdf/2008_09_annualreport/files/annual_report_200809_final.pdf>; VICTORIAN EQUAL OPPORTUNITY & HUMAN RIGHTS COMM'N, ANNUAL REPORT 2007/2008, at 25 (2008) [hereinafter VEOHRC ANNUAL REPORT 2007-08], *available at* <http://www.humanrightscommission.vic.gov.au/index.php?option=com_k2&view=item&task=download&id=436&Itemid=690>; VICTORIAN EQUAL OPPORTUNITY & HUMAN RIGHTS COMM'N, ANNUAL REPORT 2006/2007, at 36 (2007) [hereinafter VEOHRC ANNUAL REPORT 2006-07], *available at* <http://www.humanrightscommission.vic.gov.au/index.php?option=com_k2&view=item&task=download&id=424&Itemid=690>.

107. *See* AHRC, ANNUAL REPORT 2008-09, *supra* note 106, at 65; AHRC, ANNUAL REPORT 2007-08, *supra* note 106, at 60-61; AHRC, ANNUAL REPORT 2006-07, *supra* note 106, at 67-68. A similar pattern was observed for the NSW agency, though not for the Victorian agency. *See* NSWADB ANNUAL REPORT 2008-09, *supra* note 106, at 15; NSWADB ANNUAL REPORT 2007-08, *supra* note

Australian federal labor legislation has also prohibited dismissal on the ground of age since 1993, when the *Industrial Relations Act 1988* was amended to cover unfair and unlawful termination of employment, implementing ILO Convention 111 on Discrimination in Employment and Occupation.[108] Although, as noted in the Introduction, age is not covered by the ILO Convention, Australia exercised its power to include age as an additional ground of discrimination under the convention. The prohibitions applied to all employees in Australia. While the federal labor statute has been amended many times since then, often drastically, the prohibitions on discriminatory termination have always been retained and now reside in the *Fair Work Act 2009*.[109] Although the discriminatory termination of employment provisions were rarely used in the courts, their emphatic nature has probably made them more effective than anti-discrimination law.

The current federal labor legislation also includes protection against discriminatory adverse treatment extending beyond dismissal.[110] Although untested as yet, this protection seems to provide significant advantages over the anti-discrimination legislation. These "general protection" provisions allow for complaints to be investigated and pursued by the Fair Work Ombudsman (a proactive regulatory agency), and allow direct access to the federal courts which are able to issue more comprehensive remedies than under the anti-discrimination legislation.[111] A reverse onus of proof also applies, so that an employer must show that the "adverse action" was founded on reasons which did *not* include a discriminatory basis.[112]

Apart from age-specific provisions, regulation of labor conditions has been strong in Australia, although still consistent with a liberal market economy.[113] Traditionally, labor regulation in Australia was conducted

106, at 17; NSWADB ANNUAL REPORT 2006-07, *supra* note 106, at 15; VEOHRC ANNUAL REPORT 2008-09, *supra* note 106, at 13; VEOHRC ANNUAL REPORT 2007-08, *supra* note 106, at 23; VEOHRC ANNUAL REPORT 2006-07, *supra* note 106, at 35. The variations in enquiries and complaints at the federal level were before the amendments to the *Age Discrimination Act* were introduced, so cannot be explained by a change in the regulation regime.

108. *Industrial Relations Reform Act 1993* (Cth), inserting s 170DF(1)(f). Earlier protections against discriminatory dismissal, which were included as standard provisions in awards from 1984, did not include age as a prohibited ground. *Termination, Change and Redundancy Case, Supplementary Decision* (1984) 9 Indus R 115, 118 (Austl. Conciliation & Arbitration Comm'n).

109. *Fair Work Act 2009* (Cth) ss 351, 772.

110. *Id.* ss 153, 195, 351.

111. *Id.* ss 537-39, 682, 715-16, 779.

112. *Id.* ss. 351, 772; *see* Carol Andrades, *Intersections between "General Protections" Under the Fair Work Act 2009 (Cth) and Anti-Discrimination Law: Questions, Quirks and Quandries* (Ctr. for Emp't & Labour Relations Law, Univ. of Melbourne, Working Paper No 47, 2009).

113. Jones & Mitchell, *supra* note 6. On recent history of labor law changes, see Richard Mitchell et al., *The Evolution of Labour Law in Australia: Measuring the Change*, 23 AUSTL. J. LAB. L. 61

through specialist tribunals responsible for settling collective labor disputes through processes of compulsory conciliation and arbitration. Through compulsory arbitration, the tribunals made legally enforceable awards which set minimum labor standards for minimum wages, conditions and standard hours on an industry-wide basis. Since a system of "enterprise bargaining" was introduced in the early 1990s, awards have operated as a minimum "safety net" and agreements (which do not require collective representation) may be made at the enterprise or works level which can depart from award standards provided they do not disadvantage workers on an overall basis.[114]

At the same time, the role of trade unions in securing minimum conditions through collective bargaining or advocacy in award hearings has been reduced.[115] The effectiveness of regulation in guaranteeing decent work has declined with a series of changes designed to "deregulate" working conditions.[116] Most recently, the WorkChoices legislation allowed for a lowering of minimum standards by employers by effectively removing the requirement for enterprise agreements to be approved by an industrial tribunal, while relaxing the extent to which agreements could undercut established standards.[117] The introduction of the Labor government's "Forward with Fairness" policy, culminating in the *Fair Work Act 2009* (which came fully into force in January 2010), has reversed this deregulation to only a limited degree.[118]

Although there are now national minimum award standards, which are strongly enforced, the range of matters which are regulated has contracted. Many award restrictions, gained by unions and designed to ensure decent working conditions, have been removed or reduced to a common minimum. The growth of atypical forms of labor, especially casual and part-time work, has significantly dampened the impact of labor regulation,

(2010); Andrew Stewart, *Work Choices in Overview: Big Bang or Slow Burn?*, 16 ECON. & LAB. REL. REV. 25 (2006). For comparative measures of employment protection (showing that Australia has low levels of protection, comparable to the U.K. and U.S.), see *How Do OECD Labour Markets Perform?*, *supra* note 20 (scroll down to the fourth table, "Annual hours worked and averages annual wages").

114. *See* ROSEMARY OWENS & JOELLEN RILEY, THE LAW OF WORK 115-19, 334-37 (2d ed. 2011).

115. Andrew Frazer, *Individualism and Collectivism in Agreement-Making under Australian Labour Law*, *in* COLLECTIVE AGREEMENTS AND INDIVIDUAL CONTRACTS OF EMPLOYMENT 49 (Michal Sewerynski ed., 2003).

116. Colin Fenwick, *How Low Can You Go? Minimum Working Conditions Under Australia's New Labour Laws*, 16 ECON. & LAB. REL. REV. 85 (2006); Jill Murray, *Submission to the Senate Committee on Employment, Workplace Relations and Education on the Workplace Relations Amendment (WorkChoices) Bill 2005*, *available at* <http://celrl.law.unimelb.edu.au/files/jill_s_submission_nov_051.pdf> (last viewed Mar. 9, 2011).

117. *Workplace Relations Amendment (Work Choices) Act 2006* (Cth).

118. *Fair Work Act 2009* (Cth), s123.

resulting in increased wage dispersion and scope for exploitative employer practices. Casual workers, who comprise nearly one-quarter of all employees, face ready reduction in hours and are not entitled to redundancy payments or notice payments on termination.[119] For workers over twenty-five, casualization rises steadily with age and increases substantially after age sixty when it reaches 25 percent of all employees; for those aged over sixty-five, 42 percent of all employees are casual.[120] About 35 percent of workers aged fifty-five and older in "transition jobs" prior to retirement (usually part-time) were forced to move to casual or contract work.[121] Some 65 percent of older workers changed their employer when moving to part-time "transition jobs," most commonly because part-time jobs were not available with their former employer.[122] The resultant broken employment would have affected the leave and redundancy entitlements of nearly all such workers.

F. Income and Retirement Security

State-provided social security in Australia pre-dates the modern concept of the welfare state, adopting what one leading social welfare historian has described as "the wage-earner's welfare state" in recognition of the reliance on fair minimum wages (and employer-provided benefits like sick leave) to minimize poverty.[123] Beginning with the age pension, introduced nationally in 1909, state benefits have until recently tended to be universal but at minimal levels. While available to most workers, the age pension was intended to be supplemented by private savings, usually in the form of home ownership (Australia has traditionally had one of the highest home ownership rates in the world, at around 70 percent).[124] In the 1980s the then-Labor government introduced more targeted welfare support which introduced means-testing based on wealth and income. Subsequent changes by the Howard conservative government shifted the

119. *Id.*

120. FORMS OF EMPLOYMENT: NOVEMBER 2007, *supra* note 82, at 15 tbl.2. More recent breakdowns by age are not publicly available.

121. Diana Warren, *Retirement Expectations and Labour Force Transitions: the Experience of the Baby Boomer Generation* 18 (Melbourne Inst. of Applied Econ. & Soc. Research Working Paper 24/08, 2008).

122. Abhayaratna et al., *supra* note 75, at 125.

123. FRANCIS G. CASTLES, THE WORKING CLASS AND WELFARE 103 (1985); Robb Watts, *Ten Years On: Francis G. Castles and the Australian "Wage-Earners' Welfare State"*, 33 AUSTL. & N.Z. J. SOC. 1 (1997).

124. Allan Borowski, *Back at the Crossroads: The Slippery Fish of Australian Retirement Income Policy*, 43 AUSTL. J. SOC. ISSUES 311, 313 (2008); AUSTL. BUREAU OF STATISTICS, 2008 YEAR BOOK AUSTRALIA 312, 313 tbl.10.5 (2008), *available at* <http://www.ausstats.abs.gov.au/Ausstats/subscriber.nsf/0/8D6ED0E197FE38A6CA2573E7000EC2AD/$File/13010_2008.pdf>.

emphasis from entitlement to "mutual obligation" and in 2005 introduced more stringent work requirements for long-term benefit recipients.[125] Nonetheless, elements of universalism remain for the sick, aged, and long-term disabled which particularly benefit older workers.

In the last two decades, security for older workers and the retired has been shifting away from universal pensions towards employer-funded defined contribution benefits and tax concessions. Revenue-funded universal health care remains but is increasingly supplemented by private health insurance, which is also subsidized by the state.[126] So while most social security provision has remained linked to employment, it has been imposed through legislated employer obligations and taxation transfers rather than collective bargaining or individual contributions. This approach may be described as a system of "occupational welfare" in which social protection is addressed by removing barriers to workforce participation.[127] These measures, when coupled with the abolition of compulsory retirement, have provided most older Australian workers with increased freedom and security in the transition to retirement. However, since most of this security is job-linked, the benefits have been skewed against poorer workers or those prematurely forced out of work, while contributing to greater inequality in wealth and income.[128]

The age pension, which is provided to all permanent residents over sixty-five[129] is not a form of social insurance and is not dependent on participation in work or calculated by individual contributions. While modest and now regarded as a "safety net" for those unable to provide for their own retirement, its value has increased in recent years and is currently worth 32 percent of average take-home pay.[130] While the rate of benefit for

125. Terry Carney, *Neoliberal Welfare Reform and "Rights" Compliance under Australian Social Security Law*, 12 AUSTL. J. HUM. RTS. 223 (2006); Francis G. Castles, *A Farewell to Australia's Welfare State*, 31 INT'L J. HEALTH SERVICES 537 (2001); Philip Mendes, *From the Wage Earners Welfare State to the Targeted Welfare State: The Social Welfare Policies of the Australian Labor Party, 1983-97*, 52 AUSTL. SOC. WORK 33 (1999).

126. *See* Francesco Paolucci et al., *Subsidising Private Health Insurance in Australia: Why, How, and How to Proceed?* 1-2 (Austl. Ctr. for Econ. Research on Health Working Paper No. 2, 2008), *available at* <http://www.acerh.edu.au/publications/ACERH_WP2.pdf>.

127. Francis G. Castles, *The Wage Earners' Welfare State Revisited: Refurbishing the Established Model of Australian Social Protection, 1983-93*, 29 AUSTL. J. SOC. ISSUES 120, 128, 135, 138 (1994).

128. LISA MARRIOTT, THE POLITICS OF RETIREMENT SAVINGS TAXATION: A TRANS-TASMAN COMPARISON 197-98 (2010); Borowski, *supra* note 124, at 325-26.

129. The pension eligibility age is progressively being raised, and will be available at age sixty-seven for those born after 1957. *See Payments: Eligibility: Age Pension Age*, AUSTL. GOV'T CENTRELINK, <http://www.centrelink.gov.au/internet/internet.nsf/payments/age_eligible.htm> (last viewed Mar. 10, 2011).

130. The pension is indexed at 25 percent of the average wage but is not taxed unless additional income is earned. The after-tax equivalent is calculated from the Australian Tax Office, *Simple Tax Calculator*, AUSTL. TAXATION OFFICE, <http://calculators.ato.gov.au/scripts/asp/simpletaxcalc/main.

the age pension is reduced according to recipient assets and income, approximately 70 percent of persons aged over sixty-five receive a pension, 63 percent at the full rate.[131]

About 4.3 percent of the Australian age-eligible population (eighteen to sixty-four) receives a Disability Support Pension, 42 percent of whom are aged fifty-five to sixty-four, with a further 27 percent aged forty-five to fifty-four.[132] This pension, which has a disability test but no work requirements, has often been seen as a "dumping ground" for long-term unemployed older workers. Compared with all other age groups, workers aged fifty-five and over (particularly male workers) have a significantly higher probability of remaining on the disability support pension, a lower level of return to employment, and a higher likelihood of returning to the pension after leaving it for a job.[133] The disability support pension, then, often operates as a transitional step from work to retirement. Since the benefit amount received is the same as for the age pension, it provides government with a flexible means for responding to an increasing population of older workless in times of high unemployment. At several times in recent years, concern has been expressed at the ballooning cost of the disability pension, and eligibility was restricted through imposition of an "ability to work test" in 2006. However, entitlement is largely determined by an assessment of disability by private medical practitioners, and there appears to some acceptance by government of the inevitable growth in the number of older disabled recipients.[134]

asp> (last viewed Mar. 10, 2011), using average weekly ordinary time earnings for May 2010, AUSTL. BUREAU OF STATISTICS, 6302.0, AVERAGE WEEKLY EARNINGS AUSTRALIA: MAY 2010, at 1 (Aug. 19, 2010), *available at* <http://www.ausstats.abs.gov.au/ausstats/meisubs.nsf/0/80EDDA7AFB6E2C6DCA257783001B8EF3/$File/63020_may%202010.pdf>

131. A part pension is currently available to someone with regular income up to 62 percent of average weekly earnings (single rate: lower amounts per person apply to couples). *See* Austl. Dep't of Families, Housing, Cmty. Servs. & Indigenous Affairs, *Statistical Paper No. 4: Income Support Customers: A Statistical Overview 2005* (2009), *available at* <http://fahcsia.gov.au/about/publicationsarticles/research/statistical/Documents/stp4/stat_04.pdf>; Jeff Harmer, Austl. Dep't of Families, Housing, Cmty. Servs. & Indigenous Affairs, *Pension Review Report* 149 (2009) [hereinafter *Harmer Report*] *available at*: <http://www.fahcsia.gov.au/about/publicationsarticles/corp/BudgetPAES/ budget09_10/pension/Documents/Pension_Review_Report/PensionReviewReport.pdf>. Since this report, income thresholds and payment rates were increased in the 2009 budget.

132. AUSTL. DEP'T OF FAMILIES, HOUSING, CMTY. SERVS. & INDIGENOUS AFFAIRS, CHARACTERISTICS OF DISABILITY SUPPORT PENSION RECIPIENTS: JUNE 2008, at 7 (2008), *available at* <http://www.facs.gov.au/sa/disability/pubs/policy/DSP_rpt_2008/Documents/DSP_character_rtp_2008.pdf>.

133. Lixin Cai & Bob Gregory, *Unemployment Duration and Inflows onto the Disability Support Pension Program: Evidence from FaCS LDS Data*, 38 AUSTL. ECON. REV. 233 (2005); Lixin Cai et al., *Disability Support Pension Recipients: Who Gets Off (and Stays Off) Payments?*, 40 AUSTL. ECON. REV. 37(2007).

134. AUSTL. INST. OF HEALTH & WELFARE, AUSTRALIA'S WELFARE 2009, at 176 (2009), *available at* <http://www.aihw.gov.au/WorkArea/DownloadAsset.aspx?id=6442452909&libID=6442452909>.

Retirement incomes in Australia are increasingly dependent on private pensions, known as superannuation.[135] In 1992, amid concern at the aging population and the state's inability to fund future aged pension obligations, a national system of employer-funded retirement schemes was introduced.[136] The Superannuation Guarantee scheme requires employers to deposit an amount equating to 9 percent of each employee's annual wage into a government-approved superannuation fund.[137] Originally the funds were all industry-based and non-profit, with union representation on the governing boards, but recent changes designed to promote choice have led to a growth in private for-profit and self-managed funds. There are considerable tax benefits for workers who make contributions to their own superannuation accounts, although most workers continue to rely only on the compulsory employer contributions.[138]

Government policies in recent years have been designed to encourage participation in work by older Australians and reduce the incentives to cease working early. These incentives also encourage semi-retirement by allowing workers to draw from their superannuation while working part-time from age fifty-five, and recent taxation changes encourage workers to wait until sixty before drawing on their accumulated superannuation. Additional changes have encouraged people to continue working after sixty-five, by allowing them access to a part pension.[139] These changes appear to have been effective in keeping older people in work and encouraging them to manage their gradual transition to retirement.[140] However, since a substantial number of older workers retire due to involuntary reasons (principally retrenchment and ill-health), work for many in this transition phase is precarious due to unplanned circumstances.

The effect of the compulsory superannuation system has certainly been to increase retirement security for older workers, although only a low proportion of workers over fifty-five have enough superannuation to fully

135. Superannuation was progressively expanded from the 1980s through the award system which imposed compulsory levies on employers. *See National Wage Case* (1986) 14 Indus R 187, 212 (Full Bench, Austl. Conciliation & Arbitration Comm'n).

136. *Superannuation Guarantee (Administration) Act 1992* (Cth).

137. *See id.* ss 6A-15; *Guide to Superannuation for Individuals*, AUSTL. TAXATION OFFICE, <http://ato.gov.au/individuals/content.asp?doc=/content/00250233.htm> (last modified Jan. 31, 2011).

138. *See* AUSTL. BUREAU OF STATISTICS, 4102.0, AUSTRALIAN SOCIAL TRENDS 2002, at 175-77 (2002) [hereinafter AUSTRALIAN SOCIAL TRENDS 2002], *available at* <http://www.ausstats.abs.gov.au/Ausstats/subscriber.nsf/0/C0A01711EAD911BFCA256BCD007D7F10/$File/41020_2002.pdf>.

139. Diana Warren, *Australia's Retirement Income System: Historical Development and Effects of Recent Reforms* 10, 18-19 (Melbourne Inst. of Applied Econ. & Soc. Research Working Paper 23/08, 2008), *available at* <http://www.melbourneinstitute.com/wp/wp2008n23.pdf>.

140. Maggie Walter et al., *Keeping Australia's Workers in the Labour Force: A Policy Perspective*, 43 AUSTL. J. SOC. ISSUES 291 (2008).

fund their retirement.[141] However it has significantly increased the accumulated wealth of older workers, though it has also increased wealth and income inequality. For most workers, superannuation accrues through cumulative investment earnings rather than by reference to average or final salary, and is then taken as a lump sum on retirement (rather than as a pension or annuity) which is then reinvested, with the interest earned being used for self-funded retirement.[142] Paradoxically, the system may have contributed to greater anxiety and perceived insecurity, since both the level of payout on retirement and earnings afterwards are unpredictable and dependent on ever-fluctuating market earnings. There are also very significant gender differences. Because women workers tend to have interrupted careers and are concentrated in casual and part-time work, they have much lower accumulated superannuation than men.[143] This is likely to increase their vulnerability to exploitation and poor conditions resulting from exposure to precarious work.

Given the dependence of superannuation on financial and property market performance, the greatest direct impact of the global financial crisis on older workers in Australia has been the erosion of their superannuation and other savings for retirement. Average returns for superannuation funds fell by 8.1 percent in 2007-08 and 11.7 percent in 2008-09, while total fund assets declined 9.6 percent between 2007 and 2009.[144] This greatly shook worker confidence because it was the only serious decline since the superannuation scheme began. Similar to trends in the U.K. and the U.S., which will be described below, there are reports of Australian older workers deciding to continue working longer as a result of their eroded retirement savings. A telephone survey of older workers (aged fifty-five and over) indicated that over one-third (36.5 percent) had decided to

141. The average balance for workers aged fifty-five to fifty-nine is $92,460, while for workers aged sixty to sixty-four, it is $99,430. Women have only 46 percent of the average balance for male workers. ROSS CLARE, ASS'N OF SUPERANNUATION FUNDS OF AUSTL. RESEARCH & RESOURCE CTR., RETIREMENT SAVINGS UPDATE 6 (2008), *available at* <http://www.superannuation.asn.au/ArticleDocuments/116/rc0802_retirement_savings.pdf.aspx>.

142. *See* AUSTL. BUREAU OF STATISTICS, 6361.0, EMPLOYMENT ARRANGEMENTS, RETIREMENT AND SUPERANNUATION, AUSTRALIA: APRIL TO JULY 2007 (RE-ISSUE) 21-23 (June 2, 2009), *available at* <http://www.ausstats.abs.gov.au/Ausstats/subscriber.nsf/0/1A653F883363040DCA2575C8001ECB4E/$File/63610_apr%20to%20jul%202007%20%28re-issue%29.pdf>; AUSTRALIAN SOCIAL TRENDS 2002, *supra* note 138, at 175-79.

143. AUSTL. HUMAN RIGHTS COMM'N, 2009 ACCUMULATING POVERTY? WOMEN'S EXPERIENCES OF INEQUALITY OVER THE LIFECYCLE: AN ISSUES PAPER EXAMINING THE GENDER GAP IN RETIREMENT SAVINGS (2009), *available at* <http://www.humanrights.gov.au/pdf/sex_discrim/accumulating_poverty.pdf>.

144. AUSTL. PRUDENTIAL REGULATION AUTH., STATISTICS: ANNUAL SUPERANNUATION BULLETIN 39 tbl.11, 42 tbl.13 (rev'd Jan. 19, 2011), *available at* <http://www.apra.gov.au/Statistics/upload/June-2009-revised-Annual-Superannuation-Bulletin.pdf>.

postpone plans to retire, with significantly more women than men adopting this stance.[145] In the national labor force survey, there was a slight increase (1.3 percent) among those aged forty-five and over and working full-time who intended to continue working full-time between 2006-07 and 2008-09. This was accompanied by a similar-sized decline in the proportion of those who intended to switch from full-time to part-time work. There were also similar small increases in the "don't know" categories.[146]

G. Australia: Conclusions

Australia is often described (by Australians) as "the lucky country." The phrase was coined in the 1960s by political scientist Donald Horne and meant ironically, to indicate that the country's good fortune was due more to its exploitation of natural resources than to creativity and innovation.[147] The luck has continued in the economic crisis, although at least this time it has been abetted by regulation and planning.[148] For older workers, the effects of vulnerability in the labor market during the recession have been reduced by laws prohibiting compulsory retirement and, to a lesser extent, age discrimination. Perhaps more significant are the legal protections which promote general employment security (such as minimum wages and unfair dismissal laws) which are, moreover, now effectively enforced. These legal protections are supplemented by government policies introduced over the past twenty years which allow workers to plan their transition to retirement through part-time work. The risk of older workers having to endure exploitive working conditions late in their working lives has also been reduced by measures designed to secure decent living standards in retirement.

And yet these protections and policies have not been truly tested by the current global economic crisis. The mildness of the recession in Australia means that potential weaknesses have not been exposed. In particular, the reduction in centralized regulation in the labor law system,

145. Kate O'Loughlin et al., *Impact of the Global Financial Crisis on Employed Australian Baby Boomers: A National Survey*, 29 AUSTRALASIAN J. AGEING 89 (2010).

146. AUSTL. BUREAU OF STATISTICS, 6238.0, RETIREMENT AND RETIREMENT INTENTIONS: JULY 2008 TO JUNE 2009, at 18 tbl.2 (Dec. 17, 2009), *available at* <http://www.ausstats.abs.gov.au/Ausstats/subscriber.nsf/0/61A0264E827F59C4CA25768E002C8F72/$File/62380_jul%202008%20to%20jun%202009.pdf>.

147. DONALD HORNE, THE LUCKY COUNTRY: AUSTRALIA IN THE SIXTIES 209 (1964): "Australia is a lucky country, run by second-rate people who share its luck. It lives on other peoples' ideas . . . . A nation more concerned with styles of life than achievement has managed to achieve what may be the most evenly prosperous society in the world."

148. John Quiggin, *Australia and the Global Financial Crisis*, *in* GOODBYE TO ALL THAT? ON THE FAILURE OF NEO-LIBERALISM AND THE URGENCY OF CHANGE 99, 121 (Robert Manne & David McKnight eds., 2010).

associated with the decline in industry awards and their replacement by enterprise agreements, has reduced the scope for softening the impact of recession on the most disadvantaged groups of workers. In previous recessions it was possible for governments and arbitration tribunals to adopt coordinated wage and employment policies which sought to spread the costs of recovery to some extent. Instead, with a decentralized system, work and its benefits have become more unevenly distributed. As a result, if the recession had been worse in Australia, we would expect to see its effects as being more unequal and more intractable than in previous downturns.

Based on previous experience, if the recession had been deeper and longer, older workers would have been exposed to age-targeted retrenchments and declining re-employment prospects when competing with younger workers, resulting in lower employment participation.[149] Using the 1991 recession as a guide, older male workers especially would have faced underemployment, long-term unemployment and withdrawal from the labor force, the full effects of which might have taken five years or more to reverse.[150] Many of those older workers who remained in work would have faced eroding conditions in the part-time and casual jobs which they predominantly occupy. These effects would have been compounded by shrinking non-wage incomes as the value of investments evaporated and interest rates fell. Given the dependence of the superannuation scheme on the fortunes of the domestic financial sector, many older workers would have faced several more years of work beyond their preferred retirement age. Fortunately for them, older workers (by virtue of their accumulated skills, experience and wealth) have not been particularly affected. It is the older workless and underemployed for whom decent work remains out of reach particularly in straitened times.

149. SPOEHR ET AL., *supra* note 75, at 10.

150. AUSTL. BUREAU OF STATISTICS, 4102.0, AUSTRALIAN SOCIAL TRENDS: MARCH 2010, at 14 (2010), *available at* <http://www.ausstats.abs.gov.au/Ausstats/subscriber.nsf/0/ AD88F98646E88BD7 CA2576E70016C552/$File/41020_ASTMarch2010.pdf >; Kennedy & Da Costa, *supra* note 66, at 40. Some analyses argue that low skill level was a more significant determinant of job displacement than age; however low skill level is positively correlated with age. *See* Jeff Borland & James Ted McDonald, *Displaced Workers in Australia 1984-1996: Macroeconomic Conditions and Structural Change* (Univ. of Melbourne Dep't of Econ. Research Paper No 824, 2001), *available at* <http://www. economics.unimelb.edu.au/downloads/wpapers-00-01/824.pdf>.

III. UNITED KINGDOM

The European Union (E.U.), of which the U.K. is a member, has been concerned for some time with increasing the employment rate of older workers. This rate varies enormously among the member states. The Lisbon Strategy[151] called for an increase of the total employment rate within the E.U. to 67 percent by 2005 and 70 percent by 2010. This included increasing the employment rate of older workers to 50 percent by 2010.

Despite a re-launch in 2005, the Lisbon Strategy failed to achieve its objectives with respect to older workers. The overall employment rate for older workers aged fifty-five to sixty-four grew to an average of 46 percent.[152] Only twelve member states had an older worker employment rate which met the target of 50 percent and nine member states were more than ten percentage points short. These were Malta, Hungary, Poland, Slovenia, Luxembourg, Italy, Belgium, France, and Slovakia. Malta, in 2008, had the lowest rate with just 30 percent of the age group in employment.[153]

There is in the E.U. a steep fall in the employment rate after the age of fifty and the level of employment for those over sixty-five is very low. For the E.U. as a whole, approximately 85 percent of men and 70 percent of women are in employment at age fifty. By the age of sixty-nine for men and sixty-six for women, these figures fall to less than 10 percent.[154] This is partly, of course, a reflection of national policies and culture on retirement and social security systems. While the U.K., for example, is proposing to raise the state pension age to sixty-six years in the near future, the French government has faced opposition when it has proposed an increase in its pension age from sixty to sixty-two years.[155]

151. This was a strategy devised by the Council of Ministers of the E.U. following a meeting in Lisbon in 2001, where a ten year plan was conceived to make the European Community much more competitive. This process was to include increasing labor force participation rates for women and older workers; it became known as the Lisbon Strategy. Further information can be found at *Lisbon Strategy for Growth and Jobs*, EUROPEAN COMM'N, <http://ec.europa.eu/archives/growthandjobs_2009/> (archived Apr. 6, 2010).

152. *Communication from the Commission: Europe 2020: A Strategy for Smart, Sustainable and Inclusive Growth* COM(2010) 2020 (Mar. 3, 2010), [hereinafter *Europe 2020*], *available at* <http://eur-lex.europa.eu/LexUriServ/LexUriServ.do?uri=COM:2010:2020:FIN:EN:PDF>.

153. *Commission Report on the Social Situation in the European Union 2009* (Feb. 2010), *available at* <http://epp.eurostat.ec.europa.eu/cache/ITY_OFFPUB/KE-AG-10-001/EN/KE-AG-10-001-EN.PDF>.

154. *Commission Staff Working Document: Demography Report 2008: Meeting Social Needs in an Ageing Society*, SEC(2008) 2911 (Nov. 21, 2008), *available at* <http://ec.europa.eu/social/BlobServlet?docId=709&langId=en>.

155. *See, e.g.*, *Mass Protests over French Pensions Reform*, THE PARLIAMENT.COM (June 25, 2010), <http://www.theparliament.com/latest-news/article/newsarticle/mass-protests-over-french-pen

In its policy document, *Europe 2020*,[156] the European Commission described some of Europe's structural weaknesses:

> Demographic ageing is accelerating. As the baby-boom generation retires, the EU's active population will start to shrink as from 2013/2014. The number of people aged over 60 is now increasing twice as fast as it did before 2007 – by about two million every year compared to one year previously. The combination of a smaller working population and a higher share of retired people will place additional strains on our welfare systems.[157]

Perhaps more realistically than the Lisbon targets, there is a new E.U. target which relates to the working population as a whole between twenty and sixty-four years. The target aims to increase the employment rate for this group to 75 percent by 2020 "through greater involvement of women, older workers and the better integration of migrant workers in the work force."[158]

Increasing the involvement of older workers in the work force, as mandated by the new target, requires an understanding of the strengths and weaknesses of the member states' systems of labor market regulation, pensions, and other forms of social protection, and how they operate in times of economic stress. This section on the U.K. adds to that knowledge base by reviewing statistics on British older workers during the global economic crisis. Although by some measures older workers appear to have suffered less than their younger counterparts, a trend toward older employees working in non-standard positions – employed on a part-time or temporary basis or self-employed – raises concerns that they are a vulnerable working population. Facilitating their vulnerability, and undermining older worker decent work, is the existence in the U.K. of lawful mandatory retirement and, for at least a subgroup of workers, insufficient pension income.

A. Older Worker Employment and Unemployment Rates

In Great Britain there are just under twenty million people aged fifty or over. Almost nine million of these are between fifty and the State Pension Age (SPA).[159] The proportion of older workers in work has been

sion-reforms/>.

156. *Europe 2020*, *supra* note 152.

157. *Id. at* 5.

158. *Id. at* 8.

159. The State Pension Age is currently sixty-five years old for men and sixty years for women. The ages are being equalized at sixty-five years over a period ending in 2020. The U.K. government has also announced a consultation on increasing the sixty-five year limit in the near future. *See When*

increasing for some years. In the second quarter of 1999, for example, some 66.5 percent of the population between the ages of fifty and SPA and some 7.9 percent of those at SPA or above were in employment; by the second quarter of 2010 these figures had increased to 70.9 percent and 12.3 percent.[160]

In terms of employment rates, as in Australia and the U.S., the recession appears to have impacted most heavily on younger workers. The employment rate for older workers has declined less than any other age group. Indeed the rate of decline appears to increase the younger the age group. Thus for those between the ages of fifty and SPA, the employment rate has declined from 72 percent in 2008 to 70.9 percent in 2010, compared to that, say, of the eighteen to twenty-four age group which has seen a decline from an employment rate of 64.4 percent to 58.5 percent.[161] The decline for all age groups is:

Table 5

Employment Rates by Age[162]

Age group	Employment rate		
	2008	**2010**	**decline**
50-SPA	72.0	70.9	-1.1
35-49	88.7	86.0	-1.3
25-34	88.6	83.9	-2.7
18-24	64.4	58.5	-5.9
16-17	34.8	24.9	-9.9

This trend is emphasized when one considers the figures for those at or above SPA. During this same period the employment rate for this oldest age group has actually increased, from 11.6 percent to 12.3 percent. This

Should the State Pension Age Increase to 66? A Call for Evidence, U.K. DEP'T FOR WORK & PENSIONS, <http://www.dwp.gov.uk/consultations/2010/spa-66-review.shtml> (last viewed Mar. 10, 2011).

160. These statistics are taken from the web site of the Government statistics service. *Employment by Age & Sex – Statistical Bulletin Dataset*, U.K. OFFICE OF NAT'L STATISTICS, http://www.statistics.gov.uk/statbase/product.asp?vlnk=8285> (last visited Mar. 10, 2011) (scroll to "Labour market status by age group" and click to download the .xls file) [hereinafter *Employment by Age & Sex Dataset*]; U.K. OFFICE FOR NAT'L STATISTICS, STATISTICAL BULLETIN: LABOUR MARKET STATISTICS JUNE 2010 (June 16, 2010), *available at* <http://www.statistics.gov.uk/ pdfdir/lmsuk0610.pdf>.

161. *See Employment by Age and Sex Dataset*, *supra* note 160.

162. *See id.* (figures are taken from the February to April cells for each of these years).

increase is mostly the result of an increase in the proportion of female workers over SPA. The employment rate for men at or over SPA hardly changed during this period (10.7 percent to 10.6 percent), while for women the increase was from 12.2 percent to 13.3 percent. The same outcome also applied to the lower age group of fifty to SPA. The employment rate for men decreased (73.5 percent to 71.1 percent) while the employment rate for women in this age group increased from 69.9 percent to 70.7 percent.[163]

Although this superficially shows that older workers, especially female ones, have been less affected by the recession, there may be some evidence to show that this is a result of the disadvantages already suffered by older workers in the U.K. As described in greater detail below, the existence of a mandatory retirement age may have the effect of turning the older workforce into a contingent reserve workforce whose flexibility is attractive to employers in recessionary times. This is further evidenced by the increasing proportion of older women working, as it is the female workforce that traditionally makes up much of the flexible workforce.[164]

Labor force participation rates may be influenced by a discouragement effect and an added workers effect. The discouragement effect has been described as the "decision to refrain from job search as a result of poor chances in the labor market."[165] The added worker effect comes about as a result of the loss of employment by one household member resulting in another household member seeking work.[166] It can only be surmised as to whether the increase in the proportion of older female workers is the result of an added workers effect. One might hypothesize that older workers who fail to obtain employment may become discouraged workers, although, unlike in the U.S., in the U.K. there is a lack of statistical evidence to this effect.

On the other hand, as in Australia and the U.S., there are statistics which show that long term unemployment is a reality for many older workers. The figures show that longer term unemployment rates have been increasing for all younger age groups, but the rate for those workers aged over fifty has remained consistently high and appears unaffected by any recession.

163. *See id.*

164. *See infra* notes 181-83 and accompanying text.

165. Maarten Van Hamm et al., *Local Underemployment and the Discouraged Worker Effect*, 38 URBAN STUD. 1733 (2001); *see also* Maria Brown & Michael Briguglio, *Discouragement Amongst Ageing Workers in Malta within an E.U. Context*, 4 SOCIETIES WITHOUT BORDERS 45-60 (2009).

166. *See generally* Frances McGinnity, *The Labour-Force Participation of the Wives of Unemployed Men: Comparing Britain and West Germany Using Longitudinal Data*, 18 EUR. SOC. REV. 473 (2002) (describing the phenomenon and suggesting a disincentive for the effect in Britain caused by the benefit system).

Table 6

Percentage of Unemployment that Lasts for over Twelve Months[167]

	18-24	25-49	50 and over
2008	19.6	28.1	37.9
2009	17.9	25.6	31.0
2010	25.8	33.6	37.5

Clearly the prognosis for unemployed older workers is worse than for other age groups. The fragile nature of older workers' employment is exemplified in the current recession by the increasing unemployment rate for those over the age of fifty. One analysis in 2009 reported:

> Unemployment increasing at high percentage rate: There are now 367,000 older people aged 50+ out of work. While the actual numbers are low in comparison to other age groups, this is a rise of almost half (37.7 percent) over the last year. This is worrying, particularly given the pattern in previous recessions when this group was hit hard by job losses.[168]

The same analysis blamed ageist attitudes which remained a huge obstacle for older workers and found that "many people feel that the chance of finding new employment is limited because employers simply don't want to take on someone in their 50s."[169]

B. Vulnerability and Precarious Working: Part-Time, Flexible Work, Casual Work, and Self-Employment

If older workers are to be classified as a vulnerable workforce, it is because they are, both in the U.K. and the E.U., increasingly likely with age to work in types of precarious employment.[170] The historic ability of

167. U.K. OFFICE FOR NATIONAL STATISTICS, STATISTICAL BULLETIN: LABOUR MARKET STATISTICS MAY 2010, at tbl.11(2) (May 12, 2010), *available at* <http://www.statistics.gov.uk/pdfdir/lmsuk0510.pdf>.

168. AGE CONCERN, THE IMPACT OF THE RECESSION ON OLDER WORKERS (2009), *available at* <http://taen.org.uk/uploads/resources/Impact_of_the_recession_on_older_workers_media_briefing1.pdf>.

169. *Id.*

170. See Michael Quinlan et al., *The Global Expansion of Precarious Employment, Work Disorganization, and Consequences for Occupational Health: A Review of Recent Research*, 31 INT'L J. HEALTH SERVICES 335 (2001).

employers to enforce a legal mandatory retirement age has added to both the vulnerability of the older workforce and enabled employers to possibly treat them subsequently as a contingent workforce which can be exploited depending upon the economic situation. Precarious employment here is defined as being in part-time or flexible working, or casual work or self-employment, such work being more vulnerable to change in recessionary times.

Both older and younger workers may share the characteristic of not being "prime age" workers. Compared to such workers, older people are seen to have characteristics such as inflexibility and reliability that rely upon stereotypes of age. Consequently they may be regarded as a "buffer" group or as part of a labor market reserve.[171] They are, like others who suffer from negative attitudes, likely to be among the first to be dismissed when there is a need to reduce the workforce size, and among the last to be hired during periods of growth.[172]

Several characteristics are considered relevant to older worker vulnerability. First, the likelihood of being in full-time permanent employment decreases with age; older people are more likely to be self-employed or working part-time than younger age groups. Second, as noted above, once unemployed, workers over the age of fifty tend to remain unemployed for longer than other age groups. Third, older workers are more likely to be employed in precarious work as previously defined. And finally, older workers suffer from stereotyping and age discrimination; in the U.K. this has traditionally included a legal mandatory retirement age.[173]

In general terms, from January-March 2008 to January-March 2010, the number of employees, in the U.K., in full-time work fell by 876,000, but the number of employees in part-time work increased by 214,000.[174] For the same period, the number of self-employed people working full time decreased by just 17,000, while those self-employed people working part-

171. Bernard Casey & Frank Laczko, *Early Retired or Long-term Unemployed? The Situation of Non-Working Men Aged 55-64 from 1979 to 1986*, 3 WORK, EMPLOYMENT & SOC'Y 509 (1988).

172. Terence Hogarth, et al, *The Equality Impacts of the Recession* 43-44 (Warwick Inst. for Employment Research for the Equality & Human Rights Comm'n Report No. 47 2009), *available at* <http://www.equalityhumanrights.com/uploaded_files/research/47_the_equality_impacts_of_the_current_recession.pdf>.

173. *See* Malcolm Sargeant, *The Default Retirement Age: Legitimate Aims, Disproportionate Means*, 39 INDUS. L.J. 244 (2010).

174. *See* U.K. OFFICE FOR NAT'L STATISTICS, STATISTICAL BULLETIN: LABOUR MARKET STATISTICS MAY 2010, at 2 (May 12, 2010) [hereinafter LMS MAY 2010], *available at* <http://www.statistics.gov.uk/pdfdir/lmsuk0510.pdf>; U.K. OFFICE FOR NAT'L STATISTICS, STATISTICAL BULLETIN: LABOUR MARKET STATISTICS MAY 2009, at 2 (May 12, 2009) [hereinafter LMS MAY 2009], *available at* <http://www.statistics.gov.uk/pdfdir/lmsuk0509.pdf>; U.K. OFFICE FOR NAT'L STATISTICS, STATISTICAL BULLETIN: LABOUR MARKET STATISTICS MAY 2008, at 2 (May 14, 2008) [hereinafter LMS MAY 2008], *available at* <http://www.statistics.gov.uk/pdfdir/lmsuk0508.pdf>.

time increased by 82,000.[175] Thus, the British economy saw some shift into part-time working, partly perhaps because of the lack of full-time jobs. The number of people, for example, who stated that they worked part-time because they could not get a full-time job increased from 9.5 percent of part-time workers in 2008 to 14.1 percent of part-time workers in 2010.[176] Similarly, during the same period, there was an increase in those working on temporary contracts, and a jump from a figure of 25 percent of temporary workers in 2008, who were working on this basis because they could not get a permanent job, to a figure of 34.2 percent in 2010.[177] Assuming part-time work is a constituent of precarious working, one can conclude that there has been a move into precarious work by U.K. workers generally as a result of the recession and the decline in full-time employment.

As for older workers and precarious work, research prior to the recession suggests that workers over SPA in the U.K. were twice as likely to be employed in companies with one to ten employees, and far less likely to be employed in organizations with over fifty staff. People aged sixty and over were particularly likely to be employed on a temporary basis and were more likely to work in small firms with fewer than fifty employees.[178] There is no reason to assume that the recession has reversed those findings. Moreover, the likelihood of working part-time increases with age, as can be seen in these figures from the European Foundation:[179]

Table 7

Workers on Part-Time Employment Contracts in the E.U.

Age	15-24	25-34	35-44	45-54	55+	Total
All	24.7	13.5	16.3	13.4	22.1	16.7
Men	19.8	5.2	3.8	3.8	12.0	7.1
Women	30.9	23.2	31.5	25.5	37.0	28.7

175. *See* LMS MAY 2010, *supra* note 174, at tbl.3; LMS MAY 2009, *supra* note 174, at tbl.3; LMS MAY 2008, *supra* note 174, at tbl.3.

176. *Compare* LMS MAY 2008, *supra* note 174, at tbl.3 *with* LMS MAY 2010, *supra* note 174, at tbl.3.

177. *Compare* LMS MAY 2008, *supra* note 174, at tbl.3 *with* LMS MAY 2010, *supra* note 174, at tbl.3.

178. NATIONAL STATISTICS & DEP'T FOR WORK & PENSIONS, FOCUS ON OLDER PEOPLE 31 (A. Soule et al. eds., 2005) [hereinafter FOCUS ON OLDER PEOPLE], *available at* <http://www.statistics.gov.uk/downloads/theme_compendia/foop05/Olderpeople2005.pdf>.

179. EUR. FOUND. FOR THE IMPROVEMENT OF LIVING & WORKING CONDITIONS, WORKING CONDITIONS OF AN AGEING WORKFORCE 20 tbl.2 (2008), *available at* <http://www.eurofound.europa.eu/pubdocs/2008/17/en/2/EF0817EN.pdf>.

Notably, the European Foundation reported that "part-time work appears to be an involuntary choice for a considerable proportion of young and adult workers, while it seems to be much more of a voluntary choice for both older and female workers."[180] There appeared to be no gender differences among workers in the older age group in terms whether part-time work was viewed as voluntary or not. This is evidence that for at least some older workers in the E.U., part-time work is preferred to full-time work.

Within the U.K., in the age group sixteen to forty-nine years, the part-time employment rate for women averages about 43 percent and for men 9 percent. In contrast, the part-time work rate for women aged sixty to sixty-four is 70 percent and for men it is 23 percent. In short, as illustrated by Table 7, in the U.K. there is a direct relationship between working part-time and getting older.[181]

Table 8

Employment of Older Workers in Part-Time Work in the U.K. (Percent)

Age	Women	Men
50-54	42	6
55-59	51	12
60-64	70	23
65-69	85	64
70+	89	74
Total (50+)	52	16

Flexible work arrangements are also considered indicative of vulnerability since they are subject to change in recessionary times. According to an analysis by Smeaton and Vegeris, older women are more

180. *Id.* at 20.

181. Elizabeth Whiting, *The Labour Market Participation of Older People*, 113 Lab. Market Trends 285, 289 tbl.3 (2005). Wendy Loretto, Sarah Vickerstaff, Phil White 'Older workers and options for flexible work'; Working Paper Series no 31 table 2.8 Equal Opportunities Commission (2005); note the Equal Opportunities Commission has been subsumed into the Equality And Human Rights Commission; *available at* http://www.bcmeurope.com/openspace/documents/4_14_5_EOC_older_workers.pdf.

likely than older men to be in flexible working arrangements.[182] It is interesting also how the proportion of both men and women working in these arrangements decreases after the age of sixty; the exception being with regard to part-time working.

Table 9

Proportion of Employed Men and Women Using Flexible Work Arrangements 2000 and 2007[183]

Men	Flexitime		Annualized hours		Any flexible arrangements		Part-time	
Age	2000	2007	2000	2007	2000	2007	2000	2007
45-49	9	11	4	4	18	18	4	5
50-54	9	10	4	5	18	19	6	6
55-59	8	10	4	4	17	19	9	11
60-64	6	8	2	3	14	16	15	20
Women	Flexitime		Annualized hours		Any flexible arrangements		Part-time	
Age	2000	2007	2000	2007	2000	2007	2000	2007
45-49	12	15	5	5	31	32	44	43
50-54	10	13	5	5	27	30	47	42
55-59	9	11	3	5	24	27	52	47
60-64	7	10	2	5	19	24	61	80

Older workers in the U.K. were also more likely to hold a temporary employment contract. Thus some 10 percent of working men over SPA were in temporary employment compared to an average of 4 percent for the age groups below them. Similarly about 9 percent of women over SPA held temporary contracts compared to 6 percent of women between the ages of twenty-five and forty-nine and 5 percent of those between fifty and SPA.[184]

182. DEBORAH SMEATON & SANDRA VEGERIS, POL'Y STUDIES INST., EQUALITY & HUMAN RIGHTS COMM'N, RESEARCH REPORT NO. 22, OLDER PEOPLE INSIDE AND OUTSIDE THE LABOUR MARKET: A REVIEW 26-27 (2009).

183. *Id.* at 27 tbls.3.1, 3.2.

184. DEBORAH SMEATON & STEPHEN MCKAY, DEP'T FOR WORK & PENSIONS, RESEARCH REPORT NO. 182, WORKING AFTER STATE PENSION AGE: QUANTITATIVE ANALYSIS 29 tbl.3.2 (2003).

If one examines the type of temporary contract held, then it is apparent that the oldest workers are most likely to be employed in seasonal work and casual work.[185]

Finally, as noted below in the U.S. section, during recessions, increases in self-employment may be evidence that workers have lost and been unable to replace their jobs.[186] In terms of age, self-employment is more common in the U.K. among older workers than among the younger age groups. One study showed that

> 19 per cent of people aged fifty and over were self-employed compared with 14 percent of people aged 25 to 49. Older men were more likely than older women to be self-employed: 26 per cent of men aged 50 and over compared with 11 per cent of women. Gender differences in self-employment become more marked after SPA – 46 per cent of men aged 65 and over were self-employed compared with 13 per cent of women aged 60–64 in 2004.[187]

Across the E.U. there is a similar trend:[188]

Table 10

Self-employed People as a Percentage of Total Employees in the E.U.

Age	% Self-Employed
15-24	6.6
25-34	13.6
35-44	16.3
45-54	17.5
55+	28.8
Total	16.4

In all age groups men are much more likely to work on a self-employed basis than women. For the over fifty-five-year-olds in the E.U., the figures were that 72.8 percent of the self-employed were men compared to 27.2 percent who were women.[189]

185. *Id.* at 31 tbl.3.3.
186. *See infra* note 290 and accompanying text.
187. FOCUS ON OLDER PEOPLE, *supra* note 178, at 31.
188. EUR. FOUND. FOR THE IMPROVEMENT OF LIVING & WORKING CONDITIONS, *supra* note 179, at 19 tbl.1.
189. *Id.*

C. Age Discrimination and Its Connection to Weakened Job Security

Age discrimination is unlawful in the U.K. unless it can be justified as being a proportionate means of achieving a legitimate aim.[190] As in the U.S., seemingly robust protection against age discrimination nonetheless contributes to older worker vulnerability, albeit through different means.[191] More specifically, the employer's ability in the U.K. to compulsorily retire its employees renders many older workers members of a flexible and contingent workforce. Prior to 2006, compulsory retirement was effectuated, in most cases, by an express term in individual contracts of employment, which provided that employment would come to an end at a certain age, usually, but not always, sixty-five. The ability to include this term was re-enforced by legislation which took away an individual's right to complain about unfair dismissal at or after this retirement age.[192]

In 2006, the government introduced a "default retirement age" (DRA) in conjunction with regulations designed to tackle age discrimination in employment.[193] The DRA gave employers the option of forcing employees to retire at, normally, age sixty-five without the employee being able to claim age discrimination or unfair dismissal,[194] so long as the procedure mandated in Schedule 6 of the age regulations is followed. This procedure allows the employee to ask to continue working beyond sixty-five years of age.[195] The employer, following a meeting with the employee, may agree or reject the request without giving reasons.[196] Importantly, the employer may also agree to continued working for a fixed period or on a different basis.[197] This prerogative creates the potential for an employer to use older workers in a contingent way, to suit the needs of the business.

A default retirement age was a strange concept to introduce at the same time as regulations implementing a European Directive aimed at tackling age discrimination,[198] and not surprisingly, the DRA was challenged in the courts. The European Court of Justice has decided several cases challenging whether a retirement age is compatible with the

190. The Employment Equality (Age) Regulations 2006 S.I. 2006/1031, art. 3. These regulations were subsumed into the Equality Act 2010, c. 15, effective October 2010.

191. *See infra* Part IV(D).

192. Employment Rights Act 1996, c. 18, § 109.

193. The Employment Equality (Age) Regulations 2006 S.I. 2006/1031. These Regulations have now been substantially incorporated into the Equality Act 2010, c. 15.

194. *See* MALCOLM SARGEANT, AGE DISCRIMINATION IN EMPLOYMENT 119-21, 174 (2007).

195. Employment Equality (Age) Regulations 2006, sch. 6.

196. *Id.*

197. *Id.*

198. Council Directive 2000/78, Establishing a General Framework for Equal Treatment in Employment and Occupation, 2000 O.J. (L303)16.

Framework Directive on Equal Treatment in Employment and Occupation.[199] In *Palacios de la Villa*,[200] for example, the complainant claimed that he had been subject to age discrimination as a result of his dismissal at the age of sixty-five. The Court accepted that the aim of the measure which permitted the employer's action was legitimate – the aim being to check unemployment and promote employment generally – and the means were also judged to be appropriate and necessary.[201] Compulsory retirement could be a proportionate means of achieving the aim, particularly taking into account the fact that the persons concerned are entitled to financial compensation by way of a retirement pension at the end of their working life, such as that provided for by the national legislation at issue in the main proceedings, the level of which cannot be regarded as unreasonable.[202]

A second judgment concerning a mandatory retirement age was contained in the *Age Concern* case, a reference from the English High Court.[203] In that case, the European Court of Justice was asked, *inter alia*, whether the scope of the Directive extended to rules which permitted employers to dismiss employees aged sixty-five or over by reason of retirement, and whether the national regulations concerning discrimination in employment and retirement were national provisions laying down retirement ages.[204] In simple language, this claim questioned the U.K.'s introduction of the default retirement age of sixty-five years.

Age Concern, the aforementioned NGO, argued that Article 6(1) of the Framework Directive did not permit member states to introduce a general defense of justification for direct age discrimination, but allowed them to make specific provisions listing the grounds which could constitute a legitimate aim.[205] In turn, the U.K. government argued that the provisions at issue did not fall within the scope of the Directive at all.[206] The Court concluded that the Directive gives Member States the option to provide, within the context of national law, for certain kinds of differences in treatment on grounds of age if they are objectively and reasonably justified by a legitimate aim, such as employment policy, or labor market or

199. *Id.*

200. Case C-411/05, Félix Palacios de la Villa v. Cortefiel Servicios SA, 2007 E.C.R. I-8531.

201. *Id.* ¶ 64.

202. *Id.* ¶ 73.

203. Case C-388/07, Inc. Trs. of the Nat'l Council on Ageing (Age Concern Eng.) v Sec'y of State for Bus., Enter. & Regulatory Reform, 2009 E.C.R. I-1569.

204. *Id.*

205. *Id.* ¶ 36.

206. *Id.* ¶ 19.

vocational training objectives, and if the means of achieving that aim are appropriate and necessary.[207]

One of the reasons the recently defeated Labor government prevailed when the case returned to the English High Court[208] was that it proposed a review of the DRA in 2011, a review subsequently brought forward to 2010. Britain's newly elected coalition government, however, has committed itself to phasing out the DRA at an early stage.[209] This is now to take place from April 2011.[210] There will remain, nonetheless, the possibility for employers to retain an "employer justified retirement age" (EJRA), if the employer can show that it has a legitimate aim and the means for achieving that aim are proportionate.[211] Although this is likely to provide only a limited opportunity for employers, it does seem as if it will be left to the courts to decide whether an EJRA is justified. Given the wide scope for justification contained in Article 6 of the Framework Directive, it cannot be assumed that the phasing out of the DRA will inevitably mean the end of mandatory retirement in the U.K.

D. Insufficient Retirement Security

One analysis of evidence concerning the default retirement age cited an Age Concern survey in 2010 of 976 adults aged 60 to 70 which found:

> [O]f adults aged 65-70 who had retired, four per cent had been 'made to retire by their employer because of their age' in the previous year, and six per cent in the previous three years. A quarter of the age group 'know someone who has been forced to retire'; the employers of four in ten employees over 60 use forced retirement; 13 per cent of employees aged 60 to 64 definitely expect to be forced to retire.[212]

The first Old Age Pensions Act in the U.K. was adopted over one hundred years ago.[213] It introduced a universal, albeit means tested, state

207. *Id.* ¶ 8.

208. R (on the application of Age U.K.) v Sec'y of State for Bus., Innovation & Skills, [2009] EWHC (Admin) 2336, [2010] ICR 260.

209. The Conservative Party and the Liberal Democrat Party entered into a coalition agreement in May 2010 which included this commitment. H.M. Gov't, The Coalition: Our Programme for Government 7-8, 26 (2010), *available at* <http://www.cabinetoffice.gov.uk/sites/default/files/resources/coalition_programme_for_government.pdf>.

210. DEP'T FOR BUS. INNOVATION & SKILLS & DEP'T FOR WORK & PENSIONS, PHASING OUT THE RETIREMENT AGE: CONSULTATION DOCUMENT 5 (2010), *available at* <http://www.bis.gov.uk/assets/biscore/employment-matters/docs/p/10-1047-default-retirement-age-consultation.pdf>.

211. *Id.* at 10, 31-32.

212. WENDY SYKES, ET AL., REVIEW OF THE DEFAULT RETIREMENT AGE: SUMMARY OF THE STAKEHOLDER EVIDENCE 31 (Dept. for Work and Pensions, Research Report 679, 2010); *available at* http://re search.dwp.gov.uk/asd/asd5/rports2009-2010/rrep675.pdf.

213. The Old Age Pensions Act, 1908, 8 Edw. 7, c. 40.

pension for those of seventy years of age and over. It was a landmark in welfare reform and was intended to alleviate the worst poverty suffered by the poorest people in the country. Yet after a century of pension provision and pension reform, the development of pensions, and of formalized pension ages have been described by some as aspects of a process of marginalizing and degrading older people in the twentieth century, as they were progressively excluded from paid work and the social status assumed to be associated with it.[214]

In a sense, the development of the state pension system, and the creation of the state retirement age which accompanies it, creates a separate class of excluded persons, many of whom continue to live in relative or absolute poverty. This is because the U.K. pension system provides only a subsistence pension. The post-1945 old age pension arrangements were intended to allow people to retire on an income that only partially came from the state; there was an expectation that individual savings would be an important part of retirement income.[215] Indeed, the U.K. state subsistence pension is one of the lowest, as a proportion of earnings, of any E.U. member state.[216] This is very much a gender issue with only 30 percent of women who reach state pension age entitled to a full basic state pension, compared with 85 percent of men.[217] In addition, some 70 percent of the female pensioner population has no private pension at all.[218]

Nearly two thirds of all those receiving state pensions are women.[219] The following sums up the situation of women with regard to pension provision in the U.K.:

> [One] in five single women pensioners risk being in poverty in retirement . . . By 2020 it is estimated that there will be as many divorced women aged 65 to 75 as widows. Almost two thirds of divorced and separated older women have no private pension income at all . . . the number of women who are saving for retirement halves when they have a baby and the figure for men remains unchanged when they become new fathers.[220]

214. PAT THANE, OLD AGE IN ENGLISH HISTORY 385-406 (2002).

215. SIR WILLIAM BEVERIDGE, SOCIAL INSURANCE AND ALLIED SERVICES, 1942 Cmd. 6404, *available at* <http://www.fordham.edu/halsall/mod/1942beveridge.html>.

216. *See* AON CONSULTING, EUROPEAN BUSINESS LEADERS SURVEY 7 (2009), *available at* <http://www.aon.com/austria/products-and-services/human-capital-consulting/attachements/ebls_engl.pdf>.

217. PENSIONS COMM'N, PENSIONS: CHALLENGES AND CHOICES: FIRST REPORT OF THE PENSIONS COMMISSION 268, (2004), *available at* <http://image.guardian.co.uk/sys-files/Money/documents/2005/05/17/fullreport.pdf>

218. *Id.* at 62.

219. DEP'T FOR WORK & PENSIONS, QUARTERLY STATISTICAL SUMMARY 1, 17 (Nov. 11, 2009), *available at* <http://campaigns.dwp.gov.uk/asd/asd1/stats_summary/Stats_Summary_Nov2009.pdf >.

220. Equal Opportunities Commission, Parliamentary Briefing, Pensions Bill 16th January 2007,

Contributing to women's disadvantage is the traditional family care-giving role they play. Some 25 percent of all women age forty-five to sixty-four are care-givers and only 37 percent of women work full-time, compared to 60 percent of men, greatly impacting the ability of women to save for retirement.[221] The system has traditionally been based on the model of husband in paid work and wife in unpaid domestic work, a model which presently lacks correspondence to the lives of many women.[222] Linked to this is the abandonment of the principle of a non-contributory entitlement, or an entitlement not based upon the amount or regularity of contributions, and the reliance on a private pension system which is linked to earnings and periods of service.[223] Although the Pensions Acts of 2007 and 2008 sought to improve the overall levels of income and have reduced, from 2010, the qualifying period to be eligible for a full state pension,[224] there is still a legacy of large numbers of older people being reduced to poverty at retirement.

Given this weakness in the pension system, the financial imperative to continue working may be quite strong for some older workers. One international survey, which included the U.K., reported that 38 percent of respondents stated that "they will continue to work after retirement age for financial reasons; 31 percent [said] that they will work to stay involved and active, but not for financial reasons; [and] 32 percent [said] they will not seek employment after retiring."[225] According to the survey, some 21 percent of private sector employees believed that "recent economic events mean they will have to work longer before they can afford to retire. A further 10 percent expect to retire when planned but will have to scale back

Commons 2nd Reading 4.

221. JAY GINN, GENDER, PENSIONS AND THE LIFECOURSE: HOW PENSIONS NEED TO ADAPT TO CHANGING FAMILY FORMS 3 (2003) ("The disproportionate share of poverty borne by today's older women reflects the model of gender relations prevailing during much of their earlier lives, one in which a gender division of labour confined most married women to raising a family and homemaking – the male breadwinner-housewife model"); *see also*, Debora Price & Jay Ginn, *Sharing the Crust? Gender, Partnership Status and Inequalities in Pension Accumulation*, *in* GENDER AND AGEING: CHANGING ROLES AND RELATIONSHIPS 127 (Sara Arber et al. eds., 2003).

222. *See* GINN, *supra* note 221, at 3; Price & Ginn, *supra* note 221.

223. The current situation of women with regard to pensions and how this may be changing is discussed further below.

224. Malcolm Sargeant, *Gender Equality and the Pensions Acts 2007-2008,* 38 INDUS. L.J. 143 (2009). The Pensions Act 2007 reduced the qualifying period from forty-four years for men and thirty-nine years for women to thirty years for both. Pensions Act, 2007, c. 22, § 1.

225. *Recession Dents a Third of Workers' Retirement Plans*, TOWER WATSON (Apr. 20, 2010), <http://www.towerswatson.com/united-kingdom/press/1659> (reporting on the results of the company's Global Workforce Study 2010).

on their spending."[226]

E. U.K.: Conclusions

The statistics reveal that the oldest workers are more likely to be in a non-standard contractual relationship, by working on a part-time or temporary basis or being self-employed. This pattern is not unique to the U.K., but is part of a trend throughout the E.U., where higher levels of part-time working and self employment are recorded for older workers – some 22 percent of older workers work part-time, compared to an average of 16 percent for workers generally, and almost one quarter of older workers labor on a self-employed basis compared to an average of 15 percent for the general working population.[227] These are some of the characteristics of a vulnerable work force, i.e. one that might be more subject to exploitation because it does not fulfill the criteria of being in a full-time, permanent contractual relationship. This is not to say that all older people are necessarily coerced into these working arrangements. One piece of qualitative research in the U.K. suggested that significant numbers of older people actually preferred casual or temporary work compared to permanent work.[228] That research also revealed, however, that there was a desire among significant numbers of older people to remain in or enter employment.[229]

Discrimination in employment on the ground of chronological age is an issue when considering the vulnerability of older workers. There is much evidence that such discrimination exists. A U.K. government consultation, *Equality and Diversity: Age Matters*, provided some examples of age discrimination.[230] These were persons being forced to retire after reaching a certain age; not being given a job they applied for because of their age; being told their age was a barrier to general advancement; assumptions being made about their abilities due to age; and being selected for redundancy (layoff) because of age.[231] In addition, the adoption of a default retirement age in 2006 seems to have contributed to a contingent older workforce which, perversely in difficult economic times,

226. *Id.*

227. EUROPEAN COMM'N, EMPLOYMENT IN EUROPE 18 (2007), *available at* <ec.europa.eu/social/BlobServlet?docId=3068&langId=en>.

228. DEBORAH SMEATON ET AL., EQUALITY & HUMAN RIGHTS COMM'N RESEARCH REPORT 43, OLDER WORKERS: EMPLOYMENT PREFERENCES, BARRIERS AND SOLUTIONS vii, 59-64, 87, 111, (2009).

229. *Id.* at vii, 58-60, 61, 64.

230. DEP'T OF TRADE & INDUS., EQUALITY AND DIVERSITY: AGE MATTERS 9 (2003), *available at* <http://webarchive.nationalarchives.gov.uk/+/http://www.berr.gov.uk/files/file24331.pdf>.

231. *Id.*

has suffered much less proportionately in terms of employment and unemployment rates than other groups.

Regarding decent work, the U.K. falls short of at least two decent work objectives: social protection and fundamental rights at work, the latter referring to the obligation to eliminate age discrimination. Moreover, the troubling trend toward increasing part-time work and irregular employment arrangements casts a shadow on the extent to which the U.K. fulfills its obligation on employment promotion for older workers.

IV. UNITED STATES

The Great Recession[232] produced serious adverse effects for American workers of all ages. Unemployment, for example, rocketed from a November 2007 pre-recessionary rate of 4.7 percent to a high of 10.1 percent in October 2009.[233] At present, eight months into 2010, the unemployment rate is 9.6 percent, about where it has anemically hovered for months.[234] Some 14.9 million people are unemployed with 6.2 million of them categorized as long-term unemployed.[235] By one estimate, close to one-third of the American labor force is currently looking for work or has experienced unemployment sometime during the crisis.[236] That study also found that since the recession began, more than half of Americans "in the

232. Due to its severity, in terms of depth and duration, the most recent economic downturn is often referred to in the U.S. as the "Great Recession." Michael Elsby et al., *The Labor Market in the Great Recession*, BROOKINGS PAPERS ON ECONOMIC ACTIVITY, Spring 2010, at 1, *available at* <http://muse.jhu.edu/journals/brookings_papers_on_economic_activity/toc/eca.2010.1.html> [hereinafter *The Labor Market in the Great Recession*]. The National Bureau of Economic Research designates December 2007 as the beginning of the current recession in the U.S. *See* Sharon Cohany, Bureau of Labor Statistics, U.S. Dep't of Labor, *Ranks of Discouraged Workers and Others Marginally Attached to the Labor Force Rise During Recession*, ISSUES IN LABOR STATISTICS, SUMMARY 09-04, Apr. 2009, at 1 n.2, *available at* <www.bls.gov/opub/ils/pdf/opbils74.pdf>.

233. *See* RICHARD W. JOHNSON ET AL., URBAN INSTITUTE PROGRAM ON RETIREMENT POLICY, UNEMPLOYMENT STATISTICS ON OLDER AMERICANS tbl.2 (Mar. 2011), *available at* <http://www.urban.org/UploadedPDF/411904_unemploymentstatistics.pdf>.

234. News Release USDL-11-0271, Bureau of Labor Statistics, U.S. Dep't of Labor, The Employment Situation – August 2010, at 1 (Sept. 3, 2010), *available at* <http://www.bls.gov/news.release/archives/empsit_09032010.pdf>.

235. *Id.* at 1-2. The Bureau of Labor Statistics defines the "long-term unemployed" as "those jobless 27 weeks and over." *Id.* at 2. In other words, the long-term unemployed are those who are jobless and actively looking for work for over six months.

236. PAUL TAYLOR ET AL., PEW RESEARCH CTR., A BALANCE SHEET AT 30 MONTHS: HOW THE GREAT RECESSION HAS CHANGED LIFE IN AMERICA 11 (2010) [hereinafter HOW THE GREAT RECESSION HAS CHANGED LIFE]. Notably, in assessing the differences in the impact of the recession in eighty-four countries during 2009, the ILO places the U.S. in its highest category with respect to job loss – countries sustaining a very strong increase in unemployment (more than three percentage points). *See Recovery and Growth, supra* note 1, at 12 tbl.1.1; *see also* News Release, OECD, Employment Outlook 2010 – How Does the United States Compare?, 1 *available at* <www.oecd.org/dataoecd/14/57/45603148.pdf> (last viewed Mar. 14, 2011) ("Unemployment has risen more sharply in the United States following the recent global financial crisis than in most other OECD countries.").

labor force have suffered a spell of unemployment, a cut in pay, a reduction in hours or have become involuntary part-time workers."[237]

By some measures U.S. older workers, like their Australian and British counterparts,[238] are faring better than younger workers.[239] A closer inspection, however, reveals that the financial crisis has magnified older workers' existing vulnerabilities. As described below, older Americans' occupational and economic security is undercut by four factors: 1) weak job security protections; 2) weakened protections against age discrimination in employment; 3) declining retirement security; and 4) an inadequate unemployment benefit system. Although these factors are independent of the recession in a causal sense, the financial crisis highlighted vulnerabilities which must be addressed by policymakers if the U.S. is to nurture a vibrant labor market for all workers and guarantee decent work for older Americans. Before taking up those topics, however, a review of older worker employment and unemployment statistics, along with additional indicators of labor market vulnerability, is in order. These data are relevant to assessments of U.S. efforts at employment promotion, the first decent work objective.

A. Older Worker Employment and Unemployment Rates

In keeping with the trend in many countries, the U.S. population is aging.[240] In a country of about 310 million, the U.S. Census Bureau estimates that in 2010 there were just under ninety-nine million people

237. HOW THE GREAT RECESSION HAS CHANGED LIFE, *supra* note 236, at i. At the time of this writing, in the summer 2010, the National Bureau of Economic Research (NBER) had not yet declared the recession over. *Id.* at 5. The NBER, a non-profit economic research organization is considered "the quasi-official arbiter of the timing of expansions and recessions in the U.S. economy." *Id.* at 5 n.4. Shortly before submission of the manuscript to the *Employee Rights and Employment Policy Journal*, in September 2010, the NBER determined that the U.S. recession ended in June 2009. *See* Larry Swisher, *NBER Declares U.S. Recession Lasted Record 18 Months, Ended in June 2009*, Daily Lab. Rep. (BNA), A-1 (Sept. 20, 2010).

238. *See supra* Parts II-III.

239. For example, the U.S. labor force presently contains more workers aged sixty-five and over than teenagers. *See* Michael McDonough & Andy Cinko, *Elderly Workers Overtake Teens in Job Search: Chart of the Day*, BLOOMBERG (Jul. 12, 2010, 6:00 PM CT), http://www.bloomberg.com/ news /2010-07-12/u-s-workers-over-65-overtake-teens-for-first-time-since-48-chart-of-day.html. Thus, in the first half of 2010, the number of workers aged sixty-five years old and older, who were employed or actively looking for work, averaged 6.6 million while the number of sixteen- to nineteen-year-old workers in labor force averaged 5.9 million. *Id.* Indeed, there is competition for jobs between the groups in some industries, like food preparation and serving. *Id.*

240. *See* ADMIN. ON AGING, U.S. DEP'T OF HEALTH & HUMAN SERVS., A PROFILE OF OLDER AMERICANS: 2009 4-5 (2010) [hereinafter A PROFILE OF OLDER AMERICANS], *available at* http://www.aoa.gov/AoAroot/Aging_Statistics/Profile/2009/docs/2009profile_508.pdf ("Since 1900, the percentage of Americans 65+ has tripled . . . , and the number has increased more than twelve times . . . . The older population will continue to grow significantly in the future.").

aged fifty and over in the United States.[241] Not only is the population at-large aging, so is the U.S. labor force, a consequence of the aging of the baby boom generation.[242] This latter fact is relevant because, as explained below, workers vary by age in their likelihood to experience negative employment outcomes, such as unemployment.[243] Indeed, throughout the recession, U.S. younger workers were more severely affected than were older workers, a fact apparent by looking at a number of measures. Yet carefully analyzing available statistics also reveals hidden vulnerabilities among older workers that should concern policymakers.

Turning first to employment rates, or employment-to-population ratios, age-based patterns detrimental to younger workers are clearly evident. Between December 2007 and May 2010, workers aged sixteen to twenty-four experienced a drop of 6.6 points in their employment rate.[244] In comparison, the employment rate for prime age workers, those twenty-five to fifty-four, fell 4.5 points.[245] In sharp contrast, while there was minor variation during the relevant time period in the employment-to-population ratios of workers fifty-five and over, these older workers ended in May 2010 with the same employment rate they had in December 2007.[246]

241. *See* U.S. Census Bureau, THE 2010 STATISTICAL ABSTRACT, at tbl.8 (Resident Population Projections by Sex and Age: 2010 to 2050), *available at* <http://www.census.gov/prod/2009pubs/10statab/pop.pdf> . In 2008, there were a little over ninety-four million individuals aged fifty and over in the country. *See id.* at tbl.9 (Resident Population by Race, Hispanic Origin, and Age: 2000 and 2008). Individuals aged sixty-five and over numbered 38.9 million in 2008. *See* A PROFILE OF OLDER AMERICANS, *supra* note 240, at 3.

242. *The Labor Market in the Great Recession*, *supra* note 232, at 9; *see also* Mitra Toossi, *Labor Force Projections to 2018: Older Workers Staying More Active*, MONTHLY LAB. REV., Nov. 2009, at 30, 30, *available at* <http://www.bls.gov/opub/mlr/2009/11/art3full.pdf> ("With the aging of the baby-boom generation, defined as persons born between 1946 and 1964, the older age cohorts are expected to make up a much larger share of the labor force.").

243. *The Labor Market in the Great Recession*, *supra* note 232, at 9.

244. *See* AM. ASS'N OF RETIRED PERSONS PUB. POLICY INST., FACT SHEET 193, THE EMPLOYMENT SITUATION, MAY 2010: OLDER WORKER UNEMPLOYMENT AND DURATION OF UNEMPLOYMENT MOVE UPWARD 4 tbl.2 (2010) [hereinafter THE EMPLOYMENT SITUATION, MAY 2010], *available at* <http://assets.aarp.org/rgcenter/ppi/econ-sec/fs193-employment.pdf>.

245. *Id.*

246. *Id.*

Table 11

Employment Rates by Age[247]

Period	16-24	25-54	55+
Dec. 2007	52.1	79.7	37.7
Dec. 2008	49.4	77.5	37.9
Dec. 2009	44.6	74.7	37.0
May 2010	45.5	75.2	37.7
Decline	-6.6	-4.5	0

This age-based pattern comports with a common phenomenon in recessions. More specifically, during recessions, demand for younger workers declines significantly.[248] Labor economists attribute this to the lower skill and experience levels of this group.[249] Moreover, as explained further below, pressures to delay retirement – including a significant drop in retirement security – kept many older employees in the workplace during the recession, drawing a paycheck.[250] As with workers in the U.K., during the global financial crisis, the employment rate of older American workers tended not to suffer as much as that of other age groups. Thus, an initial assessment of the American system's efforts at employment promotion for older workers appears favorable. At least with respect to this group, significant numbers of a potentially vulnerable population were able to remain employed during a severe and extended economic downturn.

Unemployment rates, calculated by determining that percentage of the labor force actively engaged in a search for work, superficially indicate older workers fared better during the recession. Older worker unemployment rates throughout the recession have been lower than those for young and prime age workers.[251] This is not surprising, as older workers are typically those with the most experience and often those who have found long-term jobs.[252] A review of average unemployment rates by age

247. *Id.*

248. *See* Steven F. Hipple, *The Labor Market in 2009: Recession Drags On*, MONTHLY LAB. REV., Mar. 2010, at 3, 4, *available at* <http://www.bls.gov/opub/mlr/2010/03/art1full.pdf>.

249. *Id.* at 4.

250. *See* ALICIA H. MUNNELL ET AL., CTR. FOR RETIREMENT RESEARCH AT BOSTON COLL., ISSUE BRIEF NO. 9-2, RECESSIONS AND OLDER WORKERS 2 (2009), *available at* <http://crr.bc.edu/images/stories/Briefs/ib_9-2.pdf>.

251. *See* Heidi Shierholz, *Job Creation at a Glacial Pace*, ECONOMIC POLICY INST. (Jul. 2, 2010), <http://www.epi.org/publications/entry/job_creation_at_a_glacial_pace/> ("Older workers (age 55+) have seen the lowest unemployment rates throughout the downturn.").

252. *See* DAVID ROSNICK, CTR. FOR ECON. & POLICY RESEARCH, ISSUE BRIEF, THE ADULT

from 1981 through 2010 found unemployment rates skewed heavily toward younger workers.[253] During that period, those under twenty experienced an average unemployment rate of over 15 percent while those thirty-five and over had an average rate of unemployment of less than 5 percent.[254]

The overwhelming advantage older workers appear to possess, however, diminishes somewhat when one considers additional facts. First, older worker unemployment reached record levels in 2009.[255] In raw numbers, in 2009, on average 1.5 million employees aged fifty-five to sixty-four were unemployed each month; the 2009 monthly figure for employees aged sixty-five and over was 421,000.[256]

Second, since the global financial crisis began, unemployment has increased more for older workers than for their younger counterparts. In other words, the percentage increase in unemployment for older workers has been more dramatic than for younger or prime age workers.[257] Between December 2007 and August 2010, the unemployment rate for older workers increased by about 128 percent.

RECESSION: AGE-ADJUSTED UNEMPLOYMENT AT POST-WAR HIGHS 2 (July 2010), *available at* <www.cepr.net/documents/publications/ur-2010-07.pdf>.

253. *Id.*

254. *Id.* An accurate comparison of the unemployment rates associated with the Great Recession and those of earlier recessions requires adjusting the figures for age to account for how much the labor force has aged over time. *Id.* On an age adjusted basis, the overall unemployment rates during the current recession are the highest and have lasted longest of any recession since the Great Depression. *Id.* at 1-3.

255. *See* RICHARD W. JOHNSON & CORINA MOMMAERTS, RETIREMENT POLICY PROGRAM, URBAN INST., HOW DID OLDER WORKERS FARE IN 2009?. RETIREMENT POLICY PROGRAM, URBAN INSTITUTE, at v (2010) [hereinafter HOW DID OLDER WORKERS FARE?], *available at* <http://www. urban.org/UploadedPDF/412039_older_workers.pdf> ("The 2009 unemployment rate was 7.2 percent for men age 55 to 64 and 6.7 percent for men age 65 and older. For women, the 2009 unemployment rate was 6.0 percent at age 55 to 64 and 6.1 percent at age 65 and older.").

256. *Id.* at v. Actually, in August 2010, fourteen months after the official end of the recession in the U.S., the unemployment rate for workers aged fifty-five and over reached 7.3 percent, a new record. *See* AM. ASS'N OF RETIRED PERSONS PUB. POLICY INST., FACT SHEET 202, THE EMPLOYMENT SITUATION, AUGUST 2010: SHARP RISE IN UNEMPLOYMENT AMONG OLDER MEN 1, 2 fig.1 (2010) [hereinafter THE EMPLOYMENT SITUATION, AUGUST 2010], *available at* <http://assets.aarp.org/rgcenter/ppi/econ-sec/fs202-economic.pdf> In numerical terms, more than 2.2 million older workers were unemployed in August 2010. *Id.* at 1.

257. *See* THE EMPLOYMENT SITUATION, AUGUST 2010, *supra* note 256, at 3.

Table 12

Unemployment Rates by Age[258]

Period	16-24	25-54	55+
Dec. 2007	11.8	4.1	3.2
August 2010	18.1	8.5	7.3
% change	53.4%	107.3%	128.1%

Third, once unemployed, older American workers, like those in Australia and the U.K., tend to experience longer bouts of unemployment.[259] A recent Bureau of Labor Statistics report examined the experience of long term joblessness for different age groups. That study determined younger workers have a lower probability of remaining unemployed for twenty-seven weeks or more as compared with their older counterparts.[260] This pattern is evident throughout the recession and its aftermath. In February 2010, for example, the percent of workers aged sixteen to twenty-four unemployed twenty-seven weeks or over was 28.5 percent while for those fifty-five and older it was 49.1 percent.[261] In February 2010, the average duration of joblessness for workers sixteen to twenty-four years old was 23.3 weeks compared with 35.5 weeks for those fifty-five and above.[262] These statistics indicate significant weaknesses in the American system of employment promotion for a subgroup of older workers.

258. *Id.* December 2007 is the designated beginning of the Great Recession. *See supra* note 235.

259. THE EMPLOYMENT SITUATION, AUGUST 2010, *supra* note 256, at 2; *see also* Bureau of Labor Statistics, U.S. Dep't of Labor, *Record Unemployment among Older Workers Does Not Keep Them Out of the Job Market*, ISSUES IN LABOR STATISTICS, SUMMARY 10-04, Mar. 2010, at 1 [hereinafter *Record Unemployment among Older Workers*], *available at* <http://www.bls.gov/opub/ils/pdf/opbils81.pdf> (". . . [O]lder persons who do become unemployed spend more time searching for work.").

260. *See* Bureau of Labor Statistics, U.S. Dep't of Labor, *Long-Term Unemployment Experience of the Jobless*, ISSUES IN LABOR STATISTICS, SUMMARY 10-05, Jun. 2010, at 2, *available at* <http://www.bls.gov/opub/ils/pdf/opbils82.pdf> ("Once unemployed, however, younger workers actually have a relatively low probability of remaining jobless for a half year or more.").

261. *See Record Unemployment among Older Workers*, *supra* note 259, at 1.

262. *Id.*

Table 13

Percentage of Unemployment Lasting Twenty-Seven Weeks or More[263]

Period	16-24	25-54	55+
2007	11.9	19.9	27.7
2008	13.8	21.8	25.7
2009	23.3	33.4	39.4
2010	28.5	41.3	49.1

Age related-differences in unemployment duration, apparent not only in the U.S. but also in Australia and the U.K., are not well understood. It could be that older workers are less mobile than younger workers, may search for jobs less intensively, or may be more selective concerning available opportunities.[264] Employers may hesitate to employ older workers, fearing their wages will be too high or out of concern that older workers lack relevant skills.[265] Older workers may also be experiencing age discrimination in employment, a topic discussed below.[266]

Further complexity emerges from the unemployment statistics when one considers the gender, race, ethnicity, and educational level of older workers. Regarding gender, following the pattern for the entire labor force, older men experienced higher unemployment than older women.[267] This gender-differentiated pattern, which was larger for younger groups, is attributable to the gender composition of the industries hit hardest by the recession, including construction and manufacturing.[268]

The recession also produced far greater unemployment for older workers who are racial or ethnic minorities, and those with limited education, though the differences are greater among men than women.[269]

263. *Id.*

264. *See* RICHARD W. JOHNSON, RETIREMENT POLICY PROGRAM, URBAN INST., RISING SENIOR UNEMPLOYMENT AND THE NEED TO WORK AT OLDER AGES 6 (2009), *available at* <http://www.urban.org/UploadedPDF/411964_senior_unemployment.pdf>.

265. *Id.*

266. *See infra* section IV(D).

267. *See* HOW DID OLDER WORKERS FARE?, *supra* note 255, at 4-5. In 2009, for example, the average monthly unemployment rate for men aged fifty-five to sixty-one was 7.3 percent; the corresponding rate for women in that age range was 4.5 percent. *Id.* at 4. Similarly, during the same year, the average monthly unemployment rate for men aged sixty-two to sixty-four was 6.6 percent; the rate for women in that age group was 5.9 percent. *Id.*

268. *Id.* at 7.

269. *Id.* at 9-11.

For example, in 2009, the average monthly unemployment rate for men aged fifty-five to sixty-four was 11.4 percent for Hispanics, 9.7 percent for African-Americans, and 6.3 percent for non-Hispanic whites.[270] For women in the same age range, the unemployment rate was 8.7 percent for Hispanics, 7.1 percent for African-Americans, and 5.6 percent for non-Hispanic whites.[271]

As for educational level, in 2009, the average monthly unemployment rate for men aged fifty-five to sixty-four who did not complete high school was 12.1 percent compared with 4.7 percent for those who were college graduates.[272] The 2009 rates for women were 9.9 percent for those who did not complete high school compared with 4.5 percent for those who were college graduates.[273]

In sum, a review of employment and unemployment statistics reveals many American older workers remained in the labor force during the global financial crisis. While older worker employment rates were not affected as much as those of younger workers, older worker unemployment increased dramatically. Additionally, among older workers, unemployment struck disproportionately, with disparities often tracking factors associated with vulnerability such as race,[274] ethnicity,[275] and education level.

B. Measures of Vulnerability: Part-Time Work, Multiple Jobs, Self-Employment, Atypical Work, and Discouraged Workers

Employment and unemployment rates only provide a partial picture of the state of the labor force and the economy at-large. In this subsection several other measures are considered as indicative of economic health or hardship. The first is the rate of those employed part-time for economic reasons, also known as underemployment.[276] This measure captures those

270. *Id.* at 10.

271. *Id.*

272. *Id.*

273. *Id.*

274. For additional information on how African Americans forty-five years old and over were affected by the Great Recession see REBECCA PERRON, AM. ASS'N OF RETIRED PERSONS, AFRICAN AMERICAN EXPERIENCES IN THE ECONOMY: RECESSION EFFECTS MORE STRONGLY FELT (2010) [hereinafter AFRICAN AMERICAN EXPERIENCES IN THE ECONOMY], *available at* <http://assets.aarp.org/rgcenter/econ/economyaa.pdf>.

275. For additional information on the occupational challenges of older Hispanic workers see THE URBAN INST. & AM. ASS'N OF RETIRED PERSONS, 50+ HISPANIC WORKERS: A GROWING SEGMENT OF THE U.S. WORKFORCE (2009), *available at* <http://assets.aarp.org/rgcenter/econ/hispanic_workers_09.pdf>.

276. *See* Bureau of Labor Statistics, U.S. Dep't of Labor, *Involuntary Part-Time Work on the Rise*, ISSUES IN LABOR STATISTICS, SUMMARY 08-08, Dec. 2008, at 1, *available at* <www.bls.gov/opub/ils/pdf/opbils71.pdf>.

workers who would prefer to work full-time yet are involuntarily working part-time due to slack economic conditions causing a cut in their hours or their inability to find full-time work.[277] Such workers, especially if they are considered temporary employees or employees not provided with the benefits of full-time workers, are for the purpose of this article considered to be engaged in precarious work.[278]

Older workers considering phased retirement might willingly choose to work part-time.[279] Yet a percentage of older workers are involuntary part-time workers, and that percentage has more than doubled since the recession began. In December 2007 only 2.4 percent of American workers aged fifty-five and over were involuntarily engaged in part-time work.[280] In June 2010, 4.9 percent of workers aged fifty-five and up were involuntarily working part-time.[281] In raw numbers, this represents over 1.2 million older workers.[282]

A recent study bolsters concern about this population. Reviewing the employment status of workers aged fifty-five and over from 1987 through 2008, the study found that the percentage of older workers employed full-time/full year steadily increased through 2007.[283] The trend reversed in 2008, with older workers still more likely to work but less likely to be working full-time/full year during that first year of the economic downturn.[284] Thus, more older workers were remaining in the labor force "but increasingly in part-time rather than full-time jobs."[285]

277. *See id.*

278. *See* Frazer & Sargeant, *supra* note 76, at 3 (noting that "[p]art-time work may be relevant to the issue of precariousness as two-thirds of part-time workers are casuals.").

279. *See* THE EMPLOYMENT SITUATION, MAY 2010, *supra* note 244, at 4.

280. *Id.*

281. *See* KHARY J. COOK & PHYLLIS L. LOTT, BUREAU OF LABOR STATISTICS, U.S. DEP'T OF LABOR, EMPLOYMENT & EARNINGS, July 2010, at 37 tbl. A-27 [hereinafter EMPLOYMENT & EARNINGS], *available at* <www.bls.gov/opub/ee/empearn201007.pdf>.

282. *Id.* In the U.S., the likelihood of involuntarily working part-time diminishes with age. *See id.*; *see also* Jenny Marlar, *Underemployed Report Spending 36 % Less than Employed*, GALLUP (Feb 23, 2010), <http://www.gallup.com/poll/125960/underemployed-report-spending-less-employed.aspx> (noting that workers eighteen to twenty-nine are almost twice as likely to be underemployed as older workers).

283. *See* Craig Copeland, Emp. Benefit Research Inst., *Employment Status of Workers Ages 55 and Older, 1987-2008*, EBRI NOTES, Mar. 2010, at 2, 2 *available at* <ebri.org/pdf/notespdf/EBRI_Notes_03-Mar10.EmptStat.pdf>.

284. *Id.* The percentage of older workers employed full-time/full year increased steadily from 54.2 percent in 1993 to 66.0 percent in 2007 but declined in 2008 to 63.9 percent. *Id.* The percentage of older workers working part-time/full year remained constant in 2008 at 13-14 percent. *Id.* The percentage of older workers working only part-year (either full or part-time) increased in 2008 to 22.7 percent from 20.9 percent in 2007. *Id.*

285. *See* Press Release No. 869, Emp. Benefit Research Inst., Older Workers Trending Toward More Part-Time Work (Mar. 16, 2010), *available at* <http://www.ebri.org/pdf/PR.869.Notes.Mar-10.EmpStat.Final.pdf>.

Another indicator of economic health and hardship is the rate of those working who hold multiple jobs. Holding more than one job is an indication that a worker cannot find a job that pays sufficient wages or provides sufficient hours.[286] This rate increased for some older workers between June 2009 and June 2010. In June 2009, 4.7 percent of workers aged fifty-five to sixty-four held multiple jobs.[287] In June 2010, the rate had increased slightly to 4.9 percent.[288] In raw numbers, in June 2010 over one million workers aged fifty-five to sixty-four held multiple jobs.[289]

During a recession, an increase in self-employment is sometimes seen as a measure of economic hardship, indicating that some number of workers have lost and been unable to replace their jobs.[290] Self-employment, however, is difficult to measure because the Bureau of Labor Statistics only counts as self-employed those workers who are "unincorporated workers employed in their own business, profession, trade, or farm."[291] Once an employee incorporates his or her business, he or she is counted as an employee of that business.[292] Nonetheless, since the start of the recession, there has been a slight increase in the number of workers aged fifty-five and up who are counted as self-employed. In December 2007, a little less than 2.6 million older workers, 10 percent of older non-agricultural workers, were counted as self-employed.[293] In May 2010, close to 2.9 million older workers were counted as self-employed, 10.5 percent of non-agricultural workers aged fifty-five and over.[294]

In the U.S., there is a dearth of current data on contingent, flexible or alternative employment arrangements. Anecdotally, it appears the recession has significantly boosted the ranks of those working in jobs described as temporary or project based.[295] Some of these workers are characterized as independent contractors; others may be employees of temporary agencies or seasonal workers hired directly by their employers. It is difficult to say whether a disproportionate number of older workers fall into these

286. *See* THE EMPLOYMENT SITUATION, MAY 2010, *supra* note 244, at 4-5.

287. *See* EMPLOYMENT & EARNINGS, *supra* note 281, at 49 tbl.A-39.

288. *Id.* Interestingly, the rate of multiple job holders aged sixty-five and over decreased between June 2009 and June 2010. The rate for June 2009 was 3.4 and for June 2010 was 2.8 percent. *Id.*

289. *Id.*

290. *See* THE EMPLOYMENT SITUATION, MAY 2010, *supra* note 244, at 4-5.

291. *Id.* at 5.

292. *Id.*

293. *Id.*

294. *Id.*

295. *See* Michael Luo, *Recession Adds to Appeal of Short-Term Jobs*, N.Y. TIMES, Apr. 19, 2010, at A14 *available at*: http://www.nytimes.com/2010/04/20/business/economy/20contractor.html ("What is known as "contingent work," or "flexible" and "alternative" staffing arrangements, has proliferated, although exact figures are hard to come by because of difficulties in tracking such workers.").

categories.[296] A 2005 study, however, did find those classified as independent contractors more likely to be age thirty-five or over.[297] In terms of numbers, a 2006 Government Accountability Office report, using a broad definition of contingency – workers who do not have standard full-time employment – estimated contingent workers, including independent contractors, constituted almost one-third of the 2005 workforce or 42.6 million people.[298]

Finally, regarding the discouragement effect mentioned in the Australia and U.K. sections,[299] there has been a disturbing increase in the proportion of American discouraged workers who are older workers. These are individuals who are not in the labor force – they are not employed nor are they actively looking for work.[300] However, they report that they want a job and that their reason for not looking is discouragement over their job prospects.[301] In June 2009, workers fifty-five and over comprised 15 percent of discouraged workers.[302] By June 2010, their representation among discouraged workers had increased to almost 24 percent.[303]

The figures reviewed above evidence a labor market greatly affected by the economic downturn and cast a troubling light on U.S. efforts at employment promotion. A recent study, however, provides even more cause for concern. That study indicates that the serious labor market effects witnessed since the recession began in December 2007 are out of

296. The last Bureau of Labor Statistics study of contingent and alternative employment arrangements was published in 2005, using data from February of that year. *See* News Release, USDL 05-1433, Bureau of Labor Statistics, U.S. Dep't of Labor, Contingent and Alternative Employment Arrangements, February 2005 (Jul. 27, 2005), *available at* <www.bls.gov/news.release/pdf/conemp.pdf>. Using a common definition of contingency – workers who do not expect their jobs to last – there were 5.7 million contingent workers, about 4.1 percent of total employment. *Id.* at 3, tbl.1. Fifty-five percent of these workers "would have preferred a permanent job." *Id.* at 3. The study found contingent workers were twice as likely as their non-contingent counterparts to be young, defined as under the age of twenty-five. *Id.*

297. *Id.* at 4. In February 2005 there were 10.3 million independent contractors, 7.4 percent of total employment. *Id.* at 1.

298. *See* U.S. GOV'T ACCOUNTABILITY OFFICE, GAO-06-656, REPORT TO THE RANKING MINORITY MEMBER, COMMITTEE ON HEALTH, EDUCATION, LABOR, AND PENSIONS, U.S. SENATE: EMPLOYMENT ARRANGEMENTS: IMPROVED OUTREACH COULD HELP ENSURE PROPER WORKER CLASSIFICATION 10 (2006), *available at* <http://www.gao.gov/new.items/d06656.pdf>. A recent Bureau of Labor Statistics study of the temporary help services industry found that between 1990 and 2008, the number of workers employed in the temporary help services industry increased from 1.1 to 2.3 million people. *See* Tian Luo et al., *The Expanding Role of Temporary Help Services,* MONTHLY LAB. REV., Aug. 2010, at 3, 3, *available at* < http://www.bls.gov/opub/mlr/2010/08/art1full.pdf>.

299. *See supra* Parts II-III.

300. *See* THE EMPLOYMENT SITUATION, MAY 2010, *supra* note 244, at 5.

301. *Id.*

302. *See* EMPLOYMENT & EARNINGS, *supra* note 281, at 48 tbl.A-38.

303. *Id.*

proportion to the economic distress experienced by corporations.[304] Although real output dropped by 2.5 percent, corporate payrolls were slashed by 6 percent.[305] Looking at the period between the fourth quarter of 2008 and the first quarter of 2010, the study found corporate profits increased by $572 billion while wage payments declined by $122 billion.[306] In other words, many employers are using the recession as an opportunity for restructuring operations to maximize profits at the expense of workers.[307]

Discussions of the recession and its impact on American life frequently focus on the failure to regulate aspects of the American financial system or the overheated housing market. Less examined is another area short on regulation: the U.S. system of workplace law, which is predominantly market driven and insufficiently protective of employees' occupational and economic security, a topic relevant to evaluating the country's pursuit of employment promotion, an obligation it bears as an ILO member.[308] That subject will be addressed below with a focus on older workers.[309]

C. Weak Job Security Protection

While legal regulation might act as a brake on the shedding of workers by making dismissal costly or administratively time-consuming, as is the case in many EU countries,[310] the U.S. system of workplace law is far less

304. *See* Bob Herbert, *A Sin and a Shame*, N.Y. TIMES, Jul. 31, 2010, at A15 (quoting study author Professor Andrew Sum of Northeastern University's Center for Labor Market Studies).

305. *See* ANDREW SUM & JOSEPH MCLAUGHLIN, CTR. FOR LABOR MKT. STUDIES AT NORTHEASTERN UNIV., HOW THE U.S. ECONOMIC OUTPUT RECESSION OF 2007-2009 LED TO THE GREAT RECESSION IN LABOR MARKETS: THE ROLE OF CORPORATE DOWNSIZING, WORK HOUR REDUCTIONS, LABOR PRODUCTIVITY GAINS, AND RISING CORPORATE PROFITS 2 (2010), *available at* <http://www.clms.neu.edu/publication/documents/How_the_U.S._Economic_Output_Recession_of_20072009_Led_to_the_Great_Recession_in_Labor_Markets.pdf>.

306. *Id.* at 4.

307. *See, e.g.*, Nelson D. Schwartz, *Industries Find Surging Profits in Deeper Cuts*, N.Y. TIMES, Jul. 25, 2010, at A1.

308. *See* Edwin R. Render, *How Would Today's Employees Fare in a Recession?*, 4 U. PA. J. LAB. & EMP. L. 37, 60-62 (2001) (positing in 2001 that constraints on employee dismissal are insufficiently protective of workers in the event of a recession).

309. *See id.* (noting that scant legal protections rendered older workers particularly vulnerable); *see also* Gary Minda, *Opportunistic Downsizing of Aging Workers: The 1990s Version of Age and Pension Discrimination in Employment*, 48 HASTINGS L.J. 511 (1997) (describing a trend in increasing rates of job displacement among older workers, and arguing that the Age Discrimination in Employment Act was not an effective limitation on opportunistic, downsizing of aging employees).

310. *See generally* Paul De Grauwe, *Flexibility Is Out: Now We See Rigidity's Virtues*, CTR. FOR EUR. POLICY STUDIES, CEPS COMMENTARY, Feb. 23, 2009, *available at* <http://www.ceps.eu/ceps/download/1624> (arguing that E.U. members' job security protections and a robust social safety net are advantages in countering the global financial crisis).

protective of job security than are the systems of most developed nations.[311] Americans leave many facets of the employment relationship to the workings of the market.[312] Although this factor no doubt affects workers regardless of age, older workers are increasingly at risk of job displacement[313] and especially vulnerable to long term unemployment.[314] When coupled with general declines in retirement security, a topic discussed below, weak job security protection, and the stress it occasions, may affect older workers differently, perhaps even more severely, than their younger colleagues.[315]

The flexible system of labor market regulation in the U.S., as a legal matter, allows employers to treat non-unionized workers as expendable.[316] While employment discrimination is prohibited and some terms and conditions of employment are subject to statutory law, the vast majority of American workers – those without trade union representation, working in the private sector – are employed at will.[317] One employed at will may be terminated from employment, at any time, with or without cause, so long as no other employment prohibition, such as the ban on employment

311. The Organisation for Economic Cooperation and Development (OECD) ranks the U.S. last among developed countries in its rating of the strength of its members' protective workplace laws. *See How Do OECD Labour Markets Perform?*, *supra* note 20 (scroll to "employment protection," eighth on the page).

312. *See* ROGER BLANPAIN ET AL., THE GLOBAL WORKPLACE: INTERNATIONAL AND COMPARATIVE EMPLOYMENT LAW – CASES AND MATERIALS 100-01 (2007) [hereinafter THE GLOBAL WORKPLACE]; *see also* CHANTEL SHEAKS & MICHELLE WONG, THE SLOAN CTR. ON AGING & WORK AT BOSTON COLL., GLOBAL POLICY BRIEF NO. 5, UNITED STATES PUBLIC POLICY 13 (2009) [hereinafter UNITED STATES PUBLIC POLICY], *available at* <http://www.bc.edu/content/dam/files/research_sites/agingandwork/pdf/publications/GPB05_UnitedStates.pdf> ("In the United States, many aspects of the employment relationship are unregulated, and, instead, left to the market.").

313. *See* ALICIA H. MUNNELL, ET AL., CTR. FOR RETIREMENT RESEARCH AT BOSTON COLL., ISSUE BRIEF NO. 9-10, WHY ARE OLDER WORKERS AT GREATER RISK OF DISPLACEMENT? (2009), *available at* <http://crr.bc.edu/images/stories/Briefs/ib_9-10.pdf> (describing older workers' risk of job displacement as rising absolutely and relatively vis-à-vis prime age workers); Daniel Rodriguez & Madeline Zavodny, *Changes in the Age and Education Profile of Displaced Workers,* 56 INDUS. & LAB. REL. REV. 498 (2003) (concluding that older workers' relative risk of displacement has increased relative to younger workers).

314. *See supra* notes 259-62 and accompanying text.

315. *See e.g.* Ariel Kalil, et al., *Job Insecurity and Change Over Time in Health Among Older Men and Women*, 65B JS. GERONTOLOGY, SERIES B: PSYCHOL. SCI. & SOC. SCI. 81-90 (2010) (finding the correlation between job insecurity and health different yet salient in both older men and women, and job insecurity "a potentially important threat to older adults' health and well-being"); *see also* KENNETH A. ROOT & ROSEMARIE J. PARK, FORCED OUT: OLDER WORKERS CONFRONT JOB LOSS (2009).

316. *See* William A. Douglas, *Labor Market Flexibility Versus Job Security – Why Versus?*, NEW ECON. INFO. SERV., ORIGINAL INK, Nov. 1, 2000, <http://www.newecon.org/LaborFlexibility_Douglas.html> (arguing that abolishing job security protections promotes not labor flexibility but labor expendability).

317. *See* THE GLOBAL WORKPLACE, *supra* note 312, at 99-100. The State of Montana is the only one of the fifty U.S. states to have legislatively modified the at-will doctrine. MONT. CODE ANN. §39-2-501 (2010).

discrimination or a very limited number of other proscriptions, is violated.[318] In many cases, advance notice is not required.[319] Nowhere in the U.S., even in cases of mass layoffs or plant closings, is severance pay statutorily required.[320] Thus, it is easy and relatively inexpensive to dismiss most workers.

Before the global economic crisis, American workers' job security deficit was less tangibly evident.[321] In fact, empirical research done before the Great Recession indicates that despite the long-standing status of employment-at-will, American workers generally believed they had legal dismissal protections.[322] However, the surge in and prolonged nature of unemployment produced during the recession and its aftermath has proven revelatory.[323] And the economic impact on older workers has been

318. THE GLOBAL WORKPLACE, *supra* note 312, at 102-03.

319. Except for a federal statute requiring sixty days' notice in advance of mass layoffs and plant closings, and a few state statutes that mirror or build on its notice requirements, American non-union workers lack protection from economically-based employer decisions. The federal notice statute, the Worker Adjustment and Retraining Notification Act (WARN Act), only governs large employers – those employing 100 workers or more. *See* UNITED STATES PUBLIC POLICY, *supra* note 312, at 7; *see also* Richard W. McHugh, *Fair Warning or Foul? An Analysis of the Worker Adjustment and Retraining Notification Act (WARN) in Practice*, 14 BERKELEY J. EMP. & LAB. L. 1, 64-70 (1993); Rachel S. Arnow-Richman, *Just Notice: Re-Reforming Employment At-Will for the Twenty-First Century*, 58 UCLA L. REV. 1 (2010) (arguing for a pay-or-play system whereby employers either provide notice before discharge or pay workers for the notice period).

320. *See* THE GLOBAL WORKPLACE, *supra* note 312, at 110.

321. There was, of course, prior to the recession a "widely documented trend toward short term employment, the rise of contingent labor, the rollback of employer sponsored health plans and benefits, a reversion to external labor market practices . . . ." Rachel Arnow-Richman, *Response to Working Group on Chapter 2 of the Proposed Restatement of Employment Law: Putting the Restatement in Its Place*, 13 EMP. RTS. & EMP. POL'Y J. 143, 146, (2009) [hereinafter *Putting the Restatement in Its Place*]. Yet so long as unemployment, both long- and short-term, remained relatively low, the weakness of employees' legal protections remained to some extent theoretical. Many employers in the 1990s, for example, despite a lack of legal requirements, continued to offer "career-type jobs" with "prospects of continuity." Sanford M. Jacoby, *Kenneth M. Piper Lecture: Melting Into Air? Downsizing, Job Stability, and the Future of Work*, 76 CHI.-KENT L. REV. 1195, 1220 (2000). Those who did lose a job soon found another "career-type" position. *Id.*

322. *See* Cynthia L. Estlund, *How Wrong Are Employees About Their Rights, and Why Does It Matter?*, 77 N.Y.U. L. REV. 6 (2002); Pauline T. Kim, *Bargaining With Imperfect Information: A Study of Worker Perceptions of Legal Protection in an At-Will World*, 83 CORNELL L. REV. 105 (1997). Of course, economic hardship would be a legitimate reason for dismissal under a just cause regime. There is, however, evidence that many of the layoffs precipitated by the economic downturn were taken not due to economic hardship but in order to boost profit margins. *See supra* notes 304-07 and accompanying text; *see also* Jeffrey Pfeffer, *Lay Off the Layoffs: Our Overreliance on Downsizing is Killing Workers, the Economy – and Even the Bottom Line*, NEWSWEEK, Feb. 5, 2010, at 32, *available at* <http://www.newsweek.com/2010/02/04/lay-off-the-layoffs.html>. Unfortunately, American judges interpreting cause for discharge would be unlikely to allow human concerns to trump profit margins. *See Putting the Restatement in Its Place*, *supra* note 321, at 146 (noting that judicial innovation in support of job security is unlikely given normative "pressures to defer to businesses on their need to meet their bottom line."); *see also* David C. Yamada, *Human Dignity and American Employment Law*, 43 U. RICH. L. REV. 523, 561 (2010) (arguing for enactment of just cause protections that require employers contemplating large scale layoffs to demonstrate economic necessity).

323. U.S. workers' realization is reflected in recent surveys documenting increases in the

especially profound.[324] Other than providing protection against age discrimination, however, American workplace law does little to ameliorate the increasing vulnerability of older workers. Yet, as discussed below, recent changes in doctrinal law have weakened protections against age bias, rendering it a less effective tool for blunting the harsh economic conditions older workers face.

D. Weakened Age Discrimination Protections

The Age Discrimination in Employment Act of 1967 (ADEA) protects persons forty years old and older from employment discrimination based on age.[325] The ADEA's prohibitions apply to employers with twenty or more employees.[326] Both employees and job applicants are protected by the statute.[327] Unlike in the U.K., at the time of this writing, but in harmony with Australia, mandatory retirement is prohibited in most sectors in the U.S.[328] In the U.S., one rarely finds workers who were lawfully forced to retire.[329]

Concern that older workers might be asked to waive their protections without sufficient information prompted the U.S. Congress to pass the Older Worker Benefit Protection Act of 1990 (OWBPA).[330] The OWBPA establishes stringent requirements for the execution of enforceable waivers of ADEA claims.[331] Waivers, also known as releases, most commonly arise

proportion of Americans who feel their jobs are at risk and declines in the proportion of those professing a personal sense of job security. *See, e.g.*, Dennis Jacobe, *One in Five Americans Fear Job Loss in Next 12 Months*, GALLUP (Apr. 23, 2010), <http://www.gallup.com/poll/127511/in-u.s.-fear-job-loss-double-pre-recession-level.aspx>.

324. The recession has taken a particularly harsh economic toll on workers aged fifty to sixty-four, many of whom are still in the labor force but approaching retirement. Close to sixty percent of workers in this group report "they are in worse shape financially than they were before the recession." HOW THE GREAT RECESSION HAS CHANGED LIFE, *supra* note 236, at 42. Twenty-one percent "say they are in much worse shape." *Id.* Thus, one recent study concludes that the "age group that seems to have suffered the most" is comprised of workers aged fifty to sixty-four. *Id.*

325. 29 U.S.C. §§ 621-34 (2006).

326. *Id.* § 630(b).

327. *Age Discrimination*, U.S. EQUAL EMP'T OPPORTUNITY COMM'N, <http://www.eeoc.gov/eeoc/publications/age.cfm> (last viewed Mar. 14, 2011).

328. *See* Donald C. Dowling, *International HR Best Practice Tips: Toward a Functional Cross-Border Age-Discrimination Policy*, Int'l HR J., Spring 2009, at 1.

329. There are exceptions to the mandatory retirement ban for certain high level executives and also those whose jobs involve safety, such as firefighters and police officers. *See* 29 U.S.C. § 630(j); *see also* MICHAEL J. ZIMMER ET AL., CASES AND MATERIALS ON EMPLOYMENT DISCRIMINATION 482 (7th ed. 2008) (describing exceptions for bona fide executives, and state and municipal law enforcement officers and firefighters).

330. *See* U.S. EQUAL EMP'T OPPORTUNITY COMM'N, UNDERSTANDING WAIVERS OF DISCRIMINATION CLAIMS IN EMPLOYEE SEVERANCE AGREEMENTS, *available at*: http://www.eeoc.gov/policy/docs/qanda_severance-agreements.html > (last modified July 15, 2009).

331. The OWBPA enumerates seven factors that must be satisfied in order for age discrimination

in the context of layoffs or other terminations of employment.[332] Although no U.S. law mandates the provision of severance pay, when terminations occur, many U.S. employers attempt to stave off litigation by paying severance to workers in exchange for a release of all claims.[333]

Despite these seemingly robust safeguards, which initially indicate American defense of a fundamental right at work, there is reason for concern about older workers' legal protection from age bias. Recent U.S. Supreme Court decisions have weakened the ADEA's protections, making it more difficult to prove age discrimination than other forms of discrimination. Dianna Johnston, Assistant Legal Counsel at the U.S. Equal Employment Opportunity Commission (EEOC), recently expressed her agency's concern about the direction of doctrinal age bias law at a Public Briefing on Age Discrimination in Employment in the Context of the Economic Crisis, an event hosted by the U.S. Civil Rights Commission. Ms. Johnston noted that the Court "increasingly minimizes the significance of age discrimination," has weakened the ADEA, and has "complicated [the EEOC's] efforts to enforce it."[334]

Key decisions include *Gross v. FBL Financial Services, Inc.*,[335] a disparate treatment suit in which the Court held that mixed motives claims – claims involving both permissible and discriminatory reasons – are not cognizable under the ADEA.[336] Instead, the Court held that age discrimination plaintiffs must prove that age was a "but for" cause of the challenged employment decision.[337] In other words, unlike plaintiffs suing for other types of discrimination, age bias plaintiffs asserting disparate treatment must demonstrate that age had a decisive impact on the employer's actions, even in cases where the employer admits that age

claim waivers to be considered knowing and voluntary, a prerequisite for enforceability. *Id.* (scroll to pt. IV.A, question 6, "What makes a waiver of age claims knowing and voluntary?"). These include requirements that the waiver be supported by valuable consideration, provide for at least twenty-one days for the worker to evaluate the offer, and advise the worker to consult with a lawyer. *Id.* Additional release of claims requirements exist under the OWBPA for group layoffs of older workers. *Id.* (scroll to pt. IV.B). In such cases, employers must provide sufficient information to older workers to enable them to determine "whether older employees were terminated while younger ones were retained." *Id.*

332. *Id.* (scroll down to pt. I-II).

333. *Id.*

334. Statement of Dianna B. Johnston, Assistant Legal Counsel, U.S. Equal Emp't Opportunity Comm'n, before the U.S. Comm'n on Civil Rights 2 (June 11, 2010) [hereinafter *Johnston Statement*] (on file with the author); *see also* Transcript of Age Discrimination in Employment in the Current Economic Crisis Briefing Before the U.S. Comm'n on Civil Rights 13 (June 11, 2010) (statement of Dianna Johnston, Assistant Legal Counsel, EEOC), *available at* <http://www.usccr.gov/calendar/trnscrpt/061110ccr1.pdf>.

335. 129 S. Ct. 2343 (2009).

336. *Id.* at 2350.

337. *Id.* at 2351.

motivated its decision in part.[338] As noted by Dianna Johnson, "The *Gross* decision was a startling departure from decades of settled precedent developed in federal district and intermediate appellate courts. It erected a new, higher (and potentially insurmountable) legal hurdle for victims of age-based employment decisions."[339]

Congress is presently considering legislation that would overturn *Gross*. The Chair of the EEOC, Jacqueline Berrien, recently testified in favor of the proposed legislation, noting it would ensure age discrimination plaintiffs bringing disparate treatment claims are given the same "core protections" as plaintiffs bringing race, color, national origin, religion, and sex discrimination claims.[340]

Another disparate treatment case of concern for older workers is the Supreme Court's decision *Kentucky Retirement Systems v. EEOC*.[341] At issue in that case was a state disability retirement plan that tied benefit eligibility and calculation to normal retirement age (age fifty-five).[342] Under the plan, the plaintiff, an employee who worked beyond normal retirement age and was disabled at sixty-one years old, received no credit for imputed service, defined as years left until fifty-five, and thus had lower benefit payments than would a similarly situated younger employee.[343] Even though the state plan clearly relied on age, a prohibited factor, the Court ruled that the plan was not facially discriminatory because the employer was motivated by pension status, not age.[344] To prove age discrimination, the plaintiff would need to show animus beyond the use of age as a factor in disability retirement benefit determination.[345] This additional burden, which plaintiffs proving other forms of disparate treatment discrimination do not bear, may doom many ADEA claims because it is rare to find direct evidence of discriminatory animus.[346]

338. *Id.* at 2352.

339. *Johnston Statement*, *supra* note 334, at 5.

340. Statement of Jacqueline A. Berrien, Chair, U.S. Equal Emp't Opportunity Comm'n, at Protecting Older Workers against Discrimination Act: Hearing on S. 1756 Before the S. Comm. on Health, Educ., Labor & Pensions, 111th Cong. (May 6, 2010) [hereinafter *Berrien Statement*], *available at* <http://www1.eeoc.gov//eeoc/events/berrien_protecting_older_workers.cfm?renderforprint=1>.

341. 554 U.S. 135 (2008).

342. *Id.* 139-40.

343. *See id* at 40.

344. *Id.* at 143-48.

345. *Id.* at 150.

346. *See* U.S. Postal Serv. Bd. of Governors v. Aikens, 460 U.S. 711, 716 (1983) ("There will seldom be 'eyewitness' testimony as to the employer's mental processes."); *see also* Susan Bisom-Rapp, *Bulletproofing the Workplace: Symbol and Substance in Employment Discrimination Law Practice*, 26 FLA. ST. U. L. REV. 959, 961-62 (1999) (describing the way in which equal employment opportunity compliance strategies mask discrimination and hinder detection of workplace bias).

A final Supreme Court decision involves ADEA disparate impact claims, which allow plaintiffs to challenge neutral employment practices that fall more harshly on older workers. While the Court in *Smith v. City of Jackson*[347] approved the use of this theory, it adopted an employer defense – the reasonable factor other than age defense – that appears easier for employers to meet than the business necessity defense available in disparate impact claims brought on grounds apart from age.[348] Proving one's neutral policy or practice is reasonable will likely prove far easier than proving one's neutral practice is necessary.[349]

These three decisions, which make it more complex and burdensome for age discrimination plaintiffs to bring suit in comparison to those suing for discrimination on other grounds, indicate that at least some Supreme Court justices view age discrimination as less salient a societal problem than other forms of bias.[350] Yet there is every indication that stereotypes based on age are still prevalent.[351] Moreover, age discrimination charges filed with the EEOC have recently increased dramatically. For example, in fiscal year 2008, the number of age discrimination charges increased almost 30 percent over the prior year, representing over 25 percent of all charges received.[352] In fact, since 1998 age discrimination charges are up 61 percent.[353] In raw numbers, in fiscal year 2009, the EEOC received 22,778 age discrimination charges.[354]

In short, flimsy job security and weakened age discrimination protections render many older workers vulnerable, even when they are classified as permanent, full-time employees. That vulnerability is exacerbated by declining retirement security, addressed next, a topic relevant to social protection, and more specifically to American efforts

347. 544 U.S. 228 (2005).

348. *See* Judith J. Johnson, *Reasonable Factors Other Than Age: The Emerging Specter of Ageist Stereotypes*, 33 SEATTLE U. L. REV. 49, 51 (2009) ("[T]he Court has indicated that RFOA will not be difficult to prove, and lower courts are so holding.").

349. *Id.* at 74-77.

350. *See Johnston Statement*, *supra* note 334, at 5.

351. *See* Statement of Michael Campion, Professor of Mgmt., Purdue Univ. at the EEOC Meeting: Age Discrimination in the 21st Century – Barriers to the Employment of Older Workers (Jul. 15, 2009), *available at* <http://www.eeoc.gov/eeoc/meetings/7-15-09/campion.cfm> (discussing ageist stereotypes and how they affect older workers); *see generally* AGEISM: STEREOTYPING AND PREJUDICE AGAINST OLDER PERSONS (Todd D. Nelson ed., 2002).

352. *See Johnston Statement*, *supra* note 334, at 2.

353. *Id.* As noted by the EEOC's Ms. Johnston, not all age discrimination victims file charges and many charges are not meritorious. *Id.* at 3. The EEOC uses a merit factor rate as a gauge for assessing charge worthiness; this rate includes "all charge resolutions in which the charging party received a benefit." *Id.* Ms. Johnston noted that "[s]ince 2005, the merit factor rate for ADEA charges has averaged 19.2 percent." *Id.*

354. *Id.*

aimed at income security for older workers.

E. Declining Retirement Security

American retirement security has been declining for many years. In great part, this is due to a shift in the character of pension coverage. While in the U.S., employers need not provide pensions, modernly many do. Over the last few decades, however, there has been a precipitous decline in employers offering defined benefit retirement plans, which provide a guaranteed lifetime benefit to retirees.[355] Increasingly, those employers who provide retirement plans offer defined contribution plans, in which payments from employer contributions and/or employee deferred salary are placed into individual accounts, which are then invested, in many cases, in the stock market.[356] Defined contribution plans allocate risk away from employers and onto employees.[357]

The shift itself has been monumental. In 1985, 80 percent of those working full-time for large and medium private enterprises participated in traditional, defined benefit plans, and 41 percent were participants in defined contribution plans.[358] In March 2009, only 24 percent of those working full-time for private enterprises of all kinds were participants in defined benefit plans, while 51 percent of full-time workers participated in defined contribution retirement plans.[359]

Shifting risk and retirement savings responsibility onto employees has clearly affected older worker labor force participation in the long term, which, as noted above, has been increasing over the years.[360] The recent financial crisis, however, also produced great losses in the retirement

355. *See* ALICIA H. MUNNELL & DAN MULDOON, CTR FOR RETIREMENT RESEARCH AT BOSTON COLL., ISSUE BRIEF NO. 8-16, ARE RETIREMENT SAVINGS TOO EXPOSED TO MARKET RISK? 2 (2008), *available at* < http://crr.bc.edu/images/stories/Briefs/ib_8-16.pdf>.

356. *See* STEVEN A. SASS ET AL., CTR. FOR RETIREMENT RESEARCH AT BOSTON COLLEGE, ISSUE BRIEF NO. 10-3, WORKERS' RESPONSE TO THE MARKET CRASH: SAVE MORE, WORK MORE? 1 (2010)[hereinafter WORKERS' RESPONSE TO THE MARKET CRASH], *available at* <http:// crr.bc.edu/images/stories/Briefs/ib_10-3.pdf>; Samuel Estreicher & Laurence Gold, *The Shift from Defined Benefit Plans to Defined Contribution Plans*, 11 LEWIS & CLARK L. REV. 331, 331-33 (2007) [hereinafter *The Shift From Defined Benefit Plans*].

357. *See The Shift from Defined Benefit Plans*, *supra* note 356, at 333. Defined contribution plans also shift financial decision-making responsibility from sponsors of the plan to participants (employees), a task many participants are ill-equipped to manage. *Id.* at 334-35.

358. *See* Hilery Z. Simpson, *How Does Your 401(k) Match Up?*, U.S. BUREAU OF LABOR STATISTICS n.9 (May 26, 2010), <http://www.bls.gov/opub/cwc/print/cm20100520ar01p1.htm>.

359. *Id.*

360. *See Record Unemployment Among Older Workers*, *supra* note 259, at 1 ("[O]ne underlying reason behind the long-term rise in participation rates among the 55-years-and-older population is the move by employers to replace defined-benefit retirement plans with defined-contribution retirement plans, allowing employers to shift more responsibility for retirement income to the employee.").

accounts of American workers, and those losses affect older worker retirement planning and well-being. Between September 2007 and May 2009 – recall the recession began in the U.S. in December 2007 – the value of American retirement accounts declined by 31 percent, losing $2.7 trillion.[361]

A recent survey of workers aged forty-five to fifty-nine, found notable declines in retirement wealth tied to the financial crisis and a significant increase in the age at which the respondents expected to retire.[362] Approximately 40 percent of the respondents reported they would retire later than they had planned to before the recession[363] Similarly, a May 2010 survey conducted by the Pew Research Center found that 60 percent of workers aged fifty to sixty-one report the recession may delay their retirement.[364] A little over one-third (35 percent) of the survey's worker respondents age sixty-two and older also reported delaying retirement due to the recession.[365]

Moreover, many employees who experienced financial distress during the recession prematurely withdrew funds from their retirement accounts, with financial penalties, in order to make house payments, and pay bills and the like. One study found nearly 20 percent of American workers aged forty-five and older tapped into these funds in 2009.[366] The figure was 28 percent for Hispanics in that age group[367] and 26 percent for African Americans age forty-five and up.[368]

Further exacerbating the impact of the recession on retirement savings was the decision of many employers to cease contributing to their employees' defined contribution plans. One analysis, which found that the majority of suspensions occurred between December 2008 and May 2009, concludes that enterprise liquidity concerns – the need for cash to ensure that current liabilities can be discharged – rather than profitability concerns drove many companies to suspend their contributions.[369] That study posited

361. *See* Howard Iams et al., Fed. Interagency Forum on Aging Related Statistics, *Data Sources on the Impact of the 2008 Financial Crisis on the Economic Well-being of Older Americans*, AGING FORUM REPORT, Dec. 2009, at 1, *available at* <http://www.agingstats.gov/agingstatsdotnet/main_site/docs/DSOA_Aging_Brief.pdf>.

362. *See* WORKERS' RESPONSE TO THE MARKET CRASH, *supra* note 356, at 3.

363. *Id.*

364. *See* HOW THE GREAT RECESSION HAS CHANGED LIFE, *supra* note 236, at 69.

365. *Id.*

366. *See* REBECCA PERRON, Am. Ass'n of Retired Persons, RECESSION TAKES TOLL ON HISPANICS 45+: BOOMERS PARTICULARLY HARD HIT 6 (2010), *available at* <http://assets.aarp.org/rgcenter/econ/hispeconomy.pdf>.

367. *Id.*

368. *See* AFRICAN AMERICAN EXPERIENCES IN THE ECONOMY, *supra* note 274, at 5.

369. *See* ALICIA H. MUNNELL & LAURA QUINBY, CTR. FOR RETIREMENT RESEARCH AT BOSTON

that the ultimate impact of the suspensions, which affected at least 4.9 percent of defined contribution, or 401(k), plan participants,[370] will depend on whether the cessation is made permanent or, instead, employer contributions are eventually restored.[371] If the former, fewer workers might participate in the plans and employees overall might be unable to amass sufficient income for retirement.[372] Either way, the employer actions are a potent reminder to employees that the financial risk associated with retirement savings falls on them and not their employers.[373]

Another factor relating to retirement security is the legislatively mandated, gradual rise in the age at which full old age benefits through the government's Social Security program are available to workers. Amendments to the program passed in 1983 ushered in an increase from sixty-five years of age, for those born in 1937 or earlier, to sixty-seven years of age for those born in 1960 or later.[374] Those who retire sooner than their full retirement age see a sizable reduction in benefits. For example, a worker retiring at age sixty-two, the earliest one can retire and receive Social Security benefits, whose full retirement age is sixty-seven, will sustain a 30 percent reduction in benefits received.[375]

A final factor undercutting retirement security is a decline in the number of employers offering retirement medical insurance for their workers.[376] The disappearance of such coverage and rising medical care costs leave retired workers vulnerable to economic disaster until they reach age sixty-five, the age when the government's Medicare older worker health insurance becomes available.[377]

COLLEGE, ISSUE BRIEF NO. 10-2, WHY DID SOME EMPLOYERS SUSPEND THEIR 401(K) MATCH? 3-4 (2010), *available at* <http://crr.bc.edu/images/stories/Briefs/IB_10-2.pdf>.

370. *Id.* at 3.

371. *Id.* at 5.

372. *Id.*

373. *Id.*

374. *See* U.S. SOC. SEC. ADMIN., RETIREMENT BENEFITS 6 (2011) (explaining that those born in 1942 or earlier are already eligible for full benefits and listing the full retirement ages and how they differ for people born from 1943 to 1960 and later), *available at* <http://www.ssa.gov/pubs/10035.pdf>.

375. *See Retirement Planner: Retirement Benefits by Year of Birth*, SOC. SEC. ONLINE, <http://www.ssa.gov/retire2/agereduction.htm> (last modified Feb. 9, 2011).

376. *See* PATRICK PURCELL, CONG. RESEARCH SERV., RL30629, OLDER WORKERS: EMPLOYMENT AND RETIREMENT TRENDS 5 (2009), *available at* <http://assets.opencrs.com/rpts/RL30629_20090916.pdf>.

377. *See* U.S. SOC. SEC. ADMIN., MEDICARE 4 (2011) (explaining that Medicare is available to those sixty-five and over and to those with disabilities, permanent kidney failure, or Lou Gehrig's disease), *available at* < http://www.ssa.gov/pubs/10043.pdf>.

F. A Note on the Safety Net

As noted above, while older workers are less likely than younger workers to experience unemployment, once unemployed, older workers are more likely to remain jobless than their younger counterparts.[378] For example, in December 2009, 18 percent of unemployed workers aged twenty to twenty-four were unemployed for a year or more compared with more than 29 percent of those older than fifty-five.[379]

Unemployment benefits in the U.S., however, are only available for a maximum of ninety-nine weeks, and many of the long-term unemployed have exhausted their benefits.[380] In June 2010, approximately 1.4 million Americans had been jobless for at least ninety-nine weeks.[381] The failure of the American safety net in the face of the current recession represents a significant deviation from the notion of decent work. The system in the U.S. insufficiently addresses the obligation of social protection.

G. U.S.: Conclusions

The data reveal that vulnerability has increased for older workers during the recession and its aftermath. While employment rates are stable, unemployment rates have hit historic highs, and older worker long-term unemployment is common and increasing. A trend toward a greater proportion of older workers working part-time has appeared, while the number of older workers involuntarily working part-time has doubled since December 2007. In the last year, the proportion of discouraged workers aged fifty-five and over has increased 62.5 percent. Troubling disparities among older workers based on race and ethnicity are apparent with respect to unemployment rates and retirement savings.

While statistics on casual, temporary, and atypical work are not available, there is every reason to believe such forms of employment have proliferated. Moreover, the American system of labor market regulation provides weak job security protection for all workers, even those with full-

378. *See* SCOTT S. GREENBERGER & DOUGLAS WALTON, PEW ECONOMIC POLICY GRP., A YEAR OR MORE: THE HIGH COST OF LONG-TERM UNEMPLOYMENT 4 (2010) [hereinafter A YEAR OR MORE], *available at* <http://www.pewtrusts.org/uploadedFiles/wwwpewtrustsorg/Reports/Economic_Mobility/PEW-Unemployment%20Final.pdf>; *see also* CHRISTINE RIORDAN, NAT'L EMP'T LAW PROJECT, THE CRISIS OF LONG TERM UNEMPLOYMENT AND THE NEED FOR BOLD ACTION TO SUSTAIN THE UNEMPLOYED AND SUPPORT THE RECOVERY 6 (2010), *available at* <http://www.nelp.org/page/-/UI/2010/long. term.unemployment.fact.sheet.pdf?nocdn=1%20?nocdn=1>.

379. *See* A YEAR OR MORE, *supra* note 378, at 4.

380. *See* Michael Luo, *99 Weeks Later, Jobless Have Only Desperation*, N.Y. TIMES, Aug. 3, 2010, at A-1.

381. *Id.*

time, so-called permanent work. Age discrimination protections have been weakened, retirement security is declining, and the social safety net for the longest term unemployed is proving inadequate.

The U.S. falls short in pursuing for older workers three decent work objectives: employment promotion, social protection, and fundamental rights in the form of eliminating age discrimination.[382] Present conditions also support use in the U.S. of a more expansive definition of precarious employment than the definition used in Australia, the U.K., and many other countries. Directly responsive to the legal plight of American workers, Professor Katherine Stone includes within her definition of precarious employment not only workers in atypical employment relationships but also those steady, full-time employees who "lack a reasonable expectation of job security."[383] Such a definition is especially fitting for many American older workers, who in addition to dwindling job security and weakened age bias protection, cope with declining retirement security and an insufficient system of unemployment compensation.

V. CONCLUSIONS

In this article we have examined how older workers in three broadly similar countries have fared during the recession. The ILO's concept of decent work has been used to draw the basis of comparison in terms of four dimensions: employment opportunities and participation; conditions of work, especially precarious work; labor regulation, especially regarding discrimination; and provision for income security both before and after retirement. It remains for us to draw comparisons of the state of decent work for older workers in the countries studied, and the lessons which our study has for the concept of decent work.

A. Similarities and Differences

The recession affected each country to a different extent. In terms of the impact on general employment, Australia is regarded as one of the least affected countries, the U.K. as having been moderately affected, and the U.S. as falling in the severely affected category.[384] The response of national employers to the crisis varied significantly: in Australia, where memories

382. Consideration of the decent work agenda's social dialogue obligation is beyond the scope of this article.

383. Katherine V.W. Stone, *The New Psychological Contract: Implications of the Changing Workplace for Labor and Employment Law*, 48 U.C.L.A. L. REV. 519, 542 (2001).

384. OECD, EMPLOYMENT OUTLOOK 2010: MOVING BEYOND THE JOBS CRISIS 32 tbl.1.2 (2010).

of skilled labor shortages were fresh, employers avoided labor shedding, while employers in the U.S. were "particularly aggressive about shedding labour in response to deteriorating business conditions."[385] Despite the differences in conditions in general labor markets, the effects of the recession on older workers in each country have been strikingly similar. In terms of employment participation, older workers have been among the least affected by the recession. Employment rates among older workers during the global recession have declined slightly in the U.K. (increasing for those past retirement age), remained steady in the U.S., and increased in Australia. The low impact on both employment and unemployment among older workers has been common among industrialized countries and represents a significant departure from the experience of earlier recessions.[386] The exception here is the U.S., where older workers experienced accelerating rates of unemployment as the recession worsened. There is also evidence of a decline in hours worked, though again older workers have been affected less than younger groups.

The recession seems to have had a greater effect on the *quality* of work for older workers. For many, employment has become more fragile, inconstant, and insecure. In all three countries, older workers experience very high rates of long-term unemployment and high levels of underemployment. Older workers have been more able to stay in work than younger workers but, once unemployed, have found it much more difficult to find work, especially full-time work. It appears that the advantages of age (related to position and skills) are diminished or reversed as recession lengthens and intensifies.[387] There are also significant gender differences, with women faring better than men in keeping or gaining jobs.

Furthermore, the recession has seen an increase in the proportion of older workers living on inadequate or precarious incomes through part-time and temporary contracts. In the U.K., a disproportionately large increase in part-time employment among the oldest workers may be associated with the recession, while the recession is likely to have affected the high percentage of older workers in seasonal and casual work. In the U.S., the recession has seen a near doubling in the proportion of older workers in involuntary part-time employment.

385. *Id.* at 32.

386. *Id.* at 21.

387. For example, in the U.S., of some 14.9 million unemployed in August 2010, greater than 2.2 million are aged fifty-five or over. Almost half of those older workers fall into the category of the long-term unemployed, those out of work and actively seeking employment for six months or longer. As reported in the *New York Times*, "[t]he unemployment rate in the group [fifty-five and over] – 7.3 percent – is at a record, more than double what it was at the beginning of the latest recession." Motoko Rich, *For the Unemployed Over 50, Fears of Never Working Again*, N.Y. TIMES, Sept. 20, 2010, at A1.

Many of these effects have much to do with longer-term trends in employment among older workers, the trends being similar for all of the countries examined. People are staying in work longer, reversing the trend towards early retirement that was observable in the 1980s. This is part of a wider pattern among industrialized countries generally.[388] In Australia, the U.K., and the U.S., the increase appears to be the combined result of falling age barriers (both legal and perceptual), increased opportunities for suitable work (especially part-time), and a greater need for older workers to support themselves and their dependents. Increased participation rates at older ages are a reflection of a change in engagement in the labor force, as older workers shift towards part-time work and self-employment.

In one sense, the increase in participation by older workers simply exposes them to the same kind of insecurities faced by younger age cohorts. As they shift toward part-time and other precarious work, the pattern of participation by older workers is becoming more like that of the youngest workers.[389] Increasingly, older workers are in direct competition with younger workers for the very same jobs.[390] In the past, many older workers, men especially, had been insulated from the insecurities of precarious work by both formal and informal job protections – by laws or collective agreements restricting dismissals and by institutional lay-off practices which prioritized length of service. However many of these protections have been dismantled in the name of deregulation and efficiency.

At the same time, older workers face additional vulnerabilities related to disability and discrimination. The evidence from all three countries shows very strongly that discrimination against older workers is endemic. This is reflected statistically in the high and increasing levels of discouraged older workers: those who have withdrawn from the labor force because of the unavailability of work due to perceived age bias. For the less skilled and members of racial or ethnic minorities, the vulnerabilities of age are compounded. And where levels of precariousness are high among older workers, the dislocation effects of recession are particularly strong as working choices are further reduced. As experience from previous recessions shows, the age-related effects intensify as the period of recession lengthens.

Stronger national differences emerge when we turn to labor regulation

388. *Id.*; *see also* OECD, *Statistical Annex*, *in* EMPLOYMENT OUTLOOK 2010, *supra* note 384, at 274-82 tbl.C, *available at* <http://www.oecd.org/dataoecd/30/33/43272221.pdf>.

389. *See supra* Part IV.B.

390. *Id.*

affecting older workers. All three countries have undergone significant dismantling of labor protections in the last two decades, although the process has been more recent and less intensive in Australia, and in both Australia and the U.K., the deregulatory process has to some extent been reversed by social democratic governments. Mandatory retirement has been illegal in both the U.S. and Australia for some time; although in the U.S., effective protection against age discrimination in employment has been diminished by court decisions which make it much more difficult to challenge discriminatory discharge based on age. Effective prohibition of involuntary retirement is now also timetabled for introduction in the U.K.

However such prohibitions, by themselves, do not greatly contribute to employment security for older workers. General labor standards, such as those restricting termination and layoff or requiring severance payments, are just as important in reducing or forestalling older worker vulnerability. Americans generally have been content to leave to the market most matters affecting terms and conditions of employment and dismissal. American employers are consequently free to manage without much legal constraint. Dismissal is relatively costless and, as detailed in Part IV, during the American Great Recession employers have acted opportunistically, shedding workers in great numbers at a time when corporate profits are robust. The American case is a cautionary tale about living by market principles. Market principles are a poor mechanism for pursuing decent work.

In the U.K., dismissal is restricted but during the current crisis, mandatory retirement has been legal. This, as noted in Part III, renders older workers vulnerable, creating a kind of contingent workforce that can be flexibly deployed (or not) depending on economic circumstances. While changes are imminent in the U.K., the phasing out of the default retirement age does not necessarily guarantee the end of mandatory retirement. Thus, we see in two of the three countries profiled, aspects of legal regulation have contributed to vulnerability.

The third, Australia, is attempting to take a different road. With the Fair Work Act 2009, Australia has recently taken steps to reintroduce a measure of effectively enforced minimum conditions for vulnerable workers and has also strengthened protections against discrimination. Will the Australian approach succeed? Even if Australian statistics appear robust, it will be awhile before we can attribute such results to government policies rather than serendipity or unforeseen consequences. Keeping decent work principles in mind, however, will help us evaluate results in the future.

Regarding social security, the differences between the three countries are manifold, each having adopted a combination of approaches to retirement incomes. There are also some strong similarities. All three countries have relatively high levels of private pension provision, with retirement incomes largely provided by private pensions and investments.[391] Because of this, older workers' exposure to financial loss in these countries has been particularly high: in 2008 losses in pension investment returns were 26 percent for Australia and the U.S., 17 percent for the U.K.[392] In these countries, investments for post-retirement remain exposed to further erosion through low earnings growth.

B. Decent Work Lessons

As developed by the ILO since 1999, and restated in 2008, the concept of decent work is founded on four pillars: fundamental principles and rights at work; employment and income opportunities; social protection and social security; and social dialogue and tripartism. The ILO has recently confirmed that these four objectives of the Decent Work Agenda are "inseparable, interrelated and mutually supportive."[393] The development of the concept of decent work reflects the tendency of international labor law and the role of the ILO towards the expansion of international concern for the conditions of labor beyond minimal standards to embrace social justice and the improvement of wellbeing. Ever since the Declaration of Philadelphia in 1944, the ILO has recognized the need for working conditions to be underpinned by the protection of social security measures that provide basic levels of income and health.[394] It is now recognized that the four objectives of decent work extend well beyond minimum standards to encompass dignity, security, and social justice.

391. OECD, PENSIONS AT A GLANCE 2009: RETIREMENT INCOME SYSTEMS IN OECD COUNTRIES 30 (2009) [hereinafter PENSIONS AT A GLANCE]. For figures on private pensions, see details for each country, *Country Highlights*, OECD, <http://www.oecd.org/document/ 49/0,3343,en_2649_34757_ 42992113_1_1_1_1,00.html#country_highlights> (last viewed Mar. 15, 2011). In the U.K., about 55 percent of post-retirement incomes are privately provided. For the U.S. and Australia, the figure is about 45 percent.

392. PENSIONS AT A GLANCE, *supra* note 391, at 33-34.

393. Int'l Labour Conference, Declaration on Social Justice for a Fair Globalization, ILO art. 1(B) (June 10, 2008) [hereinafter Declaration on Social Justice], *available at* <http://www. ilo.org/wcmsp5/groups/public/---dgreports/---cabinet/documents/publication/wcms_0997 66. pdf>; *see also* Resolutions adopted by the International Labour Conference at Its 99th Session (2010), *Conclusions Concerning the Recurrent Discussion on Employment*, ¶ 42 (June 16, 2010), *available at* <http://www.ilo.org/wcmsp5/groups/public/---ed_norm/---relconf/documents/meetingdocument/wcms _143164.pdf>.

394. Emmanuel Reynaud, *Social Security for All: Global Trends and Challenges*, 27 COMP. LAB. L. & POL'Y J. 123, 140 (2006).

The concept of decent work and its pillars was elaborated by the 2008 Declaration on Social Justice for a Fair Globalization. For example, the promotion of employment involves developing the capacity of workers to be "productively occupied for their personal fulfillment and the common well-being."[395] Social protection involves extending social security to all, including a basic income and a living wage to all in need of protection. Increasing attention is being paid to the importance of taking a broad approach to social protection in the realization of decent work, one which addresses the risks of exclusion as well as the values of dignity, community (or solidarity), and equality.[396] The promotion of social dialogue includes building consensus on strategic national objectives and their effective implementation,[397] recognizing that formal law and policy is only effective when based in widespread social involvement and support. Fundamental rights at work have long been recognized as embracing the principles of non-discrimination and equal opportunity.[398]

This enhanced approach to decent work is particularly relevant for older workers. Such an approach allows for the needs of workers to be considered across the life course, so that life events like aging, disability, and dependency are provided for. The decent work agenda allows recognition of the needs of workers to develop their skills and realize their capabilities over their working lives. It also recognizes the importance of workers' ability to plan their retirement in conditions of security: security against the fear of poverty in old age; and security of income when they are no longer able to supplement their income through work.[399]

This study of older workers highlights the inseparable nature of the four pillars of the decent work agenda. For example, the promotion of decent employment opportunities has little meaning if it is undermined by a lack of social protection for those who are not able to support themselves and their dependents through work. Effective standards for securing rights at work are essential underpinnings to ensure that workers are fully enabled to support themselves without being limited by artificial barriers such as discriminatory restrictions. Social protection after retirement, to the extent

395. Declaration on Social Justice, *supra* note 393, art 1(A)(i).

396. In 2001 the ILO concluded that social security activities should be anchored in the decent work concept. *See* Alain Supiot, *The Position of Social Security in the System of International Labor Standards*, 27 COMP. LAB. L. & POL'Y J. 113, 119 (2006). On the values of dignity, solidarity and equality, see Alain Supiot, *The Outlines of A Framework Agreement on the Extension of Social Protection*, 27 COMP. LAB. L. & POL'Y J. 273 (2006).

397. Declaration on Social Justice, *supra* note 393, art 1(A)(ii), (iii).

398. Declaration Concerning the Aims and Purposes of the International Labour Organisation (Declaration of Philadelphia), ILO Constitution, Annex, art. II(a), May 10, 1944.

399. *See supra* notes 13-15 and accompanying text.

that it is increasingly dependent on worker contributions, can only be effective if it is supported by rights to full participation in work without discrimination, and by opportunities for a decent standard of living which will allow workers to accumulate savings for their own security. And, since the situations of older workers and retirees are diverse, extended forms of social dialogue are necessary to ensure that government policies are responsive and well-designed, so as to avoid unintended consequences arising from the interaction of separate policies or a failure to appreciate the needs of particular disadvantaged groups.

In all the countries examined, the demise of state-supported universal social protection has resulted in increased social insecurity, especially in times of economic instability. Following the financial crisis and recession, pressures to reduce or limit state-supported retirement security have been accompanied by setbacks to workers' private savings due to the enormous losses in financial markets. This insecurity is compounded by the spread of precarious work. As a consequence, older workers are less able to make up shortfalls in provision for retirement caused by unemployment and underemployment. They also face the likelihood of involuntary and unplanned early retirement as a result of job loss, since discrimination against older job applicants appears to be both subtle and systemic, and therefore beyond the reach of current anti-discrimination laws. An OECD report has noted that "[t]he financial and economic crisis highlights and exacerbates the issue of safety-net benefits in retirement for workers with low earnings and career gaps."[400] In countries with high dependence on private provision of post-retirement income, such as the three under examination, these inequalities are wider and the consequences for low-income workers greater, particularly for older workers who are less able to make up any shortfall in accumulated wealth for retirement.

Finally, the focus on a particular group of workers, in this case older workers, highlights the value which the concept of decent work performs in recognizing and promoting the variety of their needs. Decent work, like the capability perspective on development, promotes enhancement of "the actual opportunities of living."[401] Older workers are a diverse group. One thing that they have in common is the approaching end of work. For them, decent work has to do not only with their current experience of work, but also with their ability to plan their withdrawal from the labor force and the provision of a secure and adequate standard of living in retirement. Only a multi-faceted concept like decent work is capable of recognizing the deep

400. PENSIONS AT A GLANCE, *supra* note 391, at 38.

401. AMARTYA SEN, THE IDEA OF JUSTICE 233 (2009).

social roots and the interdependence of measures needed to secure human dignity across the course of working lives. This is never clearer than when the certitudes of market capitalism have so manifestly failed.

[7]

THE AGING OF THE AMERICAN WORKFORCE

SARA E. RIX*

INTRODUCTION

One of the great success stories of the past fifty years has been the institutionalization of retirement, the result of society's ability to support a growing nonworking population in dignity and reasonable comfort. A number of developments in the decades immediately following World War II made retirement financially feasible and attractive to the average American. These included Social Security's eventual coverage of almost the entire workforce; the introduction of automatic cost-of-living increases for Social Security benefits; the expansion of private pension coverage; the passage of Medicare legislation; and the lowering to sixty-two of the age of eligibility for Social Security retired worker benefits. The country was getting richer and choosing to use some of its increased wealth to purchase later-life leisure. Older workers jumped at the chance to retire and enjoy that leisure.

This is not to imply the absence of employment barriers confronting older workers. Age discrimination, mandatory retirement rules in many establishments, job dislocation, and skills obsolescence have long plagued the older worker. Nonetheless, the notion of what constituted acceptable activity in later life changed as retirement became respectable and workers began looking forward to it, often from relatively young ages. No longer were ill health, disability, or perhaps substantial wealth the only legitimate reasons for labor force withdrawal at older ages, although health problems have always forced some workers to retire earlier than they might have preferred. In her economic history of retirement, Dora Costa argues that retirement ceased to be a time of withdrawal and dependence on family for support and care; rather, it became one of discovery and personal fulfillment.[1] A vast leisure industry emerged to cater to increasingly affluent

* Ph.D., Senior Policy Advisor, Public Policy Institute, AARP. This Article is based on the 2005 Kenneth M. Piper Lecture at the Chicago-Kent College of Law. The views expressed in this Article are those of the author and do not necessarily represent the official policy of AARP.

1. DORA L. COSTA, THE EVOLUTION OF RETIREMENT: AN AMERICAN ECONOMIC HISTORY, 1880–1990, at 1 (1998).

retirees. Early retirement became and remains the norm; proposals to increase the age of eligibility for Social Security benefits are not popular with the public.[2]

In its recent assessment of aging and employment policies in the United States, the Organization for Economic Cooperation and Development warns of slowing economic growth, serious labor shortages, and increasing tax rates due to the rapid aging of the population.[3] Although the United States is aging less rapidly than many other developed countries, the nation's older and retired population will increase demands on public pension, health, and welfare programs. The Social Security system, for example, is currently generating more revenues than it is paying in benefits. As the boomers retire, this favorable situation will change and the trust fund reserves will eventually have to be drawn down. According to the 2005 annual report of the Board of Trustees of the Social Security Administration, the combined Old-Age and Survivors Insurance and Disability Insurance reserves will be exhausted by about 2041, at which time, the system will be able to pay only about 74% of promised retirement benefits.[4] The Medicare program faces insolvency even sooner. Fostering longer work lives, while seemingly flying in the face of prevailing patterns of behavior, could reduce the rate of growth in expenditures for these programs, contribute to economic growth, and (by giving workers longer to save and invest for retirement) help to promote workers' ultimate retirement security. Although not yet high on the policy agenda in the United States, older workers are likely to be the focus of considerably more attention on the part of lawmakers when Congress turns to specific proposals to reform Social Security.

This Article provides an overview of the weakening labor force attachment of older Americans in the decades after World War II, which was facilitated by the entrance of baby boomers and married women into the workforce; speculates on what the future holds and why more work later in life may characterize growing numbers of older workers; and discusses a

2. *See* SARA E. RIX, AARP PUB. POLICY INST., SOCIAL SECURITY REFORM: RETHINKING RETIREMENT-AGE POLICY—A LOOK AT RAISING SOCIAL SECURITY'S RETIREMENT AGE 6–8 (1999), *available at* http://assets.aarp.org/rgcenter/econ/ib40_age_policy.pdf.

3. ORG. FOR ECON. CO-OPERATION & DEV., AGEING AND EMPLOYMENT POLICIES: UNITED STATES 11 (2005).

4. *See* SOC. SEC. & MEDICARE BDS. OF TRS., STATUS OF THE SOCIAL SECURITY AND MEDICARE PROGRAMS: A SUMMARY OF THE 2005 ANNUAL REPORTS 15 (2005), *available at* http://www.ssa.gov/OACT/TRSUM/tr05summary.pdf. The Congressional Budget Office projects an insolvency date of 2052, after which scheduled revenues will amount to 78 percent of scheduled outlays. CONG. BUDGET OFFICE, UPDATED LONG-TERM PROJECTIONS FOR SOCIAL SECURITY 1 (2005), http://www.cbo.gov/ftpdocs/60xx/doc6064/03-03-LongTermProjections.pdf.

number of issues—such as labor demand and the quality of work—that must be addressed to ensure a productive aging workforce. Although the population and workforce are aging, substantially higher participation rates on the part of older persons are not inevitable.

I. BACKGROUND

Few labor force developments of the twentieth century were as pronounced or significant as the decline in participation on the part of older men.[5] Nearly two-thirds of men aged sixty-five and older were in the labor force in 1900,[6] often remaining on the job until they died or were physically incapable of doing any work at all. With the shift from an agricultural to a manufacturing economy, older men's attachment to the labor force weakened as employers sought younger and stronger workers to employ in the factories. "The growth of the factory system unquestionably accelerated the process of retirement," notes historian David Hackett Fischer,[7] a process that began well before World War II. By 1940, only 42% of men aged sixty-five and older were in the labor force.[8] The war years brought a brief hiatus to this decline, which resumed and gathered speed once the war was over.

The proportion of men aged sixty-five and older who were working or looking for work plummeted from nearly 46% in 1950 to about 16% in 1985.[9] Falling rates of participation were not limited to this age group. Over the same period, middle-aged (ages fifty-five to sixty-four in this Article) men were also showing less inclination or were provided fewer opportunities to work; their participation rate fell by nearly twenty percentage points—from 86.9% to 67.9%—between 1950 and 1985.[10] (Labor force participation rates for middle-aged and older men and women since 1950 are presented in Table 1.)

5. The official definition of labor force participation includes persons who are employed or who are unemployed and looking for work. See BUREAU OF LABOR STATISTICS, U.S. DEP'T OF LABOR, BLS GLOSSARY (2005), http://www.bls.gov/bls/glossary.htm, for the full definitions of "labor force participation rate," "employed persons," and "unemployed persons."

6. U.S. CENSUS BUREAU, U.S. DEP'T OF COMMERCE, HISTORICAL STATISTICS OF THE UNITED STATES: COLONIAL TIMES TO 1970, at 132 (1975).

7. DAVID HACKETT FISCHER, GROWING OLD IN AMERICA 143 (1977).

8. U.S. CENSUS BUREAU, *supra* note 6, at 132.

9. These data, as well as much of the other statistical data in this Article, can be found at the searchable website of the Bureau of Labor Statistics. *See* Bureau of Labor Statistics, U.S. Dep't of Labor, Labor Force Statistics from the Current Population Survey, http://data.bls.gov/PDQ/outside.jsp?survey=ln (last visited Jan. 13, 2006).

10. *See id.*

Women—at least those who are middle-aged—have moved in a different direction. The participation rate for women aged sixty-five and over (the age that one is traditionally considered "old") has fluctuated around a relatively low level over the past half century, while that for middle-aged women began to rise substantially after the war. In 1985, 42.0% of fifty-five- to sixty-four-year-old women were in the labor force, up from 27.0% in 1950.[11] Nonetheless, the increasing labor force attachment on the part of middle-aged women was not enough to offset the decline among men. As a result, from 1950 to 1985, the participation rates for the fifty-five and older population fell from 43.0% to 30.3%.[12]

Table 1 Labor Force Participation Rates, Selected Years, 1950–2004 (percent)[13]

	Ages 55–64		Ages 65+	
Year	**Men**	**Women**	**Men**	**Women**
1950	86.9	27.0	45.8	9.7
1955	87.9	32.5	39.6	10.6
1960	86.8	37.2	33.1	10.8
1965	84.6	41.1	27.9	10.0
1970	83.0	43.0	26.8	9.7
1975	75.6	40.9	21.6	8.2
1980	72.1	41.3	19.0	8.1
1985	67.9	42.0	15.8	7.3
1990	67.8	45.2	16.3	8.6
1991	67.0	45.2	15.7	8.5
1992	67.0	46.5	16.1	8.3
1993	66.5	47.2	15.6	8.1
1994	65.5	48.9	16.8	9.2
1995	66.0	49.2	16.8	8.8
1996	67.0	49.6	16.9	8.6
1997	67.6	50.9	17.1	8.6
1998	68.1	51.2	16.5	8.6
1999	67.9	51.5	16.9	8.9
2000	67.3	51.9	17.7	9.4
2001	68.3	53.2	17.7	9.6
2002	69.2	55.2	17.9	9.8
2003	68.7	56.6	18.6	10.6
2004	68.7	56.3	19.0	11.1

11. *See id.*
12. *See id.*
13. *See id.*

II. THE IMPACT OF THE BABY BOOMERS

At the same time that this was going on, the labor force experienced an eighteen-year shot in the arm as the baby boomers, born between 1946 and 1964, began entering the workforce. As they did so, labor force growth increased about 2.6% annually in the 1970s.[14] The supply of labor at least temporarily assured, employers could afford to let their older workers go. Fixed retirement ages hastened the exodus of some older workers. Employers added special incentives to their pension plans to encourage older workers to retire; retiree health benefits spread. In addition, benefit calculations in some pension plans penalized (and still do penalize) continued employment beyond an often fairly young age.[15] This happens when workers eligible for defined benefit pension payments postpone receipt of their benefits. Some find that the increase in the benefits realized as a result of delaying retirement is not enough to make up for the benefits foregone while continuing to work.[16] In such cases, the sum of benefits paid over a lifetime of retirement is less than it would have been if retirement had occurred earlier. This is hardly an incentive to keep on working.

The same has been true for workers who postpone receipt of Social Security benefits after the age of eligibility for full benefits, typically referred to as the full or normal retirement age. Workers who do so are eligible for a delayed retirement credit (DRC) that, prior to the Social Security Amendments of 1983, amounted to 3% for each year that receipt of benefits has been put off.[17] A full actuarial adjustment, however, is about 8% per year.[18] The 1983 amendments to the Social Security Act introduced a gradual increase in the DRC (beginning in 1990) that, when it reaches 8% in 2008, will be more actuarially fair.[19] Workers who postpone collecting their Social Security benefits will no longer be penalized with a loss in lifetime benefits by doing so, but until then, working longer does not fully pay off.

14. Howard N Fullerton, Jr., *The Workforce of Tomorrow*, *in* THRIVING ON AN AGING WORKFORCE: STRATEGIES FOR ORGANIZATIONAL AND SYSTEMIC CHANGE 14, 18 (Paulette T. Beatty & Roemer M.S. Visser eds., 2005).

15. *See* Laurence J. Kotlikoff. & David A. Wise, *The Incentive Effects of Private Pension Plans*, *in* ISSUES IN PENSION ECONOMICS 283, 283 (Zvi Bodie et al. eds., 1987).

16. *See, e.g., id.* at 332.

17. Soc. Sec. Admin., Legislative History, http://www.socialsecurity.gov/history/1983amend2.html (last visited Jan. 13, 2006) (providing a detailed summary of the provisions of the 1983 Amendments).

18. Michael A. Anzick & David A. Weaver, *The Impact of Repealing the Retirement Earnings Test on Rates of Poverty*, SOC. SECURITY BULL., Dec. 2000, at 3, 4.

19. Social Security Amendments of 1983, Pub. L. No. 98-21, § 114, 97 Stat. 65, 79 (codified as amended at 42 U.S.C. § 402(w) (2000)). The DRC goes to workers who delay collecting Social Security beyond the normal retirement age up to age seventy. 42 U.S.C. § 402(w)(2)(a) (2000).

Employer concerns about the costs, technological competence, and productivity of older workers have also served as employment barriers for many who might have wanted to remain at work or return to the labor force.[20] All of these factors contributed to the early retirement boom of the post-war years.

Over time, as older workers exited the labor force at younger ages and, in particular, as boomers moved into it, the workforce got younger. Between 1950 and 1985, the proportion of labor force participants who were age fifty-five or older fell from about 17% to under 13%.[21] The median age of the labor force fell from 40.5 years in 1962 to 34.6 years in 1980.[22]

III. THE LABOR FORCE IS GROWING OLDER

Eventually, most of the boomers who were going to enter the labor force had done so. In addition, the rate of increase in women's labor force participation began to slow. And, significantly, around 1985 labor force participation rates for the fifty-five and older population leveled off and then began to rise. The labor force began to age.

Since the mid-1980s, labor force participation rates for the middle-aged and older populations have been moving upward. The rate for persons aged sixty-five and over rose from 10.8% to 14.4% from 1985 to 2004, while that for those aged fifty-five to sixty-four increased from 54.2% to 62.3%.[23]

These figures for broad segments of the population obscure sizable differences by age group and sex. The participation rate for persons aged sixty-five to sixty-nine, for example, rose from 18.4% to 27.7%, or by just over 50%, between 1985 and 2004.[24] Women, particularly the middle-aged, have tended to show greater increases than men. The result has been a narrowing of the later-life male-female labor force participation gap. By 2004, the ratio of female to male labor force participation rates for those fifty-five and older was 70.6%, up from 27.6% in 1950 and 53.7% in 1985.[25]

20. *See* AARP, AMERICAN BUSINESS AND OLDER EMPLOYEES: A SUMMARY OF FINDINGS 4–5 (2000), *available at* http://assets.aarp.org/rgcenter/econ/amer_bus_findings.pdf (reporting that employers view older workers as "resistant to learning and understanding new technologies").

21. *See* Bureau of Labor Statistics, *supra* note 9.

22. Howard N Fullerton, Jr. & Mitra Toossi, *Labor Force Projections to 2010: Steady Growth and Changing Composition*, MONTHLY LAB. REV., Nov. 2001, at 21, 36, *available at* http://bls.gov/opub/mlr/2001/11art2full.pdf.

23. *See* Bureau of Labor Statistics, *supra* note 9.

24. *See id.*

25. *See id.*

Although participation rates have been rising, it would be wrong to conclude that early retirement is a thing of the past. Most workers still opt to retire early, that is, before the age of eligibility for full Social Security benefits. Ever *earlier* retirement, however, seems to have come to an end, at least for the present. Reynolds, Ridley, and Van Horn of the John J. Heldrich Center for Workforce Development go so far as to contend that "[t]he traditional notion of retirement—where one stops working completely and enjoys leisure time with friends and family—is obsolete."[26] Although it does seem as if baby boomers in particular are poised to redefine the retirement years by working longer (many of them after retiring from career jobs), most of them will undoubtedly still experience some, perhaps lengthy, period of total retirement from paid employment.

Why the declining labor force participation rate at upper ages began to change in the mid-1980s is not clear.[27] Most likely, a variety of factors came into play, affecting different workers in different ways. These include the 1967 Age Discrimination in Employment Act (ADEA) and its subsequent amendments,[28] the liberalization of the Social Security earnings test,[29] the eventual elimination of the earnings test for workers over the normal retirement age, and the growing labor force attachment of women, many of whom might be working longer to accrue pension and enhanced Social Security benefits. It is also possible that slowing labor force growth, as the baby bust generation (the cohort following the boomers) reached working age, played a role as well. Employers, particularly in industries typically reliant on an entry-level workforce, might have been experiencing labor shortages and turning to older workers as an alternative.[30]

While women's labor force participation rates may continue to rise somewhat, the extent of the increase remains to be seen. For one thing, women still assume more of the burden of informal caregiving. If women's caregiving burdens increase as the population ages, their ability to remain

26. Scott Reynolds et al., *A Work-Filled Retirement: Workers' Changing Views on Employment and Leisure*, WORKTRENDS, Aug. 2005, at 1 *available at* http://www.heldrich.rutgers.edu/Resources/Publication/191/WT16.pdf.

27. For an examination of male changes in behavior, see Richard Johnson, *The Puzzle of Later Male Retirement*, FED. RES. BANK KANSAS CITY ECON. REV., Third Quarter 2002, at 5, *available at* http://www.kc.frb.org/Publicat/econrev/Pdf/3q02john.pdf.

28. 29 U.S.C. §§ 621–634 (2000).

29. The earnings test reduces Social Security benefits for beneficiaries earning above a certain amount, which is adjusted annually. In 2005, beneficiaries below the normal retirement could earn up to $12,000, above which $1 in benefits would be withheld for every $2 in earnings. The earnings limit and benefit reduction are different for the year in which a worker reaches the full retirement age. 42 U.S.C. § 403 (2000).

30. There was some evidence of this in the fast food industry in the 1980s. McDonald's, for example, introduced its McMasters programs aimed at recruiting and training older workers.

in the labor force may be adversely affected. There is also the question of what women will do as more of them reach the traditional retirement age, having spent thirty-five or more years in the workforce. Perhaps retirement will begin to look more attractive to them—many of them have held full-time jobs in the paid workforce and in the home—especially if the retirement income they have earned during their long work lives enables them to maintain their preretirement standard of living. If so, participation rates could resume falling.

IV. WHAT THE FUTURE HOLDS

Labor force participation rates are nonetheless expected to continue rising. The Labor Department's Bureau of Labor Statistics (BLS) projects that approximately 41% of the fifty-five-plus population will be in the labor force in 2014,[31] an increase of five percentage points over the rate for 2004.[32] By 2014, more than one out of five persons in the workforce will be fifty-five or older, and the median age will be over a year higher than it is today.[33]

There are several reasons to expect that older workers will increasingly postpone retirement and that more retirees will reenter the labor force, thus resulting in labor force participation rates above those projected by the Bureau of Labor Statistics:

Stagnating private pension coverage since the 1970s. Overall only about half of all private-sector workers are covered by pension plans through their current employers, and the Center for Retirement Research at Boston College finds little change in the number of covered workers over the past thirty years.[34] Unless they have income from other sources, such as savings and investments—and many can expect little from these—workers stand to experience a substantial decline in their standard of living if they are solely dependent on Social Security in old age.[35]

The shift from defined benefit (DB) pension coverage to defined contribution (DC) coverage. Of workers whose employers do offer pension

31. Mitra Toosi, *Labor Force Projections to 2014: Retiring Boomers*, MONTHLY LAB. REV., Nov. 2005, at 25, 33 tbl.5, *available at* http://www.bls.gov/opub/mlr/2005/11/art3full.pdf.

32. *See* Bureau of Labor Statistics, *supra* note 9.

33. Toosi, *supra* note 31, at 25, 42.

34. ALICIA H. MUNNELL ET AL., CTR. FOR RET. RESEARCH, HOW IMPORTANT ARE PRIVATE PENSIONS? 2 (2002), *available at* http://www.bc.edu/centers/crr/issues/ib_8.pdf.

35. Many older Americans are completely or largely dependent on Social Security for income. It is the only source of income for 20% of the sixty-five and older population and accounts for half or more of the income of 60% of this age group. SOC. SEC. ADMIN., PUBL'N NO. 13-11871, INCOME OF THE POPULATION 55 OR OLDER, 2002, at 105 tbl.6.A1 (2005), *available at* http://www.ssa.gov/policy/docs/statcomps/income_pop55/2002/incpop02.pdf.

coverage, a declining proportion has DB coverage; employers have moved instead to 401(k) and other DC plans. The Employee Benefit Research Institute reports that as of 2001, the Pension Benefit Guaranty Corporation insured just over 35,200 DB plans, down from a 1985 high of 114,400.[36] Also as of 2001, half of assets in qualified private pension plans were in DC plans, up from 29% in 1974.[37] DC plans such as 401(k)s provide workers with investment choices, which understandably appealed to workers during the 1990s when times were good as a result of the sustained stock market boom.

One outcome of the stock market bubble of the 1990s was an increase in retirement, according to Gustman and Steinmeier.[38] But a bursting bubble could have just the opposite effect, as 401(k)s place the burden of retirement-income support squarely on the shoulders of workers themselves. Given often inadequate savings and market uncertainties, some workers do appear to be reevaluating their retirement plans. Gustman and Steinmeier report that the recent stock market bust led many workers to conclude "that it would be prudent to continue the income from working until either the market recovers or they have had an opportunity to rebuild the nest egg to a level sufficient to ensure a comfortable retirement."[39] Other research seems to confirm these observations.[40]

The year 2000 was not good for market investors, workers with pension plans among them. A survey of fifty- to seventy-year-olds who reported market losses around that time found that about 20% of workers had pushed back the date of retirement.[41] Munnell, Cahill, and Jivan estimate that workers with DC plans retire about one year later than those with DB plans.[42]

36. DAVID RAJNES, EMPLOYEE BENEFIT RESEARCH INST., EBRI ISSUE BRIEF NO. 249, AN EVOLVING PENSION SYSTEM: TRENDS IN DEFINED BENEFIT AND DEFINED CONTRIBUTION PLANS 1 (2002), *available at* http://www.ebri.org/pdf/briefspdf/0902ib.pdf.

37. *Id.*

38. ALAN L. GUSTMAN & THOMAS L. STEINMEIER, NAT'L BUREAU OF ECON. RESEARCH, RETIREMENT AND THE STOCK MARKET BUBBLE 1–2 (2002), *available at* http://www.nber.org/papers/w9404.pdf. Gustman and Steinmeier report that retirement increased by more than 3 percentage points among workers in the Health and Retirement Study. *Id.* at 27–28.

39. *Id.* at 2.

40. *See, e.g.*, S. KATHI BROWN, AARP, IMPACT OF STOCK MARKET DECLINE ON 50–70 YEAR OLD INVESTORS 2 (2002), *available at* http://assets.aarp.org/rgcenter/econ/market_decline.pdf; EMPLOYEE BENEFIT RESEARCH INST., THE 2003 RETIREMENT CONFIDENCE SURVEY SUMMARY OF FINDINGS 1 (2003), *available at* http://www.ebri.org/pdf/surveys/rcs/2003/03rcssof.pdf.

41. BROWN, *supra* note 40, at 2.

42. ALICIA H. MUNNELL ET AL., CTR. FOR RETIREMENT RESEARCH, HOW HAS THE SHIFT TO 401(K)S AFFECTED THE RETIREMENT AGE? 4 (2003), *available at* http://www.bc.edu/centers/crr/issues/ib_13.pdf.

Inadequate personal savings to supplement other sources of retirement income, particularly Social Security. Over one-third of workers report that they are currently putting nothing aside for retirement.[43] In an assessment of retirement preparedness, the Congressional Budget Office (CBO) concludes that only about half of boomers are on track to maintain their current living standards in retirement.[44] However, another CBO study suggests that much of the concern about savings in the United States could be alleviated if workers remained in the labor force until age seventy, when their Social Security benefits would be about double what they can expect at age sixty-two.[45] While workers do not have total control over how long they plan to keep working, because ill health, disability, caregiving responsibilities, or job displacement may propel them out of the workforce before they had planned, they have more say over their retirement age than they do over the vagaries of the market. A close reading of "Your Social Security Statement," which the Social Security Administration annually mails to covered persons, would make clear the impact that delayed receipt of benefits has on monthly payments.

Concern on the part of those with savings that they might outlive their money, especially in light of rising life expectancy. Today's average sixty-five-year-old can expect to live more than five years longer than could a sixty-five-year-old around the time that the Social Security system was established.[46] Life expectancy at upper ages is expected to continue increasing.[47]

The increase in the age of eligibility for full Social Security benefits from sixty-five to sixty-seven. As a result of amendments to the Social Security Act in 1983, the full retirement age began increasing gradually for workers who turned sixty-two in 2000.[48] It will continue to rise until it reaches sixty-seven for persons born in 1960 or later. Workers will still be able to collect benefits as early as age sixty-two; however, the benefits will

43. Reynolds et al., *supra* note 26, at 3.

44. CONG. BUDGET OFFICE, ECONOMIC AND BUDGET ISSUE BRIEF: THE RETIREMENT PROSPECTS OF THE BABY BOOMERS 2 (2004), *available at* http://www.cbo.gov/ftpdocs/51xx/doc5195/03-18-BabyBoomers.pdf.

45. CONG. BUDGET OFFICE, ECONOMIC AND BUDGET ISSUE BRIEF: RETIREMENT AGE AND THE NEED FOR SAVING 3 (2004), *available at* http://www.cbo.gov/ftpdocs/54xx/doc5419/05-12-RetireAge&Saving.pdf.

46. Elizabeth Arias, *United States Life Tables, 2002*, NAT'L VITAL STAT. REP. (U.S. Dep't of Health & Human Servs., Hyattsville, MD), Nov. 10, 2004, at 29 tbl.11, *available at* http://www.cdc.gov/nchs/data/nvsr/nvsr53/nvsr53_06.pdf.

47. BD. OF TRS., FED. OLD-AGE & SURVIVORS INS. & DISABILITY INS. TRUST FUNDS, THE 2005 ANNUAL REPORT OF THE BOARD OF TRUSTEES OF THE FEDERAL OLD-AGE AND SURVIVORS INSURANCE AND DISABILITY INSURANCE TRUST FUNDS, H.R. DOC. NO. 109-18, at 80 tbl.V.A3 (1st Sess. 2005).

48. *See* 42 U.S.C. § 416(l) (2000).

be substantially lower than when the full retirement age was sixty-five. Some experts doubt that this increase will have much of an impact on the actual retirement age,[49] but it is too soon to tell.

Eroding retiree health benefits. Although a long-term decline in retiree health coverage may be leveling off,[50] only 13% of private-sector employers offered health benefits to early retirees in 2002, a decline from 22% in 1997.[51] Moreover, costs to workers for the coverage have been increasing, and restrictions have been placed on eligibility.[52] Given the employer-based health system in the United States, workers who lack health-care coverage from another source may have little choice but to remain at work until age sixty-five if they are so able.

Rising educational levels. Better educated workers are more likely to be in the labor force than their less well-educated peers and to remain there later in life.[53] Although less well-educated workers may lack the resources to retire comfortably at younger ages, they are more likely than workers with more schooling to experience unemployment and work-limiting conditions such as ill health, or to find that demand for their skills has diminished. Educational attainment has also risen; among persons aged fifty-five and over, nearly 80% have four years of high school or more compared to only about 22% in 1960.[54] Nearly 90% of persons in their early- to mid-fifties are high school graduates or more.[55] All else being equal, the increase in years of formal schooling suggests continued increases in labor force participation at upper ages.

Improved health status at older ages. Ill health has long been a barrier to continued employment in old age, but declining disability rates at upper

49. *See, e.g.*, GARY S. FIELDS & OLIVIA S. MITCHELL, NAT'L COMM'N FOR EMPLOYMENT POLICY, RESEARCH REPORT SERIES 83-09, RESTRUCTURING SOCIAL SECURITY: HOW WILL RETIREMENT AGES RESPOND? 17–18 (1983); Alan L. Gustman & Thomas L. Steinmeier, *The 1983 Social Security Reforms and Labor Supply Adjustments of Older Individuals in the Long Run*, 3 J. LAB. ECON. 237, 247 (1985).

50. U.S. GOV'T ACCOUNTABILITY OFFICE, GAO-05-205, RETIREE HEALTH BENEFITS: OPTIONS FOR EMPLOYMENT-BASED PRESCRIPTION DRUG BENEFITS UNDER THE MEDICARE MODERNIZATION ACT 13 (2005), *available at* http://www.gao.gov/highlights/d05205high.pdf.

51. PAUL FRONSTIN, EMPLOYEE BENEFIT RESEARCH INST., EBRI ISSUE BRIEF NO. 279, THE IMPACT OF THE EROSION OF RETIREE HEALTH BENEFITS ON WORKERS AND RETIREES 1 (2005), *available at* http://www.ebri.org/pdf/briefspdf/0305ib.pdf.

52. U.S. GOV'T ACCOUNTABILITY OFFICE, *supra* note 50, at 23.

53. *See* STEVEN HAIDER & DAVID LOUGHRAN, RAND, WORKING PAPER SERIES 01-09, ELDERLY LABOR SUPPLY: WORK OR PLAY? 28 tbl.1 (2001), *available at* http://www.rand.org/labor/DRU/DRU2582.pdf.

54. *See* U.S. Census Bureau, U.S. Dep't of Commerce, Table A-1, Years of School Completed by People 25 Years and Over, by Age and Sex: Selected Years 1940 to 2004, at A-9 to -10, http://www.census.gov/population/socdemo/education/tabA-1.pdf (last visited Jan. 27, 2006).

55. U.S. CENSUS BUREAU, U.S. DEP'T OF COMMERCE, CURRENT POPULATION REPORTS NO. P20-550, EDUCATIONAL ATTAINMENT IN THE UNITED STATES: 2003, at 3 tbl.A (2004).

ages[56] should increase the probability that workers will remain in the labor force.[57]

Less physically demanding work. The proportion of workers in physically demanding jobs, defined as "requiring frequent lifting or carrying of objects weighing more than 25 pounds" fell from 20.3% in 1950 to 7.5% in 1996, according to the Urban Institute's Eugene Steuerle.[58] The concomitant growth of the service sector is also assumed to offer suitable employment opportunities for large numbers of older workers.

Employer demand, especially in the face of anticipated labor and/or skills shortages. There can be little doubt that the supply of *potential* older workers is rising sharply. Population projections point to slower growth in the number of younger persons available to fill the shoes of boomers who will begin reaching the age of eligibility for early Social Security benefits in 2008.[59] If they retire in large numbers at this young age—as their parents did—employers might well experience severe labor and/or skills shortages. Should that happen, the demand for older workers will increase as well. It is this potential demand for labor and skills, more than any other, that stands to have the most substantial impact on older worker employment over the next two decades.

Worker demand. Workers themselves seem poised to remain longer in the workforce and may therefore prove more resistant to retirement incentives, more willing to fight targeted downsizing, and more likely to pressure employers to offer the types of employment opportunities they say they want, such as flexible work schedules and phased retirement. Recent public opinion polls find that upwards of 60% of workers expect to work at least part-time in retirement.[60] Among boomers, the figure is as high as 80%.[61]

56. Kenneth G. Manton & XiLiang Gu, *Changes in the Prevalence of Chronic Disability in the United States Black and Nonblack Population Above Age 65 from 1982 to 1999*, 98 PROC. NAT'L ACAD. SCI. U.S. 6354, 6354 (2001).

57. *See, e.g.*, Haider & Loughran, *supra* note 53, at 11; CORI E. UCCELLO, AARP, FACTORS INFLUENCING RETIREMENT: THEIR IMPLICATIONS FOR RAISING RETIREMENT AGE 7 (1998), *available at* http://assets.aarp.org/rgcenter/econ/9810_retire.pdf.

58. Eugene Steuerle et al., *Can Americans Work Longer?*, STRAIGHT TALK ON SOC. SEC. & RET. POL'Y (Urban Inst., Wash., D.C.), Aug. 15, 1999, at 1, *available at* http://www.urban.org/UploadedPDF/Straight5.pdf.

59. U.S. CENSUS BUREAU, U.S. DEP'T OF COMMERCE, STATISTICAL ABSTRACT OF THE UNITED STATES: 2006, at 14 tbl.12 (2006).

60. PAUL YAKOBOSKI & JENNIFER DICKEMPER, EMPLOYEE BENEFIT RESEARCH INST., EBRI ISSUE BRIEF NO. 191, INCREASED SAVING BUT LITTLE PLANNING: RESULTS OF THE 1997 RETIREMENT CONFIDENCE SURVEY 4 (1997), *available at* http://www.ebri.org/pdf/briefspdf/1197ib.pdf; HUMPHREY TAYLOR, HARRIS INTERACTIVE, 3.7 MILLION PEOPLE OVER 55 NOT WORKING NOW ARE READY, WILLING AND ABLE TO WORK (1999), http://www.harrisinteractive.com/harris_poll/index.asp?PID=19; S. KATHI BROWN, AARP, STAYING AHEAD OF THE CURVE 2003: THE AARP WORKING IN RETIREMENT

Workers give a variety of reasons for why they expect to remain in the labor force, with nonfinancial reasons tending to take precedence. When pressed for the major reason, however, finances rise to the top; workers simply need the income or access to health care that employment provides. Money is also, not surprisingly, the primary reason working retirees give for remaining in the labor force.[62]

With such high—and in recent years seemingly consistent—percentages saying they plan to work in retirement, the relatively low labor force participation rates for the older population might be expected to soar. Yet the extent to which expectations and desires will translate into action is by no means clear. The average expected age of retirement is on the rise, but workers still express interest in retiring, and often at a young age. More than one-third of boomers believe that they will not want to stop working; however, more than two-fifths cannot wait to retire.[63] In fact, the average age at which boomers would *like* to stop working for pay altogether is under sixty years.[64] In other words, the retirement in which boomers expect to be working would, ideally, be a fairly young retirement.

In 2005, Reynolds, Ridley, and Van Horn reported that over one-third of workers believe that they will never be financially able to retire from full-time work or will not be able to do so until after age sixty-five; more than 70% would ideally retire at age sixty or younger.[65] Workers are also apparently less confident about their ability to retire when they want to than they were five years ago.[66]

V. EMPLOYMENT BARRIERS

Will 70 or 80, or even just 60, percent of workers remain in the workforce after the conventional retirement age? It is hard to envisage this happening if conventional retirement age is understood to be age sixty-five.

STUDY 5 (2003), *available at* http://assets.aarp.org/rgcenter/econ/multiwork_2003.pdf; Reynolds et al., *supra* note 26, at 1. *But see* CIVIC VENTURES, THE NEW FACE OF RETIREMENT: SURVEY RESULTS 9 (2002), *available at* http://www.civicventures.org/publications/surveys/ new_face_of_retirement/ 2002_surveydata.pdf (reporting that 39% of nonretired persons aged fifty to seventy-five said that they planned to work for pay at another job after they retired).

61. AARP, BABY BOOMERS ENVISION RETIREMENT II: SURVEY OF BABY BOOMERS' EXPECTATIONS FOR RETIREMENT 24 (2004), *available at* http://assets.aarp.org/rgcenter/econ/boomers_envision.pdf.

62. BROWN, *supra* note 60, at 6.

63. AARP, *supra* note 61, at 27.

64. AARP, BABY BOOMERS ENVISION THEIR RETIREMENT: AN AARP SEGMENTATION ANALYSIS 82 (1998), *available at* http://assets.aarp.org/rgcenter/econ/boomer_seg.pdf.

65. *See* Reynolds et al., *supra* note 26, at 7. Unfortunately, this survey does not indicate when workers might like to retire from *all* work.

66. *Id.*

Only about 28% of persons aged sixty-five to sixty-nine are now in the labor force.[67] To be sure, as noted above, this reflects an increase of about 50% over the past two decades,[68] but a near tripling or even a doubling of the participation over the next decade (when the first several years of the boomer cohort will be in their mid- to upper-sixties) is highly unlikely. Today's workers may expect to work in retirement—and many of them will do so—but they also indicate that they plan to work considerably later in life than today's retirees actually worked. So, for example, only 37% of nonretirees in the 2004 Retirement Confidence Survey asserted that they planned to retire before age sixty-five; however, 61% of retirees had left the labor force by that age.[69]

The CBO finds that many boomers are not waiting until sixty-five or even sixty-two to stop working.[70] As of 2004, four million boomers (the oldest of whom was only fifty-eight) had already left the labor force, most commonly because of a disability but others because they had retired. Moreover, many of the disabled were receiving benefits from Social Security Disability Insurance, a program with stringent eligibility criteria. Thus, these nonworkers would not appear to be malingerers who could work if they really wanted to. The CBO observes that if boomers "follow in the footsteps of workers now in their early 60s, perhaps one-third of the men and nearly half of the women will be out of the labor force before their 62nd birthday."[71]

Not only may disability and other problems cause workers to leave the labor force prematurely, but retirement itself may look better the closer a worker gets to it. Although the vast majority of boomers still plan to work in retirement, the proportion not expecting to work at all has increased since the late 1990s.[72]

Age continues to serve as an employment barrier for older workers, as evidenced by the duration of unemployment and wage losses experienced upon reemployment. The average duration of unemployment in 2004 was 25.8 weeks for jobseekers aged fifty-five and older, compared to 18.9

67. *See* Bureau of Labor Statistics, *supra* note 9.

68. *See id.*

69. *See* RUTH HELMAN & VARINY PALADINO, EMPLOYEE BENEFIT RESEARCH INST., EBRI ISSUE BRIEF NO. 268, WILL AMERICANS EVER BECOME SAVERS? THE 14TH RETIREMENT CONFIDENCE SURVEY, 2004, at 5 fig.3 (2004), *available at* http://www.ebri.org/pdf/briefspdf/0404ib.pdf.

70. CONG. BUDGET OFFICE, CONG. OF THE U.S., DISABILITY AND RETIREMENT: THE EARLY EXIT OF BABY BOOMERS FROM THE LABOR FORCE 1 (2004).

71. *Id.*

72. AARP, *supra* note 61, at 24.

weeks for younger jobseekers.[73] Upon reemployment older workers often experience lower wages with fewer benefits. In testimony before the Senate Finance Committee, economist Lori Kletzer mentioned earnings losses in excess of 30% for some older reemployed workers.[74] Couch has found that the average displaced worker aged fifty-one to sixty experienced an earnings loss of 39%, and the household with a displaced worker had 24% lower income.[75] The displaced are less likely to have health insurance on the new job.[76]

Older workers can perhaps take some comfort in the fact that they are less likely than younger workers to lose their jobs.[77] Nonetheless, the Bureau of Labor Statistics reports that nearly 1.7 million workers aged fifty-five and older were displaced from their jobs between January 2001 and December 2003,[78] a greater number than had been displaced during the three-year period from January 1999 to December 2001, 1.2 million.[79] Job loss can have a devastating effect. If displaced, older workers are far less likely than their younger counterparts to find work. After displacement in the January 2001 to December 2003 period, for example, 69% of workers aged twenty-five to fifty-four and 57% of workers aged fifty-five to sixty-four had found work by January 2004, but only 25% of those sixty-five and older had done so.[80] Displaced workers aged fifty-five to sixty-four were nearly twice as likely to be out of the labor force as those twenty-five to fifty-four; those sixty-five and older were nearly three times as likely as those fifty-five to sixty-four to be neither working nor looking for work.[81]

Some of these varied outcomes obviously reflect varied opportunities—older workers, especially by age sixty-five, have greater access to alternative forms of income in the form of Social Security and pensions. But they may also reflect job-seeking discouragement, whereby workers

73. U.S. BUREAU OF LABOR STATISTICS, U.S. DEP'T OF LABOR, EMPLOYMENT AND EARNINGS 242 tbl.31 (2005).

74. *Measuring the Costs of Trade-Related Job Loss: Hearings Before the S. Comm. on Finance*, 107th Cong. 89 (2001) (statement of Lori G. Kletzer, Univ. of Cal. Santa Cruz & Inst. for Int'l Econ.).

75. *See* Kenneth A. Couch, *Late Life Job Displacement*, 38 GERONTOLOGIST 7, 13–14 (1998).

76. *Id.* at 15.

77. Henry S. Farber, *What Do We Know About Job Loss in the United States?: Evidence from the Displaced Workers Survey, 1984–2004*, ECON. PERSP., Second Quarter 2005, at 13, 15, *available at* http://www.chicagofed.org/publications/economicperspectives/ep_2qtr2005_part2_farber.pdf.

78. BUREAU OF LABOR STATISTICS, U.S. DEP'T OF LABOR, WORKER DISPLACEMENT, 2001–03, at 12 tbl.8 (2004), *available at* http://www.bls.gov/news.release/archives/disp_07302004.pdf (economic news release number 04-1381).

79. BUREAU OF LABOR STATISTICS, U.S. DEP'T OF LABOR, DATA TABLES BASED ON CENSUS 2000 POPULATION CONTROLS 9 tbl.8 (2004), *available at* http://www.bls.gov/cps/disprv02.07302004.pdf.

80. BUREAU OF LABOR STATISTICS, *supra* note 78, at 2.

81. *Id.* at 12 tbl.8.

give up the job search because they think age or lack of skills makes it difficult to find a job. As officially defined, only about 84,000 persons aged fifty-five or over were discouraged in 2004;[82] however, the BLS has a particularly stringent definition of job-seeking discouragement.[83] Other research suggests that a far higher number of older workers might remain in or return to the workforce if they thought the odds of finding work were more favorable.[84]

Age discrimination remains another employment barrier for older workers. Lahey highlights a downward trend by age in the probability that a job applicant will be called for an interview.[85] Other researchers find ample evidence of the persistence of age discrimination.[86] Nonetheless, reliable data on the frequency and nature of age discrimination are unavailable.

Workers themselves believe that age discrimination is common. Nearly two-thirds of older workers say they have experienced or witnessed age discrimination in the workplace, and they think that "workers begin to face age discrimination around age 49."[87] Even though the percentage of workers reporting personally experiencing discrimination is relatively low—15% feel they have not gotten hired because of age, the highest percentage of any term of employment surveyed—the percentage has increased over time.[88] Workers who had recently looked for work were more likely to say they had experienced age discrimination, with 41% contending they had not been hired because of their age.[89]

While demographers point to impending labor shortages, shortages are by no means assured. The Wharton School's Peter Cappelli contends that

82. *See* U.S. BUREAU OF LABOR STATISTICS, *supra* note 73, at 246 tbl.35.

83. The Bureau of Labor Statistics defines discouraged workers as

> [p]ersons not in the labor force who want and are available for a job and who have looked for work sometime in the past 12 months (or since the end of their last job if they held one within the past 12 months), but who are not currently looking because they believe there are no jobs available or there are none for which they would qualify.

BUREAU OF LABOR STATISTICS, *supra* note 5.

84. *See, e.g.*, LOUIS HARRIS & ASSOCS., STUDY NO. 884030, OLDER AMERICANS: READY AND ABLE TO WORK 16 tbl.1, 25 tbl.7C (1989).

85. Joanna N. Lahey, CTR. FOR RETIREMENT RESEARCH, DO OLDER WORKERS FACE DISCRIMINATION? 3 (2005), *available at* http://www.bc.edu/centers/crr/issues/ib_33.pdf.

86. *See, e.g.*, Marc Bendick, Jr. et al., *No Foot in the Door: An Experimental Study of Employment Discrimination Against Older Workers*, 10 J. AGING & SOC. POL'Y 5 (1999); Marc Bendick, Jr. et al., *Employment Discrimination Against Older Workers: An Experimental Study of Hiring Practices*, 8 J. AGING & SOC. POL'Y 25 (1996).

87. AARP, STAYING AHEAD OF THE CURVE: THE AARP WORK AND CAREER STUDY 66 (2002), *available at* http://assets.aarp.org/rgcenter/econ/d17772_multiwork.pdf. Workers in this survey were aged forty-five to seventy-four.

88. *Id.* at 69–70.

89. *Id.* at 71.

anticipated widespread labor shortages are "accepted as articles of faith" that do not necessarily hold up when examined carefully.[90] He maintains that the problems employers face have less to do with demographic changes than with retention. Furthermore, offshoring, outsourcing, automation, and other technological developments might mitigate some labor shortages and may help explain why many employers have not introduced any policies or programs to stem the tide of retirements.[91] Labor shortages are occurring in some industries such as health care, and employers have consequently sought to attract older workers through workplace reconfiguring and alternative work schedules.[92]

Even if the labor or skills shortages materialize, there arises a question of whether they will occur in occupations that are attractive to older workers. The Bureau of Labor Statistics projects that total employment will increase by nearly 19 million jobs between 2004 and 2014.[93] Registered nurses are expected to be one of the biggest job producers, with 703,000 jobs, but nursing is also an occupation with an early exit age.[94] Among the thirty occupations with the largest projected numerical growth (which are projected to account for almost half of the new jobs), one finds nursing aids, food preparation and food service workers, janitors and cleaners, home health aides, and maintenance workers,[95] whose jobs can be very demanding physically. Also to the point is what the big job producers pay, and eighteen of the thirty occupations with the largest projected job growth currently have annual earnings that are ranked low or very low.[96] It is not clear that workers of any age are going to be attracted to some of the occupations with the largest projected job growth, so competition for the more desirable jobs may be keen.

If labor and skills shortages do materialize, employers will respond with policies and programs to entice older workers to remain in or return to

90. Peter Cappelli, *Will There* Really *Be a Labor Shortage?*, 32 ORGANIZATIONAL DYNAMICS 221, 221 (2003).

91. *See* JESSICA COLLISON, SOC'Y FOR HUMAN RES. MGMT., OLDER WORKERS SURVEY 8–9 (2003) (reporting that 32% of survey respondents indicated that their organizations had not done anything to prepare for the "possibility of a shortage of workers due to the retiring baby boom generation"). Phased retirement, believed to be an option that would cause more workers to delay retirement, is another program that, at least with respect to formal programs, has not gained much currency. ROBERT HUTCHENS & KERRY L. PAPPS, PENSION RESEARCH COUNCIL, DEVELOPMENTS IN PHASED RETIREMENT 2 (2004), *available at* http://rider.wharton.upenn.edu/~prc/PRC/WP/WP2004-14.pdf.

92. AARP, STAYING AHEAD OF THE CURVE 2004: EMPLOYER BEST PRACTICES FOR MATURE WORKERS 15, 28–30 (2004), *available at* http://assets.aarp.org/rgcenter/econ/multiwork_2004.pdf.

93. Daniel E. Hecker, *Occupational Employment Projections to 2014*, MONTHLY LAB. REV., Nov. 2005, at 70, *available at* http://www.bls.gov/opub/mlr/2005/11/art5full.pdf.

94. *Id.* at 77 tbl.3.

95. *Id.*

96. *Id.*

the workforce. For example, public opinion polls and other surveys indicate that older workers would like to reduce their work hours as they age,[97] and labor force data confirm that part-time work does increase with age.[98] Many workers maintain that they would, in fact, work longer than planned if they were able to phase into retirement.[99] To date, however, formal phased retirement programs are rare outside of institutions of higher learning, and when phased retirement is available it is generally offered on an ad hoc basis[100] that enables employers to control who takes advantage of it. Still, one anticipates that phased retirement, along with other flexible work/retirement options such as retiree rehiring, will become more prevalent if workers are needed, and if the legal and structural impediments to some of them can be eliminated. The market will talk. It has not yet done so because employers, although for the most part cognizant of the aging workforce, have not yet needed to do much about it.

VI. Responding to an Aging Workforce

There are many advantages to a voluntary extension of working life, as workers themselves admit—staying mentally and physically active, continuing to be productive or useful, helping others, contributing to the greater good of society, being around others, learning to do new things, pursuing a dream, and by no means the least important, the money.[101] Older men and women who postpone retirement continue to contribute to the nation's productive output. Further increases in Social Security's full retirement age could go a substantial way toward restoring the long-range solvency of the Social Security trust funds. Some economists argue that workers should retire later in light of the increasing life expectancy that has

97. *See* S. Kathi Brown, AARP, Attitudes of Individuals 50 and Older Toward Phased Retirement 3, 15 (2005), *available at* http://assets.aarp.org/rgcenter/post-import/phased_ret.pdf; Robert M. Hutchens, Employer Surveys, Employer Policies, and Future Demand for Older Workers 5 (March 23, 2001) (unpublished manuscript prepared for a roundtable sponsored by the Retirement Research Consortium), http://www.bc.edu/centers/crr/special_pubs/hutchens_ld.pdf.

98. U.S. Bureau of Labor Statistics, *supra* note 73, at 205 tbl.8.

99. Brown, *supra* note 97, at 3; Watson Wyatt Worldwide, Phased Retirement: Aligning Employer Programs with Worker Preferences 1 (2004); Joelle R. Weckerle & Kenneth S. Shultz, *Influences on the Bridge Employment Decision Among Older USA Workers*, 72 J. Occupational & Organizational Psychol. 317, 322–25 (1999).

100. Robert Hutchens, The Cornell Study of Employer Phased Retirement Policies: A Report on Key Findings 8 (2003), *available at* http://digitalcommons.ilr.cornell.edu/cgi/viewcontent.cgi?article=1000&context=lepubs.

101. AARP, *supra* note 87, at 9; Brown, *supra* note 60, at 6–7; MetLife Found. & Civic Ventures, New Face of Work Survey 6–8 (2005), http://www.civicventures.org/publications/surveys/new_face_of_work/new_face_of_work.pdf.

lengthened the years workers spend in retirement.[102] This argument holds that some of that increase should be "paid for" by working longer. Yet measures to increase further the age of eligibility for full Social Security benefits and to index the eligibility age to life expectancy are rarely proposed.

Older workers as such are not high on the policy agenda in the United States, and few U.S. lawmakers are actively promoting policies that would increase the labor force participation rate of older Americans. This is in stark contrast to Europe, where older workers have become a priority. For example, there is nothing comparable in the United States to the ambitious goals of the European Union (EU) that call for a five-year increase in the effective, or actual, age of retirement by 2010; an increase in the labor force participation rate of persons aged fifty-five to sixty-four from less than 40% in 2001 to 50% by 2010; and concrete action on the part of EU member states to reach those targets.[103]

For U.S. policymakers, as for employers, a pressing need to raise the age at which people leave the workforce is not evident, unlike in Japan and much of Europe where populations are substantially older and, in the case of Western Europe, public pensions are far more generous. This is because insolvency of the U.S. public pension system, Social Security, is decades away; the country is more receptive to immigrant workers than many other aging nations; and the population is increasing and aging less. Japan and many European nations will see their populations shrink. Americans are also more likely to be in the labor force, in contrast to many European countries where almost no one remains at work after the age of sixty-five.[104] The labor force participation rate for the fifty-five to sixty-four age group in the United States is well above what Europe is aiming for by 2010.[105] Less generous pension benefits, more stringent criteria for disability benefits, less comprehensive unemployment insurance coverage, and low overall unemployment rates help keep the supply of and demand for older workers relatively high in the United States.

102. *See, e.g.*, Eugene Steuerle, Urban Inst., Remarks for Tackling Social Security: Three Views (Mar. 22, 2005) (panel discussion cosponsored by AARP and the Society of Government Economists).

103. *See* SCADPlus: Increasing the Employment of Older Workers and Delaying the Exit from the Labour Market, http://www.europa.eu.int/scadplus/leg/en/cha/c11309.htm (last visited Jan. 27, 2006).

104. Of the fifteen preaccession countries, or those that had joined the European Union before May 2004, only Portugal has a higher labor force participation rate for its sixty-five and older population than the United States. SARA E. RIX, AARP, ISSUE BRIEF NO. 77, RETHINKING THE ROLE OF OLDER WORKERS: PROMOTING OLDER WORKER EMPLOYMENT IN EUROPE AND JAPAN 3 fig.3 (2005), *available at* http://assets.aarp.org/rgcenter/econ/ib77_workers.pdf.

105. *See* Bureau of Labor Statistics, *supra* note 9.

Nonetheless, although older worker employment in the United States is not the political issue that it is throughout Europe, to say nothing of Japan, a number of legislative changes over the past several decades have served to make it easier and more rewarding for older workers to remain in the labor force. These include the ADEA,[106] the Senior Citizens' Freedom to Work Act of 2000,[107] the increase in the age of eligibility for full Social Security benefits,[108] and the increase in the DRC.[109] Some businesses have also begun to target older workers for hiring and retention and have introduced exemplary practices to do that.[110]

As discussed previously, in the past several decades the U.S. government has taken steps to eliminate discrimination against older workers, thereby making it easer for people who want to remain at work to do so. The push for age discrimination legislation was perhaps motivated less by a belief that older workers represent a potential productive resource than by the conviction that discrimination against any worker is wrong and that protections afforded other minorities should be extended to the aged as well. Whatever the reason for the legislation, older workers in the United States are legally entitled to remain at work as long as they perform adequately and, of course, as long as there are jobs for them to do. The government would certainly like to see more older workers at work. But there remains the thorny issue of the desirability of the jobs—where they are, how many there are, and whether they are likely to appeal to older workers, especially those workers whose financial resources enable them to be selective about the type of work they will do.

Most of the legislative changes just highlighted make it easier or more attractive for older workers to remain in or perhaps return to the workforce, and as has been shown, some are doing that. But a substantially older workforce—or one where more older workers remain in the labor force involuntarily because they cannot afford to retire—raises a number of other questions that have not yet been adequately grappled with, even though analysts and others have been talking about the aging workforce for decades:[111]

106. 29 U.S.C. §§ 621–634 (2000).

107. Senior Citizens' Freedom to Work Act of 2000, Pub. L. No. 106-182, 114 Stat. 198 (codified as amended at 42 U.S.C. §§ 402, 403 (2000)).

108. Social Security Amendments of 1983, Pub. L. No. 98-21, § 201, 97 Stat. 65, 107–08 (codified as amended at 42 U.S.C. § 416(l) (2000)).

109. Social Security Amendments of 1983, Pub. L. No. 98-21, § 114, 97 Stat. 65, 79 (codified as amended at 42 U.S.C. § 402(w) (2000)).

110. *See* AARP, *supra* note 92, at 2.

111. *See, e.g.*, HAROLD L. SHEPPARD & SARA E. RIX, THE GRAYING OF WORKING AMERICA: THE COMING CRISIS IN WORKING AMERICA (1977).

Are jobs really so much better today that substantially longer work lives are possible? The physical demands of work may be less than when men remained employed until very old age, but work intensification, the mental stress associated with many jobs, the need to run faster and faster just to stay in place, and the growing insecurity about job tenure may undermine some of the best efforts to prolong the working lives of both men and women. Furthermore, jobs can be physically demanding without requiring heavy lifting.

What about the "healthy worker" phenomenon? Workers with health problems and disabilities tend to leave the labor force at younger ages than do those without such problems. Will we be faced with a less healthy older workforce if, for whatever reasons, workers cannot retire as early as they have been retiring? If so, what are the consequences for employer health costs, or worker performance and productivity? Available research indicates that age is a poor predictor of work ability,[112] but might that change if large numbers of less healthy workers remain employed? Some have argued that even if older workers are just as productive as younger workers, their higher wages and benefits make them more expensive for the same degree of output. To level the playing field, this argument goes, the wages of older workers should be reduced,[113] as they can be in Japan, which has substantially higher participation rates for older persons.[114] Whether U.S. workers would find this acceptable, even if it were legal under the ADEA and even if it meant improved employment opportunities, is highly questionable.

Where are the jobs going to be, and who is going to want them? It is one thing for analysts and others with good educations and rewarding and stimulating jobs to tout the virtues of working longer. It may be quite another thing for the much larger proportion of workers who check and bag groceries, care for others' aged relatives in nursing homes or assisted care facilities, serve lattes, clean offices, drive buses, or otherwise do the things that keep our world in order. Will they really want to continue working once they actually reach the age of eligibility for Social Security or pension

112. *See* NAT'L RESEARCH COUNCIL & INST. OF MED. OF THE NAT'L ACADS., HEALTH AND SAFETY NEEDS OF OLDER WORKERS 95 (David H. Wegman & James P. McGee eds., 2004); Harvey L. Sterns & Michael A. McDaniel, *Job Performance and the Older Worker*, *in* OLDER WORKERS: HOW DO THEY MEASURE UP? 27, 29 (Sara E. Rix ed., 1994).

113. *See, e.g.*, Marcus Rebick, *The Japanese Approach to Finding Jobs for Older People*, *in* AS THE WORKFORCE AGES 103, 115–16 (Olivia S. Mitchell ed., 1993); Ronald D. Lee, Univ. of Cal., Berkeley, The Graying of the Planet: Implications of the Great Global Aging Ahead, Fourth Henry Wendt Distinguished Lecture at the American Enterprise Institute (Sept. 28, 2005).

114. Rix, *supra* note 104, at 3.

benefits? Many of the jobs for which they will be qualified will not be conducive to prolonging working life voluntarily.

Do we really know what would, in fact, extend working life? As Greller and Stroh remind us, exiting the workforce (i.e., retirement) rather than remaining in it has been the focus of much of the analysis on older workers and an aging workforce.[115] Far less is known about what encourages or forces people to delay retirement or about the interventions that might keep them working longer than is known about what gets them to retire. Workers say phased retirement would keep them in the workforce longer.[116] But would it? Or would it make early retirement more attractive because workers could better afford to cut back their work hours at younger ages?

In one example of an effort to enable older workers to ease into retirement, German auto workers were given the option of working part-time for 5 years prior to retirement or full-time for 2.5 years; they all opted for full-time with the earlier retirement.[117] This response highlights the risk that phased retirement could shorten working life rather than lengthen it, which is not the outcome that many proponents of phased retirement seek.

Phased retirement and other options that might encourage people to work longer raise the question of how employers can retain only the workers they want without violating the ADEA. This suggests the need for more effective screening and weeding out at younger ages and better training and retraining throughout the work life, so that workers who want to stay on have the skills that employers need. The legal impediments to some forms of continued employment must also be dealt with. Workers who might want or need to scale back their work hours with their current employer and receive pension benefits from that employer to make up for lost wages have been prevented from doing so by an Employee Retirement Income Security Act (ERISA) regulation that prohibits the in-service distribution of pension benefits to workers who have not reached the pension plan's normal retirement age.[118]

115. Martin M. Greller & Linda K. Stroh, *Extending Work Lives: Are Current Approaches Tools or Talismans?*, *in* RETIREMENT: REASONS, PROCESSES, AND RESULTS 115, 117 (Gary A. Adams & Terry A. Beehr eds., 2003).

116. BROWN, *supra* note 97, at 3; WATSON WYATT WORLDWIDE, *supra* note 99, at 1; Weckerle & Shultz, *supra* note 99, at 322–25.

117. Gerhard Naegele, *Gradual Retirement in Germany*, 10 J. AGING & SOC. POL'Y 83, 91–93 (1999).

118. The IRS has proposed regulations that would eliminate a number of barriers to phased retirement, but as of February 2006, they had not been finalized. Distributions from a Pension Plan Under a Phased Retirement Program, 69 Fed. Reg. 65108 (proposed Nov. 10, 2004) (to be codified at 26 C.F.R. pt. 1).

Will older workers have the skills needed to qualify for the more desirable jobs that may become available? Far more attention needs to be paid to older worker training and retraining. However, it is also incumbent upon both the public and private sectors to promote life-long learning to help ensure that tomorrow's older workers do not face employment barriers comparable to those of today. And some of the burden of skills updating must fall to workers themselves.

Finally, what about the social safety net? If it becomes more difficult (e.g., costly) for workers to retire early, or if the full retirement age is further increased or indexed to longevity, mechanisms must be in place to protect those who, due to ill health, disability, unemployment, lack of skills, or caregiving responsibilities, cannot work.

CONCLUSION

What is the appropriate role for government, business, and labor in answering some of these questions about coping with and adjusting to an aging workforce? The General Accounting Office (renamed the Government Accountability Office) in 2001 called on the Secretary of Labor to convene an interagency government task force that, with input from stakeholders such as businesses and unions, would develop legislative and regulatory proposals dealing with aging labor force issues.[119] One was finally established by the Employment and Training Administration in November 2004 with the objectives of (1) "[i]dentifying and filling knowledge gaps that currently exist regarding older workers' employment opportunities"; (2) "[s]trengthening the capacity of the workforce investment system to provide comprehensive, integrated employment and training services to older workers"; and (3) "[i]dentifying and addressing the barriers to employment faced by older workers in order to increase employment outcomes for this population."[120] What recommendations this task force comes to remains to be seen; however, examples of effective collaboration among government, business, and labor can be found.

An excellent example of this tripartite cooperation is the Finnish National Program on Aging Workers (FINPAW).[121] FINPAW was one of the

119. U.S. GEN. ACCOUNTING OFFICE, OLDER WORKERS: DEMOGRAPHIC TRENDS POSE CHALLENGES FOR EMPLOYERS AND WORKERS 34 (2001).

120. Emily Stover DeRocco, Assistant Sec'y, U.S. Dep't of Labor, A National Perspective on the Aging Workforce, Remarks at the AARP Foundation Workforce Initiative Launch (February 25, 2005), http://www.doleta.gov/whatsnew/Derocco_speeches/2005-02-25-National.cfm.

121. *See* JUHA HIETANEN, EUR. FOUND. FOR THE IMPROVEMENT OF LIVING AND WORKING CONDITIONS, FINLAND 'LEADS EU' ON OLDER WORKERS POLICY (2002), *available at* http://www.eiro.eurofound.eu.int/2002/04/feature/fi0204101f.html; Rix, *supra* note 104, at 14–17.

more comprehensive and integrated older-worker programs in the world, designed and implemented to improve employment prospects for Finland's older workers. This five-year program initiated by the government sought to involve all stakeholders, including workers themselves, labor organizations, employers, managers and supervisors, employment office personnel, teaching staff, and staff of occupational health services and labor protection. Such a level of commitment is not yet evident in the United States, undoubtedly because the perceived need for it is not so obvious.

Despite the lack of a sense of urgency about the aging population in the United States, change is in the air. Seventy-six million baby boomers will obviously not all be in the labor force beyond normal retirement age—they are not all in it now. However, many millions of them will remain in the workforce until they get closer to retirement age than has been the case in recent years. And boomers, with their sense of entitlement, may expect—if they wish to remain at work in particular ways—that employers will accommodate them. Employers, for their part, might expect boomers to take advantage of the ADEA to an extent not done by their parents and grandparents. The recent Supreme Court ruling on disparate impact offers further protection to older workers.[122] As a result of that ruling, employers may more carefully assess and consequently reconsider potential personnel decisions in light of their likely, rather than just intended, impact on older workers.

Projecting into the future is a hazardous undertaking. Many economists, labor analysts, and policymakers are certain that labor shortages will eventually force employers to treat older workers with the respect they deserve. Older worker advocates and many older workers themselves are just as certain that older workers will be the ones to decide when and how working life is prolonged. Both events are likely to happen, although an appropriate match between demand for and supply of older workers is by no means assured, and there will be bumps along the way to that older (than today's) labor force. It is good to keep in mind that the older population in the United States is a heterogeneous one and is becoming more diverse. Whatever story one chooses to tell about it is likely to be correct or true for a certain proportion of that population and wrong for perhaps just as many older persons. There is no "older worker" or "aging workforce" story in the United States—there are simply many stories. Nonetheless, one can take comfort in the fact that the economy adjusted to the entrance of boomers into the workforce, and it will likely adjust to their departure—

122. Smith v. City of Jackson, 125 S. Ct. 1536 (2005).

even, or especially, if departure occurs later than it occurred for many of today's retirees.

[8]

Age discrimination in US labor markets: a review of the evidence

Scott J. Adams and David Neumark

I Introduction

Newspapers, magazines and trade publications are filled with anecdotes such as the following that paint a picture of the undervalued older worker:

> I have an M.B.A. from Columbia University and have held senior-level positions at major financial services companies. After returning to the United States at the age of 48 from three years in England, I found it impossible to find a job at anywhere near my previous level. Why? Someone my age is generally considered too old to have the dynamics to manage a group, and younger group heads don't want what they perceive as the headache of dealing with older staff. So I stay home and do all the work on my house and cars that I would otherwise have to pay somebody else to do. There are many others like me who cannot accept the diminution or the rejection of our skills. (Richmond, 1999)

There is a widespread belief that older workers are viewed differently in the workplace than younger workers. They are thought to be set in their ways and therefore less receptive to new approaches and less creative. Some evidence points to declines in acuteness of vision or hearing, ease of memorization and computational speed (see the evidence reviewed in Posner, 1995, ch. 4). Also they may be more prone to injuries and absenteeism (Finkelstein *et al.*, 1995). However, older workers may offset these declines with greater effort, and some faculties may increase with age, as others decrease. As an example, Posner (1995, ch. 7) argues that aging is associated with declines in creativity but increases in leadership ability.

The past several decades have also seen many older workers claiming wrongful treatment by their employer under the provisions of the Age Discrimination in Employment Act (ADEA) of 1967. Claims filed under the ADEA have steadily increased since 1967 and currently rival race and gender discrimination in terms of number of cases. Moreover, while wages for older workers may be high relative to young workers, there are several other areas in which older workers fare poorly. Most notably, older people who have lost their jobs face fewer opportunities for re-employment than younger workers. Also, if re-employed, they often experience greater earnings losses on the new job. Finally, in the past, many firms had explicit policies that forced workers into retirement when they reached a certain age. Even though an amendment to the ADEA in 1986 banned the use of mandatory retirement, many firms still have been successful in inducing workers to retire at certain ages.[1]

It is unclear whether these disadvantages for older people in the labor force, and their reflection in age discrimination claims, result from blatant age discrimination. For example, firms may have a good reason to remove workers at a certain age. Lazear (1979) presents a model of efficient contracting where young workers accept wages below the value of their marginal product because they know that they will be paid a higher wage later on if they continue to perform well at their jobs, although there is a date beyond which the worker's employment will be ended. This delayed payment 'contract' may in fact be an optimal way to reduce shirking among workers, and be acceptable to workers initially. However, workers earning wages above their marginal value of leisure at older ages, as happens in Lazear's model, will not want to leave their firm. Thus what may look like age discrimination is simply the enforcement of the endpoint of the implicit contractual arrangement.

With regard to the refusal to hire older workers, the part that discrimination plays is also complex. Although animus toward older workers may be a factor, a refusal to hire may also be a product of a lack of information, where applicants are assigned the average characteristics of people in their age group. This may result in statistical discrimination against individual older workers if, on average, older workers have characteristics that are less attractive to potential employers. It would be particularly worrisome if these decisions were based on negative stereotypes of older workers, some of which have no empirical evidence to support them.

In this chapter, we review the existing evidence on age discrimination and its effects in US labor markets.[2] First, we look at attempts to describe attitudes in the workplace toward older individuals and how these may affect managerial decision making. Second, we review the types of cases filed with the Equal Employment Opportunity Commission (EEOC) and assess whether this tells us anything about the nature and effect of age discrimination. Third, we document the disadvantageous positions of older individuals in the labor force in terms of central labor market barometers, including hiring, unemployment duration, re-employment wages and promotion. Finally, we look at attempts to assess whether the disadvantageous positions are the result of discrimination on the part of employers.

II Attitudes toward older workers and managerial decision making

Industrial psychologists and industrial gerontologists have conducted many studies aimed at investigating attitudes about age in the workplace, with attention to the way older workers are viewed, how these views come about, and how they shape managerial decisions. While the conclusions are mixed, some important insights arise.

First, many stereotypes exist about older workers and these appear to be used by co-workers and managers to rate applicants for jobs. Industrial psychologists use the term 'stereotypes' to refer to the association between behaviors/traits and social categories, which include age groups and particular jobs. With age, the use of stereotypes is made easier by the fact that age is not a characteristic easily hidden during the applicant screening process (Perry *et al.*, 1996).

Evidence is mixed as to whether these age-based stereotypes ultimately play a part in rating applicants, and more importantly in the decisions to hire or not to hire applicants. Several studies find no significant effect of age in selection decisions. For example, Connor *et al.* (1978) use 177 students at Loyola Marymount University to evaluate applicants using a transcript from a job interview. The raters were divided into two groups, with one group told that an applicant was young (age 24) and the other group told an applicant was old (age 63). There was almost no difference in the way the students assessed the two applicants. Other studies failing to find a significant effect of age include Locke-Connor and Walsh (1980), Triandis (1963) and Fusilier and Hitt (1983).

Other studies find evidence that younger applicants are treated more favorably than older applicants. For example, Avolio and Barrett (1987) use 156 students at a large midwestern university to listen to audiotapes of an interview of a prospective managerial hire for a temporary position. The raters were asked to evaluate an applicant. The interviews were identical, with only age being manipulated in the tapes. Participants were divided into three groups, with applicant age being identified for only two of the groups (32 and 59, respectively). Higher overall rankings were given to the younger applicant than either the older applicant or the applicant for whom no age was given. Other studies finding an age effect include Haefner (1977), Gordon *et al.* (1988) and Singer and Sewell (1989).[3]

The use of age stereotypes has been found in other areas of managerial decision making. Rosen and Jerdee (1977) conducted a study of employer behavior based on reactions to hypothetical scenarios regarding how managers would respond to various situations involving workers. Specifically, managers were presented with scenarios regarding personnel decisions (covering, as examples, unsatisfactory performance, investment in training, and promotion) and were asked how they would respond. For some survey respondents, the scenarios involved a worker that was described as young (age 32). For others, the worker was described as old (age 61). It was clear that stereotypes were considered, and the researchers concluded that they affected the elicited decisions. Several conclusions emerged. First, managers perceive older workers as less flexible and more resistant to change. Second, managers are less inclined to provide support for career development and training of older workers. Finally, promotion opportunities for older workers are more likely to be limited in jobs requiring flexibility, creativity and high motivation.

Perry *et al.* (1996) provide perhaps the most complete treatment of age discrimination in this literature. They aim to explain the underlying reasons for the use of stereotypes in decision making, and argue that the inconclusive results in previous studies may be due to the lack of appreciation of the complex ways in which other factors interact with age to influence bias. First, the use of stereotypes may be a function of the rater's bias against older workers. Other studies only consider the basic demographic characteristics of the raters. Second, there may be jobs that are perceived to be more suited for younger or older workers. This may play a part in the use of stereotypes. Finally, the preoccupation of decision makers with other aspects of their job or personal life may influence their use of age as an arbitrary decision criterion. The authors call this 'cognitive busyness'.

Using college students as hypothetical decision makers in a business environment, they measured the raters' biases against older workers. They also assigned raters to two groups, one which evaluated applicants for a job that was obviously more suited to an older worker (stamp and coin salesperson) and one that was more suited to a young worker (CD salesperson). In other tests, they assigned some raters another task to increase their 'cognitive busyness'. They find that the three factors mentioned above interact to play a role in selection decisions. However, they find no evidence that those raters who were highly biased to begin with were more likely to use age in their decision making. Although the authors did not explicitly make this point, the latter result suggests that age discrimination may be a product more of statistical discrimination than of animus. That is, raters appear to be influenced by the type of job, along with their inability to obtain more information about individual applicants (if 'cognitively busy'), rather than just preconceived negative notions about older workers.

The evidence to date has established that there exist attitudes that are unfavorable to older workers. Under certain conditions, these opinions may matter and influence firm decisions. In a recent meta-analysis, Gordon and Arvey (2004) show that these laboratory and field studies on age discrimination have revealed that older applicants and workers are evaluated less favorably than younger applicants and workers. They characterize the estimates as significant but modest. There are several important questions that remain, however. First, the studies focus on hiring decisions. As we discuss in the next section, the majority of age discrimination complaints in courts have nothing to do with the screening or treatment of job applicants. Second, most of the research is conducted in a hypothetical context, sometimes using raters with little business experience (college students). Although this evidence may mirror what occurs in actual business climates, it would be better to examine whether discriminatory activity can be observed in micro data drawn from surveys of actual employees or employers. Most important, while some of the researchers engage in conjecture about the ultimate impact of unfavorable attitudes on older workers, there is no evidence that explicitly addresses this question.

III ADEA enforcement as evidence of age discrimination[4]

Background on the ADEA

One way to gauge the nature and extent of age discrimination in labor markets is simply to review the claims that have been filed with the EEOC. In 1979, the EEOC took over administrative responsibility for the ADEA from the Department of Labor (Stone, 1980). This change was viewed as increasing the power of the ADEA, as it was accompanied by increased enforcement resources. In this section, we first describe what activities the ADEA prohibits. Second, we review recent charges filed under the ADEA and discuss whether these charges accurately reflect the state of discrimination in the US or whether they are more driven by the relative ease of establishing cases for particular types of wrongful treatment.

The roots of the ADEA lie in Title VII of the Civil Rights Act. Like Title VII, the ADEA aims to prohibit the arbitrary use of a personal characteristic in employer decision making. Specifically, age may not be used as a basis for refusal to hire an applicant, discharge an employee or setting the conditions of employment in regard to compensation, terms or privileges of employment. Moreover, the ADEA prohibits using any advertisement related to employment indicating preferences or limitations based on age. The ADEA also regulates the behavior of employment agencies and labor unions (US Code, Section 623).

The ADEA differs from Title VII in several important ways, all of which to some extent reflect the fact that differential treatment based on age may have a nondiscriminatory basis in many instances. First, it allows for seniority systems as long as such systems are not in place to evade the act. The ADEA recognizes, for example, that pension plans and other benefits are related to age and seniority, and the EEOC and the courts have established careful guidelines to clarify what is and what is not permitted. The ADEA also allows employers to use age as an occupational qualification that is 'reasonably necessary to the normal operation of a business' (US Code, Section 623). This arises out of the presumption that there may be some productivity declines stemming from age-related work limitations.[5]

In 2004, the Supreme Court decided that the ADEA could not be used by younger people to claim that they have been unfairly treated in comparison with older people, even if the younger group was within age ranges covered by the ADEA. In *Cline* v. *General Dynamics Land Systems, Inc.*, plaintiffs under age 50 (but at least 40 years old) claimed they were discriminated against because a collective bargaining agreement provided for favorable treatment to workers over 50 regarding retirement benefits. Justice Souter, in the majority opinion, wrote that 'the ADEA was concerned to protect a relatively old worker from discrimination that works to the advantage of the relatively young'. Thus, from a legal perspective, age discrimination can only be claimed by older workers regarding their treatment relative to younger workers.

EEOC claims

On its face, a review of EEOC charge data suggests that age discrimination is prevalent in the US and is on the rise. In 1968, the year following the passage of the ADEA, there were only 1000 claims of age discrimination. This was during a period of limited enforcement, however, as the Department of Labor, entrusted with administering the ADEA, did not have the resources to follow through on claims or, to some extent, the authority to follow through on claims. After the enforcement of the ADEA was switched to the EEOC, claims increased. For example, in 1982, there were 11 000 claims of age discrimination filed with the EEOC. In 2004, there were 17 837 charge receipts filed under the ADEA. This could be compared to the 24 249 charges alleging sex discrimination and the 27 696 charges filed alleging race discrimination filed under Title VII.[6]

How many of these charges have merit? Table 7.1 presents more information about charges that were resolved during the last ten years (1995–2004). The table presents information for charges under the ADEA and Title VII. It also breaks down the Title VII resolutions into those that originated from race-based and sex-based charges, respectively. Of the 166 098 ADEA charges resolved during the last ten years under the ADEA, 9282 were settled, with benefits accrued to the complainant. Another 6726 were withdrawn after the complainant received benefits. In 8149 of the remaining cases, reasonable cause was found, based on the evidence. This totals 24 157 cases reaching a merit resolution (14.54 per cent of total charges filed). The percentage of race-based and sex-based charges with merit were 13.72 per cent and 17.75 per cent, respectively. Thus the vast majority of cases are resolved in a manner that deems the claim to be without merit. Many of these were the result of administrative closures, which were caused by the failure to communicate on the part of the charging party, closure of related litigation that makes the charge futile, a determination of no jurisdiction, or a related reason. In others, no reasonable cause was established to rule that discrimination occurred.

Table 7.1 Claims filed under the ADEA or Title VII that were resolved during the last ten years (1995–2004)

	All statutes	ADEA	Title VII	Race-based	Sex-based
Total Claims	952 883	166 098	569 573	332 827	294 053
Merit resolution	153 395	24 157	90 005	45 676	52 193
Settlements	62 464	9 282	38 115	21 240	20 761
Withdrawal with benefits	38 197	6 726	21 745	10 987	13 268
Reasonable cause	52 734	8 149	30 145	13 449	18 164
Successful conciliation	14 205	1 688	7 569	3 701	4 917
Unsuccessful conciliation	38 529	6 461	22 576	9 748	13 247
Administrative closures	233 842	44 184	134 124	66 780	81 913
No reasonable cause	565 646	97 757	345 444	220 371	159 947

A review of ADEA charges also provides some information about the types of discriminatory activities that occur in firms. The most prevalent type of charge is for wrongful discharge, which comprises over one-quarter of all cases (Neumark, 2003). Not surprisingly, charges alleging pay discrimination are relatively uncommon among older workers establishing claims. Discrimination charges based on pay are more prevalent in Title VII charges. There are more charges of discrimination in benefits provision filed under the ADEA, however. Charges related to promotion or demotion issues are about equally prevalent among those filed under the ADEA and Title VII. Given the large amount of anecdotal evidence that older workers have trouble finding jobs, however, the very low number of charges alleging hiring discrimination, which comprise only about 10 per cent of total charges (Posner, 1999; Neumark, 2003), may be surprising.[7]

This does not necessarily mean that hiring discrimination among older people is not a significant problem, however. Even if hiring discrimination exists, there may be reasons why very few charges come about. First, proving that one has been discriminated against in hiring is difficult. Posner (1999) reports results from a study he conducted that found plaintiffs in hiring cases won an unimpressive 11.6 per cent of their cases. Moreover, damages in hiring cases tend to be smaller because it is difficult to believe that an applicant who truly deserved the job would earn substantially more at the new job for which he was passed over than he earns at his current job or one found subsequently, and if the worker found another job the damages may have been incurred over a short period. In contrast, wrongful termination cases are potentially more lucrative because a discharged worker can claim damages that would include the lost returns to the firm-specific human capital he has accumulated.[8]

Effects of the ADEA

If age discrimination exists, legislation that bans it (assuming it is enforced) should have an effect. There have been several studies that present evidence on the impact of age discrimination legislation. Neumark and Stock (1999) study the effects of age discrimination laws by exploiting the existence of anti-discrimination statutes in some states prior to the ADEA. Specifically, they look at changes in employment rates of older workers (in protected age groups specified by the state legislation) relative to young workers.[9] Using Census data from 1940, 1950, 1960, 1970 and 1980, and treating the federal law as binding or enforced only after the 1979 amendments, Neumark and Stock find that age discrimination laws boost employment rates of protected workers under age 60 by a small amount but boost employment rates of protected workers age 60 and over by a substantially higher amount (about six percentage points).[10]

Adams (2004) repeats this analysis using Current Population Survey (CPS) data from 1964 to 1967, a time period during which a number of states enacted age discrimination legislation. He finds employment effects that are very similar to Neumark and Stock's (1999). Adams extends this analysis to several other outcomes, including hiring and retirement. He finds no significant effects of legislation on the probability of being hired,[11] but finds that legislation significantly reduces the probability of retirement.

Taken together, these studies provide evidence that is consistent with the existence of age discrimination in the periods prior to the passage of age discrimination legislation. However, it is not conclusive. The improvement of labor market outcomes after the passage of legislation may simply be due to firms becoming fearful of litigation. They treat older workers favorably as a result, even though they may not have been discriminating against them before. Also little can be inferred from these studies about the continuing existence of age discrimination subsequent to the ADEA.

On the other hand, the review of charges filed under the ADEA from the previous subsection can establish that age discrimination (at least as defined by the law) continues to exist.[12] The thousands of cases that do reach a merit resolution are evidence of this. The geneses of the charges, however, appear heavily dependent on the likelihood of proving a case and the substantial damages that could be awarded, suggesting that there may be many other examples of age discrimination that go unreported. Moreover, the ADEA does not prohibit all uses of age as a criterion, as it recognizes that age may result in work limitations that make it impossible for a business to continue its normal operations, and that age may play a part in legitimate firm practices. To the extent that these uses of age as a criterion arise from negative stereotypes with no evidentiary basis, however, they may still represent arbitrary age discrimination.

IV Disadvantageous position

Age discrimination is an important issue to the extent that older people experience adverse outcomes in labor markets as a result of it. Here, we review a number of studies that identify an outcome or outcomes for which older workers are not well off when compared with younger workers. Although this is not evidence of age discrimination in itself, it at least points to several problem areas that call out for investigation.

Hiring

Although claims filed with the EEOC tend not to be related to hiring discrimination, the popular press contains much anecdotal evidence suggesting that older applicants are not considered on their merits alone in the job screening process.[13] Moreover, the industrial psychology literature, which we reviewed above, includes several studies that find that older applicants for a job are judged less favorably than are younger applicants.[14] The differential treatment is a problem if it is observed in micro data that older people have greater difficulty in finding work. Indeed, there is some evidence that older workers face reduced opportunities in hiring. First, the unemployment duration of older workers is typically longer. For example, according to Bureau of Labor Statistics (BLS) data on unemployment duration for 2001, workers aged 55–64 had the longest unemployment spells, with the median length being 9.8 weeks (US Bureau of Labor Statistics, 2001). As a comparison, workers aged 25–34 had a median unemployment duration of 6.7 weeks. This is suggestive of the difficulty that older workers have finding work.

Moreover, Hutchens (1988) shows that older workers face a smaller set of job choices when searching for work. In his analysis, he compares the distribution of young and old workers across industries and occupations. He defines recently hired workers as those with fewer than five years of tenure and older workers as those aged 55 years or greater. As a test, he proposes that, if older workers have fewer job opportunities, then recently-hired older workers should be clustered into relatively few industries and occupations when compared with recently hired young workers. Using the January 1983 CPS, Hutchens constructs 'segregation curves' from older and younger worker distributions by industry and occupation.[15] He finds that older workers who have been recently hired are not as equally distributed across industries and occupations as younger workers who have been recently hired or older workers in general. He cautions, however, that this is evidence consistent with fewer job opportunities, not necessarily discrimination. He does not rule out alternative explanations, some of which will be discussed in the next section.

A series of related papers investigates the experiences of workers who have been displaced from their job and have searched for a new one. Farber (1993) focuses on workers who lost or left their job because of a plant closing, a company going out of business, a position or shift being abolished, or another related reason, using the Displaced Worker Supplements (DWS) of the CPS. When linked to tenure supplements and outgoing rotation group files of the CPS, which contain information on earnings, much about the effects of displacement is learned. Using data covering separations from 1982 to 1991, Farber finds that the probability of employment among displaced workers is lower among older workers. Among displaced workers who are re-employed, the probability of full-time employment is significantly lower among those aged 55 and over, as compared with younger workers.

Farber's (1993) evidence is similar to that presented by Gardner (1995) using the 1994 DWS. Gardner reports that among workers displaced from a full-time job in 1991 or 1992 who had at least three years of tenure at that job, 60.1 per cent were re-employed at a full-time job at the time of the 1994 survey. Breaking this down by age, she finds that 70.0 per cent of those aged

25–34 were re-employed, while among those aged 55–64 only 41.3 per cent were re-employed.[16]

Promotion
Another frequently heard claim in the popular press is that older workers are passed over for promotion because of being undervalued by their employers. Herz and Rones (1989) report results of a Gallup survey conducted in 1985, in which 6 per cent of workers aged 40 and over reported that they had experienced age discrimination, mostly in the form of being denied a promotion or chance for advancement based on age. As noted above, Rosen and Jerdee (1977) found evidence of this behavior when they presented hypothetical situations to a sample of *Harvard Business Review* readers. They suggest that this behavior reduces opportunities for older workers, but no evidence is presented that explicitly establishes this. Pergamit and Veum (1999), however, do present evidence that promotions are associated with increased supervisory responsibilities and the receipt of training. Moreover, wage growth often accompanies promotions (McCue, 1996).

Incidence of displacement
While the inability of older workers to find work once displaced is suggestive of bias against hiring older workers, it may be the case that older workers are less likely to be displaced in the first place, thus mitigating the problem. After all, if a plant is downsizing, it might be expected that seniority rules or specific human capital will lead to retention of more senior workers. On the other hand, the previous section highlighted that many of the claims of age discrimination filed with the EEOC have to do with discharge. Here we review what the data show about displacement of older workers.

At one time, it was true that older workers were less likely to be displaced. Gardner (1995) reviews rates of displacement calculated from DWS data for 1984–94. Using displacements in 1981 and 1982 and the overall rate of employment for that period, she calculates that 3.8 per cent of working men aged 55–64 were displaced, while among those aged 25–34 5.0 per cent were displaced.[17] Looking at displacement and employment data for 1991–2, the overall rate of displacement was similar to that of 1981–2. There was a notable shift in the age distribution of the displaced, however. Among those aged 55–64, 4.5 per cent were displaced workers, while among those 25–34 years old the rate of displacement was 3.8 per cent. Additionally, using the 1998 DWS, Bowman and Eisenstadt (2000) find that those aged 45–54 are also beginning to make up a more substantial portion of displaced workers.

A related strain of evidence has focused on involuntary job terminations stemming from corporate restructuring and the layoffs that ensue (for example, Cappelli, 2000). Although much of this research is contentious,[18] one piece of fairly unambiguous evidence finds increased involuntary terminations of more-tenured workers (Polsky, 1999). Although this evidence has not been viewed through the prism of age discrimination, it is potentially consistent with an increased tendency to treat workers differentially according to age.

Consequences of displacement: re-employment earnings

Even though an increasing number of older workers are displaced and these workers face more difficulty getting hired, displaced older workers may be receiving income following displacement through private pensions. This should mitigate the problems associated with their displacement when compared with younger workers. Moreover, it could be the case that older workers have longer spells of unemployment because they are holding out for higher wages. Thus a review of the evidence on re-employment income, both through earnings and through other sources, is needed to determine more accurately whether older workers are hurt by their displacement.

In general, displacement is associated with lower earnings upon re-employment for all workers.[19] Among workers aged 20 or higher and re-employed full-time, Gardner (1995) found earnings to be 8.2 per cent lower on the new job. And in multivariate analyses the percentage reduction in re-employment wages is even greater (see, for example, Carrington and Zaman, 1994). Following workers for four years after displacement, Ruhm (1991b) finds that their earnings have rebounded, but still remain lower than prior to displacement.

A few studies present evidence on whether the earnings losses are greater for older workers. Gardner (1995), for example, reports that, among those aged 45–54, the percentage reduction in earnings following re-employment in a full-time job is 15.0 per cent, while among those aged 55–64 there is a 14.1 per cent reduction. As noted above, she found an 8.2 per cent reduction for all workers, and for young workers aged 25–34 a 2.1 per cent increase in earnings. In multivariate analyses, the difference by age in the estimated effects of displacement on earnings is not conclusive. This may be due to the fact that age is related to tenure and experience, factors that are often controlled for in the existing work. A few studies find disparate impacts for older workers, however. For example, Ong and Mar (1992) study the semiconductor industry and find that workers over age 54 face greater post-displacement earnings losses.

Shapiro and Sandell (1985) provide the most topical study on the re-employment experiences of older workers. They use the National Longitudinal Survey of Older Men (NLSOM), however, which predates the transfer of enforcement authority to the EEOC. They first choose a sample of involuntary job losers, and estimate a wage equation for the pre-displacement job accounting for both age and tenure. They then use this estimated regression to predict the wages on the post-displacement job, in the most relevant case accounting for the loss of tenure resulting from the job loss, and adjusting for age. Finally, they ask whether the gap between the predicted and actual wage on the subsequent job varies with age. The adjustments for age and tenure are important to control for other sources of larger wage losses among older men. Without the adjustment for tenure, the wage loss could be attributable to loss of specific human capital, which might be highest for the older workers. But, with the adjustment for tenure, loss of specific human capital should not play a role. Similarly, adjusting for age should allow for depreciation in general human capital at older ages. The findings indicate that only men aged 65 years and older appear to suffer disproportionate wage losses upon displacement.

Consequences of displacement: re-employment income

With income losses, there are several factors at work. First, many of the existing studies do not account for the lower re-employment rates when studying re-employment earnings. The lower rates of re-employment and the longer spells of unemployment of older workers suggest that earnings losses may be understated. Moreover, older workers who are displaced before their planned retirement age could see their retirement assets decline, owing both to lower contributions toward the stock of retirement assets and to a raiding of their retirement savings. The need to dip into their retirement assets becomes greater the longer their unemployment duration.

Couch (1998) uses the Health and Retirement Study (HRS) to determine how these factors play out, and assesses the ultimate impact of displacement on older workers. His HRS sample contains workers aged 51–61. He finds that, among those displaced during 1990 and 1991, the average loss in earnings was 39 per cent. This is larger than reported in the rest of the literature. Couch argues that this may be due to his inclusion of people that were not re-employed at the time of the 1992 survey, something that the rest of the literature tends not to do. This suggests that the existing estimates of the effects of displacement may be understated. Couch also investigates the extent to which other sources of income may offset earnings losses. Pension income is not an important factor. Income from other family members, however, does cushion the overall effect of the earnings decline on household economic well-being. Still, household income falls by 24 per cent for the families of displaced workers.[20]

Discrimination against younger workers

This section has outlined the disadvantageous position in labor markets faced by older workers. In many ways, however, outcomes for the old compare favorably to those of the young. For example, as discussed in the next section, older workers earn more. Moreover, while it is true that many older workers are passed over for promotion, it is also true that some young workers lose out on promotions because of their age. It is also true that older workers may be treated better on the job because of their perceived experience and accumulated skills. For example, in certain industries, customers may prefer to deal with older workers rather than younger workers.

Economists have devoted little attention to documenting the extent of discrimination against the young, however. One reason may be that age discrimination legislation does not protect younger workers against favorable treatment given to older workers, as made clear by the recent Supreme Court decision in *Cline* v. *General Dynamics Land Systems, Inc.* Moreover, the lower wages, benefits and privileges provided to younger workers often have explanations grounded in human capital models and delayed payment contract models (for example, Lazear, 1979). Workers will naturally see their wages rise as they receive training and/or progress to later stages of their incentive-based contracts with firms. In short, discrimination against the young is a problem that will correct itself as workers age, a point made in the industrial psychology literature. For example, Garstka *et al.* (2004) show that young adults differ in their responses to discrimination because they perceive their disadvantaged status as temporary. For these reasons, this section and the subsequent section focus on discrimination faced by older workers.

V Detecting effects of age discrimination

The previous section establishes that there is some evidence that older workers suffer labor market disadvantages compared with younger workers. Moreover, there is a large and growing number of older people claiming discrimination with the EEOC. The link between discrimination and these adverse outcomes, however, remains unclear. In this section, we review the unique difficulties that exist when examining this link. We then review the handful of papers that aim to detect the effects of discrimination.

Methods

Researchers attempting to detect age discrimination have found themselves in uncharted territory. One would expect the vast literature on race and gender discrimination to be a useful guide.[21] There are several reasons why applying the methods from that literature is problematic, however.

Unlike the case of race and sex, the link between age and productivity is likely much more complex. On one hand, workers may become more skilled in their work with experience. On the other hand, older workers may suffer from a diminished capacity to perform their work as age-related physical limitations arise. Researchers trying to measure the effect of age on productivity have produced mixed results. McEvoy and Cascio (1989) present results of a meta-analysis of 22 years of studies and conclude that the research tends not to show a strong link between age and job performance. However, some studies do find that age leads to diminished performance (for example, Salthouse *et al.*, 1996). A recent study of production function estimates for the manufacturing sector finds evidence of lower productivity of workers aged 55 and older (Hellerstein and Neumark, 2004).

The inability to capture the effect that age has on productivity is a major problem that researchers confront when applying the methods from the literature on race and sex discrimination to the question of age discrimination. The standard approach in that literature is to regress the log of wages on a number of individual and job characteristics that are meant to capture underlying productivity differences between individuals, and to interpret the residual as reflecting discrimination.[22] Unlike the case of sex and race discrimination, however, capturing productivity differences through other observables and attributing the remaining differences by age to discrimination is unappealing, precisely because productivity differences by age are inherently plausible (and indeed central to the human capital model).[23]

Another difficulty in using the effect of age on earnings to detect age discrimination is that age (on net) appears to influence earnings positively. In the first quarter of 2002, median usual weekly earnings for full-time workers aged 55–64 years were \$671, while median weekly earnings for workers aged 25–34 years were \$598. While this may reflect productivity differences, it has also been observed that age–earnings profiles slope upwards and more steeply than age–productivity profiles (for example, Medoff and Abraham, 1980; Kotlikoff and Gokhale, 1992).[24] The positive differentials in pay associated with age do not necessarily mean that age discrimination in pay does not exist; perhaps older workers would earn more absent discrimination. The bottom line, though, is that it is unlikely that one would or could detect age discrimination via wage regressions.

There are other outcomes that may be used as dependent variables in attempts to detect discrimination. As with earnings, however, some of these outcomes indicate that older individuals fare well when compared with younger ones. For example, unemployment rates for older workers tend to be lower.[25] Even in terms of non-labor income (Hurd, 1990), older people are in relatively advantageous positions. Thus, while one problem is the limitations of the standard regression approach to discrimination when applied to age, another is that on some dimensions older workers may in fact be in an advantaged position. While there may be good economic reasons for this apparently advantaged position (rather than 'reverse discrimination'), this suggests that we need to refocus our attention on both outcomes other than pay and methods other than regression analysis.

As an alternative to the regression approach, audit studies are a convincing way to detect race and sex discrimination in employment. These studies involve sending matched pairs of applicants with similar characteristics to employers. Differential treatment is attributed to discrimination. For example, audit studies were used to compare outcomes for Hispanic and Anglo job-seekers (Kenney and Wissoker, 1994), blacks and whites (Bendick *et al.*, 1994) and women and men (Neumark, 1996). Such an approach for older workers is fraught with unique problems, however. First, audit studies are often conducted for entry-level positions, because audit studies are most easily – and perhaps only feasibly – conducted for positions with relatively simple and quick hiring decisions, and for positions that are relatively homogeneous across employers. For older people, studies of hiring into entry-level positions might not be particularly relevant. More important, making older and younger workers look identical on paper is difficult, especially when it comes to relevant experience. As discussed above, a similar problem is encountered in the interpretation of the industrial psychology and industrial gerontology evidence.

A different technique was devised by Johnson and Neumark (1997). They used the NLSOM, which contains the question, 'During the past five years, do you feel that, so far as work is concerned, you were discriminated against because of your age?' Longitudinal information on responses to this question, and on subsequent labor market behavior, is used to study the impact of age discrimination. This approach is not without problems either, however. Specifically, underlying differences in the propensity to report discrimination may be correlated with the outcomes studied. Also workers with poor labor market experiences may be tempted to blame their employers' alleged age discrimination. Finally, some workers may simply be disgruntled with their employer and be willing to report something negative about them regardless of the truth. Since these workers are perhaps more likely to have adverse experiences, correlations between self-reported age discrimination and poor labor market outcomes may be spurious. Johnson and Neumark deal with these problems by focusing on those who switch from reporting no age discrimination to reporting age discrimination, hoping that a lagged measure of perceived discrimination controls for some of these other factors.

Evidence of age discrimination

Perhaps because of the methodological difficulties, there are only a handful of studies that speak directly to the effect of age discrimination on the ultimate labor market experiences of older workers. One study uses the audit method discussed above (Bendick *et al.*, 1996). In that study, 775 large employers and employment agencies were sent résumés for two job candidates. One of the candidates was presented as about 57 years old, and the other as about 32 years old.[26] The résumé of the older applicant received a less favorable response (on average) than that of the younger applicant. Higher growth companies were less likely to discriminate against older workers.

Attempts were made to get around the problems with using audit studies to detect age discrimination. First, the positions that were applied for were not entry-level. Second, attempts were made to render the applicants as identical as possible, while still adding to the older workers' résumés some explanation for having the same relevant experience as the younger workers. For example, in the résumés that were sent to information technology companies (about one-third of the sample), older workers and younger workers were given ten years of experience in the field. The years on the older workers' résumés between college and the beginning of the experience in the field were accounted for by giving the older applicants experience as high school math teachers. While this is a clever approach, it nevertheless may still suffer from the problem of older workers being penalized for all of the years that they were not gaining experience in the field. A younger applicant may gain favor through the fact that he 'hit the ground running' out of college. Nevertheless, the evidence is consistent with age discrimination reducing hiring opportunities.

The second study on the impact of age discrimination was conducted by Johnson and Neumark (1997), whose approach was discussed above. Their first finding is that only a relatively small percentage of older men reported age discrimination (7 per cent of the sample).[27] However, this refers to men with jobs, and hence might not cover the type of discrimination in hiring posed by age restrictions on new hires (although it could do so partially if they had searched for other jobs). More to the point, Johnson and Neumark find that those workers who report discrimination are more likely to separate from their current employer, and less likely to be employed subsequently. In addition, those who report discrimination and separate from their employer suffer a wage loss on the order of 10 per cent. Thus the evidence points to adverse consequences of differential treatment by age. It is important to note, however, that the study predates the switch in enforcement of the ADEA from the Department of Labor to the EEOC, which means that the study cannot speak directly to the existence and impact of age discrimination in today's labor market.

Adams (2002) conducts a similar analysis to Johnson and Neumark (1997), in that he uses self-reported information provided by workers about employer behavior to estimate the effects of perceived discrimination, with a couple of important differences. First, he uses the 1992 and 1994 waves of the HRS, which allows the study to speak to the question of age discrimination in the post-ADEA period. The question in the HRS that is used to infer discrimination is based on responses to the statement: 'In decisions about promotion, my employer gives younger people preference over older people.' Thus the study only focuses on one particular type of employer discriminatory behavior, albeit one that is highlighted in other evidence (Herz and Rones, 1989; Rosen and Jerdee, 1977). Finally, the study is primarily cross-sectional, which does not allow for Johnson and Neumark's (1997) approach of using multiple reports on discriminatory behavior to control for sources of a spurious relationship.[28] On the other hand, the HRS does contain variables that can be used to control for the worker's general satisfaction with the job and his employer. Adams finds that, among workers reporting that their firm passes over older workers for promotion, there is lower wage growth. In addition, such workers are more likely to separate from their employer and more likely to rate their probability of early retirement higher. These effects persist once basic individual and job satisfaction controls are added. Thus this provides more evidence that perceived discriminatory behaviors do result in poorer outcomes.

Alternative explanations

The three studies that have most directly addressed the correlation between discriminatory behavior and adverse outcomes have found evidence of a relationship. However, there are alternative explanations for this evidence, which leaves one concerned that these correlations may not be truly reflecting the impacts of age discrimination. With regard to hiring effects (as found by Bendick *et al.*, 1996), there are several alternative explanations. First, some firms may rightly conclude that older applicants cannot perform the tasks necessary for the job. This may be especially true if the job requires physical tasks that some older workers might not be able to perform as well. Second, firms may correctly assume that older workers will not remain with the firm as long as younger workers. Such differences in prospective tenure with an employer partially explain why human capital investments are more associated with younger workers, as firms have a greater incentive to invest in training the young (Oi, 1962).

Related to this argument, Lazear and Rosen (1990) conjecture that differences in promotion rates between men and women may arise because firms hold workers to a higher ability standard when deciding on a promotion if non-market abilities and opportunities are assumed to be greater. In their model, women are assumed to be as able as men in labor market activity but more able in activities outside of labor markets. The fact that they may have greater value outside of the labor market increases their chances of separation from the labor force and leads employers to hold them to a higher ability standard when deciding on their promotion. One can also argue that there are more non-market opportunities for the old than there are for the young. At the very least, their marginal disutility of work can be assumed to be greater. The promotion results found by Adams (2002) may reflect this conjecture.

A more all-encompassing alternative explanation for the alleged correlation between firm discriminatory behavior and poor outcomes is the use of delayed payment contracts modeled by Lazear (1979) and discussed in the Introduction. In particular, Hutchens (1986) investigated the relationship between the use of delayed payment contracts and hiring. He first presents a model where delayed payment contracts introduce a fixed cost into the hiring decision. Because firms delay payments to reduce worker shirking, employees fear that firms will renege on long-term arrangements and lay them off before higher wages or pensions are realized.[29] Lazear's model originally assumed that a firm was bound to the wage (and employment) path that it offered by reputation effects. In practice, however, information asymmetries exist. These may arise for a variety of reasons. Just as firms cannot costlessly observe worker output, neither can fellow workers. Thus, when a worker is fired, it is not always the case that workers can determine if the firing was justified. Moreover, firms may have to lay off workers in response to shifts in the demand curve for their product. Thus there is a possibility that firms can cheat on the contracts that they form and get away with it. As a consequence, firms must compensate workers for the expected loss in lifetime earnings from potential cheating. Regardless of the exact structure of the compensation, bonding is not costless.

In the simplest form of his model, Hutchens showed that a component of the bonding cost is fixed if workers perceive that the probability of a firm reneging on a delayed payment contract is positive and firms perceive that the probability of worker shirking is positive. This fixed hiring cost is not unlike those discussed by Oi (1962). Because of costly bonding, a firm prefers to hire those workers with the longest expected tenure so as to minimize the number of times it hires and incurs the cost. As an empirical test of the model, Hutchens constructs an index of the propensity of firms to hire older workers, which is the proportion of recently-hired workers over age 55 among total employees over age 55 in industry–occupation cells of the 1970 census. Then, using the NLSOM, he looks at whether workers in jobs with a higher index are less likely to report that their firms engaged in practices consistent with the use of delayed payment contracts (for example, pension offerings and mandatory retirement). Hutchens finds evidence consistent with the predictions of his model.[30]

As with hiring, delayed payment contracts may affect a firm's promotion decisions. In Lazear's model, payments to workers are delayed to provide incentives for good performance early in their work life. If such performance is also rewarded with promotions that are associated with pay increases as well, then under these contracts promotions among older workers may be somewhat less common and wage growth somewhat lower; in other words, under delayed payment contracts, workers may 'climb the corporate ladder' faster. Factors that coincide with delayed payment contracts, such as pensions, may also induce early retirement (Burkhauser and Quinn, 1983; Kotlikoff and Wise, 1989). Thus the two outcomes that Adams (2002) finds to be correlated with being passed over for promotion – lower wage growth at older ages and early retirement – may be explained by the relationship between promotion practices and implicit delayed payment arrangements. Indeed, Adams (2002) also finds that employees with greater tenure and those enrolled in a pension plan at work are more likely to report that their firm passes over older workers for promotion. Moreover, the negative effects on older workers become smaller and non-significant when Adams controls for worker tenure and pensions, suggesting that his effects have much to do with the presence of delayed payment contracts, rather than blatant discrimination.

For the most part, the work of Johnson and Neumark (1997) stands as the only evidence to date showing that age discrimination, apart from the confounding influences of disgruntled workers or the presence of delayed payment contacts, negatively affects older workers. Their findings that age discrimination increases job separations hold up after controls are added for employee tenure and enrollment in pension plans, as well as after correcting for some problems associated with the use of self-reported data.

VI Conclusions

Despite many conflicting results and alternative interpretations of those results, we are able to draw several conclusions about age discrimination in the United States:

- The industrial gerontology literature and the industrial psychology literature have produced more than a handful of studies showing that age is considered when making decisions about the relative worth of job applicants. Attitudes about older workers are considered in promotion decisions as well.
- The thousands of ADEA cases that are resolved and deemed worthy of merit by the EEOC indicate that age discrimination (at least as defined and recognized by the law) is a continuing phenomenon in US labor markets.
- While older workers perform relatively well in the labor market in terms of wages and employment, they perform poorly in terms of unemployment duration, the probability of getting hired, their incidence of displacement and the consequences of displacement in terms of re-employment earnings.
- Studies that estimate the link between age discrimination and adverse outcomes tend to find evidence of such a link. However, some of these studies have difficulty ruling out alternative explanations.

An additional point is worth noting as well. No study that has attempted to explain the disadvantageous position of older workers (in some respects) has analyzed empirically the motivation for the firm policies that may have caused the harm. If one can narrow the effect down to employer discrimination, there still remains the question of whether the discrimination arises out of a dislike of older workers or the application of a decision criterion based on age owing to the lack of enough credible information.

Thus future research will likely focus on whether age discrimination on the part of employers is due to animus, statistical discrimination or other economic considerations. And future policy debates are likely to wrestle with the appropriate public policy response to employers' use of age as a criterion in managerial decision making.

Notes

1. See, for example, Gustman and Steinmeier (1986), Kotlikoff and Wise (1989), Burkhauser and Quinn (1983) and Hurd (1990).
2. In focusing on the issue of evidence of labor market discrimination, this work is different from but complementary to some recent, broader surveys on age discrimination (Posner, 1999; Neumark, 2003). Both focus more on age discrimination legislation, with a great deal of information on the act, its legal interpretation and the meaning of age discrimination generally. Neumark (2003) also reviews evidence on how the legislation operates in light of existing theories on age and compensation in labor markets.
3. The studies that have looked at whether applicants are viewed differently because of their age suffer from the fact that it is impossible to present older and younger applicants equally. If the older worker is presented as having more experience, he may be treated better, even if there exist inclinations to discriminate on the basis of age. On the other hand, if applicants are given equal experience, the older worker may appear peculiar because he should have much more experience. Thus the results of these studies need to be interpreted with caution.
4. A substantial portion of material in this section is based on Neumark (2003).
5. Title VII, on the other hand, only allows exceptions with respect to race and sex in very special cases, in particular when race or sex is a bona fide occupational qualification (for example, as with actors or locker room attendants).
6. Much of the information presented in this section was calculated using EEOC enforcement data, which are available at www.eeoc.gov.
7. Hiring cases do make up a larger percentage of ADEA charges than of Title VII charges.
8. In a somewhat related recent study, Manning *et al.* (2004) note that even the decisions in court cases might be influenced by age biases among judges. They show that younger judges were less sympathetic in cases alleging age discrimination than older judges. In general, the decision patterns in age bias cases were more conservative than in race or sex cases. Epstein and Martin (2004) call their results into question, however, on the basis of a failure to stand up to alternative groupings of age categories in the data.
9. The state statutes are used because using federal legislation could attribute to the law other changes over time in factors influencing the relative employment of older workers. With the state statutes, the advent of the federal legislation can be separately identified by using states that already had an anti-discrimination statute to control for other aggregate changes in relative employment of older individuals, and using only the relative differences between these states and the other ('treatment') states to identify the effect of the policy change. In addition, because the state statutes are implemented at different times, their direct effects can be estimated to draw stronger inferences regarding the effects of age discrimination legislation.
10. They also study the effects of banning mandatory retirement but find no statistically significant effects.

11. Because the CPS surveys used do not have tenure data, Adams is forced to use transitions from non-employment (measured as of the prior calendar year) to employment (measured as of the current month). This measure is imperfect and may account for the finding of no significant effect.
12. For a skeptical perspective regarding the ability of the ADEA to address age discrimination, see Friedman (1985).
13. Shellenbarger (2001) and Weiner (2005) exemplify the articles that present such anecdotes. Common are stories about age discrimination against professionals in the field of information technology (IT). Evans (1999) painted a dire picture of the probability of IT professionals getting hired after the age of 40 during the late 1990s, citing not only the lack of necessary skills but discrimination by the younger managers making the hiring decision. Gaudin (2003) notes that this situation may be improving, as there is some evidence of more recent declines in job search times for older IT professionals. To our knowledge, however, rigorous study by economists of discrimination against older IT professionals has not occurred.
14. We also noted above that there are studies that do not find evidence of these attitudes.
15. A rigorous treatment of the properties of segregation curves is presented in Hutchens (1991).
16. On the other hand, Ruhm (1991a) offers evidence that the impact of displacement on older workers is not more severe once an adequate control group is used.
17. This calculation adjusts for tenure among employed workers and uses only those with three or more years of tenure.
18. See Neumark (2000) for a thorough review.
19. Fallick (1996) presents a thorough review of the literature on displacement.
20. Couch also shows that displaced older workers lose health insurance coverage, which may lead to more serious consequences for families of people who lose their jobs.
21. See Stanley and Jarrell (1998), Darity and Mason (1998) and Altonji and Blank (1999) for recent reviews of the literature on detecting sex and race discrimination.
22. The residual is measured either through the coefficient on a dummy variable for race or gender, or by a decomposition of race or sex differences into a component based on differences in observable characteristics and a component based on differences in coefficient estimates (for example, Oaxaca, 1973; Neumark, 1988).
23. Even with regard to sex and race, there are related problems; see, for example, Goldin and Polachek (1987).
24. There are several reasons for this. First, it may be due to the existence of efficient delayed payment contract schemes (Lazear, 1979), which were discussed in the introduction. Alternatively, it could be due to worker preferences for delaying earnings to later in life as a savings mechanism (Loewenstein and Sicherman, 1991; Neumark, 1995).
25. The Bureau of Labor Statistics provides tables in support of this point on their web page (www.bls.gov).
26. Age was not explicitly presented on the résumé but could be inferred from the year one's Bachelor's degree was received.
27. This is comparable to the polling results of Herz and Rones (1989).
28. Johnson and Neumark find that their attempts to control for heterogeneity in the reporting of age discrimination do not change their results substantially.
29. Firm opportunistic behavior in regard to delayed payment contracts has been observed by Gokhale *et al.* (1995), who showed that wage profiles flatten after hostile takeovers in firms with a more senior workforce. Orr (1998) also argues that firms use strategic bankruptcy to default on implicit contracts.
30. Although they do not test Hutchens' theory explicitly, recent findings by Hirsch *et al.* (2000) are consistent with the theory of delayed payment contracts influencing firm hiring decisions.

References

Adams, Scott J. (2002), 'Passed over for promotion because of age: an empirical analysis of the consequences.' *Journal of Labor Research*, **23**(3), 446–62.

Adams, Scott J. (2004), 'Age discrimination and the employment of older workers', *Labour Economics*, **11**(2), 219–41.

Altonji, Joseph G. and Rebecca M. Blank (1999), 'Race and gender in the labor market', in Orley Ashenfelter and David Card (eds), *Handbook of Labor Economics, Volume 3C*, New York: North-Holland, pp. 3143–3259.

Avolio, Bruce J. and Gerald V. Barrett (1987), 'Effects of age stereotyping in a simulated interview', *Psychology and Aging*, **2**(1), 56–63.

Bendick, Marc, Charles W. Jackson and Victor A. Reinoso (1994) 'Measuring employment discrimination through controlled experiments', *Review of Black Political Economy*, **23**(1), 25–48.

Bendick, Marc, Charles W. Jackson and J. Horacio Romero (1996), 'Employment discrimination against older workers: an experimental study of hiring practices', *Journal of Aging & Social Policy*, **8**(4), 25–46.

Bowman, Jan and Robert Eisenstadt (2000), 'Older workers and job displacement: what the last two decades tell us', *Southwest Journal on Aging*, **15**(2), 47–52.

Burkhauser, Richard V. and Joseph R. Quinn (1983), 'Is mandatory retirement overrated? Evidence from the 1970s', *Journal of Human Resources*, **18**(3): 337–58.

Cappelli, Peter (2000), 'Examining the incidence of downsizing and its effect on establishment performance', in David Neumark (ed.), *On the Job: Is Long-Term Employment a Thing of the Past?*, New York: Russell Sage Foundation, pp. 463–516.

Carrington, William J. and Asad Zaman (1994), 'Interindustry variation in the costs of job displacement', *Journal of Labor Economics*, **12**(2), 243–76.

Connor, Catherine L., Patricia Walsh, Debra K. Litzelman and Maria G. Alavarez (1978), 'Evaluation of job applicants: the effects of age versus success', *Journal of Gerontology*, **33**(2), 246–52.

Couch, Kenneth A. (1998), 'Late life job displacement', *The Gerontologist*, **38**(1), 7–17.

Darity, William A. and Patrick L. Mason (1998), 'Evidence on discrimination in employment: codes of color, codes of gender', *Journal of Economic Perspectives*, **12**(2), 63–90.

Epstein, Lee, and Andrew D. Martin (2004), 'Does age (really) matter? A response to Manning, Carroll, and Carp', *Social Science Quarterly*, **85**(1), 18–30.

Evans, Bob (1999), 'Age discrimination – are oldies still goodies?', *Information Week*, 5 April 1999.

Fallick, Bruce C. (1996), 'A review of the recent literature on displaced workers', *Industrial and Labor Relations Review*, **50**(1), 5–16.

Farber, Henry S. (1993), 'The incidence and costs of job loss, 1982–1991', *Brookings Papers: Microeconomics*, 73–132.

Finkelstein, Lisa M., Michael J. Burke and Nambury S. Raju (1995), 'Age discrimination in simulated employment contexts: an integrative analysis', *Journal of Applied Psychology*, **80**(6), 652–63.

Friedman, Lawrence (1985), *Your Time Will Come: The Law of Age Discrimination in Employment*, New York: Russell Sage Foundation.

Fusilier, Marcelline R. and Michael A. Hitt (1983), 'Effects of age, race, sex, and employment experience on students' perceptions of job applications', *Perceptual and Motor Skills*, **57**, 1127–34.

Gardner, Jennifer M. (1995), 'Worker displacement: a decade of change', *Monthly Labor Review*, **118**(4), 45–57.

Garstka, Teri A., Michael T. Schmitt, Nyla R. Branscombe and Mary Lee Hummert (2004), 'How young and older adults differ in their responses to perceived age discrimination', *Psychology and Aging*, **19**(2), 326–35.

Gaudin, Sharon (2003), 'Older workers becoming hot commodity', *Datamation* (obtained from www.itmanagement.earthweb.com; posted 16 October 2003).

Gokhale, Jagadeesh, Erica L. Groshen and David Neumark (1995), 'Do hostile takeovers reduce extramarginal wage payments?', *Review of Economics and Statistics*, **77**(3), 470–85.

Goldin, Claudia, and Solomon Polachek (1987), 'Residual differences by sex: perspectives on the gender gap in earnings', *American Economic Review*, **77**(2), 143–51.

Gordon, Randall A. and Richard D. Arvey (2004), 'Age bias in laboratory and field settings: a meta-analytic investigation', *Journal of Applied Social Psychology*, **34**(3), 468–92.

Gordon, Randall A., Richard M. Rozelle and James C. Baxter (1988), 'The effect of applicant age, job level, and accountability on the evaluation of job applicants', *Organizational Behavior and Human Decision Processes*, **41**, 20–33.

Gustman, Alan L. and Thomas L. Steinmeier (1986), 'A structural retirement model', *Econometrica*, **54**(3), 555–84.

Haefner, James E. (1977), 'Race, age, sex, and competence as factors in employer selection of the disadvantaged', *Journal of Applied Psychology*, **62**(2), 199–202.

Hellerstein, Judith K. and David Neumark (2004), 'Production function and wage equation estimation with heterogeneous labor: evidence from a new matched employer–employee data set', NBER working paper no. 10325.

Herz, Diane E. and Philip L. Rones (1989), 'Institutional barriers to employment of older workers', *Monthly Labor Review*, **112**(4), 14–21.

Hirsch, Barry T., David A. Macpherson and Melissa A. Hardy (2000), 'Occupational age structure and access for older workers', *Industrial and Labor Relations Review*, **53**(3), 401–18.

Hurd, Michael (1990), 'Research on the elderly: economic status, retirement, and consumption and saving', *Journal of Economic Literature*, **28**(2), 565–637.

Hutchens, Robert (1986), 'Delayed payment contracts and a firm's propensity to hire older workers', *Journal of Labor Economics*, **4**(4), 439–57.

Hutchens, Robert (1988), 'Do job opportunities decline with age?', *Industrial and Labor Relations Review*, **42**(1), 89–99.

Hutchens, Robert (1991), 'Segregation curves, Lorenz curves, and inequality in the distribution of people across occupations', *Mathematical Social Sciences*, **21**(1), 31–51.

Johnson, Richard W. and David Neumark (1997), 'Age discrimination, job separations, and employment status of older workers: evidence from self-reports', *Journal of Human Resources*, **32**(4), 779–811.

Kenney, Genevieve M. and Douglas A. Wissoker (1994), 'An analysis of the correlates of discrimination facing young Hispanic job-seekers', *American Economic Review*, **84**(3), 674–83.

Kotlikoff, Laurence J. and Jagadeesh Gokhale (1992), 'Estimating a firm's age-productivity profile using the present value of workers' earnings', *Quarterly Journal of Economics*, **107**(4), 1215–42.

Kotlikoff, Laurence J. and David A. Wise (1989), *The Wage Carrot and the Pension Stick*, Kalamazoo, MI: Upjohn Institute.

Lazear, Edward P. (1979), 'Why is there mandatory retirement?', *Journal of Political Economy*, **87**(6), 1261–84.

Lazear, Edward P. and Sherwin Rosen (1990), 'Male–female wage differences in job ladders', *Journal of Labor Economics*, **8**(1), S106-23.

Locke-Connor, Catherine and R. Patricia Walsh (1980), 'Attitudes toward the older job applicant: just as competent, but more likely to fail', *Journal of Gerontology*, **35**(6), 920–27.

Loewenstein, George and Nachum Sicherman (1991), 'Do workers prefer increasing wage profiles?', *Journal of Labor Economics*, **9**(1), 67–84.

Manning, Kenneth L., Bruce A. Carroll and Robert A. Carp (2004), 'Does age matter? Judicial decision making in age discrimination cases?', *Social Science Quarterly*, **85**(1), 1–18.

McCue, Kristin (1996), 'Promotions and wage growth', *Journal of Labor Economics*, **14**(2), 175–209.

McEvoy, Glenn M. and Wayne F. Cascio (1989), 'Cumulative evidence of the relationship between employee age and job performance', *Journal of Applied Psychology*, **74**(1), 11–17.

Medoff, James L. and Katharine A. Abraham (1980), 'Experience, performance, and earnings', *Quarterly Journal of Economics*, **95**(4), 703–36.

Neumark, David (1988), 'Employers' discriminatory behavior and the estimation of wage discrimination', *Journal of Human Resources*, **23**(3), 279–95.

Neumark, David (1995), 'Are rising earnings profiles a forced-saving mechanism?', *Economic Journal*, **105**(428), 95–106.

Neumark, David (1996), 'Sex discrimination in restaurant hiring: an audit study', *Quarterly Journal of Economics*, **111**(3), 915–41

Neumark, David (ed.) (2000), *On the Job: Is Long-Term Employment a Thing of the Past?*, New York: Russell Sage Foundation.

Neumark, David (2003), 'Age discrimination legislation in the United States', *Contemporary Economic Policy*, **21**(3), 297–317.

Neumark, David and Wendy A. Stock (1999), 'Age discrimination laws and labor market efficiency', *Journal of Political Economy*, **107**(5), 1081–125.

Oaxaca, Ronald (1973), 'Male–female wage differentials in urban labor markets', *International Economic Review*, **14**(3), 693–709.

Oi, Walter Y. (1962), 'Labor as a quasi-fixed factor', *Journal of Political Economy*, **70**(6), 538–55.

Ong, Paul M. and Don Mar (1992), 'Post-layoff earnings among semiconductor workers', *Industrial and Labor Relations Review*, **45**(2), 366–79.

Orr, Douglas V. (1998), 'Strategic bankruptcy and private pension default', *Journal of Economic Issues*, **32**(3), 669–87.

Pergamit, Michael R. and Jonathan R. Veum (1999), 'What is a promotion?', *Industrial and Labor Relations Review*, **52**(4), 581–601.

Perry, Elissa L., Carol T. Kulik and Anne C. Bourhis (1996), 'Moderating effects of personal and contextual factors in age discrimination', *Journal of Applied Psychology*, **81**(6), 628–47.

Polsky, Daniel (1999), 'Changing consequences of job separations in the United States', *Industrial and Labor Relations Review*, **52**(4), 565–80.

Posner, Richard A. (1995), *Aging and Old Age*, Chicago: University of Chicago Press.

Posner, Richard A. (1999), 'Employment discrimination: age discrimination and sexual harassment', *International Review of Law and Economics*, **19**(4), 421–46.

Richmond, Warren D. (1999), 'Retiring makes sense', *New York Times*, 22 August 1999; Sunday, Late Edition – Final, sec. 4, p. 12.

Rosen, Benson, and Thomas J. Jerdee (1977), 'Too old or not too old?', *Harvard Business Review*, **55**(6), 97–106.

Ruhm, Christopher J. (1991a), 'Displacement induced joblessness', *Review of Economics and Statistics*, **73**(3), 517–22.

Ruhm, Christopher J. (1991b), 'Are workers permanently scarred by job displacements?', *American Economic Review*, **81**(1), 319–24.

Salthouse, Timothy A., David Z. Hambrick, Kristen E. Lukas and T.C. Dell (1996), 'Determinants of adult age differences in synthetic work performance', *Journal of Experimental Psychology: Applied*, **2**(4), 305–29.

Shapiro, David and Steven H. Sandell (1985), 'Age discrimination in wages and displaced older men', *Southern Economic Journal*, **52**(1), 90–102.

Shellenbarger, Sue (2001), 'Baby boomers already getting agitated over age-bias issues', *Wall Street Journal*, 30 May 2001, p. B1.

Singer, M.S. and Christine Sewell (1989), 'Applicant age and selection interview decisions: effect of information exposure on age discrimination in personnel selection', *Personnel Psychology*, **42**: 135–54.

Stanley, T.D. and Stephen B. Jarrell (1998), 'Gender wage discrimination bias? A meta-regression analysis', *Journal of Human Resources*, **33**(4), 947–73.

Stone, Julia E. (1980), 'Age discrimination in Employment Act: a review of recent changes', *Monthly Labor Review*, **103**(3), 32–6.

Triandis, Harry C. (1963), 'Factors affecting employee selection in two cultures', *Journal of Applied Psychology*, **47**(2), 89–96.

US Bureau of Labor Statistics (2001), *Employment and Earnings*, Washington, DC: BLS.

Weiner, Steve (2005), 'Why that post-50 job is getting harder to find', *Career Journal.com* (available from www.wsj.com).

[9]

A Gap in the Agenda: Enhancing the Regulation of Age Discrimination in Employment

Michael C. Harper*

1. INTRODUCTION: THE IMPORTANCE OF AGE DISCRIMINATION

The Age Discrimination in Employment Act (ADEA)[1] has now entered its fifth decade. Since its passage in 1967 as a supplementary statute to Title VII of the 1964 Civil Rights Act,[2] the upper age limit on the ADEA's protected class has been almost completely eliminated,[3] its treatment of discrimination in employee benefit plans has been strengthened and clarified,[4] and its protections have been better insulated from prospective, coerced, or manipulated waivers.[5] Yet, as an effective tool against discrimination in employment, the ADEA still lags behind Title VII, especially in the proof methodologies that it offers[6] and in the remedies that it affords.[7] For no good policy-based

* Professor of Law and Barreca Labor Relations Scholar, Boston University School of Law. I wish to thank Jack Prior and Michaela May for research assistance.

[1] Age Discrimination in Employment Act of 1967, 29 U.S.C. §§621–633 (2006).

[2] Title VII of the Civil Rights Act of 1964, 42 U.S.C. §§2000e–2000e-17 (2006).

[3] *See* 29 U.S.C. §631(a) (amended 1986).

[4] *See* 29 U.S.C. §623(f) (amended 1990).

[5] *See* 29 U.S.C. §626(f) (amended 1990).

[6] *See* TAN 74–111 *infra*.

[7] *See* TAN 40–73 *infra*.

reason, ADEA's prohibitions of age discrimination are more difficult and less attractive to enforce for private plaintiffs than are the cognate prohibitions in Title VII. Furthermore, Congress has made no attempt since the original passage of the ADEA to fashion the statute's prohibitions against discrimination in hiring and discharge to address the special problems that employers' rational but perhaps socially costly assumptions about career paths and future productivity may pose for ADEA's protected workers—and for the achievement of the statute's goals of fair treatment and full economic utilization of these workers.[8] Where the ADEA should be based on the Title VII template, it sometimes has not been;[9] where it should depart from that pattern for purposes of regulating discrimination in hiring and discharge, it has not.[10]

Notwithstanding the obvious relative weakness of the nation's regulation of age discrimination in employment, however, little legislation to strengthen the ADEA has been introduced in recent sessions of the Congress.[11] Nor has the Obama administration yet suggested that addressing the special employment problems of our older workforce is part of its strategy for providing a stronger and fairer economic system. Contrast the relative silence of the Congress and the White House on age discrimination in employment, not only with the enactment of the Lily Ledbetter Fair Pay Act[12] in January 2009, but also with the passage

[8] *See* Age Discrimination in Employment Act, Pub. L. No. 90-202, § 2, 81 Stat. 602 (codified as amended at 29 U.S.C. § 621 (2006)).

[9] *See* TAN 40–111 *infra*.

[10] *See* TAN 112–130 *infra*.

[11] An exception is the legislation introduced in both Houses of Congress, s. 1756, 111th Cong. (2009) and H.R. 3721, 111th Cong. (2009), to overturn the Supreme Court's decision in *Gross v. FBL Financial Services*, 129 S. Ct. 2343, 174 L.Ed.2d 119 (2009). *See* TAN 97–111 and n. 111 *infra*. Another exception is § 305 of the Civil Rights Act of 2008, s. 2554, 110th Cong (2008), which would have conformed the disparate impact cause of action available under the ADEA to that available under Title VII. *See* TAN 74–96 *infra*.

[12] Lily Ledbetter Fair Pay Act of 2009, Pub. L. No. 111-2, 123 Stat. 5. This Act overturned the Court's decision in *Ledbetter v. Goodyear Tire & Rubber Co.*, 550 U.S. 618 (2007), treating the initiation of Title VII filing periods to challenge sex-based pay discrimination. The Ledbetter Act provides that "an unlawful employment practice occurs, with respect to discrimination in compensation in violation of this title, when a discriminatory compensation decision or other practice is adopted, when an individual becomes subject to a discriminatory compensation decision or other

of the Paycheck Fairness Act[13] in the House of Representatives in the same month. The latter bill, had it been able to garner the necessary 60 votes to overcome any filibuster in the Senate, would have amended the Equal Pay Act (EPA)[14] to make compensatory and punitive damages available as a remedy for the gender-related pay disparities prohibited by the EPA,[15] to include within those prohibitions most such disparities not justified by a "job-related" "business necessity,"[16] and to provide for enforcement of the prohibitions through class actions governed by Rule 23 of the Federal Rules of Procedure,[17] rather than by the more difficult to use procedures of the Fair Labor Standards Act (FLSA),[18] which remain applicable to the EPA as well as to the ADEA.[19] As I will elaborate below,[20] all of these proposed enhancements of the EPA in the Paycheck Fairness Act suggest parallel amendments to enhance the ADEA.

That no such amendments, or others of comparable potential significance, have been proposed to strengthen the ADEA may reflect the absence of any effective nongovernmental representative of the interests of older Americans as workers rather than as retired persons and consumers of public and private goods.[21] The absence of such amendments and the continuing gap between the ADEA and Title VII also

---

practice, or when an individual is affected by application of a discriminatory compensation decision or other practice, including each time wages, benefits, or other compensation is paid, resulting in whole or in part from such a decision or other practice." Pub. L. No. 111-2, § 3 (to be codified at 42 U.S.C. § 2000e-5(e)). Section 4 of the Ledbetter Act includes a conforming amendment to provide for the same initiation of the limitations period in ADEA actions, *id.* at § 4 (to be codified at 29 U.S.C. 626(d)), but the impetus for the statute was concern about the control of sex-based pay discrimination.

13 H.R. 12, 111th Cong. (as passed by the House, Jan. 9, 2009).

14 Equal Pay Act, 29 U.S.C. § 206(d) (2006).

15 H.R. 12 at § 3(a)(3).

16 *Id.* at § 3(c).

17 *See* Fed. R. Civ. P. 23.

18 29 U.S.C. § 216(b) (1938) (amended 1977).

19 *See* 29 U.S.C. § 626(b) (2006).

20 *See* TAN 40–111.

21 The American Association of Retired Persons (AARP) has been a very influential lobbying force on some issues of concern to retired rather than working older Americans.

may reflect assumptions that age discrimination is less likely to be malignly motivated and therefore less serious than are the forms of discrimination proscribed by Title VII, including race, national origin, and religion, as well as the sex discrimination also addressed by the EPA. The assumption that age discrimination is less likely to be malignly motivated indeed is supported by the findings of the Wirtz Report,[22] the report of then-Secretary of Labor Willard Wirtz that Congress in Title VII mandated to study the "factors which might tend to result in discrimination in employment because of age and of the consequences of such discrimination on the economy and individuals affected."[23] The Wirtz Report concluded that older workers did not face significant discrimination based on dislike or intolerant feelings towards the aging unrelated to assumptions about their ability to do work.[24] The Report instead found that older workers were primarily disadvantaged by a different kind of discrimination—one based on general assumptions about the ability of older workers to perform work effectively "without consideration of a particular applicant's individual qualifications."[25]

Although there is no reason to doubt these findings of the Wirtz Report, or their continuing relevance after the passage of more than four decades, the findings do not suggest age discrimination in employment is a less serious or more tractable social problem than are the forms of discrimination proscribed by Title VII. Indeed, the findings suggest age discrimination in employment may be more resilient and less subject to the progressive enlightenment of managerial decision makers than are forms of discrimination based on irrational feelings of animus or intolerance. The findings thus can be read to suggest a statute designed to eliminate age discrimination should offer aggrieved victims at least as attractive and as complete remedies and at least as favorable methodologies of proof as those offered by a statute designed to eliminate these other forms of employment discrimination.

---

[22] *See* Williard Wirtz, *The Older American Worker: Age Discrimination in Employment, Report of the Secretary of Labor to Congress Under Section 715 of the Civil Rights Act of 1964* (U.S. Dep't of Labor, 1965), *reprinted in* I EEOC, *Legislative History of the Age Discrimination in Employment Act* (1981) [hereinafter *Wirtz Report*].

[23] *Wirtz Report*, *supra* note 22, at 1 (quoting the Civil Rights Act of 1964, §715 (codified at 42 U.S.C. §2000e-14 (2006))).

[24] *See id.* at 2, 5–6.

[25] *See id.* at 6.

We should expect a form of employment discrimination based on assumptions or stereotypes about a group's ability to perform work in the present or future to be more resilient to the extent that the assumptions or stereotypes have a basis in truth. Some stereotypes about older workers may be as irrational as those on which some types of race and sex discrimination are based[26] and thus should be as subject to the progressive enlightenment of managerial decision makers, regardless of the remedies afforded to discrimination victims. There is good reason to believe, however, that age discrimination is more likely to be economically rational than are race and sex discrimination and thus less amenable to cultural or attitudinal changes without proper legal or alternative economic incentives.

Discrimination on the basis of age, for instance, often may be economically rational because, as allowed in the Wirtz Report,[27] a worker's productivity eventually will decline at some usually unpredictable age. An employer considering applicants for positions that require an investment in training or that offer necessary training or experience for later promotion to more responsible positions must make decisions on the basis of predictions about an uncertain future. It may be efficient for an employer to do so on the basis of the relative probability of older and younger workers remaining as its employees for a sufficiently long time to provide maximum returns on the employer's early investments in the workers. Even where individualized assessments of workers may provide information, beyond the simple age of the workers, relevant to future predictions about the workers' likelihood of providing future productivity for the employer, those assessments may be too expensive to justify their marginal enhancement of foresight. Other easily identifiable characteristics being roughly equal, it therefore may be efficient for employers to prefer younger workers for employment in many positions, especially ones requiring investments in training or offering the prospect of an advancing career with the employer.

This economically rational preference for younger workers may not be as strong when an employer is considering promotions or layoffs of incumbent workers, whose relevant individual characteristics it

[26] Some studies, for instance, indicate that older workers may have higher job commitment and lower rates of absenteeism than do younger workers, despite the assumptions or stereotypes of many managers. *See, e.g.*, Vincent J. Roscigno *et al.*, *Age Discrimination, Social Closure and Employment*, 86 Soc. Forces 313, 314–315 (2007).
[27] *See Wirtz Report*, *supra* note 22, at 9.

presumably can more easily assess than it can those of outside applicants. Yet, promotions to new positions also may require new skills and training and predictions about future returns; and employers may rationally decide to displace older satisfactorily performing employees, rather than younger ones, during an economic downturn because of predictions about future productivity and likely retirement dates. Furthermore, for reasons explained by economic theory and supported by empirical studies, employees with substantial seniority with a particular employer are likely to have a higher wage relative to their productivity than are employees with little seniority.[28] The former employees of course are likely to be older than the latter, and a rational employer in an economic downturn understandably faces incentives to layoff the more highly compensated, senior employees rather than the cheaper, junior employees.

The fact that discrimination against older workers is often economically rational for employers does not mean that it is not a problem for our society, however. An employer's rejection of a group of workers defined by age because the average member of the group will provide lower returns than the average worker outside the group means that all of the older workers in the age-defined group will be disadvantaged. To the extent that all employers practice the same kind of rational "statistical discrimination,"[29] older workers will be more likely to be underemployed or even unemployed at a time in their life when training opportunities and the energy to embark on new careers are lower than for younger workers. The underemployment and unemployment of older workers, moreover, is likely to be aggravated by the termination of more senior employees whose careers have produced higher wages than are justified by their current productivity. It may be rational for an employer concerned about general employee morale to layoff such workers rather than to lower their compensation or transfer them to jobs with less responsibility, but given the statistical discrimination that the workers are likely to face in the external labor market from other employers, such layoffs are likely to result in further underemployment or unemployment of still productive workers. It is telling that older

[28] *See* sources cited in note 115 *infra*.

[29] *See generally*, Edmund Phelps, *The Statistical Theory of Racism and Sexism*, 62 AM. ECON. REV. 659 (1972).

workers are more likely than younger workers to have long unemployment durations.[30]

The Wirtz Report thus appropriately concluded that age-based employment discrimination, even though primarily caused by generalizations and stereotypes rather than by intolerance or animus, leads to "the Nation's waste . . . of a wealth of human resources . . . and the needless denial . . . of opportunity for that useful activity which constitutes much of life's meaning."[31] The Report's concern with the annual economic loss of "several billion dollars" and millions of "manyears" of productive labor should only be magnified today as the first age cohort of the Baby Boom generation approaches age 65, and the median age of Americans continues to rise.[32] Keeping able and interested older Americans in productive work must be a part of any comprehensive social strategy to contend with the economic problems posed by this aging population. More work for older Americans means savings for younger Americans on income support and health insurance.

The impact of even economically rational stereotyped-based age discrimination on American society is aggravated by the injustice and frustrations felt by many older workers who perceive that they have not been treated fairly by their employers. That perception, whether or not accurate in particular cases, is reflected in the continuing growth in age discrimination charges filed with the Equal Employment Opportunity Commission (EEOC) over the past dozen years as the Baby Boom generation has aged. Those charges numbered almost 23,000 and were part of almost one-fourth of the total charges filed with the EEOC during the 2009 fiscal year, an increase of about 7,000 charges from fiscal year 1997, when less than one-fifth of the charges included allegations of age

---

[30] *See* U.S. DEP'T OF LABOR, BUREAU OF LABOR STATISTICS, EMPLOYMENT AND EARNINGS 46 (February 2010) (median weeks of unemployment for workers aged 55–64 and those aged 65 and above was 36.2 weeks and 33.4 weeks, respectively, compared to a median of 29.3 weeks for all workers 16 and older), *available at:* <www.bls.gov/opub/ee/empearn201003.pdf>.

[31] *Wirtz Report*, *supra* note 22, at 5.

[32] "[A] million manyears of productive time are unused each year because of unemployment of workers over age 45; and vastly greater numbers are lost because of forced, compulsory, or automatic retirement." *Id.* at 18. The nation's economy loses "several billion dollars" each year because of involuntary retirement. *Id.*

discrimination.[33] The perception of continuing age discrimination in the American workplace is also reflected in the results of studies conducted by social scientists.[34]

Not surprisingly, the social science literature does not clearly demonstrate the extent to which stereotypes and associated employment discrimination may have declined since the passage of the ADEA and parallel state-law prohibitions of age discrimination in employment. One analysis of studies published through 1999 found that continuing age bias "may ... be less of a problem" than it was in previous decades.[35] Some studies, however, do show clear evidence of continuing age bias in the hiring decisions of at least some employers,[36] and other evidence suggests that older workers continue to be able to find jobs only in a limited set of industries and occupations.[37] Some research even suggests that the ADEA may have led to the hiring of fewer older workers

---

[33] *See* <http://eeoc.gov/eeoc/statistics/enforcement/index.cfm>. As noted on the EEOC's website, individuals can of course file charges claiming multiple types of discrimination.

[34] *See, e.g.*, Am. Assoc. of Retired Persons, Staying Ahead of the Curve: the Aarp Work and Career Study 67 (2002), *available at:* <http://assets.aarp.org/rgcenter/econ/d17772_multiwork.pdf> (two-thirds of workers aged 45–74 responded affirmatively to the question "based on what you have seen or experienced, do you think workers face age discrimination in the workplace today"); Scott J. Adams, *Passed Over for Promotion Because of Age: An Empirical Analysis of the Consequences*, 23 J. Of Lab. Res. 447 (2002) (finding workers who believe their firms discriminate against older workers in promotion subsequently experience lower wage growth and are more likely to withdraw from labor market); Vincent J. Roscigno *et al.*, *Age Discrimination, Social Closure and Employment*, 86 Soc. Forces 313 (2007) (analysis of seemingly meritorious employment age discrimination claims). *See also*, Erdman B. Palmore, *Research Note: Ageism in Canada and the United States*, 19 J. of Cross Cultural Gerontology 41 (2004) (84% of Americans older than 60 report one or more incidents of some form of age bias).

[35] *See* Randall A. Gordon & Richard D. Arvey, *Age Bias in Laboratory and Field Settings: A Meta-Analytic Investigation*, 34 J. of Applied Soc. Psychol. 468 (2004).

[36] *See, e.g.*, Marc Bendick Jr., Charles W. Jackson & J. Horacio Romero, *Employment Discrimination against Older Workers: An Experimental Study of Hiring Practices*, 8 J. of Aging & Soc. Pol. 25 (1996); Joanna Lahey, *Age, Women, and Hiring: An Experimental Study*, xx J. of Hum Res. xxx (2009).

[37] *See, e.g.*, Barry T. Hirsch, David A. Macpherson & Melissa A. Hardy, *Occupational Age Structure and Access for Older Workers*, 53 Indus. & Lab. Rel. Rev. 401 (2000); Robert M. Hutchens, *Do Job Opportunities Decline with Age?*, 42 Indus. & Lab. Rel. Rev. 89 (1988).

in new jobs,[38] though other research suggests that the statute may have especially helped older workers retain jobs in which they and employers had made longer-term reciprocal commitments.[39]

While the nature of the reality of continuing age discrimination in the American workplace is thus not as clear as the perception of its continuing existence, and while the efficacy of the ADEA is also subject to debate, it is clear that the problem of age discrimination in employment persists and that the problem is sufficiently significant for the American economy to warrant as close attention and as strong a federal statute as that prohibiting race and sex discrimination. Further, a closer analysis of the probable nature of the barriers to the continuing productive participation of willing and able older workers in the American economy indicates that the Congress must reconsider the incentives the ADEA provides not only to workers aggrieved by age-based discrimination, but also to employers considering either the termination of senior workers whose wages may have exceeded their productivity or the hiring of new older workers in positions that may provide bridges to their retirement. Closing the remedial and procedural gap between ADEA and Title VII should be only the first part of the ADEA-reform agenda.

2. A REFORM AGENDA

2.1. Closing the Title VII Gap

2.1.1. Providing for Compensatory and Punitive Damages

Section 7(b) of the ADEA provides that in any enforcement action a "court shall have jurisdiction to grant such legal or equitable relief as may be appropriate to effectuate the purposes" of the statute, "including without limitation judgments compelling employment, reinstatement or promotion, or enforcing the liability for amounts deemed to be unpaid minimum wages or unpaid overtime compensation."[40] Despite

---

[38] *See* Scott Adams, *Age Discrimination Legislation and the Employment of Older Workers,* 11 LAB. ECON. 219 (2004).
[39] *See* David Neumark & Wendy A. Stock, *Age Discrimination Laws and Labor Market Efficiency,* 107 J. OF POL. ECON. 1081 (1999).
[40] 29 U.S.C. § 626(b) (2006).

early rulings by some district court judges,[41] however, no Court of Appeals has upheld the grant of general consequential compensatory damages for nonpecuniary and future pecuniary losses, let alone any punitive damages, under the authority of this provision.[42] Instead, successful private plaintiffs in ADEA actions have been limited to the recovery of amounts that could be treated as equitable relief, such as lost back pay and other forfeited benefits or front pay until a normal retirement age in lieu of reinstatement. ADEA plaintiffs also may recover an additional award of liquidated damages in an amount equal to any past wages or benefits lost because of the discrimination if the plaintiffs can demonstrate that an employer's violation of the statute was "willful,"[43] which the Court has held means the employer "knew or showed reckless disregard . . . whether the employer's conduct was prohibited" by the statute.[44] The availability of this liquidated damages remedy, which the ADEA incorporates from the FLSA,[45] is one reason that the lower courts have not found authority to award general compensatory and punitive damages under § 7(c)(1).

Before passage of the Civil Rights Act of 1991 (1991 Act),[46] the FLSA liquidated damages remedy, even as limited by the requirement of willfulness, offered ADEA plaintiffs more than was available to Title VII plaintiffs. Victims of race discrimination in employment, however,

---

[41] *See, e.g., Buchholz v. Symons Mfg. Co.*, 445 F.Supp. 706, 713 (E.D. Wis. 1978); *Bertrand v. Orkin Exterminating Co.*, 432 F.Supp. 952, 956 (N.D. Ill. 1977).

[42] *See, e.g., Commissioner v. Schleier*, 515 U.S. 323, 326, 326 n. 2 (1995) (noting, with citations to the First through Eleventh circuits, that "the Courts of Appeals have unanimously held, and respondent does not contest, that the ADEA does not permit a separate recovery of compensatory damages for pain and suffering or emotional distress") (citing, among others, *Slatin v. Stanford Research Inst.*, 590 F.2d 1292 (4th Cir. 1979)). *But see Shea v. Galaxie Lumber & Constr. Co.*, 152 F.3d 729, 734–735 (7th Cir. 1998) (interpreting FLSA to authorize punitive as well as compensatory damages in retaliation action).

[43] 42 U.S.C. § 626(b). Section 7(b) of the ADEA includes a proviso stating that "liquidated damages shall be payable only in case of willful violations." *Id.*

[44] *See Trans World Airlines v. Thurston*, 469 U.S. 111, 126 (1985).

[45] Section 7(b), 42 U.S.C. § 626(b), incorporates the remedy from § 16 of the FLSA, 42 U.S.C. § 216(b), but includes the proviso conditioning liquidated damages on willfulness that is not included in the FLSA.

[46] Pub. L. No. 102-166, 105 Stat. 1071.

could sue for compensatory and punitive relief through § 1981,[47] and one impetus for the 1991 Act was to provide additional remedies for victims of illegal employment discrimination who could not use § 1981. Thus, the 1991 Act added a § 1981a to Chapter 42 of the United States Code, to allow the recovery of compensatory and punitive damages for intentional discrimination that is unlawful under Title VII, but is not subject to a § 1981 action.[48] Section 1981a also provides for the same recovery of compensatory and punitive damages for intentional discrimination on the basis of disability that is unlawful under the Americans with Disability Act or the Rehabilitation Act of 1973.[49] Nothing in the 1991 Act, however, provided a new remedy for plaintiffs who could demonstrate intentional discrimination unlawful under the ADEA.

The compensatory and punitive damages remedy provided by § 1981a in most cases would provide a more valuable remedy for victims of age discrimination and thus a stronger inducement to sue and a greater deterrence of continuing discrimination than does the FLSA liquidated-damages remedy. To be sure, the § 1981a compensatory and punitive damages remedy is capped, depending on the size of the employer, from USD 50,000 to USD 300,000,[50] and in some age discrimination cases victims may have lost back wages exceeding these amounts. Liquidated damages equal to such lost wages, however, may not be available in many ADEA cases because of the conditioning of the availability of such damages on the employer's willfulness, its knowledge or reckless disregard of its violation of the Act.[51] In a typical intentional discrimination case, in which an ADEA plaintiff can prove

[47] 42 U.S.C. § 1981. The availability of § 1981 to private-sector employees had been confirmed by the Supreme Court soon after the passage of Title VII. *See Johnson v. Ry. Exp. Agency, Inc.*, 421 U.S. 454 (1975); *Jones v. Alfred H. Mayer Co.*, 392 U.S. 409 (1968).
[48] Section 1981a(a) states: "provided that the complaining party cannot recover under [42 U.S.C. § 1981], the complaining party may recover compensatory and punitive damages" 42 U.S.C. § 1981a(a)(1).
[49] 42 U.S.C. § 1981a(a)(2). *See* ADA, 42 U.S.C. § 12111, *et seq.* (2006); Rehabilitation Act of 1973, 29 U.S.C. § 705, *et seq.*
[50] 42 U.S.C. § 1981(b)(3). The cap is USD 50,000 for employees of employers with between 15 and 100 employees, USD 100,00 for employees of employers with between 101 and 200 employees, USD 200,000 for employees of employers with between 201 and 500 employees, and USD 300,000 for employees of employers with more than 500 employees. *Id.*
[51] *See* TAN 46 *supra*.

that an agent of the employer denied an employment opportunity or benefit because of the plaintiff's age, the plaintiff may be able to demonstrate such willfulness on the part of the agent. Inasmuch as the Court has treated the ADEA liquidated damages remedy as "punitive in nature,"[52] however, employers may argue that they should not be held liable for liquidated damages unless the agent's willfulness can be imputed to them under the high standards set for imposing § 1981a punitive damages on employers by the Court in *Kolstad v. American Dental Association.*[53] Those standards include showing that the "malice" or "reckless indifference" upon which § 1981a punitive damages are conditioned "are contrary to an employer's good-faith efforts to comply with Title VII."[54] The standards also seem to include showing that the agent's malice or reckless indifference—which the *Kolstad* Court interpreted as knowledge of or indifference to violating the law,[55] the same test as that for willfulness under the ADEA[56]—was authorized or approved by a managerial agent of the employer.[57] Since these may not be easy standards to meet,[58] treating the liquidated damages remedy as punitive rather than as an alternative to the

[52] *See Trans World Airlines v. Thurston,* 469 U.S. 111, 125 (1985) ("Congress intended for [the ADEA's] liquidated damages to be punitive in nature"). *See also, Commissioner v. Schleier,* 515 U.S. 323, 331–332 (1995) (holding ADEA liquidated damages punitive for purposes of calculating recipient's tax obligations).

[53] 527 U.S. 526 (1999).

[54] *Id.* at 528. (quoting *Kolstad v. Am. Dental Ass'n,* 139 F.3d 958 (D.C. Cir. 1998) (Tatel, J., dissenting)).

[55] 527 U.S. at 526–527.

[56] *See* TAN 44 *supra.*

[57] 527 U.S. at 542–543. The Court cited, apparently as a minimum condition for imputing liability for punitive damages to an employer, a four-pronged test pronounced in RESTATEMENT (SECOND) OF AGENCY, § 217 (C) (1957). 527 U.S. at 542. The tests would impute liability "if, but only if: (a) the principle authorized the doing and the manner of the act, or (b) the agent was unfair and the principal was reckless in employing him, or (c) the agent was employed in a managerial capacity and was acting in the scope of employment, or (d) the principal or a managerial agent of the principal ratified or approved the act." *Id.* (quoting RESTATEMENT (SECOND) OF AGENCY, § 217 (C)).

[58] After attempting to analyze all Title VII cases in federal district court cases during a two-year period after the *Kolstad* decision, one scholar concluded that there "are simply not a significant number of Title VII punitive damage awards finding their way into published district court decisions." Joseph A. Seiner, *The Failure of Punitive*

§ 1981a compensatory damages remedy may render it much less available and thus less valuable.

Part of the civil rights reform agenda, moreover, is the elimination of caps on the compensatory and punitive damages available to employment discrimination victims. Legislation to eliminate the § 1981a caps has been regularly introduced in Congress.[59] The inclusion in the Paycheck Fairness Act of a provision to add as a remedy for EPA violations uncapped compensatory, and where there is employer "malice or reckless indifference," punitive damages, also bespeaks the civil rights community's understanding that compensatory and punitive damages offer a more valuable alternative than the FLSA liquidated damages penalty, which is now available to EPA plaintiffs even in the absence of any showing of willfulness.[60]

Regardless of whether and at what level caps are placed on how the compensatory and punitive damages available under § 1981a are set, there is no reason why the civil rights agenda also should not include equal compensatory and punitive damage remedies for victims of age discrimination. Whether or not these victims have been subjected to malign animus or intolerance rather than mere unfair stereotyping, the types of damages they may suffer do not differ. These damages, including the "emotional pain, suffering, inconvenience, mental anguish, loss of enjoyment of life, and other nonpecuniary losses" expressly covered by § 1981a,[61] are not dependent on the type of discrimination suffered by the victims. Moreover, if age discrimination, as argued above, poses as significant a problem for our economy and society as do other forms of illegal employment discrimination, it should be subject to the same kinds of deterrence.

Damages in Employment Discrimination Cases: A Call for Change, 50 WM. & MARY L. REV. 735, 772 (2008).

[59] For example, Civil Rights Act of 2008, S. 2554, 110th Cong., §§ 441–442 (2008) (titled the "Equal Remedies Act of 2008").

[60] The EPA added a prohibition of discrimination in pay on the basis of sex, 29 U.S.C. § 206(d) to the FLSA. This prohibition thus is enforced through the FLSA's enforcement and remedial provisions, including the liquidated damages provision in § 16(b), 29 U.S.C. § 216(b). The FLSA also includes a provision, applicable to the EPA, that gives courts discretion to not award liquidated damages if the employer shows that its illegal act or omission "was in good faith and that he had reasonable grounds for believing that his act or omission was not a violation." 29 U.S.C. § 260.

[61] 42 U.S.C. § 1981a(b)(3).

2.1.2. *Providing for Rule 23 ADEA Class Actions*

Similar considerations counsel in favor of amending the ADEA to allow private plaintiffs seeking to challenge an employer's pattern or general practice of age discrimination to have the same assistance of the class action procedures of Rule 23 of the Federal Rules of Civil Procedure[62] that are available to private plaintiffs challenging patterns or general practices of race, sex, national origin, or disability discrimination under Title VII or the ADA.

Currently ADEA plaintiffs are confined to the procedures for collective actions set forth in § 16(b) of the FLSA.[63] The latter provision states that an action may be brought "by one or more employees for and in behalf of himself or themselves and other employees similarly situated."[64] It also provides, however, that "[n]o employee shall be a party plaintiff to any such action unless he gives his consent in writing to become such a party and such consent is filed in the court in which such action is brought."[65] Courts have understood this provision[66] to preclude use of a Rule 23 class action through which an employer might be held subject to liability to all victims of a practice proscribed by the FLSA or the ADEA who do not "request exclusion" from the class after "the best notice practicable" directed by the court.[67] Rather than the opt-out procedure of Rule 23, lawyers representing ADEA plaintiffs—like those representing FLSA plaintiffs, including those suing under the EPA provisions of the FLSA—thus must contact and convince prospective class members to opt in to their collective action.

---

[62] FED. R. CIV. P. 23.

[63] 29 U.S.C. § 216(b). Section 7(b) of the ADEA states that the ADEA's provisions "shall be enforced in accordance with the powers, remedies, and procedures" of the FLSA, including those in § 216(b). 29 U.S.C. § 626(b).

[64] 29 U.S.C. § 216(b).

[65] *Id.*

[66] *See, e.g., Hoffman-La Roche, Inc. v. Sperling,* 493 U.S. 165 (1989). The Court in *Hoffman-La Roche* held that district courts may allow discovery of names and addresses of employees to facilitate notice of ADEA collective actions, provided that there is no appearance of judicial endorsement. *Id. See generally* Elizabeth K. Spahn, *Resurrecting the Spurious Class: Opting-In to the Age Discrimination in Employment Act and the Equal Pay Act through the Fair Labor Standards Act,* 71 GEO. L. J. 119 (1982).

[67] *See* FED. R. CIV. P. 23(c).

The difference between an opt-out and an opt-in class is significant and has resulted in private attorneys being less able to challenge patterns and general practices of age discrimination than the forms of employment discrimination proscribed by the other federal antidiscrimination statutes. ADEA collective actions are relatively infrequent because of the difficulties lawyers face in obtaining the consents of potential plaintiffs.[68] These difficulties may be even greater than those facing lawyers assembling a group of plaintiffs victimized by some violation of FLSA's wage payment provisions. Potential ADEA plaintiffs are more likely to be dispersed and out of mutual contact if no longer employed by the defendant employer. If the ADEA challenge is to a policy, such as a promotion scheme or a layoff program, that affects incumbent workers, those workers probably will be less likely to agree to sue their employer than will those seeking some wrongfully withheld pay for overtime work.

Plaintiffs' attorneys have attempted to overcome the limitations of the FLSA opt-in procedure by including a supplemental parallel claim under state law and then requesting a Rule 23 opt-out class for this claim.[69] This strategy has sometimes been successful[70] and theoretically would be available for plaintiffs in any state with an age discrimination law that did not provide an alternative procedure for a collective action like that of the FLSA. However, a number of federal courts, most notably the Third Circuit Court of Appeals, have rejected federal jurisdiction for state wage payment claims to be litigated.[71] Furthermore, age discrimination actions based on state law, even where available as

---

[68] *See* Spahn, *supra* note 66. Average opt-in rates for FLSA collective actions may be as low as 15% of potential plaintiffs. *See* Andrew C. Brunsden, *Hybrid Class Actions, Dual-Certification, and Wage Law Enforcement in the Federal Courts*, 29 BERK. J. EMP. & LAB. J. 269, 294 (2008) ("average opt-in rate for the twenty-one cases analyzed . . . is 15.71%"); Matthew W. Lampe & E. Michael Rossman, *Procedural Approaches for Countering the Dual-Filed FLSA Collective Action and State-Law Wage Class Action*, 20 LAB. LAW. 311, 313 (2005) (estimating an average between 15% and 30%).

[69] *See generally*, Rachel K. Alexander, *Federal Tails and State Puppy Dogs: Preempting Parallel State Wage Claims to Preserve the Integrity of Federal Group Wage Actions*, 58 AM. U. L. REV. 515 (2009); Brunsden, *supra* note 68.

[70] *See, e.g., Lindsay v. Gov't Employees Ins. Co.*, 448 F.3d 416, 420–421 (D.C. Cir. 2006); *Salazar v. AgriProcessors, Inc.*, 527 F. Supp. 2d 873, 884–885 (N.D. Iowa 2007); *Brickey v. Dolencorp, Inc.*, 244 F.R.D. 176, 178–179 (W.D.N.Y. 2007).

[71] *See De Asencio v. Tyson Foods, Inc.*, 342 F.3d 301, 310–312 (3d Cir. 2003) (rejecting supplemental jurisdiction in past because of the novel issues of state law and the

opt-out class actions in federal or state court, will be limited to a class of employees defined by arbitrary state boundaries.

There is no plausible convincing rationale for this less favorable treatment of ADEA collective actions. Congress gave no particular consideration to the FLSA opt-in collective action model when it elected to use the FLSA enforcement system for the ADEA. Section 216(b) itself is a historical anomaly[72] that should be amended in the light of the development of the modern Rule 23 class action. Not surprisingly, the Paycheck Fairness Act included a provision stating that "any action brought to enforce [the EPA] may be maintained as a class action as provided by the Federal Rules of Civil Procedure."[73] The same kind of provision should be included in an ADEA reform statute.

2.1.3. *Providing an Equivalent Disparate Impact Cause of Action*

The Paycheck Fairness Act, as passed in the House of Representatives to strengthen the EPA, highlights a third way in which the ADEA should be brought to equivalence with Title VII—enacting an express cause of action to challenge ostensibly neutral employment practices that disproportionately disadvantage older workers without a job-related business justification that cannot be served by an alternative practice with neutral effects. The Paycheck Fairness Act would have provided for disparate impact actions against disparities of pay between men and women by amending the EPA to eliminate the "any other factor other than sex" defense in that statute and by substituting a "bona fide factor other than sex" defense that would require the employer to prove job-relatedness and business necessity and would

great disparity between the size of the opt-in federal claim class and the opt-out state claim class). Some district courts have held the opt-out and opt-in actions to be incompatible. *See, e.g., Woodard v. Fed Ex Freight E., Inc.*, 250 F.R.D. 178, 182 (M.D. Pa. 2008); *Herring v. Hewitt Assocs.*, 2006 U.S. Dist. LEXIS 56189 at *5 (D.N.J. Aug. 1, 2006).

[72] Section 216(b) was added to the FLSA in 1947 when Rule 23 included an opt-in requirement. Section 216(b) replaced a provision that had allowed labor unions and other entities to bring representative actions on behalf of employees. Because the opt-in provision was an explicit part of the statute, however, it did not evolve with Rule 23. *See* Brunsden, *supra* note 68, at 280–281; Spahn, *supra* note 66, at 129–132.

[73] H.R. 12, 111th Cong. (2009) § 3(c)(4) (as passed by the House).

allow a disadvantaged employee to prove the existence of an adequate alternative employment practice that the employer has refused to adopt.[74] The ADEA, unlike the EPA, however, does not seem to condemn all disparities that an employer cannot justify with a statutory defense; instead, the ADEA's basic prohibitions track the language of the original prohibitions of Title VII, in addition to providing employers a "reasonable factors other than age" (RFOA) defense not available in Title VII actions.[75] To codify an age-based disparate impact cause of action, Congress thus would have to amend the ADEA both by eliminating the RFOA defense, and by adding a provision, like that in § 703(k) of Title VII as enacted through § 105 of the 1991 Act.[76]

In *Smith v. City of Jackson*,[77] the Supreme Court, based on the RFOA defense and Congress' failure to codify a disparate impact cause of action in the ADEA at the same time it codified such an action in Title VII, held that the "scope of disparate-impact liability under ADEA is narrower than under Title VII."[78] More specifically, an employment practice not ostensibly based on age but that nonetheless disproportionately disadvantages older workers need only be a reasonable means of achieving legitimate business purposes; it does not have to be a necessary means for achieving such goals to be permissible under the statute.[79] Importantly, this means that "[u]nlike the business necessity test, which asks whether there are other ways for the employer to achieve its goals that do not result in a disparate impact on a protected class, the reasonableness inquiry includes no such requirement."[80] The Court subsequently narrowed the gap between Title VII and ADEA disparate impact actions by clarifying that since the RFOA is an affirmative defense, the burden of proving a reasonable

[74] *Id.* at § 3(a).

[75] 29 U.S.C. § 623(f)(1).

[76] 42 U.S.C. § 2000e-2(k). Without changing its meaning and therefore its legal equivalence to § 703(k), however, a new ADEA provision could be more simply and clearly stated than the negotiated, convoluted codification of the disparate impact cause of action as previously formulated by the Supreme Court.

[77] 544 U.S. 228 (2005).

[78] *Id.* at 240.

[79] *Id.*

[80] 544 U.S. at 243.

justification is on employers.[81] The gap nonetheless remains wide because disadvantaged employees in ADEA disparate impact cases, unlike those in Title VII disparate impact cases, cannot challenge justifications by offering alternative practices that do not result in a disparate impact.

Not having the option of proving the availability of less discriminatory alternative employment practices could be critical for plaintiffs in a range of potential ADEA disparate impact cases of relevance to the fulfillment of the goals of ADEA. These cases include ones challenging the use of such ostensibly neutral screening criteria for employment or continued employment as educational attainment, technological training, and scores on aptitude tests. Although the Wirtz Report recognized all of these criteria as barriers to the employment of older workers,[82] such metrics may also be useful to predict future productivity. Plaintiffs thus may be able to challenge the disparate impact of such employment criteria only by offering alternative screening standards, such as individualized assessments of past experience and technological adaptability.

Similarly, older employees disproportionately harmed by an employer's decision to discharge employees with more seniority and experience, and thus the right to higher pay and benefits under the employer's compensation system, probably only can successfully challenge the decision by offering the alternative of modifying the compensation system to afford older senior employees the opportunity to work at lower cost to the employer.[83] As the Wirtz Report also recognized,[84] one set of barriers to the employment of older workers is the higher costs that those individuals may impose on employers. Since labor costs clearly are a reasonable and legitimate business

---

[81] *See Meacham v. Knolls Atomic Power Lab,* 128 S.Ct. 2395, 2404 (2008). Clarification was necessary because the Court had stated in *Smith* that Congress' failure to amend the ADEA after its decision in *Wards Cove Packing Co. v. Atonio,* 490 U.S. 642 (1989), meant that "*Wards Cove's* pre-1991 interpretation of Title VII's identical language remains applicable to the ADEA," 544 U.S. at 229, and the Court in *Wards Cove* had pronounced that the burden of persuasion remained on plaintiffs to prove the lack of a business justification for an employment practice that disproportionately disadvantaged a Title VII protected class, 490 U.S. at 659–660.

[82] *Wirtz Report, supra* note 22, at 11, 13.

[83] Even the opportunity to offer this alternative may not be adequate for plaintiffs, however. *See* TAN 122 *infra.*

[84] *Wirtz Report, supra* note 22, at 16.

consideration, plaintiffs must be able to present some alternative way to lower labor costs to overcome this barrier to the achievement of the goals highlighted by the Wirtz Report and by the ADEA.

The policy arguments against providing a robust disparate impact mode of proof for age discrimination cases are not persuasive. Justice Stevens's opinion for the Court in *Smith* attempts to explain the RFOA provision by asserting that "intentional discrimination on the basis of age has not occurred at the same levels as discrimination against those protected by Title VII."[85] Although this assertion may be historically accurate, there is no reason to think that it is true today, especially in light of the greater economic rationality of age discrimination discussed above.[86] Furthermore, the prevalence of intentional discrimination is not directly relevant to the need for a robust prohibition of employment practices that unnecessarily aggravate a social problem, like the underutilization and premature loss of productivity of a segment of the work force. Similarly, Justice Stevens's assertion "that age, unlike race or other classifications protected by Title VII, not uncommonly has relevance to an individual's capacity to engage in certain types of employment"[87] is relevant, not to disparate impact cases challenging ostensibly neutral criteria other than age and to the need for a RFOA defense, but rather to disparate treatment cases challenging age-based classifications and thus to the ADEA's "bona fide occupational qualification" defense[88] to such classifications.

In her concurring opinion in *Smith,* Justice O'Connor makes more relevant, but still noncompelling, arguments for not applying a strong, or, in her view, even a compromised disparate impact analysis in age discrimination cases.[89]She notes that one justification for disparate impact cases is the avoidance of the perpetuation of past discrimination against a protected class,[90] but she fails to acknowledge that disparate-impact proof has been used to challenge employment practices that

[85] 544 U.S. at 241.

[86] *See* TAN 27–29 *supra.*

[87] 544 U.S. at 229.

[88] *See* 29 U.S.C. § 623(f)(2).

[89] 544 U.S. at 248, 267.

[90] *Id.* at 248, 258. Justice O'Connor cited the seminal case of *Griggs v. Duke Power Co.,* 401 U.S. 42 (1971), in which the Court first used disparate impact analysis in a case brought by disadvantaged black workers challenging educational achievement and aptitude test standards.

disproportionately disadvantage protected groups and thereby aggravate social problems even in the absence of any perpetuation of historical discrimination.[91] The fact that the "artificial, arbitrary, and unnecessary barriers to employment"[92] faced by older workers do not derive from the legacy of historical discrimination does not mitigate the social and economic problems caused by the underemployment and early withdrawal from the work force of such workers. Justice O'Connor also attempts to distinguish the relevance of disparate impact proof for age discrimination by noting that the Wirtz Report identified "advances in technology and increasing access to formal education," as real, rather than artificial, barriers to the employment opportunities of older workers.[93] Yet, as explained above,[94] even under the robust disparate impact proof afforded by Title VII, plaintiffs could not successfully challenge such barriers, or ones based on increased labor costs,[95] without offering some alternative standards for the efficient assessment of workers' productivity relative to costs. That older workers may not be able to challenge successfully employment practices that justifiably act as barriers to their employment does not justify preventing them from challenging those barriers that could be replaced with less restrictive alternatives, including more individualized assessments and adjustments of compensation levels.

Given the RFOA defense and Congress' failure in the 1991 Act to codify explicitly a disparate impact cause of action for the ADEA, it was proper for the Court in *Smith* to make it relatively more difficult for plaintiffs alleging age discrimination to press a disparate impact case. This legislative history, however, does not justify the ADEA-Title VII disparate impact gap for current Congressional policymakers. To achieve its original goals, the ADEA should be refashioned to close this gap as well.[96]

---

[91] *See, e.g.*, *Dothard v. Rawlinson*, 433 U.S. 321 (1977) (Alabama prison system violated Title VII by using neutral minimum weight and height standards for prison guards because the standards disproportionately disadvantaged female applicants).

[92] *Griggs*, 401 U.S. at 431.

[93] 544 U.S. at 259.

[94] *See* TAN 82–84 *supra*.

[95] Justice O'Connor also noted the likelihood that employee benefits and compensation "increase as an employee gains experience and seniority." 544 U.S. at 259.

[96] Such refashioning would have been accomplished by passage of § 305 of the Civil Rights Act of 2008, S. 2554, 110th Cong. (2008).

2.1.4. *Providing an Equivalent Causation Test for Disparate Treatment Liability*

By modifying through § 107 of the 1991 Act, the test for establishing liability for intentional discrimination under Title VII,[97] Congress created an additional and unwarranted gap between the ADEA and Title VII for Congress to now eliminate. Section 107 amended Title VII to provide for liability when a complaining party proves that consideration of one of the Title VII-prohibited criteria was "a motivating factor" for the challenged employment practice, "even though other factors motivated the practice...."[98] While § 107 also amended Title VII to allow an employer to avoid remedies beyond "declaratory relief, injunctive relief, and attorney's fees and costs" by demonstrating that it would have taken the same action "in the absence of" (i.e., but for) the impermissible causation,[99] the minimal causation standard for Title VII liability is now "motivating factor."

The 1991 Act, however, did not by its express terms amend the ADEA.[100] As a result, the lower courts in ADEA disparate treatment cases, relying in part on dicta in a 1993 Supreme Court decision,[101] continued to require proof that age "had a determinative influence" on the challenged decision. The lower courts in ADEA cases also

[97] Section 107(a) of the 1991 Act added a new § 703(m) to Title VII. *See* 42 U.S.C. § 2000e-2(m).

[98] *Id.* Section 703(m) provides that: "an unlawful employment practice is established when the complaining party demonstrates that race color, religion, sex, or national origin was a motivating factor for any employment practice, even though other factors also motivated the practice."

[99] Section 107(b) of the 1991 Act amended § 706(g) of Title VII. That section now provides that if an employer proves that it "would have taken the same action in the absence of the impermissible motivating factor, the court (i) may grant declaratory relief, injunctive relief (except as provided in clause (ii), and attorney's fees and costs demonstrated to be directly attributable only to the pursuit of a claim under s. 703(m); and (ii) shall not award damages or issue an order requiring any admission, reinstatement, hiring, promotion, or payment" 42 U.S.C. § 2000e-5(g).

[100] *See generally* Howard Eglit, *The Age Discrimination in Employment Act, Title VII, and the Civil Rights Act of 1991: Three Acts and a Dog That Didn't Bark*, 39 WAYNE L. REV. 1093, 1158–1172 (1993).

[101] *Hazen Paper Co. v. Biggins*, 507 U.S. 604, 610 (1993) ("a disparate treatment claim cannot succeed unless the employee's protected trait actually played a role in that process and had a determinative influence on the outcome").

continued to look to the sex discrimination decision to which Congress responded in § 107, *Price Waterhouse v. Hopkins*,[102] reading the case in effect to adopt a "but for" minimal causation standard for liability, not just for full remedies as does § 107.[103] This standard, as read by the lower courts, shifted the burden of persuasion onto employers to prove the absence of such causation where plaintiffs could demonstrate, through something Justice O'Connor in an influential concurring opinion termed "direct" evidence, that consideration of protected group status was a "substantial factor" in the decision being challenged.[104]

In June 2009, however, the Supreme Court in *Gross v. FBL Financial Services*[105]rejected *Price Waterhouse* as controlling precedent for ADEA cases. It did so not to adopt the "motivating factor" causation standard codified by Congress for Title VII cases in the 1991 Act, but rather to adopt the position taken by the dissenting Justices in *Price Waterhouse*: Proving actionable intentional discrimination requires proving that taking into account a prohibited factor was a necessary or "but-for" cause of the challenged employment decision.[106] The Court's majority in *Gross* offered no reasons, beyond those offered by the dissenters in *Price Waterhouse*, to interpret the controlling language in the ADEA differently than the majority in *Price Waterhouse* had interpreted identical language in Title VII.[107]

As a result of the *Gross* decision, there is thus now a clear distinction between the minimum level of causation for establishing liability in ADEA disparate treatment cases and the minimum level of causation for establishing liability in Title VII actions. In ADEA actions liability turns on establishing that age was a necessary or but-for cause of the

---

[102] 409 U.S. 228 (1989).

[103] *See, e.g., Sandstad v. CB Richard Ellis, Inc.*, 309 F.3d 893 (5th Cir. 2002); *Febres v. Challenger Caribbean Corp.*, 214 F.3d 57 (1st Cir. 2000).

[104] 490 U.S. at 265. The lower courts also continued to use Justice O'Connor's concurring opinion to limit the reach of § 107 in Title VII cases, at least until the Court's rejection, in *Desert Palace, Inc. v. Costa*, 539 U.S. 90 (2003), of any distinction between "direct" and "circumstantial" evidence for purposes of proving a "motivating factor" under § 107. *Id.* at 97–102.

[105] 129 S. Ct. 2343 (2009).

[106] 129 S. Ct. at 2350.

[107] For a full discussion, *see* Michael C. Harper, *The Causation Standard in Federal Employment Law; Gross v. FBL Financial Services, and the Unfulfilled Promise of the Civil Rights Act of 1991*, 58 Buff. L. Rev. 69, 105–111 (2010).

challenged decision.[108] While the exact reach of § 107 in Title VII cases remains unclear,[109] in at least some Title VII actions, by contrast, liability can be established where the plaintiff demonstrates that consideration of a prohibited status was a "motivating factor," whether or not the employer is able to limit the plaintiff's remedies by demonstrating that it would have made the same decision in the absence of the illegitimate consideration.

There is no good reason for antidiscrimination law thereby to make the proof of illegal age discrimination harder than the proof of the forms of discrimination covered by Title VII. If taking into account race or sex or national origin should be illegal, even in cases where the consideration did not make a difference in a final decision, then why should consideration of age also not be illegal, even if not determinative of a final decision? It cannot be because the other forms of discrimination are harder to prove than age discrimination and thus need a compensating lower causation threshold; if anything, age discrimination, because it is more rational and calculated,[110] might in the average case even be more difficult to prove. If age discrimination has more legitimate justifications than the forms of discrimination condemned by Title VII, then these legitimate justifications ought to support age as a bona fide occupational qualification for particular jobs.

[108] Theoretically, a distinction might be made between sufficient and necessary causation, with determinative causation referring to the former and but-for causation to the latter. This distinction could be important in cases where an illegal consideration, such as age, was sufficient to cause an adverse employment action, but was not necessary, perhaps because of the sufficiency of another illegal consideration, such as sex. The distinction between necessary and sufficient causation has not been made in the cases, however, as determinative and but-for causation have been treated as equivalent.

[109] The *Desert Palace* decision left the reach of § 107, and its motivating factor standard, for Title VII cases unclear because it expressly declined to consider "when, if ever, § 107 applies outside of the mixed-motive context." 539 U.S. at 94 n.1. Moreover, many lower courts after *Desert Palace* have continued to distinguish "pretext" proof advanced under the burden shifting system first set forth in *McDonnell Douglas Corp. v. Green*, 411 U.S. 792 (1973), from "mixed-motive" proof under the § 107 system. *See, e.g., Fogg v. Gonzales*, 492 F.3d 447 (D.C. Cir. 2007); *Wright v. Murray Guard, Inc.*, 455 F.3d 702 (6th Cir. 2006); *Griffith v. City of Des Moines*, 387 F.3d 733 (8th Cir. 2004). *See generally* Harper, *supra* note 107, at 124–132.

[110] *See* TAN 27–29 *supra*.

Such justifications, however, are not relevant to the issue of whether age was considered to any particular degree.[111]

In fact, there is no more record of Congress making a calculated decision to treat the causation issue in age discrimination cases differently than there is of Congress deciding after full consideration to treat disparate impact cases differently under the ADEA than under Title VII or of Congress deciding that opt-out class actions are not as appropriate for victims of age discrimination as for victims of the forms of discrimination covered by Title VII or of Congress deciding that some form of compensatory damages ought not to be made available to victims of age discrimination. In all these cases, the gaps between the ADEA and Title VII seem to have been a function of historical coincidences and transitional political alignments. There is no good reason why Congress should not now close all the gaps.

2.2. Encouraging the Fuller Employment of Older Workers

Our employment law should treat age discrimination as seriously as any other form of discrimination because age bias has as much of an impact on its victims and our economy. The dynamics of age discrimination may differ, however, because age, unlike most other types of status protected from discrimination, constantly changes over the course of every worker's career and accompanying job changes. Because of this change, employers may have variant incentives to treat workers differently over time. The incentives depend not only on the workers' particular age, but also on whether the workers are incumbent employees or are instead applicants from the external labor market, and on how their developing careers fit within their employers' compensation structures. These variant incentives may suggest ways that the ADEA should

[111] Legislation to overturn the Court's decision has been introduced in both houses of Congress. *See* S. 1756, 111th Cong. (2009); H.R. 3721, 111th Cong. (2009). These companion bills would clarify that the "motivating factor" causation standard applies to "any Federal law forbidding employment discrimination." Section 1756, § 3; H. 3721, § 3. The bills would thus close this particular gap between the ADEA and Title VII.

be modified further to better achieve the goals of fuller and fairer productive utilization of older workers in our economy.

Three characteristics of the incentives of employers to prefer younger workers are particularly relevant. First, the incentives against hiring new older applicants increase with the age of the applicants. This is true because the older the applicants, the more likely their skills, will decline sooner rather than later, perhaps because of an age-associated disability. The disincentive to hire older workers is probably compounded by the availability of legal remedies against age and disability discrimination, as employers rationally consider the costs of regulation and litigation in making personnel decisions.

Second, statistical discrimination against older workers based on employers' generalizations about these workers' current and future productivity is likely to be more efficient and thus more prevalent for decisions about workers in the external labor market than for incumbent workers. This is true because employers know their own workers best and can make more reliable individualized assessments of incumbent workers' not only current, but also likely future productivity. This greater knowledge about their own workers is probably particularly significant for those workers whose human capital is substantially firm-specific and thus only of use to their current employer. Employers generally are more able to place their current older employees in appropriate productive jobs than they are to place other workers from the external labor market.[112]

Third, as recognized in the Wirtz Report[113] and noted above,[114] an employer has especially strong incentives to discharge more senior incumbent workers and not to hire more experienced new workers in cases where the workers' internal or external labor market experience would command higher compensation under the employer's compensation structure than the workers' productivity would justify. An employer may prefer more junior, and thus generally younger, workers who are not more productive, but who command lower wages under

[112] Not surprisingly, studies indicate that older workers on average have lower earnings after switching jobs. *See, e.g.*, David Shapiro & Steven H. Sandell, *Age Discrimination in Wages and Displaced Older Men*, 52 So. Econ. J. 90 (1985). Older workers also have more difficulty securing new employment after losing jobs. *See, e.g.*, Hutchens, *supra* note 37.

[113] *Wirtz Report*, *supra* note 22, at 15–16.

[114] *See* TAN 28 *supra*.

the employer's pay structure. Such a pay structure may be set to offer higher wages to workers with longer tenure to encourage them to stay on the job without shirking,[115] but it provides incentives to lay off at least some more senior, older workers, especially in periods of economic contraction. Even in such periods, an employer may suffer reputational costs with more junior, younger employees if it terminates all its more senior, older employees and thus denies the promises contained in its pay structure. But if an employer retains some older workers under a kind of up-or-out system, it can still provide younger workers incentives to stay and to work hard.

Consideration of these variant incentives together highlights the special nature of the impediments to full employment of older workers. Older workers whose productive careers are aborted by the loss of employment for any reason may have greater problems continuing those careers with other employers less sure of their productivity. Furthermore, this may be true for a large group of older workers who could have continued to be especially productive for their former employers, even if not at a level justifying the compensation they once expected. Even many of those older workers who would like to work in jobs of less responsibility or intensity at lower compensation may not find employers willing to take a chance on their individual productivity because of statistical discrimination and concerns about the costs of litigation.[116]

Policymakers considering the reform of the ADEA ought to take into account these impediments and employers' underlying incentives to terminate or avoid hiring older workers. They should do so both by compelling employers to retain productive incumbent older workers and to hire new experienced older workers, regardless of the compensation previously promised to the experienced employees. Policymakers also should consider allowing employers to hire older workers for a probationary period during which the employers would be

[115] *See, e.g.*, Edward P. Lazear, *Agency, Earning Profiles, Productivity and Hours Restrictions*, 71 AM. ECON. REV. 606 (1981); Edward P. Lazear, *Why Is There Mandatory Retirement?*, 87 J. POL. ECON. 1261 (1979).

[116] The number of such workers seeking transitional bridge jobs into retirement is likely to increase as the oldest cohort of the Baby Boom generation enters the traditional retirement years. *See* David Neumark, Reassessing the Age Discrimination in Employment Act (2008), *available at:* <www.aarp.org/research/ppi/econ-sec/Other/articles/reassessing_the_age_discrimination_in_employment_act.html>.

insulated from age discrimination claims from the workers. Doing so would encourage employers to gain first-hand knowledge of particular older workers, whether the workers were hoping to start new careers or to transition to retirement by holding jobs of reduced responsibility.

2.2.1. *Qualifying the Cost Justification for Age Discriminatory Effects*

Regardless of whether it causes the displacement of older workers from jobs and workplaces in which they can be most productive, an employer's discharge of, or refusal to hire, older workers because their productivity has not kept pace with an experience-based upward incline in the employer's compensation structure is currently not an illegal age discrimination.[117] An employer who prefers one worker to another because the first worker is equally productive at a lower wage makes an individualized economic assessment equivalent to that of an employer who prefers one worker to another because the first is more productive at the same wage. Businesses legitimately judge employees, as they judge other factors of production—based on a comparison between their marginal costs and their marginal productivity.

Furthermore, older workers who are disproportionately laid off, or not hired, because an employer has adopted a policy of avoiding the employment of more senior, and thus more highly paid, employees may not be able to press successfully a disparate impact challenge to the policy. This is certainly true under current ADEA disparate impact law, as explained above,[118] because the employer's desire to reduce labor costs is among the most "reasonable" of business justifications. Even under the more robust Title VII disparate impact proof structure,

[117] The legality of such personnel decisions was confirmed by the Supreme Court's analysis in *Hazen Paper Co. v. Biggins*, 507 U.S. 604 (1293). The decision in *Hazen Paper* rejected a series of lower court decisions that had effectively interpreted the ADEA to prohibit an employer from using its own pay scale to justify terminating or refusing to hire an older worker. *See, e.g., Rivas v. Federacion de Asocianciones Pecurias de Puerto Rico*, 929 F.2d 814, 821–822 (1st Cir. 1991) (dictum); *Abbott v. Federal Forge, Inc.*, 912 F.2d 867, 875 (6th Cir. 1990) (dictum); *Metz v. Transit Mix, Inc.*, 828 F.2d 1202 (7th Cir. 1987). The reform advocated in the text would require over turning *Hazen Paper* and could be promoted as such.

[118] *See* TAN 84 *supra*.

which allows plaintiffs to suggest alternative effective business practices with less of a differential impact, most such policies might be successfully defended because employers could provide business reasons for not adopting the alternative practices. If displaced incumbent older and more highly paid senior workers suggest that the employer instead adjust its pay structure or assign the older workers to lower-paid positions,[119] for instance, the employer can claim concerns about the impact on its more junior work force, whose morale and motivation it wants to continue to buttress by the promise of increased wages.

Thus, if it is true that employment terminations, or refusals to hire, based on seniority or experience-based pay scales are inefficient for the economy, even while efficient for the employers that adopt them, these socially inefficient decisions must be addressed by a new ADEA prohibition. This prohibition should proscribe an employer discharging, or refusing to hire, an employee in the ADEA-protected class because of where the employee fits within the employer's pay structure. An employer should not be permitted to use the wages it offers, rather than those demanded by an employee or applicant, as a justification for refusing to employ.

The prohibition should not and need not also proscribe depressing the wage of a protected employee based on an assessment of past or predicted future productivity, as long as the assessment is not based in any way on age. An employer may be constrained from reducing an employee's pay by an enforceable contractual commitment to the employee or by a collective bargaining agreement, but it should not and need not be constrained by the ADEA. The ADEA's goal should be to encourage the placement of older workers in positions in which they can be most productive, not to enforce or encourage promises of increased pay with experience or seniority or to otherwise attempt to inflate the pay of older workers.

Such a qualification on the legitimacy of cost-based defenses to terminations of and refusals to hire older workers would not prevent employers from achieving the reduced turnover and increased intensity of work that can be gained from commitments to pay experienced workers more. As I have previously acknowledged,[120] qualifying the cost-based defense would "probably result in a decline in the rising

[119] *See id.*

[120] *See* Michael C. Harper, *ADEA Doctrinal Impediments to the Fulfillment of the Wirtz Report Agenda*, 31 U. Rich. L. Rev. 757 (1997).

wages offered to more experienced workers by most [non-union] employers"[121] because the option of using less experienced and thus cheaper workers would no longer be available. Hiring less-experienced and lower-compensated workers in place of the more experienced, however, may not be part of an efficient bargain, but rather the opportunistic and manipulative breach of the commitment to pay those with greater experience more. Any employer that wishes to gain the benefit of a more sharply inclined experience-wage curve can do so by enforceable contracts.

Even if such enforceable contracts, without the availability of a safety valve of preferring junior and thus cheaper workers, could not provide optimal efficiency at a particular work place,[122] however, qualifying the cost-based justification for preferring younger to older workers seems to promote efficiency for the economy as a whole because it helps avoid the unnecessary dead weight loss of unemployed and underemployed productive older workers. Most clearly, qualifying the cost-based justification helps prevent older workers from being displaced from jobs in which they may be the most productive available workers and cast out into a labor market where rational statistical discrimination is practiced by employers uncertain of how to assess their future productivity. Qualifying the cost-based justification also prohibits prospective employers from using an experience-based wage curve as a justification for such statistical discrimination against older workers, thereby helping to compel employers to provide individualized assessments of older, more experienced job applicants. Qualifying the

[121] *Id.* at 789.

[122] Professor Jolls has argued cogently that prohibiting cost-based justifications for refusals to hire and for terminations of older workers and also preventing employers from departing from their experience-based wage promises would be efficient for the general economy because it would mimic the efficient inter-employer contracting that many workers and employers would prefer but cannot reach because of transactional and legal impediments. *See* Christine Jolls, *Hands-Tying and the Age Discrimination in Employment Act*, 74 TEX. L. REV. 1813, 1830–1839 (1996). Jolls argues that such an inter-employer contract would benefit employers as well as employees because it would enable employers to more effectively use the promise of late career wages as an inducement for intense early career work. The promise could not be broken by the termination of jobs with early career employers. *Id.* For another argument that age discrimination laws can increase the efficiency of labor markets by helping to make secure long-term wage commitments, *see* Neumark & Stock, *supra* note 39.

cost-based justification does not prevent any employer from making efficient employment decisions on the basis of individualized assessments of productivity.

2.2.2. *Insulating Employers from Discrimination Litigation during a Probationary Period for Older Workers*

Any prohibition of employment discrimination against incumbent workers on the basis of some protected status provides a disincentive to hire workers of that status because doing so increases the likelihood of future regulatory and litigation costs. This disincentive is less significant for symmetrical prohibitions, such as those of race and sex generally in Title VII, because every potential employee is a member of one or another status, even if members of generally subordinated status groups are more likely to claim discrimination. Asymmetrical prohibitions like those against discrimination on the basis of pregnancy[123] and religious practice in Title VII,[124] or on the basis of disability in the ADA, however, pose potential regulatory costs that can discourage the hiring of those whom the statutes are to protect from discrimination.[125] The ADEA imposes such an asymmetrical prohibition by protecting only those 40 and older[126] and by proscribing discrimination only against older and in favor of younger workers.[127]

The disincentive for the hiring of protected workers posed by asymmetrical prohibitions of discrimination against incumbent workers does not necessarily condemn such prohibitions. The benefit that

---

[123] *See Cal. Fed. Savings & Loan Assoc. v. Guerra*, 479 U.S. 272 (1987) (finding that the Pregnancy Discrimination Act does not prevent employers from offering more benefits for pregnancy).

[124] *See* 42 U.S.C. § 2000e(j) (defining "religion" to require the reasonable accommodation of "religious observance or practice", but not requiring accommodation of secular practice).

[125] Two studies since the passage of the ADA concluded that the sometimes costly accommodation requirements imposed by that statute have led to a decrease in the employment of the disabled. *See* Daron Acemoglu & Joshua D. Angrist, *Consequences of Employment Protection? The Case of the Americans with Disabilities Act*, 109 J. POL. ECON. 915 (2001); Thomas DeLeire, *The Wage and Employment Effects of the Americans with Disabilities Act*, 35 J. HUM. RES. 693 (2000).

[126] *See* 29 U.S.C. § 631(a).

[127] *See Gen. Dynamics Land Sys., Inc. v. Cline*, 540 U.S. 581 (2004).

antidiscrimination prohibitions provide to those protected workers who are hired may more than compensate for any discouragement of the hiring of additional workers. Furthermore, prohibitions of hiring discrimination against the protected class, especially if enforced through adequate procedures and with adequate remedies, presumably can outweigh the disincentives posed by prohibitions of discrimination after hiring.[128]

Nevertheless, the asymmetrical prohibition of age discrimination after hiring in the ADEA presents an especially strong case for taking into account the disincentive effects of regulation. This is because these effects must increase with the age of the worker and the benefits of protections against discrimination after hiring must decrease after some age.

The disincentive effects of posthiring prohibitions against discrimination must increase with the age of hiring precisely because employers apply generalizations about the probable future productivity of job applicants. The older the applicant, the employer might assume, the greater the chance that the applicant will decline during his or her tenure after hiring, the greater the chance the employer will have to take adverse personnel actions, and the greater the chance that there will be litigation.

The benefits of protections against post-hiring discrimination also must decline with age for several reasons. First, employees hired at an advanced age are less likely to be on long-term career tracks with the promise of increasing compensation. Few of those on a shorter-term career track probably are given any promises of increased responsibility and pay after an age of normal retirement for the company. This explains the studies that indicate that older workers tend not to be hired in particular jobs with longer-term career paths.[129] This also indicates that employers have less incentive to discharge, rather than to redeploy, productive incumbent workers who are hired at a more advanced age.

Second, the costs to workers of discharge, or constructive discharge through adverse treatment, probably start to decline by the age of normal retirement. This is not only because the job and career opportunity being sacrificed is probably less significant, but also

[128] *See generally* Christine Jolls, *Accommodation Mandates*, 53 STAN. L. REV. 223, 273–282 (2000).

[129] *See, e.g.*, Hirsch, *supra* note 37; Robert M. Hutchens, *Delayed Payment Contracts and a Firm's Propensity to Hire Older Workers*, 4 J. OF LAB. ECON. 439 (1986).

because the level of responsibility and intensity of work desired by the employee is probably less. The kind of work that should satisfy workers after their normal retirement age thus theoretically should be more available, at least if employers could get to know the older applicants without being concerned about enlarging exposure to post-hiring anti-discrimination charges.

Policymakers therefore might consider allowing employers to require employees hired after reaching an age close to normal retirement, say 62, to waive their protection from being discharged or reassigned on the basis of age. The purpose of allowing such waivers would be to encourage the hiring of older workers by eliminating the disincentive of the threat of future age discrimination litigation. The primary underlying goal of the ADEA, we should remember, is the fuller utilization in productive employment of older workers still able and willing to work. Prohibitions of discrimination should serve, rather than impede, the achievement of that goal.

Nonetheless, there are good reasons to hesitate before allowing employers to require any older hirees to waive protection against future age discrimination. Responsible, more sophisticated employers concerned about their labor market reputations probably would be hesitant to extract such waivers, while other more opportunistic employers might use them strategically to limit their use of older employees. This strategic use could include not only rapid turnover of unprotected older hirees in certain less-desirable jobs, but also the disfavoring of job applications of older workers who are younger than the cut-off age for waiver. The latter strategy could be discouraged by lowering the cut-off age down from 62, but doing so would allow opportunistic employers to eliminate the basic protections of the statute for a larger class of older workers.

Furthermore, an allowance of a waiver would not be politically attractive, in part because it ostensibly dilutes rather than strengthens the ADEA's commands, and in part because it draws some inevitably arbitrary lines based on generalizations about the workforce and career paths. Moreover, to be effective the allowance of waivers of protection from post-hiring, post-retirement age discrimination would probably have to extend to waivers of protection from post-hiring, post-retirement age protection from disability discrimination; employers contemplating hiring older workers probably are at least as concerned about future age-associated disabilities and the costs of consequent claims of disability discrimination and for reasonable accommodations as they are about future claims of age discrimination. Yet, any proposal to compromise the ADA's commands could provoke even greater political opposition.

A more politically feasible and probably more effective compromise alternative would be to provide employers with a period of insulation from being sued for age discrimination by an employee after being hired initially after a high cut-off age, whether it be 62 or younger. During this probationary period, of perhaps a year, employers could escape their dependence on generalizations by gaining knowledge of older hirees as individuals. They could do so free of the threat of being sued after making a mistake about the productivity of the older hirees.

This compromise would not offer as much of an incentive, as would a waiver allowance, to hire workers in their most senior years because employers understand that workers' productivity may decline as they age after a probationary period. It also would not encourage as much opportunism, however, as employers would not have an incentive to disfavor workers below the cut-off age for jobs in which rapid turnover is costly and employers could not completely eliminate the statute's protections against age discrimination after hiring.

One indeed might wonder if employers should be granted a probationary period free of the constraints of the ADEA for all hirees. An employer that is willing to hire an older worker is very unlikely to discharge that worker within the first year of employment because of the worker's age, rather than because of the worker's demonstrated lack of competence. This seems especially true for any job that requires an initial period of training during which the employee is relatively overcompensated. Nonetheless, any probationary period carries some risk of insulating age-based discrimination, perhaps by different agents of the employer than those who did the initial hiring, and employers may not need the inducement of probationary hiring to consider otherwise attractive workers in their forties and early fifties. On balance then, policymakers might consider a cut-off age as low as 55, but granting employers a probationary period for all ADEA-protected over age-40 workers is probably excessive.

3. CONCLUSION

Providing employers with an insulated probationary period after the hiring of older workers, like eliminating an internal cost-based defense to age discrimination claims, might seem to modify the statute from being concerned exclusively with age discrimination, at least as narrowly defined, into a statute primarily concerned with the encouragement of the employment of older workers. Yet, the goals of the ADEA always also have included the promotion of "employment of older persons based on their ability rather than age" and helping "employers and workers find ways of meeting problems arising from the impact of age on employment."[130] Since insulating employers from concerns about age discrimination litigation encourages them to be willing to assess the ability of older workers through providing the workers with more employment opportunities, it is fully in accord with these employment goals. Similarly, eliminating the internal cost-based defense to age discrimination, by requiring employers to adjust their compensation structure to avoid the displacement of incumbent older workers, encourages employers to address a primary problem "arising from the impact of age on employment." These recommendations for an ADEA reform agenda, like the recommendations set forth in Part 2.1 to strengthen the enforcement of ADEA's current commands, thus would help secure the original goals of the statute.

[130] 29 U.S.C. §621(b).

[10]

International Comparison of Age Discrimination Laws

Joanna N. Lahey[1]

Abstract

European age discrimination legislation is discussed in the context of the U.S. Age Discrimination in Employment Act (ADEA) and related state laws. U.S. law was originally introduced to protect productive older workers from age stereotypes, but more recently preventing age discrimination has become important as a means of keeping costs down on entitlement programs as the population ages. Changes in enforcement, penalties, exemptions, length of time to file, and burden of proof have changed the effects of the laws over time. The ADEA has had both positive effects on currently employed older workers and negative effects on the hiring of older workers. Enforcement and publicity are offered as possible explanations for the strength of these positive and negative effects. Age discrimination legislation in Europe, indicated in the Framework Directive 2000/78, is driven by economic and political considerations. European legislation calls for less enforcement and more exemptions than the corresponding U.S. cases that could lead to smaller effects on employment. However, pensions, disability, unemployment, and social security potentially have a stronger effect on social norms for retirement age than does anti-discrimination legislation.

Keywords

bias, employment, international comparative study, law

---

[1]Texas A&M University, College Station, Texas, USA

Corresponding Author:
Joanna N. Lahey, George H. W. Bush School, Mailstop 4220, College Station, TX 77845, USA
Email: jlahey@nber.org

Although the United States has had federal legislation outlawing employment discrimination based on age since the 1960s, many European countries have recently had their first experiences with age discrimination laws with the advent of the Framework Directive 2000/78/EC. This directive, put in place in 2000, required member countries to design their own anti-discrimination laws by 2003, with an extension to 2006 allowed for age discrimination laws. As the baby boomer population ages, retired workers put stresses on national pension systems across the world. Given reductions in morbidity and mortality, a possible way to mitigate these stresses would be to raise the pension ages for public pensions, in effect decreasing the benefits from annuities and encouraging workers to increase the length of their working lives. However, to make these changes without decreasing the quality of life of these cohorts, employers must be willing to employ older workers.

One method to combat age discrimination in employment is to prohibit it through regulation. Although the goal of these age discrimination laws is to increase the employment of older workers, theoretically the effects of these laws are not as clear. When a worker becomes more difficult to remove, firms are less likely to take a chance on hiring that worker. Empirical work from the United States has already shown that protection laws can have unintended effects (e.g., Acemoglu and Angrist 2001; DeLeire 2000; Lahey 2008b). Viewing the new European laws within a framework developed for analyzing U.S. data can help guide EU policy makers and researchers as they attempt to grapple with ways to increase employment among these groups.

Each country in the European Union was able to create its own age discrimination law guided by the principles put forth in the Framework Directive. Although similar in many ways, a diverse set of these laws exists across the EU. The different aspects of these laws may result in different effects. Differences in enforcement, penalties, exemptions, time to file, and burden of proof influence the scope and strength of these laws, as they have influenced the effects of age discrimination laws in the United States. Additionally, some aspects of these laws, such as the effect of prohibiting age-based employment advertisements or discouraging the use of birth dates on resumes, could have a large impact but have not been formally studied.

This article introduces these new European Union laws and provides a framework for thinking about how these laws affect employment outcomes for older workers based on research that has been done in the United States on the Age Discrimination in Employment Act (ADEA).

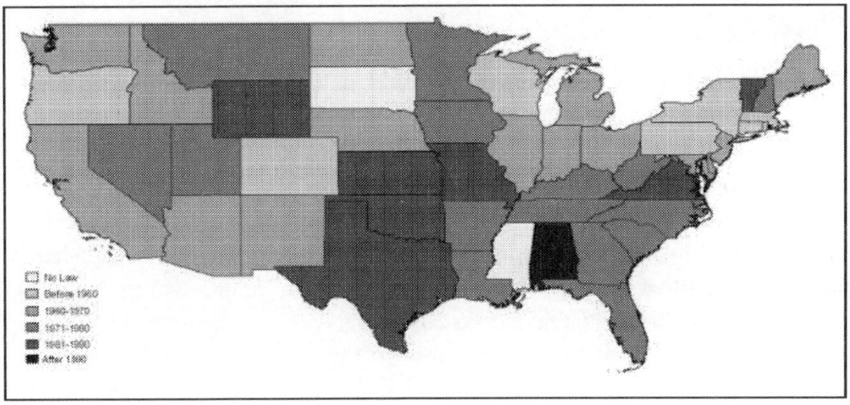

Figure 1. Implementation of state laws
Note: Information on years from Lahey 2008(b).

U.S. Discrimination Law

History

In 1965, the U.S. Department of Labor drafted a report on age discrimination in the economy that would become the basis for the 1967 federal Age Discrimination in Employment Act. This report focused on how negative and incorrect stereotypes hurt older workers and hurt the economy by keeping productive older workers from contributing. More recently, the issue of age discrimination has become of interest in most developed countries as the retirement of the baby boom generation stresses public pension programs, a problem that could be ameliorated with little loss of quality of life if older people remained in the labor force.

The ADEA protects workers and potential workers from age-based discrimination in terms of hiring, firing, and other conditions of employment. In addition to the federal ADEA, individual states have their own legislation protecting workers from discrimination based on age, beginning with Colorado's statute in 1903. Figure 1 shows the introductory dates for state legislation. Although many states essentially copied the federal law, some have had more restrictive laws. Additionally, an idiosyncrasy in the federal law provides potential plaintiffs in states with state laws additional time to bring a lawsuit compared to those in states without their own laws.

Anatomy of a Law

The original 1967 federal law protected workers age 40 to age 65 and allowed for mandatory retirement and other discriminatory behavior after age 65. In 1978, the law expanded to cover those ages 40 to 70 and in 1986 removed the upper age limit entirely. In 1978, the law also allowed the right to a jury trial and in 1979 the Department of Labor moved enforcement to the Equal Employment Opportunity Commission (EEOC), both of which strengthened the enforcement of the ADEA (Hersch and Viscusi 2004; Neumark 2001). The law included some exceptions, allowing mandatory retirement to be phased out by 1993 for workers in jobs with tenure, such as university professors. The ADEA covers workers in firms of 20 workers or more, in contrast to the more restrictive Civil Rights Act (1964) that protects those in firms of 15 or more workers from discrimination based on race, gender, national origin, or religion.

Employers are allowed to use age as a qualification in employment decisions if there is a "Bona Fide Occupational Qualification," or BFOQ, that is directly related to age. A common example given is that of an acting position. In practice, the courts have also allowed age to be considered a BFOQ in cases where public safety may be affected, including occupations such as pilots, air traffic controllers, or bus drivers. The federal law also exempts high-salaried policy-making positions (e.g., CEO) from age discrimination law.

Unlike the U.S. Civil Rights Act, which allows damages for emotional suffering and punitive damages, the ADEA limits awards to plaintiffs to "make whole" status, that is, returning plaintiffs to the point where they would have been had they not been discriminated against. These awards can include hiring, reinstating, promoting, back pay, restoring benefits, and paying lawyer fees. Lawyer fees often make up the majority of the award to ADEA recipients. Additional damages are only awarded in rare cases in which the defendant has willfully violated the law and these damages are limited to twice the amount of actual damages (Lindemann and Kadue 2003; O'Meara 1989). Because of these limits to damages, the majority of plaintiffs under the ADEA have been white male middle managers in their 50s who have lost sizeable salaries and benefits (O'Meara 1989; Schuster and Miller 1984). From the firm's perspective, if the penalties are not steep enough, it may be a profitable business decision to ignore the law and pay penalties as they occur. However, consumer backlash from publicized discrimination cases may make this type of law violation less palatable to firms.

Interpretation

The interpretation of the law in court is subject to whether or not disparate impact cases are allowed in addition to disparate treatment cases. While disparate treatment cases require intentional discrimination, in disparate impact cases a policy can indirectly impact a protected group differently than the unprotected group. A common example of a disparate impact policy would be a minimum height requirement that has a disparate impact on women, who are shorter than men on average. For age, disparate impact often involves decisions based on seniority or wages such as the decision to fire those who have the highest salaries or who have been with the firm the longest. Recently, in *Smith v. City of Jackson* (2005), the United States Supreme Court held that the ADEA authorizes recovery for disparate impact claims of discrimination. The Court also held that the "reasonable factors other than age" (RFOA) test, rather than a "business-necessity" test, is the appropriate standard for determining the legality of practices that disproportionately affect older individuals. This ruling differed from the EEOC's earlier position that an employment practice that had a disparate impact on individuals within the protected age group could not be a reasonable factor other than age unless it was justified as a business necessity.[1]

A second legal interpretation question is that of who bears the burden of proof in disparate impact cases. Generally, this question is equivalent to whether the plaintiff must prove that a policy is intentionally discriminatory or whether the defendant must prove that the policy had a bona fide business rationale. This burden of proof has shifted from defendant to plaintiff and back in age cases since the 1970s. Currently the 2005 *Smith v. City of Jackson* ruling is that

> it is not enough to simply allege that there is a disparate impact on workers, or point to a generalized policy that leads to such an impact. Rather, the employee is "responsible for isolating and identifying the specific employment practices that are allegedly responsible for any observed statistical disparities." (*Smith v. City of Jackson* 2005, quoting *Wards Cove Packing Co. v. Atonio* 1989, at 656)

Procedure

If a state has its own age discrimination statutes, the ADEA requires the claimant to file with the state Fair Employment Practices (FEP) office within 300 days of the occurrence of the incident. In the few states that do not have statutes, the claimant must file with the EEOC within 180 days. The EEOC can then dismiss the claim, at which point the claimant may pursue a civil action in court, or the EEOC can seek to settle or mediate. If the settlement or mediation is unsuccessful, the EEOC can then sue, or if it chooses not to sue, the claimant may sue (Neumark 2001). Over 95% of employment discrimination cases are brought by private attorneys, not the EEOC, and of the cases filed in federal court for employment discrimination, 92% are never brought to trial (Gregory 2001).

If the case goes to trial, the plaintiff first shows evidence of disparate treatment, that is, that there was a motive to discriminate based on age, if there is any evidence. The most common type of evidence for direct discrimination is a verbal statement of age bias as company policy. If there is no direct evidence of discrimination, then the plaintiff shows that he or she is in the protected age range, suffered an adverse reaction, was successfully performing to the employer's expectations of the work, and was replaced. Next the defendant presents one of the exceptions or defenses to the ADEA. Finally, the plaintiff attempts to establish that this defense is untrue.

Effects of the Law

Laws protecting people from age discrimination potentially have both positive and negative effects. Any law that manipulates free market decisions could have negative impacts on individual firm productivity, in this case preventing employers from making efficient hiring and firing decisions. However, if the law is fixing market failures, such as those caused by incorrect stereotypes, lack of information, or tastes for discrimination, it can improve firm productivity. Overall productivity in the economy may be increased if the law allows older potential workers who would have been unproductive in the absence of the law to become productive members of society, although resources used to follow and enforce the law may be a drain on society.

On the individual level, because it is much easier to detect discrimination once a worker has been employed, the law will have the effect of protecting those with jobs from termination and other negative actions. However, short of overt discriminatory language, it is almost impossible to detect discrimination on the hiring margin. Therefore, the law may have the effect of preventing those who might have been hired in the absence of the law from being hired; because of the law, firms may not wish to take a chance with a worker who will be difficult to fire.

Empirically, we can test which of these two competing effects, decreases in hiring or decreases in firing, dominate over time and for different groups in the labor force. Early on, the law may have even had positive effects on the hiring margin because of its effects on social norms regarding aging. The ADEA has virtually eliminated age-based language in advertising, and in the United States, it is no longer the norm to put birth date or familial status information on a resume or cover letter and work histories are generally limited to the previous 10 years. Using a differences-in-differences strategy that assumes that states with their own laws are untreated by the federal ADEA, Adams (2004) determines that the introduction of the law in 1967 caused a small positive effect on overall employment for older workers, a finding consistent with Lahey (2008b). Neumark and Stock (1999) and Jolls (1996) suggest that the ADEA may also improve efficiency during this time period in companies with long-term Lazear-type contracts because the ADEA provides a commitment device for these contracts in the absence of perfect employee monitoring; the ADEA improves employee willingness to be compensated at lower wages when first entering a firm on the promise of higher wages later.

However, the effects of the ADEA may not be fixed over time. The law was strengthened by expansions and increases in enforcement in 1978 and 1979. Lahey (2008b) exploits a difference in the legal environment that makes it easier for those in states with their own age discrimination laws to sue than those in states without their own discrimination laws. This study finds unintended negative consequences of the law on employment for older men. Men work 1.5 fewer weeks per year in states where it is easier to sue after the 1978 enforcement of the law than do men in states where it is not as easy to sue. Men are both less likely to be hired and less likely to be fired in these states, suggesting that firms take the probability of a lawsuit from older applicants into account when making hiring and firing decisions. There is no negative impact on women of the same age groups.

Other work examines the effect of changes on mandatory retirement directly. Mitchell and Luzadis (1988) find that prior to age discrimination laws in 1960, pension plans rewarded delayed retirement, but by the 1980s union plans actively encouraged early retirement while non–union plans encouraged delayed retirement. Von Wachter (2002) examines the shift of mandatory retirement to age 70 in 1978 and its end in 1986 using imputed probability of being covered by mandated retirement and finds that the labor force participation of workers age 65 and older increases by 10% to 20% in 1986 in specific industries. Ashenfelter and Card (2002) show that the abolition of retirement for college professors in 1994 reduced retirement for those age 70 and 71.

Even with stronger incarnations of the Age Discrimination in Employment Act in place, age discrimination has not been eliminated from the U.S. labor force. From 1992 to 2008, on average 15.79% of ADEA cases, for a total of 44,624 cases, were described as "merit resolutions," or successful claims, by the EEOC (author's calculations).[2] These numbers give only a lower bound because many instances of age discrimination are never litigated, and cases of hiring discrimination often go undetected. In 2002-2003, Lahey (2008a) performed an audit study, or correspondence review, experiment in Boston, MA, and St. Petersburg, FL, sending out thousands of resumes and measuring the response rate based on date of high school graduation. Because of the need to make treatment and control groups similar except for age, the study was limited to entry-level women with work histories of 10 years or less. Among this group, younger applicants (those whose date of high school graduation indicated that they were younger than 50 years old) were 40% more likely to be called back for an interview than were older applicants (Lahey 2008a).

Importance of Enforcement and Publicity

On one hand, a law has no teeth without the threat of enforcement. On the other hand, employers may be more willing to take a chance on hiring older workers if they are not concerned about the ability to remove those workers later on. Between 1967 and 1978, the ADEA was publicized but there was no formal enforcement mechanism at the federal level for violations of the law. In theory, firms were not truly constrained by the law and therefore may not have taken it into account when making hiring decisions. The positive effect on employment found by Adams (2004) could have been caused by a decrease in age-related advertisements or a change in social norms influenced by the law. However, there may have also been a decrease in firing caused by the threat of individual lawsuits; these may not have been widespread enough for firms to take them into account during the hiring decision, but could still have increased employment overall. During the later period when there was much stronger enforcement, Lahey (2008b) shows a strong relationship between the groups most likely to sue for age discrimination and the propensity for employers not to hire those workers. The hiring of women and minorities does not seem to be affected by the ADEA, and those groups are extremely unlikely to bring lawsuits during the 1978 to 1991 time period studied. Only white men older than 50, the group that brought the majority of age discrimination lawsuits (O'Meara 1989; Schuster and Miller 1984), seem to have been affected by the law; they were less likely to be hired and less likely to be fired.

Publicity, the extent to which employers and potential employees know about the laws, may also affect whether reduced firing or reduced hiring dominates overall employment of older workers. To this author's knowledge, no one has studied the trends in prevalence of advertisements that use age cutoffs or discriminatory language; however, prior to the original ADEA they were widespread and today they are much more limited. It is quite possible that removal of these age limits has increased hiring of older workers without any negative consequences, to the extent that employers are able to get more information to correct inaccurate negative stereotypes and are better able to hire older job seekers who do not fit the average profile of an older worker. Additionally, this removal could change social norms, increasing the age at which society believes that people should stop looking for work. Knowledge of age discrimination laws may also protect currently employed workers from discrimination and dismissal. However, publicity of these laws could also have negative consequences if firms react (or overreact) by increasing discrimination on the hiring margin for fear of being stuck with a worker who will be difficult to remove later.

Although the ADEA has not eliminated age discrimination from the labor market, and may actually cause some discrimination in hiring among middle-aged males, it is difficult to believe that eliminating the ADEA would result in better employment outcomes for older people, particularly if age-based advertising returns.

European Case

Directive 2000/78/EC Framework Directive

European age discrimination law is guided by the European Union's Framework Directive 2000/78. Article 13 of the 1998 EC Treaty allowed for future employment protection legislation by permitting "appropriate action to combat discrimination based on sex, racial or ethnic origin, religion or belief, disability, age or sexual orientation" (1998 European Court Reports I-621, 651; Riesenhuber 2009). The Directive 2000/78 was agreed on in 2000 and was to be put into national law by member states by December 2003, allowing member countries to request an additional three years to formulate age and disability legislation (Adnett and Hardy 2007; Bell 2002; Riesenhuber 2009). The directive only covers employment discrimination and specifically excludes state social security and social protection programs.

The European Commission's stated reasons for examining the issues of age discrimination were heavily influenced by economic reasons. The population of older people has been increasing in relation to those "working age." This increase is pressuring pension systems and other public finance systems.

Additional financing pressures for health care and old-age care will be caused by those too frail to work. The European Commission also recognized that there is a large amount of diversity among older workers—some will pressure governmental systems, but some can be tapped to contribute to these systems. The Commission thus hoped to increase the employment rate of able-bodied workers over the age of 50 in European countries through eliminating age discrimination (Sargeant 2006).

Most member countries did not have age discrimination legislation of their own prior to the inclusive legislation. Those that did generally amended or strengthened their legislation to bring it in line with the Framework Directive. Italy introduced general protection laws in 1970, but greatly strengthened them in 2003 (Radoccia 2009; Toffoletto e Soci 2009). Finland amended its penal code in 1995 to make age discrimination illegal in Penal Code Chapter 47, s 3 and passed a new Non-Discrimination Act in 2004 (Koto and Viljakainen 2009; Penal Code of Finland 2003). Poland and Romania originally implemented age discrimination laws in 1996 and 1991, respectively; however, these laws did not have "properly structured sanctions" and were updated to be in line with the European Directive in 2004 and 2000, respectively (Bazilescu 2009; Raczkowski 2009). Ireland instituted an Employment Equality Act in 1998 and amended it in 2004 (Adnett and Hardy 2007; Langford and Casey 2009). Similarly, Belgium prohibited age discrimination in recruitment and selection in a 1998 law and instituted the Anti-Discrimination Act in 2007 (Adnett and Hardy 2007; Stox 2009). Spain outlawed age discrimination with the Workers Statute in 1980, but has been one of the worst discriminators (Drury 1993); it again updated its laws in 2005 (Sagardoy 2009).[3]

Belgium, Bulgaria, Denmark, Hungary, the Netherlands,[4] Portugal, and Romania are among the states that instituted new legislation on or before the original deadline of December 2003 (Almeida 2009; Bazilescu 2009; Karacholova and Yaneva 2009; Krisch and Kürti 2009). Austria, Cyprus, Denmark, France, Germany,[5] Greece, Luxembourg, Malta, Slovakia, Sweden, and the United Kingdom are among those member states that used extension time to formulate and implement the age discrimination provisions of the Framework Directive (Banatvala and Flanagan 2009; Brincat 2009; Castagnaro and Claverie 2009; Čermák and Sturdíková 2009; Emilianides 2009; Iliadou 2009; Kliemt and Vollstadt 2009; Madsen 2009; Mertinz 2009; O'Cinneide 2005; Sands, Tour, and Truchot 2009; Stalhåmmar 2009; von Steinau-Steinrück and Vernuft 2009). In all, at least 25 countries in Europe have or will introduce legislation prohibiting age discrimination. Figure 2 groups countries by their date of original law passage.

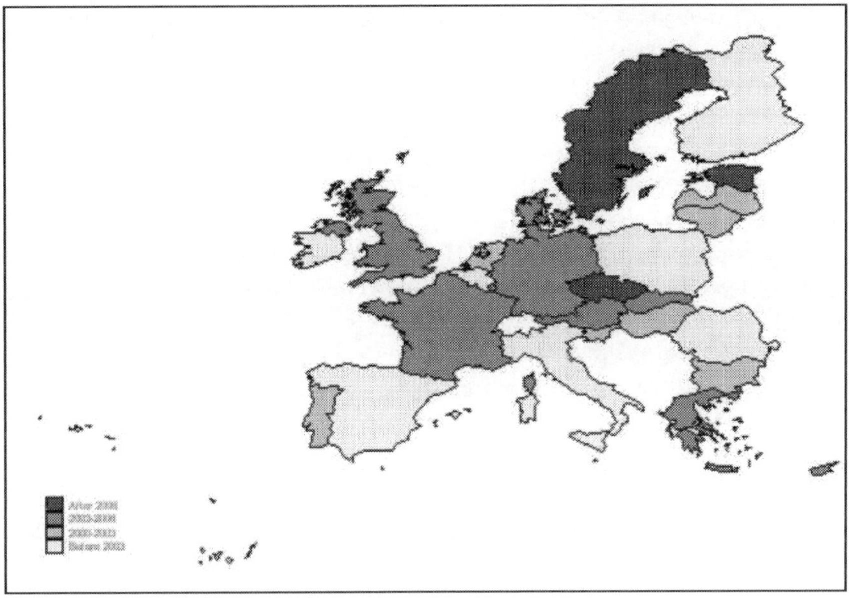

Figure 2. Timing of passage of first age discrimination law
Note: Information for figures comes from ten Bokun et al. (2010), Adnett and Hardy (2007), http://www.agediscrimination.info, European Commission (2006), Guentcheva (2006), and Drury (1993).

Modern laws prohibit explicit age limits in advertising for most occupations. Prior to the Framework Directive, some countries already prohibited age-based advertisements or had social norms that did not include them. For example, France prohibited them, and West Germany and Italy had low use in 1993. However, Spain, Greece, and the United Kingdom reported 40% of job advertisements having upper age limits (Drury 1993; Sands et al. 2009). Examining Craigslist ads, Greece and Spain still have customer service advertisements with age limits, but most of the other countries in the EU with Craigslist pages do not (author's calculations). However, in place of explicit age qualifications, advertisements in many countries did request pictures with job applications, even for occupations in which appearance should not be the predominant qualification. The request of photos with the resume is very uncommon in the United States outside of occupations for which appearance is a BFOQ, such as acting or modeling, possibly because companies do not want to open themselves up to claims of discrimination. Given that research shows that employers discriminate based on attractiveness (Rooth 2009), the request of a photograph could implicitly substitute for age bars on the hiring margin. Additionally, most applicants still include date of birth in the standard curriculum vitae (CV).

Unlike most age discrimination legislation in the United States, Directive 2000/78 does not target discrimination against older workers alone. Instead, it disallows any discrimination based on age alone, including that against younger workers. Additionally, like the early versions of the ADEA, but unlike the modern ADEA, Directive 2000/78 allows member states to specify mandatory retirement ages (Adnett and Hardy 2007; O'Cinneide 2005; Riesenhuber 2009). Because a firm would be allowed to forcibly retire an older worker at mandatory retirement age, it is plausible (though has not been thoroughly tested) that none of the other age protections would apply after the mandatory retirement age. The mandatory retirement age for many member countries is 65, although exceptions exist. For example, Ireland removed its age limit in 2004 (previously the limit was 65) and Cyprus allows a retirement age limit of 63 (formerly age 60) for civil servants (Emilianides 2009; Langford and Casey 2009; O'Cinneide 2005).

Exemptions

In addition to the potential exemptions for people over mandatory retirement age, Directive 2000/78 allows countries to make exceptions for certain industries, such as the military, judiciary, and government. It also allows exceptions for "occupational requirement," a term similar to the BFOQ in U.S. law, and for "legitimate aims." The list of potential "occupational requirements" is similar to that of the United States, primarily focusing on acting and occupations in which safety could be compromised by conditions correlated with aging. However, the list of "legitimate aims" provided in Article 6.1 to allow for direct age discrimination is much broader than the exceptions allowed in the United States, and includes items such as experience and seniority, time before retirement, and the promotion of vocational integration (Adnett and Hardy 2007; O'Cinneide 2005; Riesenhuber 2009). The United Kingdom has an even broader list of "legitimate aims" that address company planning and training goals. The Dutch Supreme Court has agreed with allowing compulsory retirement ages to ensure worker turnover and encourage younger recruits (Banatvala and Flanagan 2009; O'Cinneide 2005; ten Bokum and Hoekerd 2009).

O'Cinneide (2005) distinguishes among three different ways that member states provide guidance for exemptions. The most specific of these he terms "closed systems." These list specific circumstances for exemptions. For example, in addition to prohibitions and allowances for juveniles, Ireland specifically allows a maximum recruitment age in cases in which the job requires training or an "effective" period before retirement age. It also allows "genuine and determining occupational requirements" and exemptions for public transportation licenses (Langford and Casey 2009; O'Cinneide 2005). These exemptions are similar to case law in the United States, except for the "effective" period before retirement age. At the other end of the specificity spectrum, "open systems" provide a more vague general guideline for how to decide cases. For example, Belgium allows for differential treatment that is "objectively and reasonably justified" and Finland allows distinctions for "a justified purpose" (Koto and Viljakainen 2009; Stox 2009). Some countries such as Cyprus and Poland transplant the Directive 2000/78 language directly (O'Cinneide 2005). Interpretation of these exemptions will be based on future case law. Finally, "half-open systems" provide both a specific list and a general test. For example, the Netherlands both gives general "objectively justified" test and specifically allows for a retirement age of 65 (Holtmaat 2007; O'Cinneide 2005; ten Bokum and Hoekerd 2009).

Procedure and Punishments

The directive ensures that those who believe they have been discriminated against can bring their complaints through their national court system. Time limits for bringing a claim are set by the country and vary considerably (Adnett and Hardy 2007; Riesenhuber 2009). Austria allows up to a year for complaints depending on the type of complaint, whereas in Germany, the plaintiff must bring the case within two months (Mertinz 2009; von Steinau-Steinrück and Vernuft 2009). Article 17 of the directive allows member states to decide their own sanctions, so long as they are "effective, proportionate, and dissuasive." In practice, these penalties vary widely. For example, Austria limits administrative compensation to 360 Euros, failure to hire at 500 Euros, failure to promote at the difference in salary for three months, and hardship compensation at 720 Euros (Kunz Shima Wallentin 2009; Mertinz 2009). However, France limits to 45,000 Euro compensation and also allows for criminal charges of up to three years imprisonment (Sands et al. 2009). Several countries have compensation similar to the "make whole" legislation in the United States. Depending on the strength of the punishment, companies may make a business decision to discriminate and to pay the penalty if the expected value cost of being caught is less than that of not discriminating. However, the possibility of consumer backlash, as is argued to be the case for the Netherlands where companies are not bound by the decisions of the Committee for Equal Treatment, may make this option less attractive (ten Bokum and Hoekerd 2009).

The burden of proof rests with the complainant, although the European Court of Justice (ECJ) ruled in a 1989 sex discrimination case, *Danfoss*, that the worker only needs to show a suspicion of unequal treatment, if a practice is not transparent, to shift the burden of proof to the defendant. In practice, in cases of indirect discrimination, it is generally necessary to show that the complainant is both a different age than the comparator and better qualified. Other factors that may shift the burden of proof to the defendant include statistical differences in success rates between age groups, discriminatory comments or language, lack of transparency, a mismatch between formal selection criteria and actual selection criteria, and discriminatory questions during an interview stage (O'Cinneide 2005). In cases of direct discrimination, Directive 2000/78 includes something called a "comparator." Article 2.1.2(a) states, "direct discrimination shall be taken to occur where one person is treated less favorably than another is, has been, or would be treated in a comparable situation." In practice, this requirement is difficult to implement because it is not always easy to find a direct comparator, real or hypothetical (O'Cinneide 2005).

Once the burden of proof is shifted to the defendant, the defendant must show that "there has been no breach of the principle of equal treatment" or that the use of age was "appropriate and necessary" (O'Cinneide 2005; Sargeant 2006). Age discrimination is permitted if individual assessment is impractical (O'Cinneide 2005). It is also permitted if there is an occupational requirement or there are "legitimate aims" to the discrimination. Disparate impact cases are allowed by the directive (Sargeant 2006).

Case law and practice will determine the extent to which these new laws against age discrimination are enforced and publicized. Laws that are enforced and publicized should have greater effects, both intentional and unintentional, than those that are not. A study on Spain for www.agediscrimination.info (and confirmed in Cortadi and Aragón 2009) notes that although Spain's law is relatively strong and does not cap damages, discrimination of all kinds is still common in Spain and the courts have been reluctant to find against defendants (Cortadi and Aragón 2009; Sagardoy 2009). The study also notes that there has not been much publicity about age discrimination law.

Conclusion

In the United States, legislation prohibiting age discrimination has been in existence for decades, but its effects are still not completely understood. Prohibiting age discrimination in the United States has positive effects for those workers already employed, but has negative effects on those seeking work. The effects of age discrimination law in Europe are only now beginning to be realized. Depending on the different characteristics of these laws, they may have little effect or they may change how older people are perceived and treated by employers—for better or for worse. However strong the effects of these laws, it must be emphasized that these age discrimination laws do not work in a vacuum. There are potentially much stronger effects on the social norms surrounding older employment from eligibility for pension, disability, and social security. Mandatory retirement ages also still exist in many European countries, after which point age discrimination laws are generally not in effect.

Author's Note

The research here was prepared for the Extending the Working Life: Empirical Analyses of Legal Regulations and their Enforcement conference for the IAAEG at Trier University, Germany. I am grateful to members of that conference, M. Rose Barlow, and Ryan Beasley for helpful comments and to Jillian Boles and Effie Swanson for excellent research assistance. Any errors are my own.

Declaration of Conflicting Interests

The author(s) declared no conflicts of interest with respect to the authorship and/or publication of this article.

Funding

This paper was written while the author was a postdoctoral fellow at Rand Corporation supported by National Institute on Aging Grant T32-AG000244. All findings and conclusions are solely those of the author.

Notes

1. The recent 2009 Ricci v. DeStefano decision may have made it more difficult for plaintiffs to win disparate impact cases.
2. http://www.eeoc.gov/stats/adea-a.html.
3. Articles with information by country on age discrimination laws can be found from www.agediscrimination.info and in ten Bokum et al. (2009). Further information on these laws can be found in European Commission (2006) and information for Bulgaria is from Guentcheva (2006).
4. The Netherlands legislation came into effect in May 2004 (ten Bokum and Hoekerd 2009).
5. Note that Germany had legislation passed in 2001, the German Works Constitution Act, that regulated works councils, mandating that they "ensure that older employees are not discriminated against" (Adnett and Hardy 2007). Germany's law complied with the EU directive in 2006.

References

Acemoglu, Daron and Joshua Angrist. 2001. "Consequence of Employment Protection? The Case of the Americans With Disabilities Act." *Journal of Political Economy* 19:915-50.

Adams, Scott J. 2004. "Age Discrimination Legislation and the Employment of Older Workers." *Labour Economics* 11:219-41.

Adnett, Nick and Stephen Hardy. 2007. "The Peculiar Case of Age Discrimination: Americanising the European Social Model?" *European Journal of Law and Economics* 23:29-41.

Age Discrimination in Employment Act of 1967. Public Law 90-202, 81 U.S. Statutes 602 (1967).

Almeida, Joana. 2009. "Portugal." Pp. 271-83 in *Age Discrimination Law in Europe*, edited by N. ten Bokum, T. Flanagan, R. Sands, and R. von Steinau-Steinruck. The Netherlands: Kluwer Law International.

Ashenfelter, Orley and David Card. 2002. "Did the Elimination of Mandatory Retirement Affect Faculty Retirement." *American Economic Review* 92:957-80.

Banatvala, Sarah and Tom Flanagan. 2009. "United Kingdom." Pp. 375-90 in *Age Discrimination Law in Europe*, edited by N. ten Bokum, T. Flanagan, R. Sands, and R. von Steinau-Steinruck. The Netherlands: Kluwer Law International.

Bazilescu, Cristina. 2009. "Romania." Pp. 285-95 in *Age Discrimination Law in Europe*, edited by N. ten Bokum, T. Flanagan, R. Sands and R. von Steinau-Steinruck. The Netherlands: Kluwer Law International.

Bell, Mark. 2002. *Anti-Discrimination Law and the European Union.* New York: Oxford University Press.

Brincat, Matthew. 2009. "Malta." Pp. 233-42 in *Age Discrimination Law in Europe*, edited by N. ten Bokum, T. Flanagan, R. Sands, and R. von Steinau-Steinruck. The Netherlands: Kluwer Law International.

Castagnaro, Guy and Ariane Claverie. 2009. "Luxembourg." Pp. 217-32 in *Age Discrimination Law in Europe*, edited by N. ten Bokum, T. Flanagan, R. Sands, and R. von Steinau-Steinruck. The Netherlands: Kluwer Law International.

Čermák, Tomáš and Karin Sturdíková. 2009. "Slovakia." Pp. 309-26 in *Age Discrimination Law in Europe*, edited by N. ten Bokum, T. Flanagan, R. Sands, and R. von Steinau-Steinruck. The Netherlands: Kluwer Law International.

Civil Rights Act of 1964. Public Law 88-352, 78 U.S. Statutes 241 (1964).

Cortadi, Eva Sainz and Jesus Domingo Aragón. 2009. "Spain." Pp. 339-46 in *Age Discrimination Law in Europe*, edited by N. ten Bokum, T. Flanagan, R. Sands, and R. von Steinau-Steinruck. The Netherlands: Kluwer Law International.

DeLeire, Thomas. 2000. "The Wage and Employment Effects of the Americans With Disabilities Act." *Journal of Human Resources* 35:693-715.

Directive 2000/78/EC: Employment Framework Directive. (November 27, 2000). http://www.equalrightstrust.org/ertdocumentbank/Employment%20Framework%20Directive.pdf. Last accessed July 20, 2010.

Drury, Elizabeth. 1993. *Age Discrimination Against Older Workers in the European Community*. London, UK: Eurolink Age.

Emilianides, Achilles C. 2009. "Cyprus." Pp. 55-63 in *Age Discrimination Law in Europe*, edited by N. ten Bokum, T. Flanagan, R. Sands, and R. von Steinau-Steinruck. The Netherlands: Kluwer Law International.

European Commission. 2006. *Equality and Non-Discrimination: Annual Report 2006*. Luxembourg: European Communities.

European Court Reports. 1998. I-621, 651.

Gregory, Raymond F. 2001. *Old at a Young Age*. New Brunswick, NJ: Rutgers University Press.

Guentcheva, Rossitza. 2006. "Overview of the Status of Anti-Discrimination Legislation in Bulgaria." ASO Project Report. Retrieved July 10, 2010 (http://www.q-net.or.at/img//004ae86ae45d6cd8.pdf).

Hersch, Joni and W. Kip Viscusi. 2004. "Punitive Damages: How Judges and Juries Perform." *Journal of Legal Studies* 33:1-36.

Holtmaat, Rikki. 2007. "Country Report: The Netherlands." Retrieved March 1, 2010 (http://www.migpolgroup.com/public/docs/125.Netherlands_Discrimination-CountryReport_EN_01.07.pdf).

Iliadou, Tati. 2009. "Greece." Pp. 141-56 in *Age Discrimination Law in Europe*, edited by N. ten Bokum, T. Flanagan, R. Sands, and R. von Steinau-Steinruck. The Netherlands: Kluwer Law International.

Jolls, Christine. 1996. "Hands-Tying and the Age Discrimination in Employment Act." *Texas Law Review* 74:1813-846.

Karacholova, Maria and Tanya Yaneva. 2009. "Bulgaria." Pp. 39-54 in *Age Discrimination Law in Europe*, edited by N. ten Bokum, T. Flanagan, R. Sands, and R. von Steinau-Steinruck. The Netherlands: Kluwer Law International.

Kliemt and Vollstadt. 2009. "Germany." Retrieved March 1, 2010 (http://www.agediscrimination.info/international/Pages/Germany.aspx).

Koto, Lassi and Petteri Viljakainen. 2009. "Finland." Pp. 103-14 in *Age Discrimination Law in Europe*, edited by N. ten Bokum, T. Flanagan, R. Sands, and R. von Steinau-Steinruck. The Netherlands: Kluwer Law International.

Krisch, Imre and Nora Kürti. 2009. "Hungary." Pp. 157-70 in *Age Discrimination Law in Europe*, edited by N. ten Bokum, T. Flanagan, R. Sands, and R. von Steinau-Steinruck. The Netherlands: Kluwer Law International.

Kunz Shima Wallentin. 2009. "Austria." Retrieved March 1, 2010 (http://www.agediscrimination.info/international/Pages/Austria.aspx).

Lahey, Joanna. 2008a. "Age, Women, and Hiring: An Experimental Study." *Journal of Human Resources* 43:30-56.

Lahey, Joanna. 2008b. "State Age Discrimination Laws and the Age Discrimination in Employment Act." *Journal of Law and Economics* 51:433-60.

Langford, Kevin and Sinead Casey. 2009. "Ireland." Pp. 171-81 in *Age Discrimination Law in Europe*, edited by N. ten Bokum, T. Flanagan, R. Sands, and R. von Steinau-Steinruck. The Netherlands: Kluwer Law International.

Lindemann, Barbara T. and David D Kadue. 2003. *Age Discrimination in Employment Law*. Portland, OR: BNA Books.

Madsen, Sofie Høeg. 2009. "Denmark." Pp. 77-86 in *Age Discrimination Law in Europe*, edited by N. ten Bokum, T. Flanagan, R. Sands, and R. von Steinau-Steinruck. The Netherlands: Kluwer Law International.

Mertinz, Anna. 2009. "Austria." Pp. 1-18 in *Age Discrimination Law in Europe*, edited by N. ten Bokum, T. Flanagan, R. Sands, and R. von Steinau-Steinruck. The Netherlands: Kluwer Law International.

Mitchell, Olivia S. and Luzadis, R. Annamarie. 1988. "Changes in Pension Incentives Through Time." *Industrial and Labor Relations Review* 42:100-08.

Neumark, David. 2001. "Age Discrimination in the U.S.: Assessment of the Evidence. Pp. 43-62 in *Outlawing Age Discrimination*, edited by Z. Hornstein. Bristol, UK: Joseph Rowntree Foundation.

Neumark, David and Wendy A. Stock. 1999. "Age Discrimination Laws and Labor Market Efficiency." *Journal of Political Economy* 107:1081-125.

O'Cinneide, Colm. 2005. "Age Discrimination and European Law." European Commission. Luxembourg: Office for Official Publications of the European Communities.

O'Meara, Daniel P. 1989. *Protecting the Growing Number of Older Workers: The Age Discrimination in Employment Act*. Philadelphia, PA: University of Pennsylvania.

Penal Code of Finland. 2003. Chapter 47, Section 3.

Raczkowski. 2009. "Poland." Retrieved March 1, 2010 (http://www.agediscrimination.info/international/Pages/Poland.aspx).

Radoccia, Stefania. 2009. "Italy." Pp. 183-98 in *Age Discrimination Law in Europe*, edited by N. ten Bokum, T. Flanagan, R. Sands, and R. von Steinau-Steinruck. The Netherlands: Kluwer Law International.

Riesenhuber, Karl. 2009. "The EC Anti-Discrimination Framework Directive 2000/78." Pp. xxvii-xlvi in *Age Discrimination Law in Europe*, edited by N. ten Bokum, T. Flanagan, R. Sands, and R. von Steinau-Steinruck. The Netherlands: Kluwer Law International.

Rooth, Dan. 2009. "Obesity, Attractiveness, and Differential Treatment in Hiring: A Field Experiment." *Journal of Human Resources* 44:710-35.

Sagardoy. 2009. "Spain." Retrieved March 1, 2010 (http://www.agediscrimination.info/international/Pages/Spain.aspx).

Sands, Roselyn, Laurent-Paul Tour, and Mathilde Truchot. 2009. "France." Pp. 115-24 in *Age Discrimination Law in Europe*, edited by N. ten Bokum, T. Flanagan, R. Sands, and R. von Steinau-Steinruck. The Netherlands: Kluwer Law International.

Sargeant, Malcolm. 2006. *Age Discrimination in Employment*. Aldershot, UK and Burlington, VT: Gower Publishing Limited and Ashgate Publishing Company.

Schuster, Michael and Christopher S. Miller. 1984. "An Empirical Assessment of the Age Discrimination in Employment Act." *Industrial and Labor Relations Review* 38:64-74.

Smith v. City of Jackson, 544 U.S. 228, 241 (2005).

Stalhåmmar, Jessica. 2009. "Sweden." Pp. 347-52 in *Age Discrimination Law in Europe*, edited by N. ten Bokum, T. Flanagan, R. Sands, and R. von Steinau-Steinruck. The Netherlands: Kluwer Law International.

Stox, Yves. 2009. "Belgium." Pp. 19-38 in *Age Discrimination Law in Europe*, edited by N. ten Bokum, T. Flanagan, R. Sands, and R. von Steinau-Steinruck. The Netherlands: Kluwer Law International.

ten Bokum, Nicky and Ilya Hoekerd. 2009. "The Netherlands." Pp. 243-56 in *Age Discrimination Law in Europe*, edited by N. ten Bokum, T. Flanagan, R. Sands, and R. von Steinau-Steinruck. The Netherlands: Kluwer Law International.

ten Bokum, Nicky, Tom Flanagan, Roselyn Sands, and Robert von Steinau-Steinruck, eds. 2009. *Age Discrimination Law in Europe*. The Netherlands: Kluwer Law International.

Toffoletto e Soci. 2009. "Italy." Retrieved March 1, 2010 (http://www.agediscrimination .info/international/Pages/Italy.aspx).

U.S. Department of Labor. 1965. *The Older American Worker: Age Discrimination in Employment. Report of the Secretary of Labor to the Congress under Section 715 of the Civil Rights Act of 1964*. Washington, DC: Government Printing Office.

von Steinau-Steinrück, Robert and Cord Vernuft. 2009. "Germany." Pp. 125-40 in *Age Discrimination Law in Europe*, edited by N. ten Bokum, T. Flanagan, R. Sands, and R. von Steinau-Steinruck. The Netherlands: Kluwer Law International.

von Wachter, Til. 2002. "The End of Mandatory Retirement in the US: Effects on Retirement and Implicit Contracts." The Center for Labor Economics Working Paper, University of California, Berkeley, CA.

Wards Cove Packing Co. v. Atonio, 490 U.S. 656 (1989).

Bio

Joanna N. Lahey is a professor of economics and policy at the George H. W. Bush School of Government and Public Service at Texas A&M. She studies aging, health, savings, and the labor market. Her work on age discrimination won the 2006 W. E. Upjohn Dissertation Award for best dissertation on employment related issues.

[11]

A SOFTLY GREYING NATION: LAW, AGEING AND POLICY IN CANADA

Charmaine Spencer and Ann Soden[*]

I. INTRODUCTION

In the past half century, Canadian society has undergone substantial transformation, becoming more culturally heterogeneous, shifting from rural to urban economies, and witnessing large numbers of people living to be old. While in the 1960s and 1970s the country focussed on achieving social justice across broad populations, in the 1980s and 1990s, Canada began to awaken to a need for a special place for older adults within "A society for all ages", taking several first steps to achieve this goal. Today, the capacity of the country to recognize and respond appropriately to the social as well as legal needs and interests of older adults is continually being reshaped and tested.

A. Legal Background

Canada operates under two legal regimes: common law which is utilized in nine provinces and three territories; and a codified system of civil law, which applies within the province of Québec.[1] Since 1996, aboriginal communities have also begun to take a role in the administration of justice in a manner in accordance with their culture.

In Canada, the federal and provincial or territorial governments have specific areas of law and services over which they have constitutional responsibility. For example, the federal government is responsible for the *Canada Health Act*,[2] but provinces and territories are responsible for the administration of health care coverage. Criminal law comes under federal jurisdiction, while each province is responsible for the administration of justice.[3] Many areas of law affecting older adults, including family relations, marriage, property rights, adult protection,

---

* Charmaine Spencer, B.A., LL.B., LL.M., Adjunct Professor, Gerontology Research Centre, Simon Fraser University, Vancouver, BC, Canada; Ann M. Soden, Advocate Émérite, BCL, LL.B., Executive Director, National Institute of Law, Policy and Aging, Montreal, Canada and Commissioner, Commission of Law and Aging, American Bar Association, Washington, D.C.

[1] Canada e-Book, *Canada's legal system,* http://142.206.72.67/04/04b/04b_005_e.htm (Dec. 2, 2003).

[2] R.S., c. C-6 (1985). *See also* Health Canada, *Canada Health Act Overview*, http://www.hc-sc.gc.ca/ahc-asc/media/nr-cp/2002/2002_care-soinsbk4_e.html (Nov. 25, 2002).

[3] Criminal Code of Canada, R.S.C., c. C-46 (1985).

health consent, human rights, and employment laws fall within provincial or territorial responsibility, leading to considerable variation across the thirteen jurisdictions. The federal government, on the other hand, is responsible for income tax laws, old age security, employment insurance, standards for certain labour sectors, and the administration of the Canada Pension Plan. The federally enacted *Canadian Charter of Rights and Freedoms*[4] ("the Charter") affirms that every citizen is guaranteed certain rights and liberties consistently applied across the land, vis à vis "government" actions.

B. General Background on Demographic-Ageing

Canada has been fortunate to witness the burgeoning growth of older adults in the population over the past century. The percentage of people living to be 65 years old or older grew from 5 percent in 1901 to 7.6 percent in 1961, and to 13.3 percent in 2006. The percentage of older adults is expected to further increase to 21.4 percent by 2026 and to 24.5 percent by 2036.[5] Nonetheless, there is considerable diversity across the country in the percentage, distribution and life circumstances of older adults. For example, they represent a much smaller percentage in some groups such as aboriginal seniors.[6]

The average Canadian lifespan at birth for women grew from 65.3 years in 1931 to 82.8 years in 2001, and from 62.2 years in 1931 to 78.0 years in 2001 for men. [7] As is the case for almost every other developed nation in the world, Canada's median age has been increasing for decades, but again with important variations among groups. As of July 1, 2006, the median age of the Canadian population as a whole reached a record high of 38.8 years,[8] but was only 24.7 years within the aboriginal population.[9]

Canadian men and women also enjoy one of the longest life expectancies in the industrialized world. In 2003, Canadian men could expect to live an average of 17.4 years and Canadian women 20.8 years beyond the age of 65, an increase of 4.1 years and 5.0 years, respectively,

---

[4] *Canadian Charter of Rights and Freedoms*, Part I of the *Constitution Act*, 1982 (U.K.), being Schedule B to the *Canada Act 1982* (U.K.), 1982.

[5] Martin Turcotte & Grant Schellenberg, *Statistics Canada, A Portrait of Seniors in Canada 2006*, 11, http://www.statcan.ca/english/freepub/89-519-XIE/89-519-XIE2006001.pdf (Feb. 2007); Andrew Wister et al., *Factbook on Aging in British Columbia* 2 (4th ed., Gerontology Research Centre Simon Fraser University 2006).

[6] Statistics Canada, *Canada's Aboriginal Population in 2017*, http://www.statcan.ca/Daily/English/050628/d050628d.htm (June 28, 2005).

[7] Wister et al., *supra* n. 5, at 11.

[8] Statistics Canada, *The Daily, Canada's Population By Age And Sex*, http://www.statcan.ca/Daily/English/061026/d061026b.htm (Oct. 26, 2006).

[9] Turcotte & Schellenberg, *supra* n. 5, at 221-69.

since 1950. Average life expectancy at 85 years is also increasing (it was 5.8 additional years for men and 7.1 years for women in 2003).[10] In marked contrast, aboriginal people's life expectancy has been about seven years less on average for men and five years less for aboriginal women than for non-aboriginals. [11]

(i) Key Demographic Trends

From 1946 to 1964, Canada saw a large growth in its population. This "baby boomer" cohort now accounts for one third of the country's population,[12] leaving important social legacies for their children. Canada has witnessed decreasing family size for half a century, as women married later, had children later and entered and remained in the work force. Between 1950 and 2003, the average number of children in Canadian families decreased from 3.73 to 1.53 children.[13] While there have been political efforts during the past two decades to "offset" the potential population "imbalance " through immigration from Asia, the Caribbean, and Central or South America, immigration has been recognized as unlikely to be useful by itself in achieving population growth in Canada in the future.[14]

Although the country's success of having large numbers of persons living to be old should be considered a significant achievement, there has been a trend among governments in several parts of Canada to characterize the changing demography and indicators, such as increasing dependency ratio of the older adults to working age adults, as evidence of an impending crisis likely to cause a burden on health care and social systems. On the other hand, prominent demographers point out that while the population structure is changing, the total dependency rates of young and old combined is relatively steady and that an aging population is only one small factor in any emerging cost changes being experienced.[15]

---

[10] Statistics Canada, *Report on the Demographic Situation in Canada 2003 and 2004* 38, http://www.statcan.ca/english/freepub/91-209-XIE/91-209-XIE2003000.pdf (June 2006).

[11] Statistics Canada, *Aboriginal peoples of Canada*, http://www12.statcan.ca/english/census01/Products/Analytic/companion/abor/canada.cfm (last accessed May 3, 2007).

[12] David K. Foot, Richard A. Loreto, & Thomas W. McCormack, *Canada in the 21st Century* 4-6, http://strategis.ic.gc.ca/pics/ra/4foolo-e.pdf (Nov. 1998).

[13] Statistics Canada, *Report on the Demographic Situation in Canada 2003 and 2004* 31, http://www.statcan.ca/english/freepub/91-209-XIE/91-209-XIE2003000.pdf (June 2006).

[14] Statistics Canada, *The Daily, Canada's Population by Age and Sex*, http://www.statcan.ca/Daily/English/061026/d061026b.htm (Oct. 26, 2006).

[15] *See e.g., The Overselling of Population Aging: Apocalyptic Demography, Intergenerational Challenges, and Social Policy* (Ellen Gee & Gloria Gutman eds., Oxford University Press 2000); *see also* Monica Townson, *Status of Women Canada, Reducing Poverty Among Older Women: The Potential of Retirement Incomes Policies*, http://www.swc-cfc.gc.ca/pubs/pubspr/0662659271/index_e.html (Aug. 2000).

(ii) Politics and Participation of the Older Population

In Canada, the influence of "grey power" (the ability of older adults to shape the public discourse of ageing) is currently modest at best, at least in relation to the numbers of older persons. Indices such as attending public meetings, following news and current affairs, or voting appear to suggest that seniors in Canada are more politically engaged than younger persons. In 2003, one in five seniors reported attending a public meeting in the past year; nine in ten said they followed the news and current affairs daily. Almost 90 percent of seniors voted in the 2000 federal election.[16]

However, Canadian seniors rank well below other age groups in their participation in common political activities, such as: contacting newspapers or politicians; signing petitions; and boycotting products or participating in a demonstration.[17] Moreover, there is considerable heterogeneity of interests among seniors in Canada reflective of socio-economic, cultural, regional, gender and age cohort differences. This means that there are often competing views among older adults about what their pressing needs and priorities are, and how those goals should be achieved.

The general capacity of seniors and seniors' organizations to "have the ear of government" and promote political change or to promote their interests may be modest at the provincial or federal level.[18] Seniors' organizations face a number of significant challenges, including very restrictive tax law rules regarding political advocacy by registered charitable organizations.[19] As many seniors' organizations are registered charities, that legal status limits their ability to be strong social or political advocates. Similarly, there has been very little representation of older adults' interests (*e.g.* through intervener status) in many types of legal cases on issues that affect the lives of older adults, including prominent end of life decisions and human rights cases.[20]

Provincial government decision-making structures have shifted in recent years in many jurisdictions. There is often increased distance between policymakers and the public, and, in many cases, this distance has led to less transparency of the decision-making systems. This may

---

[16] National Advisory Council on Aging, *Seniors in Canada - 2006 Report Card* 51, Chart 5.2, Minister of Public Works and Government Services Canada (2006).

[17] *Id.* at 58.

[18] Charmaine Spencer, *Grey Power in Canada (Part 1)* 5-8, 19 GRC News 2 (2000), http://www.sfu.ca/grc/grcn_pdfs/vol19no2.pdf.

[19] *Id.*

[20] Marie Beaulieu & Charmaine Spencer, *Older Adults' Personal Relationships and the Law in Canada: Legal, Psycho-Social and Ethical Aspects* (Law Commission of Canada 1999).

make it much harder for seniors and others who support them to negotiate through systems, set or shift the political agenda in any meaningful way.

On the other hand, there is often an optimistic belief among some baby boomers that they will be able to substantially effect systematic change by virtue of their numbers, and that any previous "failure" of other generations has simply been a lack of effort. However, in reality, boomer activism has not been borne out at other points in their lifespan, except for very limited consumer purposes.[21] Late life activism tends to reflect early life involvement at a community level or in political activity or unions.

In terms of available formal structures to assure older adults' interests are advanced, one half of Canadian provinces have an advisory council on aging, including Alberta, British Columbia, Newfoundland and Labrador, and New Brunswick.[22] Others have established special seniors' secretariat (Prince Edward Island, Nova Scotia, Ontario, and Manitoba) or, as is recently the case in Québec and New Brunswick, a minister that is responsible for seniors. Typically, these only provide consultative or coordination information to other departments.[23] If department budgets are indicative of political power, the secretariats tend to have modest power at best.

The federal government established a Secretary of State (Seniors) in 2006, a position that is assigned to assist federal Cabinet ministers. In March 2007, the federal government also established a National Seniors Council to advise the Government on seniors' issues of national importance.[24] This Council replaced the National Advisory Council on Aging (Conseil consultatif national sur le troisième âge), which had been in operation since 1980, and was operationally supported by a team of federal public service employees. Its function was to assist and advise the federal Minister of Health on all matters related to the aging of the Canadian population and the quality of life of seniors.

---

[21] Charmaine Spencer, *Grey Power in Canada (Part Two)* 1-5, 22 GRC News 2 (2003), http://www.sfu.ca/grc/grcn_pdfs/vol22no2.pdf.

[22] Office of the Premier, Ministry of Community Services, *Premiers council on seniors and aging issues*, http://www2.news.gov.bc.ca/news_releases_2005-2009/2005OTP0117-000884-Attachment1.htm (Oct. 3, 2005).

[23] *See e.g., Ontario Seniors' Secretariat,* http://peel.cioc.ca/details.asp?RSN=16440 (last accessed May 3, 2007); *see also* Senior's Secretariat, *Giving Nova Scotia Seniors a Voice*, http://www.gov.ns.ca/scs/ (last accessed May 3, 2007) (In Nova Scotia, for example, the secretariat is described as the provincial government agency responsible for coordinating the planning and development of policies, programs and services for seniors).

[24] Human Resources and Social Development Canada, News Release, *Canada's New Government takes major steps to support seniors*, http://www.ccnmatthews.com/news/releases/show.jsp?action=showRelease&searchText=false&showText=all&actionFor=638726 (Mar. 5, 2007).

(iii) Gender Considerations

Gender has an important influence on aging in Canada. Because of factors such as distinctive roles and responsibilities, longevity, chronic health differences, socio and economic circumstances, as well as cumulative challenges and inequalities, older women and older men are likely to be affected by different social and legal issues. Canada has only slowly begun to explicitly recognize that undifferentiated analyses of ageing and policy can hide important differences among women and men in later life.

Canada signed the *Convention to Eliminate all Forms of Discrimination Against Women* 25 years ago. However, in broad social terms, the needs of older women have been largely under-represented in efforts to promote the rights and interests of women. While there have been some efforts to apply a "gender lens" to federal programs and policies in order to understand potential differential impacts that specific policies may have on men and women, the intersection of aging and gender is much less well recognized at the policy level.

Gender analysis needs to consider the short and long-term impact of policies and social trends across the lifespan, the cumulative impact of discrete government policies, as well as the differential impact of policies on older couples and unattached older persons (widowed, divorced, separated, ever single and living alone). For example, while the poverty rate among older couples in 2003 was relatively low at 5.1 percent, the poverty rate among unattached older women is much higher at 40.9 percent (and is approximately ten percentage points higher than among unattached older men).[25] Within a province, it is not uncommon to see the poverty rate among older women as double that of older men.[26]

For over three decades, the federal government has had a special office and program (Status of Women Canada) to promote the social, economic and political equality of women.[27] Recently, just as issues affecting the security of older women were starting to be raised, the scope of the Office changed, along with the reduced resources for promoting equality. There is a concern that this will represent retrenchment, and that future government directions may focus largely

[25] National Council on Welfare, *Poverty Profile 2002 and 2003* 39, http://www.ncwcnbes.net/documents/researchpublications/ResearchProjects/PovertyProfile/2002-03Report_Summer2006/ReportENG.pdf (Summer 2006).

[26] *Id.*

[27] Andree Coté, *History of the Status of Women's Canada: Women's Program and Why It Matters*, http://www.fafia-afai.org/files/Backgrounder%20on%20SWC%20Womens%20Program%20and%20Why%20It%20Matters%20Sept%2014%202006.pdf (Sept. 2006).

on formal equality, not substantive equality for women, a result which can have significant negative implications for older women. There have also been some beginning efforts at the grassroots level in recent years to build the knowledge of middle aged and older women about the feminization of poverty and the key issues affecting their income security in later life.

II. THE PLACE OF ELDER LAW

Elder law is a relatively new development in law and policy in Canada. Since the 1980's, a number of legal issues that form part of the field and practice of elder law have been offered at some Canadian universities within gerontology, criminology, and health sciences courses. These have typically focused on mental capacity, guardianship and end of life issues. While traditional fields of legal practice such as Wills and Estates have a long history of serving predominantly older clients, the legal field in Canada has only relatively recently begun thinking about law and aging as a special field of practice, or to consider aging as another important lens to understand the law and its effects.

In May 2007, the Supreme Court of Canada held that there is no overall constitutional right to legal counsel, although a right to counsel may be recognized in specific and varied situations under the *Charter.*[28] This recent decision has important implications for older adults. Legal services are largely beyond the financial capacity of many older adults, leaving many without access to justice or to rely on "self help." Within the last few years, some provincial public legal education organizations began offering basic legal information for older adults. These written materials typically focus on provincial or federal benefits and services for seniors, or on victimization issues, and may be available in several languages in some jurisdictions.[29] Public legal education in Canada tends to remain a passive system, where older adults must know where to seek information. Legal information on the Internet remains marginally accessible to most seniors, even if one assumes some are in contact with people who will have access to this technology.[30] With the possible

[28] *British Columbia (Attorney General) v, Christie,* 2007 S.C.C. 21 (May 25, 2007).

[29] *See e.g.*, Legal Services Society, *When I'm 64: A Guide to Benefits and Services for People Aged 60 and Over,* http://www.lss.bc.ca/assets/resources/pubs_w/wi64.pdf (Jan. 2006).

[30] For a discussion of public legal education's potential in meeting the needs of low income persons through Internet presence, *see* Lois Gander, Lecture, *The role of public legal education in poverty law services,* http://www.legalresourcecentre.ca/docs/povjun03.doc (June 2003); *see also* Lois Gander, Lecture, *The role of the internet in providing public legal education services to disadvantaged individuals and communities,* http://www3.extension.ualberta.ca/lsp/povjun03.doc (last accessed May 3, 2007). And, for an illustration of the type of information available, *see* Older Adults

exception of poverty lawyers working in some jurisdictions, legal aid in Canada has not covered many of the legal issues commonly affecting older adults. Moreover, older adults' incomes may be slightly over financial thresholds for legal aid eligibility. Legal aid typically focuses on family law and defense of criminal charges. The Advocacy Center for the Elderly ("ACE") is the one notable exception to this general lack of legal aid services.[31] Serving the City of Toronto in Ontario, ACE began providing the first specialized legal aid services to older adults in 1985 and is still unique within the country.[32] ACE has helped develop promising practice approaches, critical thinking and systemic advocacy in a number of key areas, including housing issues affecting older adults, abuse and neglect issues, and care facility rights.

The national development of elder law skyrocketed after 2002, when the Canadian Bar Association ("CBA") first recognized it as new area of legal practice. CBA's formation of the National Elder Law Section ("NELS") led to significantly more opportunities for private and public sector lawyers and their support staff to become informed and sensitized to legal and related issues of aging. They now have access to online and in person courses,[33] provincial and national conferences, as well as national exchanges such as "Elder Member Listserv." The NELS has now grown to over 1000 members. Also, for the first time, Canadian lawyers became engaged as an association with provincial and federal governments to consider, advocate, and elaborate on new laws, policies and law reform, sometimes joining with colleagues in other professions such as medicine, social work, and gerontology, many of whom had long been involved in these issues.

Unlike the development of the elder law practice in the United States, which was given impetus in the early 1980's and financial viability by assisting older clients with later life planning, Medicaid eligibility and private guardian/conservatorship services, Canada's subsidized health care system, its system of public guardians or public trustees (and in Québec Public Curator), along with the absence of a culture or industry of lawyers acting as private guardians or trustees, may explain, in part, the later start to the development of elder law as a

---

Knowledge Network's focus on abuse, http://www.oak-net.org/index.html (last accessed May 3, 2007).

[31] *See* Advocacy Ctr. For the Elderly, http://www.advocacycentreelderly.org (accessed June 1, 2007).

[32] Legal aid clinics exist in some form in all provinces. These are subsidized by provincial government funding for persons with revenues and/or assets under a certain threshold, usually the poverty line. *See* Advocacy Ctr. For the Elderly, *About ACE,* http://www.advocacycentreelderly.org/nav/about.htm (accessed June 1, 2007).

[33] E.g., Legal Education Society of Alberta (LESA), available at http://www.lesa.org (accessed June 1, 2007).

special practice area in Canada. Canada, however, has been quickly catching up.

Although it is too early to determine, the private practice of elder law would likely challenge most lawyers to market and sustain financially as a stand alone practice. That may change for some in time as the aging population grows and elder law becomes better known. In the meantime, elder law is being marketed and practiced in conjunction with, or as a complement to, other specializations, notably wills, estates and trusts and health law, as a way to provide a more complete, holistic, package of services to a growing older clientele.

To help meet that knowledge demand among lawyers and other professionals, the first national comparative law text was published in 2005 on basic issues of elder law.[34] Selected issues of law and aging (which were previously taught as occasional courses or course sections in health or gerontology within faculties of medicine or social work) are now beginning to be taught as comprehensive courses of law. This new trend started first at McGill University's Faculty of Law in 2005 with a national comparative law course. Courses soon followed in three other provinces (Saskatchewan, Alberta and British Columbia). The first elder law course for provincial, territorial and federal judges was offered through the National Judicial Institute in Ottawa in 2005.

While at least one university has been giving some of its law students experience with older adults through law clinics for several years, the first comprehensive clinical course in Elder Law was introduced in the spring of 2007 at McGill's Faculty of Law through the Centre for Legal Information on Aging/Centre légale d'information pour les aînés ("CLIA"). This *pro bono* clinic will be supported by students and senior lawyers and notaries, and is an initiative of the National Institute of Law, Policy and Aging/Institut national du droit de la politique et du vieillissement ("NILPA"), in alliance with the Faculties of Medicine and Social Work at McGill University, and the Institut universitaire de gériatrie de Montréal.

Research on legal issues has also increased at universities and within governments as the urgency of addressing the complex set of needs, rights and benefits of older Canadians and the impact of aging on society is given greater priority and receiving more government and institutional funding. In this regard, two specialized legal centers dedicated to research, education and advocacy, have been established -- the Canadian Centre for Elder Law Studies, which is affiliated with the British Columbia Law Institute, and NILPA, based in Montreal.

---

[34] Ann Soden, *Advising the Older Client* (1st ed., LexisNexis Canada 2005).

III. THE ELDER LAW LANDSCAPE IN CANADA

A. *The Right to Social Security*

Unlike some countries, Canada has not entrenched a "right to social security" in law *per se*.[35] However, Canada has established a relatively robust three-tier retirement system comprised of: (a) a contributory employment-based pension (Canada Pension Plan (CPP)/ Québec Pension Plan (QPP)); (b) a basic social security program (Old Age Security/Guaranteed Income Supplement); and (c) where available, workplace pensions and self contribution retirement savings. The maturation of public pensions, in particular, has helped to significantly reduce the poverty rate of Canadian seniors in the past quarter century.[36] Nonetheless, the income gap between men and women in later life remains very evident and reflective of life long disparities. For example, in 2004, the mean *before-tax* income of women over 65 was 67 percent of that of men.[37]

(i) Canada Pension Plan (CPP)

First developed in 1966,[38] this employment-based pension plan provides a monthly income, a lump sum death benefit, survivor benefits and disability benefits in cases of "permanent disability."[39] The province of Québec provides an equivalent Québec Pension Plan (QPP) for its residents.[40] The CPP/QPP is funded by contributions by employees and employers, not by general tax revenues.

The pension amount received starts after a person applies (normally at age 65). However, a person can apply as early as 60 (and will receive a permanently reduced amount), and as late as age 70 for an enhanced amount. Low income people aged 60 and over who receive social assistance are typically required by provincial law to apply for CPP benefits early, but with the permanently reduced amounts.[41] The CPP is recognized for having a number of important benefits over

---

[35] *See e.g.*, International Covenant on Economic, Social and Cultural Rights, Art. 9.

[36] Turcotte & Schellenberg, *supra* n. 5, at 66.

[37] The constant before-tax income difference between men and women in 2004 was $10,800 ($21,400 vs. $32,500), virtually unchanged from 2000, Turcotte & Schellenberg, *supra* n. 5, at 29.

[38] Human Resources Development Canada, *Pension Timeline*, http://www.civilization.ca/hist/pensions/cpp-timeline_e.html (last accessed May 3, 2007).

[39] Canada Pension Plan, R.S.C., c. C-8 (1985).

[40] Régie des rentes Québec, *A retirement pension under the Québec Pension Plan*, http://www.rrq.gouv.qc.ca/en/retraite/rrq (last accessed May 24, 2007).

[41] Lillian Zimmerman & Charmaine Spencer, *Bismarck meets the Boomers: Does mandatory retirement have a future* (Gerontology Research Centre, Simon Fraser University forthcoming).

workplace pensions: it covers all sectors of the economy; is completely portable; covers part-time and self-employed workers; and accommodates family responsibilities to some degree.[42]

The CPP is intended to replace about 25 percent of the person's income.[43] The average CPP pension for women in October of 2005 was approximately $334 (or 63 percent of the average $527 received by males). Couples can split their CPP benefits to reduce the payable tax, if they desire. The pension credits may also be divided upon marriage dissolution.

(ii) Old Age Security (OAS)

This is a federally administered public pension program enacted by the *Old Age Security Act.*[44] It provides older adults with a modest monthly pension at age 65 if they have lived in Canada for at least 10 years, and a partial pension for immigrants once they have met the 10-year requirement.[45] The OAS is fully indexed to annual cost of living. The program is financed from federal general tax revenues. Although often considered a "universal benefit," it is gradually "clawed back" at higher levels of income.[46]

Low income seniors (predominantly older women and immigrants) [47] who receive the Old Age Security may also be eligible for the Guaranteed Income Supplement (GIS). Close to one half of women aged 80 and older depend on the GIS. This may, however, under represent the level of need. As a result of lack of awareness of the GIS benefit and the cumbersome annual renewal process, persons aged 80 and over are the group of older adults most likely to not receive the GIS even though they are eligible. In some jurisdictions, more than 60 percent of seniors received GIS, and this rises to 80 percent of women aged 80 and older.[48] OAS and GIS benefits amount to a total of about

---

[42] Townson, *supra* n. 15.

[43] National Council on Welfare, *A Pension Primer 1999*, http://www.ncwcnbes.net/documents/researchpublications/OtherPublications/1999Report-PensionPrimer/ReportENG.htm (last accessed May 26, 2007).

[44] R.S., c. O-9 (1985).

[45] Human Resources Development Canada, *Overview of the Old Age Security program*, http://www.hrsdc.gc.ca/asp/gateway.asp?hr=/en/isp/oas/oastoc.shtml&hs=ozs (last accessed May 3, 2007).

[46] *Id.*

[47] National Advisory Council on Aging, *supra* n.16, at 33.

[48] National Advisory Council on Aging. *supra* n.16, at 34.

$28 billion per year—14 percent of the federal government's total yearly spending.[49]

Receipt of the GIS is often a springboard for other provincial or territorial government benefits. There is also an Allowance for 60 to 64 year-old spouses or common-law partners of pensioners who receive GIS, as well as a survivors' Allowance payable to 60 to 64 year-old widowed spouses or common-law partners.[50] Canada has international social security agreements with a number of countries to enable people who have lived or worked in another country to be eligible for benefits in Canada or in that other country.[51]

While this public pension system of OAS/GIS has improved the poverty situation of seniors in Canada, seniors' organizations have recommended a number of needed improvements. These focus on: coordinating programs; improving adequacy to meet at least basic poverty lines such as Low Income Cutoffs;[52]and redressing the punitive nature by which the GIS is "clawed back" from seniors who have small amounts of income above the identified income thresholds.[53]

Many recently immigrated seniors are more likely to have low incomes, reflective of the 10-year residency requirement before they can apply for Old Age Security and the GIS.[54] As a result, they must manage without these and other important government benefits throughout that period.[55] When a family member or other person sponsors an older adult to come to Canada, that individual is fully responsible for that person's needs. If the sponsorship breaks down, and the older person becomes in need of social assistance, the social assistance payments by government now become a debt that the sponsor must repay.

There has been little litigation on the public pension system. However, in 1995, the Supreme Court of Canada heard *Egan v. Canada* ("*Egan*"),[56] an equality rights case involving federal legislation that denied old age security benefits to persons in same-sex relationships. In *Egan,* the Court found that federal legislation violated Section 15 (discrimination based on sexual orientation) of the *Charter*, but upheld

[49] Office of the Auditor General of Canada, *Old Age Security-Human Resources and Social Development Canada and Service Canada,* http://www.oag-bvg.gc.ca/domino/reports.nsf/html/20061106ce.html (Nov. 28, 2006).

[50] Human Resources and Social Development Canada, *Income Security Programs*, http://www.hrsdc.gc.ca/en/gateways/nav/top_nav/program/isp.shtml (accessed May 3, 2007).

[51] Service Canada, *International Benefits,* http://www.hrsdc.gc.ca/asp/gateway.asp?hr=en/isp/ibfa/intlben.shtml&hs=sya (last accessed May 3, 2007).

[52] National Advisory Council on Aging, *supra* n.16, at 18.

[53] *Id.*

[54] *Id.* at 33.

[55] *Id.* at 33.

[56] [1995] 2 S.C.R. 513.

the specific measure under consideration as a reasonable limit in Canadian society. This case was the first time where a majority of the Supreme Court recognized that sexual orientation is a prohibited ground of discrimination under Section 15. Over the next five years, however, the federal government made changes to pension eligibility to the Old Age Security program and the Canada Pension Plan to include common law relationships and people in same-sex relationships, subject to having lived together for a specified time.

(iii) Workplace (Employment, Occupational) Pensions Plans

Less than 50 percent of seniors receive monies from a private (workplace) pension plan, directly or through survivor benefits.[57] Historically, there have been important differences for men and women in the Canadian labour force, both in terms of having access to workplace pensions and the adequacy of those pensions. In 2001, over 60 percent of women in the workforce did not have access to workplace pensions.[58] The majority of women continue to work in sectors that have lower rates of workplace pensions and women's work trajectory is often different with more time spent out of the workforce. On average, women working fulltime earn only 71 cents for every $1 men earn,[59] reflecting significant structural inequities.[60] These economic realities have long-term implications for them in later life. Immigrants are also much less likely to have private (workplace) pension plans than non-immigrants.

In 2003, workplace plans represented 41 percent of older men's incomes but only 26 percent of older women's, with the remainder being made up of OAS/GIS, CPP, or savings. Only 12 percent of immigrants aged 60 or older in 2003 had any private pension income; and this pension money accounted for only 13 percent of their total income. While divorced or separated women have been legally entitled since the 1970s to claim a portion of their former spouse's workplace pension as a divisible family asset, most still do not, which may increase their risk of poverty in later life.

---

[57] National Advisory Council on Aging, *Aging in Poverty in Canada 2005,* 13, http://dsp-psd.pwgsc.gc/Collection/H88-5-5-2005E.p-df.

[58] *Id.* at 11.

[59] Statistics Canada, The Daily, *Women in Canada,* Mar. 7, 2006, http://www.statcan.ca/Daily/English/060307/d060307a.htm.

[60] Some of the challenges of trying to achieve and legally enforce pay equity can be seen in the Supreme Court of Canada decision in *Newfoundland (Treasury Board) v. N.A.P.E.,* [2004] 3 S.C.R. 381, 2004 SCC 66.

B. *Personal Retirement Savings*

Since the mid 1970s, the federal government has promoted individual saving for retirement by providing an income tax deduction for retirement savings registered in special plans. These plans largely benefit higher income individuals, reducing their marginal taxes more. Unlike workplace pension vehicles, these retirement savings are not a "pension plan." The policy has been criticized on several fronts: as abdicating public responsibility; as a major tax diversion that reduces taxes to government to the detriment of funding for social programs for low income persons;[61] and for being promoted to low income earners who actually risk losing benefits in later life by having these savings.

C. *The Right to Health Care*

(i) Receiving Health Care

Canada has a universal Medicare program under the *Canada Health Act.*[62] Passed in 1984, the *Act* serves as a foundation for the provision of health care services in the country. It set out two major categories of health care services: (1) Insured Health Services (these traditional health services are defined as medically necessary hospital services, physician services and surgery-dental services provided to an insured person); and (2) Extended Health Care Services, which include nursing or long-term residential care, home care, and ambulatory health care services.

Provinces have assumed responsibility for the extended health care services. Each jurisdiction has individually determined the types and level of services they will provide. This contributes to the variability among provinces in terms of regulations, range and extent of services available, models of service delivery and funding models and user charges.[63] Each province sets priorities and sets up its own health system in different ways.

---

[61] *See e.g.* Claire F.L. Young, Status of Women Canada, *Women, Tax and Social Programs: The Gendered Impact of Funding Social Programs Through the Tax System,* 42-43, http://www.swc-cfc.gc.ca/pubs/pubspr/066265028X/200010_066265028X_e.pdf (Oct. 2000).

[62] R.S., c. C-6 (1985).

[63] *See* Marcus Hollander et al., The Identification and Analysis of Incentives and Disincentives and Cost-Effectiveness of Various Funding Approaches for Continuing Care (Technical Report No. 1), http://www.hollanderanalytical.com/downloads/id-tech-1.pdf (May 2000); *see also* Marcus Hollander, *Unfinished Business: The Case for Chronic Home Care Services, A Policy Paper,* http://www.hollanderanalytical.com/downloads/unfinished_business.pdf (Aug. 2003); Karen Parent et al., *Analysis of Interfaces Along the Continuum of Care, Technical Report No. 2,* http://www.hollanderanalytical.com/downloads/continuum-tech-2.pdf (Feb. 2002).

Reflective of the universal Medicare system, 95 percent of seniors in Canada have access to a regular family doctor.[64] Only a small percentage of seniors (6.6 percent) report unmet health needs, mainly attributable to long waiting times or accessing specialized services for a newly-diagnosed medical condition.[65] However, the country has been experiencing a "health care gap" between need and appropriate resources across age groups and the population. A high median age among health care professionals, significant lack of physicians and nurses who specialize in geriatrics and a growing trend to substitute nursing care with less formally skilled practitioners in institutional settings can significantly affect older adults' ability to receive appropriate and good quality care, and may increase the likelihood of some to experience medical neglect.[66]

During the past decade, there has been pressure at the political level to allow a greater level of privatization into the health care system, a move which has met significant public resistance. In 2005, the Supreme Court of Canada considered a case involving a provincial government's prohibition of private insurance for health care procedures covered under provincial Medicare.[67] In that case, the Court ruled that a province could not prohibit persons from obtaining this type of private insurance, and identified the problem of health service delays. Although the specific issue involved in the case was fairly narrow, it has been politically characterized in some quarters as "evidence" to legally permit increased health care privatization.

(ii) Discrimination in Health Care

Older adults' medical care can be negatively affected by direct and indirect discrimination. Although each province and territory has human rights legislation that prohibits discrimination in terms of "services ordinarily available to the public," at least one province does not offer age discrimination protection in the area.[68] There have been few, if any, human rights cases put forward by older adults to help shape the understanding of what this term means in the context of health care.

---

[64] Charmaine Spencer, *A Way Forward: Abuse Prevention in Institutional Settings - National Snapshot* (University of Toronto: Institute for Life Course and Aging forthcoming).

[65] *Id.*

[66] *Id.*

[67] *Chaoulli v. Québec (Attorney General)* [2005] 1 S.C.R. 791, 2005 SC 35.

[68] *See e.g.* Alberta's *Human Rights, Citizenship and Multiculturalism Act*, [RSA].1980 c, H-14, § 4; British Columbia's *Human Rights Code*, [RSBC 1996] c.210, s. 8(1); Saskatchewan *Human Rights Code*, SS 1979, c. S-24.1 (includes "age " as a protected category, but defines it as only including persons aged 18 to 65).

Older adults in many jurisdictions may experience forms of individual or systemic discrimination in terms of accessing appropriate health services (for example, limits on number of health conditions to be discussed in an appointment; physicians discharging patients with multiple health problems to manage their workloads, or discharging smokers from their patient list). Older adults are generally disadvantaged in equality cases, as litigation of human rights cases does not survive the person.

(iii) Advance Care Planning and Living Wills

The right of the capable individual to consent or refuse treatment is well established in Canadian common law. Included is the right to identify in advance what types of care the individual might want or not want in the event of incapacity. For over a quarter century, Canadian common law has stood by the legal principle that a doctor is not free to disregard a patient's advance instructions.[69] Across the country, there are a wide range of legal tools that have been created to aid personal decision-making in the context of health care, personal care and end of life care. Each province and territory has its own structure and systems for these decisions. Depending on jurisdiction, these may include: statutorily recognized temporary substitute decisionmakers; use of personal care directives; instructional directives (without or without also naming a proxy); and the choice of nominating someone to speak on the behalf of the person who is now unable to communicate his or her own wishes. As a result, these legal instruments now play important roles in planning for incapacity.[70] All Canadian provinces and territories have legislation dealing with advance health care directives except Nunavut, which provides for powers of attorney for property and financial matters only. Most advance directives cover health care and personal care, such as hygiene, nutrition and where the person will live or receive treatment.

There is concern among some legal practitioners that acute care and long-term care staff often misunderstand the purpose of advance care planning instruments and there is a real risk of their misuse.[71] The matter

[69] *See Malette v. Schulman* (1990) 72 O.R. (2d) 417 (C.A.); *Fleming v. Reid* (1991) 4 O.R. (3d) 74 (C.A.).

[70] *Advising the Older Client, supra* n. 34, at 109 (contributor Gerald Robertson's article, *Enduring Powers of Attorney and Health Care Directives*).

[71] Jane E. Meadus, Judith A. Wahl, & Pauline Rosenbaum, *Written Submission to the Standing Committee on Social Policy on Bill 140, An Act respecting long-term care homes* 2, http://www.advocacycentreelderly.org/pubs/Nursing/Submission.pdf (Jan. 17, 2007). "A 2004 research study of advance directive policies in long term care homes in Ontario found that "policies regarding advance directives in long-term care centres in Ontario generally do not comply with the spirit or the letter of the applicable laws". *Id.* at 53. *See also* Judith Wahl, *Testimony to the Special*

of *requiring* advance care planning by seniors, especially as a condition for receiving services, has been receiving increased attention in Canada at a policy level. This may be driven less out of respect for personal autonomy in making decisions, and more by the mistaken belief that advance directives will help reduce health care costs.

(iv) Euthanasia

In Canada, active euthanasia is prohibited under the Criminal Code of Canada ("the Criminal Code").[72] Those who help hasten a person's death risk being charged with: aiding or abetting a person to commit suicide;[73] failing to provide the necessaries of life;[74] or second degree murder (manslaughter).[75] The legal issues of euthanasia and assisted suicide were subjected to considerable public discussion at the Senate level in Canada in the mid-1990s, following a *Charter* case.[76] The case involved a woman with a severe disability (Lou Gehrig's Disease) who was seeking medical assistance to end her life at a future point. Any physician who aided her would have risked being charged under section 241 (b) of the Criminal Code. The Court concluded that although the Criminal Code effectively denied her right to security of the person (as the law did not permit her personal autonomy to control how long and how she lived), this denial was considered in accordance with the Canadian principles of fundamental justice.

Subsequent to the case, the country installed a Special Senate Committee on Euthanasia and Assisted Suicide, leading to important hearings on end of life care.[77] As a result of those deliberations, Canada developed a special Secretariat on Palliative and End of Life Care and a national palliative care strategy.[78] Since then, there has been private

---

Senate Committee on Aging, May 28, 2007, http://www.parl.gc.ca/39/1/parlbus/commbus/senate/Com-e/agei-e/44655-e.htm?Language=E&Parl=39&Ses=1&comm_id=600.

[72] R.S.C., c. C-46 (1985).

[73] Criminal Code of Canada, R.S.C., c. C-46, § 241(b) (1985) (aids or abets a person to commit suicide).

[74] Criminal Code of Canada, R.S.C., c. C-46, § 215 (1985) (duty of persons to provide necessaries).

[75] *See e.g., R. v. Latimer,* 2001 SCC 1 (2001), a case involving active euthanasia by a father against his disabled child. Robert Latimer was charged with second degree murder.

[76] *Rodriguez v. British Columbia (Attorney General),* [1993] 3 S.C.R. 519.

[77] Parliament of Canada, Special Senate Committee on Euthanasia and Assisted Suicide, *Of life and death - Final report,* http://www.parl.gc.ca/35/1/parlbus/commbus/senate/Com-e/euth-e/rep-e/LAD-TC-E.HTM#Tablepercent20ofpercent20Contents (June 1995).

[78] *See* Health Canada, *Canadian Strategy on Palliative and End-Of-Life Care,* http://www.hc-sc.gc.ca/hcs-sss/alt_formats/hpb-dgps/pdf/pubs/2005-strateg-palliat/2005-strateg-palliat_e.pdf (last accessed June 2, 2007).

member bills put forward to amend the Criminal Code to legalize active euthanasia, but these have not been put to a vote.

D. *The Right to Adult Protection*

(i) Abuse and Neglect Protections

Abuse and neglect of older adults is a complex social and legal issue, with multiple dimensions and a diverse typology.[79] In community settings, the perpetrators may be the person's spouse, one or more family members, paid care providers, or casual acquaintances. The abuse may be recent or long standing (having begun earlier in a relationship and continued into later life). While some abuse or neglect cases involve older persons who may have limited or deteriorating mental capacity, the vast majority do not. As a result, the response to preventing or addressing abuse and neglect in later life does not easily fit within one type of legal or social approach.

Most Canadian jurisdictions integrate the protection and legal interventions for abused or neglected older persons through the use of: (a) family violence protection laws (restraining orders, peace bonds); (b) mental health, adult guardianship and substitute decision-making laws (to aid mentally incapable adults); (c) public guardian and trustee law (for cases involving financial abuse and mental incapability); and (d) in the case of Québec, into its human rights law.[80] Regional networks as well as a national network have developed in Canada to help communities work together to better understand and address the underlying causes of abuse and neglect of older adults in appropriate ways.[81]

Many of these provincial or territorial laws use criteria other than older age as the threshold for protection and government intervention.

---

[79] Some Canadian academics have drawn a conceptual distinction between frauds or other criminal matters where older adults are victimized by strangers as distinct from "abuse" and "neglect" by persons in positions of trust, power or authority. *See e.g.* Canadian Network for the Prevention of Elder Abuse, *What is senior abuse, http://www.cnpea.ca/what_is_abuse.htm.*

[80] Québec Charter of Human Rights and Freedoms, R.S.Q. 2006 c. C-12, Part I, Chapter IV, § 48, http://www.cdpdj.qc.ca/en/commun/docs/charter.pdf (Apr. 19, 2006) ("Every aged person and every handicapped person has a right to protection against any form of exploitation. Such a person also has a right to the protection and security that must be provided to him by his family or the persons acting in their stead.").

[81] *See e.g.*, Canadian Network for the Prevention of Elder Abuse, http://www.cnpea.ca (accessed June 2, 2007); The Ontario Network for the Prevention of Elder Abuse, http://www.onpea.org/en/Home.htm (accessed June 2, 2007); Réseau québécois pour contrer les abus envers les aînés, http://www.rqcaa.org/accueil.php?lang=en (accessed June 2, 2007).

Unlike the United States, but similar to England,[82] most Canadian jurisdictions have steered clear of requiring mandatory reporting for abuse or neglect of adults in the community. Moreover, special adult protection laws geared to addressing some aspect of abuse, neglect or self neglect among "vulnerable adults" exist in five provinces and one territory and vary in definition and scope.[83] These special statutes first developed in the 1970s.

Although there have been private members bills put forward from time to time, there is no specific criminal charge of "elder abuse" in Canada. This reflects a belief that the existing criminal law provisions are sufficient, a recognition of the underlying paternalism of a criminal offence premised on the assumption that older adults are necessarily vulnerable,[84] and the lack of concrete evidence from other jurisdictions that special criminal laws for abuse in later life reduce the likelihood of harms occurring or effectively remedy the harms. Under the Criminal Code, the court may consider a number of circumstances in determining the appropriate sentence for theft, assault, manslaughter or any other criminal matter. Special circumstances may include whether the crime involved abuse of a spouse or partner,[85] a relationship of trust or authority,[86] or whether it was motivated by prejudice, bias or hatred of an individual or group, based on a number of listed factors, including age and disability.

The country has made major efforts since the mid 1990s to better understand and address the underlying causes of abuse and neglect of older adults. The overall development of services and resources for abused or neglected older adults is improving but still lags significantly behind other areas of family violence prevention. In 2004, in the case of *Nova Scotia (Minister of Health) v. J.J.*,[87] the Supreme Court of Canada considered the role of the provincial courts in scrutinizing services being provided to vulnerable adults under adult protection laws.[88] In *Re: J.J.*, the Family Court judge declined to authorize a plan to transfer the protected adult to a facility out of the region. The Supreme Court of

[82] *See* Rachel Filinson, *"No Secrets" and Beyond: Recent Elder Abuse Policy in England*, 18 J. of Elder Abuse & Neglect 1 (2007).

[83] These are Yukon, British Columbia, New Brunswick, Nova Scotia, Prince Edward Island, and Newfoundland and Labrador.

[84] For a general discussion on assumptions about age, capacity and vulnerability across the lifespan, *see e.g.*, Law Commission of Canada, *Does age matter? Law and relationships between the generations* (Feb. 2004).

[85] Criminal Code of Canada, R.S.C., c. C-46, § 718.2 (ii) (1985) ("Other sentencing principles").

[86] Criminal Code of Canada, R.S.C., c. C-46, § 718. 2 (iii) (1985) (arguably, this would include professionals and paid caregivers).

[87] [2005] 1 S.C.R. 177.

[88] *Nova Scotia (Minister of Health) v. J.J.* [2005] 1 S.C.R. 177, 2005 SCC 12.

Canada determined that the courts were not limited to accepting or vetoing care plans put before them by the adult protection services; judges also had a responsibility to determine whether the plan was consistent with the best interests and welfare of the protected person.

To reduce barriers within the justice system and better aid older adults who have been victimized by family or others, there have been efforts in some jurisdictions to build the knowledge of police, victim services, Crown Prosecutors and the judiciary, especially to actively avoid the stereotyping of older adults as incapable, mistaken or unreliable persons. These educational efforts also often focus on nurturing a sound understanding of the dynamics of abuse or neglect in later life, both in community and institutional settings, as well as its impact on the individual, family and communities.

The availability of new technology such as video recording to tape victims statements have helped police efforts in some municipalities to improve the likelihood of securing a conviction in the event the older adult subsequently becomes ill or becomes mentally incapable. The recent Supreme Court of Canada case *R. v. Khelawon*,[89] an assault case involving hearsay evidence of a deceased resident of a care home, highlights the real risk of perpetrators simply outliving their older victims.

"Elder neglect" is uncommon in Canada as a criminal matter. However, when extreme neglect occurs, it may lead to a charge as failing to provide necessaries of life where one person is physically or otherwise dependent on another, or, as happened in a recent case, indirect contributions to the person's death may be raised to manslaughter.[90]

With regard to abuse in care facilities, most provinces have enacted or incorporated policies to deal with abuse in institutional settings such as *licensed* care facilities. However, there are far fewer safeguards for unregulated collective settings such as retirement homes or personal care homes, or assisted living, and these types of facilities increasingly comprise the bulk of units where physically or mentally frail older adults will receive care and support in later life.[91]

In licensed care, these safeguards include general quality of care standards, mandatory reporting for abuse, some type of inspection process or general oversight process. Depending on jurisdiction, these may or may not be incorporated into statutes or regulations. A few provinces have enacted special recognition (bill of rights) for residents in

---

[89] [2006] S.C.R. 57.

[90] Peter Brieger, *National Post, Son guilty of manslaughter for neglect of elderly mom*, http://www.canada.com/nationalpost/news/story.html?id=edcc6f00-4413-4a74-9320-ad2c6558906b (Feb. 8, 2007).

[91] Spencer, *supra* n. 64.

the care facilities, along with residents', users' or family councils.[92] Two jurisdictions (Alberta and Manitoba) have enacted special laws for the protection of persons in care, and have established a special office to oversee this.[93] However, the legal thresholds for abuse and neglect under these laws result in two thirds of the cases being deemed "unsubstantiated."[94]

(ii) Guardianship

Canada uses a wide terminology for guardianship, which can include trusteeship, committeeship, guardianship, and protective supervision. The procedure for obtaining guardianship of the physical person and or the estate (property, assets and financial affairs) of a mentally incapable person is set out in provincial and territorial "mental incompetency" and adult guardianship laws and related legislation.[95] The field of guardianship and substitute decision-making has undergone considerable change in the past 25 years.[96]

All provinces except one provide some form of statutory guardianship that uses certificates declaring the person as mentally incapable.[97] The advantage of these tools is ease of use; but there is considerable difficulty for the person to later regain control over finances. The statutory guardianship orders may contravene the *Charter* as not meeting basic principles of fundamental justice.[98]

Court-ordered guardianship is intended to be used as a last resort. Legislation in several jurisdictions requires that less restrictive and intrusive alternatives to court-ordered guardianship be explored.[99] Alternatives to guardianship now include: adult protection legislation for short-term intervention by health and social services personnel; health care consent legislation codifying the common law of consent; and enshrining the use of an adult's spouse, near relatives or friends as substitute decisionmakers. In some cases, imaginative and innovative use of the law of trusts, particularly the creation of income and discretionary trusts, may provide for the financial needs of the incapable adults. These are usually created for aging intellectually disabled persons by their

[92] For an overview of the legislative and regulatory schemes within Canada, *see* Spencer, *supra* n. 64.
[93] *Id.*
[94] *Id.*
[95] Soden, *Advising the Older Client, supra* n. 34, at 82-107 (contributor Robert M. Gordon, *Guardianship of the Person and Estate*).
[96] *Id.* at 105.
[97] *Id.*
[98] *Id.*
[99] *Id.* at 86-91.

parents.[100] Enduring powers of attorney are seen as valuable for their ease of use and not requiring judicial intervention, but are also recognized as open to abuse.[101] Some provinces have put legal safeguards in place to reduce these potential risks.

Canada has made significant efforts to use guardianship as a last resort, and to find less intrusive but as effective means of meeting older adults' needs. There have also been efforts to tailor the guardianship so that it only covers specific needs, such as over finances or the person. The Civil Code of Québec[102] provides several protective measures that offer legal protection to older persons who become unable to take care of themselves or their property. These take the form of mandate, curatorship, tutorship or advisership.[103] Guardianship by government representatives has been largely actively avoided at a policy level because of the cost to the public coffers. However, the approach is sometimes criticized as creating the risk of accepting almost anyone as a guardian, including unscrupulous persons.

E. The Right to Institutional Long-Term Care

In 2001, 7.4 percent of Canadian seniors and 32 percent of those aged 85 and over lived in facilities that provided health care as well as personal support or assistance.[104] Access to publicly funded long-term care (skilled nursing) facilities is typically controlled by health and social services that utilize an assessment process. Increasingly, in many parts of the country, only the frailest and medically compromised are being admitted to the licensed skilled care facilities.

As previously mentioned, provinces tend to draw a legal distinction between skilled nursing care facilities and other congregate environments such as assisted living or other supportive care environments. The former tend to have certain minimum standards, and the latter tend to operate in a relatively non-regulated environment.[105] In several Canadian jurisdictions, assisted living and supportive housing for seniors is specifically excluded from basic landlord tenant law protections, leaving residents to rely on operator drafted adhesion contracts.[106] Quebec and Ontario are two notable exceptions.[107]

---

[100] *Id.* at 105.

[101] Robertson, *supra* n. 70, at 113.

[102] S.Q. 191, c. 64.

[103] Soden, *Advising the Older Client, supra* n. 34, at 186-196 (contributor Pierre Deschamps, *General Planning for the Older Client (Part III - Québec)*).

[104] National Advisory Council on Aging, *supra* n. 16, at 10.

[105] Spencer, *supra* n. 64.

[106] Soden, *Advising the Older Client, supra* n. 34, at 317 (contributors Margaret Hall and Charmaine Spencer's article, *Assisted Living*).

There are currently significant systemic legal issues arising in long-term care that may undermine older adults' rights and harm their care. Among these are: inappropriate admission to care; inappropriate terms in admission contracts; failure to obtain proper health care consent; abuse of residents (including rights violations); resident neglect; inappropriate use of physical and chemical restraints or improper use of "secure units"; and misuse of advance care planning documents.[108] In the past decade, there have been increasing concerns about the quality of the care in the facilities, the staffing levels and training, and the lack of qualified dementia care across the care and housing continuum.[109]

F. The Right to Community Based Long-term Care

(i) Home Care

As previously mentioned, home care falls under provincial jurisdiction as extended health care under the Canada Health Act.[110] Provinces and territorial governments largely operate under the policy assumption that formal government services only act as a default safety net for persons without any family support. While provincial governments' spending on home care has increased significantly within the past decade, a smaller proportion of seniors now receive government subsidized home care, and those receiving home care can still have important unmet needs.[111]

Over 80 percent of care is provided by family (usually the aging spouse); and at a policy level, this has largely been treated as "cost free" care.[112] This ignores the heavy costs to middle aged and older women who are predominantly the caregivers.[113] In particular, it has been noted

---

[107] Residential Tenancies Act, 2006, S.O. 2006, c. 17, Part IX (Care Homes); Civil Code of Quebec, Q.S.Q. 191, c. 64, arts. 1892 to 1978. Note, however, the Quebec Civil Code provisions do not include any room "situate in a health or social services institution."

[108] Meadus, Wahl, & Rosenbaum, *supra* n. 71, at 2.

[109] Spencer, *supra* n. 64.

[110] R.S.C., c. C-6.

[111] Gisèle Carrière, *Statistics Canada, Seniors' Use of Home Care*, 17(4) Health Report, 43-50, http://dsp-psd.pwgsc.gc.ca/Collection-R/Statcan/82-003-XIE/82-003-XIE2005004.pdf (2006).

[112] Janet Fast, Deanna L. Williamson & Norah Keating, *Hidden costs of informal elder care 1999*, J. of Family and Economic Issues, Vol. 20(3), 301-326, 322, Sept. 1999. For a general discussion on the economic impact of elder care in Canada, *see also* Janet Fast, Jacquie Eales & Norah Keating, *Economic Impact of Health, Income Security and Labour Policies on Informal Caregivers of Frail Seniors*, March 2001, http://www.swc-cfc.gc.ca/pubs/pubspr/0662654765/200103_0662654765_2_e.html (accessed May 3, 2007).

[113] Marika Morris et al., Canadian Research Institute for the Advancement of Women (CRIAW), *The Changing Nature of Home Care and Its Impact on Women's Vulnerability to Poverty*, http://www.swc-cfc.gc.ca/pubs/pubspr/0662280857/199911_0662280857_1_e.pdf (Nov. 1999); *see also* Janet Fast et al., *Status of Women Canada, Economic Impact of Health, Income Security and*

that employed women, those who have concurrent child-care responsibilities, those who live at a moderate distance from their care receiver, and family caregivers are served the least well by existing policy approaches to informal caregivers.[114]

(ii) Filial Responsibilities

The old age security system is seen as the primary financial support to older adults. However, each provincial and territorial jurisdiction has a form of law that requires some degree of filial financial responsibility to parents.[115] There has been very little litigation in this area and the laws may be considered as vestigial to the 1930s Depression, when governments had difficulty providing for older members of the population.

The courts have interpreted an adult's responsibility to his or her parents as secondary to the adult's responsibility to support his or her children and spouse. Courts avoid judging the quality of the family relationship in childhood to determine how "deserving" older adults might be for financial support, and some analysts note use of these laws can destroy already fragile ties between family members.[116] Recently, after a review of the function and application of the financial responsibility provisions of the law, one provincial law reform body called for its repeal.[117]

Section 215 (1) of the Criminal Code of Canada also imposes a duty on certain persons to provide the necessaries of life to another who is "unable by reason of detention, age, illness, mental disorder or other cause to withdraw self from that charge and is unable to provide self the necessaries of life."[118] The person may be subject to a criminal charge if he or she fails in that duty and the failure endangers the life of the person or is likely to permanently endanger the health of the other person. These charges are rarely laid.

Labour Policies on Informal Caregivers of Frail Seniors, http://www.swc-cfc.gc.ca/pubs/pubspr/0662654765/200103_0662654765_e.pdf (Mar. 2001).

[114] Fast et al., *supra* n. 113.

[115] Soden, *Advising the Older Client*, *supra* n. 34, at 380 (contributors Nicholas Bala et al., *Family Law for the Canadian*).

[116] Christa Bracci, *Ties that bind: Ontario's Filial Responsibility Act*, 17 Canadian J. on Fam. L. 455-500 (2000).

[117] British Columbia Law Institute, *Parental Support Obligation in Section 90 of the Family Relations Act*, BCLI Report No. 48, at 42 (Mar. 2007), http://www.bcli.org/pages/projects/parentalsupport/Parental_Support_FRA_section_90_Report.pdf (accessed June 2, 2007).

[118] Criminal Code of Canada, R.S.C, c. C-46, § 215 (1) (1985).

(iii) Support of Family Care (End of Life)

In January 2004, the federal government enacted changes to employment insurance law to permit eligible workers to receive compassionate care (employment insurance) benefits. The benefits are only paid for a maximum of six weeks to a person who has to be absent from work to provide care or support to a gravely ill family member at risk of dying within the next 26 weeks.[119] The policy requires family to obtain a medical certificate of impending death from the physician. The definition of "family member" was expanded in 2006.[120] However, the scope and other eligibility criteria such as substantial diminution of weekly income significantly limit its use by family.[121] On the other hand, almost every province permits some *unpaid* compassionate care leave in its employment standards,[122] as does the federal government under the Canada Labour Code in its standards for federally regulated employees.[123]

G. The Right to Labour

Labour is a shared federal-provincial responsibility, with each government regulating those sectors for which it has constitutional responsibility.[124] Canada has provided a number of protections for workers in employment laws and human rights laws to safeguard them from discrimination in the workplace. In some provinces, such as British

---

[119] Service Canada, *Employment Insurance (EI) Compassionate Care Benefits*, http://www1.servicecanada.gc.ca/en/ei/types/compassionate_care.shtml (May 8, 2007).

[120] Service Canada, *Employment Insurance Compassionate Care Benefits - who is considered a family member?,* http://www1.servicecanada.gc.ca/en/ei/types/compassionate_care.shtml#family (accessed May 26, 2007).

[121] Katie Osborne & Naomi Margo, Health Council of Canada, *Compassionate Care Benefit: Analysis and Evaluation*, 20, 28, http://www.healthcouncilcanada.ca/docs/papers/2005/Compassionate_Care_BenefitsEN.pdf (accessed May 30, 2007) (while the government estimated that there might be up to 270,000 compassionate care claimants a year, in 2004/5, only 7,150 claim benefits were paid across the country).

[122] *See e.g.*, Laws of Manitoba, The Employment Standards Code Amendment Act, http://web2.gov.mb.ca/laws/statutes/2003/c00703e.php (accessed June 2, 2007); Legislative Assembly of British Columbia, *Employment Standards (Compassionate Care Leave) Amendment Act*, 2006, http://qp.gov.bc.ca/38th2nd/1st_read/gov08-1.htm.

[123] Canada Labour Code, R.S.C., c. L-2, § 209.2 (1985); *see generally* Yosie Saint-Cyr, *Compassionate Care EI Benefits-A Reminder*, http://www.hrinfodesk.com/Articles/compassionatecarebenefitsandleave.htm (accessed June 2, 2007).

[124] Michel Fourzly & Marc Gervais, *Human Resources and Social Development Canada, Collective Agreements and Older Workers in Canada* (Human Resources and Social Development Canada Labour Program 2002), 6, http://www.hrsdc.gc.ca/en/lp/spila/wlb/pdf/caowc-dftaccc-en.pdf (2002).

Columbia, this protection only goes to age 65.[125] Even with age-based equality rights, older adults who work are in a vulnerable position in hiring and employment, as well as in work conditions. Sponsored older immigrants who tend to have low education and lack English or French language skills may be particularly vulnerable to labour exploitation.

More than 22 percent of recent retirees return to some paid work after a "first retirement," and for over one third of them, it is for financial reasons.[126] The "official" unemployment rate among seniors is low compared to other age groups, but is growing.[127]

(i) Mandatory Retirement

No Canadian law specifically endorses mandatory retirement. However, a combination of lack of human rights protections or employment standards against age discrimination in some jurisdictions and high court judicial interpretations created a legal environment in the late 1980s and early 1990s that effectively permitted mandatory retirement as reasonably justified across many occupations. During that period, the Supreme Court of Canada heard a series of legal challenges under the *Charter* to mandatory retirement policies in union and university contracts, with significant differences in views evidenced among the judiciary. Mandatory retirement policies have increasingly been recognized as having a differential negative impact on women and recent immigrants, as both groups tend not to have the traditional work force trajectory of men.

In 2006, Ontario removed the upper age limit in its human rights law, effectively abolishing a significant proportion of mandatory retirement in that jurisdiction.[128] Mandatory retirement was already banned in several provinces and territories, including Alberta, Manitoba, Quebec, Prince Edward Island, Nunavut, the Yukon and the Northwest Territories. However, today, even where age protection exists, older employees may be required to retire in some occupations if it is deemed a *bona fide* occupational requirement.

It has been suggested that the driving force for changes to mandatory retirement in Canada will be business economics, not human rights considerations.[129] In 2002, about 14.5 percent (one in seven) of

---

[125] Human Rights Code, R.S.B.C., c. 210, § 1 (1996); *see also* Saskatchewan Human Rights Code, S.S. 1979, c. S-24.1, § 2 (1).

[126] National Advisory Council on Aging, *supra* n. 16, at 53-54.

[127] National Advisory Council on Aging, *supra* n. 16, at 53-54.

[128] Human Rights Code R.S.O., c. 19, § 10 (1990) (as amended).

[129] Soden, *Advising the Older Client*, *supra* n. 34, at 251-304 (contributor Charmaine Spencer, *Discrimination- the law and older adults* in *Advising the Older Client*).

seniors "indicated they were forced into retirement because of mandatory retirement policies."[130] An additional 25 percent "involuntarily" retire for health reasons, or because of job disruptions such as layoffs or restructuring.[131] Older workers' knowledge and skills often do not match current business needs, impeding potential re-employment. Although this has been recognized for almost two decades,[132] at a policy level, there have been relatively weak efforts in the federal and provincial employment training schemes or within private industry to effectively retain or retrain older workers.[133] Moreover, there has been little if any legal discussion of the inequity underlying this omission.

(ii) Early Retirement

Until recently, the trend in Canada has been towards early retirement (i.e., before the age of 65), particularly among people who had pensionable benefits.[134] Early retirement was often encouraged during periods of high unemployment, particularly among older workers, in the hope of creating more job openings for younger workers. The proportion of older workers receiving unemployment benefits includes many who have not been able to find employment, and for all intents and purposes, are involuntarily "retired."[135] This is often the case for manual workers for whom demand is low and who are often in poor health.[136]

(iii) Phased Retirement

The Income Tax Regulations[137] regarding employees accruing pension benefits under a defined benefit Registered Pension Plan (RPP)

---

130 National Advisory Council on Aging, *supra* n. 16, 52.

131 National Advisory Council on Aging, *supra* n. 16, 53-54.

132 *See e.g.* Mary Trueman, *Training of Older Workers in Canada, Training Discussion Paper No. 22* (ILO Publications 1989).

133 Marjorie Armstrong-Stassen & Andrew Templer, *Adapting Training for Older Employees: the Canadian Response to an Aging Workforce*, 24 J. of Mgt. Dev. 57 (2005).

134 *See* Patrick Kieran, *Early retirement trends, Perspectives on Labour and Income, 2* (9), Statistics Canada Cat. No. 75- 001-XIE, 7-13, http://www.statcan.ca/english/studies/75-001/archive/2001/pear2001013004s4a01.pdf (accessed May 29, 2007).

135 Geoff Rowe & Huan Nguyen, *Older workers and the labour market, Perspectives on Labour and Income*, 3 (12), Statistics Canada Cat. No. 75- 001-XIE, 23-26 (2002), http://www.statcan.ca/english/freepub/75-001-XIE/0120275-001-XIE.pdf (accessed May 29, 2007). *See also* Wendy Pyper & Philip Giles, *Approaching retirement, Perspectives on Labour and Income, 3* (9), Statistics Canada Cat. No. 75- 001-XIE, 5-12 (2002), http://www.statcan.ca/english/freepub/75-001-XIE/0090275-001-XIE.pdf (accessed May 29, 2007).

136 Wendy Pyper, *Aging, health and work, Perspectives on Labour and Income, 7* (2), Statistics Canada Cat. No. 75- 001-XIE, 5-15 (2006), http://www.statcan.ca/english/freepub/75-001-XIE/10206/art-1.pdf (accessed May 29, 2007).

137 C.R.C., c. 945 (enabled by Income Tax Act, R.S.C. 1985, c. 1 (5th Supp.)).

currently prevent employers from offering phased retirement programs that would permit older workers to continue working part-time, while at the same time receiving a partial pension. Amendments to the Income Tax Regulations were proposed in 2007 to allow an employee to receive pension benefits from a defined benefit RPP and simultaneously accrue further benefits, subject to certain constraints. These changes will be in effect for the first time in 2008.

H. Income Tax Law

Income tax policy and the laws supporting it carry a number of special provisions for older adults. In addition to the basic "personal tax credit," seniors benefit from an "age credit" to help reduce the amount of taxes owing.[138] Some may also be eligible for disability credits in case of permanent disability, and deductions for out of pocket medical expenses.[139] On a spouse's death, registered retirement benefits can be "rolled over" to the surviving spouse without triggering tax consequences.[140] Very recently, changes to income tax regulations have begun permitting income splitting for seniors.[141]

IV. FUTURE TRENDS

Several needs related to older adults are beginning to be recognized and addressed in Canada. There is a substantial and growing need for continuing education on issues of law and aging available for the legal profession and professionals in other disciplines who represent or serve older people. There is a pressing need to better inform/educate the general public about issues affecting older adults and families or others who may be helping them. This begins with raising public awareness about rights, obligations, benefits, and resources relevant to the lives of older adults. This can occur in many different ways, including consumer guides and handbooks, internet sites, group presentations and individual counselling through specialized legal information clinics. While 'self-help' tools and resources available at no

[138] *Income Tax Act,* R.S.C. 1985, c. 1 (5th Supp.). For general description, *see* Canada Revenue Agency, "What you can deduct," http://www.cra-arc.gc.ca/tax/individuals/topics/income-tax/return/completing/deductions/menu-e.html (accessed May 29, 2007).

[139] *Id.*

[140] Canada Revenue Agency Income Tax Interpretation Bulletin, IT 500 R, "Registered Retirement Savings Plans -- Death of an Annuitant", § 27-28 (Dec. 18, 1996), http://www.cra-arc.gc.ca/E/pub/tp/it500r/it500r-e.html (accessed May 29, 2007).

[141] Department of Finance Canada, "Tax relief for seniors", http://www.fin.gc.ca/pensioncalc/factsheet_e.html (accessed May 29, 2007).

or a nominal cost will be an increasingly valuable aid to many older adults, these courses depend on the individual's ability to access and utilize the tools. In recent years, a number of Canadian guides have been under development by non-profit associations to aid the understanding of older adults, family caregivers and persons working with older adults of general legal and ethical issues related to care giving, end of life, filial support, and substitute decision making.[142]

There is an ongoing need to improve access to justice for older Canadians. Older adults on fixed incomes often have their legal needs overlooked, and can find access to legal remedies highly problematic. They often have little or no means to afford legal assistance for relatively simple, but sometimes time-consuming, legal matters. Many older adults may experience difficulties communicating in English or French, or may lack basic literacy, let alone the capacity to achieve good legal literacy to understand and enforce their rights. At present, general purpose legal aid clinics, where they exist, are not set up to address the types of issues or to meet the often complex set of needs of older adults in a multidisciplinary and holistic manner. As a result, there is a pressing need for specialized government-subsidized legal aid clinics in each province to provide formal legal advice and representation for older adults on individual matters, as well as advocacy on systemic issues, drawing on proven models such as that of the Advocacy Centre for the Elderly.

There is strong need for critical legal analysis in the areas of law affecting older adults, whether that is a feminist analysis that looks beyond middle age or other critical approaches. Among other things, this analysis will need to examine the intersection of aging, gender, ability, race and other statuses in the context of social policy and law. The law is seldom neutral or objective in its application to the lives of older adults, and aging is a highly gendered issue.

The practice of elder law in Canada is likely to continue, in large part, in conjunction with other fields of law. Although it is an approach which has not yet been widely adopted in the country, future elder law practice may need to draw on multiple disciplines. There are several different models to consider, including case management approaches to addressing client files that present a combination of legal, accounting, tax, health and social issues. For example, a lawyer may act as the primary "point person" for the coordination of service delivery by a

[142] *E.g.* guides produced by the Canadian Palliative Care Association, http://www.chpca.net/home.htm (accessed June 2, 2007); Caregivers Coalition, http://www.ccc-ccan.ca/ (accessed June 2, 2007).

variety of professionals whose services are independently engaged by the client. Some practitioners may consider opening professional multidisciplinary practices comprised of lawyers, accountants and others such as social workers. Future practice might include the sale of ancillary products such as long-term care insurance and financial investments for the delivery of a one-stop, full service to older clients. However, all of these options will need to be carefully considered for their practicality and adherence to provincial codes of conduct, the ethical implications, and potential liability for representations made by other professionals to one's clients.

Canada has begun to see important legal and practice research unfold in recent years. This research will affect older adults and practitioners. For a decade, the country has been implementing promising practices for addressing abuse and neglect of older adults in the community and institutional settings, and may be starting to consider some national strategies in the area. Capacity assessment guides for lawyers, judges, physicians and social workers that are adaptable to the laws of each jurisdiction are likely to become more commonplace. The Western provinces have been considering the development of uniform power of attorney legislation for the common law provinces of Canada.[143] There are slowly developing efforts to raise understanding about advance care planning, along with its underlying laws and ethical principles, among lawyers, doctors and social workers. Over time, the country will likely see the development of best professional practices in the advising and drafting of legal instruments in the planning for incapability.

Several new issues are being explored and identified, including: the legal needs and matters affecting special populations of older adults, including older women, older sponsored immigrants and ethnic seniors; older adults in the penal system; older Inuit and First Nations persons; older adults with developmental disabilities; and older adults who are gay, lesbian, bisexual or transsexual. Increasingly, older adults and others are seeking information and advice from a variety of professionals on the wide range of supportive housing and long-term care facility matters, and a specialized practice in long-term care law is likely to develop over time. Many traditional areas of contract and administrative law well may be reviewed, using an aging lens in the future.

---

[143] Western Canada Law Reform Agencies, *Enduring Powers of Attorney: Areas for Reform, Consultation Paper #1* (June 2004), http://www.law.ualberta.ca/alri/docs/wclraCP1.pdf (accessed May 29, 2007).

There are some existing and potential areas of conflict among professions when it comes to legal issues and the respective scope of practice will need to be clarified over time. For example, practitioners find that real estate agents, social workers and other housing and care professionals, as well as gerontological consultants, sometimes offer what may appear to be legal advice to clients, or practice illegally within the fields of other professions, but without the requisite education, licensing or recognition of potential liability.

Various Canadian stakeholders such as the Canadian Bar Association, Canadian Centre for Elder Law Studies, and the National Institute on Law, Policy and Aging have a variety of comparative law studies in various stages of planning or development. They are also beginning to examine matters on a cross-jurisdictional or an inter-provincial level. In addition, they have begun working internationally with bodies such as the Commission of Law and Aging in Washington D.C. and the faculties of law at Wake Forest University and Stetson University's Centre for Excellence in Elder Law.

V. CONCLUSION

Canada has witnessed a number of significant changes in social policy and law during the past four decades. One of the important bright notes is the reality that life is more financially secure for many older adults, as a result of the maturation of the Canada Pension Plan and enhancements to the public pension system. Yet, inequities remain for subgroups of older adults, including many older women and minorities. Retrenchment in the area of public pensions continues to loom, creating the prospect of a much less secure future for many.

There has been progress made in recent years to better recognize the diversity of relationships among adults, with expansion of policy definitions of 'spouse' and 'family'. However, these policy changes have often been reactive -- reflecting of the efforts of interested individuals pushing for change, rather than proactive direction in social policy planning. Further, many of these changes maintain the *status quo,* leaving the bulk of social responsibility for caregiving resting on individuals and family, and not treated as a collective (state) responsibility. While there have been significant advancements in individual rights in areas of substitute decision making and alternatives to guardianship, collective rights to affordable and appropriate housing and adequate health care have lagged across the lifespan.

Other areas such as protection of older adults' human rights in key areas of employment, accommodation, health care and other services have also lagged significantly, and with very little discourse in these areas as to how to balance interests. Ageism is still manifest in the country, although hidden from view. Mechanisms to engage the public discourse on what the future of aging and intergenerational relationships *might look like* and *should look like* are at continued risk. It is in this mixed environment that the capacity of the country to recognize and respond appropriately to the social as well as legal needs and interests of older adults will continue to evolve.

While law and aging policy in Canada may face many challenges and more transitions in the future, the future of elder law in Canada looks very encouraging as the country softly greys.

[12]

The Amendment of the Employment Measure Act: Japanese Anti-Age Discrimination Law

Ryoko Sakuraba

Kobe University

The Employment Measure Act, which was enacted in 1966 and proclaimed the general principles of Japan's labor market policies, was revised in 2007. This paper sheds light on the meaning and effect of Article 10, to which much attention was paid as Japan's first anti-age discrimination regulation. Article 10 stipulates that firms must provide equal opportunities to workers in relation to recruitment and hiring irrespective of age, thereby making a former 'duty to endeavor' into a 'legal duty.' As a result, job offers with age limits may be rejected by employment placement organizations and discriminated workers may claim damages in tort suits.

However, there are some doubts as to the effectiveness of Article 10 due to its broad exemptions, including hiring only 'new graduates.' Therefore, in view of its constitutional basis and policy objectives as well as limited outreach, this paper observes that anti-age discrimination regulations in Japan still indicate the nature of the employment policy approach rather than the human rights approach. Regulations on age-based treatment appear to be merely a patchwork rather than a conclusive anti-age discrimination law.

Apart from the anti-age discrimination provision, in order to improve the employment management of youth and foreigners, the 2007 revision added an obligation of employers to report to Public Employment Security Offices in the event of the employment and separation of foreign workers. It also adopted 'duty to endeavor' provisions and guidelines, both of which recommended employers to take various measures, such as the introduction of a recruitment process for old graduates, employment of youth as regular workers, support of foreign workers in claiming for workers' compensation benefits, and so forth. This paper provides an analysis that though these measures based on 'duty to endeavor' have only weak legal effects, they seem an appropriate means to attain their policy objectives while not giving rise to the issues of 'reverse discrimination' or 'intrusion into freedom of contracts.'

I. Introduction

The Employment Measure Act (hereinafter, the EMA), which was first enacted in 1966 and proclaimed the general principles of Japan's labor market policies, was revised in 2007 with the amendments taking effect as of October 2007. Among the changed and newly introduced articles, the 'anti-age discrimination in relation to recruitment and hiring' provision (Article10) attracted special attention.[1] In addition, this amendment created a

[1] Regarding the developments of the EMA, see: Noboru Yamashita, *Boshu Saiyo ni okeru Nenrei Seigen Kanwa to Chukonenreisha no Saishushoku*, Rodo Horitsu Junpo 21 (No. 1525, 2002); Keiichiro Hamaguchi, *Nenrei Sabetsu*, 79 Horitsu Jiho 53 (No.3, 2007); Takeshi Yanagisawa, *Atarashii Koyo Taisaku Hosei*, Kikan Rodo Ho 110 (No.218, 2007). Regarding the regulations on

duty of employers to endeavor to improve the employment management of youth and foreign workers. Furthermore, the system of mandatory notification was introduced, in which employers are obligated to notify the Public Employment Security Offices in the event of the employment or separation of foreign workers.

This paper begins with an explanation of the major features of the amended EMA (Section II). In particular, it sheds light on the meaning and effect of the 'anti-age discrimination in relation to recruitment and hiring' provision. Section III is devoted to the analysis of the provision's nature from the perspective whether it deals with an age equality issue or an employment policy issue. Finally, issues remaining after the amended EMA and the possibility of its future developments are addressed in Section IV.

II. Features of the EMA 2007 Revision

1. Anti-Age Discrimination in Relation to Recruitment and Hiring

(1) Backgrounds and Contents of the EMA 2001 Revision

Regulations against age limits for recruitment and hiring have been gradually reinforced in Japan in recent years. The first step was the revision of the EMA made in 2001.

After the collapse of the bubble economy in the 1990s, persons above the age of 40 and once unemployed as a result of their company's restructuring found it difficult to obtain new jobs for the following two reasons. First, the typical recruiting practices in Japanese firms had an adverse impact on unemployed middle-aged or older workers. In the case of long-term regular workers, recruitment activities customarily began during the spring of the year prior to graduation of high schools, colleges or universities. New recruits entered their companies immediately following graduation and started working without specification of the jobs in which they would engage. They were expected to acquire occupational skills through on-the-job training and work reassignments over a long time, and would gain promotion from within. Thus, persons above the age of 40 and who had graduated from school many years ago found it quite difficult to obtain new jobs. Second, mid-career hiring, which refers to hiring those who have worked elsewhere, is becoming prevalent recently; however, even those companies that have opened their doors to mid-career hiring often set age limits for recruitment and hiring, such as "No one above 40 admitted."[2]

---

setting mandatory retirement age, see: Hideyuki Morito, *Graying Japan, Swaying the Policymaker*, 16 The International Journal of Comparative Labour Law and Industrial Relations 25 (No. 1, 2000); Noboru Yamashita, *Act Concerning Stabilization of Employment of Older Persons*, 4 Japan Labor Review 71 (No. 3, 2007); Makoto Fujimoto, *Employment of Older People after the Amendment of the Act Concerning Stabilization of Employment of Older Persons: Current State of Affairs and Challenges*, 5 Japan Labor Review 59 (No.2, 2008).

[2] According to the white paper of the Ministry of Labor in 2000, the average age limit for recruitment was 41.1 years of age.

Under these circumstances, labor economists and trade unions began to contend that Japan should introduce anti-age discrimination laws to abolish the practice of imposing such age limits. Accordingly, the EMA was first revised in 2001 to provide that proprietors must, when regarded as necessary in order for workers to effectively display their abilities, 'endeavor to provide equal opportunity' to workers in relation to recruitment and hiring irrespective of age (Former Article 7); also, ten allowable reasons for age limits were set out by the guidelines of the Ministry of Health, Labor and Welfare. Therefore, without any of those allowable reasons, firms were required to make an effort not to impose age limits on recruitment or hiring.

The allowable reasons could be divided into three types. First, age limits for recruitment and hiring were considered justifiable as occupational qualifications in cases where:

a-1. There is a requirement for smooth business with customers in the particular age brackets whom the proprietor targets in selling goods and providing services.

a-2. There is a requirement for authenticity in the arts or entertainment.

a-3. There is a requirement for the prevention of accidents and ensuring safety at work in view of the frequency of accidents at that workplace.

a-4. A certain level of physical functions including strength or eyesight, which generally deteriorates as a result of aging, need to be maintained to perform job duties smoothly.

Second, age limits could be set in order to comply with statutes. Firms could set age limits when:

b-1. They employ only persons aged 60 years or older, or persons in certain age brackets, the employment of which is encouraged by employment policies including the provision of subsidies.

b-2. There is a statutory age limit for that particular work.

Third, even in the following cases where age was not relevant as an occupational qualification, age limits were allowed to be set in order to maintain typical Japanese employment practices, namely recruitment from new graduates, long-term employment until the mandatory retirement age[3] and age-based pay systems, where:

c-1. Proprietors recruit and hire persons in particular age brackets, such as 'new graduates,' in order to provide them with skills development over a long period of service.

c-2. Proprietors recruit and hire persons in particular under-represented age brackets in order to restore and maintain the workforce's age balance, and thus maintain their continued business and succession of skills and knowledge.

c-3. Proprietors recruit and hire persons in particular age brackets in consideration of their

[3] A 'mandatory retirement age' signifies a system that causes employment contract relations to terminate automatically, regardless of the worker's wishes, when the worker reaches a certain age.

mandatory retirement age and necessary periods between hiring and retirement, in order for workers to display their ability effectively or develop the ability to perform their work duties.

c-4. Proprietors recruit and hire persons in particular age brackets where wage systems for existing workers would have to be modified due to age-related pay systems in the establishments being not suitable for hiring middle-aged or older persons.

These guidelines were criticized for putting in place too many allowable reasons.[4]

(2) Legal Effects of the Duty to Endeavor under the EMA 2001 Revision

In addition, the legal effects derived from the 'duty to endeavor' were considered weak for the following reasons. Where a firm offered Public Employment Security Offices, which provided free employment placement under the Employment Security Act (hereinafter, the ESA), to post their job offerings while imposing an age limit on job seekers, officials could ask the firm to repeal the age limit; or where the firm did not repeal it, to give one of the ten allowable reasons for the maintenance of the age limit. However, offers for posting job offers setting age limits without any of the allowable reasons may not be rejected under the 'duty to endeavor' provision of the EMA in 2002. Article 5-5 of the ESA provides that "Public Employment Security Offices and employment placement business providers shall accept all offers for the posting of job offerings; this is provided, however, that such offers may be rejected if their contents violate any laws or regulations." Meanwhile, offers setting age limits without any of the allowable reasons, which violate not a legal duty but only a 'duty to endeavor,' should be accepted.

Moreover, in the case of firms refusing to employ workers on the grounds of their age without any allowable reasons, these refused workers were not interpreted to have rights to claim for employment or damages. Article 3 of the Labor Standards Act (hereinafter, the LSA) of 1947, which states the principles of equal treatment applicable to labor contracts, prohibits only discrimination by reasons of the nationality, social status and creed of workers. The Japanese constitution promulgated in 1946 contains the guarantee of equality under the law, but prohibition of discrimination is limited to that on the grounds of race, creed, sex, social status or family origin (Article 14, Paragraph1). Age discrimination, which is not clearly prohibited by these laws, nevertheless could be arguably interpreted to be unlawful as an unreasonable and differentiating treatment violating the general principle of equality derived from these provisions, and in the spirit of the former Article 7 of the EMA. However, this interpretation was not adopted by labor law scholars in light of the Supreme Court decision in the *Mitsubishi Jushi* case.[5]

The *Mitsubishi Jushi* case involved denial of employment to a worker who did not

[4] Hideyuki Morito, *Koyo Seisaku to shite no Nenrei Sabetsu Kinshi*, in *Shogai Geneki Jidai no Koyo Seisaku* 85, 126 (Atsushi Seike ed., Nippon Hyoronsha 2001). Thus, the 2004 revision of the OPESA also obliged proprietors to explain their reasons for imposing age limits on applicants.

[5] The *Mitsubishi Jushi* Case, Supreme Court, Dec. 12, 1973, Minshu 27-11-1536.

disclose his history of campus activism at a job interview. The firm refused to formally hire him because it emerged that he had told a lie at the interview. Denial of employment for such reasons was alleged to run counter to the principle of equal treatment in the LSA, as well as the constitutional guarantee of freedom of beliefs (Article 19) and the equality clause (Article 14). However, the Supreme Court stated that the fundamental human rights prescribed by the constitution did not directly apply to the acts of private persons. Moreover, the court held that the principle of equal treatment in the LSA was limited to post-hiring working conditions and was not applicable to the process of hiring. The Court stressed that the principle of freedom of contracts should be applied to cases where there was no contravention of statutory or other special restrictions on hiring practices.

As such, age discrimination, which was not explicitly enumerated as prohibited grounds under the Constitution or the LSA and had just started to be regulated by the 'duty to endeavor,' was not interpreted to be unlawful.[6] Thus, former Article 7 and the guidelines were criticized for being in its nature a 'duty to endeavor' and setting forth too many allowable reasons.

(3) Reinforcement of Regulations by the EMA 2007 Revision

Apart from unemployed older workers, youth unemployment[7] had begun to be recognized as a social challenge at the time of the amendment made in 2007. Normal recruitment practices based on age barred persons in their 20s or 30s from stable jobs, including those who had received a higher level of education. Some persons in their late 20s or 30s—so-called 'older-younger persons,'—who had graduated from school following the burst of the economic bubble and found it quite difficult to secure work of their choice at that time, had been looking for a stable job while working at a temporary job. Some of them had not been able to obtain stable employment since their graduation. In addition, movement between jobs is not rare among the younger generation these days. It was reported in the 1990s that 50% of high school graduates and 30% of university graduates leave their first jobs within 3 years.[8]

Older-younger workers and youth unemployment were recognized as urgent social issues, with increasing concerns about the enlarged income gap among nations and rapid progress of the aging population.[9] Therefore, in June 2007 the following provision of the EMA was made compulsory:

---

[6] Yamashita, above n.1 (concerning the EMA), at 25.

[7] According to the OECD report published in 2008 (Jobs for Youth: Japan), the unemployment rate of persons 15 to 24 years of age was 7.7% (twice that of those 25 to 54 years of age) in Japan in 2007 and below the OECD average of 13.4%. However, the long-term unemployment rate rose to 21% among those 15 to 24 years of age and was over the OECD average of 19.6%.

[8] Regarding youth employment, see Yuki Honda, *"Freeters": Young Atypical Workers in Japan*, 2 Japan Labor Review 5 (No.3, 2005).

[9] According to the white paper of the Ministry of Welfare, Labour and Health in 2006, the population aging rate (the percentage of persons aged 65 or over) was 20.8 % in 2006.

Article 10: Proprietors must, when it is regarded as necessary under the Ordinance of the Ministry of Health, Labour, and Welfare, in order for workers to effectively display their abilities, provide equal opportunity to workers in relation to recruitment and employment irrespective of age, in accordance with the Ordinance of the Ministry of Health, Labour and Welfare.

This provision has the following legal effects. First, the Minister of Health, Labour and Welfare may give advice, guidance or recommendations to firms violating this Article (Article 32). Second, when a worker is treated unfavorably on the grounds of age in relation to hiring, he or she may follow the procedures of the Act on Promoting the Resolution of Individual Labor-Related Disputes to solve her or his dispute, asking for assistance (advice and guidance) from the Prefectural Labor Bureau (Articles 1 and 4).[10]

These two enforcement systems are not totally new, since they could be taken under the former 'soft-law approach.' However, under the new 'hard-law approach' there are two additional routes to rectify age limits. Where firms provide job offers setting age limits to employment placement organizations (Public Employment Security Offices or private employment placement providers), in light of the provision's strengthened mandatory character, they may decline to post their offers under Article of 5-5 of the ESA, which stipulates that job offers violating statutes may be rejected.

When a firm fails to employ a person on the grounds of age and as a result that person files a lawsuit, the court will not order the firm to hire that person in consideration of the principle of freedom of contracts. This provision merely obliges employers to give equal opportunity, and does not give individuals the right to demand employment.[11] However, the court may order the firm to pay some consolation money for non-economic damages to the discriminated worker in tort suits (Civil Code, Article 709) where appropriate, as in the case of violation of the Act on Securing, etc. of Equal Opportunity and Treatment between Men and Women in Employment (hereinafter, the EEOA) comprehensively prohibiting sex discrimination in employment.[12]

(4) Justifiable Reasons for Age Limits under the 2007 Revision

It should be noted that the Ordinance issued on this article maintained some of the former exemptions while also deleting other exemptions, in accordance with the decision accompanying the bill that the exemptions should be reduced as much as possible. In the following six cases, proprietors can:

a. Set age limits for hiring workers in accordance with mandatory retirement age.
b. Set age limits for hiring workers where there is a statutory age limit for the

[10] They cannot ask for mediation by the Dispute Adjustment Commission, since the act excludes disputes in relation to hiring from mediation process (Article 5).

[11] See, Yanagisawa, above n. 1, at 116.

[12] Discriminated workers are not considered entitled to claim for employment; however, failure to hire by reason of sex is interpreted to constitute a cause of action under the tort provision.

particular work.

c. Recruit only new graduates who are youth, or below certain ages, in order to give them the opportunity to develop and improve their occupational abilities over a long period of service.
d. Hire persons in particular under-represented age brackets in order to maintain the succession of occupational skills and knowledge.
e. Set age limits for hiring where there is a requirement for authenticity in the arts or entertainment.
f. Employ only persons aged 60 years or older, or persons in certain age brackets, the employment of which is encouraged by the state's employment policies.

As a result, the following four reasons under the former Article 7 were not included in the new Ordinance, that is smooth business with customers, prevention of accidents at work, maintenance of workers' physical functions, and maintenance of age-based wage systems.

The remaining six justifiable reasons have the following meaning. According to exemption (a), for example, where companies have a mandatory retirement age at 60 years and they want to hire workers under contracts for an indefinite period, they can set limits for hiring at age 60 in accordance with the mandatory retirement age. In order to understand this exemption, one should know the regulations against setting a mandatory retirement age under the Act Concerning Stabilization of Employment of Older Persons, which was enacted in 1971 and amended in 2004 (hereinafter, the OPESA). The OPESA stipulates that when an employer sets a mandatory retirement age, it cannot be below the age of 60 (Article 8). In light of this, companies can maintain the mandatory retirement age at 60 years or over to the extent that they comply with the regulations for workers over the age of 60; according to Article 9 of the act, when an employer fixes the retirement age it shall conduct any one of the measures listed in the items below in order to secure stable employment for older workers until the age of 65:

a. Raising the mandatory retirement age;
b. Introduction of a continuous employment system (refers to the system of continuing to employ an older person who wishes to keep working following their mandatory retirement); or
c. Abolition of the mandatory retirement age.

'Continuous employment systems' include the system under which employees meeting certain objective requirements, such as a certain level of physical strength,[13] following the employee's mandatory retirement, are given the opportunities to conclude fixed term contracts with their employers again. Against this legal background, many companies maintain the mandatory retirement age at 60 years and provide workers between the ages of

[13] The selection criteria can be set forth by a labor-management agreement, which is concluded between an employer and a union organizing a majority of the workers at an establishment or, in its absence, a person representing a majority of the workers.

60 -65 years opportunities to work under fixed term contracts.[14] In such cases companies can set limits for hiring at the age of 60 years, in accordance with the mandatory retirement age.[15]

According to exemption (b), when persons in a particular age bracket are prohibited from engaging in certain jobs by statutory provisions, firms can set age limits for hiring based on the provisions. 'Minors,' which refers to persons under the age of 18, are considered, when compared to adults, physically and mentally immature and technically unskilled to require special safety and health protections. Based on that idea, an employer is not permitted to employ a person under the age of 18 between 10:00 p.m. and 5:00 a.m (Article 61 of the LSA), to have persons under the age of 18 work underground (Article 63 of the LSA), and to engage such persons in hazardous and harmful duties (Article 62).[16] The Security Service Act also prohibits persons under the age of 18 from working as a security guard and prohibits security service companies from engaging such persons in security service (Article 14). The Explosives Handling Act prohibits persons under the age of 18 from handling explosives and stipulates that any individual shall not engage such persons in handling explosives (Article 23).

According to exemption (c), when a firm hires workers under indefinite contracts, it is permitted to set age limits for hiring on the grounds that the firm requires workers to develop their job skills through long-term employment.[17]

The meaning of exemption (d) is somehow complex and would be better understood

---

[14] In the survey conducted by the JILPT in 2006 on firms with 300 workers or more, more than 90% of them introduced the continuous employment system rather than elimination or extension of the mandatory retirement age. Also, around 70% of these firms established selection criteria. More than 80% of these firms use fixed term contracts to employ older people beyond the mandatory retirement age. See Fujimoto, above n. 1.

[15] This exemption is applied in the case of employment under indefinite terms. In the case of employment under fixed term contracts, age limits for hiring cannot be set in accordance with the mandatory retirement age. The age limits must coincide with the mandatory retirement age. For example, where firms set the mandatory retirement age at 60 years, they cannot set the age limits for hiring at 55, on the grounds that a 5 year period is necessary for workers to develop occupational skills until the mandatory retirement age is reached.

[16] Hazardous duties include cleaning, oiling, inspecting or repairing the dangerous parts of any machinery or power transmission apparatus while in operation, putting on or taking off the driving belts or ropes of any machinery or power transmission apparatus, operating a crane driven by power, engaging in any other dangerous work as specified by the ordinances, or handling heavy materials as specified by the ordinances. Harmful duties include the handling of poisons, powerful drugs or other injurious substances, or the handling of explosive, combustible or inflammable substances, or in places where dust, powder, harmful gas or radiation is generated or where there are high temperatures or pressure levels, or other places which are dangerous or injurious to the safety, health, or welfare of workers.

[17] It is to be noted that an employer is not permitted, when attempting to justify setting age limits on the grounds of this exemption, to require workers to have job experiences or satisfy the upper age limits, such as 'persons between the ages of 20 and 30 years,' and 'persons below the ages of 30 years with 5 years experience in similar jobs.'

through the use of some illustrations. For example, firms wishing to hire system engineers under indefinite contracts are permitted to set age limits for recruitment as 'persons aged between 30-34 years.' This is in the case where firms currently employ only 20 system engineers between the ages of 30-34 years, while also employing 50 system engineers between the ages of 25-29 and 45 system engineers between the ages of 35-39 years; thus, system engineers aged between 30-34 years can be considered underrepresented for the job. The age range, which is used to decide whether workers at certain ages are underrepresented, must be 5-10 years between the ages of 30-49 years. The job category is to be specified in accordance with the small occupational category provided by the Ministry of Health, Labour and Welfare, such as 'system engineers,' rather than the general term 'engineers.' If the number of workers belonging to certain age brackets in certain jobs is less than half the number of persons belonging to the upper and lower age brackets in that undertaking, they are deemed to be 'underrepresented.' Accordingly, the new guidelines made it more difficult for firms to meet the requirements of this exemption.

According to exemption (e), firms can set age limits when they want to hire an actor who is to play a child's part. However, they cannot set age limits for clothes salespersons on the grounds that their shops target customers in certain age brackets, since this reason does not constitute 'requirements for authenticity in the arts or entertainment.'

The exemption (f) allows firms to employ only persons aged 60 years or older, or persons in certain age brackets, the employment of which is encouraged by employment policies. One example of 'the employment encouraged by employment policies' is 'Trial Employment,' under which the Public Employment Security Offices refer persons who experience considerably difficulty in finding new jobs because of their experience, knowledge and their personal categorizations such as 'younger persons' (persons under the age of 40 years) or 'older persons' (persons over the age of 45 years). Firms can employ these workers temporarily, and they can receive certain wage subsidies for three months; when the firms finally decide to hire those workers after three months, they can receive other subsidies in certain cases.

(5) Effectiveness of the Anti-Age Discrimination Provision

There is a survey showing that recruitment practices with age limits are being reduced.[18] Despite this, some labor law scholars doubt the effectiveness of the new anti-age discrimination provision. The Ordinance maintains still broad exemptions, such as hiring only 'new graduates.'[19] In the case of denial of employment on the grounds of age without any of justifiable reasons, the remedy for discriminated workers will be nominal, such as the provision of consolation money or compensation for some transportation expenses. No

[18] According to the survey conducted by Zenkoku Kyujin Joho Kyokai in the fall of 2008, the rate of job offerings without age limits on job seekers increased from 55.3% to 76.3% after amendment of the EMA. http://www.zenkyukyo.or.jp/pdf/age_release.pdf

[19] Yanagisawa, above n.1, at 116.

doubt it would be quite difficult to adduce sufficient evidence to establish that age motivated a firm's failure to hire, where they do not at face value set age limits for recruitment and there are no direct effects. Moreover, Article 10 does not clearly cover indirect age discrimination. For example, age-neutral practices with discriminatory effects on youth or seniors, such as imposing the requirements of certain periods of occupational experience on job applicants, would not, per se, be construed as being unlawful.

2. Measures to Promote Youth Employment

As seen before, while normal recruitment practices targeting new graduates have had positive effects on the smooth transition from school to employment, they have also presented a high hurdle for those who once deviated from the normal hiring tracks. A series of reforms have been introduced in recent years to combat youth unemployment, including setting up a one-stop service center for young job seekers (so-called job cafés), 'Trial Employment' and so on. One measure included in the EMA to combat youth unemployment is the prohibition of age limits in relation to recruitment and hiring (Article 10) as discussed above. Another measure is the creation of a new provision imposing the following 'duty to endeavor,' and setting guidelines titled 'the guidelines for proprietors to take appropriate measures for securing employment opportunities for younger workers.'

According to Article 7 of the revised EMA, proprietors must endeavor to ensure employment opportunities for youth in consideration of their roles in the future industry and society. To this end, proprietors are expected to take measures for the improvement of employment management. These include a change in their methods of recruitment and hiring as follows. According to the guidelines, first, in order to legitimately make the hiring decisions of firms depending on an individual's ability and experiences, firms are expected to clarify the information of job contents, working conditions, required occupational abilities and skills development. Second, firms are also required to give job opportunities to those who have already graduated from school (hereinafter, 'old graduates'), and set forth year-round recruitment procedures or recruitment procedures in fall as well as normal recruitment procedures in spring. These measures would enable job opportunities to be provided to those who did not follow the typical spring recruitment processes.

In order to prevent youth unemployment, firms must also endeavor to take necessary measures to improve the stability of the workforce among the younger generation. According to the guidelines, firms are required to clarify the information of job contents, working conditions, and so forth, thereby preventing disappointed young persons from leaving their jobs. Employers are also required to give younger persons in non-regular work, such as temporary or part-time jobs, opportunities to move into regular work. In order to facilitate the development and improvement of practical occupational abilities, employers are required to conduct both on-the-job and off-the-job training.

In short, this 'duty to endeavor' provision (Article 7) was expected to improve the youth employment situation by rectifying traditional employment practices, such as hiring only new graduates on a voluntary basis. Based on a soft-law approach, the legal effect of this provision is weak from one perspective; firms not performing the duty may merely have advice or guidance from the Minister of Health, Labor and Welfare. These firms are subject to neither criminal penalties nor civil liability. However, from another perspective, this provision and the guidelines recommend recruitment with specified job contents, year-round or fall recruitment procedures, and extension of job opportunities to old graduates, thereby inevitably intervening in the freedom of companies to determine recruitment methods, that is the 'principle of freedom of contracts.' Furthermore, where employers give only youth opportunities to move from non-regular work into regular work, it might arguably constitute 'age discrimination' against seniors. Presumably because of these concerns, legislators took a soft-law approach in calling for an improvement in recruitment and hiring methods.

3. Measures for Foreign Workers

(1) Findings Surrounding Foreign Workers

According to a survey on the employment situation of foreign workers conducted by the Ministry of Health, Labor and Welfare in June 2006, one fourth of 223,000 foreign workers in Japan are in precarious employment situations, such as dispatched workers or contract-based workers.[20] As for compulsory state-run insurance programs,[21] the rate of coverage was not high among foreign workers.[22] Under these situations, the 2007 revision of the EMA introduced two measures; one is the system of mandatory notification of the employment and termination of foreigner workers, and the other is the duty to endeavor to improve the employment management of foreigner workers.

(2) Notification of the Employment and Termination of Foreign Workers

When a firm hires a worker whose nationality is not Japanese, or when such a worker leaves them, they bear an obligation to confirm the worker's name, status and terms of residence as specified by the Immigration Control and Refugee Act, as well as their date of birth, sex and nationality by checking their passports or any other identification materials, and submit a written form on these matters to the Chief of the competent Public Employment Security Office (Article 28, Paragraph 1). Foreigners who are already employed on October 1, 2007 are also covered. Any proprietor who has violated this article shall be punished by way of a fine not exceeding 300,000 yen (Article 38).

---

20 Regarding measures for foreign workers, see Kazuaki Tezuka, *Foreign Workers in Japan: Reality and Challenges*, 2 Japan Labor Review 48 (No.4, 2005); Chizuko Hayakawa, *Gaikokujin Rodo no Hoseisaku* (Shinzansha 2008).

21 Employees meeting certain requirements must enroll in employee health insurance and employee pension insurance. Employers must pay insurance premiums for the employees.

22 According to the employment management survey on foreign workers conducted by Nomura Soken in 2002, around half of workers were not covered by social insurance programs in companies with 50 or more workers who are mostly of Japanese ancestry.

On receipt of the preceding notification, the State shall endeavor to improve the employment management of the foreign workers concerned, and also promote the re-employment of terminated foreign workers by taking the following measures (Article 28, Paragraph 2). The Public Employment Security Offices shall provide firms with necessary guidance and advice to facilitate the proper employment management of foreign workers. In order to promote the re-employment of separated foreign workers, the Offices shall provide the foreigners with employment information and placement, and search for job offers for these workers. Occupational training shall be implemented for them through public vocational training agencies.

The notification system is also intended to be used for immigration control. The Minister of Health, Labor and Welfare shall, when the Minister of Justice makes a request in order to confirm certain matters with respect to the residence of a particular foreigner and take some measures specified by the Immigration Control and Refugee Act, shall submit the information on the foreign workers provided by their employers (Article 29).

Until the amendment made in 2007, notification of the employment of foreign workers was operated on a voluntary basis once a year in June at companies with 50 or more employees. The new notification system was made compulsory for all employers with one or more foreign workers, and a notification duty is imposed each time one or more foreigners enter or leave employment at their workplaces. The reinforced notification duty is expected to contribute to the improvement of the employment management of foreigner workers, as is discussed below.[23]

(3) Improvement of the Employment Management of Foreigner Workers

According to the newly introduced Article 8, proprietors are imposed with a 'duty to endeavor' to improve the employment management of foreign workers employed by them. It includes measures to facilitate adaptation to their occupation, thereby enabling them to effectively display their abilities. In addition, when foreign workers leave firms as a result of dismissals or other reasons and wish for reemployment, firms must endeavor to take necessary measures to support their reemployment. In order to put this 'duty to endeavor' into effect, 'the guidelines for proprietors to take appropriate measures with respect to the improvement of employment management of foreign workers' has been issued by the Ministry of Health, Labor and Welfare.[24] The contents are as follows.

---

[23] By contrast, in the legislative process it was feared that the mandate of notification, which possibly requires employers to investigate the nationality of employees, might be taken as an infringement upon the right of privacy for employees and discrimination against foreigners. The guideline explained below emphasizes that such discrimination would not be allowed.

[24] As for foreign workers, 'the guidelines with respect to the terms and conditions of employment of foreign workers' has already been put in place since 1993 as a circular notice for labour inspectors and officials of Public Employment Security Offices. The meaning of Article 8 of the EMA and the new guidelines, therefore, is the introduction of a clear statutory base for both the regulations of foreign workers as well as the addition of new contents.

Firms must comply with labor laws and social insurance laws equally applied to foreign workers. It should be repeated here again that proprietors shall not engage in discriminatory treatment prohibited under Article 3 of the LSA,[25] that is discrimination by reason of nationality in relation to the terms and conditions of employment. In addition, proprietors shall not impose a worker's nationality as a condition on recruitment when they post job offerings to Public Employment Security Offices and private employment placement service providers (Article 3 of the ESA). Apart from these legal duties, according to the guidelines, proprietors must 'endeavor' to hire workers through 'fair selection' within their residence status. Failure to hire foreigners on the grounds of their nationality, as mentioned above, has not been construed unlawful under Article 3 of the LSA; however, the guidelines implicitly recommend firms to conduct the selection of workers without special consideration of their nationality.

Second, proprietors are required to treat foreign workers appropriately in consideration of their limited knowledge about language, culture, employment and job seeking practices in Japan, and any other special circumstances as follows. In relation to recruitment, proprietors are required to present the terms and conditions of employment of foreign workers in written forms or e-mails where appropriate, and for workers living foreign countries, a share of the travel expenses and arrangement of residence in addition to these items. Proprietors shall not hire foreign workers who cannot engage in work legally under immigration control. Special recruitment and hiring processes for foreign students are also recommended.

In regards to working conditions, in order to secure health and safety at work, firms are required to teach foreigners the Industrial Safety and Health Act, machineries and equipments used by them, safety devices and protective equipment, verbal instructions and body signs for the prevention of accidents and the firm's safety regulations, through methods that can be easily understood by foreign workers including illustrated postings or signs. With respect to social insurance systems, firms shall let foreign workers know the relevant acts and their procedures, and enroll them in these systems. When foreign workers leave workplaces, firms shall go through the legitimate procedures and inform them of Public Employment Security Offices through which workers can obtain unemployment benefits, as well as provide them with any other support as required. It is also necessary for firms to support a foreign worker's claim for benefits from Industrial Accidents Insurance.

In relation to the prevention of dismissals and promotion of reemployment, employers are required to refrain from dismissals and in cases of redundancy they are required to support the reemployment of foreign workers, such as the introduction of any other group companies, implementation of occupational training and provision of information on job

[25] It provides that "An employer shall not engage in discriminatory treatment with respect to wages, working hours or other working conditions by reason of the nationality, creed or social status of any worker."

offerings.

These regulations have no mandatory effect on labor contracts between employers and employees. Firms violating these regulations, however, might receive advice, guidance, or recommendations from the Minister of Health, Labor and Welfare (Article 32). Moreover, in cases where a foreign worker meets with an industrial accident and the employer's instructions on safety were insufficient or difficult for them to understand, the worker may file a lawsuit to the court. In this case, the court might order the employer to compensate the worker for damages not covered by the benefits from Industrial Accidents Insurance, on the grounds that violating the guidelines constitutes negligence under the tort (Civil Code, Article 709).

III. Age Discrimination: Equality Issue or Employment Policy?

Are the regulations on setting age limits for recruitment and hiring and the treatment of youth, to which much attention was drawn as the first step toward Japan's anti-age discrimination law, based on a human rights approach?[26] Or perhaps on an employment policy approach?[27] The human rights approach regards differences of treatment based on prohibited grounds, such as sex and race, as a violation of the human rights of the individual to equal treatment. Any exception to this principle is strictly construed so as to interfere with the rights of individuals as little as possible. In contrast, the 'employment policy approach' uses a variety of policy instruments to support individual workers, paying attention to their different attributes. When certain treatments based on certain grounds are regulated to attain policy objectives, those regulations take on a patchwork aspect.

The anti-age discrimination provision included in the revised EMA can be deemed to be based on the employment policy approach rather than the human rights approach. This conclusion is obtained in light of the EMA legal basis, policy objectives, ways of regulations and comparison with sex discrimination law, as follows.

---

[26] See Kazuo Sugeno, *Discrimination in Employment: Dynamism and the Limits of Harmonization in Law*, in *Discrimination in Employment XV World Congress of Labour Law and Social Security* 5, (Roger Blanpain ed., Peeters 1998); Takashi Araki, *The Impact of Fundamental Social Rights on Japanese Law*, in *Social and Labour Rights in a Global Context: International and Comparative Perspectives* 215 (Bob Hepple ed., Cambridge University 2002).

[27] Regarding the analysis of age discrimination law from this perspective, see Colm O'Cinneide, *Comparative European Perspectives on Age Discrimination Legislation*, in *Age as an Equality Issue* 195 (Sandra Fredman and Sarah Spencer eds., Harts 2003); Bob Hepple, *Legislation against Age Discrimination in Employment: Some Comparative Perspectives*, JILL Forum Special Series (No. 19, 2004); Ryoko Sakuraba, *Nenrei Sabetsu Kinshi no Hori* (Shinzansha 2008); Ryoko Sakuraba, *Employment Discrimination Law in Japan: Human Rights or Employment Policy?*, in *New Developments in Employment Discrimination Law* 233 (Roger Blanpain, Hiroya Nakakubo, Takashi Araki eds., Wolters Kluwer Law & Business 2008).

1. Constitutional Basis

First, the statute prohibiting age discrimination in respect to recruitment and hiring was the EMA, a statute categorized under the 'Labor Market Law'; this fact itself shows that the new provision for rectifying age limits is based on the employment policy approach rather than being treated as an equality issue. The basis for the development of Japanese employment law after World War II was the constitutional provisions.[28] In addition to human rights, the Constitution also prescribes fundamental social rights. Article 27, Paragraph 1 proclaims that all people shall have the right to work and thus obliged the State to give workers suitable employment opportunities. This obligation of the State is fulfilled through the 'Labor Market Law,' which consists of the ESA that regulates employment placement services, recruitment and labor supply businesses, the OPESA and other acts including the EMA.

2. Policy Objectives

The second feature is the policy objectives of the revision. The 'anti-age discrimination in relation to recruitment and hiring' provision was first introduced in 2001 as a 'duty to endeavor' as explained above. The then act's title, which including the phrase 'cope with economic and social changes by ensuring smooth reemployment', was reflective of its policy objective. To this objective, the relaxation of age limits on hiring was considered necessary to promote job matching depending on the ability of workers. The policy objective was extended to efforts to combat youth unemployment in the 2007 revision. The employment of youth and elderly is promoted by the revised EMA as well as that of women, persons with disabilities and foreigners. All of them are expected to participate in the labor market and contribute to the reinforcement of the State's financial foundation in the midst of a progressing aging society.

It is noteworthy that the EMA as of 2007 can be characterized as the symbol of transformation of employment policies in Japan. The development of 'Labor Market Law' in Japan can be divided into three stages; first, right after World War II, where the main objective of employment policies was to facilitate the function of external labor markets and a smooth labor transition; second, following the oil shock of the 1970s, when employment security within a company was given priority; and third, in the post-bubble economy, during which Japan's employment policy shifted its emphasis to flexible labor movement once again in the midst of rising unemployment rates. The subsequent revisions of the EMA, therefore, were part of the measures to diversify employment policies in order to cope with changing economic and social conditions.

---

[28] Regarding the Constitutional basis of Japanese employment and labour law, see Araki, above n. 26.

3. Methods of Regulations

Third, regulations on age-based treatment appear to be merely a patchwork rather than a conclusive anti-discrimination law. Since the EMA regulates only age limits for recruitment and hiring, a mandatory retirement system at the age of 60 years remains lawful. Setting such a mandatory retirement age is lawful if it satisfies the requirement of the OPESA as seen above. Apart from age limits for recruitment and hiring and the mandatory retirement age, employers have the possibility of maintaining age-based practices as follows.

Is redundancy targeting older workers unlawful? It depends on the application of the adjustment dismissals doctrine. The 'abuse of dismissal rights' doctrine was codified in the Labor Contract Act (Article 16) in 2007.[29] With regards to employment adjustment dismissals, judicial decisions have been handed down stating that any adjustment dismissal is an abuse of the right to dismiss unless it meets the following four requirements: there must be a business necessity, the employer is obliged to take various measures to avoid adjustment dismissals such as the implementation of transfers, the selection of those workers to be dismissed must be made according to reasonable criteria, and proper procedures must be taken.

Redundancy targeting older workers triggered a discussion on whether or not the selection criterion of 'older workers' was reasonable, and if it satisfied the third requirement. In one case, the court refuted the dismissal on the grounds that older workers usually found it difficult to secure new jobs, their ability did not deteriorate as a result of aging, and their disadvantages should at least be compensated by special early retirement allowances.[30] On the other hand, there have been several cases where the reasonableness of dismissal was affirmed. The judges ruled that the dismissal of older workers was necessary to save money as the wages of such workers were relatively high.

Another example of disadvantageous age-based practices is the wage-cut system for the elderly.[31] In recent years, traditional age or length of service-based wage systems are being transformed into performance-based pay through changes of work rules or the conclusion of collective agreements. The 'Daishi Ginko Case' was the first instance where the Supreme Court decided on this issue.[32] The wages of those between the ages of 55-60 years were reduced in exchange for an extension of the retirement age from 58 to 60 years. The court considered the advantages of employment extension and consequently viewed the reduction of wages as a reasonable modification having a binding effect on workers. On the

---

[29] Regarding the development of this doctrine, see Takashi Araki, *Labor and Employment Law in Japan* 17*ff* (The Japan Institute of Labour 2002).

[30] The *Varig Nihon Shisha* case, Tokyo District Court, Dec. 19, 2001, Rohan 817-5.

[31] Regarding the work rules doctrine, see Araki, above n.29, at 51*ff*; Shinya Ouchi, *Restructuring of Enterprises and Protection of Working Conditions of Middle-Aged and Elderly Employees in Japan*, Kobe University Law Review 29 (No. 30, 1996). This doctrine was codified in Articles 7, 9 and 10 of the Labor Contracts Act, which was adopted in November 2007.

[32] The *Daishi Ginko* case, Supreme Court, Feb. 28, 1997, Minshu 51-2-705.

other hand, in the second Supreme Court case[33] in which the wages of the elderly were cut by 30%-40% of those paid under the former system while the wages of younger workers were increased, a decision was reached that the disadvantages were too great and unfair in that only older employees were disadvantaged.

Thus, in cases of redundancy or reduction in wages targeting older employees, since there are no statutes explicitly prohibiting these practices and the tests applied here are no more than reasonable tests, some age practices have remained lawful.

4. Comparison with Sex Discrimination Law

Fourth, its character as an employment policy is made clear if it is compared to the EEOA prohibiting sex discrimination in employment in Japan. The EEOA states its aim as securing equal opportunity and treatment between men and women in employment 'in accordance with the principle in the Constitution of Japan of ensuring equality under law' (Article 1), and thus clearly indicates that it deals with the issue of equality.

The EEOA enacted in 1985[34] still indicated its character of the employment policy approach, since employers were merely obliged to 'endeavor' to treat men and women equally during the processes of recruitment, hiring, assignment and promotion while provisions with respect to training and education, fringe benefits, and retirement and dismissals were mandatory. However, the 'duty to endeavor' clauses were effective in changing workplace culture and building a social consensus that women should be given equal employment opportunities. Accordingly, the EEOA was strengthened in 1997 with the addition of a mandate of equal treatment at the time of recruitment and hiring, assignment and promotion. In June 2006, the material scope of regulations was extended to 'placement' including the 'allocation of duties' and 'granting of authority,' the 'demotion' of workers, 'change in job type or employment status,' 'encouragement of retirement' and 'renewal of the labor contract' (Article 6), as well as recruiting and hiring (Article 5), promotion, education and training, fringe benefits, and retirement and dismissal (Article 6). Therefore, employers should not discriminate on the grounds of sex at almost all stages of employment unless they can demonstrate legitimate reasons justifying differential treatment.

The guideliness issued by the Ministry of Health, Labor and Welfare allow only narrow justifications. The following acts are permitted as positive actions and occupational requirements:

a. Favorable treatment for women in employment categories where women are substantially under-represented (positive action).

b. Unfavorable treatment against men or women if:

---

[33] The *Michinoku Ginko* case, Supreme Court, Sep. 7, 2000, Minshu 54-7-2075.

[34] Regarding the development of the EEOA, see Takashi Araki, *Equal Employment and Harmonization of Work and Family Life: Japan's Soft-Law Approach*, 21 Comparative Labor Law & Policy Journal 451 (No. 3, 2000); Hiroya Nakakubo, *"Phase III" of the Japanese Equal Employment Opportunity Act*, 4 Japan Labor Review 9 (No. 3, 2007).

b-1-1. requirements of authenticity call for the assignment of a man or woman only in the arts or entertainment;

b-1-2. requirements of security call for the assignment of a man only in a guarding role;

b-1-3. any other occupational characteristics, such as those of a religious or moral nature, or work in a sports competition, calls for the assignment of a man or woman only and where there is the same degree of necessity as in the aforementioned items.

b-2. statutes prohibit employers from assigning a man or woman to particular work.[35]

b-3. a job requires work in a particular foreign country whose manners and customs are so different that a man or a woman could not exercise his or her ability.

In summary, it can be analyzed that revisions of the Act brought a shift from the employment policy approach to the human rights approach, in that its application was extended to all aspects of employment in order to effectuate 'the principle in the Constitution of Japan of ensuring equality under law.'

By contrast, the EMA merely prohibits recruitment and hiring discrimination. Moreover, age limits for hiring can be set when they fall under the listed exemptions; (a) in accordance with a mandatory retirement age; (b) there is a statutory age limit for a particular work; (c) recruiting only young persons to give them skills development over a long period of service; (d) hiring persons in a particular under-represented age bracket; (e) there is a requirement for authenticity in the arts or entertainment; (f) employing only persons in certain age brackets, the employment of which is encouraged by employment policies.

Among these, (b), (d) and (e) are recognized as justifiable reasons even under the EEOA. On the other hand, there are special justifiable reasons for age limits (a), (c) and (f). The exemptions (a) and (c) can be explained as those included to respect traditional employment practices in Japan. Exemption (f) was added to put into effect the EMA objective of promoting the employment of youth and the elderly. Thus, in light of its limited outreach, age discrimination regulations contained in the EMA are far from being based on the human rights approach derived from the equality principle.

IV. Conclusion: Current State of Affairs and Future Issues

1. Anti-Age Discrimination and Promotion of Youth and the Elderly

As the foregoing indicates, it can be said that the revised EMA took the employment policy approach by allowing relatively broad exemptions. Also, it might be criticized for taking only lukewarm measures. It seems, however, a suitable means to attain its objective of promoting the employment of older and younger persons in a gradual process while

---

[35] The LSA provides that an employer may not have a woman engaged in underground work, work involving lifting heavy materials and work in places where harmful gas or dust such as lead is generated (Article 64 (2) and 64 (3), Paragraph 2); furthermore, only women could be licensed to perform as midwives (Health Nurses, Midwives and Nurses Act, Article 3).

considering the possible impacts of strengthened regulations on employment practices. Setting a mandatory retirement age and hiring only new graduates have been considered an integral part of the Japanese long-term employment system. It is feared that prohibiting these practices as unlawful age discrimination would result in the collapse of Japanese employment management. Attempts to rectify the practice of hiring only new graduates would inevitably curtail the 'freedom of contracts' of employers to some extent; firms would be required to take pro-active measures for the improvement of employment management. As such, the practice of hiring of only new graduates is expected to be modified through the firms 'duty to endeavor' to introduce an all-year-round process of recruitment or recruitment covering old graduates.

In regards to the treatment of age, the employment policy approach, which allows for flexibility in selecting policies in view of built-in employment practices, would be suitable. Generally, age discrimination can be seen as an area in which employers should enjoy a relatively broad margin of discretion, since age-based treatment affects everyone in society and is reasonable in some cases. Matters relating to age equality in Japan are therefore addressed through the employment policy approach rather than the human rights approach. Seemingly weak regulations, such as the 'duty to endeavor,' have played an important role in the development of Japanese anti-discrimination law, as shown in the case of the EEOA. As such, in the future there is the possibility that administrative efforts based on such clauses will contribute to consensus building among labor, management and citizens for the reinforcement of regulations on setting age limits for hiring.

Another controversial future issue would be whether or not Japan should introduce comprehensive anti-age discrimination law beyond the current regulations on age limits for hiring. With the influence of the anti-age discrimination laws both in the US and the EU, there is an increasing number of theorists arguing in favor of this.[36] Careful deliberation of the possible impacts on Japanese employment practices would be necessary, in view of the special character of age discrimination.

2. Improvement of the Employment Management of Foreign Workers

Subsequently, the question would arise as to whether or not measures for foreign workers, which are also addressed through the 'duty to endeavor,' are legitimate. Is the protection given to foreigners not sufficient, in spite of the character of nationality, which relates to the identity of workers and cannot be chosen freely by their own will? Or on the contrary, is there too much protection that constitutes 'reverse discrimination' against domestic workers?

In regards to the first question, emphasis should be put on the contents of the 'duty to endeavor.' They include namely proactive measures such as a special recruitment process for foreign students, explanation of Japanese labor laws for foreign workers, and support of

[36] See, Takeshi Yanagisawa, *Koyo ni okeru Nenrei Sabetsu no Hori* 241*ff* (Seibundo 2006).

foreign workers claiming for workers' accident compensation benefits. In a sense, recommending these measures would invade the freedom of the employment management of firms. Therefore, here again, a soft-law approach based on Article 8 and the guidelines seems appropriate. It is expected that the employment management of foreign workers would be improved, and they would be more integrated into the labor force through administrative efforts based on this Article.

As for the second concern, it is certain that the special treatment of foreigners as recommended by the guidelines, in which domestic workers could not be included, can be seen as reverse discrimination against Japanese workers. However, attention should be paid to the different attributes of foreigners, such as their limited knowledge about the language, culture and employment practices in Japan. Legislators presumably thought that the special treatment of foreigner workers by employers in accordance with the guidelines would be allowed as a positive action; this would compensate for their real difficulties in employment while at the same time being not so disadvantageous for domestic workers, and would not constitute unlawful nationality-based discrimination.

The most serious current legal issue would be whether or not discrimination by reason of a worker's nationality in relation to hiring, which has been interpreted to not violate Article 3 of the LSA on the basis of the Supreme Court's decision, should be banned. With the increasing labor mobility and strengthened regulations on hiring practices such as prohibition of age or sex discrimination, it would not be surprising that nationality-based discrimination in relation to hiring may be prohibited by revision of the EMA or LSA, or adoption of comprehensive anti-discrimination laws in the future.

[13]

Age Discrimination and the European Court of Justice: EU Equality Law Comes of Age

Colm O'Cinneide
Reader in Law
UCL

Introduction

Age discrimination in the field of employment and occupation is now subject to legal controls imposed under Directive 2000/78/EC, which limits the circumstances in which the national law of member states may permit employers to subject employees to different treatment on the grounds of age. The prohibition of age discrimination in the Directive received a general (if vague) welcome across the EU. There appeared to be an assumption that the EU should follow other jurisdictions such as the United States, which had enacted legislation prohibiting age discrimination.[1] In addition, the possibility of European legislation on age discrimination appeared to open new opportunities for enhancing protection against prejudice, inequality and the denial of human rights, while also advancing key elements of the EU's Employment Strategy (the EES, often better known in its revised form as the 'Lisbon Strategy'), in particular its focus on securing access to employment for older persons.[2] As a result, many member states implemented the Directive into their national law without appearing to give the matter too much consideration.

However, the text of the Directive left many key issues unresolved. In particular, the status of the prohibition on age discrimination was left uncertain. Was age to be treated as a full ground of discrimination, similar to gender or race, or as a lesser, secondary non-discrimination ground? Would the prohibition on age discrimination be treated as touching on fundamental rights, or was it a regulatory measure which should be applied by courts with a light touch, respectful of the important role age distinctions often play in national social and employment policy?

The emerging case-law of the European Court of Justice (ECJ) on these issues has proved to be controversial, far-reaching and perhaps surprising to many. The Court has affirmed the importance of the prohibition on age discrimination, while also linking it with the general principle of equal treatment which it now recognises as a fundamental norm of the EU legal order. This case-law is worth close consideration, because of how it shows how the Court's emerging equality jurisprudence will take shape in the years ahead, even in the contested and difficult field of age discrimination.

---

[1] See e.g. the Age Discrimination in Employment Act 1967 (USA).

[2] See European Council, 2000, Lisbon Presidency Conclusions, 23-24 March 2000; European Council, 2005, Brussels Presidency Conclusions, 23-24 March 2005; European Commission, 1993 *White Paper on Growth, Competitiveness and Employment: The Challenges and Ways Forward into the 21st Century*, Bulletin of the European Communities, Supplement 6/93; European Commission, 1997, *Green Paper on the Organisation of Work*, Bulletin of the European Union, Supplement 4/97; J Kenner, *EU Employment Law: From Rome to Amsterdam and Beyond* (Oxford: Hart, 2003); C Barnard, *EU Employment Law* (Oxford: OUP, 2006).

The Age Discrimination Provisions of Directive 2000/78/EC

The EU was given competency to legislate on to prohibit discrimination on a series of new grounds, including age, by the Treaty of Amsterdam in 1997, which inserted Article 13 into the EC Treaty.[3] The enabling power contained in Article 13 was subsequently used as a basis for the enactment of Council Directive 2000/78/EC of 27 November 2000 establishing a general framework for equal treatment in employment and occupation (the 'Framework Employment Equality Directive', referred to in general in what follows as 'the Directive').[4]

Article 2 of the Framework Employment Equality Directive has the effect of prohibiting direct and indirect discrimination in employment and occupation on the grounds of age, as well as on the other non-discrimination grounds covered by the Directive, namely sexual orientation, religion or belief and disability.[5] Age is therefore classified under the Directive as a fully protected ground of non-discrimination, and the Directive places similar restrictions on the use of distinctions based on age as are imposed in respect of the other non-discrimination grounds recognised in EU law, at least in the sphere of employment and occupation.[6]

However, age differs from other non-discrimination grounds covered under EU law in certain important aspects. To begin with, there appears to be a greater range of circumstances where age may constitute be a rational and legitimate reason for distinguishing between different groups of persons than is the case for the other non-discrimination grounds. Age-based distinctions are often based upon stereotyping and prejudice. However, the use of such distinctions may also at times be rooted in rational considerations and serve valuable social and economic objectives: the same is rarely true of the other non-discrimination grounds such as sexual orientation, gender, race or religion.[7]

---

[3] Article 13 permitted the European Council, acting unanimously on a proposal from the Commission and after consultation with the European Parliament, to take 'appropriate action to combat discrimination based on sex, racial or ethnic origin, religion or belief, disability, age or sexual orientation.'

[4] Article 13 was also used as the legislative basis for Council Directive 2000/43/EC of 29 June 2000 implementing the principle of equal treatment between persons irrespective of racial or ethnic origin (the 'Race Equality Directive'). For analysis of Article 13, see M. Bell, *Anti-discrimination Law and the European Union* (Oxford: OUP, 2002).

[5] Article 2 also prohibits harassment on the grounds of age, as well as instructions to discriminate, while victimisation as a result of bringing an age discrimination claim is prohibited under Article 11.

[6] The Race Equality and Directive 2004/113/EC implementing the principle of equal treatment between men and women in the access to and supply of goods and services extend protection against discrimination on the grounds of race and gender beyond the scope of employment and occupation. The European Commission has proposed a draft directive on extending protection across the discrimination grounds covered by the Framework Equality Directive beyond employment: see Proposal for a Council Directive on implementing the principle of equal treatment between persons irrespective of religion or belief, disability, age or sexual orientation {SEC(2008) 2180} {SEC(2008) 2181}, COM/2008/0426 final, CNS 2008/0140.

[7] The ground of disability gives rise to particular difficulties, as reflected in the provisions governing reasonable accommodation as set out in Articles 2(2)(b)(ii) and 5 of the Directive.

In particular, age may be a useful and fair method of selecting which groups of individuals may benefit from particular measures, or to identify groups for differential treatment, especially when age serves as a rational 'proxy' or indicator that particular groups possess certain characteristics in general, such as experience, maturity, good physical capability, or financial stability. Age is often used in such cases to categorise groups in very general and sweeping terms: however, such generalisations are often necessary in the field of social and employment policy and experience indicates that it is harder to avoid the use of age in making these generalisations than it is for the other non-discrimination grounds.

As a result, age discrimination legislation must establish a framework for distinguishing between circumstances where the use of age to differentiate between individuals is justified, and when it is not. That framework is provided by Article 6 of the Directive, and in particular via the provisions of Article 6(1), which provides that differences of treatment on the grounds of age which would otherwise constitute direct discrimination may be permitted in national law, if it can be shown that their use is objectively justified as appropriate and necessary to achieve a legitimate aim.

> 'Notwithstanding Article 2(2), Member States may provide that differences of treatment on grounds of age shall not constitute discrimination, if, within the context of national law, they are objectively and reasonably justified by a legitimate aim, including legitimate employment policy, labour market and vocational training objectives, and if the means of achieving that aim are appropriate and necessary.'

The references to 'legitimate employment policy, labour market and vocational training objectives' in Article 6(1) provide an indication of the type of legitimate aim that may be put forward to justify the use of distinctions based on age. The text of Article 6(1) also takes the unusual step of providing some examples of the type of differences of treatment based directly on age that may be objectively justified.[8]

Article 6(1) thus permits employers to make use of age-based distinctions if the use of these distinctions can be shown to be objectively justified and based upon legitimate aims.[9] This marks age as different from other non-discrimination grounds, as direct

[8] These include 'the setting of special conditions on access to employment…for young people, older workers and persons with caring responsibilities in order to promote their vocational integration or ensure their protection'; the 'fixing of minimum conditions of age, professional experience or seniority' for access to employment'; and 'the fixing of a maximum age for recruitment…based on the training requirements of the post in question or the need for a reasonable period of employment before retirement'.

[9] For detailed analysis of Article 6(1) and the age discrimination provisions of the Directive, see C. O'Cinneide, *Age Discrimination and European Law* (Luxembourg: Office for Official Publications of the European Communities/European Commission, 2005), pp. 1-57, available at http://europa.eu.int/comm/employment_social/publications/2005/ke6805147_en.pdf: also, H. Meenan, 'Age Equality after the Employment Directive' (2003) 10 *Maastricht Journal of European and Comparative Law* 9-38; S. González Ortega, 'La Discriminación por Razón de la Edad' , 59 *Temas Laborales,* 2001, pp. 93-124.

discrimination based on the other grounds is not permitted.[10] This difference in legal terms reflects the special characteristics of age as a non-discrimination ground and the manner in which the use of age-based distinctions appears to be justifiable in more situations than appears to be the case with the other non-discrimination grounds.

The Uncertain Status of the Prohibition on Age Discrimination

However, the provisions of Article 6(1) also give rise to a more fundamental question: does the special status of age mean that it should be treated as a lesser or subordinate form of discrimination? Should age discrimination be treated as intrinsically less serious and less 'suspect' than gender or race discrimination, or even perhaps other forms of discrimination such as discrimination on the basis of sexual orientation or religion and belief? If so, should national courts applying the provisions of the Directive and the ECJ interpreting its scope grant Member States considerable discretion when they choose to make use of age-based distinctions, or permit employers to differentiate on the basis of age?

This key question also gives rise to wider issues about the extension of EU anti-discrimination law across the new non-discrimination grounds as set out in Article 13 of the EC Treaty. EU law on gender discrimination is rigorous, highly developed and demanding: gender equality is recognised both in the text of the EC Treaty and in the case-law of the ECJ as a fundamental right. However, should some or all of the 'new' non-discrimination grounds be treated in a similar manner?

The 2000 Directives appeared to establish a 'hierarchy of protection' between race and gender discrimination, on the one hand, and the other discrimination grounds on the other.[11] Did this mean that age, sexual orientation, religion or belief and disability are to be treated as second-class discrimination grounds, in contrast to race or gender? Should all these 'new' grounds be treated as 'suspect' and treated in a similar manner, or should distinctions be recognised to exist between each ground, reflecting the very different structures of prejudice that have generated the different types of discrimination that EU law now attempts to redress? Crucially, should the structural elements of EU anti-discrimination law, such as the objective justification test, the reversal of the burden of proof, and the ability for employers to show that a protected characteristic constituted a 'genuine occupational qualification' be applied differently across the different grounds,

---

[10] Other differences exist between age and the other non-discrimination grounds within the framework of the Directive. Under Article 6(2), member states are permitted to allow occupational security schemes to fix age limits for admission of new potential beneficiaries, or to set age limits as to when beneficiaries may become entitled to retirement or invalidity benefits (which can include fixing different ages for employees or groups of employees), or to use age criteria in actuarial calculations in such schemes, provided that this does not result in sex discrimination. No similar exception exists for the other grounds. Article 3(4) also specifically permits member states to exempt their armed forces from the age provisions of the Directive: of the other grounds covered by the Directive, such an exception only also exists for disability.

[11] See M. Bell, *Anti-discrimination Law and the European Union* (Oxford: OUP, 2002), 32; M. Bell and L. Waddington, Reflecting On Inequalities in European Equality Law' (2003) 28(3) *European Law Review* 349-364.

with varying levels of rigour and intensity depending on the non-discrimination ground at issue?

These general uncertainties become particularly prominent when it came to age. In contrast to the other discrimination grounds, including sexual orientation, religion or belief and disability, few EU member states had taken action to prohibit age discrimination prior to agreement being reached on the text of the Directive.[12] There was no substantive jurisprudence from the European Court of Human Rights on equality issues related to age, and little if any jurisprudence from national courts on this subject either. Age discrimination was not seen as a priority issue in most of the EU, and it was not seen as a core area of concern for discrimination law.

As a result, it was unclear as the transposition period of the Directive neared its end whether the European Court of Justice would apply the objective justification test under Article 6(1) with a similar rigour and intensity of review as it did when applying this test in other areas of discrimination law, such as indirect sex discrimination, or where free movements rights are at issue. In particular, would the ECJ treat age-based distinctions as 'suspect', and subject their use to close and exacting scrutiny, or would it adopt a more flexible and permissible approach, allowing the use of age to differentiate between different categories of employees when it was reasonable to do so?

The Contested Nature of Age Discrimination

It was possible to make arguments both in favour and against treating age as a 'suspect' ground, of similar status to the others. In the eyes of some commentators, age discrimination constitutes an intrinsically less serious form of discrimination than other types of unequal treatment. As already noted, the use of age-linked requirements to differentiate between employees is common, and can be often rational and justified: therefore, the argument can readily be made that age discrimination is not as serious a form of inequality as other forms of discrimination.[13]

In addition, age discrimination is not linked to historical oppression or to large-scale deprivations of human dignity, unlike the other forms of discrimination. There has been no clear age-linked historical experience to equate to the poisonous legacy of racism and anti-Semitism, or the long centuries of ingrained sexism and homophobia, or the embedded disadvantages faced by many persons with disabilities.[14] In the age discrimination case of *Massachusetts Board of Retirement v. Murgia*, the US Supreme Court stated that 'old age does not define a "discrete and insular' group ... in need of 'extraordinary protection from the majoritarian political process.' Instead, it marks a stage that each of us will reach if we live out our normal span.'[15]

[12] C. O'Cinneide, 'Comparative European Perspectives on Age Discrimination' in S. Fredman and S. Spencer, *Age as an Equality Issue: Legal and Policy Perspectives* (Oxford: Hart, 2003), 195-218.
[13] See the general discussion of the 'sceptical case' against age discrimination in N. Bamforth, M. Malik and C. O'Cinneide, *Discrimination Law: Theory and Context* (London: Sweet & Maxwell, 2008), Ch. 15.
[14] George Rutherglen has similarly argued that the ADEA 'cannot be justified in terms of opening opportunities to a historically disfavored group.' See G. Rutherglen, 'From Race to Age: The Expanding Scope of Employment Discrimination Law' (1995) 24 *J. Legal Studies* 491.
[15] (1976) 438 US 285.

Therefore, it is possible to make the argument that age constitutes a lesser form of discrimination, which was less serious than other forms of discrimination and in respect of which a less demanding approach could be adopted when applying the objective justification test set out in Article 6(1) and other elements of European anti-discrimination law. The fact that the Directive provided that direct age discrimination could be objectively justified, in contrast to the other discrimination grounds, could be seen to support this argument. In the United States, Richard Posner has gone so far as to argue that the range of circumstances in which age discrimination is a necessary tool for effective decision-making in employment is so considerable as to justify the repeal or substantial dilution of the US age discrimination legislation.[16]

In addition, the argument could be made that there is also a need to recognise the importance of 'intergenerational solidarity', which can be defined as the set of intertwined obligations of social support that the generations owe each other. Age discrimination laws could create the risk that the status and exiting entitlements of older workers would be unfairly protected at the expense of younger workers. It also could mean that promotion paths could be blocked and older workers left to occupy senior posts at the expense of younger employees, while employers are left to deal with the declining productivity levels that may be associated in some employment contexts with older workers.[17] Therefore, these concerns could again be cited to justify a 'light-touch' approach to age and a flexible application of Article 6 and other elements of the Directive when the use of rational age-based criteria by employers and national governments was at issue.

However, alternative arguments could also be made, to the effect that age discrimination should be treated as a 'suspect' form of discrimination and be subject to similar rigorous levels of judicial scrutiny as are applied when applying the objective justification test to other forms of discrimination, such as gender and race. Age-based differences in treatment are often based on generalised assumptions or casual stereotypes, which are often highly inaccurate and based upon misleading and unfair stereotypes that do not reflect the true diversity of individuals within the age groups affected.[18] Both younger and older persons may be affected by such stereotypes: for example, younger persons are often assumed to lack maturity: older persons are often assumed to lack flexibility, motivation and the ability to absorb new ideas.[19] When individuals are subject to discrimination as a result of these demeaning stereotypes, they

[16] R. Posner, *Aging and Old Age* (University of Chicago Press: Chicago, 1997).

[17] See the detailed argument made in S. Issacharoff and E. W. Worth, 'Is Age Discrimination Really Age Discrimination? The ADEA's Unnatural Solution' 72 N.Y.U. Law Rev. 780.

[18] The Irish age discrimination case of *Byrne v FAS*, DEC-E2002-045 (2002), is a good example of a case involving discriminatory and unfair assumptions. The case found that a 48-year old woman was refused a vocational training place, and was told at interview that older students were less successful at technical drawing and had more conflict with family commitments. The Equality Officer in finding for the claimant observed that no objective evidence to support these comments had been produced, and the interviewer seemed just to have applied a series of discriminatory assumptions in refusing her a place.

[19] See S. Fredman, 'The Age of Equality', in S. Fredman and S. Spencer, *Age as an Equality Issue: Legal and Policy Perspectives* (Oxford: Hart, 2003) 21-70, especially 22-35.

are denied equality of treatment and respect.[20] Therefore, applying a rigorous approach to age discrimination could be said to advance the fundamental right to equality.

Age discrimination also produces negative social consequences. Groups who are subject to age discrimination often suffer social exclusion, high levels of poverty and the denial of access to basic goods and services, which in turn imposes substantial economic and social welfare costs upon society at large.[21] In many European states, older workers who lose their jobs and younger job-hunters who lack extensive work experience often are effectively excluded from the job market, with serious social consequences.[22] Therefore, applying a rigorous approach to age discrimination could be said to advance pressing social objectives, linked to the achievement of the European Employment Strategy.[23]

The ageing population of Europe is also a relevant factor. The age structure of the EU population is expected to change dramatically in coming decades due to shifting patterns in fertility, life expectancy and migration rates. The combined EU population is projected to be slightly larger but much older in 50 years' time than it is now, with population expected to decrease in about half of the EU Member States and the overall EU median age projected to rise from 40.4 years in 2008 to 47.9 years in 2060.[24] Older persons are expected to make up an ever-increasing share of the population, due to continued gains in life expectancy: however, at the same time, the younger proportion of the population will decrease due to below-replacement fertility rates.

As a result of these trends, the EU is expected to move from having 4 working-age people for every person aged over 65 at present to a new ratio of 2 to 1 by 2060.[25] Unless older workers are able and encouraged to remain in the workforce, and younger workers enabled to gain work experience and move onto the career ladder, productivity in Europe may radically decrease over the next few decades, which will make supporting the European social security systems much more difficult. The prevention of age discrimination may therefore be an important element in meeting the challenge of

---

[20] See the discussion in Fredman, *ibid*: see also C. O'Cinneide, 'Comparative European Perspectives on Age Discrimination' in Fredman and Spencer, *Age as an Equality Issue*, 195-218, especially 214-5; Australian Human Rights and Equal Opportunity Commission, *Age Matters: A Report on Age Discrimination* (Canberra: HREOC, May 2000); Ontario Human Rights Commission, *Discrimination and Age: Human Rights Issues Facing Older Persons in Ontario* (Toronto: 2000).

[21] See for example the analysis in UK Employers' Forum on Age, *The Cost of Ageism* (London: EFA, 1998): see also H. Meenan, 'Age Discrimination in the UK' (2000) 4 *International Journal of Discrimination and the Law* 247-292.

[22] See UK Employers' Forum on Age, *The Cost of Ageism* (London: EFA, 1998), quoted in H. Meenan, 'Age Discrimination in the UK' (2000) 4 *International Journal of Discrimination and the Law* 247-292

[23] See B. Hepple, 'Age as Discrimination in Employment', in S. Fredman and S. Spencer, *Age as an Equality Issue* (Oxford: Hart, 2003), 71-96.

[24] European Commission (DG ECFIN) and the Economic Policy Committee (AWG), *The 2009 Ageing Report: Underlying Assumptions and Projection Methodologies for the EU-27 Member States (2007-2060)* (European Economy), Brussels, 7th December 2008, Brussels, available at http://ec.europa.eu/economy_finance/publications/publication13782_en.pdf (last accessed 20 January 2010). See also Giuseppe Carone and Declan Costello, 'Can Europe Afford to Grow Old?'(2006) *International Monetary Fund Finance and Development Magazine*, available at http://www.imf.org/external/pubs/ft/fandd/2006/09/carone.htm (last accessed 20 January 2010).

an ageing society, again pointing towards the need for the rigorous application of the age discrimination provisions of the 2000 Directive.[26]

Therefore, a combination of factors rooted both in social values and public policy support could be cited as supporting the rigorous application of age discrimination legislation by the courts, but other arguments could be made in an opposite direction.[27] The justifications in favour of a rigorous approach to age discrimination appear to be primarily rooted in anti-stereotyping and public policy concerns, and less in a concern for human dignity, which is often advanced as a justification for a rigorous approach across the other non-discrimination grounds.[28] Nevertheless, prohibiting age discrimination can be seen as protecting autonomy, and freedom from age inequality is recognised as a right in Article 21(1) of the EU Charter of Fundamental Rights. However, the counter-arguments already outlined question the ultimate importance of prohibiting age discrimination, and draw attention to the possible negative consequences that rigorous enforcement of age discrimination law may bring about.

An Overview of the ECJ's Age Discrimination Case-Law

As such, when the Directive came into effect in 2003 (or in 2006, for Member States which had taken advantage of the extended transposition period permitted to implement the Directive's provisions on age and disability), it was unclear exactly how the ECJ would strike the balance between these conflicting considerations in applying its age discrimination provisions. This uncertainty was compounded by the absence of substantial national jurisprudence on age discrimination, and the lack of detailed academic commentary on issues of age equality.

This context makes the ECJ jurisprudence on age discrimination that has emerged since the seminal *Mangold* decision in 2007 all the more striking, controversial and significant. The ECJ has surprised many commentators by its strong insistence on the suspect nature of age as a discrimination ground and the need to apply the objective justification test with rigour in age cases.[29] Despite suggestions from several different Advocate-Generals that age should not be treated as equivalent to gender and other 'suspect' forms of discrimination (see below), the Court has clearly indicated in its *Mangold,*[30] *Palacios de la Villa*[31] and *Age Concern* judgments that the prohibition on age discrimination is to be applied with similar rigour as are other anti-discrimination

[26] For a comprehensive analysis on this point, see H. Meenan, 'The Future of Ageing and the Role of Age Discrimination in the Global Debate' [2005] *The Journal of International Aging, Law & Policy* 1-41.

[27] For a critical analysis of these debates, see N. Bamforth, M. Malik and C. O'Cinneide, *Discrimination Law: Theory and Context* (London: Sweet & Maxwell, 2008), Ch. 15.

[28] Christine Jolls has suggested that a prohibition on age discrimination 'cannot be justified on traditional distributive or rights-based grounds', but can be justified on the grounds of fairness and social policy: see C. Jolls, 'Hands-Tying and the Age Discrimination in Employment Act', (1996) 74 *Tex. L. Rev.* 1813, at 1814.

[29] For the Court's explanation of how this test should be applied in the context of gender discrimination, see Case C-170/84 *Bilka Kaufhaus* [1986] ECR 1607.

[30] Case C-144/04, *Mangold v Helm*, [2005] ECR I-9981.

[31] Case C-411/05, *Félix Palacios de la Villa v Cortefiel Servicios SA* [2007] ECR I-8531.

norms. It has also not hesitated in its decisions in *Mangold* and *Kücükdeveci*[32] to treat the prohibition on age discrimination as an integral aspect of a general principle of equal treatment, which the Court considers to constitute a core value of the EU legal order and which appears to encompass all of the non-discrimination grounds now protected in EU law.

In other words, the Court has chosen to treat age as equivalent as other non-discrimination grounds, and in general to confer the status of superior norms upon the provisions of EU anti-discrimination law in general. In doing so, it has even been willing to depart from its previous reluctance to give directive direct effect in private relationships in order to ensure the effective implementation of the general principle of equality, and the anti-discrimination law that gives expression to this principle.

At the same time, the Court's age discrimination decisions have recognised the distinctive nature of age discrimination. The Court has given a relatively wide margin of discretion to Member States wishing to make use of age-based distinctions, where States can make reasonably strong objective case exists to support the use of these distinctions. It has therefore both affirmed the status of the prohibition on age discrimination and the fundamental importance of anti-discrimination norms in general, while developing a workable and nuanced jurisprudence in the field of age equality.

In discussing the evolution of this case-law, it is worth noting that the age discrimination provisions have generated more preliminary references to the ECJ from national courts than all the other 'new' (post-2000) discrimination grounds taken together, including race and religion. Thus far, the ECJ has made eight significant decisions in the field of age discrimination, compared to one decision in the field of race discrimination,[33] two in the field of disability,[34] one in the field of sexual orientation[35] and none thus far in the area of religious discrimination.

This perhaps reflects the uncertainty that surrounded age discrimination, and the lack of comparable national case-law on the topic: in the absence of clear guidance in the text of the Directive or from other authoritative sources as to how to apply its age discrimination provisions, national courts have repeatedly referred difficult cases to Luxembourg. As a result, the age discrimination provisions of the Directive have thus far generated much more legal controversy than was anticipated in many quarters. Far from being a sleepy backwater of European anti-discrimination law, age has proven to be a difficult and contested area of law.

The ECJ judgments on age discrimination have also been of considerable important in clarifying both how the Directive is to be interpreted in general. The judgments in

[32] Case C-555/07, *Kücükdeveci v Swedex GmbH & Co KG*, ECJ, Grand Chamber, Judgment of 19th January 2010.

[33] Case C-54/07, *Centrum voor gelijkheid van kansen v Firma Feryn NV* [2008] 3 CMLR 22.

[34] C-13/05, *Chacón Navas v Eurest Colectividades SA* [2006] ECR I-6467; Case C-303/06, *Coleman v Attridge Law* [2008] ECR I-5603.

[35] Case C-267/06, *Tadao Maruko v Versorgungsanstalt der deutschen Bühnen*, ECJ, Grand Chamber, Judgment of 1st April 2008.

Mangold, *Bartsch*[36] and *Kücükdeveci* have clarified that the Directive should be interpreted as giving effect to a general principle of equal treatment, which the Court considers to be part of the quasi-constitutional framework of core principles that underpins the EU legal order in its entirety. The Court's judgment in the *Wolf* case has clarified how the genuine occupational requirement exception set out in Article 4 of the Directive is to be interpreted,[37] while the scope of the Directive and its applicability to national laws governing retirement ages have been explained in the *Palacios de la Villa* and *Age Concern* judgments.

The age discrimination case-law of the Court is also proving to be increasingly important in clarifying wider issues of EU law. The ECJ decision in *Mangold* has been of particular importance, as well as being particularly controversial, as here the Court recognised the existence of a wide principle of equal treatment encompassing all the different discrimination grounds currently recognised in EU law.[38]

Furthermore, the *Mangold* decision, as clarified by the recent ECJ decisions in the age discrimination cases of *Bartsch* and *Kücükdeveci*, appears to have established that national courts must give effect to this general principle of equal treatment by disregarding national laws linked to the transposition of Directives and other elements of EU law which conflict with this principle. As Advocate General Bot noted in his opinion in *Kücükdeveci*, the requirement for national courts to disapply national laws that conflict with EU legal norms is not wholly new, as it dates back to the *Simmenthal* decision.[39] However, these cases appear to have developed this doctrine and taken its implications one stage further, by clarifying that national courts must disapply national laws in the case of conflict with this general principle of equal treatment, even where this has the result that in practice the Directive will become applicable in 'horizontal' disputes between private parties. This jurisprudence marks a departure by the Court from its traditional reluctance to avoid giving horizontal direct effect to Directives within national law: now, it appears that Directives may be directly applicable as between private parties when they embody and give effect to fundamental principles of EU law.

In these cases, the Court has therefore re-fashioned key elements of EU law: it has insisted upon the inclusion of the prohibition of age discrimination as a component element of the general principle of equality and non-discrimination in EU law, and used age discrimination cases to give new life, dynamism and status to this principle, establishing it as a core value of the European legal order. Far from being a marginal backwater of EU anti-discrimination law, age discrimination has become a major artery for its development and legal expression.

---

[36] C-427/06, *Bartsch v Bosch und Siemens Hausgeräte (BSH) Altersfürsorge GmbH*, ECJ, Grand Chamber, Judgment of 23 September 2008.

[37] C-229/08, *Wolf v Stadt Frankfurt am Main*, ECJ, Grand Chamber, Judgment of 12th January 2010.

[38] See Case C-144/04, *Mangold v Helm*, [2005] ECR I-9981.

[39] Case C-555/07, *Kücükdeveci v Swedex GmbH & Co KG*, ECJ, Grand Chamber, Judgment of 19th January 2010, Opinion of Bot AG, para. 55.

What is also particularly striking in examining the evolution of the case-law is that the Court's views appear to have been often developed in contrast to the perspective put forward by successive Advocate Generals, who have adopted a more cautious approach to age discrimination. Therefore, it is possible to characterise this case-law as driven by the Court's conscious decision to treat age discrimination as having equivalent status as other ground, and to give wide-ranging effect to the principle of equal treatment.

Why exactly the Court has taken this stance is a question worthy of examination. But, before turning to this point, it is useful to describe the development of the case-law in broad chronological order. Two main strands exist in the case-law: the development of the Court's interpretation of the age discrimination provisions of Directive 2000/78/EC, and its analysis of the relationship between these provisions and the general principle of equal treatment. These two strands appeared woven together initially in *Mangold*, the Court's first decision in respect of the Directive, as well as its first decision on age discrimination. The controversial question of the link between age discrimination and the principle of equal treatment was then left to one side as the Court focused on interpreting the age provisions of the Directive, before the two strands were woven together again in the recent *Bartsch* and *Kücükdeveci* decisions of the Court.

First Steps: The *Mangold* Decision

The *Mangold* case concerned an age-based exception to the general provisions of the German Labour Code that concern fixed-term contracts, which provide that the use of fixed-term employment contracts of more than two years duration, or which are renewed more than three times within two years, must be shown by the employer to be objectively justified. To encourage greater employment of older workers, these general provisions were amended in 2002 by legislation which gave employers the freedom to conclude fixed-term contracts in certain circumstances that were not subject to these limits with workers over the age of 58 (and with workers over the age of 52 until December 2006) without having to show objective justification.[40]

This measure was challenged on the basis that it subjected older workers to lower levels of employment protection and therefore constituted unjustified age discrimination. However, the claimant was faced with the obstacle that the Directive's age discrimination provisions were not in effect in Germany at the time the legal action was commenced, as Germany had taken advantage of the 2006 extended deadline to implement these provisions. To circumvent this obstacle, the claimant argued that the legislation in question was contrary to the obligations of the German government to take effective measures to implement the age discrimination provisions of the Directive by December 2006 and not in the interim to take action which would conflict with the goals and purpose of the Directive.

[40] The relevant provisions were para. 14(3), fourth sentence, taken together with para. 14(3), first sentence, of the *Gesetz über Teilzeitarbeit und befristete Arbeitsverträge und zur Änderung und Aufhebung arbeitsrechtlicher Bestimmungen* (TzBfG). The use of fixed-term contracts which were essentially a continuation of, or a substitution for, existing permanent contracts of employment was not permitted, an element of the case which should perhaps have received more attention in the judgment of the Court.

In its judgment, the ECJ agreed that the less favourable treatment afforded to older workers by the 2002 legislation constituted a difference of treatment on the grounds of age. It went on to find that this could not be objectively justified, rejecting the German government's argument that the special discriminatory measures were justified by the goal of ensuring greater employment of older workers.

In the view of the Court, reducing employment protection for individual workers over a particular age could not be objectively justified by reference to vague arguments that this could improve their employability as a collective group.[41] The Court acknowledged that national governments had wide discretion in deciding and giving effect to national employment policies. It also accepted that promoting the 'vocational integration of unemployed older workers' could constitute a legitimate aim in assessing whether the legislation under challenge was justifiable.[42] However, it considered that the use of age as the sole criterion for identifying the affected persons who would lose important forms of employment protection, and the absence of reference in the legislative scheme to other relevant considerations such as the structure of the specific labour markets in question and the personal circumstances of individuals seeking work, had the result that the measure under challenge went well beyond what was permitted under the objective justification test set out in Article 6(1).

What is striking is this part of the judgment is the rigour with which the objective justification test set out in Article 6(1) was applied. This aspect of *Mangold* has often been overlooked in the controversy that surrounded the other elements of the judgment. However, in its analysis of the Directive's provisions, the Court emphasised that Member States would have to show clear objective justification if age limits were used to limit the legal protection available to particular groups. In addition, in para. 65 of its judgment, the Court made explicit reference to the gender discrimination case of *Lommers*, thereby indicating that the objective justification test will be applied to age in a similar manner as it is applied to other discrimination grounds, a point subsequently confirmed in the following cases.

However, the controversy generated by *Mangold* stemmed not so much from the Court's interpretation of the age discrimination provisions of the Directive, but from the extra elements of the Court's analysis in this case. Following this conclusion that the German legislation in question was not in conformity with Article 6(1) of the Directive, the Court proceeded to describe the prohibition on age discrimination set out in the Directive as an expression of a general principle of equal treatment, which it classified as a fundamental norm of the Community legal order.

Specifically, in paragraphs 74–77 of *Mangold*, the ECJ stated that Directive 2000/78 set out a 'general framework' for giving effect to the general principle of equal treatment in the field of employment and occupation, which was a fundamental norm of the EC legal

---

[41] From a social rights perspective, *Mangold* is an interesting judgment on account of the Court's evident scepticism that measures which limit employment protection can be justified because of how it might make that group more employable as a whole.

[42] See paragraphs 59 and 60 of the judgment, [2005] ECR I-9981.

order. The Court considered that this principle was embedded in various international treaties and in the constitutional traditions common to the Member States. It then went on to say that 'the principle of non-discrimination on grounds of age' was an aspect of this wider principle, appearing to elevate the prohibition on age discrimination to the status of a basic norm of the Community legal order by virtue of its link with the more general principle of equal treatment. By infringing the provisions of the Directive, the Court considered that the national law in question was also incompatible with this general principle of equal treatment: the age discrimination provisions of the Directive were interpreted as an authoritative legislative expression of the general principle.

The Court then went one step further, and concluded that national legislation which conflicted with this general principle of equal treatment should be disapplied by national courts, even if the relevant provisions of the Directive itself were not yet legally binding on the country concerned. In reaching this conclusion, the Court partially relied upon what is often described as the '*Inter-Environnement* doctrine', whereby member states must, during the period set aside for national implementation of a directive, 'refrain from taking any measures liable seriously to compromise the result prescribed'.[43] However, the Court also introduced a new element into its reasoning, finding that 'observance of the general principle of equal treatment, in particular in respect of age, cannot as such be conditional upon the expiry of the period allowed the Member States for the transposition of a directive intended to lay down a general framework for combating discrimination…' In other words, the German legislation not alone could be considered to undermine the proper implementation of the Directive, it also conflicted with the general principle of equal treatment and should therefore be disapplied in the context of the private dispute between employer and employee at issue in this case, even though the Directive itself was not as yet legally binding.

Taking all the elements of the *Mangold* decision together, the Court in one sweeping judgment established i) the status of age-based distinctions as 'suspect' criteria whose use in the context of employment and occupation must be shown to satisfy the exacting requirements of the standard objective justification test, while ii) also recognising that the prohibition on age discrimination was an integral aspect of a more general principle of equal treatment, which iii) national courts were obliged to respect by disapplying conflicting national laws.

The Post-*Mangold* Backlash

The implications of this were far-reaching: in requiring the German courts to disapply the relevant legislation at issue in *Mangold*, the Court effectively ensured that direct effect was given to the Directive's provisions, notwithstanding the fact that the implementation date had not yet passed, and also irrespective of the fact that the Court has traditionally been reluctant to give horizontal direct effect to the provisions of directives.[44] As a result, the *Mangold* decision has generated serious controversy in Germany and other member states. The question of whether the German courts should respond to *Mangold* is at the time of writing before the German Constitutional Court in

[43] Case C-129/96 *Inter-Environnement* [1997] ECR I-7411.

[44] See e.g. Case C-91/92 *Faccini Dori* [1994] ECR I-3325.

a case brought by the company directly affected by the decision in that case, *Honeywell Bremsbelag GmbH*, and the correctness of the judgment remains very controversial.

The Court's judgment has also been subject to severe academic criticism on a variety of grounds. Some of this criticism was directed at the perceived departure from the rules limiting the horizontal direct effect of directives.[45] Others criticised the concept of a general principle of equal treatment, on the basis that the enabling provisions of Article 13 of the EC Treaty could not be treated as sufficient grounds for the recognition of a free-standing principle in Community law, or argued such a general principle lacked sufficient content and precision to be applied as the Court did in *Mangold.*[46]

More specifically, strong criticism was directed by some commentators at the inclusion of age within the scope of this general principle, given the lack of protection offered against age discrimination in national law across the EU. Some commentators have argued that the limited scope of protection offered against age discrimination under the Directive, in particular the potential for direct age discrimination to be objectively justified under Article 6(1) and the lack of protection outside of the field of employment and occupation, means that age should not be seen as covered by the general principle of equal treatment. [47]

In particular, the former President of the German Republic and President of the German Constitutional Court, Roman Herzog, strongly criticised the inclusion by the ECJ in *Mangold* of age within the scope of the general principle of equal treatment in a newspaper article attacking what he argued was excessive judicial activism on the part of the ECJ. [48] He argued that it was a 'fabrication' on the part of the Court to treat age discrimination as contained within the general principle of equal treatment, on the basis that age discrimination was not treated as linked to the equality principle in the vast majority of the constitutional traditions of the member states, or in any international treaty.[49] He also argued that as issues of age discrimination gave rise to little or any

[45] See e.g. Editorial Comments, *CML Rev.* 2006, pp. 1–8.

[46] See e.g. the discussion in F. Kuitenbrouwer, *Onbescheiden Rechters*, NRC Handelsblad, 7 February 2006, summarised in J. Jans, 'The Effect in National Legal Systems of the Prohibition of Discrimination on Grounds of Age as a General Principle of Community Law' (2007) 34(1) *Legal Issues of Economic Integration* 53–66, 58-60. See also D. Martin, 'L'arrêt Mangold – Vers une hiérarchie inversée du droit à l'égalité en droit communautaire?', *Journal des tribunaux du travail*, 2006, pp.109-116 ; J. Cavallini, 'De la suppression des restrictions à la conclusion d'un contrat à durée déterminée lorsque le salarié est un senior', *La Semaine Juridique Sociale*, 2005, pp. 25 to 28; O. Dubos, 'La Cour de justice, le renvoi préjudiciel, l'invocabilité des directives: de l'apostasie à l'hérésie?', *La semaine juridique*, 2006, pp. 1295 to 1297; O. Le Clerc, 'Le contrat de travail des seniors à l'épreuve du droit communautaire', *Recueil Dalloz*, 2006, pp. 557 to 561; E. Dubout, on 'Mangold' in *Revue des affaires européennes* 2005, pp. 723 to 733; A. Masson and C. Micheau, 'The Werner Mangold Case: An Example of Legal Militancy' *(2007) European Public Law* 587-593.

[47] L.A.J. Senden, *Over idealen en ideale rechtsvorming in de Europese Unie*, inaugural lecture, University of Tilburg, 10 March 2006. The text is available on the website at: http://www.uvt.nl/webwijs/show.html?anr=687502, and is discussed in J. Jans, 'The Effect in National Legal Systems of the Prohibition of Discrimination on Grounds of Age as a General Principle of Community Law' (2007) 34(1) *Legal Issues of Economic Integration* 53–66, 60.

[48] This article can be found in English translation: R. Herzog and L. Gerken, 'Stop the European Court of Justice', *EU Observer*, 10th September 2008.

[49] See also L. Gerken et al., *‚Mangold' als ausbrechender Rechtsakt* (München: Sellier, 2009).

'trans-boundary' impact, the ECJ should defer to national decisions as to how to deal with this problem and not apply the objective justification test with the rigour it did in *Mangold.*

It is clear that some elements of the *Mangold* decision are vulnerable to criticism. In particular, the Court's reasoning that the German legislation conflicted with the general principle of equality, even though the specific legislative framework through which that principle was expressed, Directive 2000/78/EC, had given countries the option of delaying full implementation was open to question. In addition, key elements of the judgment, in particular the source of the general principle of equal treatment, are not always clearly expressed. However, strong arguments can be made that *Mangold* is less of a departure from previous ECJ case-law than was assumed by many commentators. The judgment of the Court can be seen as simply involving a logical extension of the well-established doctrine of the supremacy of EU legal norms over national law, and as adding yet another situation to the circumstances in which the Court recognises that directives may have direct effect in national legal systems.[50]

The Court had also in previous cases indicated that a general principle of equal treatment existed in EU law,[51] and the inclusion of age within the scope of this general principle appears to be entirely consistent with the text of the Recitals of Directive 2000/78/EC, which link the protection conferred by that Directive against discrimination to national and international human rights standards governing equality and non-discrimination, and which do not differentiate between age and the other non-discrimination grounds.[52] In addition, the arguments cited by Roman Herzog as to the lack of 'trans-boundary' effects associated with age discrimination are very problematic, as similar arguments could be made for all forms of discrimination: there is nothing that distinguishes age in this respect from gender and other forms of discrimination.

It could be argued that the reaction to *Mangold* may to some degree stem from a deep unfamiliarity with age discrimination, and even perhaps with anti-discrimination norms in general beyond the well-established gender discrimination case-law. In any case, the case-law of the ECJ on age discrimination has continued to evolve. The ECJ has not renounced its approach in *Mangold,* despite criticism of the vague and uncertain nature of the general principle of equal treatment by Advocate General Geelhoed in his opinion

---

[50] See the excellent analysis in J. Jans, 'The Effect in National Legal Systems of the Prohibition of Discrimination on Grounds of Age as a General Principle of Community Law' (2007) 34(1) *Legal Issues of Economic Integration* 53–66.

[51] See the discussion of the relevant case-law in the essays collected in A. Dashwood and S. O'Leary (eds.), *The Principle of Equal Treatment in EC Law* (London: Sweet & Maxwell, 1997).

[52] Advocate General Bot makes this point in his Opinion in the subsequent *Kücükdeveci* case: see para. 76. He also suggests rightly that the Court would have strengthened its case in *Mangold* had it placed emphasis on the specific guarantee of the right to freedom from age discrimination contained in the 'equality clause' of Article 21(1) of the EU Charter of Fundamental Rights. For a favourable analysis of *Mangold* from an equality rights perspective, see D. Schiek, 'The ECJ Decision in Mangold: A Further Twist on Effects of Directives and Constitutional Relevance of Community Equality Legislation' (2006) *Industrial Law Journal* 329-341.

in the *Chacón Navas* case[53] and Advocate General Mazak in his opinions in the *Palacios de la Villa* and *Age Concern* cases.[54] Instead, the Court in the age discrimination cases that have followed *Mangold* has re-affirmed that age will be treated similarly as other forms of discrimination, and that the prohibition on age discrimination in the Directive is an expression of the general principle of equal treatment which requires conflicting national laws to be disapplied even where this results in horizontal direct effect being given to the age discrimination provisions of Directive 2000/78/EC. However, the Court has introduced some more nuanced elements into its approach, which do not represent a departure from its general stance towards age discrimination in *Mangold*, but rather constitute a clarification of the position adopted in that decision.

Lindorfer and *Palacios*: New Directions?

At first, in the aftermath of *Mangold*, the direction of the Court's jurisprudence on age discrimination appeared uncertain. In the *Lindorfer* case, which concerned an appeal from the Court of First Instance concerning claims that the claimant's years of pensionable service had been calculated by in a way that constituted discrimination on the grounds of sex and age, Advocate General Jacobs in his initial Opinion written before delivery of the *Mangold* judgment suggested that age could not be treated as equivalent to gender or other forms of discrimination.[55] Subsequently, the Grand Chamber of the Court, having taken over this case from the First Senate of the Court and re-opened the proceedings in the wake of *Mangold*, resolved the case without any reference to age discrimination or even to the general principle of equal treatment, despite seeking the views of parties on both matters and having the benefit of further discussion in a second opinion, by Advocate General Sharpston, on these points.[56] The Grand Chamber was able to do this, as the sex discrimination arguments represented the real substance of the case. However, the absence of any discussion of the general principle of equal treatment, or of age discrimination, in the judgment appeared to cast some doubt over the approach adopted by the Court in *Mangold*, and indicated that perhaps the Court was less than sure of its position.

This perception was reinforced by the criticism of the *Mangold* decision made before the *Lindorfer* decision was handed down by Advocate Generals Geelhoed and Mazák in their Opinions on the *Chacon Navas* and *Palacios de la Villa*[57] cases respectively. As mentioned above, both Advocates General suggested that the general principle of equal

[53] C-13/05, *Chacón Navas*, [2006] ECR I-6467, Opinion of Geelhoed AG, para. 54.

[54] Case C-411/05, *Félix Palacios de la Villa v Cortefiel Servicios SA*, [2007] ECR I-8531, Opinion of Mazák AG delivered on 15 February 2007, para. 86.

[55] Case C-227/04 P *Lindorfer* v *Council*, [2007] ECR I-6767, Opinion of Jacobs AG, delivered on 27 October 2005, paras. 84-91.

[56] The case was been reopened by Order of the Court of 26 April 2006, with the second Opinion delivered on 30 November 2006 by Advocate General Sharpston, and Judgment was delivered by the Grand Chamber on 11 September 2007. The Opinion by Sharpston AG was more ambiguous and nuanced on the question of the status of age discrimination and its relationship with the principle of equal treatment, but nevertheless echoed the views of Jacobs AG to some extent.

[57] Case C-411/05, *Félix Palacios de la Villa v Cortefiel Servicios SA*, [2007] ECR I-8531

treatment was too uncertain a legal concept to be applied in the manner that the Court had done in *Mangold*.

As a result of their concern that the Court had over-reached itself in *Mangold*, both Advocate Generals also called for the Court to adopt a 'restrained' approach to the application of the provisions of Directive 2000/78/EC, with Mazák AG in his opinion in the second age discrimination case to be decided by the Court, *Palacios de la Villa*, arguing in particular for a very cautious approach to be adopted by the Court in applying the age discrimination provisions of the Directive.[58] However, the Court in *Palacios* chose to adopt an alternative approach, effectively re-affirming the general approach to the age discrimination provisions of the Directive that it had adopted in *Mangold*, while however leaving the issue of the relationship between the prohibition of age discrimination and the general principle of equal treatment open.

The *Palacios* case concerned a reference by a Spanish court concerning the provisions of a national collective agreement which established that employees in workplaces covered by the agreement would cease to be employed at the fixed retirement age of 65, subject to a condition that the employees affected had made sufficient contributions under the national social security scheme to become entitled to a full retirement pension. Legislation in 2005 had permitted the inclusion of such compulsory retirement age provisions in collective agreements, after a process of extensive debate as to the potential impact of the abolition of retirement ages on the operation of the Spanish labour market. Therefore, this case not alone re-opened the question of the status of age discrimination, but also raised the question of whether the Directive applied to national rules governing retirement ages, which remained another issue left apparently unresolved by the text of the Directive.

In his opinion, Mazák AG argued that age should be distinguished from other forms of discrimination, as follows:

> So far as non-discrimination on grounds of age, especially, is concerned, it should be borne in mind that that prohibition is of a specific nature in that age as a criterion is a point on a scale and that, therefore, age discrimination may be graduated. It is therefore a much more difficult task to determine the existence of a discrimination on grounds of age than for example in the case of discrimination on grounds of sex, where the comparators involved are more clearly defined….What is more, whilst the application of the prohibition of discrimination on grounds of age thus requires a complex and subtle assessment, age-related distinctions are very common in social and employment policies.[59]

Mazák AG then proceeded to suggest that the Directive should be interpreted as not extending to national rules governing retirement ages, on the basis that the application of the prohibition on age discrimination to such rules was not justified, and that Recital 14 to the Directive recognised this by, as discussed above, providing that the Directive

[58] Case C-411/05, *Félix Palacios de la Villa v Cortefiel Servicios SA*, [2007] ECR I-8531, Opinion of Mazák AG delivered on 15 February 2007.

[59] Paras. 61-63.

was 'without prejudice' to retirement ages. He argued that 'it would... be very problematic to have this Sword of Damocles hanging over all national provisions laying down retirement ages, especially as retirement ages are closely linked with areas like social and employment policies where the primary powers remain with the Member States...[60]

In effect, in his opinion in *Palacios*, Mazák AG was arguing both for age to be treated in a very different manner than gender as a ground of discrimination, and for the Directive to be given a restrictive and cautious interpretation, especially where national rules retirement ages were concerned. In so doing, he was effectively challenging the approach adopted by the Court in *Mangold* that age discrimination should be treated as essentially 'not different in substance' from other forms of discrimination.

However, the Court in its judgment in *Palacios* declined to follow this lead. The Court considered that legislation establishing rules relating to employment came squarely within the scope of the Directive, with the result that rules governing retirement ages were subject to the Directive's age discrimination provisions.[61] In so doing, the Court implicitly rejected the argument made by Mazák AG that the uncertain status of age discrimination justified a narrow interpretation of the Directive in this context.

The Court also emphasised that national measures which were based on age had to meet the high standards of the objective justification test, which it applied in a similar manner as it is applied in other areas of discrimination law. However, the Court nevertheless took the view that considered that the retirement age provisions in question could be regarded as objectively justified under Article 6(1) of the Directive, on the basis that they were objectively and reasonably justified by a legitimate aim relating to employment policy and the effective functioning of the Spanish labour market, and the use of a fixed retirement age did not appear to be inappropriate and unnecessary to achieve this aim in the circumstances.

In particular, the Court at paragraph 53 of its judgment highlighted that the measure in question 'was adopted, at the instigation of the social partners, as part of a national policy seeking to promote better access to employment, by means of better distribution of work between the generations'. The Court also went on to note that the measure took into account both the age of employees and also their pension entitlements, as well as allowing collective agreements to modify the operation of the retirement age scheme. Therefore, it concluded that the national legislation in question could be regarded as coming within the 'broad discretion' accorded to member states in setting and implementing employment policy and as objectively justified under Article 6(1). Given this finding, the Court considered there was no need for it to comment on the

[60] Paras. 63-65.

[61] At para. 44, the Court made the following observations about the interpretation of Recital 14: 'It is true that, according to recital 14 in its preamble, Directive 2000/78 is to be without prejudice to national provisions laying down retirement ages. However, that recital merely states that the directive does not affect the competence of the Member States to determine retirement age and does not in any way preclude the application of that directive to national measures governing the conditions for termination of employment contracts where the retirement age, thus established, has been reached.'

compatibility of the Spanish provisions with the general principle of equal treatment mentioned in *Mangold*.

Thus, in *Palacios*, the Court implicitly rejected the suggestion by Mazák AG that age should be treated as substantially different from other forms of discrimination, in particular gender. However, the Court in applying the objective justification test in a rigorous manner was nevertheless willing to find the Spanish law governing retirement ages to be in conformity with the Directive. The Court thus re-affirmed the rigorous nature of the prohibition on age discrimination set out in the Directive, while accepting that the complexity of the policy issues which surround the difficult issue of retirement age justified granting states a relatively wide margin of discretion in this area of employment policy. However, it left further consideration of the link between age discrimination and the principle of equal treatment for the future, leaving the status of this aspect of the *Mangold* judgment open. In other words, the analysis of the age discrimination provisions of the directive adopted by the Court in *Mangold* was re-affirmed, while the analysis of the relationship between age discrimination and the general principle of equal treatment also adopted in the case was left to one side.

Age Concern: The Status of Age Discrimination Re-Affirmed

Subsequently, the Court adopted a similar analysis in the UK case of *R (The Incorporated Trustees of the National Council on Ageing (Age Concern England) v Secretary of State for Business, Enterprise and Regulatory Reform.*[62] This reference again concerned the complex question of retirement age, an issue on which there was been extensive debate in the UK. Previously, UK law had provided that workers over the age of 65 could not bring claims of unfair dismissal if they were employed, which effectively enabled employers to terminate their employment contracts after this date. The provisions of the UK Employment Equality (Age Discrimination) Regulations 2006, which implemented Directive 2000/78/EC into UK law, extended protection against unfair dismissal to employees over 65, to ensure conformity with the prohibition on age discrimination. However, the new Regulations introduced new provisions which permitted employers to terminate the employment contracts of employees who are older than 65: employees who wish to continue to work after this 'mandatory retirement age' can request to stay on, and if they continue to work are protected against unfair dismissal, but employers need only 'consider' this request.

The UK Government justified the existence of this retirement age provision on the basis that many employers wanted to have clarity as to when employees would retire, to assist their recruitment planning and workforce management. However, the strong and prominent network of age equality NGOs in the UK challenged these provisions, on the basis that the use of mandatory retirement ages by employers violated principles of age equality and was not objectively justified under EU law.

This case differed from *Palacios* in three important respects. Firstly, the UK Government cited the workforce management needs of employers to justify the

[62] Case C-388/07, *Age Concern England* [2009] ECR I-0000, ECJ (Third Chamber), Judgment of 5th March 2009.

retirement age provisions: however, this is not specifically listed as a legitimate aim in the list of examples of legitimate aims set out in the text of Article 6(1) (see above), unlike 'employment policy', the aim cited by the Spanish Government in *Palacios*. Secondly, unlike the case in *Palacios*, age was the sole criterion taken into account in the application of the UK retirement age provisions: employees could be dismissed at 65 if an employer wished to make use of the mandatory retirement age provisions, even if they had not made enough contributions to qualify for a full pension under the relevant social security legislation. Finally, the UK retirement age provisions had not been agreed through a process of consultation with the social partners.

In their arguments before the ECJ, the coalition of age equality NGOs argued that these differences between the UK and Spanish situations meant that the UK retirement age provisions could not be considered to be objectively justified. In adjudicating this case, the ECJ was also asked by the referring national court to clarify whether the objective justification test to be applied when direct age discrimination was alleged was of similar scope and rigour as the objective justification test to be applied when indirect discrimination on other grounds was at issue. *Age Concern* thus gave rise to more fundamental issues as to the nature of the prohibition on age discrimination set out in the Directive.

Therefore, it was no surprise when Mazák AG in his Opinion took the opportunity to reiterate some of the views he expressed in his opinion in *Palacios*, arguing that age should not be treated as a 'suspect' ground of discrimination and therefore the objective justification test should be applied in a less demanding manner than in other contexts. Again, his arguments are worth reproducing in detail:

> Age is not by its nature a 'suspect ground', at least not so much as for example race or sex. Simple in principle to administrate, clear and transparent, age-based differentiations, age-limits and age-related measures are, quite to the contrary, widespread in law and in social and employment legislation in particular. At the same time, age is fluid as a criterion. Whether differential treatment constitutes age discrimination may not only be a question of whether it is founded directly or indirectly on age, but also a question of what age it relates to. It may therefore be much more difficult than for example in the case of differentiation on grounds of sex to establish where justifiable differentiations on the basis of age are ending and unjustifiable discrimination is starting…
>
> By providing for a specific and additional possibility of justification, Article 6(1) aims to take account of the specific nature and difficulties of age discrimination. It is obviously intended to enable Member States to retain age-based employment practices and to set or preserve age limits in so far as they are justified by a legitimate employment or social policy aim…
>
> Accordingly, and contrary to what Age Concern England appears to suggest, the possibilities under the directive of justifying differences of treatment based on age are more extensive than those based on the other grounds mentioned in Article 1 of the directive. That should, however, not be interpreted as putting age

> discrimination at the bottom of a perceived 'hierarchy' of discrimination grounds under the directive. Rather, it constitutes an expression of the material differences between those grounds and in the way they function as legal criteria. It is not a matter of value or importance, but a matter of how to entrench the scope of the prohibition of discrimination adequately.[63]

Mazák AG went on to express his view that the UK legislation on retirement ages could in principle be objectively justified.

In its judgment, the Court agreed that the UK legislation could in principle be considered to be objectively justified, but referred the matter to the national court for final determination.[64] In particular, the Court took the view that the fact that the UK had justified its legislation on the basis that it ensured that employers could conduct effective workforce planning was not necessarily fatal, as this could be considered to constitute a general legitimate interest. The Court also reiterated that Member States enjoy a broad discretion in the area of national employment policy, and took the view that the differences between the Spanish measures at issue in *Palacios* and the UK legislation at issue in *Age Concern* were not so significant as to establish that the UK law was clearly not in conformity with the Directive.[65]

The Court therefore in *Age Concern* placed much less emphasis on the social factors that it had taken into account in *Palacios*, and appeared willing to accommodate the desire of the UK to make life easer for employers. However, despite this shift in emphasis, the Court again implicitly rejected the suggestion by Mazák AG that age discrimination should be analysed as a 'non-suspect' form of discrimination. In particular, the Court emphasised at paragraph 67 of its judgment in *Age Concern* that 'Art. 6(1) imposes on Member States the burden of establishing to a high standard of proof the legitimacy of the aim relied on as a justification', and in paragraph 51 that while Member States enjoy broad discretion, 'that discretion cannot have the effect of

---

[63] Case C-388/07, *Age Concern England* [2009] ECR I-0000, Opinion of Mazák AG, delivered on 23 September 2008, paragraphs 74-76. The Italian Government made similar arguments in its intervention before the Court in this case. Advocate General Ruiz-Jarabo Colomer made a broadly similar suggestion in *Maruko*, arguing that the 'essential character' of the right to non-discrimination on the ground of sexual orientation is of a different order to that which the Court attributed to the principle of non-discrimination based on age in *Mangold*.

[64] Case C-388/07, *Age Concern England* [2009] ECR I-0000, Judgment of 5th March 2009. In the UK, the High Court subsequently held that the retirement age provisions could be regarded as objectively justified in the light of the general approach adopted by the ECJ: however, Blake J., the judge who decided the case, expressed considerable doubts as to whether the UK Government had shown sufficient justification for its selection of 65 as the appropriate retirement age, given changes in employment patterns: see *R(Age UK) v Secretary Of State For Business, Innovation & Skills* [2009] EWHC 2336 (Admin). The retirement age legislation is currently the subject of a review by the UK Government, which is considering increasing the age to 68 or even perhaps abolishing it in its entirety.

[65] The Court also clarified that measures could be justified by legitimate aims which were not specifically included in the list of examples of such aims set out in Article 6(1) of the Directive, as long as they served 'legitimate social policy objectives' that were 'distinguishable from purely individual reasons particular to the employer's situation, such as cost reduction or improving competitiveness': see paragraph 46 of the Judgment.

frustrating the implementation of the principle of non-discrimination on grounds of age'. It continued:

> Mere generalisations concerning the capacity of a specific measure to contribute to employment policy, labour market or vocational training objectives are not enough to show that the aim of that measure is capable of justifying derogation from that principle and do not constitute evidence on the basis of which it could reasonably be considered that the means chosen are suitable for achieving that aim (see, by way of analogy, Case C-167/97 *Seymour-Smith and Perez* [1999] ECR I-623, paragraphs 75 and 76).

This part of the *Age Concern* judgment is particularly significant. It clarifies that the Court will require a rigorous application of the objective justification test in the context of age, notwithstanding the greater possibilities of justifying the use of age-based distinctions permitted by the Directive. The reference to the *Seymour-Smith* judgment also indicated again that case-law from other areas of discrimination law can provide guidance on how the test will be applied, thereby implicitly suggesting that the prohibition on age discrimination can be seen as analogous to other forms of discrimination law.

Palacios and *Age Concern* are important judgments. They confirm the Court's general approach to the age discrimination provisions of the Directive that was initially set out in *Mangold.* In both cases, the ECJ have clarified that age discrimination is to be treated similarly as other forms of discrimination, and the objective justification test is to be applied with similar rigour across the different discrimination grounds. However, the Court also made it clear in both cases that the specific nature of age discrimination would be taken into account in applying this objective justification test, and Member States enjoy wide discretion in areas where legitimate aims relating to national employment policy and other general interests were at issue. Age is thus treated as both similar and different to the other discrimination grounds: it is treated as a 'suspect' category which warrants the rigorous application of the objective justification test, but nevertheless the special nature of age and the potential for age-based distinctions to serve rational ends is also factored into the application of this test.

Applying the Court's New Template: *Hütter*, *Petersen* and *Wolf*

Palacios and *Age Concern* have therefore established a general template for how the Court will interpret the age discrimination provisions of the Directive, which echoes the Court's initial approach in this area in *Mangold.* This template does not rely upon the link between age discrimination and the general principle of equal treatment established by the ECJ in *Mangold*: it is based primarily on the text of the Directive, as interpreted by the Court. This template has subsequently been applied in a series of cases, which have further clarified how the discrimination provisions of the Directive should be interpreted and understood.

In the case of *Hütter v Technische Universität Graz,* a preliminary reference from Austria raised the question of the compatibility with the Directive of Austrian legislation which provided that periods of work under the age of 18 were excluded when calculating an employee's grading for salary purposes.[66] In its judgment, the Court initially considered that this constituted a clear difference of treatment based on age. Turning then to the question of objective justification under Article 6(1), the Court observed that the Austrian Government had suggested that the law in question was designed to achieve two legitimate aims, namely encouraging those under 18 to stay in secondary education, and simultaneously promoting the integration of young people who have pursued vocational training into the labour market, by encouraging employers to train apprentices without later having to incur extra salary costs. The Court considered that while both could constitute legitimate aims, they appeared to be contradictory, as the law could not both encourage students to remain in full-time secondary education and also encourage the full integration into the labour market of those who chose to leave.

In addition, the Court questioned whether the law could be said to rationally advance either aim: the age limit applied irrespective of whether students had staying in secondary education or undergone vocational training, while it also could 'lead to a difference in treatment between two persons who have pursued the same studies and acquired the same professional experience, exclusively on the basis of their respective ages'.[67] Therefore, the age limit 'did not single out a group of persons defined by their youth in order to give them special conditions of recruitment intended to promote their integration into the labour market', and therefore could not be said to advance the aim of integrating particular groups of younger workers. As such, the national law could not be said to be objectively justified under Article 6(1).

Hütter demonstrates the willingness of the Court to apply the objective justification test under Article 6(1) with rigour. In the subsequent case of *Petersen v Berufungsausschuss für Zähn für den Bezirk Westfalen-Lippe*,[68] the Court demonstrated a similar concern to enure that the use of age-based distinctions was clearly directed towards achieving a legitimate aim, but also indicated it willingness to accommodate measures designed to advance broad considerations of public policy, including policies designed to ensure fairness of opportunity across different age groups.

This reference from the German labour courts concerned an age limit of 68, after which dentists providing public care under the German health insurance system lost their authorisation to continue this work. However, this age limit did not apply to dentists in private practice, who were not subject to any upper time limit. The German Government attempted to justify the age limit on two separate grounds. Firstly, it argued the time limit was justified and necessary in order achieve the legitimate aim of protecting the health of patients obtaining dental care under the national statutory health insurance

---

[66] Case C-88/08, *Hütter v Technische Universität Graz*, ECJ, Third Chamber, Judgment of 18 June 2009. The claimant in this case, Hütter, recruited by the Technische Universität Graz (TUG) as a contractual public servant after having completed a period of apprenticeship as a laboratory technician: however, the professional experience he had acquired before the age of 18 was not, however, taken into account in his grading.

[67] Para. 39.

[68] Case C-341/08, *Petersen v Berufungsausschuss für Zähn für den Bezirk Westfalen-Lippe*, ECJ, Grand Chamber, Judgment of 12th January 2010.

scheme, as 'general experience' indicated that dentists suffered a decline in performance after the relevant date. Secondly, the Government also justified the measure as necessary to give effect to the legitimate aim of ensuring the stability and continuity of the system for insuring providers of public health insurance care: the age limit served to open up new places on the panel of dentists providing public care are to younger dentists, thereby sharing opportunities fairly across the different generations.

In its judgment, the ECJ took the view that the protection of public health could constitute a legitimate aim, but that the German Government had failed to establish that the time limit was justified and necessary on that basis, as no similar age limit had been imposed upon dentists in private practice. It was inconsistent to argue that an age limit was necessary to protect patients against possible decline in the skills of dentists, but not to apply this protection to patients receiving private practice, and this inconsistency called into question the legitimacy and necessity of the age limit.

However, the Court went on to say that the age limit could in principle be objectively justified on the basis of the second alleged legitimate aim, i.e. on the grounds that it was necessary to maintain an equitable balance between older and younger dentists, and to keep open paths of career progression within the public health panels. The necessity for such an age limit would depend on the circumstances of the specific labour market in question and the extent to which there was an excess of dentists wishing to occupy places on the public panel: however, the Court considered that whether these conditions were satisfied in the circumstances of the case was a matter for the national courts to determine.

Petersen is interesting for a number of reasons. The rigour of the objective justification test is demonstrated by the Court's refusal to accept that the age limit could be justified as necessary to protect the health of patients on the grounds that it did not apply to dentists in private practice. However, the willingness of the Court to accommodate aims rooted in broad policy considerations can be seen in its acceptance of the second argument based on the need to open up opportunities for younger dentists. This also illustrates that the Court may be willing to give Member States a wide margin of discretion when the use of age-based distinctions are used to advance 'inter-generational solidarity'.[69]

Petersen is also notable for the Court's apparent willingness to accept the contention by the German Government that the skills of dentists deteriorated with age. This argument was based on reference to 'general experience', rather than on specific medical studies. There is a concern here that arguments based on 'general experience' in the age context may simply involve stereotyping: while the matter was not decisive in *Petersen*, it remains to be seen whether the Court will require more extensive evidence of links

[69] This decision echoes that of the UK Employment Appeals Tribunal in *Seldon v Clarkson Wright and Jakes* [2009] IRLR 267, where a law firm's desire to open up partnership opportunities for younger solicitors was held to constitute a legitimate aim that could potentially justify a retirement age of 65.

between age and decline in performance than was offered in this case, or whether it will be in general willing to accept generalisations in this context.[70]

Similar issues of competency and the link between age, physical performance and genuine occupational requirements were at issue in the case of *Wolf v Stadt Frankfurt am Main*,[71] another reference from the German courts which the Grand Chamber of Court decided at the same time as *Petersen*. This case concerned a law which prevented individuals over the age of 30 applying to the fire service. The German Government argued that this measure was designed to achieve a legitimate aim, namely ensuring the operational capacity and effective functioning of the professional fire service. It also argued that the measure in question was justified and necessary to achieve this legitimate aim, on the basis that evidence showed that few fire service employees over the age of 45 years of age would have sufficient physical capacity to fight fires effectively and rescue persons in danger, and that the age limit ensured that individuals recruited to the fire service could perform these tasks for a sustained period of time before they were assigned to less physically demanding duties.

The Court accepted that an age limit in these circumstances could be objectively justified under Article 6(1), but crucially also accepted that it could constitute a genuine occupational requirement under Article 4(1) of the Directive. The Court supported its reasoning in this respect by referring to Recital 18 to the Directive, which provides that the Directive does not require emergency services to recruit or retain persons who cannot carry out the range of functions that they may be called upon to perform in their job. In the view of the Court, high physical capability was a genuine and determining occupational requirement for the posts in question, and the imposition of a maximum age limit served as an adequate and effective 'proxy' for the required level of physical fitness.

Again, as in *Petersen*, the Court seems to be willing to accept a link between age and physical capacity for the purpose of determining what constitutes a genuine occupational requirement. This is significant, as it may mark a departure from the Court's traditionally rigorous approach to determining the existence of a genuine occupational requirement: a narrow application of Article 4 would treat physical capacity as the sole occupational requirement in this case, and the use of age limits would have to be justified solely under Article 6(1).[72]

---

[70] There is a need for great caution in assuming that performance declines with age: medical evidence demonstrates that this is not necessarily the case: see J. Grimley-Evans, 'Age Discrimination: Implications of the Ageing Process', in S. Fredman and S. Spencer, *Age as an Equality Issue: Legal and Policy Perspectives* (Oxford: Hart, 2003), pp. 11-20.

[71] *C-229/08, Wolf v Stadt Frankfurt am Main*, ECJ, Grand Chamber, Judgment of 12th January 2010.

[72] This judgment contrasts with a decision of an UK employment tribunal in the case of *Baker v National Air Traffic Services*, ET/5596/60, which considered that an upper age limit of 36 in recruitment of air traffic controllers could not be considered to be objectively justified, on the basis that the employer had failed to show that the age limit was necessary to achieve similar legitimate aims as those cited in the *Wolf* case. However, in the *Baker* case, there was no evidence that the performance of air traffic controllers generally declined with age, unlike the case with the fire fighters in *Wolf*.

In this respect, *Wolf* along with *Petersen*, *Palacios* and *Age Concern* may again be said to demonstrate the Court's willingness to accommodate the proportionate use of age limits to serve rational legitimate aims by Member States, even while the decision in *Hütter* shows that the Court remains committed to the rigorous application of the age discrimination provisions of the Directive.

Back to *Mangold* – *Bartsch* and *Kücükdeveci*

This rigour has been recently on sow again in the Court's recent decision in *Kücükdeveci v Swedex GmbH & Co.*[73] This reference, again from the German labour courts, concerned the second sentence of Paragraph 622 (2) of the German Civil Code (the *Bürgerliches Gesetzbuch,* the BGB), which provided that periods of work under the age of 25 would not be taken into account in calculating minimum notice periods for termination of employment, which were in general based on length of service. This had the effect of ensuring that worker aged under or about 25 years of age had shorter notice periods than other workers: in this specific case, the claimant, Ms Kücükdeveci, had worked for Swedex GmbH & Co for ten years since she was 18 years of age, but when she was dismissed, the employer calculated the notice period as if she had three years' length of employment.

The German Government argued that this measure was objectively justified, as it was necessary to ensure greater flexibility in the labour market and to encourage greater employment of younger workers. The Court accepted the legitimacy of these aims, in line with its judgments in *Palacios*, *Age Concern* and *Hütter*. However, again consistently with its existing jurisprudence, the Court held that the age limit at issue could not be considered to be a justified and necessary measure to achieve these aims, as it applied to all employees who were 25 when they began their employment, regardless of their age or length of service at the time of their dismissal. In other words, the measure in question applied a rigid age-based criterion without reference to the different circumstances of the individual employees affected and their varying lengths of service, and therefore in line with *Hutter* could not be considered to be objectively justified.

Kücükdeveci represents the Court's latest re-affirmation of the rigour of its approach to the age discrimination provisions of the Directive. However, the Court also uses this judgment to link its developing case-law on the age discrimination provisions of the Directive back to the general principle of equal treatment recognised in *Mangold*, and returns to the issues of the supremacy of EU law and horizontal direct effect initially analysed in *Mangold*. In effect, the ECJ in *Kücükdeveci* re-affirms its *Mangold* judgment, and takes the opportunity to clarify the impact and consequences of that earlier decision, as well as the relationship between the provisions of the Directive, the requirements of the general principle of equal treatment, and national law.

---

[73] Case C-555/07, *Kücükdeveci v Swedex GmbH & Co KG*, ECJ, Grand Chamber, Judgment of 19th January 2010.

While developing its case-law on the age discrimination provisions of the Directive, the Court had returned to the controversial terrain of the *Mangold* judgment in yet another preliminary reference from the German courts, *Bartsch v Bosch und Siemens Hausgeräte (BSH) Altersfürsorge GmbH.*[74] This case concerned an application by Mrs Bartsch following the death of her husband to his employer for a survivor's pension. According to the rules of the employer's pension fund, no survivor's pension would be paid out if the surviving spouse was more than 15 years younger than the deceased former employee, a provision which was compatible with the relevant domestic law. Mrs Bartsch was 21 years younger than her husband and therefore was refused payment. She challenged this on the basis that it constituted age discrimination, and the German courts referred the matter to the Court of Justice.

Significantly, Mrs Bartsch's husband had died before the transposition period of the Directive had expired in 2006. Therefore, the question at issue was not whether the age discrimination provisions of the Directive applied, but whether any age discrimination that had taken place constituted a violation of the general principle of equal treatment recognised by the Court in *Mangold*, and if so whether the national courts were obliged to disapply the relevant national laws that applied in this situation and give direct effect to the prohibition on age discrimination. In other words, *Bartsch* opened again some of the issues at stake in *Mangold*, which had remained untouched since the earlier decision as the subsequent age discrimination cases had all clearly come within the period inn which the Directive's age provisions had been in force.

Sharpston AG in her Opinion used this opportunity to propose an approach which would retain the essence of the *Mangold* decision while clarifying its scope and meeting some of the concerns the judgment had generated. She noted that the Court's evolving age discrimination case-law had developed without reference to the general principle of equal treatment, and suggested that the Directive constituted 'detailed legislative intervention' designed to give expression to a new and emerging understanding of the appropriate scope of the general principle of equal treatment.[75]

Sharpston AG then proceeded to argue that national legislation enacted to implement or give effect to Community law, or to take advantage of a derogation permitted under Community law, should comply with this general principle of equal treatment even when the detailed provisions set out in the Directive were not yet in force, as such laws could be said to come within the substantive scope of Community law and therefore could be required to conform to its fundamental norms, including the general principle of equality. She gave the example of the legislation at issue in *Mangold* as an example of such a law, as it had been initially enacted to implement a Community law obligation (the transposition of Directive 1999/70, concerning the framework agreement on fixed-term work concluded by ETUC, UNICE and CEEP (OJ 1999 L 175, p. 43). National

[74] Case C-427/06, *Bartsch v Bosch und Siemens Hausgeräte (BSH) Altersfürsorge GmbH*, Judgment of Judgment of 23 September 2008.

[75] At paragraph 58 of her Opinion, she commented that '[I]t is precisely *because* the general principle of equality has now been recognised also to include equality of treatment irrespective of age that an enabling legislative provision such as Article 13 EC *becomes* necessary and is duly used as the basis' for legislation in the form of the Directive.

laws which however remained outside the scope of Community law and which were not yet required to comply with the Directive could not however be required to comply with the general principle, as they lay at that time outside the scope of application of Community law: the laws governing survivors' pensions at issue in *Bartsch* came within this category. Therefore, Sharpston AG argued that, unlike *Mangold*, this case fell outside the scope of Community law and therefore the general principle would not apply to require the national courts to disapply the offending domestic law.[76]

In its judgment, the Court essentially agreed with this analysis, perhaps grateful for an opportunity to clarify its earlier decision. It concluded in its short judgment that the allegedly discriminatory treatment in question in this case had 'no link with Community law', in contrast with the legislation at issue in *Mangold*, which was linked to the implementation of a Directive. Therefore, in *Bartsch*, the Court both signalled its intent to continue to adhere to the full scope of the *Mangold* decision, while also clarifying that its impact was confined to matters that came within the general scope of Community law, thereby providing reassurance to some of its critics.

However, while *Bartsch* provided welcome clarity, it did not address the issues surrounding horizontal direct effect and whether giving effect to the general principle of equal treatment required that national courts disapply conflicting national law, even if it applied in the private sphere. In contrast, the Court's 'return to *Mangold*' in its *Kücükdeveci* judgment addressed these issues head on, as it had been requested to do by the national court that made the reference.

In his Opinion in *Kücükdeveci*, Bot AG suggested that the 'indissociable' link between the Directive's provisions and the general principle of equal treatment meant that the Directive should be given horizontal direct effect, as its 'primary purpose' was to give effect to this fundamental norm of the EU legal order which should apply across the substantive scope of EU law. In its judgment, the Court agreed, describing the age discrimination provisions of the Directive as 'giving expression' to the general principle of equal treatment, which the Court suggested should be the 'basis' of examining the effect of the Directive's provisions. On that basis, and also taking into account Art 21(1) of the EU Charter of Fundamental Rights, which prohibits any discrimination on the grounds of age, the Court took the view that national courts must disapply national laws that conflict with the Directive's age provisions, even in a case involving proceedings between private individuals.

The Court's judgment on this point in *Kücükdeveci* is a little opaque, but appears to complete the post-*Mangold* picture, while simultaneously opening a new front in EU law. The Court in this judgment appears to confirm that the age discrimination provisions of the Directive can be regarded as giving expression to the general principle of equal treatment, and clarifies that the fundamental nature of this principle within the

[76] Sharpston AG went on to suggest that the general principle of equal treatment could not be given horizontal direct effect in areas that lay outside the scope of Community law and therefore would not be applicable in this case, even if the disproportionate impact of the age-linked restriction in question, and in particular how it operated to deprive Mrs Bartsch of any pension, would not be objectively justifiable under the Directive, in her opinion. The Court did not address these issues in its judgment.

EU legal order requires that national legislation which conflicts with the Directive must be disapplied, even if this ensures that the Directive in effect is given horizontal direct effect. The essence of the *Mangold* decision, as re-interpreted and clarified in *Bartsch*, is thus re-affirmed in *Kücükdeveci*, which also confirms the close link between the prohibition on age discrimination, other areas of anti-discrimination law, and the fundamental values of the EU legal order. In this way, *Kücükdeveci* re-unites the two strands of the Court's age discrimination case-law, and unifies them into a single thread.

Future Directions

It remains to be seen how the Court will interpret and apply the age discrimination provisions of the Directive in other contexts. Several new preliminary references that concern age discrimination are currently before the Court. Of particular importance are three German cases: the *Rosenbladt* case, which asks the Court whether national laws that enable collective agreements to fix a mandatory retirement age of 65 are compatible with Article 6(1) of the Directive;[77] the *Bulicke* case, which concerns the time-limits within which age discrimination claims can be brought and whether a reduction in these time-limits from those previously applying in gender discrimination cases can be said to constitute unlawful 'regression' under the Directive;[78] and the *Prigge* case, which concerns the mandatory retirement age of 60 imposed on pilots in the interests of public safety.[79] The latter case will be particularly interesting, as the wide scope given to the genuine occupational requirement test in *Wolf* will come under new focus.[80]

Additional issues of particular concern to age discrimination also remain to be resolved. It is unclear whether the discriminatory dismissal of an employee in order to prevent the employee obtaining age-related benefits or employment rights might be capable of justification,[81] or when age discrimination to maintain the financial integrity of pension schemes may be acceptable.[82] It also is uncertain how the comparator requirement will be applied in complex age discrimination cases, when the courts should be willing to make an inference that age-related discrimination has taken place, or how the burden of

[77] Case C-45/09, Reference for a preliminary ruling from the Arbeitsgericht Hamburg (Germany) lodged on 2 February 2009 - *Gisela Rosenbladt v Oellerking Gebäudereinigungsgesellschaft mbH.*

[78] Case C-246/09, Reference for a preliminary ruling from the Landesarbeitsgericht Hamburg (Germany) lodged on 6 July 2009 - *Susanne Bulicke v Deutsche Büro Service GmbH.*

[79] Case C-447/09, Reference for a preliminary ruling from the Bundesarbeitsgericht (Germany), lodged on 18 November 2009 - *Reinhard Prigge, Michael Fromm and Volker Lambach v Deutsche Lufthansa AG.*

[80] The issues discussed in *Petersen* concerning the need to provide younger employees with opportunities for promotion and advancement will also be important in *Prigge*: the Dutch courts have taken the view that requiring pilots to retire at a comparatively early age is justified and necessary to ensure younger pilots receive sufficient opportunities. See Dutch Supreme Court, 8 October 2004 , Nr. C03/077HR, *16 Pilots v. Martinair Holland NV and the Vereniging van Nederlandse Verkeersvliegers*; 8 October 2004, Nr. C03/133HR, *Applicant v. Koninklijke Luchtvaartmaatschappij NV (Royal Dutch Airlines) and the Association of Dutch Traffic Pilots.*

[81] This was discussed by the UK Employment Appeal Tribunal (EAT) in the case of *London Borough of Tower Hamlets v Wooster*, UKEAT/0441/08, which is currently under appeal.

[82] See for example the UK case of *Bloxham v Freshfields Bruckhaus Deringer*, 2205086/2006 (ET), where an Employment Tribunal upheld the introduction of special transitory pension arrangements for partners of a leading London law firm over the age of 55 on the basis that this measure was objectively justified as necessary to maintain the financial well-being of the law firm's pension scheme..

proof provisions of the Directive should apply. It also remains to be seen when the use of age-based distinctions to identify groups targeted for positive action will be deemed to be proportionate and justified, and in what other circumstances will arguments rooted in 'inter-generational solidarity' be deemed to be objectively justified.

Beyond the scope of age discrimination, the Court's judgments in *Mangold*, *Bartsch* and *Kücükdeveci* will in all likelihood continue to generate new developments. The age discrimination provisions of the Directive are one type of expression of the equal treatment principle: by logical extension, the other provisions of the Directive, and the provisions of the Race Equality and revised Gender Equality Directives are also expressions of this principle and therefore conflicting national legislation must be set aside in their case as well. It remains to be seen what impact this will have in the context of horizontal private relationships post-*Kücükdeveci*.

It also remains to be seen what other general principles of EU law exist that require directives which give expression to their provisions to be given effective horizontal direct effect via the disapplication of conflicting national legislation. If the Data Protection Directive gives expression to a general principle of privacy, should conflicting national laws in line with *Kücükdeveci* be disapplied, and the Directive applied directly as between private parties? Does this also apply to directives giving effect to social rights, or to directives that can be interpreted as protecting rights set out in the EU Charter of Fundamental Rights? Bot AG at paragraph 90 of his Opinion in *Kücükdeveci* has highlighted the issues that arise in this context:

> … given the ever increasing intervention of Community law in relations between private persons, the Court will, in my view, be inevitably confronted with other situations which raise the question of the right to rely, in proceedings between private persons, on directives which contribute to ensuring observance of fundamental rights. Those situations will probably increase in number if the Charter of Fundamental Rights of the European Union becomes legally binding in the future…

The age discrimination case-law of the Court has opened new terrain in EU law: it remains to be seen how it will be filled.

Conclusion

The Court has surprised many commentators in how it has interpreted the age discrimination provisions of Directive 2000/78/EC, and how it has linked these provisions with the general principle of equal treatment, which is now classifies as a fundamental norm of the EU legal order. Some of this surprise was directed at the Court's willingness to treat age discrimination as a 'suspect' ground of discrimination and to apply the objective justification test with similar rigour as is done with the other non-discrimination grounds, even if in its case-law it grants Member States some degree of discretion when age-based distinctions are used to achieve legitimate aims. There was also surprise at the Court's willingness to give horizontal direct effect to the equal treatment within the scope of Community law, and therefore to the age provisions of the

Directive. *Mangold* and *Kücükdeveci* indicate that EU anti-discrimination norms have a special status, on account of their link to the equal treatment principle: along with gender equality, which is well-embedded in the EU legal order, the new non-discrimination grounds set out in Article 13 seem to be coming of age through the provisions of the 2000 Directives and the overarching equal treatment which they express and embody.

It is interesting to speculate why the Court has chosen to protect the age ground with the rigour it has, given the debates that surround its status and legitimate concerns about the impact of age discrimination law, while also insisting in the face of strong criticism on the link between the prohibition on age discrimination and the principle of equal treatment. It may be the case that the Court is eager to make clear the commitment of the EU legal order to non-discrimination norms, at a time when equality and discrimination issues loom large across Europe, and the European Court of Human Rights has begun to develop its own historically neglected discrimination case-law. The rhetorical and moral significance of the language of equality, the recognition of a right to equal treatment in Article 21(1) of the Charter, and the Court's strong commitment in the past to gender equality may all also be playing a role. What is apparent is that the emerging ECJ case-law on discrimination is going to be dynamic, and may disrupt existing assumptions as to the state and scope of EU law. Perhaps unexpectedly, the age discrimination case-law appears to be leading the way.

Note

This article was originally published in 2009–10 by *Revue des Affaires Européenes*, **2**, pp. 253–76.

[14]

The New UK Retirement Regime, Employment Law and Pensions

CLAIRE KILPATRICK*

1. INTRODUCTION

This article provides a critical assessment of the new retirement unfair dismissal regime, introduced by the Age Regulations[1] in October 2006, to implement the UK's obligations under the age strand of the EU Framework Equal Treatment Directive.[2] It argues that the new retirement regime is an unfortunate and unnecessary step on the road to dealing with the relationship between dismissal and age. It demonstrates this by placing the new retirement regime in a broader relevant public policy context, first by linking it with ongoing developments in employment law and then by looking at its relationship with state and private pension provision in the UK.

After detailing the new retirement regime, it is evaluated within an employment law context. The argument is made that, like the statutory dispute resolution procedures, the new retirement regime is an overly complex and ill-conceived New Labour experiment. It is a substantial and ill-fitting extension to the law of unfair dismissal which is unlikely to contribute to a smooth transition towards a more wide-spread disappearance of mandatory retirement. Instead, its more predictable outcomes are the generation of widespread uncertainty, larger employment advice bills for workers and businesses alike and increased workload and difficulties for the courts and tribunals.

However, my critique of the new retirement regime has a broader basis and a longer term perspective. I demonstrate first that it is difficult coherently to understand or to design employment law retirement regimes without fully considering the pension context in which they operate. From a pensions perspective, in terms of both process and outcome, the Government's action on the new UK retirement regime was not its finest hour. In terms of process, placing the employment law retirement regime in what I consider to be the essential context of pensions reform reveals the poor, unprincipled and reactive nature of the Government's action. This was very far from being an example of 'joined-up' government or a coherent policy consensus. Instead,

* Law Department, London School of Economics, email: c.kilpatrick@lse.ac.uk. This is a revised version of a talk given to the Industrial Law Society in London in April 2007. I am extremely grateful to all those who commented on that occasion.

[1] SI 2006/1031.

[2] Directive 2000/78/EC.

the careful and impressive public policy consensus built up in relation to pension reform by the Turner Commission was not replicated or connected sufficiently with the parallel and contemporaneous debate on age discrimination in employment law. In terms of outcomes, while the new regime endures, the result of this policy mismatch between employment law and pension reform is to allow employers easily lawfully to dismiss older workers, increasing numbers of whom may not, precisely because of the parallel changes to state and occupational pension policy and practice, have access to an adequate alternative source of income. This cannot be considered to be a socially desirable or just outcome for older workers and it is a cruel paradox that it results from a measure aimed at combating age-related discrimination and disadvantage.

2. THE NEW UK RETIREMENT REGIME

The new UK retirement regime, like its predecessor, rotates around two key concepts: normal retirement age (NRA) and statutory retirement age (SRA)/default retirement age. NRA is an employer-set retirement age—more precisely it is the age at which employees in the employer's undertaking who hold, or have held, the same position as the employee in question are normally required to retire. In both the old and new regimes, the SRA of 65 operates as a default age in the sense that it operates only where the employer sets no NRA. The old regime was in operation for three and a half decades.[3] In that regime, the NRA and the SRA closed the door on a finding of unfair dismissal, by making access to a tribunal dependent on being dismissed before the NRA or, in its absence, the SRA (age 65 years).[4] Both regimes are concerned with allowing employers to dismiss older workers on grounds of age by modifying the application of the general law of unfair dismissal to such dismissals.

The new regime, introduced by the Age Regulations 2006, and effective from 1 October 2006, is much more complex than its predecessor. It is necessary carefully to outline its key features before turning critically to examine it.[5]

Regulation 30 of the Age Regulations, the 'exception for retirement', is the key provision setting up the overall design of the new retirement regime. It provides:

> (2) Nothing in Part 2 or 3 [of the Age Regs] shall render unlawful the dismissal of a person to whom this regulation applies at or over the age of 65 where the reason for the dismissal is retirement.
>
> (3) For the purposes of this regulation, whether or not the reason for a dismissal is retirement shall be determined in accordance with sections 98ZA to 98ZF of the 1996 Act.

[3] In relation to unfair dismissal (1971–2007). It operated, under a modified formula, for a longer period (from 1965 to 2007) in the context of redundancy dismissals.

[4] For detailed analysis of the original retirement exclusion see C. Kilpatrick, 'Age, Retirement and the Employment Contract' (2007) 36 ILJ 119.

[5] This is a much extended version of the briefer account in Kilpatrick, ibid.

The age of 65 identified in Regulation 30(2), the Default Retirement Age (DRA), in fact signals a more complex regime of justification of retirement ages. The second interlinking dimension of the new regime is the imposition of procedural duties in relation to retirement dismissals—these are fleshed out in Schedule 6 of the Age Regulations. The key features of both these dimensions are outlined below.

Both these feed into the design of the new provisions on unfair dismissal in ss 98ZA–98ZF of the Employment Rights Act 1996. In terms of unfair dismissal, unlike its predecessor, the new regime operates by making 'retirement' a potentially fair reason (PFR) for dismissal. This is done by adding a substantial new, and semi-autonomous, chunk to the unfair dismissal chapter in the ERA 1996. Dismissal must take place at a retirement age deemed lawful and comply with certain procedural duties to be fair.

A. Retirement Ages and Justification in the New Regime

Like the old regime, the new one places great emphasis on the employer not dismissing before any NRA it has set or used. In the new regime, dismissing an employee before the NRA makes the dismissal unfair. However, as jurisprudence under the old regime shows, ascertaining what the NRA is or whether indeed there is one, is not a simple task. The jurisprudence, and the issues remaining unresolved in that case-law on determining the NRA, under the old regime will remain a valid and central source of reference in the new regime. That case-law shows that there is a rebuttable presumption that the NRA is the contractually agreed retirement age. Absent a contractually agreed retirement age, it is difficult to sustain the existence of an NRA. The NRA can be higher then the contractual retirement age, by showing a different (higher) age at which employees in the relevant group could reasonably be compelled to retire, though this has proved difficult to establish before the courts. Whether (following the same test) the NRA can be lower than the contractual retirement age has been a matter of lively judicial dispute.[6] We shall look again at the significance of how the NRA is set when we consider below significant recent empirical studies of how employer operate retirement policies.

Unlike the old regime, in the new regime certain NRAs have to be justified in order to be lawful. This is the primary manifestation of the age discrimination dimension of the new regime. The effect of the Age Regulations is that employers with NRAs below 65 years will always have to justify their use in retiring employees to avoid unfair dismissal claims being taken against them.[7] That justification is set

[6] For detailed discussion, see Kilpatrick (2007) above n 4.

[7] The details of the unfair dismissal regime make it clear that NRAs of under 65 will have to be justified irrespective of the age at which dismissal of the employee actually takes place: see s 98ZE ERA 1996. One can envisage therefore cases in which an employee dismissed at 65 contends that an NRA of say, 64, was in place while the employer, to escape the need for justification, will contend that no NRA was in place, and that dismissal occurred at the (lawful) DRA.

out in Regulation 3(1) Age Regulations which requires employers to show that their prima facie directly discriminatory treatment on grounds of age is nonetheless lawful because it is 'a proportionate means of achieving a legitimate aim'. No further detail is given in the Age Regulations as to what might constitute an objective justification for an NRA of, say, 60 years. All this is left to the courts.

Where the relevant age is 65 or over (the National Default Retirement Age), Regulation 30(2) provides that the dismissal is lawful where the reason for dismissal is retirement. This applies both to those situations where an employer sets an NRA of 65 or over and to instances where the employer does not have an NRA, making the state-set DRA of 65 applicable. A second justification question arising under the new retirement regime is therefore what might constitute objective justification by the UK for this National DRA of 65—is it compatible with the prohibition on age discrimination in Directive 2000/78/EC? In introducing the regime, the Government undertook to review in 2011 the need to exempt retirement ages of 65 or over from the requirement of objective justification.[8]

B. Procedural Duties in the New Regime

Turning to the extensive procedural duties structuring the new retirement regime, the duty to inform is the starting point. The main duty to inform[9] requires the employer to do two things. First, it requires the employer to inform the employee in writing of the intended date of retirement (IDR) between 6 and 12 months before it occurs. Second, it requires the employer to inform the employee of his or her right to request not to retire. Should the employer fail to comply with the main duty to inform, it remains under a continuing duty to inform the employee of the IDR and of their right to request not to retire up until 14 days before the IDR.[10] Additionally, the legislation provides sanctions for failure to comply with the main duty to inform. Failure to comply with the main duty to inform gives the ET a statutorily structured discretion to find that the PFR of retirement has not been established.[11] The employer is also subject to a free-standing sanction for failure to comply with the main duty to inform—an employee can obtain compensation of up to eight weeks' pay from an Employment Tribunal.[12]

One of the dual functions of the duty to inform is to set the IDR. The regime is designed so that dismissing the employee before the IDR will make the dismissal

[8] Patricia Hewitt, Secretary of State for Trade and Industry, HC, 14 December 2004: 'the legislation, which will come into force in autumn 2006, will provide for a national default retirement age of 65 and a right for employees to request working beyond the set retirement age. The decision to have a national default retirement age will be reviewed after five years'.

[9] Regulation 47 Age Regulations gives effect to Para 2, Sched 6 Age Regulations.

[10] Para 4, Sched 6 Age Regulations.

[11] See below text accompanying nn 32–4.

[12] Para 12, Sched 6 Age Regulations.

unfair. Given the cardinal importance this gives the IDR, we need to consider further how this date is established. There are three different ways in which an IDR can be established.[13] The first is that the employer properly notifies that date under the main duty to inform, that is to say, the employee is informed no more than twelve months but no less than six months before that date of her IDR. As we have seen, the legislation strongly encourages the IDR to be set in this way by sanctioning the employer for failure to comply with the main duty to inform.[14] The second way of setting the IDR is that the employer notifies it under the continuing duty to inform—this can be as little as two weeks before the IDR. Finally, the IDR can also be set by the employee—where the employer fails to notify the IDR under the main or continuing duty to inform, an employee can make a request not to retire and is required, where he has reasonable grounds to believe what the date of retirement will be, to identify an IDR in their request.[15] One can envisage this occurring in a workplace where employees in the particular employee's position are routinely retired at 65; not having heard anything by the time she is 64½ years old, an employee could proceed to make a request not to retire and identify her 65th birthday as the IDR. Once established, an IDR can also be altered to an earlier date (by agreement between employer and employee) or a later date (by agreement or as a result of an employer's response to a request made by an employee not to retire on the original IDR established).[16] Should an IDR not be established in any of these three ways, it appears that the dismissal would not then be for reasons of 'retirement' and, at present at least, would be automatically unfair for failure to follow the statutory disciplinary procedure.[17]

The second function of the duty to inform is to alert the employee of their right to request not to be retired on the IDR. The employer is placed under a corresponding duty to consider such requests. Where an employer has complied with the main duty to inform, an employee wishing to make such a request must do so not less than three months but not more than six months before the IDR.[18] The employer must consider an employee's request not to retire, normally at a meeting and, if not granted, at an appeal. Where a meeting is held, the employee has a right to be accompanied.[19]

[13] Para 1(2), Sched 6 Age Regulations.

[14] See above nn 11–12 and below text accompanying nn 32–4.

[15] Para 1(2)(c) and para 5(2), Sched 6 Age Regulations.

[16] Para 3, Sched 6 Age Regulations.

[17] Section 98A(1) ERA 1996. On the future of the statutory disciplinary procedure see below n 41.

[18] Para 5, Sched 6 Age Regulations. Where employees have benefited from full employer compliance with the duty to inform they must make requests more than three months but less than six months before the IDR (para 5(5)(a), Sched 6); in all other cases no more than six months before the IDR (para 5(5)(b), Sched 6).

[19] But, as with the right to request flexible working, no right for that companion to be a full-time trade union official: para 9 especially (2)(b), Sched 6 Age Regulations; Regulation 14 especially para (3) Flexible Working (Procedural Requirements) Regulations 2002. Denial of the right to be accompanied is sanctioned by giving the employee recourse to the ET to claim a maximum of two weeks' pay as compensation—para 12, Sched 6 Age Regulations.

The employer must notify the employee of its decision in each case. Requests by employees and notifications by employers must be in writing.[20] Employees' requests must also specify that they are making a request under paragraph 5 of Schedule 6 of the Age Regulations.[21] We will see below that while failure to comply with the duty to inform is relevant at both the potentially fair and the fairness stages of the new retirement regime, the duty to consider requests to retire is, with one exception,[22] only taken into account at the second, fairness, stage.

Having outlined the building blocks of the new regime, we can examine further how it operates by looking at how retirement ages and procedural duties are combined within the new retirement regime in different ways so as to identify when employers definitely establish the PFR of retirement, definitely do not establish it and possibly establish it. Where the PFR of retirement is established, the new regime also introduces a retirement-specific test of fairness.

C. Definitely PFR of Retirement

There are three ways of definitely establishing the PFR of retirement. In all instances, the main duty to inform and the IDR must be respected. In addition, retirement must have taken place not below an NRA of 65 or more,[23] in accordance with an NRA of under 65 which has been justified,[24] or, where there is no NRA, at the DRA of 65 or over.[25]

Although where these conditions are met the dismissal is only *potentially fair*, retirement dismissals have their own separate definition of fairness, hence our description above of this regime as being semi-autonomous from that of the general law of unfair dismissal. The Tribunal does not determine whether the dismissal is fair or unfair in the usual way according to s 98(4). Instead, s 98ZG ERA contains a modified fairness test for retirement dismissals. In essence, this

[20] Paras 5–10, Sched 6 Age Regulations.

[21] Para 5(3), Sched 6 Age Regulations.

[22] See below n 33.

[23] Section 98ZD(2) ERA 1996. It is well worth noting that the NRA and the Intended Date of Retirement do not have to coincide. To benefit from the retirement PFR, the legislation merely requires that dismissal take place on or after the NRA. In relation to NRAs of 65+, the current regime therefore gives employers considerable discretion in treating members of staff differently when it comes to determining their actual exit age. Provided it fulfils the procedural requirements, it could, for instance, dismiss most employees at 65 but keep some on until a later date. Given past judicial interpretation of what constitutes an NRA, it is unlikely that such actions by the employer will make the NRA the higher age.

[24] Section 98ZE(4) ERA 1996.

[25] Section 98ZB(2) ERA 1996.

deems fair all retirement dismissals which fall into the 'definitely potentially fair' category, provided the employer has complied with the duties associated with requests by the employee not to retire.[26]

D. Definitely Not Retirement

There are two ways in which the dismissal will definitely not constitute the PFR of retirement. In the first, the NRA or the age dimension does not respect the regime rules. This can be because dismissal occurs before the NRA,[27] the NRA is under 65 and is not objectively justified[28] or it can be because there is no NRA and the employee was dismissed before the DRA of 65.[29] In the second, the IDR has not been respected and dismissal occurs before the IDR.[30] It is noteworthy that compliance by the employer with the main duty to inform will not stop such a dismissal falling outside the 'retirement' PFR category.[31] This confirms the cardinal importance for employers of not dismissing before the IDR.

E. Possibly Retirement

Here, the NRA and age dimensions are both respected, dismissal has occurred on the IDR *but the main duty to inform has not been respected.*[32] The Tribunal is given the discretion to decide whether the PFR of retirement is established by looking in particular at whether the employer, though not complying properly with the main duty to inform, has in any event complied with the continuing duty to inform the employee up to two weeks before the IDR and whether it has held a meeting to consider an employee's request not to retire.[33] Rather strangely, the

[26] Section 98ZG also makes the fairness of dismissals contingent on consideration of whether the employer has complied with its continuing duty to inform. However, this is redundant in those instances where the PFR of retirement is definitely established as, to establish the PFR, the employer must have fully complied with the duty to inform. It is therefore only relevant in those situations where the legislation states that the PFR of retirement is possibly established, considered below.

[27] Section 98ZC ERA 1996.

[28] Section 98ZE(2) ERA 1996.

[29] Section 98ZA ERA 1996.

[30] Section 98ZD(4), 98ZB(4), 98ZE(6) ERA 1996.

[31] Section 98ZD(3), 98ZB(3), 98ZE(5) ERA 1996.

[32] Section 98ZB(5), 98ZD(5), 98ZE(7) ERA 1996.

[33] Section 98ZF ERA 1996. This is then the exceptional situation where any part of the duty to consider is relevant at the, first, potentially fair, stage of the fairness enquiry. The Government's *Employment Equality (Age) Regulations 2006: Notes on Regulations* (paras 277–8) also indicates that s 98ZF may be used by ETs to decide whether a dismissal is potentially fair when the main duty to inform has been complied with but dismissal occurs after the IDR: this situation is not expressly dealt with in the legislation.

ET then has to consider almost, though not quite, identical factors in order to ascertain whether the dismissal is fair.[34]

F. A Smart Retirement Regime?

Having outlined the new retirement regime in some detail, we can stand back from it a little and question whether the Government needed to introduce such a complex regime, particularly in light of its own recognition that one significant part of the regime design, the DRA of 65, might be short-lived as it would be subject to review in 2011, a point to which we shall again return below.[35] Keeping the desired policy to be that of maintaining a retirement exception when transposing an EU age discrimination prohibition, simpler alternatives were clearly available. The Government could, for instance, simply have amended the old regime to require NRAs under 65 to be objectively justified in order to benefit from the exclusion of unfair dismissal jurisdiction. It could have retained its (potentially) transitional nature by warning employers that, beyond 2011, retirement dismissals at all ages, not just those below 65, might require objective justification.

One's response to this depends essentially on how valuable or otherwise one considers the procedural duties introduced by the new regime to be: the duty to inform the employee of the IDR, the need to respect that date and the right to have requests not to be retired considered at a meeting and an appeal. Complexity is not in itself a bad regulatory attribute, but only if that complexity serves some useful regulatory purpose.

Looked at in employment law terms, the new procedural duties which mark out the new retirement regime have got two possible competing 'New Labour' comparators: the right to request flexible working[36] and the Statutory Dispute Resolution procedures.[37]

[34] Section 98ZG ERA 1996: to decide whether a dismissal is fair, the ET should consider the employer's compliance with the duty to inform, and whether it considered any request not to retire, including by holding a meeting and an appeal.

[35] See above n 8 and below n 82.

[36] The right to request flexible working was introduced for parents of children under six (where the child is disabled under 18) in the Employment Act 2002, effective as of 6 April 2003. It is contained in ss 80F-I ERA 1996, the Flexible Working (Procedural Requirements) Regulations 2002 SI 3207 and the Flexible Working (Eligibility, Complaints and Remedies) Regulations 2002 SI 3236. The right was extended to carers by the Work and Families Act 2006, s 12.

[37] These were introduced by the Employment Act 2002, effective as of 1 October 2004. They are contained in s 98A ERA 1996, the Employment Act 2002, ss 29–33 and Sched 2, 3 and 4 and the Employment Act 2002 (Dispute Resolution) Regulations 2004 SI 752.

We consider first the Government's chosen comparator: the right to request flexible working.[38] On this view, the new retirement regime is akin to the rights to request flexible working by parents and carers because it is a well-designed transitional regime which, through application of a 'light touch' regulatory approach, will help change employment cultures away from fixed mandatory retirement ages. This reading of the new retirement regime leans particularly heavily on one element of it: the consideration of employee's requests not to retire. In relation to flexible working, the view is that employers often fail to accommodate their employees' desires to work different patterns simply because of lack of awareness of their needs. When alerted to those needs by an employee request, they are generally happy to accommodate them when the current work pattern is not underpinned by any particularly compelling rationale. Similarly then, it is argued, employers somewhat mechanically operate retirement ages, and employees accept them, but a request by an employee who wishes to keep working will suffice in many cases to alter the employer's position. Indeed, the regulatory nudge can apparently be even gentler in the case of retirement: this must be why, unlike the right to request flexible working, the employer is not required to give any reason for its refusal to accept the request not to retire while it is so required when it refuses a parent or carer's request to work flexibly.[39] It is this possibility of gently reworking mandatory retirement, which explains the maintenance, for the time being at least, of a DRA of 65, and the complex interaction and multiple permutations of ages, retirement dates, procedural duties of information and consideration and the right to request in the new retirement regime which has been detailed above.

[38] Patricia Hewitt (then Secretary of State of what was (pre-Brown) Trade and Industry), announcing the decision to introduce a right to request not to retire in the House of Commons on 14 December 2004, stated, 'This right will follow the model of the right to request flexible working for parents with young children, where it has been successful in changing the culture towards more family friendly working. This policy will ensure that employers listen to employees who want to keep working and think about whether they can agree. In doing so, it will help promote a culture change including on workforce planning and the design of employee benefits, and move towards a position where fixed retirement ages are relied on only where they can be objectively justified by the employer': Hansard HC vol 428, cols WS 126ff.

[39] Where an employer refuses a flexible working request, it must state which of a list of grounds specified in s 80G(1)(b) apply (eg inability to recruit additional staff, detrimental impact on quality) and give a sufficient explanation of why those grounds apply in relation to the employee's application: Regulation 5(b)(ii) Flexible Working (Procedural Requirements) Regulations 2002. Compare this with a refusal to accept a request not to retire, 'Where the decision is to refuse the request, confirm that the employer wishes to retire the employee and the date on which the dismissal is to take effect': Para 7(7)(b), Sched 6 Age Regulations. Davies and Freedland comment on this feature of the Age Regulations: 'it is highly unusual for such a duty to be framed in such purely procedural terms; the regulatory touch upon the employer's discretion is at that point truly as light as a feather': *Towards a Flexible Labour Market: Labour Legislation and Regulation since the 1990s* (Oxford University Press, 2006) p 86.

However, in my view, the more apt regulatory comparator is the Statutory Dispute Resolution Procedures. Unlike the right to request flexible working, the new retirement procedures operate by altering the general law of unfair dismissal. True, the new retirement regime is much more semi-detached from the general law of unfair dismissal than the Statutory Dispute Resolution Procedures, especially the statutory disciplinary procedures, are. Nonetheless, in both instances, it is the employer's power of dismissal which is made subject to following certain formal steps of information provision, meetings and appeals. Moreover, in the case of the retirement regime, and unlike the right to request flexible working, before the right to request not to retire is normally triggered,[40] the employer must already have consciously made a decision in relation to that employee, and that decision is a decision to dismiss on a determined date, effected by informing the employee of their IDR. Surely, the employer must be considered less open to acceding to requests to alter a concrete decision it has made, particularly when the duty to consider does not require it to give the employee any good reasons for its refusal to depart from its original decision. Instead, the critical first step in the procedure, as in the Statutory Disciplinary Procedure, is taken by the employer and that decision is a decision to dismiss.

The Statutory Dispute Resolution Procedures, effective only as of 1 October 2004, have recently been the subject of the Gibbons Review, on behalf of the Government.[41] Quite spectacularly, that Review has recommended their complete repeal. Some of the problems the Gibbons Review identified are worthy of note in considering the new retirement regime: 'the requirement to express problems in writing can act as a trigger for greater conflict rather than a route to resolution' and 'complexity drives users to seek legal advice earlier with associated increased costs'.[42] The complexity of the retirement regime and its interaction with the fairness of dismissals is likely to have two effects, similar to those of the Statutory Dispute Resolution Procedures, neither of which fulfil the desired regulatory aim of easing UK workplaces smoothly and gradually towards a position in which mandatory retirement is minimised.

Employers will naturally be concerned to make their retirement decisions unfair dismissal proof. One response employers may accordingly have to navigating the new regime is to find a straightforward and sure-fire method of

[40] In the exceptional case where the right to return is triggered by the employee, the employer has simply failed to comply with its procedural duties to inform under the retirement regime. See above n 15.

[41] M. Gibbons, *Better Dispute Resolution: A Review of Employment Dispute Resolution in Great Britain* (March 2007, DTI, 60 pp). The Government immediately launched a consultation on the Review: *Success at Work: Resolving Disputes in the Workplace: A Consultation* (March 2007, DTI). The outcome is an Employment Bill, aimed to have Royal Assent in Summer 2008, which will *inter alia* repeal the Statutory Dispute Resolution Procedures.

[42] Gibbons Review, n 41 at 25. For requirements to place requests etc in writing under the new retirement regime, see above nn 20–1.

making retirement dismissals fair. The most straightforward method of doing that is to make the NRA,[43] or where there is none the age of 65, the IDR for all employees, automatically trigger notification of that date six months before it and stick to that date in all instances, especially because failure to respect it makes the dismissal unfair. This means, of course, refusing all requests not to retire but, provided the employer goes through the formal steps of meetings and appeals, there can be no comeback. And requests may dwindle if none is successful. One perverse effect of the new retirement regime may be to lead fewer employers to accede to requests not to retire than occurred before its entry into force.

Alternatively, employers and employees may struggle to operate the new regime. This is likely to lead to mass non-compliance, or ambiguous compliance, by employers and employees, with particular procedural steps. Again, such difficulties breed litigation, the demand for legal advice, and a focus on securing procedural compliance, but may achieve less in the way of smoothly shifting expectations and outcomes about mandatory retirement.

In terms of evaluating the potential impact of the new retirement regime, we can turn to a survey, commissioned by the DTI, which looked at just over 2000 establishments' policies, practices and preferences relating to age between November 2004 and May 2005.[44] Of these establishments, 37% employing over half of the total number of employees had formal compulsory retirement ages for at least some of their staff.[45] Those more likely to have compulsory retirement ages were larger private sector organisations and the public sector. Assuming that these 'formal compulsory retirement ages' are found to be contractually agreed, as discussed above, it is likely that they will constitute the NRA for the employees they cover.[46] Three sets of employers (and employees) can be distinguished: those with a formalised retirement age of 65, those in which that formalised age was under 65 and those with no formalised retirement age (in retirement regime parlance, no NRA). The first group is the largest: 65 was in fact the most common (maximum or fixed) compulsory retirement age. For these employers, the main challenge the new retirement regime represents is compliance with the procedural duties.[47] Those belonging to the second group, with formalised retirement ages

[43] Though where the employer wishes to maintain an NRA under 65, it will have to face the hurdle of justification. Employers wishing to maintain an NRA of less than 65 are likely to be particularly averse to permitting exceptions to the stated NRA, for fear that it may jeopardise the cogency of their justification arguments. This, of course, militates against the declared regulatory objective of adjusting retirement policies to employee preferences wherever possible.

[44] H. Metcalf and P. Meadows, *Survey of employers' policies, practices and preferences relating to age* (DTI, 2006, pp 240).

[45] Table 4.2.

[46] See above s 2A.

[47] An additional significant challenge, considered below at text around nn 50–52, is uncertainty about the lawfulness of the 65-age pivot under EU law. If this is found to be unlawful, each employer with a retirement age, whatever that may be, will have to be able objectively to justify its use.

below 65, are mainly public sector employers and financial intermediaries.[48] These employers, under the new retirement regime, need either to modify upwards the age at which they dismiss (retire) people on grounds of age or find a way to justify that age. But the new retirement regime does not only affect the predominantly large employers with formal compulsory retirement ages: it must also be complied with by the third group, populated by smaller employers. A small employer, which does not set a retirement age, will automatically fall foul of the Age Regulations and the new retirement regime if it dismisses an employee because of age at any age below 65. But even at 65 or above, the dismissal will still fall outside the fair retirement dismissal category constructed by the retirement regime unless it jumps through the procedural hoops the new regime creates, leaving the employer liable both for unfair dismissal and age discrimination.

The initial impact of the Age Regulations has been examined in a study by law firm Berwin Leighton Paisner of more than 50 private and public organisations, with a combined staff of almost 80,000. This found that a third of employers had still to introduce retirement procedures, with small businesses particularly struggling to cope with the requirements under the new legislation. At the same time, more than 40% of employers, 'possibly as a result of increased pressure on pensions', had received requests from employees to work past retirement age.[49] These early indications on use of the right to request not to retire are most revealing. Employees using this route may legitimately feel short-changed when they discover that the introduction of age discrimination legislation has not given them a right not to be dismissed on grounds of age, nor even a right to reasons as to why an age-related dismissal is necessary, but simply a right to request not to be dismissed on grounds of age, a request which can be rejected for no reason, provided the employer goes through the steps of a meeting and an appeal.

This signals one very important respect in which the new retirement regime must be compared unfavourably with the Statutory Dispute Resolution Procedures. Indeed, all our employer and employee strategies, considered above, for dealing with the new retirement regime, must be read and reconsidered in the light of this very significant difference. Unlike those procedures, the new retirement regime came, as the Government was well aware, with an obvious EU-legality health warning. This is one reason the Government promised to review the DRA of 65 in 2011. Yet that review, designed in part to help protect the UK retirement regime from a successful legal challenge under EU law, may well be pre-empted by a successful legal challenge to either the UK regime itself or in a decision by

[48] Metcalf/Meadows above nn 44, 75.

[49] As reported in the *Financial Times*, 28 June 2007, 5. On the reasons for increased pressure on pensions see below, s 4A.

the ECJ on retirement rules in another Member State or for EU staff.[50] Indeed, the ink had barely dried on the Regulations when Heyday, part of Age Concern, a campaigning charity, had taken judicial review proceedings against, among other things, the National DRA in the Age Regulations, and this has resulted in the High Court making a reference to the ECJ.[51] From the outset, therefore, some employers and employees have known that it is entirely unclear whether the new regime will be found by the ECJ to comply with the Framework Directive, so that the expenditure of time and effort on careful compliance with the new regime by employers may be wasted, as employees unhappy with the result are being advised to bank claims with Employment Tribunals pending some direction from the ECJ.[52] The combination of procedural complexity and legal uncertainty associated with the new retirement regime is a deeply unhappy one. The new retirement regime seems more likely to produce a bumpy, difficult and expensive transition rather than an orderly and light-touch transition towards a diminishing use of mandatory retirement, although it was precisely this latter regulatory goal which justified the complexity of the new regime.

This is because a key difference between its two New Labour comparators and the new retirement regime is agreement on the policy aim. All those involved in the Gibbons review agreed that the policy goal—to encourage early dispute resolution inside workplaces—was sound, disagreement focused on whether the statutory dispute resolution procedures were a good means of achieving that goal. Similarly, allowing employees the amount of flexible working consistent with effective businesses is uncontentious (though the details of what that means may well be). Yet both the policy aims behind the retirement regime, and the mode of delivering those aims, are contested. In particular, it is disputed whether

[50] A series of cases concerning application of the prohibition of age discrimination to retirement dismissal and pension rules are being decided by the ECJ: in the first, the Court found no age discrimination because of a lack of comparability, Case C-227/04P *Lindorfer v Council*, judgment 11, September 2007, Opinion AG Jacobs, 27 October 2005, Opinion AG Sharpston, 30 November 2006 (note the Court asked for a second AG Opinion in this EU staff dispute on age and gender discrimination in pension rules following its decision in *Mangold* in November 2005). In Case C-411/05 *Palacios de la Villa* v *Cortefiel Servicios* the Court found a Spanish retirement regime to be an instance of justified direct age discrimination. These cases also provide the next episodes in the Court's development of age discrimination launched by the earlier, and highly controversial, *Mangold* decision: [2005] ECR I-9981. Both indicate that a more cautious stance is now being taken by the Court towards the development of age discrimination.

[51] Case C-388/07 *The Queen on the application of the Incorporated Trustees of the National Council for Ageing (Age Concern England) v Secretary of State for Business, Enterprise and Regulatory Reform* (pending). This case is also referred to as *Heyday*.

[52] See the advice on the Age Concern Web site (http:/www.ageconcern.org.uk): 'What can you do if you are forced to retire? If you are age 65 or over … you can take the following action: Inform your employer of the *Heyday* case that has been referred to the ECJ. Explain that there is a possibility that the ECJ will find that mandatory retirement ages are unlawful.' It continues with detailed advice about banking a case before an Employment Tribunal.

employers should, subject to compliance with the new procedural standards, be able to continue to dismiss employees over 65, *simply because of their age*, without employees being able to challenge that either as age discrimination or as an unfair dismissal.[53] One reason for that contestation is, of course, the statutory recognition of age as a prohibited ground of discrimination. But although this prohibition at EU level is an important cause of pressure on regulation of dismissals for retirement, in a sense this prohibition is merely one symptom of a broader set of pressures on how labour market exit is conceived and regulated. Such pressures come both from changes in the labour force and changes in firm organisation. With dramatic increases in healthy life expectancy, which regularly continue to defy actuarial prediction, new exit ages and pension design are needed. These changes in the labour force have combined with changes in firm design, and particularly firm-level pension provision, to create new challenges for public policy concerning retirement. We turn now to evaluate the new employment law retirement regime within this broader context.

3. THE RATIONALE AND DESIGN OF RETIREMENT REGIMES: PENSIONS, RETIREMENT AGES AND THE OLD RETIREMENT REGIME

It is useful to start at the beginning and ask: where did mandatory retirement ages and employment law retirement regimes originate? What is their rationale? The starting-point is not legislative rules but the prior development of rules on retirement by employers. Employer-set compulsory retirement rules were extremely rare in the nineteenth century. However, as internal labour markets and managerial hierarchies developed in the larger firms of the early twentieth century increasingly companies began to compel the retirement of employees, often at fixed ages, and the existence of a pension fund made such a policy feasible if not always popular. Indeed, it was the introduction of compulsory retirement ages which stimulated the increasing generosity of occupational pension schemes (OPSs). As Leslie Hannah has argued in his illuminating historical analysis of occupational pensions and retirement in Britain, 'the pension at retirement is the most potent factor in reducing and sweetening the retirement decision or in smoothing the path of mandatory retirement enforcement'.[54]

Why did these firms want mandatory retirement ages? Mandatory retirement ages with generous OPSs allowed firms to manage employees' expectations of long-term employment and the particular difficulties of demoting or dismissing those high up in the management hierarchy. Defined benefit pension schemes

[53] Unless the employer itself has set a higher retirement age.

[54] L. Hannah, *Inventing Retirement: The Development of Occupational Pensions in Britain* (Cambridge University Press, 1986) 114.

based on final, rather than average, salary are particularly good at making mandatory retirement at a fixed age palatable, especially for employees who have progressed upwards inside the firm. There was a huge expansion in both employer-set mandatory retirement ages and OPSs throughout a good part of the twentieth century. This is reflected in the fact that in the early-mid 1990s, well over 10 million UK employees, fairly equally split between public and private sector, were members of final salary Defined Benefit (DB) pensions.[55] The critical point to note is that, in their genesis, mandatory retirement ages were very strongly articulated with a pension promise of income linked to average or final salary. The mandatory retirement—defined benefit occupational pension nexus in turn formed an important component of the successful construction and operation of internal labour markets.[56]

The old retirement regime (upper age limit) for unfair dismissal introduced in the UK in 1971 therefore simply reflected these developments. However, it is significant to note that no formal relationship was ever forged between OPS entitlement and application of the old retirement regime making the latter very over-inclusive in its application.[57] Even at their peak, occupational pensions barely covered half of the UK's working population and covered many fewer women than men.[58] Yet all employees, not just those with access to a decent occupational pension, were subject to the old retirement regime, which blocked those employees' access to tribunals to make unfair dismissal claims. It is of the highest importance that this significant design flaw has not been addressed in the new retirement regime, despite a new pensions context within which increasingly fewer workers benefit from the mandatory retirement—defined benefit occupational pension benefit nexus.

4. THE RATIONALE AND DESIGN OF RETIREMENT REGIMES: THE NEW CONTEXT

Two parallel sets of debates of great importance for workers have recently been taking place in the UK: one on pension provision and the other on employment

[55] Pensions Commission, *First Report*, 114. There are additional and significant reasons for the dominance, and generosity, of final salary defined benefit pensions in the UK system such as: incomes policies, inflation-proofing, the exceptionally strong performance of the equities market between 1974 and 2000.

[56] In the public sector, a stronger—and distinctive—deferred salary rationale may be present.

[57] Note, however, that the setting of a lower DRA for women than men (60 rather than 65) in the old retirement regime reflected a link with the age of entitlement to state pension, so that women could be lawfully dismissed at 60 while man had the right not to be unfairly dismissed until 65. The ECJ found this to be unlawful gender discrimination in Case 152/84 *Marshall* [1986] ECR 723. As a result, the NRA in the old regime was equalised at 65 for women. It is also the case that from the post-WW2 welfare settlement until 1989, receipt of state pension was subject to retirement from employment.

[58] OPS coverage peaked in 1967, at 49%, having extended rapidly post WW2: see L. Hannah above n 54 at 65, 31–2.

law reform in light of the need to implement the age strand of the 2000 Framework Equal Treatment Directive. The latter led to the new retirement regime considered above. We have seen that the new employment law retirement regime has constructed an elaborate regime protecting employers' right to dismiss at 65, and the legality of formalised mandatory retirement at younger ages provided justification is available. The first part of my analysis has critiqued this regime from an internal employment law perspective. In this second part of the analysis, it is argued that the policy decision to introduce the new retirement regime looks bizarrely myopic, to say the least, when we see that all around this decision, exceptionally well-informed policy decisions were being taken to make a definitive break with labour market exit at 65 in state pension design and to deal with the fall-out from the abandonment by large numbers of UK employers of the mandatory retirement—defined benefit occupational pensions nexus. The key issues connecting pension provision to retirement ages are set out before concluding by critically comparing the pensions debate with the parallel debate on the new employment law retirement regime.

A. Pension Provision Reform Debate

In 2002, the Government set up a Pensions Commission (chaired by Lord (Adair) Turner) with the remit of reviewing the longer term challenges faced by the pensions system and making recommendations for reform. This Commission produced three reports[59] and, through impressive research and argumentation, focus-group discussions with affected people and businesses, as well as an effective public communications strategy, has managed to generate a radically new pensions settlement for the UK. Most of its key recommendations have been accepted by Government and are being implemented in a series of White Papers and legislative acts.[60] Perhaps, the most remarkable feat achieved by the Pensions Commission has been to bind employers' organisations into a settlement which, for the first time, entails compulsory contributions by all employers to workers'

[59] *Pensions: Challenges and Choices. The First Report of the Pensions Commission* (October 2004); *A New Pension Settlement for the Twenty-first Century: The Second Report of the Pensions Commission* (November 2005), *Implementing an Integrated Package of Pension Reforms: The Final Report of the Pensions Commission* (April 2006).

[60] White Paper, *Security in Retirement: Towards a New Pensions System*, Cm 6841 (Department of Work and Pensions, May 2006, pp 222), responses in Cm 6960 (October 2006, pp 101), Pensions Act 2007 (primarily focused on state pension reform). See also the White Paper *Personal Accounts: A New Way to Save*, Cm 6975 (Department of Work and Pensions, December 2006, 174 pp), responses in Cm 7971 (June 2007, 102 pp) and the Bill introduced in November 2007.

occupational pensions.[61] The Pensions Commission also successfully urged a new clarification of the roles the state and private parties should play in pension provision, a clarification which will be accompanied by the (gradual) dismantling of many accumulated complexities in the UK pension system. It recommended in particular the withdrawal of the state as a provider of earnings-related pensions as a back-up to employer-provided pensions.[62] This role played by the state is itself due to the comparatively early and strong presence of occupational pensions voluntarily provided by employers in Britain compared with other industrial countries. Instead, the Pensions Commission recommended that in future the State's role in pension provision should be primarily that of providing a flat-rate basic state pension, aimed at poverty prevention.[63] At the same time, all workers should be given a realistic opportunity to create a pension income comparable to their previous earnings. The State should enable and encourage this by introducing a semi-compulsory occupational pension. It is semi-compulsory because all employees not covered by better occupational schemes will automatically be enrolled, although they have the right to opt-out. Employers will also be obliged to contribute with a 3% employer contribution[64]—this has, most remarkably, been accepted by the government in the face of employer opposition.[65] This is an important turning-away from the principle of voluntarism which has hitherto dominated the actions of UK governments, not least New Labour, in relation to occupational pensions. Employers will no longer be able to choose whether or not to contribute to the private pensions of their workforces.[66] The new

[61] It can be usefully contrasted with New Labour's previous 'light-touch' intervention on pensions provision—the 'stakeholder' pension introduced in 1999. This required all employers with five or more employees, which had no employer-contributing scheme in place, to nominate a pension scheme to which workers could contribute—no employer contribution is required. This has, predictably, not produced impressive results: 80% of all employer-designated stakeholder schemes are 'empty shells'—nominated schemes but with no members: Pensions Commission, *Second Report*, 48.

[62] This led to the introduction in Britain of the graduated retirement pension (1961), then the State Earnings Related Pension Scheme (1978) and finally the State Second Pension (2002). Various private schemes have always been allowed to contract out of the various state earnings-related systems, though the variety of schemes so permitted was extended extensively in 1987 to include DC schemes and Approved Personal Pensions.

[63] The linking by the Thatcher Government of the Basic State Pension since 1981 to price rather than wage increases has led to it not fulfilling this role of poverty prevention (its value fell from about 20% average earnings in the late 1970s to 15% in 1997); this has been alleviated by means-tested supplements under New Labour. Because, *inter alia*, of the perverse incentives means-testing has on savings behaviour, the Pensions Commission recommended however restoring a earnings-linked Basic State Pension which, in itself, and without means-testing, delivers a minimum income.

[64] Alongside 1% from the state in tax relief and 4% from the employee. This 8% total constitutes the minimum contribution base.

[65] Although the Government has conceded a three-year phasing in period during which the employers' contribution will increase annually from 1% up to 3%: see its response to the May 2006 *Security in Retirement* White Paper Consultation above n.60.

[66] See above n 64.

pensions settlement concerns therefore both state and private pensions.[67] Further consideration of state and private pension reforms and changes demonstrates the poor fit of the new retirement regime with those reforms and changes.

(i) State Pension Reform

The key conclusion reached in this regard by the Pensions Commission is that longer working is required (extending working lives) for reasons of public expenditure, intergenerational fairness and preventing pensioner poverty. As the Commission noted in the Foreword to its Second Report, 'One of the useful roles of an independent commission is to present society with difficult but unavoidable choices'. A useful starting-point is estimates by the Government Actuarial Department that the ratio of people aged over 65 to those aged 20–64 will increase from 27% today to 47% in 2050.[68] This will have a dramatic impact on public expenditure on state pensions. Though dealing with the impact of this demographic challenge solely by increasing average retirement age would be unacceptable (for instance, men's average retirement age, to keep costs stable, would have to increase from 64 today to 69.6 in 2050, ie faster than the increases in life expectancy[69]) some part of the state response to the demographic challenge must involve an adjustment upwards of the state pension age. Otherwise, either too much money must be spent by current workers on supporting pensioners or pensioners must become poorer. Neither of these outcomes respects the principle of inter-generational fairness, and the latter is unacceptable from a basic welfare provision perspective too. Instead, the Pensions Commission recommends that the social decision on how to set state pension age should be based on the following proposition:

> Each generation should enjoy the same proportions of adult life spent contributing taxes to support state pensions and spent receiving state pensions. There is therefore a strong case that state pension ages should rise over time at least proportionately in line with life expectancy.[70]

The Pensions Commission accordingly recommended an alteration of state pension entitlement rules designed in different ways to encourage longer working. Some of these recommendations have already been legislated for. The

[67] Two further important areas of focus of the Pensions Commission, which it is beyond the scope of this article to explore, were the reduction of gender inequality in pensions outcomes and the need to compensate for persistent socio-economic differences in life expectancy in designing state pensions (in the UK, men from the lowest socio-economic class live five years less than men in the highest).

[68] Pensions Commission, *Second Report*, 88.

[69] Ibid, 96.

[70] Ibid, 98. The proportion of adult life spent in retirement has increased dramatically from the 1950s as average retirement age has decreased and life expectancy has increased: see *Second Report*, 97.

most noteworthy is the increase in state pension age recently legislated for in the Pensions Act 2007. Following equalisation of the state pension age for men and women at 65 in 2020,[71] State Pension Age will increase in 2024–26 from 65 to 66, in 2034–36 from 66 to 67 and in 2044–46 from 67 to 68. A second set of recommendations concerns incentives for deferring the state pension. Recent reforms already in the pipeline prior to the Pensions Commission Report had introduced deferral incentives likely to be attractive to, in particular, lower earners. Hence, from 2005, deferring Basic State Pension for two years affords entitlement either to a 20% weekly increase in the state pension paid or a tax-free lumpsum of £10,000. The Pensions Commission proposed making deferral options more flexible by extending the current deferral/non-deferral position to include partial deferral options. This would allow, for example, a worker to draw part of their state pension while continuing to work part-time. The Government has promised to keep under review more flexible deferral options.[72]

The Pensions Commission also drew the obvious implication from the upwards shift in state pension age resulting from these two linked sets of reforms: if people cannot expect to obtain income via a state pension, then it is important to ensure that their place on the labour market is as secure as those of workers of any other age; 'as pension age increases, it is vital that jobs are available for those who wish to work longer'.[73] This is not just for reasons of social justice. From a public expenditure perspective, if pensionable age increases and average retirement ages do not, pension expenditure will simply be substituted in many cases by non-pension benefit expenditure such as Incapacity Benefit or Job-Seeker's Allowance.

It is the decisive move away from 65 and towards longer working in relation to state pension design which is worth noting. This shift is also apparent, though in different ways, in private pensions changes and reforms.

(ii) Private Pension Reform

Beyond state pension, the Pensions Commission took the view that individuals should be allowed to make their own trade-offs between additional saving, working longer and level of income in retirement. Its recommendations focused therefore on making alterations to the current UK pensions system so that people are placed in a position where they are both genuinely enabled and encouraged to provide a standard of living in retirement comparable to that they previously enjoyed.

[71] Legislated for in the Pensions Act 1995: the SPA for women will increase by 6 months each year between 2010 and 2020.

[72] White Paper, *Security in Retirement* (May 2006), para 4.15.

[73] Pensions Commission, *Second Report*, 35.

In terms of considering how provision of occupational pensions reflects upon the continuing protection of mandatory retirement ages in the new retirement regime, especially at or after the age of 65, the critical contrast to draw here is between the employment exit pattern encouraged by DB schemes and that encouraged by Defined Contribution (DC) schemes.

DB schemes offer benefits that are fixed by reference to a member's salary. Such schemes encourage exit at a fixed age—indeed they are often deliberately designed so that there are penalties for working beyond that age. This helps them fulfil their internal labour market function. Moreover, final salary formulas in particular encourage cliff-edge retirement—going straight from a full-time career salary pinnacle (because it is upon this that the pension income will be calculated) to leaving that employment at a fixed age. As explored above, DB schemes, and latterly final salary schemes, were the most common form of OPS in the UK throughout the twentieth century. Hence, in 1995, more than 80% of private sector pensions (covering over five million employees) were calculated using a final salary defined benefit formula. Roughly five million public sector employees are still covered today by final salary DB schemes.

In contrast, DC schemes do not fix benefits: instead contributions by members and employers are determined and the pension benefits obtained will depend on what can be purchased, normally an annuity, with the contributions accumulated in the pension pot. DC schemes certainly create greater variety in retirement ages and may also encourage longer working. The reasons for this are evident. An employee-member of a DC scheme approaching retirement may look at the annuity rates applicable to her pension pot and decide that she cannot afford to retire.[74] Delaying retirement has got two possible favourable consequences for her annuity rate. First, annuity rates may change for the better if she holds on. Second, the longer the individual delays retirement, the older they become so, subject to life expectancy for someone her age not increasing in the meantime, her annuity rate should be more favourable because she will be expected to require it for fewer years.[75]

Moreover, rising life expectancy is likely to accentuate the tendency towards longer working for those in DC schemes. Increases in life expectancy will mean that rates for annuities bought at any given age will fall, leaving individuals with

[74] See Pensions Commission, *First Report*, 34: 'The fall in equity markets and thus in the size of individual pension funds since 2000 and the significant reduction in overall annuity rates since 1998, are likely to have encouraged a significant number of people in DC schemes to delay retirement.'

[75] See the eg given by the Pensions Commission comparing two men, one 65, the other 60, with the same savings rate, both of whom decide to retire and annuities an accumulated pension fund on 20 October 2005: the 65-year old could enjoy a pension 52% higher than the 60-year old: Figure 8.1, *Second Report*, 329. See also J. Banks and S. Smith, 'Retirement Ages in the UK', (2006) 22 *Oxford Review of Economic Policy* 40, 47–50.

the choice between increased savings, a lower pension income, or an increase in the age at which a pension is drawn. The latter is, of course, usually linked to a later age of exit from the workforce.

Given these tendencies produced by DC schemes, their increasing prevalence should be of the utmost interest in designing an employment law retirement regime. It is well known that the last decade or so has seen a truly spectacular flight away from DB schemes in the UK private sector. From around five million in 1995, today, well under two million private sector employees are in open DB schemes and the Pensions Commission has concluded that, 'It is difficult to see private sector DB provision, certainly final salary in form, playing more than a minimal role in the future UK pension system'.[76] One reason for the flight away from DB schemes is, of course, that in those schemes, unforeseen pre-retirement costs of rising life expectancy are borne by the pension provider, while in DC schemes, this cost is borne by the pension recipient. Another is that the rationale for DB schemes—maintenance and effective functioning of internal labour markets—is a key feature of firm design in much fewer firms than it was before. In a recent contribution to a collection of essays in honour of Sir Bob Hepple, Paul Davies and Mark Freedland note the development of an 'internal disintegration of production whereby the worker is more strongly individuated, in a more atomised patterns of relations *within* the producing enterprise, than was previously the case. The worker within the firm is often now subjected to a more elaborately personalised set of incentives and risks than in the previously typical pattern',[77] which was 'directed at constructing and maintaining (whether on a unitary or on pluralistic basis) a coherent and solidaristic sense of institutional identity of and within the employing enterprise'.[78] To the extent that OPSs provide a weather-vane for the emergence and incidence of internally integrated and disintegrated firms, the rapid flight from DB schemes in the UK backs up this analysis to a quite astonishing degree.

Moreover, the spread of DC pensioning will be further bolstered by the new semi-compulsory private pension system, which (following the Pensions Commission) we have seen the Government proposes to introduce for all employees aged over 22 and with earnings over the Primary Earnings Threshold (currently around £5,000) in 2012. This will be a defined contribution system in which an estimated 10 million employees will automatically be enrolled.[79] If DB

[76] Pensions Commission, *Second Report*, 48. DB pension provision remains in place for almost all the 18% of UK workers who work in the public sector.

[77] 'Changing Perspectives Upon the Employment Relationship in British Labour Law' in C. Barnard, S. Deakin and G. Morris (eds), *The Future of Labour Law* (Hart, 2004) 129.

[78] Davies and Freedland, ibid, 151. See also the interesting analysis by G. L. Clark, 'The UK Occupational Pension System in Crisis' in H. Pemberton, P. Thane and N. Whiteside (eds), *Britain's Pension Crisis: History and Policy* (Oxford University Press for The British Academy, 2006).

[79] White Paper, *Security in Retirement* above nn 60, 45.

schemes were the occupational pensions of the twentieth century, the twenty-first century looks set to belong to DC schemes.

What is critical is that, overall, the clear thrust of these developments and reforms in state and private pensions is towards a later, more flexible, and, in relation to earnings-related provision, less certain moment at which retirement income will come on stream. The point to be stressed is that all these developments fit extremely poorly with mandatory retirement ages whether those be employer or state-set. The link between mandatory retirement ages and a pension promise of adequate replacement income *at that same age* has been broken for almost all workers in the private sector and the reforms being introduced in the new pensions settlement are not designed to reconnect that severed link. This is why the Pensions Commission strongly recommended having no DRA:

> The Pensions Commission strongly recommends however that there should be no default age beyond which age discrimination legislation does not apply, and believes that removing it will send a powerful signal that increases in State Pension Age will be accompanied by changes in practice and culture towards older workers.[80]

B. Age Discrimination and Retirement Ages Debate

Contrast that with the parallel universe of the consultation on age discrimination, remembering always that these consultation processes took place at the same time. In its consultation on the introduction of age discrimination legislation, the Government originally proposed circumscribing when retirement ages would be allowed very tightly. Initially, it contemplated possibly allowing employers to exceptionally justify mandatory retirement and possibly to allow, at most, a DRA of 70.[81]

A year and a half later, a Government U-turn was announced in the House of Commons by Patricia Hewitt, and then Secretary of State for Trade and Industry. A DRA of 65, coupled with a right to request, was introduced.[82] Yet,

[80] Pensions Commission, *Second Report*, 135.

[81] *Equality and Diversity—Age Matters* consultation (July 2003): 'Retirement ages that employers set for employees will be unlawful under the Directive, unless they can be objectively justified. We are seeking views on whether the legislation should provide for employers, exceptionally, to be able to justify mandatory retirement ages according to their own circumstances and by reference to specific aims. We are also asking for comments on a DRA of 70 at or after which employers could require employees to retire.'

[82] 14 December 2004, House of Commons, The Secretary of State for Trade and Industry (Patricia Hewitt): 'The treatment of retirement age is an important aspect of the implementation of this legislation [Directive 2000/78/EC]. We have consulted widely on this issue, both formally and informally, and have listened to a range of strongly held views. We have carefully balanced the arguments on all sides, and have decided that the legislation, which will come into force in autumn 2006, will provide for a national default retirement age of 65 and a right for employees to request working beyond the set retirement age. The decision to have a national default retirement age will be reviewed after five years.'

the Government had no strong principled basis for the new retirement regime. Instead, it was primarily a pragmatic concession to employer lobbying in the course of consultation on implementation of the age strand of Directive 2000/78/EC, balanced by offering employees a right to request not to retire and a promise to review it in 2011. It is a lesson for employment law reform to compare this buckling before employer pressure in relation to the new retirement regime with the cleverly constructed pressure placed on employers' organisations to accept the need for compulsory employer pension contributions in the new pensions settlement proposed by the Pensions Commission.

It is true, as the Pensions Commission noted, that *on average*, those retiring now and over the next decade or so are in a historically good position, with the really acute problems with pension provision, if the system is left unaddressed, coming on stream from around 2020. It can therefore be argued that the Government will be able to sort out the problems with the new retirement regime well before then—for instance, in its planned review in 2011. Moreover, it can be argued that special factors made this not in fact the truly golden opportunity to link employment law reform and pension reform it might at first glance appear to be.[83] One such factor was the need to have age discrimination legislation in place by the transposition deadline laid down in Directive 2000/78: this militated against designing the employment law rules to fit with the outcome of the pensions debate. Another was that although the Pensions Commission's view on the undesirability of the legality of mandatory retirement was clear from 2004—two years before the Age Regulations came into force—it was very far from certain that the recommendations of that Commission for a new pensions settlement would prevail, especially given the powerful opposition of Gordon Brown, at that time Chancellor of the Exchequer, to some of its key proposals. It would therefore have been politically difficult for the DTI (as it then was) to base its age discrimination retirement regime on the policy proposals being put forward between 2004 and 2006 by the Pensions Commission.

Nonetheless, it remains the case that the Government failed to connect these two clearly linked public policy debates more closely together to build up a stronger and more principled consensus, especially among employers, on how employment law regulation of retirement ages and changes in pension provision might fit together. Not only did the Government enact a complex regime which poorly fits the new labour market exit context but it also failed to enact the innovative measures needed to enable workers to continue working longer but, if

[83] I am grateful to the Editor for discussions on this point.

desired, in an altered pattern. Note on this again the strong recommendations of the Pensions Commission:

> [A]s pensionable age increases ... it is vital that jobs are available for those who wish to work longer both up to pensionable ages and, if they want, beyond. It is also essential that the options available to people are as flexible as possible (eg a gradual step-down from full-time work to part-time work to full retirement). Achieving these objectives is a major challenge: government policies to facilitate their achievement are a high priority.[84]

The Government could have made its comparison of the new retirement regime and the right for parents to request flexible working ring true had it introduced a regime in which mandatory retirement ages would only very exceptionally be permitted and in which those over a certain age would have a right to request flexible working. Exceptional mandatory retirement could have been deployed as a much-needed carrot to encourage private sector employers to retain decent DB schemes. Instead, we have a regime in which mandatory retirement ages remain across the board (though susceptible to various kinds of judicial challenge), while ever-increasing numbers of employees are not promised an adequate pension at that age.

[84] *Second Report*, 35. For reflections prior to the Age Regulations on the interaction between mandatory retirement and pensions see B. Hepple, 'Age Discrimination in Employment: Implementing the Framework Directive 2000/78/EC' in S. Fredman and S. Spencer (eds), *Age as an Equality Issue: Legal and Policy Perspectives* (Hart, 2003) 71, 89–93.

Name Index